D1016506

STRIPPING BARE THE BODY

ALSO BY MARK DANNER

The Secret Way to War:
The Downing Street Memo and the Iraq War's Buried History

Torture and Truth:
America, Abu Ghraib, and the War on Terror

The Road to Illegitimacy:
One Reporter's Travels Through the 2000 Florida Vote Recount

The Massacre at El Mozote: A Parable of the Cold War

STRIPPING
BARE THE BODY

Politics Violence War

MARK DANNER

NATION
BOOKS

Published by Nation Books, A Member of the Perseus Books Group
116 East 16th Street, 8th Floor
New York, NY 10003

Nation Books is a co-publishing venture of the Nation Institute and the
Perseus Books Group

Books published by Nation Books are available at special discounts for bulk
purchases in the United States by corporations, institutions, and other
organizations. For more information, please contact the Special Markets
Department at the Perseus Books Group, 2300 Chestnut Street, Suite 200,
Philadelphia, PA 19103, or call (800) 810–4145, extension 5000, or e-mail
special.markets@perseusbooks.com.

Editorial production by The Book Factory.
Composition and design in Adobe Garamond Pro by Cynthia Young.

Library of Congress Cataloging-in-Publication Data

Danner, Mark, 1958-
    Stripping bare the body : politics, violence, war / Mark Danner.
        p. cm.
    Includes bibliographical references and index.
    ISBN 978-1-56858-413-3 (alk. paper)
    1. Military history, Modern—20th century.   2. Military history, Modern—
21st century.   3. Violence—Political aspects.   4. Torture—Political aspects.
5. Haiti—History—1986–   6. Balkan Peninsula—History—1989–   7. Iraq
War, 2003–   8. United States—Foreign relations—1989–   9. United States—
Military policy.   10. Militarism—United States.   I. Title.
D858.D36   2009
355.0209'045—dc22

                                                            2009026666
10 9 8 7 6 5 4 3

For my mother,
in partial answer
to her favorite question:
Why can't you go
somewhere nice
for a change?

POLITICAL VIOLENCE strips bare the social body, the better to place the stethoscope and track the life beneath the skin.

—Leslie F. Manigat, President of Haiti,
February–May 1987

Contents

Foreword by Louis Begley

THE PUBLICATION OF *Stripping Bare the Body* is a timely act of public service and a literary event, bringing together Mark Danner's luminously intelligent and engaging narratives and stories from the world's war zones. They include a compelling report from Haiti on the cycle of violence which engulfed that country following the military coup in 1986, in which Jean-Claude ("Baby Doc") Duvalier was deposed after fifteen years of bloody misrule; the genocide in the Balkans unleashed by Milosevic, Mladic, and Karadzic after the implosion in 1991 of the Yugoslav federation; and the catastrophic mismanagement by the Bush administration of the conduct of the war in Iraq and what it named the global war on terror. Taken together, they are a moral history of America's engagement with the world over the last generation as well as an account of a twenty-three years' journey through hell on earth by an ideal observer: Danner is endowed with a passion for truth, great physical courage (as witnessed by the near death experiences in Haiti and the marketplace of Sarajevo related in the Afterword to this volume), a muscular writing style, and a heart as big as a barn.

Tucked in between the sections on the Balkans and Iraq is a brilliant long essay, "Marooned in the Cold War," Danner's penetrating discussion of former President Clinton's feckless decision to expand NATO to include former Warsaw Pact nations. Danner deplores the expansion, seeing it as the epitome of the bungling by successive U.S. presidents of post–Cold War relations between the United States and Russia, and the proclivity of American leaders to let rhetoric outrun available means of action. Danner's analysis is prophetic, as we now see President Obama struggle with the conundrum created by former President Bush's foolish decision to base an anti-missile defense on Polish and Czech territory. Alas, the global war on terror shows little sign of abating either in Iraq, where it may spawn a civil war among the Shia majority, Sunnis, and Kurds, or in Afghanistan where a resurgent Taliban enjoys—thanks in no small measure to the Bush administration's neglect of the need to strengthen civil structures in Pakistan—sanctuaries and access to recruits. Nor has President Obama, despite his resolve and intentions, yet finished cleaning out the stable of Augeas that the Bush administration has left for him at Guantánamo. Danner will not be lacking in opportunities to continue his vitally important work.

Danner was born in 1958. His first report from Haiti included in the present volume was published in the fall of 1989 when he was barely thirty-one. It is hard to believe the scope and superlatively sustained quality of his writings since then. Soon after his travels in Haiti, he reported on the mass murder by U.S.-trained Salvadoran troops of the Indian villagers of El Mozote (in an extensive article published in *The New Yorker* and issued in book form as *The Massacre at El Mozote: A Parable of the Cold War*), and, before beginning his coverage of the war on terror, he found time to write about the stealing of the 2000 presidential election. Those marvelously vivid articles have been republished in a volume entitled *The Road to Illegitimacy: One Reporter's Travels through the 2000 Florida Vote Re-Count*.

A common reality underlies the human and political disasters to which Danner is drawn so irresistibly: man's unchanging capacity to do evil, manifesting itself in acts of horrific sadism. Without it, the *parenthèse* between the coup that overthrew Baby Doc and yet another coup that carried General Prosper Avril to the presidency could not have degenerated into two years of assassinations by machete-wielding killers, castrations, dismemberments, arson, and looting. Danner's narrative breaks off in 1988, when Avril takes power, but Haiti's agony continued through successive rounds of bloody repressions of political parties, labor unions, individual political opponents, and students. A pause in the violence came in February 1991, upon the installation as president of Father Jean-Bertrand Aristide. The election he won had been monitored by the O.A.S. and the UN, and by Haitian standards was not significantly tainted by fraud and violence. But the respite was not long lasting. Killings and massacres continued through Aristide's ouster and return to power, and the bumbling and timorous attempts by the O.A.S., the UN, and the United States to stabilize the country and relieve its starving population.

Man's capacity for evil is on full display in the slaughter, beginning in 1992 by Bosnian Serbs of their Muslim neighbors, ethnic cleansing by rape and terror of Muslim cities, towns, and villages, and in Omarska, the Serbian Auschwitz, in which Serbian military and volunteers carried out by hand, with clubs, guns, and revolvers, the work that at Nazi Germany's Auschwitz was largely entrusted to gas chambers and crematoriums. Danner's descriptions of the agony of Srebrenica and Sarajevo, and the diabolical duplicity of General Mladic—the jovial hands-on manager of massacre after massacre—leave one shaken to the core. But Milosevic, Mladic, and Karadzic did not invent ethnic cleansing in the Balkans. Those atrocities had a powerful local precedent in the mass killings, beginning in 1941, of Serbs and Jews by the dreaded proto-fascist Croatian Ustashas (an SS like formation). The murder of Bosnian Serbs in their extermination camps, and prisons, fields and forests, nearly fulfilled the wish of Croatia's leader, Anton Pavelić, to kill the two million Serbs living inside Croatia. He hoped thereby to make Croatia better able to hold its own against neighboring Serbia. These murders were revenged first by Chetniks, a rightwing Serb militia that equaled Ustashas in ferocity, and subsequently by Serb communist partisans' massacres of Ustashas, Chetniks, and other political opponents in May 1945 as they tried to escape to Austria from a Yugoslavia governed by Tito.

Torture is evil's purest expression. As Danner shows in his groundbreaking pages on the Report of the International Committee of the Red Cross, the revelations contained in the Report, coming as they do on top of other overwhelmingly damning evidence, foreclose any pretence that the "enhanced interrogations" or "alternate sets of procedures," to use Bush administration speak, practiced on detainees identified in the Report and many others as well are anything but torture. As Danner reminds us, the "twelve basic techniques," going from "suffocation by water" through "prolonged stress standing positions," "beating and kicking," and "prolonged shackling" in stress positions, painstakingly catalogued in the Report, have their roots in the methods used by the Soviet G.P.U and the Chinese military during the Korean War for the principal purpose of obtaining false confessions. Anyone thinking that it is possible to put a more benign construction on what was done to the detainees should read the description of the extensive interrogation of Abu Zubaydah, admittedly an al-Qaeda operative, and then ponder the meaning of his treatment not just to Zubaydah but also to the interrogators. The utilitarian justification—the claim that inflicting such torment was the optimal means of preventing a greater evil, in the form of terrorist attacks on the United States—does not hold water. It has been punctured not only by statements of FBI interrogators and others familiar with the results obtained by torture, but perhaps even more tellingly by the pervasive and revolting brutality with which *all* U.S. detainees have been treated, including those who had no intelligence value. The nascent smirk on former Vice President Cheney's face when he affirmed that waterboarding is "a no-brainer for me" reveals the dirty secret of sadism.

DANNER'S BLISTERING DENUNCIATION leaves no doubt that "the most senior officers of the U.S. government, President George W. Bush first among them, repeatedly and explicitly lied about [the use of torture by the United States] both in reports to international institutions and directly to the public. The president lied about it in news conferences, interviews, and, most explicitly in speeches intended to set out the administration policy on interrogations before the people who had elected him." We also know that torture of specific detainees was approved step by step and choreographed by highest government officials, a group that often included Condoleezza Rice, Donald H. Rumsfeld, Colin Powell, and the vice president. Sanction for specific procedures—the "gold shield" that was to provide immunity for acts of such savagery—was sought and ostensibly obtained in a pair of memoranda, alternatively smug and breezy, produced by two Office of Legal Counsel lawyers, John Yoo, and Yoo's superior, Jay Bybee, who declared them legal under U.S. law, including U.S. obligations under treaties. Yoo is now a law professor at Boalt Hall; Bybee is a judge on a Federal Court of Appeals. They are peaceable men. One hesitates to accuse them or (with the exception of the former vice president) the other highly civilized senior government officials of sadism.

That leaves one with a question: What went through their minds, what were the feelings, of Rice, Rumsfeld, Powell, and Cheney when they met in a White House conference room and permitted or ordered a detainee be beaten, kicked, slammed against a wall, made to stand with his arms shackled above his head for extended periods of time (in the case of one detainee who had lost one leg apparently for as long as two weeks, apart from two or three times when he was allowed to lie down), or subjected to the "no brainer" of waterboarding? How is it possible that, in so far as it is known, not one of them stood up and demanded that these outrages stop? Would they be equally passive if in the street they saw a man being savagely beaten? It is just barely possible that they had come to believe so firmly in the greater good theory that even as they measured fully the outrage they considered it their duty to repress all stirrings of pity. The more likely explanation is that words used to denote these tortures, or even videos if they had seen them, did not make them connect with the human beings in such extreme distress. The carapace of indifference was too thick—they lacked empathy, the quality without which we are moral idiots, incapable of apprehending the humanity of other men.

The massacres and savage individual assaults in Haiti often pitted the ascendant, high yellow mulattoes against the blacks of lower standing and vice versa. As the long and shameful history of slavery, oppression of minorities, and genocide after genocide shows, the indifference to the suffering or agony of our *frères humains*—the lack of empathy—comes easiest if they are unlike us, whether by reason of racial, ethnic, or religious differences. The cards were stacked against the detainees captured in Bush's global war on terror. Those of "high value" were implicated in monstrous crimes, and had claimed the religious duty to kill infidels in the name of Islam. They reaped the hatred they had sown. The others, just because they are Muslims, whether or not they were guilty of crimes, can be perceived easily as soldiers in the jihad against the United States and the West. It would have been surprising if their captors—or for that matter, the American public—had been ready to treat them like brothers.

Danner argues very persuasively that the ultimate assurance against the repetition of the shame of Guantánamo can be obtained through "a broadly persuasive judgment, delivered by people who can look at all the evidence, and can claim bipartisan respect on the order of the Watergate Select Committee or the 9/11 Commission, on whether or not torture made Americans safer." He believes that this is the only way "we can come to a consensus about torture. By all accounts, it is likely that the intelligence harvest that can be attributed directly to the "alternative set of procedures" is meager. But whatever information might have been gained, it must be assessed and then judged against the great costs—legal, moral, and political—incurred in producing it. Torture's harvest, whatever it may truly be is very unlikely to have outweighed those costs."

I confess I cannot be optimistic about the outcome of such an inquiry or its effect. The history of the torture by the Gestapo of underground fighters against Nazi Germany, to take but one example, shows that men and women who could not be broken, who did not give names of others in the underground, were extraordinarily few. I fear that a bipartisan or nonpartisan inquiry into the "harvest" will either find some successes or will be ambiguous enough for Cheney and others of his ilk to tout the practical necessity of the actions that we hope will never be repeated. The sad but inescapable truth is that only the restraint of laws can counteract our propensity to do evil. President Obama in his Inaugural Address on January 20, 2009, charted the path clearly: "As for our common defense, we reject as false the choice between our safety and our ideals. Our Founding Fathers, faced with perils that we can scarcely imagine, drafted a charter to assure the rule of law and the rights of man—a charter expanded by the blood of generations. Those ideals still light the world, and we will not give them up for expedience's sake."

Strict and vigilant enforcement by the U.S. government of compliance with the obligations of the United States under international law, including the Geneva Conventions and the UN Convention Against Torture, as well as with the laws of the United States that make torture a felony will be required to make the president's words become our reality.

—July 14, 2009

Introduction

Confronted with murder, death, destruction, we are compelled to stare: The instinct is part of what makes us human. Often we don't want it to be: it seems savage, archaic—uncivilized. Lot's wife, transformed into a pillar of salt because she could not resist gazing back on the massacre of Sodom, embodies the conflict. Plato, several hundred years later, narrates it:

> Leontius, the son of Aglaion, was going up from the Piraeus under the outside of the North Wall when he noticed corpses lying by the public executioner. He desired to look, but at the same time he was disgusted and made himself turn away; and for a while he struggled and covered his face. But finally, overpowered by the desire, he opened his eyes wide, ran toward the corpses and said: "Look, you damned wretches, take your fill of the fair sight."
>
> —*The Republic*, IV[1]

Violence horrifies us, transfixes us, draws the eye and ignites the passions; "overpowered by desire," we have no choice but to look. Traffic cops know it. Film directors know it. News producers know it. Its reality is built into our news, into what we understand to *be* news—"if it bleeds, it leads"—and from there into our politics. For leaders in a democracy, charged with crafting a foreign policy that can attract consensus or at least acquiescence, the instinctual power exerted by the spectacle of violence is a reality to be managed and sometimes feared.

For the teller of stories, whether he assembles them from "facts" in the world or ghosts in his imagination, violence offers, beyond the inherent emotional charge, the lure of resolution. To suspense, the engine of narrative, violence supplies climax and catharsis. From political conflict, the melding of thesis and antithesis that moves history, violence extracts synthesis. Whether by war, coup d'etat, revolution, or terror, violence is the continuation of politics by other means. When power re-emerges from society and embodies itself as violence the underlying realities of politics are laid bare. Thus the governing metaphor of this book: Violence strips bare the social body.

This stripping bare—according to the dethroned Haitian president to whom I owe the figure—produces a "moment of nudity" that presents an opportunity both fleeting and priceless: to place the stethoscope against the naked skin and listen to the reality beneath. Want to understand a society, comprehend the roots of its injustices, trace the structure of its power? Examine it at a moment of intense political struggle, when leader assassinates leader, party militia battles army, death squads liquidate rivals, paramilitaries massacre the defenseless—and above it all power, that great distinguished thing, suddenly disembodied and contested, floats free, bobbing up and down above the roiling crowd like a brightly colored ball, ready to be seized and claimed by the strongest, the most clever, the luckiest.

This book, telling as it does stories of violence and political conflict from around the world—from Haiti, the Balkans, and Iraq; from the secret "black sites" of Asia and the air-conditioned conference rooms of Washington, DC—is a gathering of those moments of nudity: a cycle of narratives that attempt to piece them together, slowly and deliberately, "as they actually happened."[2] Not only to draw out, from the dense tangle of event, the what and the who and the how, but to convey the excitement and life-heightening passion of being there and struggling to construct a comprehensible but faithful narrative from a welter of conflicting and bewildering signs. From far away, such stories come to us with an order readily imposed, often a moral or ideological one: good versus bad, developed versus underdeveloped, us versus them. The closer one gets, the less certain things become. When you pass through the looking glass and stagger into the scene, what you see and hear takes on a confusing and multifarious complexity. The innocent eye is overwhelmed with impressions. The senses and the intellect come alive. Every new bit of information strips away certainty. Ignorance becomes radical, disorienting: delicious. After a few weeks or days of looking and listening and learning, you realize that despite all the work, *you know nothing*. Then truth dawns: it is *because* of all the work that you know nothing. You have stripped away the borrowed preconceptions and secondhand conclusions and attained a cherished state. From here you might begin to understand—*for yourself*. Reaching this point, making a clawing start on advancing beyond it, is the voluptuous pleasure of reporting.

A gathering of stories, then, beginning in "points of nudity" brought on by violence: massacre, genocide, terror, torture, war. These stories come together to begin to tell a larger one, a moral history of America as a world power over the last quarter-century: America as it emerged victorious from the Cold War, stumbled haltingly through the bloody "post–Cold War" world, burst like a bellowing crusader into the evangelical dreams of the War on Terror, and now, amid the ruins of ideological certainties, struggles to emerge from the moral and political crisis of the "state of exception"—the de facto martial law imposed after the attacks of September 11, whereby torture, warrantless surveillance, and other emergency measures were introduced as permanent realities of American life.

Haiti and The Late Cold War:
Beyond the Mountains

It is no accident that our presiding metaphor of politics and violence comes from a Haitian intellectual *cum* politician, for Haiti is the great exotic hothouse of politics, a tiny land vast in its complexity a few hundred miles off America's shores, which has seen many times its share of rulers: kings, emperors, dictators, presidents for life. Violence is the motor of Haiti's politics, the means of regime change, the method of succession. The struggle for power is ongoing and endless, permeating all aspects of life and implicating any Haitian of wealth and reputation. "If a man does not go into politics," says the former president who gave me this book's title, "then politics itself comes to him." A professor, intellectual, and writer from an illustrious political family, he attained power thanks to the military after a bloody, aborted election, and lost it a few months later in a tumultuous coup d'etat.

Occasionally there comes a leader powerful, ruthless, and bloody-minded enough to put an end to the ceaseless churning of political struggle and impose his will on the land. Duvalier proved himself a virtuoso of terror, perfecting a kind of grandiose public violence—blackouts, sirens, massacres both targeted and random with bodies left lying in the street—that obliterated his enemies and drove abroad those who managed to survive. Though his bloodthirstiness made him an embarrassment to successive U.S. administrations, he played brilliantly on the presiding fixation that drove U.S. policymakers during the Cold War: the containment of communism. Fear of communist influence trumped all other concerns, certainly human rights, and the dictator was a master at ratcheting up that fear among Americans and gaining from them the forbearance that allowed his survival. He understood American preoccupations, was more realistic about American interests than the Americans were themselves. It is often the case: The United States gazes out upon the world with a self-satisfied confidence in the superfluity of its power; the mistakes flowing from its ignorance it can and does survive, for the costs are borne by the objects of its gaze. They, for their part, look back at us clear-eyed, with calculation and cunning: they know us much better than we know them. They have no choice.

I came to Haiti at the fall of the regime, after the old dictator's clownish son was flown out of the realm he had inherited in an American military jet, courtesy of officials of the Reagan administration (who weeks later would perform a similar service for Ferdinand Marcos of the Philippines). I meant to cover Haiti's "transition to democracy"—a phrase much beloved by the Reaganites, some of whom, as officials in the George W. Bush administration, would carry it to the Middle East. For me Haiti was a laboratory, a training ground in the mechanics of political struggle,[3] as a great efflorescence of parties and newspapers and radio stations sprouted up, covering in a rich new fauna the desert left by three decades of dictatorship, while the soldiers and militiamen who had ruled the land looked balefully on. By this time, most American officials believed, in one form or another, in the "transition to democracy": with the end of the Cold War in sight, what, after all, was America's interest in Haiti beyond "stability," and would not a freely held election and the popular government it produced be the best way to secure it? This is the bedrock of the American political faith, resting in its turn on an idealized version of our own self-image: that on one sacred day people rich and poor, famous and obscure, can come together at the ballot box and, each bearing equal power—the power of one vote—freely choose who leads them. Power resides in the people, equally divided; leaders take it in trust from their hands. If only the illegitimate dictator can be removed, the political infection excised, democracy will harness and express the natural forces of freedom and cure the polity of its ills.

It is a beautiful vision and we would see an effort to put it into effect on a much greater scale two decades later in post-Saddam Iraq. Alas, in neither place did new polities spring, fresh as newborns, from the sacred ballot box. People, even when they share equally in the ballots, do not divide equally a nation's power. The shadow of the dictator, the darkness of the old order, looms everywhere. A Duvalier, a Saddam—such leaders are the expressions of political dysfunction, not their causes. In Haiti, the vast disparities of rich and poor, the spectacular concentration of wealth and power among a very few, the grinding, elemental poverty of the vast majority, meant a truly free election would likely place in the palace a leader of the poor. Such a leader might gain the most votes but, despised and feared by the country's elite, he would be far from wielding power. That he would be obliged to take. To those who had always fought among themselves for power in Haiti, a free and fair election would be, in effect, the launch of a revolution.

The consequences of this conundrum played out in step after bloody step during the weeks and months described in this book, leading up to the election day massacre of 1987 and the "tin can elections," revolutions and coup d'etats that followed. These events form the preface to the historical tragedy of the next two decades, which included the rise of the populist leader Jean-Bertrand Aristide, his ascension by ballot box, his fall by coup d'etat, his restoration by American invasion, and his fall and exile by yet another coup.[4] The Americans, exerting their overwhelming power to reshape the politics of a tiny immiserated land, failed disastrously in Haiti. They underestimated the nationalist response that would accompany their every move, blundering about in the complex mechanism of Haitian politics like a watchmaker blinded by his own shadow. The flamboyance of its violence, the bright garish glow of the foreground, led policymakers impatient with obscurity to scant the looming ghosts of Haiti's past: In their majority illiterate and unschooled, Haitians nonetheless walk in history, among the ghosts of past leaders. But the Americans failed to listen to the life beneath the skin. Even sending twenty thousand U.S. troops failed to alter the fundamental dynamic, not least because President Clinton, knowing the mission lacked political support but unwilling to spend political capital to build it, chose to forgo any action that might risk American casualties. U.S. soldiers did not confront the militiaman, who retained their weapons, went underground. A U.S. helicopter flew President Aristide back to the Presidential Palace; a decade later a U.S. plane flew him out again. Haiti, twice occupied by the Americans in the last century, would remain impervious to the impatient fickleness of the American gaze.

The Balkans and the Post–Cold War:
The Saddest Story

The post–Cold War world arrived in a great telegenic festival of freedom, as democratic revolution swept through the ancient capitals of the East. The governing narrative told of a near miraculous reaffirmation of America's cherished faith: a mystical turning toward "the city on the hill." President Reagan—standing defiantly in Berlin, shouting "Mr. Gorbachev, tear down this wall!"—offered the annunciation. And word became flesh. The Wall came down. Democracy and capitalism had triumphed. By the simple force of his "moral clarity"—by showing himself willing to call the Evil Empire what it was—Ronald Reagan had ended the Cold War. And now that the End of History had truly arrived, it was only a matter of time before its triumph would sweep the world.

Such was the official myth. The reality, of course, was that the Revolutions of 1989 had much more to do with Mikhail Gorbachev, the true world-historical force driving the Cold War's end. Had the Soviet leader chosen to respond to the first murmurings of revolution by dispatching the Red Army, as his predecessors had repeatedly done, the United States would have again stood by and done nothing. Communist regimes could tumble in the East not least because the man holding power in Moscow had chosen to let them. And he felt himself forced to make that choice not because of an exhortation shouted in Berlin but because of the slow coming to fruition of a policy of containment that had been devised in Washington four decades before. George F. Kennan, the father of containment and one of the figures looming over the pages that follow, had prophesied the moment with his customary elegance: "Soviet power, like the capitalist world of its conception, bears within it the seeds of its own decay," Kennan wrote in 1947; the West could hasten that decay by a "long-term, patient but firm and vigilant containment of Russian expansive tendencies" consisting of "the adroit and vigilant application of counter-force at a series of constantly shifting geographical and political points, corresponding to the shifts and maneuvers of Soviet policy."[5] It was a realist policy par excellence: The Soviets would inevitably push outward and, whenever and wherever they did, the West must push back. It is a revealing irony that Kennan's call for an "adroit and vigilant" statesmanship—a statesmanship consisting not of "sporadic acts that represent the whims of democratic opinion but only by intelligent long-range policies"—had to be introduced to the country via the Truman Doctrine, a highly ideological clarion call to fight communism by supporting democratic peoples around the world. Kennan, the arch-realist, hated the speech; but the appeal to "the whims of democratic opinion" he found so distasteful was the chosen solution to what I have called the Athenian Problem: the challenge of building and sustaining support among a democratic polity for an imperial foreign policy. In order to gain public forbearance for a policy of global ambition that truly could challenge the Soviets "at a series of constantly shifting geographical points," a senator told Harry Truman, the president would have to "scare the hell out of the American people." Americans would be fighting not just Russia but communism. Americans would be fighting for freedom. And the anti-communist crusade in which containment was eventually couched did indeed gain public support—but at the cost of embedding the country's foreign policy in an ideological prison: The fear of being labeled "soft on communism" became a driving force in domestic politics and insinuated itself into the country's policies abroad, limiting the flexibility and freedom of action of American leaders and sometimes bringing catastrophic consequences, most obviously in Vietnam.

The triumph of containment in 1989, trumpeted as a reaffirmation of American democratic, free-market ideology, catapulted the country into a post-ideological age. George H. W. Bush and his team, consummate foreign policy realists, took pleasure in managing the transition in Europe with cool professionalism. Struggling the next year to build support among Americans to fight Saddam Hussein in what was a classic "realist" war—a fight to protect access to strategic resources and the sanctity of the existing sovereign state system—Bush would finally be forced to denounce Saddam as "worse than Hitler" and dub the limited war to expel him from the autocracy of Kuwait a crusade for freedom. This reversion to the familiar music goosed the poll numbers, but when the smoke cleared the Kuwaiti emirs had been restored to their golden palaces and Saddam remained in power.

The post–Cold War world was an era without a name, dubbed by default with one of those colorless labels that, like "nonfiction," define a thing only by what it is not. Americans, having long sheltered under a comforting ideological canopy, where evil enemies were identified and the cause clearly defined, had stumbled into a post-ideological age. Both Bush and Clinton struggled to fill the vacuum, offering the pale consolations of the New World Order and the Expansion of Market Democracies; neither doctrine, each nearly empty of ideology, acquired a following. Neither offered a clear guide to U.S. interests in that great time of victory for freedom, democracy, and capitalism, when America, supreme and unchallenged, bestrode a "unipolar world."

Looking back at that post-ideological interregnum between Cold War and War on Terror, perhaps one might christen it the Era of Genocide. Two arrived in quick succession, including, in the Balkans, the first genocide to unfold in "real time" before the world's television viewers. Day after day, month after month, Americans and Europeans watched soldiers and militiamen slaughter the innocent in the Balkans; the shelling and the cleansing and the massacres all played out across the electronic screen, enacted in bright and vivid color. Television cameras were admitted to the Bosnian camps, and those images of emaciated prisoners staring out from behind barbed wire, clanging as they were with historical echoes, brought outrage and anger and almost no action at all. The "CNN effect"—the Western public staring transfixed at emaciated prisoners, at dismembered corpses of those who had been shelled while they waited in line for water or bread—brought some pressure for Western leaders to act, but this they managed to relieve by sending NATO warplanes to patrol the skies above and by dispatching NATO troops, in the "blue helmets" of the United Nations, to deliver food to the besieged below—a policy the recipients dubbed "feeding the dead."

The comforting ideological canopy of the Cold War had vanished: What exactly were American interests? In what cause should the country deploy its unchallenged power? To ensure the continued flow of oil from the Middle East? Certainly. To guard the bodies of thousands of innocent civilians from genocidal killers? The answer to this, finally, was no. In retrospect the Vietnam Syndrome had not been "buried beneath the sands of the Middle East," as President Bush had proclaimed after his Gulf War triumph. During the Balkan Wars the ghosts of Vietnam walked everywhere, haunting, most prominently, Colin Powell, a product of the Vietnam-era Army who enumerated the war's lessons in what came to be known as the Powell Doctrine, according to which the U.S. military should intervene only when it has a clear and limited mission, demonstrated public support, a well-delineated "exit strategy," and the freedom to bring to bear overwhelming force. [6] The Gulf War, a quick and wildly popular triumph, was its perfect expression. The Balkans, alas, was a mess—no way to conceive a clear mission, let alone an exit strategy. Though after the Gulf victory the United States' military authority was at its height, and though one could conceive any number of limited interventions in the Balkans that would have saved thousands of lives and perhaps prevented genocide, among leaders paralysis emerged instead, and the fascinating phenomenon of "self-deterrence." Since the mission was unclear, and American interests uncertain, overwhelming force would not be deployed. Since overwhelming force would not be deployed, any action, even one well short of overwhelming force, must be foreclosed. Taking even a small action was thought to engage U.S. prestige; its failure, risking a loss of that prestige, might lead the country down the perilous road of "mission creep," compelling it to take further actions and perhaps drawing it gradually into the full involvement it had earlier foresworn.

And so any and all use of force was "taken off the table," defanging American and Western policy. A lame-duck George H. W. Bush, smarting from the criticism of his failure to prevent the killings, sent U.S. soldiers to bring food to starving Somalis instead. That mission, built on a confused rationale and benefiting from little public support, led under Bill Clinton to the debacle of "Black Hawk Down": eighteen soldiers dead in Mogadishu, which brought a hasty and embarrassing American retreat. The lesson drawn was to avoid "mission creep" at all costs, a lesson that would lead Clinton officials to dismiss out of hand taking action to stop the killing in Rwanda—indeed, in effect to block interventions by its allies, notably the Canadians, out of fear that the dreaded "mission creep" might force the United States to rescue them. For American policymakers, ideologically untethered, wary of the impatient public, genocide in Bosnia had led to humanitarian intervention in Somalia, fiasco in Somalia to enforced aloofness toward Rwanda. In fact, Rwanda and Somalia had nothing to do with one another; they were joined only by their unfortunate association in the mind of the superpower. That association, fortuitous and meaningless as it might have been, proved to be everything for the Rwandans, eight hundred thousand of whom died in ninety days.

Iraq and the War on Terror: Lost in the Forever War

Certainly this gross disparity between the fact of unrivaled American power and the lack of moral purpose in its deployment—the appalling image of a genocide perpetrated in Europe while the television cameras rolled and the superpower's warplanes patrolled impotently overhead—had much to do with one of the more perplexing political developments of the post–Cold War era: the decision on the part of the majority of the liberal elite to support George W. Bush in launching a war of choice against Iraq in 2003. There was a felt need to match moral purpose to power: in the face of dictatorship and terror the United States must protect the innocent, advance human rights.[7] That need, as it turned out, dovetailed with the ideology of freedom George W. Bush set forth in the days after the attacks of September 11, 2001.

That ideology, of course, was not new. Within nine days, President Bush had transformed the terrorists into "the heirs of all the murderous ideologies of the twentieth century . . . follow[ing] in the path of fascism, and Nazism, and totalitarianism." The ideological canopy had been restored. Terrorists, who "hated our freedoms," became the new communists. And America had a new but familiar mission: to destroy terror and advance freedom. The War on Terror would become the new Cold War. Like a slightly threadbare but still functional suit of clothes, the old ideology had been hastily dragged from the closet, refurbished, and thrown on.

Unfortunately it didn't quite fit. It was effective, of course, in building public support: Americans knew the anti-communist music well; they had been hearing it for generations. But the words did not match the new threat. Terrorists were not communists: they controlled no state, commanded no armies. The threat the jihadists posed was largely ideological, designed to persuade young Muslims, confronted with an image of the godless, imperialistic, repressive superpower, to join the fundamentalist struggle, whose targets, first of all, were American autocratic allies in Cairo and Riyadh and the Gulf. Faced with this George W. Bush proposed his Iraq adventure as a first step in a crusade of breathtaking ambition: He would use America's unrivaled power to transform the Middle East, to set off a "democratic tsunami" that would sweep away the old order and leave in its wake a region of allies newly free. Trumpeting the threat of Saddam's weapons of mass destruction, he led the country to invade and occupy Iraq—and did it with a thoroughgoing incompetence that stands unmatched in U.S. history, managing in an occupation that was almost entirely improvised on the spot to set off a wave of violent insurgency and civil war that left a hundred thousand Iraqis dead and served as a laboratory for the development of a new, deadlier generation of "asymmetric warfare," an arsenal of improvised explosive devices, car bombs, and creatively deployed terror now making itself felt in Afghanistan. Indeed, Afghanistan, the chaotic wellspring of 9/11 abandoned by George W. Bush when he hurried off on his Iraq adventure, now threatens to become the latest failed American experiment in nation-building, presided over by a young president determined to prove he spoke truth when he prefaced his opposition to Iraq as "a dumb war, a rash war" with repeated assertions that "I don't oppose all wars." As I write, the troops have begun to flow to "the right war" in Afghanistan, and yet among Americans the troops' dispatch brings not determination and resolve but apprehension and doubt: The Iraq War ended the illusion of overwhelming American power and the dream of the "unipolar moment." America's power to destroy, dependant on its peerless military technology, is unmatched; its power to build amid the destruction a new and lasting order, which depends on wisdom, statesmanship, planning, and a commitment to foster and sustain the support of the public, is limited indeed.

In launching his "War of the Imagination," George W. Bush managed to fulfill every expectation and dream of the new enemy. Post-9/11 America became the America the jihadists depicted: an imperial, aggressive, blundering power that managed, by means of lurid, deathless images of tortured Muslims, to prove to the world that all of its purported respect for human rights and freedom was nothing but base hypocrisy.

The Black Sites and the State of Exception

American attention, that great spotlight, has moved on from Iraq. It is the blitheness of power: the privilege to push the cost of one's mistakes, the damage wrought by the extravagance of one's dreams, onto the accounts of others. Iraq remains violent, divided, and unstable, but the American gaze has moved on.

Iraq destroyed Bush and made Obama possible. But though Bush has gone, we are living still in the "state of exception" he imposed.[8] It is not the first such period in American history; one can list the constriction of liberties during other times of crisis: the Alien and Sedition Acts of the late eighteenth century, the Palmer Raids and deportations during World War I and afterward, the mass internments of Japanese Americans during World War II. George W. Bush's "state of exception," though one can speak about warrantless wiretapping and other surveillance, about the use of immigration laws to imprison aliens indefinitely, about the general untrammeled expansion of executive power, has had as its signal attribute the torture of detainees. Soon after the attacks of September 11, the American government established a network of secret prisons, or "black sites," "disappeared" detainees there, and tortured them secretly.

And then not so secretly. Americans have known about the "stress and duress tactics" since late 2002, about the use of waterboarding in particular since the middle of 2004.[9] Torture has been revealed and revealed and revealed. This is surely one of the agonizing attributes of our post–September 11 age: the unending need to reaffirm realities that have been proved, and proved again, but just as doggedly denied by those in power, forcing us to live trapped between two narratives of present history, the one gaining life and color and vigor as more facts become known, the other growing ever paler, brittler, more desiccated, but sustained by the life support of official power. When it came to torture, scandal did not unfold according to the model we have taken for granted since Watergate, with revelation leading to investigation and finally to expiation and punishment. Torture survived its exposure. Apart from a handful of hapless soldiers who allowed themselves to be photographed at Abu Ghraib, no one has been punished for instituting a policy of torture. We have had a score or more investigations, but none has had the power to declare the policy illegal and punish those who designed and implemented it. Torture quickly became a "frozen scandal," doomed to be revealed again and again in an endless cycle of self-reinforcing stasis.[10] Even as I write, we await the revelation of new documents from the CIA and the Department of Justice. Though the new president has declared we will no longer practice it, torture has become a much discussed and debated part of recent American history that has never been officially renounced. Indeed, the former vice president makes public appearances to express his support for torture and to charge that the new administration has left the country vulnerable to attack by discontinuing its use. One of our major parties supports it unequivocally—while not, of course, calling it torture.

That the debate over torture has become an enduring part of our politics is perhaps the most important legacy of the Bush administration, for it cuts to the heart of who we are as Americans. Look again at the photographs: Hooded Man, Leashed Man, the piles of naked men, the exposed figures cowering before the teeth of the lunging police dogs, the lines of men grasping their genitals, forced to masturbate. These are encounters choreographed to assert power and dominance through systematic degradation, humiliation, and shame. The torturer exerts his or her power by the forced draining of the power of the other. Hooded, stripped, exposed, the tortured becomes pure object, bereft of control over even the most basic and intimate areas of life. Deprived of sight, shelter, cover, his body belongs to someone else, who is free to manipulate it, strike it, shame it, place it under stress; even his sexuality is wrenched away from him and used as a weapon against him.[11]

Go beyond laws broken and treaties violated. It is hard to think of a dynamic more corrosive of the liberal idea of government: a government limited in its power, prevented by its basic philosophy and its laws from violating the autonomy of the individual. These images came before us in 2004, accompanied by the usual defense of the nation that tortures—they depicted only the activities of a "few bad apples." Their outlandish grotesquerie helped make this argument plausible: Surely only a handful of sadists, acting without supervision, could have been responsible. After a momentary outcry, and a dozen or more investigations—none of which confronted the responsibility of those who made the policies and those who gave the orders—the question of torture receded, metamorphosing from shocking revelation to ongoing story. And, from revelation to revelation, we have declared our shock and disgust and learned to live with it.

Stripping Ourselves Bare

Like Plato's Leontius, we struggle not to look, paralyzed by our own disgust at our attraction to the violent and the grotesque; but look we do. There was a time when that inherent shame might have expressed itself, redeemed itself, by animating a push to punish the wrongdoers and wipe the society free of torture. But the political dynamic introduced with such boldness and confidence in the wake of 9/11—the faith that Republicans "can go to the country on this issue" of terrorism, because Americans "trust the Republican Party to do a better job . . . protecting America," as Karl Rove put it a few months after the attacks[12]—remains with us still. The Politics of Fear is nothing new in American life; the structure of its argument, the pattern of its use, is not much different from what used to be called "red-baiting." The leader unwilling to apply torture, according to the former vice president, is the leader who simply doesn't understand the magnitude of the threat. He is naïve, soft: a dupe. He will put the country at risk. He is, through his own gullibility, a traitor.

So that "moment of nudity" has returned to our own shores; the stethoscope rests on us. The stories that follow, selected from the work of two decades and left pretty much as I wrote them,[13] have led back here, to this place. I would not have expected it, and yet there is something perversely pleasing in it, too. Some of the earliest writing I ever did on politics, as a college student in the late 1970s, took up the methods of Argentina's "dirty war"—in particular the use by its military and intelligence services of their version of waterboarding: *el submarino*. Argentina of the Dirty War, where tens of thousands were tortured and "disappeared," remains far from America of the War on Terror. But not as far as it once was. Not far enough. The looming symmetry disturbs; the comparison is uncomfortable. But one draws narrative pleasure nonetheless from the comfort of a return, of the closing of a circle. That is the thing about stories. You never know where they might lead.

—Grizzly Peak, Berkeley
August 2009

I.

Beyond the Mountains

Deye mon, gen mon
Beyond the mountains, more mountains
—**Haitian proverb**

La parenthèse

MORNINGS in Port-au-Prince, just before dawn, as the last, scattered gunshots faded in the distance and the outlines of the city began to take shape in the dirty air—tiny houses, painted aqua and salmon; the huge and ghostly National Palace, gleaming white; gray and rust-colored slums, canopied in smoke—my colleagues and I would go off in search of bodies. This was during the days leading up to Sunday, November 29, 1987, the day of the election that was to bring democracy to Haiti. Each morning, we would meet in the darkness in front of the Holiday Inn, near the glass doors of a newly opened press center, through which we could just make out banks of telephones and telexes and stacks of cheerful red-and-blue election press kits. During those last days, foreign correspondents and international observers and election experts poured into the country, and the afternoons were filled with solemn press conferences, but the real story unfolded at night. It was a loud and violent conversation, meant to be overheard: One followed its progress by charting the gunshots echoing over the city, then read the results by cruising the streets at daybreak to count the corpses.

On the Tuesday before the election, we set out in the white early morning, skirting the Champ de Mars park, and passing beneath hundreds of little blue-and-red flags that hung limply from the telephone wires, celebrating Haiti's new democracy, and under banners stretched across the main streets exhorting Haitians to vote. Following the brown smoke billowing in the distance, we drove slowly through the waking capital, and soon, as we circled the perimeter of the great *bidonville* ("tin-can city") of La Saline, already covered over in brown cooking smoke and blurry in the rising heat, we found the first remnant of the night's conversation. Not far from rows of brightly colored *camionnettes*, called "tap taps," just in from the countryside, where shirtless, sweating men were unloading baskets of mangoes and bunches of green bananas and great dirty bags of charcoal to feed the tens of thousands of cooking fires in the vast slum, we came upon a clump of chattering people—a sight that in Haiti that week invariably meant a body.

Pushing through the crowd, we discovered a tall, lean young man, several hours dead, laid out carefully on Haiti's Route Nationale 1. His body had been prepared for its role: A rope had been twisted about his neck, and above the frayed noose a metal necklace had been pulled tight around his chin, but most of it had disappeared into the gaping maroon slashes around his mouth and throat. Distinct, deep machete cuts in a V-shaped pattern above and below the mouth, they seemed almost an attempt to construct for the victim, after death, a parody second mouth. A partly smoked cigarette had been placed between his lips, a charred wooden match balanced jauntily on his chin. Within easy reach next to his stomach, which, left exposed, was already dense with flies in the rising heat, were a handful of rice, a can of tomato sauce, and a slab of cheese, all displayed on a scrap of brown cardboard. "That's so he can eat," an old man said, laughing, bringing on the laughter of the crowd. "And the cigarette, that's to keep him happy." There was no blood on his shirt, the old man said, because when they spotted him near the La Saline marketplace early that morning, as gunshots echoed in the distance, this tall young man had been wearing a dress—the all-purpose Haitian disguise—and carrying a can of gasoline. He was a Tonton Macoute, they said, a member of Jean-Claude Duvalier's militia—one of the thousands who had gone into hiding after the fall of the dictator, nearly two years earlier, and who now, during the months of growing violence, had begun to reappear in the neighborhood. He had come to spread terror by bringing to the people of La Saline what they dreaded most: a fire that in seconds would roar through the dense labyrinth of dry scrapwood hovels, leaving scores of people dead and thousands homeless.

But the *brigades de vigilance*—neighborhood committees that had formed themselves in these last days of terror—had been watching. And when the Macoute appeared in that dark and now deserted marketplace, wearing his dress and carrying his can of gasoline, the brigade slum boys let out a shout and gave chase, pursuing him down the tiny alleyways, over the ditches filled with pale-green waste, until at last they caught him, dragging him to the ground beneath the black mountains of the vast charcoal yard. There, in front of the angry, shouting crowd, the slum boys stunned him with their machetes, then lynched him. They prepared the body and left it on the road for Guédé, the *vodou* lord of the Crossroads to the Underworld, to attend to in his own good time—for Guédé, despite his great power, often appears as a poor wandering beggar, a famished traveler who would be sure to look kindly on the sumptuous meal of rice and sauce and cheese that had been left beside the young man's lifeless hand.

Fire was the chosen means of night terror in that election week. A few hours before dawn the previous day, a mob of men armed with heavy clubs had stormed into the Marché Salomon, a huge, lofty building, with concrete arches and a sheet-metal roof that since the late nineteenth century had housed one of the city's main public markets. Shouting and screaming in the darkness, the men had used their clubs to beat the people sleeping there—mostly market women from the country, who were guarding their precious merchandise, and the usual complement of beggars. The men had chased them off, then carefully, methodically poured out their gasoline and torched the building. The enormous blaze roared until dawn, reddening the night sky and covering the capital in a pall of smoke that reeked of burned bananas and charred meat. At dawn, one could see amid the smoking rubble scores of beggars and market women staggering about, moaning and wailing as they picked through the tons of blackened, stinking food. I watched a frail old man probe around, then straighten up and let out a shout: He held up a piece of charred meat in triumph before stuffing it into his mouth as his colleagues raced toward him through the rubble.

A woman with a red kerchief on her head pulled something from the black waste and rose up straight, showing me what had once been her prized hen. By now, others had gathered around me, hoping that this white man with his notebook might be moved by their litany of losses and somehow make it right.

"I lost some beans and some bananas."

"I lost three chickens."

"I lost some beef."

A little white-whiskered man, in blue jeans and a white shirt, cut short the voices. "Yesterday, many people went to bed hungry, but today we'll have food," he said. He held up a burned piece of beef and gestured, grinning, toward the black landscape. "There's food in Haiti now, because things are starting to boil."

IN AN EARLIER predawn darkness, on February 7, 1986, Jean-Claude Duvalier took the wheel of his BMW and, with his elegant mulatto wife, Michèle Bennett, coolly smoking a cigarette at his side, drove to François Duvalier International Airport, boarded an American military jet, and fled to an opulent exile in the south of France—there to rejoin an expatriated fortune estimated at more than $250 million (equivalent to more than Haiti's annual budget).

For fifteen years, he had ruled the land, and his father fourteen before him. It was Dr. François Duvalier, known as Papa Doc, who had painstakingly created the intricate dictatorial system that came to be called Duvalierism, and installed himself at its apex, as president for life. The engine of Duvalierism was the Tontons Macoutes, a "volunteer" militia that was part mass political party, part paramilitary force, part extortion ring, and part storm troop. In their tens of thousands—no one knew the exact number—the Macoutes, wearing dark glasses, red neckerchiefs, and blue denim, covered the land, searching out any potential threat, be it a student with contacts among the exiled opposition, a merchant reluctant to surrender a kickback, or, most threatening of all, a restive army officer pondering a coup.

In 1971, Papa Doc died in office; by one count, he had survived eight invasions and attempted coups and at last departed the palace only, as he had vowed, "to the salute of cannon." His power at the end had been such that, having obliterated all opposition, he could install as his successor a slow-witted nineteen-year-old distinguished only by his great bulk and his glassy stare—and bequeath to him, by sheer force of will and the fear evoked by his name, a reign that endured a year longer than his own.

But after a decade of Jean-Claude's rule in this impoverished land—the poorest in the hemisphere and one of the poorest on earth, where nine people in ten live on less than a hundred and eighty dollars a year, where four in five cannot read, and where the life expectancy barely exceeds fifty years—the economy had begun to spiral even further downward. And in the fifteenth year of Jean-Claude's rule the young dictator came under attack.

The explosion took place in November 1985. In the desolate port city of Gonaïves, during a peaceful demonstration against food shortages, Duvalier's security forces killed four schoolchildren, and those deaths—four murdered Haitians out of the tens of thousands killed over the past three decades—unleashed something uncontrollable. Overnight, the four children were transformed into martyrs. Around the country, young Haitians were suddenly marching, students refusing to attend classes; Catholic priests were publicly urging them on, with Radio Soleil, the church station, serving as the revolt's nervous system. Duvalier's Macoutes responded by shooting demonstrators, and the regime moved to imprison some prominent people, and to close Radio Soleil. But American officials, who under Jean-Claude had become the dominant foreign presence in the country, reminded the president that their aid during this difficult time would depend, as always, on his "human rights" comportment. And the army officers, sensing the weakness of the regime and the ambivalence of the Americans, seemed to be holding back, biding their time. The young dictator, unsure of himself, wavered; he was not the man his father was, had never shown the same mastery of the techniques of unremitting terror. And he had allowed the Duvalierist political base—built on black-power nationalism and anti-Americanism—to weaken and fragment. Over the years, the rich and pampered Jean-Claude had become, to the disgust of many of Papa Doc's old *noiriste* henchmen, an ally of the mulattoes, and had grown increasingly dependent on the Americans and their aid. He enjoyed the money and the parties, the perquisites of power, but when the moment came he had little stomach for the fight—for fully unleashing the repressive apparatus his father had carefully constructed.

When the people began to march, he hesitated, reshuffled advisers, fired ministers; the Americans applied pressure, and soon many of those he had jailed were released, and Radio Soleil was reopened. The Tontons Macoutes were eager to crush the revolt, and strained against the leash, but they were mostly held back. Then, while Haitians filled the streets, and opposition roadblocks began to spring up, the Americans gave a final push: In a critical damning gesture at the end of January 1986, Reagan administration officials announced they would refuse to certify to Congress that the Duvalier regime was improving in its respect for human rights—a decision that would cut off American aid.

THE OMINOUS MEANING of the gesture was clear. "We told them," an American diplomat said later, "we weren't going to certify unless they did things—start political parties, release prisoners, keep Radio Soleil open— they really couldn't do and still keep power." Soon afterward, the American ambassador spelled matters out in a chat with the Haitian foreign minister: The United States preferred President Duvalier's early departure, provided he left the country in the hands of the military. ("Duvalier saw the handwriting on the wall," an American diplomat put it later. "But the U.S. helped translate it for him.") On February 6, the ambassador was summoned to the palace, where the exhausted dictator inquired whether an American plane could be found for him and his family. The envoy, thinking of the difficult "transition" ahead, had a request of his own: Could the president do something to "neutralize" his Macoutes, to prevent a spree of killing after his departure? Duvalier promised to put them under the control of the army; then, at the urging of his foreign minister, he dictated the names of six men he would leave in his place to rule the exploding country. ("He left the way he wanted to leave," the diplomat said. "Otherwise he might not have left at all. He still had repressive mechanisms at his disposal.") A few hours later, Duvalier was gone.

It fell to General Henri Namphy, a stocky, bullnecked, moon-faced mulatto, who had been the armed forces' chief of staff under Duvalier and now became the senior member of the hastily formed junta, to take control during *la parenthèse* that would follow—the "parenthesis" of disorder, political jockeying, and sporadic violence that traditionally bridged the fall of one Haitian ruler and the rise of the next. Such crises had punctuated the story of independent Haiti, a span of a hundred and eighty-two years during which thirty-five men had come to power and ruled the land, then left it in their various ways: one executed, one a suicide, two assassinated, one blown up along with the National Palace, six dead in office, eighteen violently overthrown. "A revolution in Haiti," ex-President François Légitime (overthrown in 1889) explained to readers of the London *Herald* in 1911, "does not have the same meaning as it would have here. It is our only way of changing administrations. Here you have an election; down there they have a revolution."[1] On February 7, 1986, the latest *parenthèse* began in jubilation. The street in front of the National Palace overflowed with thousands of delirious Haitians—Haitians dancing, singing, swigging rum, honking their horns, abandoning themselves to a tumultuous national celebration. Amid it all stood General Namphy, a gruff officer who had served virtually his entire career under the Duvaliers but who, despite his position as chief of staff, had held little real power—for it was a tenet of Duvalierism to keep the army fragmented, divided, and thus able to recognize as its one real master only the dictator himself. It was over this ill-trained, ill-led force of seven thousand men that General Namphy now uncertainly ruled, and through it proposed to rule the 6 million citizens of the newly christened *Haiti Libérée*.

Soon after the dictator's flight, Haitians heard General Namphy announce that his regime would ensure a "firm, just, and good transition to democracy," heard him vow (in his ferocious, shouting speechmaking style, the only way Namphy could overcome a lifelong stutter) that his transitional government would help "build a new Haiti, based on reason, social justice, tolerance and freedom." They heard the American secretary of state proclaim that the United States remained "committed to the development of democratic government and respect for fundamental human rights in . . . Haiti," and they saw the Americans follow through by first restoring the crucial foreign aid and then more than doubling it.

Yet no sooner had Namphy taken power than assertions and demands and accusations began sprouting everywhere like weeds, spreading across the aqua and salmon walls of Port-au-Prince in a lush growth of misshapen letters and misspelled words. The graffiti were dominated by one idea, which instantly became the presiding ideological concept of post-Duvalier Haiti's *bamboche démocratique*, or "democratic spree"—an inescapable, insistent demand to *déchoukay*.

Déchoukay is a Creole word meaning to uproot, and during the next two years uprooting would loom as the guiding principle of the Haitian opposition. These calls to uproot, to rip out, soon became the ground over which the various factions of the opposition battled one another, thereby exposing the central paradox of the *parenthèse*: The measure of a leader's credibility, and thus his mass popularity, had quickly become his vow to "uproot" the existing system—the very system that still controlled Haiti's governmental apparatus and that alone, could give that leader power.

Having *déchoukayed* Jean-Claude Duvalier, his hated wife, and all their despised, decadent hangers-on, the Haitian people pushed further: not only the omnipresent Duvalierist slogans, the photographs, and the streets named for the Duvaliers but also the Macoutes, the high officials, the mid level bureaucrats, the collaborators—all traces of the regime that for thirty years had dominated the country, had co-opted, obliterated or exiled its national culture, and had insinuated itself into every interstice of national life—were to be instantly destroyed.

Perhaps the most memorable image of Operation Déchoukaj was the uprooting of the Macoutes: angry crowds of poor Haitians surrounding an unlucky militiaman—usually a frightened, pleading man, by now in civilian clothes, having hurriedly discarded his blue denim uniform—and beating him to death with sticks, or stoning him to death, or covering him with gasoline and burning him alive, and leaving his remains lying in the sun to be further abused, or else parading them triumphantly through the neighborhood.

Those who opposed the uprooting would be uprooted in their turn. For had not the people uprooted Duvalier? Had they not accomplished what had come to be called *la révolution sans armes*? Operation Déchoukaj, it was said again and again, more and more insistently, during the first months of the *parenthèse*, had only just begun.

Letting the violence take its course was the officers' attempt to satisfy the overwhelming political emotion of that time: the people's desire for revenge. "I stood and marveled at the justice of the people," Father Jean-Bertrand Aristide, an influential priest and proponent of the "unarmed revolution," told me passionately.

But how, I asked, could he, a priest, a moral leader of the Haitian people, call such acts "justice"?

"Our consciences should be clear," Father Aristide said heatedly. "These Macoutes were Satan, Satan incarnate." And there was still great great danger, six weeks after the flight of Duvalier, he said. "The people must continue to show how strong they are, how strong they can be! They know about the Duvalierist presence in the cabinet, the presence of Duvalier in the public administration, in the army, even in the church. It is not enough that those people say they've changed their *mentalité*. They are Duvalierists! And the people will remove them, one by one, as they did Duvalier."

What mattered was not just that General Namphy and the others in the junta—with the sole exception of Gérard Gourgue, a lawyer and human rights activist—had served Duvalier in the past. Or even that, after a dictatorship of three decades, everyone with any authority in the government, in the public administration, and in the army was, at least by the loosest definition, a Duvalierist. What mattered was that the people thought they had made a revolution, and demanded justice as their fair reward. But justice was the one thing that the officers could not give them, for in their view what had brought down Duvalier was their coup d'état, and it was a coup based on a compromise: Duvalier would leave quietly if his "associates" were protected; the Macoutes would let the army assume power quietly if their leaders were protected, if their rank and file were permitted to fade away without pursuit or prosecution.

So this became "the compromise with power that weighs on the country to this day," in the words of Haitian political scientist and politician Leslie F. Manigat. For not only did the officers stand aside while the "justice of the people" was administered to those "little Macoutes" who, of the thousands of Macoutes in flight, were unlucky enough to get caught; they also looked the other way while a number of notorious officials made their escapes. Mme. Max Adolphe, the leader of the Macoutes and a onetime commandant of the infamous Fort Dimanche prison, disappeared, rumored to have escaped the country disguised as a nun or, in another account, secreted in a crate of mangoes. (Her pleasant split-level on the Pétionville Road, with its signature stone shark grimacing open-mouthed in the swimming pool, was thoroughly *déchoukayed*.) Albert Pierre, Jean-Claude's former secret-police chief, popularly known as Ti Boulé (Little Flame), because of his preferred method of torture, was allowed in late February to leave the country and take refuge in Brazil—an official move by the government which elicited general indignation, with even Justice Minister Gourgue calling it "shocking and offensive to the nation."

Shortly afterward, Gourgue resigned from the first junta, becoming for a time the most popular political leader in the country and, having forced Namphy to reconstitute his tottering regime, earning the general's undying enmity. Within a few weeks of Duvalier's departure, demonstrators had begun to shout, "Down with Namphy!" and within two months the slogans of the gathering opposition had taken shape: the interim government was "Duvalierism Without Duvalier," which meant "The Revolution Has Not Yet Finished."

THROUGHOUT THE EXHILARATING first months of the *parenthèse*, each day seemed to bring a new demonstration or strike, the announcement of a new political party or mass organization or human-rights group, the christening of a new newspaper or magazine. Each flight from New York or Paris or Miami brought a celebrated dissident returning with a bit of Duvalierist history—a family massacred, colleagues executed, months spent in Duvalier's torture chambers—and a score to settle with the Duvalierists. The counter-elite, so long exiled, had returned to fight for power.

For three decades, the Haitian political world had been fallow and moribund; with a few exceptions, those politicians and intellectuals who had not been killed had long since fled. "Under Duvalier, if you had any talent or ambition and wanted to stay in Haiti, you had two alternatives," a Frenchwoman, long a resident in Port-au-Prince, told me. "You could let yourself become totally corrupted or you could be killed. That was it." A large part of the intelligentsia chose exile. Although pressure from the Carter administration had brought a brief but hesitant political opening (slammed shut within days of Reagan's election), by 1986 one in every six Haitians was living abroad, including the overwhelming majority of professionals: More Haitian economists and technicians were working in Africa than in Haiti, and many more Haitian professors were teaching outside their country than within it.

One such professor was Leslie Manigat, who had built a distinguished academic career studying the workings of Haitian political crises. That career had begun as early as 1953, when Manigat, a twenty-three-year-old Sorbonne student, dissected the first Haitian *parenthèse* in his thesis, "The Liquidation of Saint-Domingue as a French Colony"; it continued after the young scholar returned to Haiti to take up a position in the foreign ministry. Then, in 1957, his career really took off, for in that year, at long last—after six years of corrupt rule by Paul Magloire, a high-living black officer in the pocket of Haiti's mulatto elite—Dr. François Duvalier had emerged from hiding and, after a chaotic nine-month *parenthèse* in which five governments rose and fell, was elected, with the army's help, president of the republic.

Dr. Duvalier was a black nationalist, a *noiriste*—a "soft-spoken country doctor" who "knew the people." And Manigat, brilliant, energetic, ambitious, and singled out as one of Papa Doc's young favorites in those exciting times, shortly became the foreign ministry's director of political affairs, and, at the same time, the founder of Haiti's National School of Advanced International Studies.

But after just a few years of Duvalier's increasingly bloody "political revolution" the inevitable falling out came (over Professor Manigat's support of a student strike), and there followed in 1961 the weeks spent in a "forced visit to the Duvalierist prisons" (as the professor jokingly described it later), then asylum with his family in the Argentine Embassy, and finally, a safe-conduct having been grudgingly granted, years of celebrated exile. Across three continents, the honors followed one upon another, at the University of Paris; at the University of the West Indies, in Trinidad; and then at Simón Bolívar University, in Caracas.

Through it all, he continued to publish prolifically—an outpouring of books and monographs and articles. But the key texts orbited around a fixed point, and returned to one overriding goal: to analyze minutely virtually every major *conjoncture* (as he called these periods of crisis) in Haitian history. And in almost all of these fascinating, exhaustive studies he deftly inserted, like an interconnecting thread, one version or another of a favorite Manigat dictum: that the political crisis might be considered "a moment of nudity, propitious for applying the stethoscope to the social body."

Now, for this latest "moment of nudity," Professor Manigat could at last be present. As the leader of the seven-year-old Rally of National Progressive Democrats, he had become one of dozens of Haitian presidential candidates walking a tightrope between the anti-government popular movement, which claimed to voice the sentiments of "the people," and the widely hated but still all-powerful officers.

He had expected a triumphant welcome, and there was no lack of cheering supporters at the airport. But the press was strangely absent. It was only later that he discovered what had happened; for it was April 26, the anniversary of one of Papa Doc's bloodiest days of terror twenty-three years before. Outside Fort Dimanche, the opposition had held a large demonstration, and Namphy's men had fired into the crowd, leaving six dead and a hundred wounded.

So it was into a world of confrontation, heightened rhetoric, and frenzied political activity that Manigat returned. After the shootings, the country erupted again, and various popular leaders demanded that the Namphy government relinquish power. General Namphy had announced no plans for elections, had brought no Macoutes to trial (indeed, it was widely believed that scores of them had been integrated into his army), and had done little to bring about the kind of wholesale reform that the people were loudly demanding. On the contrary, the army—its command structure wholly unaltered from what it had been in the last days of Duvalier's rule—seemed quite willing to shoot Haitians down in the streets.

In what had been a political and intellectual desert, the floodgates had opened, and suddenly politics had become a growth industry. Overnight, a small, dead country had been transformed, in the words of the Haitian sociologist Laënnec Hurbon, into "an immense social and political laboratory."

"THE CRUCIAL, urgent task here is to build political institutions—real, lasting political institutions," Rosny Desroches, a schoolmaster who had been named the interim government's minister of education, told me. "I'm talking about the parties and the unions that will stabilize our political life. When you don't have political parties, for example, that a president can lead after he leaves office, he wants to stay president forever."

As Desroches spoke, parties and committees and groups were indeed being created, but in fantastic profusion. Acronyms—the MIDH, the KID, the LHID, the PAIN—were flourishing, as any Haitian of note or weight seemed to be starting a political party or a mass organization or a political committee or a magazine. It was all an exciting venture in the rhetoric of politics, politics as full-dress theatre, operatic politics, politics by declamation: an honored—if, by definition, sporadic—Haitian tradition. But the work of coalition-building, of the subjugation of personal ambition so necessary to a party, was mostly absent. With one important exception, the political parties were built largely around single personalities. When it finally came time to hold an election, thirty-five candidates applied to run for president.

The overriding role of personal ambition and the resulting factionalization were nothing new in the world of the Haitian *parenthèse*. "The most striking feature of the Haitian system is the intensity of political activity," Professor Manigat had written in 1964, observing François Duvalier's Haiti from exile in Washington. "Everything is political and may become involved in the struggle for power. . . . The reputation earned by an engineer in his special field is regarded as a political trump. The prestige that a professor gains among his students may represent a political threat to the government. . . . Such is the encroachment of politics on all aspects of life that if a man does not go into politics, politics itself comes to him."[2]

In the months after Jean-Claude Duvalier's fall, amid an unruly urban mass population, a frightened and insecure elite, and a disaffected and isolated peasantry, Haiti Libérée's political spectrum began to take shape. At one end was the government, run by the army and managed largely by the same corrupt administration that had served Duvalier, with a few respected civilians brought in to fill cabinet posts.

Exerting a strong influence on the government were the harder-line Duvalierists (powerful businessmen who had benefited from the regime; retired officers; influential former Duvalier ministers), who sought to crush any move toward political reform by working through their connections within the army and the government, by paying for strikes and demonstrations to pressure the regime publicly, and by employing the now underground Macoutes to attack and disrupt the opposition—all the while remaining in the background themselves.

At the other end of the spectrum were the mass organizations, what Professor Manigat called "the counter-power in the streets": hundreds of loosely organized groups that, depending on the occasion, could mount a demonstration in a matter of hours or minutes, and were headed by "popular leaders," many of whom had been in exile during the Duvalier years. It was impossible to estimate the "permanent" membership of these organizations; they thrived on the growing distrust of the Namphy government and the disdain most people felt for the "traditional" politicians. By mounting strikes and demonstrations, these groups pushed for the resignation of certain "Macoute" members of the government—carrying on the process of uprooting Duvalierism which Father Aristide called "peeling the onion, layer by layer."

Caught in between were the various "traditional" politicians—*les candidats*, as they became somewhat derisively known—all of whom wanted desperately to be president and thus found themselves forced to scurry back and forth, denouncing the government during times of crisis, in order to curry favor with the "popular movements," but striving always to avoid alienating the army officers who still controlled the transition.

In June, General Namphy, warning that the country was "on the edge of anarchy," at last announced an electoral calendar, thereby pleasing the Americans and the candidates but leaving most of the popular groups, who believed a fair election was impossible under Namphy, unappeased. When it came time for the first event—the election of a constituent assembly the following fall—less than one in twenty Haitians stepped forward to vote.

Instead, the people turned their attention to a menacing image: that of several of Papa Doc's old henchmen smiling at a press conference as they announced the establishment of a neo-Duvalierist party.

Protesting Haitians poured into the streets in the largest demonstrations yet, and two weeks later the new party was forced to disband.

Meanwhile, in the red-carpeted hall of the Palais Législatif, sixty-one forgotten delegates had begun to debate a new constitution. Almost before anyone noticed, they had produced an extraordinary document: a constitution that, in its litany of absurd and brilliant and, finally, Machiavellian provisions, must have surprised the people of Haiti as much as it surprised the government, which had thought that everything was under firm control and now found itself presented with a populist and wildly popular document that stripped the officers of the one power that was the only power in the Haiti of the *parenthèse*—the power to conduct elections. On March 29, 1987, the constitution went to the voters, and this time more than 1 million Haitians turned out, and more than 99 percent voted yes.

Two key provisions led to this astonishing vote. The first created an independent Provisional Electoral Council, which would write the electoral law and oversee the coming elections—that is, count the votes. The second stipulated that for ten years no "architects of the dictatorship" could be candidates for public office. In a country where almost all power had depended, in the end, on the government, the Duvalierists—who, rich and prosperous, now saw themselves with so many enemies and so much to lose—were to be stripped of power entirely. The constitution had become a mechanism to de-Duvalierize and de-Macoutize the country; it had become a version of Father Aristide's unarmed revolution—a version made solely of paper. The opposition, in the guise of the constitution, had taken over the official process.

In June, the Namphy government made a clumsy move to steal the key electoral power back, by claiming that it alone had the authority to supervise the elections. Once again, people poured into the streets, and this time Namphy's troops shot them by the score. After a week of protests, the general backed down. But the opposition, hoping to build on its victory, now issued the call "*Raché manyok*"—"Pull up the manioc!" Or, in the full phrase, "Pull up the manioc and leave the field clean!"—in other words, overthrow the government.

It was a critical miscalculation. In the days that followed, more demonstrators died in the streets; but though the army had been there to push out Duvalier, there was no one to push out the army. The Americans, after warning pointedly against any "perversion of the democratic process," nonetheless reaffirmed their support for the Namphy government. When the smoke cleared, General Namphy remained in place, but he was now deeply antagonistic toward the Provisional Electoral Council and its vaunted "independence." Like the Duvalierists, he viewed the council as a vehicle for failed revolutionaries to put themselves in power.

In August, a leader of a minor party, campaigning in the countryside, was hacked to death by angry peasants; someone had denounced him as a Communist, a word that in Haiti for thirty years had been a synonym for "devil." In October, a well-known presidential candidate, an exile recently returned from Manhattan, stood before the Port-au-Prince police station, his lawyer's gown draped over one arm, and began a speech demanding the release of a prisoner within. Suddenly, two men burst through the crowd of reporters, and one of them placed a pistol at the candidate's temple and fired. No charges were filed.

On November 2, the Provisional Electoral Council announced a list of twenty-three "acceptable" presidential candidates—thereby in effect disallowing the twelve others, on the ground that they had, "by excess of zeal," been architects of the dictatorship. But, having circumvented the army, the council was left with only the constitution to protect it; and, as a Haitian proverb has it, "Constitutions are made of paper, bayonets are made of iron."

Hours after the council's decision was announced, a group of armed men blocked off the Rue Pavée, a main street within a few hundred feet of the police station and the army headquarters, and set about ransacking and then burning the council building. The men seemed in no particular hurry;

indeed, they seemed determined to be thorough—some witnesses said they used a flamethrower. Neither the police nor the soldiers lifted a hand.

Thus as Haiti, for the first time in thirty years, moved toward elections, it became increasingly apparent that power had assumed two distinct forms: the heretofore mute power of numbers, who saw in the elections a chance for change; and the power of those with guns and influence, who saw in them a direct threat.

NOW, SIX DAYS before the election, I left the smoking ruin of the Marché Salomon and drove to Jean-Claude Bajeux's Ecumenical Center for Human Rights, on the bougainvillea-lined Rue de Marguerites. Bajeux was a key figure in the Front National de Concertation, or National Togetherness Front, a moderate-left party that was really not a party at all but an ad-hoc coalition joining KONAKOM—a loosely organized congeries of unions, peasant groups, mass organizations, and church groups that had emerged from the Congress of Democratic Movements earlier that year—to the small Socialist Party and several other party-like organizations. It was, in short, a popular front, and its foot soldiers were the lay workers and the priests of the Ti Legliz, the Liberation Church. Since the Front, unlike traditional Haitian political parties, was formed from the bottom up, it seemed to many Haitians the organization most likely to be able to marshal countrywide, grass-roots support, and also, crucially, to have its people present at all or most of the thousands of isolated polling places.

"We don't know what will happen from moment to moment," Bajeux told me, leaning forward in his chair, his hands tightly clasped—a tall, thin, light-skinned man with a round bald spot that looked almost like a tonsure, making him resemble the friar he had been in another life. "We don't know if the army will back the terrorists or will move to neutralize them. They know them, of course—know who did this, know their cars. But so far the army is like this." He crossed his arms. "The soldiers want to prove that the Electoral Council is unable to conduct organized elections. In the streets, the people say the army is doing this; I am less categorical—I say the army is *letting* the Macoutes do it. If the army doesn't act, if it doesn't arrest some people, it means they want the disorder, they don't want the elections to go forward." Bajeux paused. "It's time for the Americans to act. It's time for the embassy to"—he clenched both hands, thumbs down, turned them—"tighten the screws."

And if they didn't? If the Americans didn't put pressure on the army?

"If the army doesn't arrest anyone before this evening, *they*"—the Macoutes—"will burn other things, kill other people, maybe some of us."

At that moment, as if on some absurdly well-timed cue, shots rang out in the street outside—two or three single shots, then a burst of automatic fire—followed by screaming and yelling, then the screech of tires. Bajeux's eyes widened slightly, and he looked at me: The shots seemed to come from just outside the door. But almost at once he gently dropped his hands in a movement of resignation and rose slowly to his feet. He led his secretary and another guest to a little room in the back of the office, then turned and sat down. "Now we wait," he said softly.

It was in 1964, when he was a young member of the Fathers of the Holy Spirit, that Bajeux had run afoul of Papa Doc. The dictator had summarily expelled the entire Jesuit order; he was then in full, raging *Kulturkampf* against the Catholic Church—terrorizing the largely French and Canadian clergy and defying the Vatican, which excommunicated him. (His victory in this struggle was one of Papa Doc's proudest accomplishments—and also constituted his poisoned legacy, for the nationalized church made use of its enhanced prestige to encourage the revolt that overthrew his son.) Father Bajeux signed a letter to his bishop protesting the expulsion of the Jesuits; the bishop turned it over to the dictator, and the young priest was expelled to the Dominican Republic, where he began ministering to Haitian exiles. His mother and brothers and sisters continued to live in Port-au-Prince, in a pretty, pale-orange gingerbread house on the Rue Berne.

In Haiti, that summer of 1964 was a climax of the period's turmoil and terror. In August, thirteen young exiles invaded in the south. Swarms of Tontons Macoutes and soldiers hunted them down; two were taken alive and sent to the capital, where they were tied to stakes in the National Cemetery and—before huge crowds of children—executed in a televised ceremony.

Earlier that summer—about the time Father Bajeux was opening his mission in Santo Domingo—another exile had led a hit-and-run operation over the Dominican border. "There was some confusion, because the radio talked about both events, and my name came out," Bajeux recalled. "In Port-au-Prince, some people told my mother she was in danger. She went to see the secretary to the papal nuncio, who told her that everyone in Haiti was threatened, so he didn't see why she should be specially threatened. She went to the French ambassador, who told her the same thing, and said, 'Really, I can guarantee that nothing will happen to you; there is nothing to fear.' That was at eleven in the morning. At eleven that night, they all disappeared—my mother, two sisters, and two brothers. And the house stayed open—the doors open, all the lights on—for a month.'"

It was more than two decades—time spent working and teaching in the Dominican Republic, Mexico, and Puerto Rico—before Bajeux stepped off a plane in Port-au-Prince, a few days after Jean-Claude Duvalier boarded his, and returned to his mother's house.

"It was still there, but ruined, destroyed," Bajeux said. "You see, after the house had stayed open a month, some Macoutes came and occupied it. And it was only twenty-two years after, when I arrived in February, that I put them out. I came into the house and I did like this"—he clapped sharply three times—"and they said, 'We were waiting for you. We knew you were going to arrive.' And the Macoutes handed me their papers, one of which said, 'This house was given to us by Mme. Max Adolphe.' I heard later how at police headquarters my family were beaten up, raped. Other prisoners saw them at Fort Dimanche, but after that . . ."

Now, twenty-three years later, the Macoutes were still here, and there was shooting outside his door. In the street, I found scores of people still running in panic, but the gunmen had sped off; a Haitian friend of mine who had been waiting at Bajeux's gate told me that there were three or four of them in a small white car, plus a young man on a brown-and-white motorcycle. They had stopped in front of the gate and jumped from the car—one man brandishing an Uzi, the others drawing pistols—and fired into the air. Then they had raced down the street and turned the corner.

As my friend and I drove toward that corner, we could see a commotion on the Avenue Jean Paul II: Perhaps thirty or forty tough-looking, muscular young men, in T-shirts and slacks, all with clubs or rocks or machetes in hand, were surging down the busy street, bellowing furiously, swinging their clubs, thrashing people who hadn't run away fast enough. Some of the gang were throwing rocks through store windows and smashing windshields on parked cars, and, as we approached, driving slowly, a young black man raised a jagged chunk of concrete high above his head and, screaming wildly, was on the point of heaving it through the windshield until he saw I was white, whereupon he shouted for me to back up, to stay away or take the consequences.

The gang moved rapidly on, sweeping down the thoroughfare in a few minutes of shouting and tumult, and then melted away, leaving behind a deserted street littered with smashed cars and broken glass from the storefronts—one of which belonged to the Movement to Install Democracy in Haiti, the party of Marc Bazin, a longtime World Bank official and a leading presidential candidate. Bazin, an articulate economist, had led a highly publicized crusade against corruption during a brief stint as Jean-Claude Duvalier's finance minister, in 1982 (the dictator had fired him after five months), and was popularly thought to be "the American candidate," or, sometimes, "the Haitian Kennedy," for his good looks and dynamic style. But the carborne terrorists seemed no more impressed by World Bank conservatives than by leftist intellectuals; they had taken care to spray his headquarters with gunfire.

In the distance I heard shouting and the sound of tires, and within minutes the streets leading to the wealthy suburb of Pétionville were jammed with people trying to escape what had suddenly become a "hot day" in town (a reverse and more frenzied version of the procession of Mercedeses, BMWs, and Peugeots that early each morning dropped the kids off at school and brought the fathers to their government offices). Farther downtown, merchants were pulling down their shop grates. On one main corner of the Avenue John Brown, on the way up to Pétionville, I found a tire and some other rubble burning—a hastily built barricade—and was told by several bystanders that a man wielding a rifle had appeared suddenly, chased people away, thrown the barricade together, then disappeared; and, they added, almost as an afterthought, the man had been wearing a dress.

ON THE ROUTE DE DELMAS, in the middle of the ugly commercial clutter that was the main legacy of Jean-Claude's vaunted Decade of Development, I found the new headquarters of the Electoral Council, where, behind sandbags and credentials checks and a mandatory search at a metal gate, there was an air of embattled chaos. "We have no security whatsoever," René Belance, the public-relations director, told me. "Before, we had two policemen, but now the government has pulled them. When we ask for security, they don't answer. Last night, we were attacked again. Did you see? There are sixteen bullet holes downstairs."

Through a window I could see two young men shoveling gravel into canvas sacks: more sandbags to protect the building. Behind Belance, volunteers were perched on a stepladder, working to install a new drop ceiling in what until a few weeks before had been a factory. Council officials, mostly young men neatly dressed in sports shirts, hurried back and forth among the various offices—one each for the nine council members, plus special rooms marked "Computers," "Public Relations," "Press." In the center of the main room, journalists milled about, waiting for yellow press passes. The foreign reporters were treated with an efficiency—a deference, even—unusual for Haiti but befitting what the council recognized as their central role: with the increased pace of the killings and burnings, the foreign press and observers had become a lifeline for the isolated council, carrying its message (who could resist the appeal of "free and fair elections" in Haiti?) to the outside world.

In a small office, Louis Roy, a white-haired, distinguished-looking mulatto physician of seventy-one, was telling a group of journalists, "It is those who don't want the elections to come off who have the force, who have the ammunition, who have the money to buy people and send them into the street, as they did this morning." During the early years of François Duvalier, Roy had served as the head of Haiti's Red Cross, bravely protesting the dictator's illegal arrests until one day someone tossed a bomb into his front yard, almost killing his young son. Roy spent the remainder of the Duvalier years in Montreal, and returned in the spring of 1986 to play a key part in writing the constitution. "It is not only a question of scaring people so they don't vote," he was saying. "It is that we may not be able to send all the material to the polls. For example, today we had fifty-six student volunteers who were supposed to pick up the ballots from the printer. But because of the situation they didn't show up."

In a mountainous country with very few roads and the great majority of the people scattered in inaccessible villages, many of which can be reached only on foot or by donkey, six thousand polling places had to be supplied with ballots enough to offer 3 million eligible voters a chance to vote for one of the twenty-three presidential candidates. And, since four out of five of those voters were illiterate, it was essential that ballots printed with clear photographs of the candidates were delivered to all the polling places. Desperate, the council had tried to rent helicopters from private companies in the United States but failed. "No helicopter owner wants to rent his helicopter in this situation," Roy said.

Outside, volunteers were loading cartons of ballots onto trucks. As I was examining one cargo, I was warned off by a young man. "It is not the time for that sort of curiosity," he told me dryly. And why should they not be suspicious—paranoid, even? The council was isolated, unarmed, unprotected, and, as Sunday drew nearer, the government's attitude became increasingly clear: The people wanted the army out of the election, and out of the election the army would be; the election was the council's business—let it try to carry the thing off by itself, with only the help and protection of its foreign friends, if it could. All around the council headquarters were inspiring signs of its foreign support. New computers to count the votes—on which earnest young volunteers were furiously practicing—had been donated by the French. Gray plastic ballot boxes—eighteen thousand of them—had been donated by the Canadians, who had also given gas lanterns to light the polling places in the many towns and villages without electricity. Registration forms had come from the Venezuelans.

And, of course, there was money. About $1 million, Roy said, had come from the Japanese. But the money to pay for the printing and the pens and paper, the banners and posters, as well as the picture books showing how to vote in easy cartoon lessons, and the television and radio commercials and cassette tapes that explained the procedures in careful Creole, and for the many other things needed to stage an election in a land that hadn't seen one in three decades—including now the sandbags and heavy steel sheets nailed in place over Roy's windows, which, as he proudly pointed out, had already been dented by a burst of gunfire—the bulk of all this money had come from the Americans. Those same Americans who had supplied the military plane that carried off Jean-Claude Duvalier, who had doubled their foreign aid to help Haiti through the difficult "transition" that followed, had now become the main backers of Haiti's democratic election, having donated something on the order of $8 million. Small wonder that Jean-Claude Bajeux was waiting impatiently for the embassy to "tighten the screws"; the election—like the tottering Haitian economy—was largely an American-financed production.

"WE HAVE SPOKEN with the government about the lack of security," an American diplomat said on Tuesday. "And, remember, an army or police unit did show up at Bazin's headquarters yesterday." The diplomat, precise and expressionless in his light-blue cotton suit, was giving a "not for attribution" briefing to a roomful of reporters assembled at AID headquarters, a sprawling, pale-orange building on the Boulevard Harry Truman, not far from the city's harbor. Almost all pronouncements from American officials in Haiti were not for attribution. "Our actions have such a magnified effect here, mainly because of the weight Haitians give them," a senior envoy had explained to me. "You don't need to do or say much, so you have to be very,

very careful. A little muscle twitch over here gets magnified many, many times."

As for the identity of "the terrorists," the diplomat was now saying cautiously, "I assume we are talking about people associated with some of the rejected candidates." That seemed reasonable, I thought, remembering the second of the bodies I had seen that morning, a plump, shoeless corpse that had been left like a bouquet in front of the Institution Secondaire Gérard Gourgue. In all likelihood, the victim was thoroughly uninterested in politics and had simply made the mistake of venturing out on the streets at night during a difficult time, when people "associated with some of the rejected candidates" stumbled across him, shot him in the stomach, heaved him into the back of their jeep, and dumped him in front of the candidate's door—just far enough from a "GÉRARD GOURGUE PRESIDENT DE TOUS LES HAITIENS" poster to make their message clear without overdoing the sarcasm.

"Essentially, the kind of violence we've seen shows the strength of terrorist-type actions," the American diplomat was saying. "That is, a few people can cause a great deal of disruption." Then, in response to a question about army involvement, he said, "No, I have seen no concrete evidence of it."

The person in the best position to have such evidence, of course, would have been the victim. As it was, army jeeps passed by the corpse two or three times while I was present, though the soldiers did not bother to stop, contenting themselves with exaggeratedly fierce looks directed at the assembled bystanders and photographers. It seemed likely that the man would lie there in the sun all day, or longer, in what one bystander referred to as "the old Papa Doc way—leave them lying there to teach people a lesson." No Haitian, certainly, would move to touch him. ("Are you just going to leave him *lying* there?" I heard an exasperated American reporter demand of a teacher in the Gourgue school. He had to repeat the question several times before the gaping young man managed to stammer back, "Well, yes, yes, I will"—staring at the American as if he were crazy.)

But if the army wasn't involved, the American diplomat was asked at the briefing, then why didn't the army—that is, the government, of which, after all, the United States was the main foreign supporter—do something to stop what seemed a clear effort to disrupt these elections, of which the United States was also the main foreign supporter?

"Well," the diplomat said, after a pause, "remember that all this is rooted in the antipathy that exists between the Namphy government and the council. The people made it clear that the election was the affair of the council. So the government is saying, 'O.K., don't ask for help from us when you have a problem.'"

Americans at the Embassy had been making this point for some time—that the confrontation was rooted in the behavior of both sides. And the point was certainly well taken. But it was also true that only one side had the guns, and thus the army's continued "neutrality" could lead only to one result: the Duvalierists' scuttling the election. This brought to mind what another American spokesman, during the early, rocky days of the Namphy regime, had told me: "Look, Namphy is not a politician; none of these guys are. They're army men, they don't like politics, don't understand it, don't trust it. They are trying to hold the country together." It had seemed a reasonable view then, a few weeks after the departure of Jean-Claude, but as the *parenthèse* continued it had seemed increasingly threadbare. Namphy not a politician? The statement depended, of course, on how you defined politics, and it gradually became clear to me that under the Americans' definition Duvalier would not have been a politician, either; nor, for that matter, would most of the Haitians now running for president.

From the beginning, the Americans had trusted in General Namphy and the army. As an embassy official told me shortly after Duvalier's fall, "There are only two nationwide institutions in this country that could have taken power: the army and the church. And the church doesn't want it." Having seen to Duvalier's departure with what they viewed as admirable efficiency, the Americans were faced with the question of what to do with this poor, mysterious country. And what other choice was there but to rely on the army to "broker the transition"?

The diplomat had begun to grow impatient with the barrage of questions about why the United States did not "apply pressure." Still, it was clear—to take the most sympathetic interpretation of General Namphy's motives—that there were already pressures on him, and that they were mounting. From the two hundred or so Haitians who within months of Duvalier's fall had announced their intention to run for president, four had now been designated—by some subterranean process affected by *telediol*, the fabled Haitian rumor mill, and then affirmed by the radio stations and the newspapers (and to the intense irritation of Leslie Manigat and several others)—the "major" candidates.

One of the four, Sylvio Claude, was an untutored, rabble-rousing Baptist preacher, who had been repeatedly jailed and beaten during Jean-Claude's reign. ("Here Is the Martyr!" was his election slogan.) He was wildly popular in the Port-au-Prince slums and therefore totally unacceptable to the Haitian elite and the army that supported it (and, for that matter, to the Americans; the diplomat shook his head when Claude's name was raised). Another was Marc Bazin, who during his few months as Duvalier's finance minister had sniffed out and attacked corruption—an accomplishment for which he was remembered much more warmly by the Americans than by the Haitian officers and their wealthy friends. A third, Louis Déjoie II, fondly nicknamed Ti Loulou, was the scion of an old mulatto-elite family, and a direct descendant of both a founder of the country and a key nineteenth-century president. Ti Loulou was the son of Senator Louis Déjoie, the very man whom François Duvalier, with the electoral help of this selfsame army (including Second Lieutenant Henri Namphy), had defeated in the hard-fought election of 1957—whereupon the senator, never admitting defeat, had gone into bitter exile, where he and his followers (including his son) had passed the years plotting to overthrow the dictator. Finally, there was Gérard Gourgue, the human-rights advocate who had been badly beaten by Macoutes under Jean-Claude, and whom Namphy, according to diplomats who knew him well, hated "pathologically." Many Haitians believed that Gourgue, powered by the Front's nationwide network of priests and lay workers, had a very good chance of winning the election.

And then there was the election itself; no doubt—as the diplomat now conceded—there would be "irregularities." For General Namphy, however, the irregularities were unlikely to present the major problem. More worrying by far were the thousands of volunteers all around the country who would be running the election—all of them supporters of the constitution and therefore by definition anti-Duvalierist and at least partly anti-army. In previous presidential elections, it had been the army doing the counting. Now the army had been frozen out. But if the army wasn't counting the votes it still had the guns and the power to keep order and protect the process—or not. Of course, keeping order might well involve shooting at Duvalierists, Macoutes—whatever—some of whom happened to have strong connections in the army; indeed, some of whom, since the fall of Duvalier, happened to be *in* the army (particularly in the Dessalines Battalion: Its powerful commander, Colonel Jean-Claude Paul, was known to have welcomed a number of Macoutes into the battalion and to have extended his protection to others who had remained in hiding). For General Namphy—as his right-hand man in the junta, General Williams Régala, had stressed to me—preserving the "institutional integrity" of the army was paramount, because only the army could "hold the country together when all the civil institutions collapsed."

Could General Namphy really be expected to risk that "institutional integrity"—risk soldiers shooting at soldiers or, worse, risk seeing his commands ignored, his own position undermined? And for what? For the Electoral Council? For Gérard Gourgue?

The American diplomat could see this line of reasoning, but he, like the other American officials I had spoken to, appeared not to accept it. Indeed, the Americans couldn't afford to accept it. They had to believe in Namphy, the large-hearted non-politician General Namphy. Namphy was *theirs*, they told themselves (refusing to recognize that, in reality, they were *his*). The general clearly didn't care about power, the Americans insisted; he was a simple man, who liked nothing better than to drink and play cards with his buddies. He wanted out, and he could read the balance sheet: When it came down to it, after all, the country couldn't function without the Americans. (Without American aid, an embassy man had told me patiently, "the Haitian government collapses—poof!") If it weren't for the Americans, Namphy wouldn't be there. And for the Americans everything hinged on "democratization," as Namphy was well aware. What could the general do? As always, he had to hold the situation together.

Now, toward the close of his briefing, the American diplomat was asked what would happen if Namphy *couldn't* hold things together. "You mean, if anything happens to . . . derail . . . the democratic process, shall we say?" he said slowly, and paused. Then he responded firmly, "An immediate cutoff of all U.S. aid. That's in the law." As for Bajeux's hope—that the embassy would "tighten the screws"—the embassy appeared to think the screws were tight enough.

Give the General time. It was a complicated place, Haiti; its problems were never-ending. (The Haitian proverb *"Deye mon, gen mon"*—"Beyond the mountains, more mountains"—had been helpfully emblazoned on the embassy's press kits.) In any event, was it not evident, at least, that the general and the Americans understood one another? "The judgment that we have is that violence is not on a high enough level to disrupt the elections," the American diplomat went on. "Now, if there were daytime violence generalized over the country, I think that could pose a real threat. Daytime violence would be a more troubling thing."

AS WE DROVE downtown from the briefing under a brilliant midday sun, we heard the squeal of tires, two or three rapid machine-gun bursts, screams, then the roar of a panicked, stampeding crowd. By the time we reached the Rue Pavée, almost within sight of the burned council headquarters, people had begun to poke their heads out from doorways and from behind boxes, where they had dived for cover. On one of the galleried sidewalks lay a young man of perhaps twenty-five, his arms spread out amid a pile of cassettes; he had been dead only seconds, but he looked as if he'd been frozen there forever, precisely posed, in gray pinstriped pants, white T-shirt, and fancy green-white-and-red knit shoes.

He had been sitting on the sidewalk selling smuggled cassettes, like the hundreds of other contraband merchants clogging the downtown area, when a Pajero jeep—the classic Macoute vehicle—screeched by, an Uzi firing out the window. There was no reason, no warning, no sense, and, before he could move, a bullet had ripped open his stomach and another had pierced his right eye, and he was likely dead before he hit the ground, scattering his cassettes in all directions.

Now a crowd of jostling photographers, mostly white, quickly encircled him—supplying the Télé Nationale news clip for that night. ("*Terreur générale en centre-ville,*" the anchor intoned, but the viewer saw only the swarm of white photographers, their safari vests bristling with extra lenses, and here and there a glimpse of one of the dead man's fancy shoes.) Down the block, moans were rising: Two others had been badly wounded.

"I am revolted by this act," Marc Bazin said on that same newscast. Interviewed outdoors, he squinted behind his steel-rimmed glasses; even in a short-sleeved blue *guayabera*, without his World Bank executive's elegant suit, he remained the self-assured statesman, big-shouldered, deep-voiced. "The terrorists' strategy is negative—to burn, to spread terror, chaos, to prevent a better life for Haitians," he said. "But the elections are the will of the people, and I think they will come off." Bazin had told me earlier in the day—on which, among other things, his headquarters had been machine-gunned again, and his main rival had had bestowed upon him a corpse outside his door—that he would do no more campaigning for the rest of the week.

On the broadcast, after a public service advertisement showing a woman carefully choosing, then casting, a ballot, with a voice-over offering step-by-step instructions in Creole (courtesy of the Electoral Council, whose staff was no doubt now watching the news, holed up for the night in its sand-bagged, bunkerlike headquarters), came a Louis Déjoie commercial: To the strains of a sprightly "*Déjoie, Déjoie*" ditty the candidate—a big-bellied, light-skinned Ti Loulou—dances his way through an assortment of wretchedly poor neighborhoods, the crowds mobbing him, kissing him, poking him, and, most endearingly, putting their hands all over his bald head. He seems to love it, the dancing, gyrating candidate; his smile dazzles as he pulls a plump market woman into his arms and waltzes her about.

On Sunday, I had waited for the Déjoie campaign amid a large crowd gathered in a parking lot in Croix des Bouquets, not far from the capital. Suddenly, all was chaos: People began running, and then a singing, swaying parade of dancing drummers and bamboo-flute players split the crowd as the procession arrived, at its head the candidate's large white jeep, his bald pate and fat torso poking through the sunroof, his big arms waving. Amid the crush of people, everyone was now dancing and singing ("*Déjoie, Déjoie!*"), and rum bottles were being passed. The singing went on and on, as the candidate climbed heavily to the roof of his jeep, waited for the microphone to be passed hand to hand over the swaying crowd, sang and danced along for a few verses, and at last began to speak.

Like most political speeches, this one was long on slogans and short on policies, but it was delivered in the brilliant, colorful Creole for which Déjoie was famous, and it kept the crowd laughing. He pledged to represent the peasants, for his party stood for "the politics of the earth," and he told his cheering audience that the thirty years of *krazé-zo*—literally, "breaking bones," or repression—was over.

Near the end of the speech, he attacked two of his rivals, arguing that Bazin and Hubert de Ronceray, because they had served Duvalier (de Ronceray as minister of labor and social affairs), should have been excluded as Duvalierists. Déjoie's attack delighted the crowd, but it jolted me; for this argument tended to undermine the legitimacy of the electoral process itself—and as such upheld a key tenet of the Duvalierists, who pointed to the presence of the two former ministers as proof of the council's political bias.

IN THE LATE AFTERNOON of the Tuesday before the election, I began my round of visits to those important but less vocal candidates—those whose influence was felt mainly after dark. With two Haitian friends, I began the ascent up John Brown, retracing the route of the panicked motorists. As the road climbs higher and higher above the swarming city, the air grows cooler, the skins grow lighter, and the ranks of the great houses begin. Here cluster the main players of Haiti's traditional political game—those who took lead roles in this *conjoncture*, as their fathers had in those before.

Just off the Canapé Vert, for example, lies a neat white two-story house of glass and concrete: the home of Clovis Désinor, a lifelong associate of François Duvalier, who served Papa Doc faithfully as political strategist, speechwriter, minister of finance, minister of commerce, and who, until the Old Man shocked Haitians by bequeathing power to his famously dense teenage son, had been judged by many to be Duvalier's rightful heir. Early in 1985, the mysterious and widely feared Désinor, a stooped-over seventy-year-old black man, broke publicly with Jean-Claude, and he was believed by many to be the strongest Duvalierist presidential candidate. But now the council had banned him from the elections—after he had been out of government, a private citizen, for seventeen years.

No, M. Désinor would not speak to me, a somewhat exasperated young man told me at the gate. No, it made no difference that he had spoken to me once before. (That had been during the weeks after Jean-Claude fell, when Désinor, winking and craftily grinning, had warned of the "tendency toward disorder" growing in Haiti, "a disorder that serves no one," he said. "Order is the spinal cord of any nation, and Haiti's spinal cord has been broken. We will see what happens.") But now, the young man went on, M. Désinor was not speaking to the press, and particularly not to the American press. Not while his case was in court. Didn't I know he was appealing the council decision? Didn't I know he was going to sue Mike Wallace, after that setup on *60 Minutes*? (Désinor had unwisely let Wallace interview him in English, a language he didn't know well, and had found himself goaded into declaring, with perfect telegenic ferocity, that he was a Duvalierist, and that he was "proud of it." He meant, of course, a *true* Duvalierist, the sort that had not held power since the death of Papa Doc. But how could stupid Americans be expected to understand such distinctions? Désinor now blamed Wallace for helping the council ban him.)

By the time we entered the lovely upper-class neighborhood of Debussy, it was growing dark, and one of my Haitian friends insisted that I let him out of the car. Traffic had fallen off, and the few pedestrians on the street were hurrying home; in half an hour, the streets would be deserted. It was not a time for visits—especially not there.

A scant half mile from chez Désinor, behind a high wall, stood the large, rambling white-and-aqua house of General Claude Raymond, a godson of Papa Doc. As a young officer in the heady, bloody days of the "Duvalier Revolution," during the early 1960s, Raymond had commanded the Presidential Guard and been a leading figure in the Tontons Macoutes; upon Papa Doc's death, he had served as the armed forces' chief of staff, keeping a watchful eye during the critical early years of Jean-Claude's regime—before the young dictator, having found new allies, abruptly sent him off to Spain as ambassador in 1973. But General Raymond, now retired, had many supporters, who saw in him a link to the Old Man, to true Duvalierism. And though his presidential candidacy had also been disallowed, these friends had not abandoned him.

During those violent weeks, many would notice that the general's house had become the scene of curious nocturnal gatherings. Just before nightfall, its large garden would gradually fill with men, who passed the time lounging about among a half-dozen four-wheel-drive vehicles parked in the driveway. Near midnight, it was said, the cars moved out onto the deserted streets.

Tonight, five days before the election, the parking area behind General Raymond's gate was crowded with jeeps and cars and, leaning against a pillar, one small chocolate-and-white motorcycle. "That's it!" my Haitian friend said. "That's the one from yesterday morning." He had been waiting outside Bajeux's office when the gunmen came: four in a small white car, and one on a brown-and-white motorcycle.

Just inside the gate, perhaps forty young men, neatly dressed in slacks and sports shirts, were sitting on the steps or leaning against the cars, almost all of them black, muscular, and very tough-looking. They were murmuring to one another in low voices, but when I passed through the gate, holding my press card in front of me, there was a silence, and not a friendly one; it persisted as a bearded young man rose and ambled toward me. No, he said, the General was not there. No, he could assure me he wasn't. The general was very busy, you see. No, no, waiting for him was out of the question.

Under the silent stares of the general's assembled supporters—they did not share the council's fondness for the foreign press—I walked back to the car and drove slowly down the deserted street. "You interrupted them," my friend said, pulling himself up so his head could once more be seen through the window. "They were cleaning their guns."

NOT LONG BEFORE the shooting began that night, the weather-beaten black face of Clovis Désinor appeared on the television screen, and the old Duvalierist proceeded to address his Haitians in a frightening, mesmerizing speech. The style—the dark, raspy voice and rhythmically nodding head; the hypnotic chanting repetition of cryptic, powerful phrases; the exaggerated raising and lowering of the voice; the frequent dramatic climaxes—was pure Papa Doc, as were the words, evoking conspiracy, betrayal, foreign manipulation.

"Haïtiennes! Haïtiens!" Désinor began, with a fearsome look. "Nothing is hidden that will not be uncovered." And throughout his speech he repeated this dark and obscure accusation like a mantra. He spoke of the "excess and abuse of power cynically practiced by the members of the Electoral Council," noted that "these collaborationists . . . have invited or accepted foreigners," including "the financial aid of the United States," to hold the elections, and declared flatly that the council "plotted the ruin of our sovereignty; for . . .

the council members will rig the votes in order to fulfill the desires of their . . . investors."

Toward the end of the long and rambling discourse, Désinor spoke of God. "God alone . . . our compass" had advised "Clovis Désinor, His creature" to tell his followers to stay away from the polls Sunday: "*Abstention totale*! Don't cover yourselves with shame and ridicule by participating in these criminal operations of the Electoral Council, who betray us . . . by conniving with these foreigners." Then, leaning forward into the camera, the man who had loyally served as the sturdy right hand of Papa Doc solemnly concluded, "Nonviolence remains de rigueur."

AROUND MIDNIGHT, as we sat on the veranda of the Grand Hotel Oloffson, we heard the shooting begin. But tonight the bursts of fire had acquired an odd accompaniment. After each shot, a great metallic clanging rose up, underlaid by a low, mournful howling—hundreds, then thousands of human voices forming a steady bass under the chaotic high-pitched smashing of metal against metal. The whole city seemed to be in an uproar. Listening intently to the din, which had been joined by the barking of scores of hungry dogs, we managed to isolate one of its sources—the "hot" slum neighborhood of Carrefour Feuilles.

We crept quietly through the dark garden and peered out into the street. Under the single street light, several boys had begun to construct a barricade, dragging hunks of concrete from a building site across the street, lugging part of a rusted car chassis, rolling into place old stumps and pieces of wood, and piling up an arsenal of stones.

There was a burst of gunfire nearby, and immediately a great clanging rose up; fifty yards down the block we could make out the darkened profile of a tall, emaciated figure smashing a metal rod against a light pole and howling into the air. The noise died away, and the figure emerged from the half shadows and began to stride back and forth—shoulders thrown back, posture almost absurdly erect, metal rod thrust under one arm—and then to chant, rhythmically, in a haunting, otherworldly tone: "*Toi! Toi! Toi! Lève-toi!*" Over and over he chanted in his eerie voice, striding back and forth, pausing only to smash his metal rod against the pole after every burst of gunfire: "*Toi! Toi! Toi! Toi qui dors! Lève-toi!*"—"You! You! You! You who sleep! Rise up!" It was the *bat tènèb*, the "tenebrous beating" by which the Haitian masses, powerless but for their numbers, had traditionally called to one another to wake, to rise up and defend their homes. As I watched this bizarre figure moving in and out of the shadows, I realized he was wearing, over a dirty T-shirt, an old and ragged flowered dress.

Now a great furor arose in the middle distance: the squeal of tires, then gunshots, a crescendo of panicked voices, screams, and the sound of a charging crowd. The steady roar continued. After the nights in which bursts of gunfire had kept the darkened streets deserted, the city now had come to life—a strange and violent life played out under the street lights.

My companions and I got in our car, and, making sure those manning the first barricade had seen us and knew we were "press" (knew that we were *blans*, white foreigners), we drove slowly through the gate and into this night world. We moved carefully, the car idling along at walking speed, interior light left on to expose our white faces and yellow press passes. In this way, shouting "*Journalistes! Journalistes!*" all the while, we inched cautiously from the first barricade to a second, and on to a third, each time hoping that the grim-faced young men at the next barrier would be reassured to see us pass by their colleagues, and hold off throwing their stones or charging with their machetes until we came close enough for them to see our faces.

Most streets were barricaded—with oil drums and scrap lumber, with cinder blocks, with wrecked cars. At most of the barricades, four or five young men stood by, some with machetes and clubs, some with stones, ready to surround and smash the car if the shouted commands to stop, to wait, weren't heeded. Once, when we turned a corner, screams, clanging machetes, and a hail of stones forced us to retreat.

Beyond the barricades, the streets were awake but strangely silent; families sat stone-faced on their steps or in their doorways, seeming—with their machetes and clubs, their metal rods, their faces garishly lit by the sulfurous lights—like ghoulish parodies of urban propriety. On one street, five or six boys played, between two barricades, a vigorous but silent game of soccer with an unraveling ball of twine.

As we passed into a large intersection, we heard music, and saw across the way a group of young people frenziedly dancing the merengue. To the pulsating music blasting from a small cassette player, a young woman and three men were thrusting their blue-jeaned hips, shaking their machetes overhead, and bending, whenever they heard shots, to smash them against the curbside in a great scraping of sparks. As we approached, one dancing young man, sweat running down his neck, proffered his rum bottle and gestured, finger to his lips, that he would not speak; then, machete under one arm, he took my notebook and slowly wrote, in painstaking French, "We were obliged to do this, because the government is not on the side of the people. They burned the market. They hurt us. Despite everything, we will vote Sunday." Finally, at the entrance to a little square not far from the National Cemetery, our car was stopped, surrounded, and engulfed by a screaming, stampeding mob. Hands yanked open the doors and pulled us from the car, then hustled us forward into the square, which was packed with people, all of them motioning for us to move forward.

At the end of a long aisle of grinning people was a grotesquely battered hulk of metal that had been a car; on its caved-in roof lay the mutilated remains of what moments before had been a man. Our handlers pushed us forward to see the body, which was tightly ringed by smiling faces. The man had been stripped and pummeled by many hands; there were long slashes about the trunk, where part of his intestines had tumbled out, and on the youngish face a series of deep cuts, several in the peculiar parody-mouth pattern I had noticed that morning; but the climax had been a tremendous machete blow directly to the crown of the bald head which had released, in one great sweep from base of skull to forehead, a three-inch ruffle of brains. His arms were extended outward, and his hands had been hacked off. An elderly man, his face pressed close to the body, caught my stare, smiled, and shrugged, as if to say, "I didn't take them!" Then, as my eyes moved to a bloody machete he cradled, he said aloud, "We must look for more game tonight!"

Around the smashed car, the people were pushing in upon the body, eager to talk:

"We are *flattered* to see you," a young man in a T-shirt, makeshift club in hand, kept saying, to nods from those beside him.

"You must understand that we are able now to watch over our neighborhood," another young man said, in halting French. "You must understand that we are civilized." The car had come on fast, he said, careering into the square (we had heard the tires). As the people had closed in around it, the driver—"the Macoute"—had waved a revolver but had had no chance to use it before the mob dragged him from the car. How did they know he was a Macoute?

Angry protestations. Hadn't he had a gun?

Yes, I said, but perhaps he had panicked on seeing the crowd, and tried to defend himself?

Well, in any case, he was "unknown in the neighborhood."

"You must understand that we are *civilized*," the young man said again, to approving nods. "We waited for the car to come."

"We were forced to do this," an old man said. "The government forced us to do this."

"We'd had *enough*," a woman said fiercely.

Others repeated with her, "*We'd had enough!*"

"We joined together to protect ourselves," a man said, and then, leaning forward, explained, with patient emphasis, "When I am hit, it causes pain. I learn to hit back."

Then why not go to the source—perhaps to Désinor's house, or Claude Raymond's?

"No, no!"—vehemently. I had got it all wrong. "We don't involve ourselves in political things."

All at once, the crowd was running, stampeding across the square, and we were pressed against our car. More shooting in the distance, more shouting, then a siren, whining its way closer.

Cautiously, we drove back through the neighborhood, from one barricade to another, past the silent people on their steps, past the young men with machetes standing like statues on their corners, past the little group dancing the merengue, and the silent footballers still playing, a wrecked car serving as barricade and goal. When we neared the hotel gate, we found the tall, thin man still there, striding back and forth in his ragged dress, chanting into the darkness. As we passed around the barricade, he halted and said softly, in a raspy, high-pitched voice, "We have done good work tonight—at last."

BY THE TIME WE CREPT out again, just after dawn, he had vanished, as had most of the barricades in the now deserted streets. In the murky gray light of the square, only the smashed car remained, seeming very small now. The corpse had disappeared.

Driving through the waking city, we found the night's other victims. On the Grande Rue, a clump of chattering passersby marked a mutilated corpse: a well-known Macoute from the *quartier*, the excited people said, Luc Altidor, known as Café Amè—Bitter Coffee. Last night, he had appeared after midnight, gasoline can in one hand, revolver in the other. But his neighbors had been ready. A snickering young man gestured to where the corpse, naked now but for a shredded T-shirt, had been castrated, then pointed across the street, where a crowd of laughing people were parading above their heads in triumph the missing bits of flesh.

In the huge, swampy shantytown of Cité Soleil, crowds surrounded two partly dismembered corpses, which lay next to an almost unrecognizable jeep. "They were working for Namphy," a young man told me, pointing to one of the bodies. "He was getting a bag of rice and fifty dollars every month. We made him talk before we killed him." But as I looked at the jeep—a thirty-thousand-dollar vehicle pounded to rubble by a mob of frenzied people, few of whom saw a hundred dollars in a good year—I noticed a distinctive marking and, leaning closer, saw printed there "Corvington Courier & Escort Security Service." Wasn't it possible that these private security guards had driven uncomprehending into this rabid, frightened crowd, and panicked when their uniforms didn't show the people that they were making a terrible mistake? The question remained open for several days (until members of the Cité Soleil neighborhood brigade appeared on Télé Nationale to apologize for their unfortunate error); but to the celebrants in that early morning it was a victory. As we made our way slowly through the narrow streets, a smiling market woman shouted at the *blans*, "Tell America Cité Soleil is doing its work!"

"During this crisis, the people have shown a great maturity," Marc Bazin intoned gravely at a press conference that morning. "In their vast majority, the Haitian people have made their peace with Jean-Claude Duvalier and his family. And those who want to block this election will fail—because the people want the election and there is no way to stop it."

What about the government, the army?

"The government has an air of powerlessness," Bazin said carefully, after a significant pause, "but we don't know if it's incompetence, impotence, even indifference."

Shortly before, in the heart of the commercial cacophony of the Route de Delmas, we had passed a burned vehicle that proved to be an army jeep.

Three intruders had come in it early that morning. They wore civilian clothes, but one brandished an army I.D. card. They fled before the neighborhood committees, taking refuge in a "Macoute house," from which they managed, with guns, to hold off the crowd until, according to several people, "twenty or so soldiers came in a truck" and rescued them.

Which proved—what? Only that some officers were definitely helping the Macoutes. But if the army as an institution was ostentatiously keeping its nose out of things, as the American diplomat had suggested, then perhaps—perhaps—the elections could come off.

At the new council headquarters, where the young people were still practicing on their computers, Louis Roy told me, "The army is waiting. It will let the Duvalierists and the neighborhood committees fight it out, let the terrorism continue. It's all a show for the Americans, to convince them that only the army is able to keep order in the country."

When I passed the mangled Macoute on my way back along the Grande Rue, the remains, now less feet and hands, were surrounded by a swarm of photographers. By early afternoon, when I was heading for the bustling Iron Market downtown (into which, moments before, four men had casually strolled, only to draw automatic weapons and fire into the crowd), the corpse had been dragged to the middle of the busy boulevard and set afire, to the cheers of a small crowd. Half an hour later, as I headed to the Hôpital Général (at least four people had been badly wounded in that shooting), the corpse was still burning. And an hour later, as I walked down the steps of the capital's main morgue (one of the Iron Market victims had died), an ambulance pulled up and two overworked attendants carefully extracted a stretcher with the carbonized, scattered, almost unidentifiable last remains of Café Amè, the neighborhood Macoute.

THAT EVENING'S TELEVISION had the usual strange jumble of news shows and interview programs: a talk with a presidential candidate; film of the Iron Market shootings; increasingly urgent appeals from the council ("We need trucks to transport the ballots into the provinces, people to drive and to provide security").

Then came a bizarre interview with another presidential candidate, the usually mild-mannered law professor Grégoire Eugène, who took the occasion to lash out at the council, claiming that it was infested with leftists controlled by Gourgue; that it favored the Front National and therefore was incapable of running a fair election; that "peasants or fellows with only basic education" would be easily tricked into voting however those running the polls wanted them to. And, he hinted, the neighborhood *brigades de vigilance* were in fact controlled by the council—or, at least, run by those on the left who also ran the council.

The argument itself was just another version of the classic Duvalierist attack, denouncing the elections as what one frustrated candidate called, in a felicitous phrase, a *coup d'état des urnes*—a ballot-box coup d'état. It was strange to be hearing it from Eugène, who was a founder of the Social Christian Party and a longtime Duvalier opponent. But it was clear now that, although he was desperate to become president ("Grégoire," an American diplomat told me with a sigh, "Grégoire's for rent"), he had little following. He was, then, just the respectable but malleable sort the officers might have preferred had they been in a position to choose a *président marionette*. And what Eugène was sketching out, I realized as he concluded his scathing attack, was the perfect rationale for a real coup d'état.

After this interview, the programming was interrupted, and a long typed announcement scrolled slowly up the screen: "The situation has been aggravated by the appearance of groups of peasants known as *comités de vigilance*, which . . . only serve to sow confusion and to render the task of the forces of order more difficult. . . . In these conditions, the Minister believes it is his duty to remind [Haitians] that the maintenance of order and public security is the direct and exclusive responsibility of the armed forces of Haiti. . . . Major General Williams Régala." The army had at last weighed in.

In the dark, deserted streets of the capital, the troops were moving out. From a small covered carport in front of the Holiday Inn, we watched truckloads of soldiers pass by, rounding the front of the spotlit National Palace, circling the Champ de Mars. Around midnight, shooting began, and we tried to follow its progress, but tonight there was no clanging of machetes, no low moaning, no chanting, and we didn't dare to venture out.

At dawn, it did not take long to see that everything had changed. On a little street in Carrefour Feuilles we found our first body: a heavyset man lying face down in a mud puddle, his arms outstretched, the blood on his shirt still bright red. In his back were four entry wounds, closely grouped, and only his own digging footprints marked the mud: He had apparently been shot with an automatic weapon as he tried to run away, probably from a car or a jeep, and probably less than an hour before. This time, there were no onlookers eager to talk. People hurried by, the women balancing buckets of water on their heads, the men carrying their bundles, reluctant even to look at the man face down in the mud. Who was he? Did you know him? Not even a word in reply now; just uneasy glances and a mumbled "*Pa konnin*"—"Don't know."

At the corner of Dessalines and the Rue Chareron, amid a group of silent people, we found a young man lying—also shot in the back, also very recently. A woman approached, crying, and shrieked when she saw the body. It was her son; she was quickly pulled away. An old man told me quietly that soldiers in an army truck had shot him. No one else would say a word. Two blocks down, another small, silent crowd surrounded the body of a skinny old man: He was curled up on his side, blood staining his white shirt, a red wool cap still on his head. He, too, had died very recently, in this early-morning sweep meant to ensure that Haitians on their way to work would not miss the message. When I asked who had done this, I got no answer until, finally, a man burst out, "It was the soldiers! They were alone in the streets."

ON THE AVENUE Martin Luther King, not far from the airport, a neatly dressed man in his early thirties lay with a neat tattoo of bullet holes etched up his spine and neck. The crowd of murmuring people surrounding him suddenly broke apart and ran in a panic, and I turned to find an army truck approaching. But the soldiers passed by, with only a few mildly interested glances at the corpse and a few stern looks at the fleeing crowd.

Back in Carrefour Feuilles, a handful of people stood near some porch steps, at the top of which was posed a slumped and ghoulish figure: a cadaver, his black face painted as if with some dirty theatrical whiteface, glinting metal nails protruding from his nostrils. Here, instead of just driving off, the killers obviously hadn't been able to resist having a bit of fun. So there sat the white-faced corpse as the residents of Carrefour Feuilles hurried by, trying not to look. Had this, too, been the work of the soldiers, intent on driving home to the people that "the maintenance of order and public security is the direct and exclusive responsibility of the armed forces"?

That Thursday, for the first time all week, there was no daytime terror in the capital. As darkness fell, cautious, determined young men pushed open the gates of the council building, looked carefully about, then signaled, and big trucks rumbled slowly out into the street, carrying cartons of ballots to cities and villages around the country. Around midnight, the shooting began.

Friday morning, though, there were no bodies. The army had indeed put down the brigades—but to what purpose? The soldiers would not countenance the challenge of the neighborhood committees, but would they let the election come off? In Cité Soleil, just after dawn, kerchiefed women were lined up before the tank truck that sold water to the slum dwellers, each in turn paying her ten cents and then walking off slowly, effortlessly, majestically, the big sloshing bucket balanced on her head. The women were stocking up for the weekend, not knowing what would happen.

Wandering down the black-earth streets of the vast slum, stepping over the sewage ditches, threading our way through the labyrinthine passageways that separated the sheet-metal hovels, we asked the people crouching in the doorways about the voting. But the soldiers had been there the night before, walking down these streets, emptying their automatic weapons into the air or into the dirt, and the people were frightened.

In the stinking quarter called Cité Carton (Cardboard City), a man told me shyly that he would vote for Sylvio Claude, and another brightened and agreed: Sylvio, the poor black man, the tap-tap driver who had lived through Duvalier's torture—"They beat him, put him in prison." In the swampy section called Brooklyn, a skinny, shirtless young man who was feeding old automobile parts into a caldron of molten metal, making pots to be sold at the market, wiped the sweat off his brow, dug a paper out of his pocket, and thrust it at me: "He, he will be our next president!" It was the poster of Sylvio ("Here Is the Martyr!"), the squat, square-jawed man in the thick spectacles and ill-fitting cheap suit who had declared to me two days before that only he, Sylvio Claude, was a *candidat authentique*, "authentic" meaning, in the peculiar color code of Haitian politics, not just "man of the people" but *black*—the true black of the masses.

That afternoon, Ernst Mirville, the council president, conceded, to a room packed with journalists, "The council has had many difficulties, and many of the technical problems derived from the political ones." The latter, he said, could be easily summarized: "The government and the Council do not see things the same way. The council is a completely new institution—I conceive of it as a revolutionary institution in Haitian politics."

AT DAWN THE NEXT DAY, the day before the election, some colleagues and I waited quietly in our car at a crossroads north of the capital until, rumbling out of the ground fog like a great sea monster, a big tractor-trailer emerged on the road before us. From its cab the driver waved nervously, for he was carrying dangerous cargo: cartons of ballots marked for the Artibonite Valley, one of the "hottest" areas of the country. Several council trucks had been attacked during the last few days. We fell in behind him as he cautiously headed north, passing through Cabaret, through paddy fields in the Artibonite, past a series of gasoline-drum-and-sapling roadblocks—unmanned at this hour, as we had hoped.

At the election bureau in Gonaïves, a crowd was waiting; amid much shouting and running about, a score or so of young men hurriedly unloaded the big truck, transferring some of the cartons to a smaller one for the trip into the Artibonite. Soon we were on the dirt road to Verrettes; the sun was up, and we were enveloped in a moving cloud of dust that entirely covered three straw-hatted Haitians who sat with their legs dangling from the truck's open back. Here and there, peasants working in the fields straightened, machetes in hand, to watch the truck pass; they knew what it carried. When we stopped, however, they would not speak. One wrinkled old man, almost toothless, his bare feet buried in wet mud, mumbled in response to every question, general and specific, the classic words of the Haitian peasant confronted with an outsider, who, well intentioned or not, can only bring him trouble: "*M'fè pa politik*"—"I'm not interested in politics."

In Verrettes, young men, watched over by a local priest, rapidly unloaded the cartons, handing them over one by one to a small cinder-block building, where they were neatly stacked. The town seemed very tense: People watched the proceedings from their houses, and a young soldier in olive green, a carbine slung over his shoulder, stood silently by, looking uncomfortable.

Would there be trouble tomorrow?

"Everything will pass in orderly fashion" was all he would say, over and over. A middle-aged man wearing wire rimmed glasses, who was directing the unloading, would say only, "We are determined to do the elections efficiently—and without the army." He would not give his name.

As we left, we passed an army jeep cruising slowly ahead of its trail of dust. A few miles away, in the village of Borel, a small blue pickup rumbled past crammed with eight soldiers, all looking warily out, their guns at the ready. Along the road, people stood like statues before tiny mud houses, or leaned over the peculiar green fences (formed of a strange succulent that grew heavily over a wooden frame) that separated their bare yards from the dirt road. All watched tensely as the soldiers passed.

We pulled to a stop near a group of villagers and were surrounded by people anxious to talk. There had been a massacre here, they said excitedly. On Monday, some Macoutes had burned down the local election bureau. Wednesday evening, some soldiers from the Verrettes barracks—they had first taken off their uniform shirts so they couldn't be identified—drove into Borel shooting; they killed a horse and strafed the local church. Later, when the truck they had requisitioned came back, the furious villagers seized it and burned it. Thursday morning, the soldiers returned, accompanied this time by several armed civilians. Without a word, they opened fire on the villagers, killing a fifty-six-year-old man and two youths, aged seventeen and fifteen, and some livestock, and then burned two houses.

"We can't vote, because there is no polling place now," a teenager in a Michael Jackson T-shirt said. "All the people want to vote, but we don't think the army will let us."

We heard the rumble of an approaching vehicle, and the villagers moved away from our car. It was the blue pickup again, moving even more slowly this time. Now two young women were standing among the soldiers in the back, both leaning forward and scanning the scene, occasionally pointing to this or that house. We followed at a distance.

After a mile of halting progress, the truck came to an abrupt stop, and suddenly, in a wholly unexpected burst of movement, the soldiers leaped out, their rifles held high against their chests, fingers on the triggers, and, fanning out, charged a little mud house as if they were assaulting a bunker.

We had pulled up about fifty yards back and got out of the car; now we stood in the middle of the road, transfixed. All at once, the soldiers became conscious of us. They froze in their charge, then turned to face us. Everything seemed to stop: The slender young men in olive green stared at us over their automatic rifles, their faces impassive, and we stared back, pens poised over notebooks, cameras clutched at chest level. No one moved. Finally, very deliberately, the lead soldier moved his rifle in a wide arc, back and forth, at the level of our chests—once, twice, three times. That was all it would take. It would be that easy. They stared for one beat more, then turned, climbed silently back into the truck, joining the two staring female informants, and drove off. We were left flat-footed in the road, fifty yards from the still unmolested house. No one had come out. Whoever had been about to be beaten or killed would have at least a few more minutes to enjoy life in Borel.

As night fell, we returned to Gonaïves, the old City of Independence, where we found Victor Benoit, the Front's senate candidate from Borel, in a small apartment off the main square. He had hidden behind his house when the soldiers came, he said, then fled into the hills, where "the peasants protected me." Then he had traveled secretly, floating down the Artibonite in a banana boat. Now, he told us, the council had just issued a *communique*, canceling the voting in Verrettes and several other towns nearby. "They haven't been able to organize; the polling places have been burned," he said, and he went on, "Here, where the democratic sector is strong, and the Macoute structure remains strong as well, there is a struggle between two worlds: the old Macoute world and the democratic world that is fighting to be born."

AT MIDNIGHT, THE WAR BEGAN. All night long, the machine-gun fire was incessant; it seemed to come from all around us, sometimes from very close. At times we heard large explosions, then what sounded like grenades; then rifle shots; then more automatic fire. On the road, only the occasional jeep, its headlights dark, moved slowly past. Gonaïves seemed to be in the grip of a great battle. At dawn on election day, we drove out cautiously. The streets were mostly deserted. It was in Raboteau, the enormous slum from which the entire popular movement that overthrew Duvalier had emerged, that the night travelers had concentrated their attention: They had strafed houses, burned and smashed the few cars on the streets, set fires here and there.

In front of the squat cinder-block building where we had left the ballots the day before, a noisy crowd had already gathered. It was growing light; one could see where the election bureau's facade had been freshly raked with bullets. But soon the polls would be open, and the people, despite it all, had come to vote.

A few blocks away, we stopped and turned on the radio for the news from the capital. Radio Haiti Inter was utterly silent. So was Radio Soleil. We moved rapidly through the dial. Silence. (Hours earlier, armed men had smashed Radio Haiti Inter with grenades, had machine-gunned Radio Antilles, had blown up Radio Soleil's transmitter.) Only one station, finally, Radio Métropole, seemed to be broadcasting, and it played only marches.

In the distance, suddenly, there was shooting, then screams.

We found the corner in front of the election bureau, which not five minutes before had been crowded with hundreds of jostling people, absolutely deserted. In the middle of the empty street, a white motor scooter lay on its side, one of its wheels still turning. In the intersection, a fire was burning: Four or five of the cartons we had seen delivered the day before had been stacked up, with handfuls of ballots stuffed around them as kindling, and set afire. Through the flames, among the crumpled, charred ballots, I could make out the faces of Marc Bazin and Gérard Gourgue. The fire burned fitfully. Apart from its gentle rustling, there was silence.

I moved to the building and, stepping over the threshold, had time to glimpse the stacked cartons, each with a single ballot taped to its side, and to think, they missed so many, before the shots began. A black sedan, seemingly dropped out of the sky, came hurtling around the corner, guns firing from windows on both sides. I fell down inside the small open vestibule, heard bullets hit the facade, the shots echo. Focusing my eyes on the floor tiles against my nose, I heard the screeching tires fade, and the revved-up engine; then nothing.

As I came out on the porch, locking eyes with my colleagues, who were just emerging from behind a parked car across the street, all of us brushing ourselves off, the black sedan was there again, just as suddenly, just as loudly. I fell face forward on the stoop and heard the bullets strike against the building just above me, *felt* them strike, and felt a shower of plaster dust gently falling on my back and neck.

Again, the car was gone. I got up, ran across the street, and joined my friends, who were crouched behind some pillars. After a few moments, we moved tentatively out into the street, and instantly there were shots, this time single shots, from somewhere overhead: a sniper or snipers in the window of one of the buildings nearby.

It had all been very well prepared. It was clear that no one, not even nosy white journalists, would get near the Gonaïves voting bureau on this election day.

We made a last pass through Raboteau and found people standing warily in their doorways, or huddled together on their porches. There was no more defiance. "Haitians will not vote today!" one man shouted. All the speculation, the musings about whether the elections would come off, the embassy briefings and the candidate interviews and the rest, suddenly seemed absurd; it had all come down to who had the guns and who did not, who was willing to use them and who was not. Passing the mustard-yellow barracks, we saw the soldiers sitting, standing, milling about. They seemed tense, solemn, as they watched us drive by. As we headed into one of the slum's main streets, a woman shouted to her friends, "Here come the Americans to save us!" and there was bitter laughter.

At the town of L'Estère, in the Artibonite, we saw peasants waiting in a long line that snaked past the Church of the Immaculate Conception: women in kerchiefs, men in straw hats—perhaps a hundred of them—all waiting to reach a small shed opposite the church. As we walked toward it, there was shooting, and we flinched, and the crowd laughed and pointed at us in delight. Up on the road, the soldiers were striding by, firing. But here the people would not be frightened.

Inside the shed, five people sat calmly behind old wooden school desks on which stacks of white paper were arranged—more than a score for the presidential candidates alone. Next to the stacks stood three of the gray plastic ballot boxes donated by the Canadians. As I watched, a young man at the head of the line stepped forward, paused, looked around, then said shyly, in a soft voice, "Sylvio." A woman behind the desk picked a paper from one of the stacks and handed it to him. He folded it slowly and put it in one of the boxes, then waited while the poll workers ceremoniously plucked a ballot from each of the remaining stacks and handed them to him, so he could tear them up and throw them in the wastebasket. The woman took his hand and dipped his little finger in a small, rusted can full of red ink. As he left, smiling at his red finger, the next man came forward. I watched for several minutes. Sylvio seemed to be doing rather well.

The voting in L'Estère had begun at 6 A.M., and already seventy-four people had cast their ballots. (A man was marking crosshatches carefully on a scrap of paper.) But hadn't they heard—as we just had, on the one radio station still functioning—that the election had been cancelled? It didn't matter. In L'Estère, the voting would go on.

The trip back to the capital—a lovely and familiar drive, between sea and palm trees, on a beautiful day—was taken at breakneck speed and filled with strange and frightening interruptions: roadblocks manned by grimfaced soldiers, who plainly didn't know what to do with us; a pickup truck carrying a bloody, badly wounded *brigade de vigilance* member (shot by soldiers the night before) and his weeping brother; makeshift roadblocks thrown up by armed and angry men whose loyalties, and purposes, were obscure.

South of Saint-Marc, at Freycinau, we were stopped by a crowd of furious peasants armed with machetes. They were manning one roadblock (a newly felled tree) and were backed up by a second—a tractor-trailer truck jackknifed across the road, which, we realized with a sickening feeling, was the very truck we had escorted north the morning before.

The shouting peasants surrounded our car, smashing it with their machetes, and pulled us out; we raised our hands with our press passes and shouted, "*Journalistes! Journalistes!*" but they were inflamed, frightened, crazy. "*Communistes! Communistes!*" I heard several yell. (Hadn't someone yelled that the past summer, at the political leader as he tried to speak, just before the peasants swarmed over him and hacked him to pieces?) As they were raising their machetes and feinting forward, I caught the eye of an old peasant in a red shirt, who was raising his machete a few feet from me—he didn't seem interested in the press pass I held out in front of my chest like a pitiful shield—and all at once I pictured the handless man lying on the car roof and thought, My God, just like this? In this place? Then: And what a story *that* would make—imagining the photographers jostling about. (I learned only later that a CBS crew had come up behind us in their car and had kept their camera running as it lay on the dashboard, and that the confrontation would appear on the news that night.)

We were still standing paralyzed, press passes against machetes, praying that no one would strike first, when a four-wheel-drive appeared from the other direction. The driver, a well-heeled Haitian, shouted to the peasants, demanded to know what they were doing, told them we weren't Communists, and persuaded them to let us go. The disgruntled peasants demanded money, and took a few dollars and a camera or two before letting us proceed slowly around the big truck.

AT DAWN ON THAT ELECTION MORNING, Port-au-Prince had been blanketed in gray smoke. On the grounds of the National Palace, the troops of the Presidential Guard were drawn up in their morning muster, receiving orders from their commander. On their patrols this fateful day, Colonel Charles Louis told them carefully, they were "not to interfere" and, above all, "not to fire on 'the cars' in the street, no matter what you see"—an order that, according to the Guardsman who later described this scene, "everyone understood to mean not to interfere with the attacks."

A few blocks away, armed men were invading the Sacré Coeur, smashing the altar and beating the priests and several worshippers with machetes and rifle butts. Outside the home of General Claude Raymond, a mysterious Sunday-morning traffic jam had formed, as a contingent of four-wheel-drives struggled to make its way through the general's narrow gate. A young European woman, driving down the street in her own jeep, became caught up in the jumble; an angry driver cursed and, as she passed the gate, shot her in the back.

Not long afterward, near one of the busiest corners of the city, where the Avenue John Brown, sloping up toward Pétionville, meets the Avenue Martin Luther King, a great crowd of men surged forward, moving down the main streets and transforming a pleasant, fairly prosperous neighborhood into a bloody anarchy that hadn't been seen since the heyday of Papa Doc.

Most of the men were armed with machetes and clubs, though some had guns, and they were smashing cars and beating people who fled before them. In the midst of this roiling mob moved a gray Daihatsu Charade and a blue Suzuki jeep, which circled methodically as the men inside fired weapons from the windows. The cars were "like the center point . . . of the Macoutes' activities there," said Geoffrey Smith, an Australian freelance photographer who, with a Haitian friend, had found himself in the neighborhood. "The gray Charade was just circling around, firing and circling, as if it were a radio-controlled toy."

On a corner, a small white car had been run up on a sidewalk, its windshield shattered, its driver, slashed with a machete, lying dead beside it, his wife shot and wounded. Not far from the corner of John Brown and Martin Luther King, three pedestrians, presumably on their way to vote, were shot where they stood. Suddenly, an army truck loaded with soldiers turned on to the Avenue John Brown. And there, not far from the Ruelle Vaillant—a cul-de-sac at the end of which lay the École Argentine de Bellegardes, a little gingerbread school that today had become a polling place crowded with voters—the army truck pulled up next to the gray Charade, and the car's occupants chatted for a moment with the soldiers. (Whether these were

Presidential Guardsmen, punctiliously following their orders "not to interfere," or troops of the Dessalines Battalion is not known.) Whereupon the soldiers drove off and the mob of Macoutes, with their machetes and clubs and guns, moved down the Ruelle Vaillant.

What happened next was sketched out, as so often that week, by the outline of the corpses. As the first victims were shot on the road leading to the school, the people waiting to vote—who, sheltered in the school's closed-in courtyard, had been oblivious of the chaos on the street outside—began to run away in terror. Finding no exit, they poured into four tiny, open-air classrooms to the right, pushing and clawing, burrowing under the benches, crouching behind cartons, pulling over them any furniture or boxes that came to hand.

And so the Macoutes, advancing steadily on the terrified, unarmed people, could kill at leisure. When the men with machine guns had emptied their weapons, their machete-wielding colleagues moved in, hacking off limbs, decapitating at least one woman, turning the small courtyard for a few nightmarish moments into a howling slaughterhouse.

Then the men were gone and strangely, were almost immediately followed by two fire trucks, bristling with soldiers, and three ambulances. Geoffrey Smith was one of the first to reach the school. The army's subsequent arrival was "very quick, too quick," Smith told me. "They didn't want witnesses, you see."

The plan seemed to be to remove most of the bodies immediately, leaving just a few, "to make people believe only this happened"—that is, to lessen the scale of the massacre. The bodies would be whisked away and would disappear into a secret grave. The Ruelle Vaillant would be a massacre but, at least for the world press, a small one—four or five people, perhaps.

Smith and others, however, chanced to be nearby. Moving from room to room, they saw about twenty people, shot to pieces. In one classroom, in particular, Smith said, "The people had huddled around the wall, and in two other classrooms there were people underneath the benches. They'd heard shooting in the street, they'd run in here thinking it was safe. But because they were all literally around the wall, it was just a simple matter of spraying them with gunfire. The two women who had been running the elections were the persons with their faces shot half off, lying there with the pamphlets and everything all over the floor. In the room with the most people—about ten—there was one woman screaming in the corner, and another woman over near the far wall was just . . . shaking around. And as the soldiers moved from room to room they found more people still alive, who were pretty well buried under the school desks and the bodies, still lying there in the pools of blood.

"There was such an ambience of palpable evil and cold, cold fear. I mean, the poor people who'd somehow survived were there screaming simply out of a state of absolute shock. I'm talking about people who were stood in front of a wall and were sprayed with bullets, and were then lying in a mass of bodies. That fear pervaded the whole area—an extremely strong ambience, as if an evil plague had swept through, like a wind or something."

By this time, with the camera crews and photographers arriving, the ambulances, packed to capacity with corpses and a few survivors, drove off, and the soldiers left. As the journalists stood amid the remaining bodies, a green Volvo station wagon pulled up, and four men got out and started shooting. The journalists fled toward the school, retracing the bloody path taken by the voters less than half an hour before, then struggled in terror to scale the walls behind the school. The Macoutes moved forward, firing steadily. Smith was shot in the leg. Three members of an ABC News crew were wounded. A Dominican cameraman, just getting out of his car, raised his hands in bewildered surrender and was shot at point-blank range, collapsing and then (as one fleeing witness, looking back over his shoulder, glimpsed him) "literally swimming, hand over hand, in a lake of blood, groaning, 'Help me, help me.'" He died later in the hospital. A photographer, Jean-Bernard Diederich, who was scrambling over a high wall, looked back and saw a man taking aim. "I couldn't see his face," he said, "but it was definitely a soldier." Several witnesses later claimed to have recognized the olive-green-clad troops of the Dessalines Battalion.

BY MIDMORNING, Port-au-Prince, with its almost 1 million inhabitants, had taken on the uniquely sinister aspect of a great metropolis that stands unaccountably deserted under a shadowless light. Only in front of the cathedral was there a human presence: a young man lying in a little pool of blood, staring up at the bright sun. Arms splayed, shirt torn, this peaceful, sun-warmed corpse had seemingly become the capital's sole resident.

His living compatriots, having been transported with awful abruptness back to a time that many of them remembered all too well, cowered indoors. Hiding as well were the members of the Electoral Council, including its president, Ernst Mirville, who, shortly after the Ruelle Vaillant massacre, had telephoned Radio Métropole from an undisclosed location to announce that the elections had been postponed "to a later date."

For Haitians, the limits to wholesale brutality—the unflinching daylight massacre of innocents—that had been drawn since the fall of Duvalier had in a few minutes been swept away. The streets of the capital empty at midday, the sirens wailing, the corpses of men, women, and children lying in pools of blood, all the taut aftermath of a convulsion of unbridled violence—"All this brings back Duvalier, the father, I mean," a well-to-do woman told me over the telephone. "People who were here then are flipping out now. Those who can are trying to get out. You see," she said after a pause, "*you* think it was a massacre, but this was just a normal day under Duvalier."

So the people stayed inside, where, in the afternoon, they could see an angry General Namphy appear on Télé Nationale to launch, hours after the massacre, a stinging attack on the Electoral Council. His face ominous behind his tortoiseshell glasses, his deep voice almost shouting as he struggled to master his stutter, the general denounced the council for "inviting foreign powers to meddle in the internal affairs of the country." He had decided "to put an end" to the council but vowed his "determination to conduct to the end . . . the democratic process which must culminate in the installation on February 7, 1988, of a president freely elected by the Haitian people." Those final words—"*librement elu par le peuple haïtien!*"—the general barked out, emphasizing each syllable, while he stared into the camera with a baleful grimace, as if daring his viewers to challenge him.

That evening, before the shooting began, a tired representative of the "foreign powers" to which the General had referred appeared at the Holiday Inn before the assembled journalists, who assailed him with angry questions. Jeffrey Lite, the American Embassy spokesman, looked wan and pale as he announced that the United States had "terminated all military assistance to Haiti." This amounted to $1.2 million, most of it already spent. An additional $106 million, which, together with the World Bank and International Monetary Fund money tied to it, floated the Haitian economy, "was being reviewed." (That night, Washington announced the cutoff of the bulk of that—about $62 million, or all but "humanitarian aid," which was mostly food shipments.)

To the cascade of questions Lite had little new to say. The United States had supported the "rapid, orderly, and peaceful transition to democracy in Haiti." And while it had been "apparent that the government and the council were at loggerheads for many months—still, we thought . . ." His voice trailed off.

Could it be that the embassy, with all its sources, had had no warning of the attacks?

"Today," Lite said slowly. Then he paused, closing his eyes briefly. "Today was a surprise."

And now not only had the whole jerry-built transition so carefully shepherded by the embassy collapsed in a spectacular mess but the Americans found themselves forced to do what they had dreaded doing, even as a last resort: They were forced to cut off their aid. "We've fired that bullet now," an American diplomat told me, with a sigh, several days later. "Now that chamber—the biggest chamber—is empty." The Americans, having carried out their threat, had nothing else to threaten. And General Namphy had nothing else to lose.

Namphy would now pick his own council. That meant that the army would be running elections and would control their result, which in turn meant that the "popular" candidates—not only Gourgue but probably Claude, Déjoie, and Bazin as well—seeing in such an arrangement nothing for themselves except the destruction of their popular credibility, would decline to run.

Sunday night, truckloads of soldiers moved out into the city. On that and subsequent nights, the shooting was heavy. In Carrefour Feuilles and the other slums where the *brigades de vigilance* had been strongest, the soldiers moved in in force, emptying their clips and rounding up any young men they found. There were persistent rumors—never confirmed—of secret executions, even massacres, in Fort Dimanche. And why not? After all, it had happened many times before.

DURING THE WEEKS that led up to a second election, on January 17, the process of exclusion accelerated. Sylvio Claude was accused of urging an American invasion—a lethal charge in Haiti. (In reality, he had asked for an international force to observe any future vote.) Télé Nationale played and replayed film reports of ballot-stuffing—the heart of a campaign to discredit the November 29th election and, thereby, all four major candidates. The four candidates, for their part, made it clear that they wouldn't participate in Namphy's election. ("We don't oppose elections," Bajeux told me. "We oppose elections with this government. The country is now being run by a herd of murderers.") Defiantly, they issued a call for a general strike against the government. But the people did not halt their business in a great show of revulsion against Namphy and the election violence; they did not respond to the four candidates who claimed to represent them. No doubt, as Bazin told me, "They were scared to death." But there was something more. "After the uprising failed last summer," a young Liberation priest told me, "the people saw the elections as the only way to uproot the Macoutes. It was like a religion." And now, in a few moments of horror, the Macoutes had proved that religion false, powerless. And they had lost their faith. "The people are psychologically and economically exhausted," Michel Soukar, a leading figure in the Front, conceded. "We don't think the people have the means to get rid of the Namphy government unless they have help on the international level—as they did to get Duvalier out."

Seeking "help on the international level"—to isolate the Namphy regime, and force it out before it could hold its own elections—quickly became the strategy of the four candidates, thus, paradoxically, lending some truth to the government propaganda. Déjoie flew to the United States, met in Washington with administration and congressional figures, and delivered a rousing address to a crowded meeting hall on the Upper West Side of Manhattan, where several hundred Haitians of the diaspora, incongruous in heavy coats and scarves, delighted in his colorful Creole and bold rhetoric. Of the coming election he said, "Any candidate [who wins] would be chosen by the army, and he wouldn't be able to govern, I'll tell you that. We will not accept this government! We will continue our fight!" It was like the old days, when his father, in the same city, had said the same things about Duvalier.

"THERE IS NO ALTERNATIVE—it's as simple as that," an American diplomat said, when asked why the embassy was ignoring Déjoie's call for further sanctions, why it was letting the Namphy electoral process run its course.

"Actually," a second diplomat put in, leaning back in his chair, "from Duvalier's departure on, that fact has defined the situation here: There is no alternative."

The first diplomat paused and took a spoonful of grapefruit. The three of us were sitting in the pleasant, leafy garden of the first diplomat's house, not very far from the Ruelle Vaillant. "The embassy has been pushing to get the four big candidates together for a long time," he said. "Finally, in mid-December we received the four candidates at the embassy. We said, 'Look, we'd like to do something for you. But you have to prove you're leaders in order for us to back you—leaders as well as vote-getters. You have to show that the 90 percent of Haitians who supposedly follow you will really hearken to your call.'"

"And they couldn't do that," the second man said. "At least one strike would have had to stick, but the strikes were failures, jokes. These guys have voters, not followers."

The first diplomat leaned forward. "Look, in the end, politics is compromise, cooperation, coalition-building—and, to be frank, Haitians have never shown a talent for any of those," he said. "What is it they say? 'There's a bit of Macoute in every Haitian.'" He took a sip of coffee. "So now, of course, all you hear them saying is 'It's the *Americans*' fault.' The centrist politicians say, 'We know you Americans could make it stop, you could make Namphy behave and the Macoutes disappear, if only you'd apply *pressure*.'" I thought of Bajeux. "And the radicals say, 'This whole slaughter here is your fault, because, in fact, they did it with your support.' And the hardliners—within the government, in the army, wherever—they say, 'Why the hell aren't you Americans supporting us? I mean, we're fighting Communists here!'"

"Of course, in the end I don't think Mr. Castro is very interested in Haiti," the second diplomat said. "This country is like a very old patient in a hospital, and he's on the machine, but even though the doctors see no sign of recovery, they don't pull the plug—they try to do what they can. So we tried to do that, and maybe we should have done it differently. But that might not have worked, either. Intervention is a very complicated thing, and it usually doesn't work out the way you think."

ON DECEMBER 30, Professor Leslie Manigat appeared on television. He made, everyone agreed afterward, an extraordinary speech—elegant in language, brilliant in argument. Manigat noted that the army "constitutes, in any case, an institution without which—still less against which—no workable political solution can be found." He mocked the strategy of the so-called four major candidates—noting that though each claimed to control 60 to 70 percent of the vote, making their collective support at least 240 percent of the Haitian electorate, they had been unable to bring off a general strike a week after the massacre. Then this man who had been so long in exile, so long a fighter for Haitian democracy, announced that his party—"the party of the opening" ("*le parti de l'ouverture*"), punning on the name of the country's founder, Toussaint Louverture—had decided to take part in the army's elections.

During the first weeks of January, the discussion came to center on whom the officers would choose. Would it be Grégoire Eugène, a mild and seemingly malleable man? Or Hubert de Ronceray, who had served many years as Jean-Claude Duvalier's minister of labor and social welfare before jumping ship to become an "opposition leader" several months before the dictator fell? Or Leslie Manigat, the prestigious intellectual?

On January 17, the voting was very light throughout Port-au-Prince; in many places, the polls seemed to be empty or nearly so all day. Outside one small polling place, I heard music and, glancing inside, saw a radio sitting on a desk with its stacks of ballots, next to which two soldiers were dancing the merengue, holding their automatic rifles above their heads as they thrust their hips. North of the city, my colleagues and I found near-empty polling places as well, though in Saint-Marc we watched a group of young men— few of them looked old enough to vote—push forward to cast their ballots in a little school. Several objected angrily when the poll worker tried to mark their fingers with red dye. Curious, we followed them as they piled into a pickup truck and drove to a pretty house a mile or so away and disappeared inside. When they reemerged, they were all wiping their hands: They had washed off the red. They piled into the truck to vote again.

They were voting for Manigat—a fact that was not hard to discern, for, as at most places that day, the ballots were distributed outside the polls by young men who stood in a group and competed for the attention of the prospective voter. When he had marked his ballot, the voter handed it to a poll worker, who thereupon scrutinized it, often announcing the choice, and placed it in the ballot box.

That morning, in a polling place across from the National Palace, a soldier had told me his colonel had given an order: "Manigat is the man of the army. Vote for Manigat." The next day, a bitter Grégoire Eugène said to me, "I had known two days before that the elections would be a joke. I gave fifty thousand of my ballots to a candidate for mayor for him to have distributed around Port-au-Prince. Then I learned he had Manigat's ballots distributed instead. I called him and was told, 'As an old soldier, I had to follow orders.' We assumed he was referring to the head of the army."

Most Haitians seemed to agree with Eugène that the elections were "a joke"; but what, exactly, made them so? That there had obviously been cheating? True, but it was impossible to tell how much. That a number of evidently popular candidates had boycotted the vote? Yes, but they had done so of their own accord. That so few people had voted? Yes, but those people, too, had acted voluntarily, and, in any event, the government later claimed that 35 percent of the Haitians had voted, insisting that in the provinces, especially in places one could not reach in a day without a helicopter, the turnout had been very high indeed. And, of course, it could have been true: There was no way to tell, just as there was no real way to be sure, in a country without polls, with few roads, and with an illiterate population, that the four "major candidates" still controlled more than 90 percent of the vote.

And so, behind the closed doors of Namphy's council headquarters— journalists had been hustled out at gun point—the counting went on, and on. And finally the council members announced that they had completed their work and had determined that in this difficult, dangerous election, held under such perilous conditions, one man had somehow managed to secure a majority—miraculously, a bare 50.27 percent, thus making a runoff unnecessary. The victor was an intellectual, an academic of international reputation, the scion of a distinguished family, a man all Haitians could be proud of—and on whom other countries, in time, might well look kindly.

Thus, on February 7, 1988, the second anniversary of the glorious fall of the dictator Jean-Claude Duvalier, in the sullen, exhausted country, its foreign-aid lifelines severed, its economy collapsing, its people angry, Leslie F. Manigat, the master of the *conjoncture*, came to power.

The New Yorker, November 27, 1989

The Legacy

A FEW WEEKS AFTER the fall of Jean-Claude Duvalier, in February, 1986, the statue of Christopher Columbus presiding over the harbor of Port-au-Prince was seized and thrown into the sea by persons unknown, who left fastened on the empty pedestal a sheet of paper with a simple scrawled message: *"Pa de blans en Hayti!"*

In Creole, the word *blans* means foreigner as well as white: Haitians applying the slogan "No foreigners in Haiti!" to Christopher Columbus is a little comedy, and one that begins to convey a sense of the Byzantine inter-twinings of Haitian history, culture, and ideology; for when Columbus landed, in 1492, on the north coast of the island of Hispaniola (the western third of which is now called Haiti), his arrival predated that of the first black by almost a quarter century. It was only after the Spanish had virtually exter-minated some half-million native Arawak Indians through forced labor, unfamiliar disease, and indiscriminate brutality that they imported their first African slaves—an expedient authorized by the Spanish Crown partly at the urging of Bartolomé de las Casas, a Dominican missionary priest who was appalled at the treatment of the Indians. When, three centuries later, the descendants and successors of those African slaves wrenched control of the country from Napoleon's troops, they would rename the now independent colony of Saint-Domingue with an Arawak word, *hayti*—"mountainous"—which, apart from a few antiquities, is pretty much all that remains of the island's first inhabitants.

In the Musée du Pantheon National, a sleek, modern, mostly under-ground structure built by Jean-Claude Duvalier across the street from the National Palace, the visitor is confronted with rusty iron manacles, chains, branding masks, muzzles, pokers, and other implements, carefully arranged behind a sheet of glass. "For three centuries," reads a nearby placard, "our ancestors were subjected to the humiliation of being bought and sold at pub-lic markets, branded like beasts, and exposed to forced labor and punish-ment of an indescribable horror. . . . Thanks to the sweat of these slaves, the

47

Western part of the island, which little by little was occupied by buccaneers and baptized Saint-Domingue, became the richest colony of the New World, accounting for one-third of the commerce of the French Kingdom."

That figure may be an understatement. During the nine decades between Saint-Domingue's official passing to French hegemony under the Treaty of Ryswick, in 1697 (the eastern part of the island remained under Spanish control, as Santo Domingo), and the outbreak of the French Revolution, in 1789, it became the world's richest, most productive, and most coveted colony—an enormous slave-powered export factory that produced almost two-thirds of the world's coffee, almost half of its sugar, and large proportions of its cotton, indigo, and cocoa. In 1789, Henry Adams wrote, "Paris swarmed with Creole families who drew their incomes from the island, among whom were many whose political influence was great; while, in the island itself, society enjoyed semi-Parisian ease and elegance, the natural product of an exaggerated slave-system combined with the manners, ideas, and amusements of a French proprietary caste."[1]

By that revolutionary year, the colony's forty thousand or so white Frenchmen—landed planters and a middle class of tradesmen and suppliers—were ruling over almost five hundred thousand African slaves. And since blacks on the plantations tended to reproduce at an unnaturally low rate and to die young, and it was thus cheaper for a planter to import an adult African than to "breed" a slave and raise him from birth, as many as two-thirds of the half-million blacks had made "the middle passage" from West Africa to the Caribbean; that is, at the time of the revolution two slaves in three had been born and raised in Africa, spoke an African language, practiced an African religion, and retained vivid memories of a life lived in freedom, which made the brutal life of the plantations all the more painful. Justin Girod-Chantrans, a Swiss traveler who visited the island on the eve of the revolution, gave this description of a slave gang at work:

> They were about a hundred men and women of different ages, all occupied in digging ditches in a cane field, the majority of them naked or covered with rags. The sun shone down with full force on their heads. Sweat rolled from all parts of their bodies. Their limbs . . . fatigued with the weight of their picks . . . strained themselves to overcome every obstacle. A mournful silence reigned. Exhaustion was stamped on every face . . . several foremen armed with long whips moved periodically between them, giving stinging blows to all who, worn out by fatigue, were compelled to take a rest—men or women, young or old.[2]

How did forty thousand whites enforce such discipline on five hundred thousand blacks? By terror: The ugly iron implements now on display in the glass case saw frequent use. The reports of contemporary visitors are filled with accounts of how slaves were lashed and beaten, how they were forced to wear tin masks to prevent them from eating sugarcane, how recalcitrant slaves were maimed or mutilated, or roasted over slow fires, or filled with gunpowder and blown to pieces.

Apart from the whites in the manor houses and towns and the blacks in the fields, there gradually arose a third class in Saint-Domingue, whose numbers grew rapidly, to the point where by the time of the French Revolution they almost equaled those of the whites: the free mulattoes. At the pleasure of his father, a "true mulatto" child could be declared free—a "true mulatto" being defined, in the complicated race theology devised in Saint-Domingue, as the offspring of a "pure white" father and a "pure-black" mother. This system, according to which "colored" offspring were divided into ten classes, depending on the "color mix" of the past seven generations, was set out clearly in the standard contemporary source, the *Description Topographique, Physique, Civile, Politique et Historique de la Partie Francaise de l'Isle Saint-Domingue,* of 1797, by M.L.E. Moreau de Saint-Méry (himself a white or possibly *sang-mêlé* colonial):

noir	0–7 parts white
sacatra	8–23 parts white
griffe	24–39 parts white
marabou	40–48 parts white
mulatre	49–70 parts white
quarteron	71–100 parts white
métif	101–112 parts white
mamelouc	113–120 parts white
quarteronne	121–124 parts white
sang-mêlé	125–127 parts white[3]

Thus, the product of, say, a white man and a *mulâtresse* was a *quarteron*—a result that, as C. L. R. James writes in his 1938 account *The Black Jacobins,* could also be "produced by the white and the *marabou* in the proportion of 88 to 40, or by the white and the *sacatra,* in the proportion of 72 to 56 and so on all through the 128 varieties."[4]

By the late eighteenth century, many mulattoes owned plantations, and a good number had been educated in Europe. As a class, they had become rich and, particularly in the south, powerful. Yet as their power grew they were subject to increasing discrimination from the whites—especially those with less money; at the same time, they hated and feared the blacks, for, as James bluntly puts it, "the advantages of being white were so obvious that race prejudice against the Negroes permeated the minds of the Mulattoes who so bitterly resented the same thing from the whites."

The loyalties of the mulattoes were, perforce, divided: between, on the one hand, their black slave mothers and relatives still working in the fields, with whom they shared the condition of less than full citizenship and the contempt, steadily increasing, of the whites; and, on the other, their white, European fathers, whose culture and way of life the mulattoes envied and imitated, and who, like them, had property to protect, including slaves—property that would be threatened if freedom were to be granted the slaves, on whom, after all, the colony's prosperity was founded. Indeed, the divided loyalties of the mulattoes and the whites' ambivalent attitude toward them—they needed the mulattoes as allies against the slaves, yet to grant them the full citizenship they demanded, to admit that they were truly and completely men, would, by undercutting the ideology of color, seem to lead ineluctably toward granting the black slaves the same—proved to be a critical factor during the political and military maneuverings of the Haitian revolution. And the legacy of those divided loyalties has hovered like a noxious cloud over the history and politics of Haiti.

THE EVENTS MAKING up the Haitian revolution, which lasted, off and on, from 1790 until 1804, were intimately bound up with political developments in the mother country and with France's military campaigns in Europe; it was as if Saint-Domingue served as a kind of funhouse mirror across the Atlantic, complicating and distorting the already complex struggles of revolutionary France. At one time or another during those fourteen years, black slave soldiers fighting for their freedom found themselves battling not only their white masters but the armies of France, Great Britain, and Spain, and both white- and mulatto-led black armies in the south as well. In the end, the glorious revolution would stand as "the only successful slave revolt in history," as all the histories note, yet it effected a bloody and incomplete metamorphosis of the slave system, leaving Haiti not only with its peculiar social structure and violent, autocratic politics but with an entire stock of heroes and symbols that gave flesh to the enduring themes of Haiti's history: brutal repression, often foreign-aided; heroic revolt; miraculous liberation. Each class—each color—reads this chronicle in its own way, and each successive leader aspiring to power is faced with the task of appropriating it.

For the mulattoes, the war began in 1790, when, led by a wealthy planter with good connections to the Friends of the Negro, an abolitionist society in Paris, they demanded that all rights of French citizenship—and the newly christened revolutionary Rights of Man—be granted them (but not the blacks). Their forces were crushed, and the mulatto leaders, whose fine looks, upright bearing, and fiery eloquence had made a great impression in revolutionary Paris, were horribly tortured, broken on the wheel, and beheaded (this operation being performed, as the sentence stipulated, on the opposite side of the parade ground from that on which whites were executed).

For the blacks, the war began the following year, when a series of secret nocturnal vodou gatherings was organized under the leadership of a huge vodou high priest known as Boukman. They culminated in a celebrated meeting during a thunderstorm, in a wood known as Bois Caiman, in the northern mountains above Cap Français (today Cap Haïtian). A few days later, a signal was given, and the slaves rose up, massacred their masters, and fired the plantations across the northern plain, transforming in a night one of the wealthiest agricultural regions of the world into a vast, hellish confla-gration. Boukman's secret vodou gathering has served as a fount of Haitian revolutionary, nationalist, and—sometimes—pro-black, anti-mulatto imagery. It was at Bois Caiman that, as a placard in the Musée du Pantheon National puts it, "*la négritude* rose to its feet for the first time, showing where our first roots lay and marking with its seal the foundation of our eth-nicity and of our culture."

However potent *la négritude*, the masses of unschooled slaves would never have been able to do what they did without the rise of a class of extraordi-nary leaders, and of those none was more extraordinary than Toussaint Lou-verture. Before the revolution, Toussaint Bréda was a privileged slave, a cattle steward, on large northern plantation. An ugly man, short but powerfully built, he had been born in the colony to the son of an African chief and impressed all who met him by his imposing dignity. His skill as a horseman was legendary (he was nicknamed the Centaur of the Savanna), and he had also managed to learn to read. He acquired his military strategy, legend has it, from a close study of Caesar's *Commentaries*.

When the slaves rose up in the north, Toussaint, by now a free man, was in his mid-forties. He joined the slaves a month into the rebellion and quickly became a leader. Maneuvering a fiendishly complicated world where alliances could shift abruptly, often in response to distant events, Toussaint first led his men alone against the colonists; then joined the Spanish, fighting under the banner of the French royalists against the ruling Republicans; and then, some months after Louis XVI was executed in Paris, joined the French Republicans and fought with them to push the Spanish from Saint-Domingue. Finally, Toussaint and his troops were instrumental in clearing the island of the British, who had hoped to profit from France's turmoil by stealing its richest colony.

In 1800, soon after Napoleon became First Consul, Toussaint Louverture (he had adopted this surname in 1793 to mark the "opening" of freedom to the black slaves) became the governor of what officially remained a French colony—but one that made its own laws to govern its own population, which consisted almost entirely of former slaves. Already ruler of the colony in all but name, Toussaint plainly wanted to retain this relationship with France; Napoleon, however, determined to put an end to the upstart, for rea-sons both strategic and personal. It was Toussaint who stood in the way of the First Consul's New World Empire. "Toussaint exercised on [United States] history an influence as decisive as that of any European ruler," Henry Adams wrote. "Before Bonaparte could reach Louisiana he was obliged to crush the power of Toussaint." This circumstance was all the more irritating because observers had begun to point out similarities between the two mili-tary geniuses. Adams again: "The same abnormal energy of body and mind; the same morbid lust for power and indifference to means; the craft and vehemence of temper; the same fatalism, love of display, reckless personal courage . . . [This] parallelism roused Napoleon's anger, and precipitated a conflict which had vast influence on human affairs. . . . Toussaint seemed naturally to ape every action which Bonaparte wished to make heroic in the world's eyes. There was reason to fear that Toussaint would end in making Bonaparte ridiculous; for his conduct was, as it seemed to the First Consul, a sort of negro travesty on the consular *regime*."[5]

In 1801, after Toussaint named himself governor-general for life, Napoleon resolved to put him in his place. In November, he sent a huge fleet to the island, carrying more than ten thousand crack troops under the command of his brother-in-law General Charles-Victor-Emmanuel Leclerc. Their mission was to reconquer the colony, unseat Toussaint, and restore slavery in Saint-Domingue. If France had recognized black rule in Saint Domingue, Napoleon wrote Talleyrand, then "the sceptre of the New World would sooner or later have fall into the hands of the blacks."[6] It was to be a war of counter-revolution.

THE FATE OF THE NEWLY FREED SLAVES rested with Toussaint—and much now else besides. If the blacks were defeated, Adams wrote, "The wave of French empire would roll on to Louisiana and sweep far up the Mississippi." For Napoleon to succeed in his New World ambitions, Toussaint must be removed. "Rid us of these gilded Africans," the First Consul wrote General Leclerc, "and we shall have nothing more to wish."

It was not to be; General Leclerc and the majority of his troops would soon be dead. By the time the war ended, in 1803, with the disembarkation of the bloody remnants of fifty-five thousand French soldiers, the former colony had been devastated and depopulated: Cap Français, Saint-Marc, and many other cities and towns had been burned to the ground; most of the plantations had been destroyed; all but a few of the surviving whites had fled to France or the United States; and a third or more of the blacks were dead. These included Toussaint himself, who died not by force of arms but by treachery, having been lured to a meeting by the French, then captured and shipped back to France, where he succumbed to pneumonia while imprisoned in a fortress in the Juras.

The war had been characterized by astonishing brutality on all sides: Not only were towns and plantations methodically looted and burned but prisoners were regularly tortured and killed and their heads mounted on the walls of stockades or on pikes along the roadsides. Rape and massacre of noncombatants were the rule. According to several accounts, the French used dogs to rip black prisoners to pieces before a crowd assembled in an amphitheatre. During the last, desperate phase of the war, General Jean-Jacques Dessalines, an illiterate and ferocious former field slave, who had succeeded Toussaint as leader, gave his troops a now celebrated order: "*Koupé tet, boulé kay!*"—"Cut off heads, burn houses!"

But when it was over—when General Dessalines had ripped the white middle from the French tricolor to form the Haitian flag, and the French colony of Saint-Domingue had become the independent nation of Haiti—

an astounded world faced an undeniable fact: Half a million illiterate African slaves had defeated the armies of the most powerful nation on earth and created the world's first (and at that time its only) independent black republic. To the nations of Europe and to the United States it was a terrifying and threatening fact, for Haiti was not only the second independent nation in a hemisphere still crowded with the possessions of Britain, France, Portugal, and Spain but a republic of rebellious slaves surrounded by a great number of colonies and one independent nation where slavery remained a basic economic fact of life.

In Europe, the miraculous phenomenon was an inspiration to the Romantics: Wordsworth addressed a celebrated poem to Toussaint, the "miserable Chieftain" ("Though fallen thyself, never to ride again, Live, and take comfort. Thou hast left behind Powers that will work for thee"), and Kleist wrote a famous story, "Betrothal in Santo Domingo." ("Now in 1803, as the world knows, when General Dessalines was advancing against Port-au-Prince at the head of thirty thousand Negroes . . .").[7] The reaction among political leaders, however, was simple panic: To them, Dessalines represented the nightmare of incipient revolution. (A modern historian has aptly dubbed him "the Castro of his time.")

The panic was not discouraged by Dessalines, one of whose first acts as the ruler of independent Haiti was to order the massacre of all the whites remaining on the island. A contemporary observer wrote of "piercing shrieks" that resounded one night as squads of soldiers moved from house to house, killing whole families, and noted that the next day the rivulet running through Cap Français was "literally red with their blood." After the massacre, Dessalines issued a proclamation: "Never again shall colonist or European set foot on this soil as master or landowner. This shall henceforward be the foundation of our constitution." When Haiti's first constitution was written, in 1805, those words were included, and the formal prohibition was retained in successive constitutions until 1918, by which time American Marines had occupied the country. (Before writing the Act of Independence, at Gonaïves, Dessalines's secretary, Boisrond-Tonnerre, had made a famous vow, known to every Haitian since, literate or not: "For our declaration of independence we should have the skin of a white for parchment, his skull for inkwell, his blood for ink, and a bayonet for pen!") The constitution, drawing on both the extreme centralization of the French colonial system and the military instincts of the Haitian leaders, made Dessalines ruler for life, an autocrat with the power to choose his successor. It also tried to head off the imminent conflict between the educated and propertied mulattoes and the newly freed black slaves by declaring that all Haitians, regardless of color, were henceforth to be considered "black," and it formalized Dessalines's earlier nationalization of the plantations, declaring all land the property of the state.

None of these steps—and particularly not the massacre of the whites and the appropriation of French-owned land—did much for the former colony's image abroad, or helped breach its economic and diplomatic isolation. The hemisphere's other revolutionary state, the United States, seemingly a natural ally, refused to recognize its newly independent neighbor, partly because of French pressure but mainly because southerners feared that Haiti's example might influence American slaves. Vice President John C. Calhoun pointed out in 1826, "It is not so much recognition simply, as what must follow it. . . . What would be social relations to a Black minister in Washington? . . . Must his daughters and sons participate in the society of our daughters and sons? . . . Small as these considerations appear to be they involve the peace and perhaps the union of the nation." Calhoun's words were prophetic: "The land of the free" recognized Haiti only in 1862, during the Civil War administration of Abraham Lincoln.

It was during the first two decades of independence in a devastated, isolated country, its rivers clogged with corpses, its fields and towns charred ruins, where the ability to read and technical skills were almost nonexistent, that the peculiar Haitian social structure took shape. The new country's isolation increased its self-absorption and its nationalism, and deepened its internal divisions, cultural and economic, and its suspicion of the colonial powers. The country possessed a ready-made elite, in the mulattoes and smaller number of black freedmen, and to these was added a fabricated one, drawn from the country's new rulers—Dessalines and his fellow black officers. Otherwise, the nation consisted of an illiterate population of Africans who in their years in the New World had known nothing but plantation work under the lash and a decade and a half of apocalyptic war.

During that war, Toussaint had tried to reestablish the export economy by using forced labor on the plantations, many of which were leased to army officers. Now the emperor—not to be outdone by Napoleon, Dessalines had crowned himself Jacques I in October 1804—followed suit, instituting a system of quasi-serfdom, in which military officers again leased the former estates, and worked them with indentured ex-slaves. The workers were legally restricted to specific plantations and were forced to labor in conditions of such harshness that they soon recognized in the system a virtual restoration of slavery, and they began to desert and flee to the mountains in large numbers. There they joined the many communities of *marrons*—runaway slaves who had escaped the plantations in colonial times and become squatters, making their homes on remote slopes and cultivating small subsistence plots.

The members of the new Haitian elite were also dissatisfied with Dessalines's policies, especially his nationalizing of the plantation land, which the mulattoes claimed as their rightful inheritance. The mulattoes rose up in the south. Dessalines, who detested the mulattoes, thundered, "How does it come to pass that since we have chased away the colonists, their children are claiming their property? The Blacks whose fathers are in Africa will then have nothing? Be careful of yourselves, Negroes and Mulattoes . . . the property we have conquered in spilling our blood belongs to all of us; I insist that it be shared with equity."

But Dessalines, whose regime had become increasingly corrupt ("Pluck the chicken, but don't make it scream," he advised his ministers), was unpopular even among many of his black officers, who regarded the fertile land as their spoils of war. On October 17, 1806, Jacques I, Emperor of Haiti, known to the people as Papa Jacques, was ambushed by a group of mulatto officers near Port-au-Prince, dragged from his horse, and bayoneted. After his body was stripped and castrated, the fingers hacked off to yield up their golden rings, it was left to rot in the sun on the Place d'Armes.

THE ASSASSINATION OF DESSALINES, the father of the country, plays the part of the Fall—of original sin—in Haitian history. His name is synonymous with black power, black independence, Haitian nationalism: After the flight of Jean-Claude Duvalier in 1986, the portly, tricorne- and braid-bedecked, sword-bearing figure of Dessalines could be seen as the central character in countless nationalist murals celebrating Haiti's "second liberation." And 1806 serves black Haitians, in particular, as a kind of shorthand for the moment when Haitian history—set on the path of political and economic independence and black self-rule by a leader who, however corrupt and autocratic, at least attempted to speak for the disinherited and to break down the walls of color and class inherited from the colony—began to go terribly wrong. But 1806 means something very different to mulattoes, who "have been ever since victims of a paralyzing complex of guilt because of the assassination of Dessalines," in the words of Haitian scholar Lyonel Paquin. "The Blacks did a good job of feeding that complex," Paquin continues, "ceaselessly accusing the Mulattoes of the crime. It is an historical blackmail which lasts to this day."[8]

After 1806, a leadership struggle ensued, which developed into a civil war between black- and mulatto-led factions, and the country split in two: In the south was a mulatto-ruled Republic of Haiti, under General Alexandre Petion; in the north a black-ruled State of Haiti, under General Henry Christophe. In 1811, Christophe, a former slave, crowned himself King Henry I and proceeded to create an aristocracy of Haitian princes, dukes, counts, barons, and knights, who became the ancestors of today's "black bourgeoisie of the north." He also built, not far from Cap Haitien, an opulent palace known as Sans Souci, and the Citadelle La Ferriere, a huge castle, set high on a mountain, that from the air looks like a vast stone ship knifing through giant waves. To impress visitors, legend has it, the king would parade his soldiers on the fortress's lofty battlements and demonstrate his authority and power by ordering whole squadrons to march straight ahead toward the sheer wall, where, unquestioningly, having received no command to halt, they would disappear over the edge, plummeting a thousand feet into the valley below.

Christophe granted some estates to his newly created aristocrats, and late in his reign he began to distribute land in smaller parcels, but in general he followed Dessalines in trying to reinvigorate the export economy by keeping the large plantations intact and maintaining a forced-labor system. In the south, the mulatto president Pétion, faced with a shortage of labor and money, and with stagnant agricultural production, decided on radical land reform: He broke up all the plantations into small parcels and sold them for nominal sums or granted them outright to his officers and soldiers. Although many of the old mulatto elite did manage to retain or amass estates, Pétion went on distributing small tracts of land to common soldiers until his death in 1818. Jean-Pierre Boyer, a mulatto general, succeeded him and, after the death of King Henry (the king, seeing his regime about to collapse in the face of internal rebellion, committed suicide in 1820, supposedly with a silver bullet), reunited the country; Boyer eventually applied the land-reform policy throughout Haiti.

The reforms took about forty years in all, and when they were complete, what had been an international, export-led economy driven by large-scale agricultural production had been transformed into a nation of benighted smallholders. Sugar, which had been the key to Saint-Domingue's wealth, virtually disappeared as an export crop, and coffee—easily cultivated, or even collected, for it grew wild on Haiti's isolated mountains—replaced it as the country's most remunerative export, a cash crop that was grown by small cultivators along with the bananas, yams, and corn they fed their families. Haiti's may be the only revolution in history to have turned a modern (albeit slave-powered) trading state into a largely peasant country. The small landholdings created by Pétion and Boyer, which became ever smaller as they were divided equally, in the new French fashion, among the children of each succeeding generation; the rapidly growing peasant population; the consequent exhaustion of the soil and erosion of the land; and the succession of Haitian rulers, members of the urban-based elite, who cared little and did less about these rural problems—these factors led directly to the spectacular poverty of Haiti today.

By creating a nation of smallholders, the land reforms helped determine the future development of the elite and the type of governments—despotic, unstable, corrupt—they would form. Since the Haitian elite's wealth and power, unlike those of the elites elsewhere in Latin America, could not be based on land—even those who had managed to secure or retain large estates were forced by lack of available labor to parcel their land and lease it to tenant farmers—the land reforms, as the economist Mats Lundahl put it in a study of Haiti, made government "the most lucrative source of incomes in the country." Thus, writes Lundahl, "The administration was turned into a generator of legal and illegal incomes accruing to the followers of the politicians who happened to be in command at the moment, and the supremacy of this group was always contested by others fighting for their turn."[9]

The intra-elite fights were so frequent as to seem almost continuous, were often bloody, and were frequently complicated by the involvement of one or more foreign powers. But from Dessalines to Duvalier the political struggles in Haiti can be said to have had two relatively constant characteristics: They tended to involve the great mass of Haitians as a marginal or, more often, instrumental force, usually brought into play by a leader to help remove the country's current ruler from power; and they turned, either overtly or covertly, and often in the most intricate ways, on the great burden bequeathed by colonial Saint-Domingue: the critical fulcrum of color.

WHEN ADMIRAL COLUMBUS was asked by Isabella to describe his newly discovered island of Hispaniola, so the story goes, he reached for a sheet of paper from the queen's writing desk, crumpled it, dropped it on the table, and said, "It looks like that." Today, Haiti's ratio of population to arable land is one of the highest in the world, with the result that, as a favorite statistic of AID people in Port-au-Prince has it, while only 30 percent of Haiti's land is cultivable, 40 percent is under cultivation. All over Haiti one sees on impossibly steep mountainsides rows of sticks hammered into the earth, looking like the leavings of some primitive mountaineer. In fact, they are the footholds that a Haitian farmer relies on in cultivating his property. Perhaps only in Haiti do farmers hurt themselves falling off their fields.

The denuding of the hillsides, not only by overcultivation but by the peasant's never-ending search for wood for charcoal (which is rapidly becoming his major cash crop), eventually led to catastrophic erosion; from the air, the blue water around the island is seen to be clouded with dirt—tons of Haiti's precious topsoil, trickling down day after day, month after month, to the bottom of the ocean. Large parts of the country have been transformed into virtual desert, and, despite tree-planting efforts by the many "development groups" working in Haiti, are being so transformed still. This has gradually forced the peasants off the land. During the last three decades particularly, more and more of them have been piling into buses and coming to the cities, adding to the squalor of the urban slums. (And since the early 1970s, increasing numbers have boarded rickety boats and braved the open seas and the United States Coast Guard, in the hope of reaching the riches of south Florida, six hundred miles away.)

The migrations to the cities represented the coming together of two worlds that had previously been separate. One was the so-called "low world" of the countryside—a world made by the freed black field slaves who flooded into rural Haiti, became peasants either by squatting or by receiving land during the land reforms, and, isolated and unschooled, created what C. L. R. James called "Africa in the West Indies." Even today, eight Haitians in ten still live in that world. All along the car-choked streets of Port-au-Prince, signs of it are everywhere—most notably the ubiquitous peasant women just in from the country, carrying their produce to market in great baskets balanced effortlessly on their kerchief-bound heads.

Within a few miles of the capital, the market women's husbands, strawhatted black peasants, are working tiny plots—an acre, two, four, often widely separated—with little more than a machete, just as their great-grandfathers did. Like their great-grandfathers, they are illiterate; speak only Creole, in a country whose official language was always French; practice vodou, in country whose official religion was always Catholicism; live with their woman—or if they can afford it, their several women—in *plaçage*, or common-law marriage; react with suspicion and sullen fear to outsiders (a category that includes Haitians from the city as well as the almost never glimpsed foreigner); and know the authority of the dreaded state only through a military *chef de section*, or sheriff, who functions as an all-powerful proconsul. The *chef de section*'s word is law, the more so since the peasant is mute before the French-speaking official world of courts and government. In the case of a land dispute—and land disputes are constant, for most peasants hold no written titles to their property—his muteness may leave him defenseless before the powerful city man, who covets his fields, speaks French, and has friends in the government.

This city man is part of Haiti's "high world." Perched in lovely houses in Pétionville, Laboule, and Kenscoff, high above Port-au-Prince, the Haitian elite, though tiny in numbers, are a formidable group: As the peasants are culturally African, the elite are culturally European—foreign educated, French speaking, well traveled—and a larger and larger proportion of them, as one moves up the income scale, are light-skinned. They live in the cities, and hold jobs in the bloated bureaucracy, or in other, more indirect ways draw income from the government, which traditionally (until the advent of foreign aid) funded itself by taxing the produce of the peasants. Government in Haiti thus evolved as a huge extractive mechanism, sucking funds from the masses on the countryside and channeling them to the elite in the cities.

MUCH OF HAITI'S HISTORY can be understood as the struggle within the elite—often, but not always, divided very roughly into mulatto and black factions—to achieve and retain political power, and thus control access to the spoils. During Boyer's reign, the mulatto grip on the government solidified and tightened. "The aristocracy of the high-yellow skin has been erected on the ruins of the aristocracy of the white skin," the French sociologist Victor Schoelcher reported bluntly in 1843. Spenser St. John, a British envoy on Haiti some time later, observed, "Every one who mixes on Haytian society is struck by the paucity of black gentlemen to be met with at balls, concerts, or the theatre, and the almost total absence of black ladies."

In 1843, an impatient younger generation of mulattoes overthrew Boyer, and over the next several years there developed what came to be called *la politique de doublure*, or "the politics of understudies," on which an old, distinguished, and malleable black general would play the part of president, thereby smoothing the ruffled feathers of the blacks, while "understudies"—

the predominantly mulatto factions of the elite—wielded the real power behind the scenes. This continued until 1847, when the mulattoes, as Paquin dryly puts it, "picked the wrong man."

His name was Faustian Soulouque, and at the time of his elevation he was the commander of the Palace Guards. An illiterate black, he was regarded as stupid and easy to control. Like François Duvalier, who was to rule Haiti more than a century later, he was fatally underestimated by his opponents, and was able to turn their low opinion of him into his greatest strength; he knew how to appeal in ideological terms to the black Haitian masses (he was the first and perhaps the only Haitian ruler to organize official vodou ceremonies); he counterbalanced the army by setting up a secret police militia force loyal only to him, and also organized the *zinglins*, a company of illiterate, brutal peasants; he tended to distrust and turn on those who most helped him gain and retain power; and he massacred the mulattoes and then set loose the black masses to loot and destroy their businesses and property. In 1849, he crowned himself Emperor Faustin I, and created a large black aristocracy of his own. But Emperor Faustin eventually bled the country dry by the expensive pomp of his court and by his several attempts to conquer neighboring Santo Domingo, and he was overthrown in 1859 by a mulatto general, Fabre-Nicolas Geffrard.

Here, Haitian history begins to grow more and more complicated, increasingly obscured by a dense growth of insurrections, revolutions, coups d'état, civil wars, with peasant armies marching back and forth across the land, the general political chaos punctuated by the screams of massacres and the smoke of fired and looted cities. During this period, which, with interruptions, lasted until 1915, the army tended to be made up largely of illiterate peasants who had been forced into service. Recruiting, the Haitian writer Frédéric Marcelin declared in the 1890s, "Whether it's carried out brutally in the streets or mildly by letter, is at bottom nothing more than a means of coercion. Our army is nothing more than a vast prison turned inside out."

Many of the battles fought by these reluctant revolutionaries involved some degree of foreign intervention—at first British or French, and then, later in the century, German and American as well—as one faction or another preferred to witness foreign gunboats shelling Haitian cities rather than see its political opponents victorious; as, in the growing chaos, one or another nation felt bound to protect its nationals; or as France and, later, Germany and the United States felt called upon to "encourage" the Haitians to resume payment on their huge foreign debt, which Boyer had been forced to incur in 1825 in order to pay the immense reparations that France demanded in exchange for its recognition of the new nation. Throughout the century, debt payments constituted a major drag on Haiti's development and a further threat to its stability. During the forty-eight years between the overthrow of Geffrard and the landing of the marines in 1915, sixteen presidents served; two completed their terms.

IN 1907, IN A MODEST HOUSE not far from the National Palace, François Duvalier was born. As Bernard Diederich and Al Burt note in their study *Papa Doc*, this was "during the military dictatorship of Nord Alexis," though when François "was one year old General Antoine Simon overthrew Alexis."

> He was four when a revolution ousted Simon and five when an explosion reduced the old wooden Palais National and President Cincinnatus Leconte along with it to splinters. Duvalier was six when President Tancrède Auguste was poisoned; his funeral was interrupted when two generals began fighting over his succession. . . . One Michel Oreste got the job, but he was overthrown the following year by a man named Zamor, who in turn fell a year later to Davilmar Théodore.[10]

President Théodore lasted barely three months before Vilbrun Guillaume Sam marched a detachment of irregulars down from the north and overthrew him; President Sam had reigned five months when, with another revolution spreading from the north, he ordered 167 political prisoners, most of them members of elite families, massacred, and took refuge in the French Embassy—whence, on the following day, a mob dragged him out, impaled him on the embassy's spiked fence, and tore his body to pieces.

Enter the United States Marines. They came to put an end to the chaos—or at least, that was the reason given publicly. Perhaps more important was concern about the repayment of a large New York bank loan and worry about possible encroachments by the Germans, whose nationals by then controlled much of the country's importing businesses, and who, embroiled as they were in the First World War, might welcome the chance to interfere in a country whose strategic value had just been greatly increased by the opening of the Panama Canal.

When the marines marched ashore, François Duvalier was a child of eight; by the time they left, he was a nationalist intellectual of twenty-seven; a young physician who had worked widely in rural Haiti; an amateur ethnographer and anthropologist with a strong interest in vodou and peasant culture; and, like many of his contemporaries, a burning *noiriste*. Rekindled nationalism, a product not only of the occupation itself but of the Americans' preference for ruling the country through mulatto politicians, proved to be one of the major legacies of the occupation, along with a few new schools, a telephone system, and repaired roads (this last, courtesy of forced-labor gangs toiling under white marines—for Haitians, a painful echo of the slavery their forebears had endured).

Another important legacy was the "professionalized" Garde d'Haiti, which, though it had been trained by United States Marines to be disciplined, hierarchical, and, above all, "nonpolitical," soon came to serve as the key to political power. And the better roads and more efficient communications helped concentrate political power in the capital and made possible a much more efficient exploitation of the countryside. (For the marines, starving the regional centers had served as a useful tactic in combating an anti-American guerrilla movement known as the Cacos, who were peasant irregulars led by Charlemagne Péralte, a legendary hero. Péralte was eventually betrayed by a spy and assassinated by a marine; a famous photograph, picturing the dead leader tied upright to a door, Christlike, has taken its place as an icon of Haitian nationalism.)

Duvalier understood these legacies, as he did the Americans' belief that a Haitian democracy must be built on a strong middle class—the tiny group among which Duvalier, the country doctor son of a minor magistrate, numbered himself.

FRANÇOIS DUVALIER, a serious and somewhat awkward little man who wore thick spectacles and affected formal dark suits, seems to have impressed most people who encountered him, from his years in college and medical school to his time in the cabinet, as a taciturn, even enigmatic, figure of uncertain intelligence and ability.

His student years during the twenties and thirties were a time of great intellectual excitement in Haiti. The return of whites to power had always been Haiti's ultimate nightmare, and the occupation gave rise to unceasing, anguished self-analysis. Political and intellectual groups of all ideological hues sprang up, issuing declarations and manifestos, publishing short-lived journals and newspapers. All the groups, whether Communist, Fascist, ultranationalist, or racist, had a common goal: accounting for what had befallen the independent Republic of Haiti, and formulating a plan for its political future.[11]

By the time the marines departed in 1934, Duvalier had become a founding member of a group called Les Griots (meaning The Bards in Guinean). Building on an "ethnology movement" of the 1920s, these young men pressed for frank recognition of the role that African traditions had played in Haiti's history: They embarked on careful studies of peasant life, emphasizing, among other things, the importance of vodou. For ambitious intellectuals in a country where the official language was French, the official religion was Roman Catholicism, schooling had long been the preserve of the mostly European Catholic clergy, and so-called "high" culture had always looked to Paris, this was a controversial view. For the Griots, and especially for Duvalier, the "valorization," as he called it, of Haiti's African character had clear political implications—implications that were being made bitterly clear even then, in the immediate aftermath of the American occupation, by the wholesale *mulâtrification*, or "mulatto-ization," of the government and the army, and that became even clearer during the early 1940s, when the government, in collaboration with the Catholic Church, launched an "anti-superstition" campaign against vodou.

Duvalier developed his ideology in a series of articles, essays, and pamphlets published during the thirties and forties, many of them written with

Lorimer Denis, a black lawyer and mystic reputed to be a *houngan*, or vodou priest. These writings are voluminous, contradictory, and at times rather obscure, but the main line of thought, expressed most fully in his and Denis's treatise *The Class Problem Throughout Haitian History* (1946), may be said to follow from a frankly racist premise: that Haiti is a nation whose people are overwhelmingly of African descent, and thus share a particular cultural and political disposition. (In building on this premise, Duvalier sometimes cited European racist theorists like Alfred Rosenberg, chief ideologist of the Nazis.) Despite this clear racial disposition, Duvalier argued, Haiti had since its founding been dominated, politically and culturally, by a mulatto, Europeanized elite (either directly or by means of *la politique de doublure*). In other words, since its inception the social system of independent Haiti had in fact been nothing more than an extension of Saint-Domingue's. The black elite (with a few important exceptions) had largely collaborated, and in so doing had shown themselves to be traitors to their true allies: the black masses—the peasantry, who embodied in their daily lives the culture and religion of Africa.

For Duvalier, the political solution, which he often framed as a quasi-mystical "saving" of the nation's soul, using terms that recall the European Fascist rhetoric of the period, could come only with a true revolution that would wrest power from the old elite. "All revolution, if it is to be profound and durable," Duvalier and Denis wrote in 1946, "must have as its object the redemption of the masses." But how was such a redemption to be effected? "There must rise up, as long before in Saint-Domingue, one or more of those representative individuals of whom Carlyle speaks and who, by means of their personal synthesis, polarize the agonies, the hopes, and also the desire to endure of a class of men who can create the Toussaint Louvertures, the Dessalineses, the Christophes, founders of Empires and of Nations." This "representative individual" could arise only from the black middle class, since, as Duvalier wrote somewhat later, he must be a "descendant of peasants, emerging from the matrix of the history of the race," while also laying claim to "a sufficient level of intellectual culture" to counterbalance the elites and manage the revolution.

As the Haitian sociologist Laënnec Hurbon explains, the stipulation that the black savior must have sufficient "intellectual culture" provides a clue to something rather strange in Duvalier's populism. His revolution would not be a cultural reformation of Haiti; it would not seek to replace the French spoken by educated Haitians with Creole, or to replace Roman Catholicism with vodou, or, indeed, to direct the Haitian state to concern itself with helping those who had always been ignored—the peasants. Rather, Duvalier's "redemption of the masses" would seek to put, and retain, a black in power, and to promote the black middle class into prime places in a system that had always been closed to it. This shift in political power—which must be permanent, which must endure, unlike all previous "revolutions" in Haitian history—would itself constitute the redemption of the masses. The basic lineaments of the system—the extreme cultural and economic division of the country into "two worlds"—would remain largely unaffected.

AS PRESIDENT, THEREFORE, Duvalier, the redeemer of the masses, would follow all other Haitian rulers in speaking to the nation mostly in French, though 90 percent of his people were unable to understand him. On taking office, Duvalier, the great champion of vodou, would receive the traditional Te Deum in a Catholic church. Though he would make great use of vodou—both by projecting himself as the incarnation of a frightening vodou *loa* ("spirit") named Baron Samedi, who was the guardian of the graveyard, and by recruiting to his cause vodou priests in the countryside as a means of exerting local power—vodou itself would never become anything like Haiti's official religion.

As a result of the tumultuous events known as the Revolution of 1946, "the black man in power" became a reality. A student strike against President Elie Lescot, an elite mulatto, expanded into a general strike, which, in turn, provoked a *coup d'état*, headed by three army officers. After a raucous seven-month *parenthèse*, Dumarsais Estimé, a black deputy who had served as minister of education during the thirties, became president. And Estimé, a man from a humble peasant family in Verrettes, presided over an infusion of blacks into the public administration, many of them the very middle-class intellectuals who had been calling for a *noir au pouvoir*.

Duvalier, who had been working in an American-sponsored campaign against the tropical disease yaws in rural Haiti (and, under the program's sponsorship, had spent two semesters at the University of Michigan, in Ann Arbor), entered the government as director of public health, later advancing to under-minister of labor, and then to minister of public health and labor. During Duvalier's time in office, the government raised the minimum wage, passed unprecedented labor and health laws, enacted a statute forbidding foreigners to teach Haitian history; it also worked to increase tourism and foreign investment by sponsoring an international fair. Under the nationalist banner, the arts flourished, especially Haitian painting; it was the beginning of what came to be known as the Haitian Renaissance.

The atmosphere of intellectual excitement and nationalist renewal was heady, but it didn't last. Though Estimé succeeded in bringing money into the country, a great deal of corruption came with it; a group that had always been excluded from the traditional fruits of power was eager to make up for lost time. There were scandals in the banana industry and in several projects connected with the international fair. The old elite, unaccustomed to being locked out, began to plot with the army.

In 1950, faced with growing turmoil and encouraged by an impatient elite, the three officers who had deposed Lescot four years before overthrew Estimé, forcing him—in a scene that Duvalier would never forget—to walk between a double column of soldiers on his way to a ship that would carry him to exile. One of these officers, Colonel Paul Magloire, a black man strongly backed by the traditional elite, made a triumphant tour of the country and shortly thereafter was elected president.

To Duvalier, Magloire represented return to business as usual, a black officer once again working only to fill his own pockets and those of the elite, in yet another version of *la politique de doublure*. From his position in the cabinet, Duvalier had watched Estimé's downfall, had observed how the elite conspired with the army and how both profited from the growing popular agitation on the left. He had added a useful course in the practical realities of Haitian politics, and a number of valuable contacts in the labor unions, to his knowledge of Haitian history and peasant culture.

Duvalier spent the Magloire years working for the American sanitary mission, acquiring political allies, and, during the later, more repressive period of Magloire's rule, hiding from the police. (While underground, according to legend, Duvalier made an intensive study of Machiavelli.) By 1956, when Magloire tried to extend his term and was brought down by yet another general strike and by the intervention of his own army, the soft-spoken little country doctor—scholarly, unassuming, apparently even honest, having declined, unlike virtually all his colleagues, to profit from his four years in office—was in a position to put himself forward as the rightful heir to Estimé's black revolution.

THE *PARENTHÈSE* OF 1956–1957 was a spectacular exercise in prolonged political crisis, a nine-month period during which Haiti was ruled by five governments, all of them pushed, pulled, manipulated, and, finally, destabilized by the four men who held the real power—the four major candidates for president.

In many ways, the events of the *parenthèse* that brought Duvalier to power loomed over the one that followed the overthrow of his son twenty-nine years later: In both, an enormous burst of political activity—an explosion of political parties, new magazines and newspapers, popular organizations and committees—was packed into a very short period bracketed by repression; in both, the real work of winnowing out the candidates and determining the eventual winner was decided largely in the maneuvering before the election itself; in both, the unforgivable sin for any candidate was offending the power in place, the army; and, in both, the losing candidates refused to recognize the man who eventually became president as the legitimate winner, thereby ensuring continued political instability.

In 1957, both François Duvalier and his major opponent, Senator Louis Déjoie, boasted national reputations and could claim whole regions of the country as strongholds. Déjoie—a handsome, European-educated aristocrat who liked to dress for dinner—was the scion of a wealthy mulatto family that included General Nicolas Geffrard, a major figure in the war of independence, and his son, President Fabre-Nicolas Geffrard; he was backed by the traditional elite, which by then included not only the powerful Catholic

Church and a large part of the officer corps but virtually all the country's significant businessmen. Meanwhile, Daniel Fignolé, tall, slim, good-looking, and blessed with a talent for rousing Creole rhetoric, wielded enormous power in the capital, where he could unleash adoring masses to do great damage. Many black soldiers also favored him, and some officers. Clement Jumelle, Magloire's finance minister, claimed significant support within the public administration and among the professional class. And, finally, Duvalier, issuing his call for black salvation in halting, somewhat mystical terms, had a strong following in the north and throughout the countryside, and was a favorite not only of many black soldiers but of key black officers. And though it was known that a group of operatives he had assembled was planting bombs and concocting other violent "dirty tricks," he managed to retain his benign image: Papa Doc, the slightly dotty country doctor.

As the four candidates fought each other through the rise and fall of five governments, through general strikes, mass demonstrations, bombings, attempted assassinations, and political violence of every sort, it gradually became clear that Duvalier had an all important advantage: "the impossibility of any electoral victory on the part of his opponents," as the political scientist and future president Leslie Manigat observed. Jumelle had been wholly discredited by the corruption and scandals of the last regime; Fignolé was a populist rabble-rouser whom the elite would never countenance; and Déjoie, the strongest of the three, was an elite mulatto facing three blacks in an overwhelmingly black and highly race-sensitive country.

The deciding event was the "civil war" of May 25, 1957, when the army split in two. A Déjoie faction broke off and took up positions across the Champ de Mars from the bulk of the military, in the Dessalines Barracks behind the palace. As crowds gathered to watch, artillery bombarded the barracks, and snipers fired back, picking off several of the gunners. (Within the barracks, according to the memoirs of Colonel Pressoir Pierre, a Duvalierist, the soldiers were "overcome with panic" under the artillery barrage, but a young second lieutenant named Henri Namphy "went—in peril of his life—directly to the line of fire seizing control of the situation and restoring confidence to his men.")

When the "civil war" was over, seventeen soldiers and perhaps a hundred civilians were dead and the Déjoie faction had been defeated. Some of the leading "rebel" officers were cashiered and a few imprisoned. With Déjoie weakened, Duvalier moved to deal with Fignolé, joining with Jumelle to support the appointment of the young firebrand as provisional president.

On the day of Fignolé's inauguration, Port-au-Prince was the scene of delirious celebration; the following dawn revealed that the facades of many of the city's houses and other buildings had been emblazoned with the Fignolé insignia and the slogan "We have taken power for 25 years!"

"The speed with which the slogans had been printed frightened me," Colonel Pierre notes in his memoirs. The high command's fears were not eased when the young president ordered a reshuffling of officers that would send certain loyalists of May 25 to posts outside the capital, and announced, without consulting the high command, that he was doubling his soldiers' pay. Fignolé's days were numbered.

ON JUNE 14, the soldiers of the Dessalines Barracks were pleased to learn that a double feature would he shown in the barracks that evening. As they filed into the theatre, they were asked to leave their rifles outside, "to prevent accidents." Having enjoyed two Westerns, the now unarmed soldiers were loaded into trucks and driven out of the capital. Meanwhile, in the palace, there came a sharp knock at the door of the cabinet room, and a group of officers burst in, machine guns in hand, and marched the provisional president down the hall, out of the building, and to a wharf, where his family had been assembled on a waiting launch; the Fignolés were on their way to twenty-nine years of exile in New York. Before his supporters had any inkling of trouble, "the cowboy-movie coup" ended the political career of the populist president. He had ruled for nineteen days.

When it dawned on the slum dwellers of Port-au-Prince that they had been deprived of their idol, they reacted first with shocked paralysis and then, two nights later, with fury. A rumor—that crucial weapon of Haitian politics—began to race through the city that Fignolé was still in Haiti, that he was being held in Fort Dimanche prison, that he would soon be executed.

In the dark slums of the capital, a huge, howling mob rose up, making a roar that, in the words of Maurepas Auguste, then an army officer, "could have terrified the most courageous: a formless and mournful tumult, like that signaling the approach of a hurricane, by tens of thousands of people screaming to raise the dead and accompanied by a sinister clashing and smashing of all sorts of objects." This was the *bat ténèb*, the "tenebrous beating": The screaming crowd pounded machetes, knives, pots, and pans against the lampposts, smashing the streetlights block upon block as they advanced, plunging the entire city into a deafening darkness.

General Antonio Kébreau, the army chief of staff, unleashed his troops. The city had become "a jungle," he explained to journalists the next day. "You heard, gentlemen, those cries of savage beasts, those electric poles resonating, that infernal noise." From Fort Dimanche, soldiers directed heavy-machine-gun fire into the crowd; then, behind armored cars and tanks, they advanced into the slums, massacring the people in the streets and later moving from house to house to slaughter those who had taken refuge.

The next day, the soldiers brought in trucks and loaded up the bodies, and with them came the firemen, to hose down the blood-soaked streets. Since the soldiers dumped their truckloads into secret graves, no one knows how many died during the *nuit rouge*; estimates range from five hundred to several thousand. Whatever the number, the slums had been quieted.

On September 22, the mild-mannered country doctor was elected president for a six-year term, carrying into office with him a solidly Duvalierist legislature. Though Déjoie outpolled him in Port-au-Prince, Duvalier showed overwhelming support outside the capital; indeed, in some places the number of votes helpfully delivered by the officers well exceeded that of the local population. But though fraud was certainly widespread, there could be no question of Duvalier's popularity.

To the defeated candidates, Duvalier's election was merely another step in the *parenthèse*—merely the latest move in the political struggle that had racked the country for nine months. Déjoie insisted that he was the true winner (and his son was still making that claim thirty years later). From exile, Fignolé claimed that he remained Haiti's constitutional president (and he continued to say so until his death, in 1986). Both, along with Jumelle's supporters and the many still loyal to the exiled Magloire, vowed to continue the struggle. All expected that Duvalier would soon be overthrown, and wanted to be in a position to seize the opening when it came.

Within a few days of the election, bombs began exploding around Port-au-Prince, fires erupted in the countryside, ambushes were laid. In one incident, an army post near the capital was attacked and several soldiers were murdered, most while they slept; the attackers, never identified, were widely believed to be pro-Déjoie renegades. When Déjoie supporters launched a commercial strike, however, soldiers and armed Duvalierist toughs forced open the doors of the shops and welcomed in the hungry crowds to pick the shelves clean.

It is tempting to speculate about what Duvalier would have become had he not been obliged to wage, from the moment he took office, "two years of permanent struggle. Against a conspiracy of all sectors . . . plots, conspiracies, invasions," in the (admittedly self-serving) words of General Gérard Constant, a close Duvalier associate who eventually served as his chief of staff. "Conspiracy was permanent," Constant said in a published interview with Haitian writer Michel Souker. "The Fignolists were on a war footing. . . . They were like the first Christians who were waiting for the return of the Messiah. . . . The subversion helped to give birth to Duvalier, and the ferocity of the regime. Power makes the man, and power reveals the man. But would there have been occasion to exercise his ferocity if everything that happened hadn't taken place?"

At the end of 1957, said Constant, Duvalier found himself faced with two alternatives: Either "he would be incapable of ruling, and in three or six months he would fall," or he would succeed in "making his rule perennial. The rule of a single class." The choice was obvious. "It was decided, therefore, to oppose this terrorism with a terrorism of the State."

To retain power in the fragmented world of Haitian politics became Duvalier's obsession, and the steps he took to do so would dominate the country's politics for more than three decades.

After receiving the presidential sash from General Kébreau, on October 22, Duvalier pledged to "guarantee the exercise of liberty to all Haitians" and "to reconcile the nation with itself." As for his "enemies," the mumbling country doctor said, "I have no enemies except those of the nation."

DURING THE FIRST YEARS of his regime, Duvalier's consuming need to solidify his power combined with a series of plots, conspiracies, and invasions to produce a complicated repressive apparatus that Manigat has called "the Fascism of underdevelopment." In time, the various organs of the predatory state—the secret police, the Presidential Guard, the factionalized army, and, above all, the Tontons Macoutes—reached into every cranny of the country, nourished by a vast system of informers. But the system was designed not to foster a totalitarian, class-destroying revolution but to ensure at all costs, the longevity of Duvalier's rule. As the president later said of his beloved Macoutes, they "have but one soul: Duvalier; know but one master: Duvalier; struggle but for one destiny: Duvalier in power."

The core of Duvalier's machinery of repression had taken shape during the campaign, when he assembled the group of bomb-makers, *saboteurs*, *agents provocateurs*, dirty tricksters, and strong-arm men. These terrorists then put together a rank and file of young Duvalierist toughs, drawing on the virtually inexhaustible supply of manpower in the slums. A dominant member of the early group was Clément Barbot, a slender black man given to severely elegant suits and dark glasses who became the head of Duvalier's secret police (he was said to hand out business cards identifying him as such) and later played a leading role in setting up the militia.

Soon after Duvalier's inauguration, while the country echoed with bombings and calls to revolt, a squad of heavily armed, hooded men burst into the home of a well-known pro-Déjoie journalist, manhandled her teenage children, then carried her off; she was raped, savagely beaten, and left sprawled half-naked and near death on the roadside. Barbot and his group had assumed a new, more frightening shape—that of sinister *cagoulords*. In the coming nights, these "hooded ones" paid visits to other prominent members of the opposition; some were beaten, some were carried off to Fort Dimanche and other prisons, some disappeared entirely.

The Duvalier method quickly became clear: attack swiftly and on all fronts, always maintaining the initiative; move to crush, then co-opt, any independent power center; respect no boundaries in administering terror, liquidating not only adversaries but their families and friends, and in as spectacularly brutal a fashion as possible; and, above all, trust no one—and particularly not those who seem to be loyal allies. Independent power in itself was anathema, even if it might appear to be perfectly loyal at the moment; all independent power must be obliterated.

Jumelle had already gone underground, and Déjoie did the same, slipping out of the country and eventually making his way to Cuba, where, with the support of the newly installed Fidel Castro, he began training Haitian exiles to mount an invasion. Fignolé traveled from New York to Cuba and engaged in similar pursuits. In New York, General Magloire plotted and kept in touch with exile groups. In Washington, exiled Haitian politicians were soon remonstrating with desk officers in the State Department and the C.I.A., soliciting support for the liberation of the homeland. Spies were everywhere in the rapidly growing exile communities, as Haitians plotted and planned, against Duvalier and against one another. And in Santo Domingo the crafty old Dominican dictator Rafael Trujillo was wining and dining the Haitian chief of staff, his good friend General Kébreau, as if Kébreau, and not Duvalier, were the Haitian head of state.

In a touching ceremony soon after he took office, the president had bestowed on General Kébreau an unheard-of six-year term as army chief. Barely five months later, Duvalier, whom many officers openly disdained as a figurehead, abruptly transferred most of Kébreau's principal allies out of Port-au-Prince. Having long held him in contempt, the officers were not prepared for his decisiveness or ruthlessness, or the skill with which he played on their lingering jealousies and rivalries. Once Duvalier had exiled Kébreau's men, he wasted no time in purging Kébreau himself. The first the powerful general heard of his fall was a thirteen-gun salute accompanying the appointment of his successor, whereupon he sought asylum in the Dominican Embassy.

Kébreau's successor lasted only nine months. Again and again, Duvalier moved to purge the upper ranks of the army, at one point shooting a number of officers after a coup plot came to light, at others abruptly retiring or imprisoning the Old Guard, or sending officers into exile to various foreign embassies. He sniffed out plotters or simply removed figures he suspected might one day become plotters. Even those older men who had been his staunchest allies were mercilessly purged, for they commanded the one thing that could not be allowed to exist: independent power. All the while, Duvalier continued to advance much younger black officers rapidly through the ranks. He rewarded his favorites handsomely, promoting brutal, ambitious men like Claude Raymond, his godson, and Gracia Jacques, whom Duvalier had known since he was a child.

The goal was to factionalize, weaken, and thereby neutralize the military as an institution capable of any independent action: to "Duvalierize" it. And Duvalier's most important tool, here, as in other areas, was his genius for exploiting the jealousies and vanities of others, setting the already divided officers against one another, spreading suspicion and intrigue. He methodically emasculated the officer corps by reaching around the chain of command, telephoning minor provincial officers personally and without bothering to inform their superiors. Promotions were dependent on the whim of the president alone. He put Raymond in charge of the newly created Presidential Guard, an elite unit of several hundred men, every one of whom became well known to Duvalier, took orders directly from him, and lived and worked within the palace grounds.

Finally, he moved the army's main store of weapons into the basement of the palace. "Last June, one visitor was shown how Haitian military logistics operate," Richard Eder, of the *New York Times*, later wrote. "He was sitting with Duvalier in his office when an aide came to tell the president that guerrillas had landed at Saltrou and the army needed ammunition. Silently the president took a gold key from his pocket and took out a revolver. He got up, tiptoed to the door and cocked the revolver, opened the door and peered out. A secretary appeared and he gave her the gold key."[12]

The crucial event both for the military and for the future of Duvalier's regime was *l'affair Pasquet*, also known as "the Dade County Deputy Sheriffs' Invasion." It was the first and, in its way, the most serious of a succession of buffoonish attempts to overthrow Papa Doc—an eight-man invasion launched from Florida which, in its sheer, comic-opera absurdity, almost succeeded. It was led by Captain Alix Pasquet, a well-known mulatto officer who had been close to Magloire. Two mulatto officers with similar pedigrees joined Pasquet, as did five American mercenaries, including two Florida deputy sheriffs.

Late on the night of July 28, 1958, during Duvalier's ninth month in power, the invaders disembarked from a motor launch north of Port-au-Prince and fought a short engagement with a military patrol, killing three soldiers. The three Haitian officers and five Americans piled into a commandeered "tap-tap" *camionnette*, drove into the capital, and, bluffing their way past the guards, managed to seize the Dessalines Barracks, adjacent to the palace. Placing the troops under guard, they settled in and began to make telephone calls, informing various commanders that they had taken control and demanding their support, then calling Duvalier directly to tell him the game was up. As the dictator later recounted in his memoirs:

> Awakened by the firing and the cannon reports, I donned the uniform of a soldier . . . and called the commander of the barracks. Instead of the commander, a voice answered. "This is Alix Pasquet. There's no general here." Pasquet then arrogantly demanded that I give my name, title and rank. "President of the Republic and Supreme Chief of the Armed Forces,' I answered. Whereupon the little maniac dared to order the Chief of State to put down his arms and present himself at the gate of the Dessalines Barracks with a white flag. . . .
>
> I hung up the telephone, picked up my rifle and my steel helmet. Surrounded by Duvalierist allies, male and female (the core of the future militia), loyal officers, the men of my secret police, I waited until dawn . . . to order [the assault].[13]

Actually, according to other accounts, the president of the republic panicked, packed his bags, and, in the tradition of tottering Haitian heads of state, made ready for a run to a foreign embassy. However, the position of the invaders, who might well have taken the palace if they hadn't paused to telephone first, was becoming shakier each moment, and became hopeless when Duvalier learned that the invading force numbered only eight. (One of the rebel officers, unable to control his urge for a Haitian cigarette, had nonchalantly sent a captive soldier out to fetch some, and the man had been quickly interrogated.) And Duvalier already knew something the rebels did not—that the nation's cache of arms, which they thought they controlled, was in the palace basement.

As dawn broke over Port-au-Prince, François Duvalier—a slight, owlish man with thick black spectacles, looking more than usually incongruous in his fatigues and steel helmet, with a .45 in his belt—marched out with Claude Raymond and Gracia Jacques and a number of other friends, and laid siege to the barracks. The palace's emergency sirens wailed, rallying calls went out to loyal Duvalierists over the radio, and it wasn't long before Captain Pasquet and his accomplices in the barracks were surrounded by a mob of bloodthirsty partisans.

The rebels' calls to important commanders having met with no success—they were waiting to see which way the wind blew—the eight now had no allies and no options. When the gang of soldiers and Duvalierist irregulars charged the barracks behind a hail of bullets and grenades, the rebels had nowhere to go. Pasquet and four others, including three of the Americans, died in the barracks; their bodies were stripped and battered by the attackers. The remaining three were tracked down nearby; a soldier shot one American, and the crowd tore the two other men to pieces, paraded their remains triumphantly through the streets, and later carried them into the palace to present to their president.

Duvalier, resplendent in his fatigues and helmet, and flanked by his gun-waving young officers and partisans, seemed a very different man; he had become, in the words of General Constant, "an implacable monster, unpitying in everything that concerned his power."

BY THIS TIME, the Duvalierist legislature had voted the president full emergency powers. Duvalier was ruling by decree: The country was under a state of siege, and a nighttime curfew had been imposed. The *cagoulards* were continuing their nocturnal visits, and the newspapers and radio stations they had not destroyed were muffled by government censorship. At moments of heightened stress, armed Duvalierists—tough-looking black men wearing dark glasses, with pistols bulging under their suit jackets—patrolled the streets checking identification papers. Now, after the Pasquet affair, Duvalier moved to create what might be called the single defining institution of his regime: the Tontons Macoutes.

From the beginning, the Macoutes were a strange amalgam of popular militia, religious sect, mass political organization, secret police, protection racket, and terrorist unit. And though the organization itself was new, the Macoutes worked by infecting already existing structures of authority, thereby enabling the Duvalier partisans to multiply their power a hundredfold.

In the countryside, for example, the *chefs de section* very often became leading Tontons Macoutes. And the vodou priests, usually the most powerful men in their villages or towns, who had mostly been key supporters of Duvalier during the campaign, as well as the *gros nègs* of a given community—the better-off peasants, who could hire labor and lend money to their fellows—often became leading Macoutes as well.

Duvalier had created his own mass movement, devised to repel invaders and to fight the *apatrides*, "the countryless ones" (Déjoie, Fignolé, and the other plotters had been deprived of their citizenship, and their property confiscated). Macoute Day, on which huge mobs of Macoutes, in uniforms of blue denim, with red neckerchiefs, would pour into the grounds of the palace, listen to their leader's peroration, then swarm out into the capital, firing their weapons (and often killing number of people), was July 29, in remembrance of the Pasquet invasion.

While the most powerful Macoutes were often the *chefs de section*, vodou priests, and *gros nègs*, the bulk of the force—its foot soldiers—came from the slums and the villages. They were illiterate blacks, poor and wholly unsentimental; Duvalier, in raising them up to be Macoutes, had given them overwhelming power, for the first time in their lives, and they wielded it without pity, especially when it came to those elites who had theretofore despised them.

The Macoutes' reason for being—indeed, their only hope of ensuring their own survival—was to keep Duvalier in power. They did this by growing and spreading; Macoutes emerged in every neighborhood and every institution, in every ministry of the government and every school, and as taxi drivers, bartenders, and bus drivers. Though the most frightening Macoutes were the fierce men in blue uniforms and dark sunglasses who waved their guns about, abused people on the street, killed with impunity, and terrorized the capital during crises, there were many more who did not wear uniforms but nonetheless belonged to the militia, carried "the card," informed on their colleagues, and remained vigilant guardians of Duvalierism. No one knew how many there were (after Jean-Claude Duvalier fell, the newspapers' estimates varied from fifteen thousand to three hundred thousand). In time, the Macoutes permeated everything in Haiti, including the Haitian mind.

For the Haitian child, "Tonton Macoute" has always been the dark side of Christmas: If you have been a good boy, Tonton Noël (Uncle Christmas) will come and reward you with wonderful gifts from his treasure-laden sack; if you have been a bad boy, Tonton Macoute (Uncle Knapsack) will come and grab you, throw you in his sack, which is huge and dark, and carry you off into the night. The figure of the frightening bogeyman carrying off naughty children is probably universal, but in Haiti, where secret societies ruled the night in the countryside, where in some areas people knew they could not travel after dark without a "safe conduct" granted by these unofficial, vodou-linked authorities, and where stories of travelers vanishing in the darkness were common, it took on a deeper resonance. This was especially true for the peasants, and for the urban masses, most of whom were transplanted peasants or their children. For them, the Macoute was not just a brutal man with a gun; he was evil and all-powerful. As every Haitian knew, Papa Doc was the incarnation of Baron Samedi, the vodou *loa* who trafficked with the dead. And the Macoutes were his creatures.

"You know what my very first memory is?" a Haitian friend asked me. "It was a Sunday, and my father had taken me to church. We walked out into the big market at Carrefour—he was holding my hand, I remember, and it was bright sunshine. And then suddenly, across the market, appeared Ti Bobo"—a huge, dreaded Macoute—"and people saw him, and heads turned. And suddenly, just like that, the people ran *like mice*. The whole crowd—everybody—just ran, in panic. Ti Bobo just stood there laughing."

TI BOBO PASSED INTO the realm of legend in 1967, when a soldier he had abused checked a machine gun out of the barracks armory, searched out Ti Bobo, and methodically cut him in half. Duvalier gave Ti Bobo a state funeral. Many other Macoutes have also attained legendary status, thanks to their creative achievements in brutality. (Several women are among them, the most prominent being Mme. Max Adolphe, a celebrated sadist and connoisseur of pornography, who was a leader of the Macoutes and a warden of the infamous Fort Dimanche, where she is said to have delighted in mutilating the genitals of her male prisoners.) Any Haitian can tell you Macoute stories. They are carved in his mind, like the memory of a unique force of nature.

The Macoutes were Papa Doc's instruments; by virtue of him they were above the law. The overwhelming majority of them were not paid—officially, they were called National Security Volunteers—and depended for their living on extortion. As Laënnec Hurbon has written, they were "a mode of inscription of the president as the sole legitimate owner of the nation." Hurbon quotes an expatriate Haitian worker: "If somebody touches a militiaman, it is Duvalier he touches."[14] The Macoutes *were* Duvalier; they need answer only to him.

A Macoute would take his food from the market without paying for it, ride free in buses and taxis, demand that peasants bring in his harvest, and press the wealthier residents of his neighborhood to make contributions to his upkeep. A Macoute's demand that somebody hand over his car, his land, even his house was often preceded by the suggestion that the owner seemed a bit disloyal to Duvalier. A refusal to give up what was desired would be interpreted as an act hostile to Duvalier, and a reluctant owner could be beaten, imprisoned, even killed on the spot; there was no appeal, no recourse to a higher authority. In many cases, wealthy Haitians were forced into exile, and stripped of their nationality and their property. Macoutes who infested the public administration not only drew several monthly checks, in the time-honored fashion of Haiti's public servants, but used their posts to acquire public property.

In time, the Macoutes became so insatiable, Hurbon writes, that "in villages the development of Macoutism caused certain businessmen and small producers to reduce the volume of their businesses, to avoid working for the sole profit of the Macoutes."[15] There was only one sure way of protecting oneself—by becoming a Macoute. Not necessarily a gun-toting militiaman but an informer, a member of the organization; for there were no part-time Macoutes. A good Duvalierist, as the ardent Duvalier minister Luckner Cambronne put it, "stands ready to kill his children, children to kill their parents." Through the pervasiveness and omnipotence of the Macoutes, Duvalier would proclaim himself "the lord and master of this land of Haiti."

DURING THE REGIME'S first three years, the army was purged and cowed, the independent press was destroyed, and those opposition figures who had not been murdered were imprisoned, driven underground, or forced into exile. The leadership of the Haitian "counter-elite" that customarily fought for power was left to expend its energies in plotting invasions and coups.

Beginning with the Pasquet affair, a rhythm was established which would be further refined with each invasion: While militiamen and soldiers rushed to meet the invaders, sirens wailed in the capital, and a curfew was declared. Heavily armed Macoutes raced about the city, setting up roadblocks (where they demanded "tolls" of passing motorists), beating or imprisoning anyone who looked slightly "suspicious," murdering anyone who resisted. The embassies began to fill with Haitians seeking asylum. In Fort Dimanche, political prisoners were summarily executed. Families of the invaders, if they were unfortunate enough to have remained in Haiti, were tracked down and massacred. Villagers who had had contact with invaders were also massacred. Corpses were left lying on the street for days, and when the police or Macoutes finally picked them up they were not returned to the families.

During these crises, the capital was often blacked out, the nights were full of unexplained shooting, and rumors were the only source of news. Duvalier would disappear into the palace for weeks at a time, and forbid his family to venture out—a restriction that was particularly hard on his three small daughters. "The Macoutes would come and wake me in the middle of the night and tell me he had sent for me," a beautiful mulatto woman who had been a dressmaker in Port-au-Prince told me. "They would take me to the palace. I had no way to refuse. I would find these poor little girls waiting for me, tired and bored out of their minds. They hadn't been out of the palace in weeks, and now their father, who adored them, had promised that they could have new dresses. It was dark outside, there was shooting, everyone was home scared out of his wits, and there I was in the palace with these little girls, measuring them, showing them patterns and material, doing anything I could to amuse them. I felt sorry for them. I was called there many times, but I remember seeing *him* only once. He was up on a balcony, looking down at us. He looked and looked, then he smiled a little."

Within months of the Pasquet affair, the smiling Duvalier's Macoutes and soldiers tracked down Charles and Ducasse Jumelle, brothers of the former candidate, and murdered them while they slept. (For the benefit of the press, their bodies were dragged outside and posed with pistols in their hands.) Less than a year later, Clément Jumelle himself staggered into the Cuban Embassy, mortally ill of uremia, and died there. His funeral procession provides a famous scene of those years: As the Jumelle cortège moved slowly toward Sacré Coeur, a car filled with machine-gun-toting Macoutes, siren wailing, cut in front of the hearse. The Macoutes dragged out the coffin and heaved it into the back of an accompanying pickup truck. Then they roared off, siren still wailing. Jumelle was given a secret burial, with Macoutes the only mourners, in his home town of Saint-Marc.

A little more than a year after Pasquet's coup attempt, a squad of thirty Cubans, led by an Algerian associate of Déjoie, landed on the southwestern tip of the island. The invaders were quickly contained by Haitian soldiers and by peasants. (The peasants were offered large rewards for the invaders' heads.) All but five of the Cubans were killed, as was the Algerian, and the survivors were paraded in the capital and eventually returned to Castro.

In this instance, the Haitian soldiers were being advised by the United States Marines, whom Duvalier had invited in to help retrain his army. This action had surprised the Americans and shocked the Haitians, for they were well acquainted with Duvalier's proclaimed views on the American influence in Haiti's history. But the American mission not only helped Duvalier immobilize the army but also allowed him to confront his opponents with what seemed strong American support for his regime.

From the beginning, Duvalier's relationship with the Americans was complicated and contradictory. It had been generally thought that the embassy favored Déjoie, though Duvalier had enough prominent American supporters to let him suggest that the Americans were actually backing him. Yet the ex-presidents Magloire and Fignolé did their plotting from bases in New York, and the Pasquet invasion had set off from Florida, which Duvalier did not let his supporters forget. Finally, Duvalier's invitation to the marines put Americans squarely in the middle of his struggle with the army, and his attempts to use them to train the militia launched a series of struggles that would end, in 1963, with the withdrawal of the marine mission after four years.

But the major issue between the two countries was foreign aid. The prolonged political chaos had left Haiti's treasury empty; 90 percent of its people remained illiterate; and, during the years since the occupation, its roads and bridges had fallen into a disastrous state of disrepair. These conditions worsened under Duvalier, whose regime by 1963 was spending more than half its budget on the Presidential Guard and the Macoutes, and siphoning off much of the rest in an enormous spree of corruption. Funds were pilfered directly through unbudgeted accounts attached to the Régie du Tabac, the government tobacco monopoly, which included taxes on cotton, sugar, and other products. Import licenses, franchises, and monopolies were sold to businessmen willing to pay substantial kickbacks.

Such measures, which would be vastly expanded under Papa Doc's son, were, in effect, ways to suck more money from the peasants and the urban poor, by both reducing their income from commodity exports and increasing the price they had to pay for staple imports. (The system became known as *pèzé-sucé*—"squeeze and suck"—after a popular frozen treat.) Though the bureaucrats were now in many cases drawn from the black "middle classes," the techniques through which they filled their pockets were the same as the ones that the elite, both mulatto and black, had used in Haiti since the war of independence.

IN 1960, American aid represented about 30 percent of the country's budget, the following year about half. Duvalier was demanding that the Americans greatly increase the amounts, and also that the money be offered without conditions, which he claimed violated Haiti's sovereignty. The Americans, wary of seeing their money flow into the hands of Macoutes or Duvalierist ministers, insisted on having some say in how the funds were spent.

The rise of Castro added to this diplomatic poker game a crucial new card, and Duvalier used it skillfully throughout his reign. Haiti lay fifty miles east of Cuba, next door was the Dominican Republic, and from there it was a short hop east to Puerto Rico. If these facts of geography were lost on American planners, the Cuban leader's several attempts to intervene in the Dominican Republic and the presence of Haitian exiles undergoing training at Cuban bases served to remind them.

Whenever Duvalier's aid requests were not satisfied, he responded with lightly veiled threats, the most famous being the "Appeal of Jacmel," a 1960 speech in which the dictator demanded a "massive injection of money" from the United States, and went on to muse about "the two great poles of attraction in the world today" between which small states like Haiti (as the Cuban experience showed) were forced to make a difficult choice. To underline his threat, Duvalier received trade missions from Poland and Czechoslovakia, and played an adroit cat-and-mouse game with Haitian Communists, whose presence he needed to make his threats credible. Duvalier allowed leftist students to agitate now and then, and, to disturb the already nervous Americans further, maintained in his government a number of Haitians with Communist backgrounds.

Against a United States administration obsessed with Castro and his growing influence in Latin America, this sort of blackmail was a potent weapon. Sometimes it was less than subtle; in 1962, when the member nations of the Organization of American States met in Punta del Este, Uruguay, for the famous conference that excluded Cuba, the United States needed Haiti's vote for a two-thirds majority. "The foreign minister of Haiti . . . calmly remarked to [Secretary of State Dean] Rusk that he came from a poor country in desperate need of aid," and "obviously this need would affect his vote," Arthur Schlesinger, Jr., who was a delegate at the conference, wrote later. "We finally yielded to blackmail and agreed to resume our aid to the airport at Port au Prince."[16]

WITHIN HAITI, Duvalier continued his attack on the opposition, the definition of which had now been expanded to include the labor unions, students, and the Catholic Church. His tactics remained the same. Recalcitrant labor leaders were beaten and imprisoned, and replaced with Macoutes. The drivers' union, which retained the power to paralyze the country and was thus by far the most important, was thoroughly Macoutized, the drivers serving as useful source of intelligence for the regime. Students went on strike, and many were imprisoned.

Duvalier also moved against the country's priests, three-quarters of them foreigners (mostly French and Canadian), whom he saw—with some reason—as representatives of the elite, allied with the students, in opposition to the regime. In 1959, to make it dramatically clear that men of the cloth enjoyed no special dispensation, Macoutes invaded the Port-au-Prince cathedral during Sunday Mass, beat scores of people senseless, including priests at the altar, then arrested them. He began summarily, sometimes brutally, expelling priests, including two archbishops of Port-au-Prince.

For the Vatican, it was too much. The papal nuncio was withdrawn, Duvalier excommunicated. No matter. Macoute priests took the places of many of those expelled. Macoutes also took control of Haiti's only university. Professional people began to flee the country in a great flood, making the diaspora, and many of the new countries of Africa as well, far richer in Haitian doctors, nurses, lawyers, economists, and other technicians than Haiti itself.

In April 1961, Duvalier held an election for the legislature, as his constitution required. The regime's propaganda apparatus kicked into high gear, distributing to peasants who were trucked in from the provinces thousands of straw hats hearing the slogan "*Vive Papa Doc!*" Each ballot, as was customary, read at the top, "*Republique d'Haiti Dr. François Duvalier, President de la Republique.*" When the results were in, to no one's surprise the all-Duvalierist slate had been handsomely returned to office. ("Army men with guns forced everyone emerging from church to go to the polls," *Commonweal* reported. "All were handed the ballot of just one candidate and informed that the . . . others had been jailed the night before.") But the president went a step further, announcing to his astonished fellow citizens that in fact this had been a presidential election as well, that the official-looking name at the top of every ballot actually meant that every vote cast had been a vote for Duvalier himself—and that he was pleased to accept the wish of all Haitians to return him to office for another six-year term (though the current one still had two years to run); the vote was 1,320,748 to zero.

It was a preposterous move, audacious and absurd. But it was brilliant as well, for it avoided the turmoil that inevitably accompanies the last year or two of a Haitian president's term, when he tries to extend his mandate and the various powerful elements of the country fight to dislodge him. Now Duvalier had declared his intention of remaining, and claimed the support of the Haitian people for doing so—and he had done it, as usual, in a manner calculated to keep the opposition off balance.

Probably the height of Duvalier's terror came in the months before and after May 1963 when he had been scheduled to give up power. April began with the discovery of another plot in the military, and soon the horribly beaten body of one officer was lying in the sun on the parade ground, providing a lesson to his friends. Duvalier's main opponent was now his own ruthless former secret-police chief, Clément Barbot, whom the dictator, sniffing disloyalty, had thrown into Fort Dimanche. Although Duvalier finally released him, and presented him with a new automobile to show there were now no hard feelings, Barbot eventually went underground.

The climax of the terror came on April 26, when a person or persons unknown (Barbot, it turned out) assassinated the two bodyguards and the driver of Jean-Claude Duvalier and one of his sisters as they were being dropped off at school. The operation was precise—one shot to each man— and the children were not harmed (the goal may have been to lure Duvalier to the scene, in order to assassinate him). But, in the palace, Duvalier exploded in rage, and Port-au-Prince became a bloodbath. Macoutes and Presidential Guards swarmed over the city, shooting down anyone unfortunate enough to be driving a car similar to that driven by the attacker, and murdering ex-military officers, who were thought to be the only ones capable of such marksmanship. Hundreds of people were arrested and carried off to Fort Dimanche; few of them ever reappeared. Roadblocks sprang up everywhere, and in the chaos that had descended on Port-au-Prince anyone foolish enough to be found on the street invariably spent most of his time standing with his hands in the air and a machete poised above his neck, being searched by a Tonton Macoute.

Meanwhile, Duvalier had become convinced that the attacker could only have been the award-winning army rifleman Lieutenant Francois Benoit— even though Benoit had by then been in asylum in the Dominican Embassy for days. A heavily armed gang of Macoutes and Presidential Guards stormed the officer's house and machine-gunned his parents, the servants, the family dogs, and a neighbor who happened to be chatting with the old couple. Then the gang set the house on fire; Benoit's infant son perished in his crib inside.

The Macoutes and Presidential Guards sought out Benoit's other relatives, and beat and imprisoned them. (They murdered, among others, a lawyer named Benoit Arthaud, whose only crime appeared to be his first name.) They invaded and searched the Dominican Embassy building, then moved to the ambassador's residence, where those seeking asylum were sheltered, surrounded it, set up machine-gun positions, and prepared to invade.

In Santo Domingo, President Juan Bosch issued an ultimatum: Haiti would either order its forces out of the grounds of his embassy or face the consequences. Dominican tanks moved to the border. American warships patrolled Haitian waters.

There ensued a lengthy diplomatic crisis in which virtually everyone believed that Duvalier was finally finished—that whether it took an American or Dominican invasion, an exile assault across the border, or a successful operation by Barbot, the president would not last out the spring.

DUVALIER BROKE RELATIONS with Bosch, and decided to declare a carnival. With corpses still littering the capital, he brought truckloads of peasants into the city, distributed free rum, arranged for floats and troupes of dancers. As Diederich and Burt report, when a mediating committee from the O.A.S., arrived, Duvalier appeared before them and the roaring crowd. "I am here to continue the tradition of Dessalines and of Toussaint Louverture,' he told the crowd. "I am the personification of the Haitian fatherland. . . . No foreigner is going to tell me what to do. . . . Bullets and machine guns capable of daunting Duvalier do not exist. . . . *I am already an immaterial being.*"

A few days earlier, Dr. Jacques Fourcand, Duvalier's physician, who was also the pistol-toting head of the Haitian Red Cross, had given a famous peroration: If foreigners tried to overthrow Duvalier, he warned, "Blood will flow in Haiti like a river. The land will burn from the north to the south, from the east to the west. There will be no sunrise and no sunset, just one great flame licking the sky. There will be a Himalaya of corpses, the dead will be buried under a mountain of ashes. It will be the greatest slaughter in history." As in the revolution, foreign whites were trying to retake the land the slaves had died to win, but Duvalier, the son of the great Dessalines, would slaughter those foreign invaders as had the father of independent Haiti before him.

The United States briefly "suspended" relations with Haiti and made plans for a provisional government. Disappearances continued in Port-au-Prince, as did the blackouts and roadblocks. But as the crisis dragged on American diplomats began to wonder who among the eternally divided opposition could take over the country; while Bosch, unsure of the support of his own military (which, indeed, overthrew him shortly thereafter), slowly let the crisis cool. Most important, Bosch moved to stop a planned invasion by a pro-Déjoie and pro-Fignolé exile group that the Dominican generals, apparently unbeknownst to their president, had been sponsoring near the border. And Clément Barbot and his brother, who, after installing their families in embassies, had been conducting a prolonged campaign of bombings, assassinations, and ambushes (and had infuriated Duvalier by calling him on his office telephone to tell him he wouldn't last long), were finally trapped in a cane field outside the capital. A combined force of Presidential Guards and some of the Tontons Macoutes whom Barbot had once commanded set fire to the cane and shot the two as they tried to escape.

Once again, Duvalier had won. Soon a pro-government newspaper ran a curious montage on its front page: a picture of Jesus Christ with His hands placed on the shoulders of François Duvalier, above the caption "I have chosen him." An electric sign began to flash on and off over the often blacked-out capital, bearing the message "I AM THE HAITIAN FLAG, ONE AND INDIVISIBLE. FRANÇOIS DUVALIER." Finally, the dictator—bowing, he said, to "popular demand"—declared himself president for life, and was pleased to see his selection confirmed by a plebiscite, in which Haitians were generously allowed to cast as many ballots as they wanted.

The rhythm of plotting, invasion and retribution continued. During the summer of 1964, thirteen members of the exile group Jeune Haiti—mostly young mulatto aristocrats—invaded near the southwestern city of Jérémie, hoping to incite an insurrection. Most were tracked down and murdered by Macoutes, but two were captured alive, sent to the capital, and, after weeks of torture, executed at the National Cemetery in a televised ceremony attended by crowds of children whom Duvalier had ordered brought from the schools. Meanwhile, Duvalier took action against the families of the invaders. Down Jérémie's lovely main street, with its stately galleried buildings, were marched naked the city's richest and most prominent mulatto families—the Sansaricqs, the Drouins, the Villedrouins. These cultivated, European-educated aristocrats, powers of the city for generations, were forced to endure the jeers of the crowd, then were herded along to the barracks, and from there to the airport to be massacred—a task gloatingly performed by Macoutes, who killed the infants and little children first, by dagger, to inflame their parents, and the women next, to inflame their husbands. And then the great houses of the families were thrown open to sack, and the people of Jérémie poured in and took all they could carry.

None of the exile groups ever succeeded in provoking a general uprising. They met with a reluctance on the part of the peasants which resulted not only from their fear of Duvalier's bloody retribution but also from the great gulf that separated the mostly elite invaders and the suspicious peasantry.

Trouble also continued within the army. Late one night during the summer of 1967, officers of the General Staff were called to the palace and then driven to Fort Dimanche. There they found nineteen of their colleagues tied to stakes. The officers were issued rifles, and, under the hard gaze of Duvalier and his Macoutes, ordered to fire. Several days later, Duvalier gave another of his memorable speeches: "Duvalier is going to do something. He is going to take a roll call. . . . Major Harry Tassy, where are you? Come to your benefactor. . . . Absent. Lieutenant Joseph Laroche. . . . Absent." And so on, through the nineteen names. Then, after a pause and with a little laugh, "All of them have been shot."

The officers had apparently been plotting a coup, reportedly the brainchild of Colonel Max Dominique, who had married Duvalier's daughter Marie-Denise and was involved (he thought) in a struggle over the succession with Luc Albert Foucard, the brother of Duvalier's powerful secretary, who had married Nicole, another Duvalier daughter. In any case, Duvalier, presumably out of devotion to Marie-Denise, allowed his son-in-law to take part in the little nocturnal drama at Fort Dimanche on the side of the firing squad, not on that of its targets. After watching the colonel shoot his former co-plotters, the dictator named him ambassador to Spain.

Despite these distractions, by the late sixties Duvalier was firmly in place. The army was divided and enfeebled, its upper ranks occupied by Duvalier loyalists. Those members of the counter-elite who survived remained in exile in New York, Miami, and Santo Domingo, where they went on squabbling and plotting, mostly against one another. Those who remained paid their specially calculated "taxes" to the regime. The bulk of the country's professionals also remained in exile, practicing in New York, Montreal, Miami, and Paris. Newspapers and other media that didn't slavishly support the regime had been suppressed. Macoutes had infiltrated all areas of the public administration, including the university and the remaining labor unions. In the legislature, the deputies competed in the fulsomeness of their praise for the *Président à vie*. A great many priests had been replaced with Macoutes. Several foreign embassies, including Great Britain's, had been reduced to consular level; the United States, which had been by far the largest supplier of foreign aid, had cut off all direct assistance in 1963.

In 1966, a period of consolidation began. The Vatican lifted the excommunication of Duvalier and presented him with one of his greatest victories: The Haitian head of state was granted power to approve the appointment of an indigenous hierarchy, the first ever in Haiti. By now, the traditional elite had learned that, despite Duvalier's lusty rhetoric of class conflict, he had little interest in upsetting Haiti's two-world system. Peasants were trucked in from the countryside to provide mass demonstrations of support, but the money continued to flow from the countryside to the city, and the traditional means of repression were merely absorbed into the Macoute network.

Duvalier smashed and domesticated the institutions by which the elite traditionally guarded its power, but he did not smash the elite itself (except those who threatened him); he merely opened it somewhat, making room for a new black elite, drawn from his cherished "middle class." While in 1957, writes Michel Soukar, "The country was dominated by thirty or so families, twenty-five years later the World Bank mentioned two hundred millionaire families. The Duvalierist Revolution is characterized by this increase in the number of the privileged."[17] Though Duvalier drew many of his Macoutes from the poor quarters, he did nothing to bring money to those neighborhoods—or, indeed, to better the lot of the peasants he so often cited as the base of his support.

After a decade of Duvalier, the greater part of Haiti's business sector had actually come to appreciate "a regime under which strikes are not tolerated, wages do not rise and the social obligations of the labor code can be bypassed by private 'arrangements,'" as Leslie Manigat wrote in 1971. The business class gradually joined the church in coming to "a rapprochement with the regime, in exchange for its own depoliticization."[18] To the elite, as rumors grew of Papa Doc's declining health and of a growing succession struggle, the prospect of a stable, continuing "Duvalierist Revolution" began to look increasingly attractive.

In June of 1969, this sentiment was strengthened when Duvalier liquidated his sole remaining opponents: the Haitian Communists. In an early-morning raid on a safe house on the Avenue Martin Luther King, soldiers murdered almost the entire Central Committee, and increased the number of dead by executing several who had been brought to the scene from Duvalier's prisons. A month later, when Nelson Rockefeller, governor of New York, visited Haiti on a tour of Latin America, Duvalier told him to inform President Nixon how he, Duvalier, had proved his staunch anti-Communism. Then he and the governor went out on the balcony, where the two men greeted a huge, enthusiastic crowd. A photograph of Papa Doc, white-haired and frail, leaning on Rockefeller as both men smiled and waved to the Haitian masses, was widely distributed; the rapprochement with the United States had begun.

Soon a new American ambassador, a black man, arrived, and before long he was openly advocating the resumption of United States aid. Duvalier, who was suffering increasingly from diabetes and heart disease, crushed several absurd attempts to overthrow him, and purged a few cabinet members. The gossip grew over the struggle for the succession.

IN JANUARY, 1971, Haitians were startled to learn that Jean-Claude Duvalier—the immensely fat, famously stupid nineteen-year-old son of the dictator, well known for his preoccupation with cars and girls, and referred to by his schoolmates as *tête-panier* (Basket-Head)—was to be their new ruler. "We all know," Papa Doc told his people, "that Caesar Augustus was nineteen when he took into his hands Rome's destiny, and that his reign remains 'the century of Augustus.'" More soberly, Jean-Claude wrote his father that he understood Papa Doc wanted to "avoid fratricidal fights, mortal for the future of the country [and] assure the perenniality of the revolution."[19] After fourteen years of Duvalierist revolution, these were goals on which the church, the elite, the army, and the Americans could all agree.

The constitution was duly changed to lower the age of eligibility for the presidency from forty to eighteen, and a referendum was held, so that Haitians could overwhelmingly affirm (2,391,916 to zero, according to the official tally) that Jean-Claude was their choice. Meanwhile, the American ambassador had won his campaign for renewed American financial assistance: A new AID contingent was on its way.

On April 21st, François Duvalier died. The American ambassador was called in, and the Duvalier family requested that United States naval forces guarantee the security of the coastline, to prevent rebel landings. Three days later, François Duvalier was buried in an immense ceremony, full of tolling church bells and marked by scenes of weeping and hysteria among ordinary Haitians. At one point during the funeral, a great wind suddenly rose up, and the crowd took cover in panic—it was, many said, the soul of Duvalier leaving the great man's body.

At the Te Deum celebrating Jean-Claude's ascension, Papa Doc's hand-picked archbishop, François Wolf-Ligonde, told the expressionless young man, "Your authority is a participation in divine authority. . . . Chief of State, you are not a simple delegate of the community, Excellency, but its guide, in the pursuit of its highest goals. . . . The years we will live under your accession . . . will constitute a special period in the history of our country. Because, for the first time since our glorious Independence Day, Power is confided to Youth."

A few months before, Papa Doc had claimed the same intention: to "hand the government over to Youth." But he had had a simpler motive, the one that had been his goal all along. After fourteen years of steady attack, of constantly reshuffling cabinets, purging all rivals, rooting out any who might be conceived as pretenders to the throne, he stood alone, supreme and unchallenged. His overarching ambition had been to depart the palace only "to the salute of cannon," and this he had done. But he left no one who could claim the loyalty of his followers. Only a cipher, armed merely with his name and his blessing, could hope to succeed him. "In a way, it was the Old Man's last thumb in everyone's eye," one of Jean-Claude's former officials told me. "Because, you know, all of them—the generals, the priests, the elite—had thought of him as a joke. But he had smashed them, killed them, destroyed them all. And, finally, when only he stood there, and nobody dared challenge him, this was his way of rubbing their noses in it. Because what was Duvalier really saying in picking this fat stupid kid? 'No one can touch me, even in death. Watch: Even in dying, I will force you to take this . . . this *boy* as your ruler. *And you will accept him!*'"

A poster familiar to Haitians had reappeared around Port-au-Prince. "I HAVE CHOSEN HIM" was once more the caption, but this time it was a white-haired Papa Doc who stood in Jesus Christ's place, his frail hand placed on one immense shoulder of his son, Jean-Claude, the mountainous, brooding boy-king in a shiny suit.

The New Yorker, December 4, 1989

The Mountains

O N FEBRUARY 7, 1986, the day the dictator Jean-Claude Duvalier and his wife, Michèle Bennett, flew off to exile in France, a
crowd of jubilant Haitians invaded the National Cemetery, a vast
expanse of concrete crammed with bright-colored tombs—ivory and
turquoise and rose—bearing the names of Haiti's great families. At the surprisingly modest memorial of François Duvalier, Jean-Claude's father, who
had ruled from 1957 to 1971, the crowd converged, extinguished the eternal
flame, swarmed over the white brick structure, and began pounding on it
frenziedly with thousands of stones. Within minutes, the tomb had been
reduced to a dusty ruin: a crumpled roof balanced precariously on four battered struts. But when the doors of the vault beneath were finally ripped
open, it seemed as if the great dictator, fifteen years dead, had played a final
joke on his poor Haitians: The tomb was empty. Some said that the son had
made room for his father aboard the plane filled with expensive luggage, others that Papa Doc had never been buried there at all; still others simply
looked frightened and moved away.

Several months later, I passed through the yellow gates of the cemetery a
little after dawn, when in the gray early light scores of emaciated Haitians,
the graveyard's living inhabitants, were just beginning to stir, crawling out
in their rags from the shelter of the graves. A sweet high voice was singing a
strange, corrupted Latin, and in a moment I saw the *houngan*, a tall young
vodou priest dressed severely in white shirt and black slacks. As he sang the
prayer in a sinuous, eerie voice, half a dozen of the faithful stood nodding
behind him, all facing an old cemetery building—roofless now, its stone
stained and rusty brown—that was jammed with a great confusion of
wooden planks and splinters, coffins and parts of coffins. In a window,
affixed to a sill splattered with white and black wax, a black candle flickered, and next to it stood a skull: It was Saturday, Baron Samedi's day, and
the faithful were honoring him, the *loa* who watches over the land of the
dead.

On the low walls surrounding the ruined tomb of Papa Doc—who, with his black suits and hats and his solemn undertaker's manner, had embodied Baron Samedi for so many Haitians—the graffiti had by now grown into a barely legible palimpsest. Some of it was standard political stuff—"We was must punish all the bloodthirsty ones!"—but most was obscene: coarse words scrawled in degraded Creole ("Michèle Bennett is an old used whore!" "Jean-Claude is a faggot!" "Going with faggots, snorting cocaine—no more in Haiti!"). Yet among the insults and crude drawings there was hardly a reference to the tomb's former occupant, almost nothing about Papa Doc himself—the man who had killed the great majority of the forty thousand Haitians estimated to have been murdered during the Duvalier years. "The father was tough, very tough," one of the worshipers explained. "He killed many, many. But he cared for the people. In the morning, he would give a speech saying the prices were too high, and in the afternoon the prices would go down. And"—he chuckled, touching his temple—"he was smart, so smart."

A tall, thin man wearing only a pair of filthy brown trousers, who was reclining on a rose-colored tomb nearby, did not hesitate when I asked who had been the better ruler, father or son. "The father, the father," he said. "The father gave us bread."

THE FATHER HAD BEEN a Haitian ruler—the bloodiest in Haiti's bloody history, but still a Haitian. He had made himself "sole lord and master" of a land where the overwhelming majority of the people, descendants of slaves, are still haunted by "the specter of the master," where the people nod in mute unsurprise when their rulers emerge as tyrants, and where those who wield power are themselves imprisoned in the relentless logic of the slave master, who must regard all those beneath his lash as potential rebels. But if the father had been awesome yet comprehensible, the son, inheriting power as nineteen-year-old cipher, had gradually emerged as something else, something foreign and decadent. By the end of his fifteen-year rule, Jean-Claude and his wife had become the ultimate bourgeois, the consummate arrivistes, ready to sell the country to the highest bidder. The National Palace had become the scene of opulent costume parties, where the young *Président à vie* appeared dressed as a Turkish sultan to dole out ten-thousand-dollar jewels as door prizes, while the rabble outside were invited to watch the festivities on televisions that had been set up in the parks where they slept.

From the outset, Jean-Claude's regime had been a "free-spinning wheel," relying on the momentum conferred by his father's power and, increasingly as time went on, by the United States. At Papa Doc's death, the American ambassador was called and asked to detail United States Navy ships to patrol Haitian waters in order to ensure a peaceful transition. Soon the Americans were providing more than ships, for Haiti's economic crisis was accelerating. Larger and larger numbers of starving peasants were migrating to the cities. Haiti's soil had been eroding for decades, and, with it, the basis of the extortionist "squeeze and suck" economy on which the government rested; the countryside simply offered less and less to squeeze.

Papa Doc's response had been to reinforce and strengthen the existing apparatus of repression, mainly with his ubiquitous Tontons Macoutes militia, and to close off Haiti from foreign influence. With the accession of Jean-Claude, the country was thrown open. During the first four years of his regime, foreign aid increased tenfold, and it continued to rise sharply. By 1981, when Haiti's entire operating budget had just barely reached $150 million, the country was receiving well over $100 million in foreign aid. Having taken the money from the Americans and their International Monetary Fund and World Bank colleagues, Jean-Claude was forced, to some extent, to take their advice along with it. And the prescription of the planners, while simple in outline, was revolutionary in its implications. Haiti's only hope, they said, lay in its becoming an export economy—what one enthusiastic Agency for International Development administrator described as "the Taiwan of the Caribbean." In the countryside, Haiti must shift from a smallholder system to agroindustry: large-scale agriculture intended to produce winter fruits and vegetables for the American market. Haiti's peasants would have to bow to the inevitable fact that, as a World Bank report said in 1983, "Haiti's long run future will be urban." As an AID report had conceded earlier, "such a drastic reorientation of agriculture will cause a decline in income and nutritional status, especially for small farmers and peasants" and "a 'massive' displacement of peasant farmers."

So the migration already begun would be accelerated; the slums would swell. Out near the Port-au-Prince airport, industrial parks sprang up, rows and rows of hangarlike buildings laid out behind chain-link fences, home to the American sporting-goods and clothing and electronics firms that, encouraged by tax breaks and other incentives, quickly arrived to make use of Haiti's growing pool of cheap labor. Planes flew in each day with plastic and silk, and flew out each night with radios and brassieres. Before long, the assembly industries were employing sixty thousand Haitians, which meant they probably supported a quarter of the population of Port-au-Prince. The Black Republic, independent Haiti, was on its way to becoming a great productive engine, supplying labor to assemble products for American consumers, and depending on imports from American farms for its food. The heir of the Duvalierist revolution had turned the cradle of black nationalism into the world's leading manufacturer of baseballs.

Successfully carrying out such a wrenching economic and cultural revolution, with all its dislocations and anti-nationalist implications, would have demanded the greatest political talent, a skilled and efficient public administration, a consistently strong American economy, and a good deal of luck; Jean-Claude, as it happened, had none of these. The repressive instruments of the regime remained in place, but gradually, under American pressure, the terror died down, and its arbitrary character lessened. Subject to intense human-rights scrutiny by the Carter administration, Jean-Claude let various independent power centers that his father had crushed regain some of their strength: the army, whose position had been bolstered by the creation (under American auspices) of the elite Léopards counter-insurgency battalion; the traditional, largely mulatto elite, many of whom had been exile under Papa Doc, but whose technocratic expertise the young dictator now needed; the church hierarchy, which, thanks to Papa Doc, was now mostly Haitian born; the intellectuals, who used the outlets provided by the church radio station and Jean-Claude's new state television and radio stations to push the political "opening" to its limits. When the father's old-line *noiriste* henchmen—the Duvalierists *pur et dur*—made known their disapproval of these developments, they found themselves out of favor with the son.

Though within days of Reagan's election the opening was slammed shut—a number of intellectuals were rounded up and imprisoned or, in some cases, expelled—Duvalier's Haiti had become a more predictable police state. The regime no longer murdered huge numbers of people; now it preferred to corrupt them.

THE FIRST FAMILY of Jean-Claude's new, showily corrupt elite was unquestionably the Bennetts. They had risen very fast, bursting into prominence in 1980, with Jean-Claude and Michèle's wedding. This huge celebration, in which everything was imported from Paris (gowns, food, hair stylists, fireworks) at a reported cost of millions of dollars, would be remembered as the young dictator's symbolic declaration of independence: It was nothing less than an out-and-out alliance with the mulatto elite—the very families Jean-Claude's ferocious father had decimated. Papa Doc's widow, Simone Ovide, had been vehemently opposed to the match, and in this she joined almost all of the "dinosaurs," the Duvalierist Old Guard. After all, Michèle, a former New York secretary, was not only a divorcée, who was much gossiped about among the Haitian elite for her reputed promiscuity, but, worst of all, she had previously been married to the son of Captain Alix Pasquet, a well-known mulatto officer who in 1958 had led the Dade County Deputy Sheriffs' Invasion, the first of many buffoonish attempts to overthrow Papa Doc.

After the marriage, first father-in-law Ernest Bennett, who had never been a terribly successful businessman, became very wealthy very quickly and very conspicuously. He took advantage of his presidential connection to extend his interests into almost every sector of the economy, from his BMW dealership, to his coffee and cocoa export concerns, to the tiny but surprisingly lucrative Haiti Air, whose planes the now untouchable Bennett was reportedly using to transship, among other things, the most remunerative cargo of all: cocaine.

Such blatant corruption did not amuse Jean-Claude's American sponsors. In 1982, Frantz Bennett, Michèle's brother, was arrested in Puerto Rico for drug trafficking, and began a three-year jail term. That same year saw the appointment, after vigorous pressure from the Americans and their friends at the lending agencies, of Marc Bazin, a former World Bank official, as finance minister. Bazin did not wait long before earning the nickname Mr. Clean, announcing that no less than 36 percent of the government's funds was being stolen, confiscating eighty luxury cars from wealthy families pending payment of duty, and refusing to purchase five thousand tons of sugar that Bennett had generously proposed to sell to his son-in-law's government at roughly double the world price. Such "outrages" continued for almost five months before the dictator fired his finance minister and sent him into exile.

"Haitians have been undemocratic not because they are inherently Fascist but because they are dishonest," Bazin told me four years later. "The whole bloody business of repression, torture, and killing was developed to stay in office, in order to make money."

The country has always been a "kleptocracy." The elite occupy the powerful positions in the government bureaucracy, running the import and export firms, investing in the assembly industries—and paying very few taxes. Traditionally, the government has been supported by commodity and import taxes—paid disproportionately by the poor—and, more recently, by foreign aid. Peasants sell their coffee and other products to speculators at artificially low prices, and they in turn sell them to the exporters (the most powerful of whom, during the later Jean-Claude years, was Ernest Bennett, who, according to some reports, accounted for as much as 40 percent of coffee exports).[1] The taxes that cut into the peasants' profits go to fill the government coffers, and thence flow to the elite: squeeze and suck.

Upon this bedrock are constructed various levels of corruption. The first level is on display in any government ministry, where, in the tiny offices and hallways, hundreds and hundreds of idle people loiter, "working" only a few hours a day. "I went to see a friend of mine in the education ministry," an acquaintance told me, "and I stuck my head through the door of her office and found about twenty people sitting there. So I said, 'I'm sorry, are you busy?' They all looked at one another and burst out laughing." "Oh, you must try the agriculture ministry," a foreign economist told me. "An absolute swamp. Crowds in the hallways, masses of people milling about. It's like out in the street." During Jean Claude's rule, the number of government employees doubled, to thirty-two thousand—officially, that is. A World Bank report estimated that in reality the government employed almost twice that number, noting delicately that "there are many nonexistent and non-performing employees on the public payroll." Many public servants never come to work at all; many receive several checks, made out either in their own names or in the names of dead people: "zombie" checks.

Another level of corruption is hidden in the inflated prices that all Haitians pay for products, including many staples—inflated not only because of high government taxes but because powerful people in the government have awarded import franchises and monopolies to their friends and relatives in the importing business, who then charge Haitians what they please. Under Jean-Claude, so-called "national industries"—state monopolies of sugar, cooking oil, flour, and cement—quickly became sink-holes of corruption. In 1982, for example, the Haitian government pur-chased from an Italian company a prefabricated sugar mill, originally intended for Uganda. The Italians had managed to sell it to Haiti, in part by paying a huge "consultant's fee"—reportedly more than $10 million—to Jean-Claude himself. The mill, unsuited to Haiti's sugar crop, could never have been profitable; set up in Darbonne, south of the capital, and encumbered with many unneeded employees and with costly secondary contracts doled out to the dictator's friends, it soon took its place as yet another perpetual drag on government funds—its losses consuming, together with those of the other "national industries," almost 4 percent of the country's entire gross domestic product from 1982 to 1985.

FINALLY, THERE IS THE inelegant but time-honored technique of just plain stealing. Between 1978 and 1984, Jean-Claude, in addition to receiv-ing an annual expense account of $2.4 million and a supplemental account of $2 million, drew off an estimated $30 million from the Régie du Tabac, which collected commodity taxes. In 1980, the I.M.F. gave Haiti $22 mil-lion in budgetary support; $20 million simply vanished from the govern-ment's account, to be used, as a 1981 United States Congress report put it, "for unknown purposes." Under the Food for Peace program, AID donated to the Haitian government millions of dollars each year in food, including surplus wheat, which was then made into flour at the state mill. The flour was supposed to be sold to Haitians at low prices. In fact, it was sold at prices that were up to 27 percent higher than what imported flour would have cost, in part because to each sack was added a ninety-three-cent surcharge, which went directly to the Duvaliers.[2]

During the early 1980s, the risks of the American-designed develop-ment program became clear. Though a shakeout among computer manu-facturers in the United States helped slow and then halt the growth of the assembly industries, the migrants continued to swell the slums. The num-bers of desperate Haitian "boat people" streaming toward Florida increased dramatically. The discovery of African swine fever among Haitian pigs led to an American-sponsored eradication program that further devastated the countryside. ("When the pigs were destroyed, the school population dropped 60 percent," a United States government anthropologist told me. "For a peasant, a pig was a savings account: He'd slaughter a pig just before school started, and use the money to buy kids' clothes and so on.") The appearance of AIDS among Haitians, and rumors—bitterly resented by Haitians—that the disease had come to the United States from Haiti, led to the abrupt collapse of the tourist industry.

For Jean-Claude's proclaimed "Decade of Development" the results were grim: From 1980 until Jean-Claude's departure, six years later, the Haitian economy shrank by about 15 percent. His father's regime, built on brutal repression applied by absolutely loyal retainers, might have withstood such a strain, but Jean-Claude's government now depended on the support of the elite, a much more fickle and self-centered group. In the cities and towns, the old Duvalierists had already been partly cut out of the spoils, and in the countryside they were being dramatically impoverished. This impoverishment widened the fault line in the Duvalierist coalition into a gaping crevasse and exacerbated the cultural schizophrenia that had plagued the country since independence.

"Jeanclaudism was nothing more than a perversion of Duvalierism," General Claude Raymond, Papa Doc's godson and faithful aide, told me in January of 1988. "When you go into the countryside, as I have, and you see the lot of the peasants, growing more miserable, and poorer, and more desperate, every day, you know this is not Duvalierism. When you hear of the fifteen hundred *houngans* murdered in the countryside during the last two years, you know this is not Duvalierism."

A BLOCK OR TWO from the National Cemetery stands an enormous house, four stories high, flat-roofed, of concrete painted yellow and orange and green. It serves as the home and the *houmfort,* or vodou temple, of Mme. Pierre Toussaint, a.k.a. Mme. Pierrot, one of the richest *mambos,* or vodou priestesses, in Haiti, and an early casualty of the vodou wars that broke out during the spring of 1986, in the aftermath of the fall of Jean-Claude Duvalier.

Mme. Pierrot is a striking figure: a short, heavyset elderly woman with eyes so glaucous they appear almost entirely opaque; thick, fat lips that look bruised and swollen; and a disconcerting way of seizing her interlocutor's arm and leaning in very close when she wants to make a point. When I spoke to her that April, she told me how, within days of Duvalier's departure, two thousand people had invaded her house and stayed several days, looting and destroying. "It was when the priests began to preach against vodou that they began to pillage," Mme. Pierrot said, leading the way through the dozens of empty rooms, with bits of wire still peeping out from the walls where the light switches had been, and twisted shreds of cable remaining from television antennas. "You see, the Catholics, they made Duvalier leave, they made him fall," she explained. "And now they have a lot of power, they're organized."

She pointed to graffiti—"Down with Vodou!" "Liberation of Zombies!"—and laughed grimly. "They came here to steal, that's all, to take things," she said. "You know, 90 percent of the Haitians practice vodou; but very often they are ashamed—especially the richer ones—and they come at night." She opened the door to the *houmfort* itself and pointed. It was a large room, with a center post and a carefully smoothed dirt floor, and it had hardly been disturbed.

"Everyone knows Duvalier killed a lot of people, but there are a lot more crimes now than under Duvalier, and the government"—the interim government of General Henri Namphy, the former army chief of staff, whom the dictator left to rule in his place—"the government does nothing. No one talks about that," she said bitterly.

Thirty feet from Mme. Pierrot's front door, I was stopped by two teenagers. They had helped sack that house, they said. Didn't I know that she was the richest *mambo* in the city, that she had been the preferred priestess of the Duvalier ministers? Yes, Roger Lafontant, the interior minister, used to come to Mme. Pierrot; even Jean-Claude himself came once. Didn't I know that all the *houngans* had been in league with Duvalier?

IN JÉRÉMIE, the beautiful City of Poets, on the tip of Haiti's southern peninsula, I met a young lay worker named Bernardin Fleurvil, a pleasant-faced black in a button-down shirt and neatly pressed slacks. "You want to know about uprooting vodou priests?" Fleurvil asked in response to my question, flashing a bright smile. "We did it ourselves. It was good work," he went on, smiling again, and leaning back against the pale-orange wall of Ste. Hélène Church. "We crushed their *houmforts* and we forced them to recant. You see, all the *houngans* are evildoers. They make people sick, then demand money from them to make them well. And they kill people. All the time. And you know"—Fleurvil lowered his voice—"Duvalier was tied to the *houngans*. That's how he was able to remain in power—he had an arrangement with the *houngans*. Everyone knows that."

And so the *déchoukaj*, or uprooting, of Duvalier was directly followed by the *déchoukaj* of vodou. Throughout the country, during the three months after Duvalier's departure, many *houngans* died—hundreds, probably, though some said thousands. That much is clear, but from there on, as so often in Haiti, motives and ideologies become twisted, tangled, difficult to follow. "Beyond the mountains, more mountains." After the fall of Duvalier and the destruction of those who had served him—Macoutes, *houngans*, or, as was often the case, both—came the eruption of a deep-seated religious and cultural struggle that had inflamed the countryside for more than a century. To the churchmen, it was another battle in a war to the death, pitting their God-fearing Children of Light against the benighted peasants' vodou Children of Darkness, an ideological struggle to which the recent rise of the church as a political opposition force had given fresh energy. To the vodou practitioners—which is to say all the peasants and most of the poor of the cities, as well as nationalist intellectuals—vodou was the central, life-giving force of Haitian culture, its wellspring. The vodou priest was not only the Haitian peasant's holy man but his wise man, his adviser, his artist, and—in those thousands of towns and villages that had no hope of ever glimpsing a medical doctor—his healer. But to churchmen, and to many development specialists, vodou was a retardatory superstition that would disappear with "development."

Fleurvil, twenty-one years old, was a member of Jérémie's Jeunesse Chrétienne, a Catholic youth group. Sitting in the pews of Ste. Hélène's lovely pale blue-and-white nave, he and several other young lay workers—Marie Danois, Pierre Décembre, Joël Paul—eagerly told me how they had carried out what they called their "moral uprooting, uprooting without killing," against the vodou priests.

"Right after Jean-Claude left, the people had been very brutal," Fleurvil said. "In the countryside the people killed many *houngans*. Here in this parish, though, we killed only two evildoers—an old woman and a boy. The old woman had killed many, many people; everyone knew it. She was burned alive. Right in the middle of the street—it was a spectacle. Then the boy was decapitated."

"And his ears—" Marie Danois put in.

"Yes, yes, his ears were cut off and dragged behind," Fleurvil said.

Four days after Jean-Claude left, Fleurvil and his friends had a meeting. "We met here in Ste. Hélène School," he told me. "And finally we worked out a method of 'moral uprooting' that would give a moral lesson, that would motivate the *houngans* and the evildoers to abandon their craft. Then we went to see the bishop."

One Saturday in late February, a large crowd of young people, accompanied by a priest and a Protestant pastor and two soldiers in olive green, had proceeded down the narrow streets of Ste. Hélène parish, moving from *houmfort* to *houmfort*, demanding entrance and destroying what they found. "The *houngans* knew if they didn't let us do this they would die," Fleurvil said. "We crushed the *houmforts*. We smashed all the instruments of their craft—the rocks and powders, the little dolls, the bottles filled with foul-smelling liquids. We also found *laissez-passers*—secret passports for traveling at night. The writing on them was horribly deformed."

"And we found a list of names," Pierre Décembre said excitedly. "A hundred and sixty-three names—of those the evildoers had condemned to death. Three of them were already dead."

"Of course, now we had destroyed their *houmforts*," Fleurvil resumed, "but we knew that the craft itself remained in their heads. So we talked to them, and they agreed to give up their craft, to begin serving the church. Thirteen came here and appeared before the congregation during mass and rejected that profession."

Had the priest cooperated in all this, I asked.

Fleurvil smiled. "Oh, yes," he said. "Père Côté went everywhere with us, walking with us all day, from house to house. He is a priest who is very determined in carrying out his mission."

IN A FINE TWO-STORY house perched on a knoll in Jérémie, overlooking the Gulf of Gonâve, sat Père Lucien Côté, a tough Québécois priest in his sixties, stocky, with a full head of iron-gray hair, and a big silver cross fastened to his buttonhole. "The people here have always been afraid of these . . . persons," he began, in a gravelly voice, rocking back and forth in an old wooden rocking chair on a second-floor porch. "Whenever anyone dies, they say one of these people has 'eaten' them—that's the expression. After Duvalier left, ten were killed in Privilé, another ten in Buvet—they had been burned or ripped apart. Terrible. I remember I saw one boy riding his bicycle, and he'd tied something to the handlebars with some string, and when I looked closely it turned out to be two ears he was dragging behind him. Anyway, in my parish thirteen of these persons were supposed to die. When I heard, I said, 'We can't do that. There must be another way.' So I gathered twenty of my young people and the Protestants—they are anti-Satanists par excellence, you know—and we paid them visits, moving over them one after another, like a great wave. We said, '*Bonjour!* We know there are some who want to kill you. But we want to help you.'

"We not only destroyed the *houmforts*," Père Côté went on, "but smashed the oratories and the altars, the small drums they used to call their friends, and the big drums for the ceremonies. We found their hidden bottles of herbs, their potions, their images of Erzulie—she's the double of the Virgin Mary."

ERZULIE, THE BLACK VIRGIN, is one of the key *loas* of the vodou pantheon; the earth itself was born through her breast, as Christ was born to the Virgin. Yet Erzulie is a flirtatious, capricious romantic lady who adores fine presents, wine, perfume, chocolates. During ceremonies, she descends the center post in the *houmfort* to "mount" or take possession of her worshippers, as do all the *loas*. Indeed, Père Côté would have found other familiar figures in the *houmforts*—bright chromolithographs, torn from Catholic prayer books, of St. James the Elder, clad in his steel helmet, who doubles for Ogu, the warrior god; St. Anthony the Hermit, who doubles as Legba, the lord of the road and the interpreter between men and spirits. Vodou, as Père Côté well knew, is a syncretic, encompassing religion, which, upon its arrival with the slaves from West Africa in the sixteenth century, began to absorb the Catholic iconography into its own practice. In Haiti today, the vodou practitioner tends to think of himself as, above all, a good Catholic. Does he not, after all, worship one Bon Dje, one Good Lord, through the intercessions of his *loas*, his saints?

But the church has always felt otherwise. So as Père Côté and his young helpers marched through Jérémie they would have torn down those pictures of their saints, and destroyed them along with the drums and the potions.

"And then," Père Côté was saying, "we found the powders, made from the bones of children they killed. People said that Duvalier and his father used to ask these persons to give them the bones of babies so they could make ceremonies that would ensure the power of the government.

"But our purpose in all this was to make the people's fear of these persons disappear," Père Côté went on. Only progress would eliminate these superstitions: "Gradually, as the people here become more enlightened and aware, they will abandon them. Literacy, for example, will bring us many gifts, and not the least of them will be that the people will be more scientific in their outlook."

So, in the end, was vodou just a matter of ignorance, benightedness, lack of education?

"Oh, no!" Père Côté said, raising his voice and leaning forward in his rocking chair. "It's not only a psychological fact—it's a *spiritual* fact! I do a great many exorcisms, and when I exorcise these spirits I know that after-ward these people are healed. Healed! I know that the spirit is in them. I know because it *speaks* to me!"

Talking rapidly, Père Côté told of a religious meeting in a village near Les Cayes, on the southern peninsula, in which a twenty-six-year-old woman suddenly collapsed to the floor, possessed. "She thrashed about on the floor and tried to scratch me with her fingernails and to pull off my cross," the priest said. "I began to pray, in Latin, and, of course, this peasant girl knew nothing of Latin. 'Spirit, what is your name?' I said, in Latin, and instantly from her mouth came a low voice intoning the word 'Agwe.' Of course, they have a spirit called Agwe; so I knew who the spirit was and I prayed and prayed, and finally"—Père Côté grasped the cross he wore—"finally, I cast him out. And at last the girl stood up—she was healed. The spirit was gone from her. And then I asked her in Latin what her name was, and if she knew Agwe, and, of course, she didn't understand a word."

The priest silently rocked back and forth for a moment or two, his eyes closed. Then he looked at me and said, slowly and carefully, "I see these spirits as Satan, another form of Satan. Their own spirits could not act with so much spiritual force. You see, these people"—he swept his arm about to take in the tiny, crude houses below—"believe that they can't talk to God, that He is too far, and that only these spirits can serve as intermediaries. Everything for them derives from their belief that God is too far away."

"THE PRIEST CAME AND SAID, 'Now Duvalier is gone and there are no more *houngans*,'" Camoniè, an ancient *houngan*, told me several months later. "He said that it was the *houngans* who had made the Duvaliers monkeys"—given them power. "And then the priest took the drums."

Camoniè is a small, wiry old man—perhaps seventy-five, perhaps older, he doesn't know—who lives in a hut set on the edge of a deep gorge near the tiny village of Sainte-Rose, which lies on a footpath high above Marbial. Marbial itself is a cluster of houses in the mountains above Jacmel; only a few miles separate it from that beautiful city, on Haiti's southern coast, but one needs a very sturdy four-wheel-drive jeep, a dry season, perfect weather, and a good deal of luck to make the teeth-chattering trip between them in two hours. Crunching over fields of sun-whitened boulders, constantly plowing back and forth through the quick-flowing river, one slowly climbs into the valley—into what feels like a prehistoric landscape, its steep walls molded into bizarre volcanic shapes. At Marbial, one leaves the overheated jeep and begins the long hike to Sainte-Rose, following the narrow, twisting path up the mountains. Three hours later, one arrives sweat-drenched at the Church of Ste. Rose. It is here, in a tiny white stone building with red doors and a sheet-metal roof—before which a scattering of malnourished, listless people loiter, watching roosters peck about and skeletal dogs bask in the sun—that the vodou drums and other "instruments" of Camoniè and his colleagues were stored in the weeks after the fall of Duvalier.

Three days after the fall of Duvalier, a peasant sitting in front of Ste. Rose confirmed, Père Marat Guiran had come up from Marbial, gathered the people at Ste. Rose, and announced that "anyone who didn't bring in his drums would be uprooted." And when Père Guiran stopped to see Camoniè, the oldest and wisest *houngan* in the region, Camoniè did what he was told. "I didn't argue, because he is a priest," he said. "After all, I have no right to say what the state does." For Camoniè, living high up in the mountains, there is no real difference between a priest and the state. Both are distant, both draw their power from outside, neither is to be argued with.

Along with the other *houngans*, Camoniè, who was old enough to remember the church's last great "anti-superstition" campaign, in the early 1940s, had gone to Ste. Rose two weeks later, and had appeared at a big mass where all the *houngans* promised they would no longer "serve Guinée"—that is, serve Africa, by practicing vodou.

"They say we have no right to serve Guinée," Camoniè told me, waving a hand across the great gorge. "But it's something they can't take away. I was born into this law. It's what I am; it can't be changed. It's useless to try."

Franck Étienne, a well-known Haitian novelist and painter, had told me, "Haitians live in a dream; they are a mysterious, mystical people. Theirs is the opposite of the Western mind, where all is rational, devoted to progress—which means, in the end, profit, 'development.' Our culture is not really a Western culture at all; and the source of it, the wellspring of the art and the way of life in Haiti, is vodou."

AT THE HEIGHT of the vodou wars, a *houngan* named Max Beauvoir established a command center at his home, a large stone house and *houmfort* south of the capital. A handsome, articulate black man, Beauvoir was part politician, part crusader, part self-promoter, part charlatan. Educated in Paris and New York as a biochemist, he had returned to Haiti when his grandfather, a well-known *houngan*, died, having designated his grandson his successor. Though Beauvoir styled himself a radical *noiriste*—a fervent defender of vodou and Haitian peasant culture against the encroachments of foreign influence—he was best known for performing vodou "spectacles" in Port-au-Prince which were well frequented by tourists.

Ensconced in his study—its gray stone walls draped with beaded vodou flags, its shelves lined with classics on religion and anthropology—Beauvoir worked at a computer, compiling a list of *houngans* who had been killed or attacked, printing out transcripts of inflammatory remarks that had been broadcast on Radio Soleil and Radio Lumière (the Catholic and Protestant stations), and, above all, keeping in touch with the press, both Haitian and international. To Beauvoir, the central issue was clear: The Catholic priests and, even more actively, the Protestant pastors were seizing their chance to wipe out vodou once and for all.

One day that spring, I drove with Beauvoir to a *houmfort* near the town of Bognotte, in the sugarcane-growing region of Léogâne. An old *houngan* named Dieusibon came forward to greet us, and offered us chairs under a tree in front of his temple, a small mud building with walls gloriously painted in pale, chalky blue and salmon, covered with the gorgeous figures of Erzulie and her friends—a tribute from the old *houngan* to his *loa*.

Beauvoir listened intently as Dieusibon told how a group of five young people had come to his *houmfort* and demanded money "or else they would crush his place." He had told the gang he had nothing to give but had begged them not to destroy his *houmfort*, promising to have some money when they returned.

"This is how they do it," Beauvoir said to me. "They'll come back later and take his money, then kill him." He leaned forward and asked Dieusibon where the youths had come from, and received in response a gesture: over that hill. He asked again, and after hesitating the man said that he thought they had come from La Colline and, after more prodding, that they had been sent by a "Pastor Harris." Beauvoir looked at me in triumph—La Colline was also known as Chrétienville, after its large Protestant mission.

Beauvoir handed the old man a card and instructed him to call if he had more trouble. "I can be here in an hour," he said. "And if they come back, blow on the *limbé*"—the age-old Haitian tocsin, inscribed in the iconography of the Revolution: The black slaves blew on their conch shells, summoning their fellows from the plantations to revolt.

LA COLLINE WAS A SMALL TOWN, but it had at its center a large new church, of pale-orange stone, and a sign informing the visitor that he had arrived in "CHRISTIANVILLE—JIM AND CAROL HERGET, DIREC- TORS." I asked a well-dressed, smiling young Haitian where I could find Pastor Harris and after a bit of discussion he led me up a little hill to a pretty American-style ranch house, built of the same orange stone. There I met Jim Herget, a plainspoken American in his mid-fifties from Buffalo, New York, who introduced himself as a founder and director of Christianville, a mission of the Churches of Christ.

Herget was proud to show me around the mission, pointing out the fish- pond, the chicken houses, and the pig farm, all the buildings so trim and new that they looked incongruous in the Haitian landscape, as did the smil- ing, well-scrubbed young Haitians walking about. In Christianville, Herget told me, they had established Haiti's first 4-H Club; in the Christianville school they taught six hundred children; in Christianville's special feeding program they cared for four hundred undernourished children. Two thousand meals a day were served at Christianville, Herget said; some of the food was raised right there, but much of it was supplied through Catholic Relief, the Church World Service, and other "nongovernment organizations" and "private voluntary organizations"—NGOs and PVOs in development lingo—supported by American foreign aid.

I asked Herget about Dieusibon's charge—that the youths who attacked him had been sent from Christianville. The missionary laughed. "These witch doctors," he said, chuckling and shaking his head. "Well, it's true we haven't heard much of those drums these last few months." He laughed again, then looked at me. "No, seriously, I don't know anything about that. Look, we hope here that if these kids learn a little they won't need that kind of superstition. Here we try to teach people reading and writing—real basic. We try to see they get fed every day. We try to teach sewing and cooking and other useful things."

They *were* useful things, and many would certainly argue that Christianville greatly benefited this part of Haiti, as did other Protestant missions that had sprung up in the country during the past few years, spurred on by the available American aid and welcomed by what a 1985 number of Christianville's cheery newsletter, *The Evangel*, called "the beautiful 'open door' given missionaries by the Haitian Government." *The Evangel* observed, in its boosterish tone, "Our 'Missionary army' in Haiti is gaining strength"—an observation that, however ominous it might sound to Beauvoir, meant that the missionaries were feeding more people, helping to clothe them, trying to educate them.

But in so doing, of course, they were creating God-fearing Protestants. As a self-questioning technician at one of the international agencies bluntly put it, "When I hear myself tell someone I'm 'in development,' I always try to remember that what I'm really in is the culture-busting business."

No other Caribbean country can boast a culture with the vibrancy of Haiti's, the purity of its African heritage; and, of the beautiful canvases in the galleries of Port-au-Prince, many of the best come from *houngan* painters and use the iconography of vodou. And yet, the blunt missionary might have asked, do pretty pictures feed Haitians? "The poor are always with us," André Pierre, a *houngan* renowned for his painting, told me, smiling a serene smile. "He who doesn't live among the poor the *loa* doesn't visit." Which is why Pierre so hated the Protestants. "These pastors are rich," he said angrily. "That's all they think about—making money. They don't truly believe in the spirit." For Pierre, as for all Haitian peasants, to believe in the spirit is to believe in the earth—*la terre*. "Everything comes from the earth," he told me, "Everything—even man. That is Haiti: agriculture, working the earth. The inspiration for the paintings," he said, sweeping his hand about a small room, next to his *houmfort*, where an unfinished painting of Ibolélé, the cock *loa*, stood, "comes from the earth, from agriculture. Without it, I could not paint with the hand of God."

THIS INDOMITABLE SENTIMENT was now fighting against the accelerating decline of the countryside—against erosion, overpopulation, and the pressure of the "development experts," the "culture-busters" from AID and the World Bank and elsewhere, who saw it as inevitable that impoverished, peasant Haiti would become an "urban country." And yet thus far Haiti had had mostly slums and political upheaval to show for their efforts. "I don't know any country that has moved toward this kind of development without crushing its own culture," said Max Paul, the director of the Bureau of Ethnology, a large institution in Port-au-Prince which had grown, like Duvalier's *noirisme*, out of the ethnological movement of the 1930s. "Televisions, big cars—is that development?" he asked. "We have some of it now, in any case."

At bottom, he said, development was a political question. "Foreign industries of the sort Jean-Claude wanted come here only when you give them dirt-cheap labor, no unions, low taxes. This is a difficult combination to produce in a democracy. That is why we had *la paix jeanclaudiste*—no unions, no labor unrest, etc. The political system guaranteed it."

And that is why, after the fall of Jean-Claude, strikes were not long in coming to the assembly plants, with the strikers demanding wages of up to six dollars a day—double the going rate—and why a fair number of factories responded, with predictable alacrity, by closing down. During the violent months following Jean-Claude's departure, at least ten thousand jobs were lost. And more disappeared when Leslie Delatour, a young University of Chicago–trained finance minister appointed by General Namphy's interim government, took advantage of the opening provided by the transition and the increase in American aid to close the Darbonne sugar mill and other corruption-ridden remnants of "Jeanclaudism."

For Delatour and his American sponsors, as for the American sponsors of Jean-Claude Duvalier, Haiti represented an economic problem to be solved, and the only solution was the American market.

"Look, first, this country will not be able to survive without extensive foreign aid," a high-ranking American diplomat told me. "Foreign assistance is just a fact of life for Haiti. And if you want jobs real quickly, the quickest way to do it is bring in factories. It's that simple."

But what about the overwhelming power it gives the United States?

The diplomat smiled and looked at the ceiling. "Look, I mean, let's face it: America doesn't really need Haiti," he said. "The American interest in Haiti is to prevent things from getting really bad, to get a decent life for Haitians, so we can prevent all the things that could happen if we don't: Haitians killing one another, Haitians killing Americans in Haiti, more Haitian boat people heading to Florida."

When Haitians looked at the results of Jean-Claude's rule, they saw not the new assembly plants but a ravaged countryside and a plundered economy. And when they looked at the interim regime of General Namphy they saw the same policies being applied with what seemed to be more efficiency and even more drastic results: Large state-owned enterprises summarily closed, throwing Haitians out of work.

Another result was the wave of contraband, much of it from the United States, that suddenly flooded through the now "liberated" ports, thereby helping Delatour in his efforts to "liberalize" the heavily protected Haitian economy. In Gonaïves, Miragoâne, Saint-Marc, and other ports, ships from Miami would tie up at piers crowded with eager Haitians, and unload cargoes of cheap American rice, or used refrigerators, or secondhand bicycles, or even used Mercedes sedans. For each item that passed through his port the local army commander would receive a fee: ten dollars, it was said, for each bicycle, from two to four dollars for each bag of rice, as much as a thousand dollars for each car. Though Delatour had stamped out some of the corruption tied to the state industries, smuggling provided the delighted officers with an entirely new cash flow—one that bypassed the government entirely.

Others were not so pleased. Delatour's layoffs led to large demonstrations. The contraband rice and other products ruined Haitian farmers; peasants began attacking the convoys of smuggled Miami rice as they made their way to the capital. Namphy's policies seemed only a more effective—and harmful—version of those of Jean-Claude Duvalier.

That is why it makes more sense to understand the real anti-Duvalier "revolution" as having happened not in 1986, with Jean-Claude's fall, but in 1971, with his ascension. As the arch-Duvalierist General Claude Raymond told me bitterly, "Duvalierism died in 1971, along with François Duvalier." A decade later, the extreme unpopularity of his son's policies, and the corruption attached to them, had begun to engender a nationalist reaction in the countryside and the provincial cities. "The revolt started among the displaced peasantry," Jean-Jacques Honorat, an agronomist and development theorist, told me. "In the slum of Raboteau, in Gonaïves, for example, it started among the displaced peasants."

But this nationalist reaction produced only the interim regime of General Namphy; the strong nationalist aspirations that had helped overthrow Jean-Claude were left unfulfilled, and various groups sprang up to lay claim to them. Most prominent was the "democratic sector"—the intellectuals, organizations, and peasant groups that eventually formed the leftist Front National de Concertation.

There was also a darker claimant—an old-line Duvalierist counter-movement, which had begun as a movement of Duvalierists *pur et dur* against Jean-Claude and the American and mulatto encroachment he welcomed. These staunch black nationalists did not interpret the public disgust with

Jean-Claude as extending to *them*; on the contrary, Jean-Claude's policies disgusted them as well. And at least some of these Duvalierists actually believed that they could win an election.

Nine months after Jean-Claude's flight, the old-liners tried to start a "neo-Duvalierist"—that is, "true Duvalierist"—party. But Haitians poured into the streets in huge protests—protests the Duvalierists believed were orchestrated by the left-wing opposition. The Duvalierists were forced to disband. They watched angrily as the opposition gained control of the electoral process, by drafting a constitution that stripped the army of its power to run elections and gave it to an independent Electoral Council. Then, when the council barred Clovis Désinor, Claude Raymond, and the other Duvalierists from competing in the elections, and when the army under General Namphy stepped ostentatiously aside—to show that it would not defend the electoral process the council was conducting—the Duvalierists at last had their say: In bloody massacres on election day, November 29, 1987, in which at least thirty-four people were killed as they waited to vote.

After the massacre, the Americans withdrew their aid from the traumatized country, and the four most popular candidates announced that they would refuse to take part in a second election, which the army was hastily organizing. The officers would use this second election, many Haitians believed, to bring an old-line Duvalierist to power. But the officers, after three decades of serving Duvaliers, had little desire to see Désinor or Raymond in the palace. Shortly before the election, an army-controlled Electoral Council shocked Haitians by disallowing the Duvalierists' candidacies once again. The Duvalierists' ambitions were left unsatisfied.

In the days leading up to the new election, Haitians passed the time speculating about whom the army would choose as its *président marionette*. The candidates scurried and postured, making pronouncements and courting influential officers at diplomatic receptions. On January 17, 1988, perhaps one Haitian in ten stepped forward to vote, and after a delay proper to the gravity of the occasion it was announced that a world-renowned political scientist, scion of one of Haiti's most distinguished families, a political leader who had spent a twenty-three-year exile struggling to achieve democracy in his homeland, had been elected Haiti's thirty-seventh ruler. And thus, two years to the day after Jean-Claude's fall, Leslie F. Manigat came to power.

To SAY THAT MANIGAT came to power is to simplify matters somewhat, of course, for it was the very question of his power that had yet to be decided. On inauguration day, the new president sat behind a tiny table in the Salle des Bustes, on the main floor of the National Palace, beaming as the *chef de protocole* brought forward well-wishers. As he waited, Manigat, looking less portly than usual in a smart black suit, toyed absently with the blue-and-red presidential sash—placed over his shoulder only an hour before by General Namphy.

During the ceremony, the general's light-colored moon-shaped face had repeatedly crinkled into a broad grin; indeed, it was remarked later that he had spent a good part of what was meant to be a solemn occasion smiling, even laughing—that he had seemed to regard it all as a big joke. After the ceremony, while the president finished greeting the well-wishers in the Salle des Bustes, General Namphy waited upstairs, in the Salon Jaune. The general, who was beginning a three-year term as commander-in-chief of the Haitian armed forces—a position to which he had prudently appointed himself three months before—watched as servants arranged three Louis XVI chairs carefully on the gold carpet: one for the new president; one for the smiling commander-in-chief, at his right hand; and, at his left, one for General Williams Régala, who for two years had served as General Namphy's deputy in the interim regime, and also as his minister of the interior and of defense. As holder of the latter position, General Régala—a handsome black man with an intelligent, if permanently smirking, face—had authority over the army, the police, and the security services.

So the scene in the Salon Jaune—the newly elected president flanked by his self-proclaimed commander-in-chief and his minister of defense, as he greeted Haitian and foreign dignitaries—illustrated a central problem confronting Manigat: How, as a president who came to power in an election run by the military, in which so few eligible Haitians voted, could he find the support to counterbalance the generals and become anything more than their puppet?

As the men took their seats, a heavily built, very black officer with a frighteningly impassive face stepped forward and stood beside General Namphy: Colonel Jean-Claude Paul, the commander of the Dessalines Battalion, housed in the Casernes Dessalines, the mustard-colored barracks adjacent to the palace. Today, however, Colonel Paul was serving as General Namphy's bodyguard; he held, discreetly, almost swallowed up in one enormous hand, an Uzi submachine gun. Colonel Paul was known to be a great friend of many of the old Duvalierists; it had been his olive-green-clad troops who had stood by while voters were shot and hacked to pieces on November 29. He was rumored to be involved in drugs, and would soon be indicted by a Miami court for cocaine trafficking. The new president, in his inaugural address, had surprised Haitians by lashing out at drug trafficking—an activity known to have become a lucrative pastime for a number of senior officers, and thus a preoccupation of Reagan administration officials who had so far refused to restore American aid.

For President Manigat, assuming control of a country whose economy was being slowly strangled for lack of hard currency, Colonel Paul and his Uzi thus represented an interesting complication, as they also did for at least one member of the diplomatic corps who would shortly be brought forward to toast the new president: The American ambassador, Brunson McKinley, a tall, distinguished, but on this occasion rather sheepish-looking man whose dexterous efforts to avoid speaking to the new president were later remarked upon by several guests. Only the week before, the ambassador's boss, Secretary of State George Shultz, had told Congress that the United States, in evaluating its support, would be waiting to see whether President Manigat would "in some way assert himself so that he isn't simply a spokesman for the military."

Others were waiting to see that question answered as well. Formidable scholar of Haitian history that he was, the new president undoubtedly recognized his predicament as a variation on what during the 1840s had come to be called *la politique de doublure* ("the politics of understudies"), whereby certain powerful elements in Haitian society would choose as figurehead a malleable person, through whom it would be convenient to rule. On the last occasion, in 1957, the army had had the misfortune to choose François Duvalier. As a protégé of Duvalier, Manigat had been on hand to see that episode played out. He had seen how the supposedly feeble Papa Doc moved swiftly to replace the preening chief of staff who had brought him to power, how he had cleverly played one officer off against another.

Of course, the officers (including Namphy, then a young second lieutenant) had seen it all as well. They chose Manigat at least partly because, having been so long in exile, "he was the one who had no electoral support, who had no one behind him," as a former high official in Jean-Claude Duvalier's interior ministry told me. But of all the candidates Manigat was the last one anybody would pick as a malleable puppet. He was famously brilliant, famously charming, famously strong-willed. With so many politicians eager for a chance at the puppet's role, why did Generals Nemphy and Régala single him out? Because, in the words of Leslie Delatour, "He was the most respectable, and his international connections were fantastic." After the November 29th massacres, Haiti had become an international pariah. Who better than Manigat to bring the country in from the cold? But that, of course, raised the awkward matter of Ambassador McKinley and, behind him, the officials of the Reagan administration, who were so concerned about drugs.

From what sources would Leslie Manigat be able to draw power? There were only three: from outside the country, by restoring the foreign-aid lifeline; from within, by somehow proving to Haitians that, despite the manner of his coming to office, he was an independent leader; and from the military itself, by playing the officers off against another. These strategies, as would soon become apparent, were irreconcilable. It was as if a kind of cat's cradle had formed, an intricate trap that during the next months would shift and move, assume different configurations, but would always hold entangled at its center the struggling figure of the brilliant Leslie Manigat.

EVEN BEFORE MANIGAT'S VICTORY was officially announced, he had launched an appeal to the other candidates to join him in "a coalition," which would include "not only those who took part in these elections but those who didn't." But the most popular of the opposition candidates remained aloof, demanding that the new president prove his good intentions by moving quickly to liberate political prisoners, halt the continuing arrests in the countryside, and appoint independent commissions to investigate the election violence. Meanwhile, "popular leaders" like Père Jean-Bertrand Aristide, a charismatic priest lionized by his parishioners in the slums of Port-au-Prince, immediately began denouncing Manigat's "*gouvernement diabolique*," and warning ominously that "from now on the people will refuse to take to the streets empty-handed."

This was just the sort of talk that the November 29 massacre had been meant to stifle. It was sure to be unpopular with the officers—especially men like Colonel Paul. After the fall of Jean-Claude Duvalier, the colonel had disarmed at least one large unit of Macoutes and brought them back to the Dessalines Barracks, absorbing a substantial number into his battalion, according to a young lance corporal and former Macoute. And he employed hundreds of others as "attachés" of the army.

And now Franck Romain, the newly reelected mayor of Port-au-Prince, established another Duvalierist power center, at City Hall. Romain, himself a former army colonel and a Papa Doc protégé, had built up his own Macoute organization, drawn from the Cité Soleil slum.

Soon after Manigat took office, the capital began to endure what came to be called a "climate of insecurity." Cars were stopped at roadblocks, and their occupants searched at gunpoint, there were arbitrary arrests, searches of opposition figures, armed robberies; and corpses littered the streets each morning. In the countryside, the extermination had continued steadily since the twenty-ninth. "They have cut off the heads of the democratic organizations that had emerged," Père Freud Jean, a liberation priest from Belladère, a town near the border, told me. "Those organizations that existed have been systematically destroyed." In the Artibonite region, a local priest said the *chefs de section* were going after democratic leaders with machetes.

Manigat could do nothing about any of this; he had little power over his commander-in-chief or his minister of defense and, in any event, the nation's recently adopted constitution gave the president no power to remove the army commander before the end of his three-year term. The constitution had envisaged a weak presidency and a strong legislature. Unfortunately for Manigat, his legislature had come to power the same way he had: The officers had had the council declare those candidates most congenial to them the new senators and deputies. Since virtually all the deputies therefore owed their jobs to General Régala, Manigat's own defense minister could reach around the president and block legislation as he saw fit.

The endless quarrels that resulted were carried on in an atmosphere of economic collapse. Though Manigat's government would eventually obtain promises of small amounts of aid from France, Italy, Taiwan, and Japan, the Americans wouldn't budge. The congressmen insisted on "free and open elections," which the new president of Haiti was not in a position to provide. As a senior American diplomat told me, "We began the process of trying to do something for Manigat, but while we convinced the executive branch we couldn't convince Congress; the people in the opposition whom Manigat had not managed to bring around had too strong an influence there." The congressmen also demanded the extradition of Haiti's allegedly No. 1 drug dealer—a man who also happened to command the most powerful unit in the Haitian Army. "Each time I met with the American ambassador, he asked about Jean-Claude Paul," Martial Celestin, Manigat's prime minister, told me. "They were obsessed with him." Of course, Manigat couldn't deliver Colonel Paul; only other powerful officers could do that.

IN MAY 1988, President Manigat—with his treasury almost empty, no American money in sight, and his troubles with the legislature increasing— began to move against contraband and corruption. He appointed a customs official for the port city of Saint-Marc and fired the heads of the state flour mill—a notorious source of corruption—and Téléco, the state telephone monopoly. In Saint-Marc, Captain Ernst Ravix, the local army commander, responded by organizing a demonstration against his president in which some three thousand residents marched, chanted, and burned barricades. In the capital, coup rumors flew, for the two executives Manigat had fired were associates of General Namphy. More than thirty corpses appeared on the capital's streets during May alone.

Early in June, Gérard Latortue, the foreign minister, visited Washington and asked State Department officials and members of Congress "to come to see and assess the situation" before they took further action against the Manigat government. He urged the United States to consider the alternatives: "If we go, it will not be democracy that comes."

On June 14, General Namphy summoned Colonel Paul and informed him that he was being "promoted" to head of intelligence at military headquarters—that is, to a desk job. There were rumors that Reagan administration officials, who had been heavily criticized for the United States' inability to unseat Panama's Manuel Noriega, had promised Latortue a partial resumption of aid if Paul was transferred. Some people said that Namphy, annoyed by Manigat's recent actions and impatient with his lack of results in dealing with the Americans, was preparing the ground for a coup against the president; others that Namphy had ordered the transfer at the urging of the president, who was setting a clever trap for the general.

In any event, Colonel Paul—no doubt with American prisons on his mind—left the general's office and, finding the entrance to the Dessalines Barracks blocked by soldiers loyal to Namphy, went to the palace and told his president that he would not accept the transfer. He then climbed over a wall of the barracks, regained control, and barricaded himself inside with his men. Paul's vulnerability had provoked a split in the army; at last, Manigat's chance had come.

Early on June 15, Manigat issued a communiqué. "To avert a major crisis," it began, "from which democracy and the country will suffer the damage, I am ordering the withdrawal" of the transfer order, which, he said, violated the constitution, because General Namphy had not informed the president of it beforehand. This was bald defiance, and the capital braced for action; but now Manigat had the cornered Paul on his side, and the thousand Dessalines troops. A few hours later, the general publicly backed down, issuing a communique that rescinded Paul's transfer "for the moment."

The next day, Manigat told journalists that his action had had nothing to do with "individuals" but was a matter of "the supremacy of civilian power and respect for constitutional norms." Yet the president's demeanor seemed to belie his words. "He was all puffed up, pumped up with his power," Jean-Claude Bajeux, a National Front leader, said later. "You could see it, this feeling of 'Now, at last, I—I have taken power!'" And he immediately began to use it. On the evening of June 17, Haitians were astonished to learn that Manigat, the puppet president, had fired General Henri Namphy, commander-in-chief.

It was a Friday night. "What I heard at parties that night from everyone was 'Oh, Manigat's a big man, he did it!'" a longtime Port-au-Prince resident told me. "A lot of people started to respect him a little, because he had got rid of Namphy." And though the streets of the capital quickly emptied in the expectation of trouble, there came not a sound from the officers of the Haitian armed forces, the powerful men who only four months before had installed the powerless Manigat in office.

But while the officers sat paralyzed in their houses there was anger in the ranks; among the troops of the Presidential Guard it had been brewing for a long time. From the beginning, the arrogant intellectual from the diaspora had shown little talent for the peculiar blend of condescension, diplomacy, and patriarchal largesse—the essence of military politics—that had bound Haiti's praetorian guard, created under François Duvalier, to its president. The soldiers were mostly uneducated young men from the slums, peasants, or sons of peasants. Papa Doc had made sure he knew each soldier's name, had listened to his problems, and, most important, had personally handed him his money, adding special bonuses to help pay for a corporal's new house or for the care of his sick child. Jean-Claude had continued this tradition, and so had General Namphy.

The troops who were stationed at Manigat's house, a private told me later, "weren't even given a place to sleep." And he added, angrily, "His wife didn't respect the soldiers of the Presidential Guard." Mme. Manigat, he said, on being told by one soldier that his daughter was about to take her first communion, reached into her purse and handed him a dollar. The guardsmen were not impressed with the president's high-toned "foreign" scruples; in a country where power traditionally binds its servants fast with condescension and cash, they felt themselves spurned and deprived. And now, in siding with Paul over Namphy, the president had "favored the troops of the Dessalines Battalion" over those of his own guard, and thereby upset the delicate balance of rivalries that held the Haitian armed forces together.

Saturday morning, hours after Manigat fired General Namphy, Paul sent about eighty of his soldiers to Namphy's home, a walled house north of the city, where the general sat brooding. The Dessalines men, clad in their olive-green combat uniforms, surrounded both the house and Namphy's regular contingent of twenty-three khaki-clad Presidential Guards. General Namphy was effectively under house arrest, imprisoned by the forces of the man he had tried to unseat only four days before.

By midmorning Sunday, the disgruntled Presidential Guardsmen had gathered in the inner courtyard of the National Palace. "You know, Manigat's never done a thing for us, and Namphy's done a lot," one corporal told the men, according to several soldiers. "Let's go out and get him." The men agreed, resolved to rescue their chief, and spent the rest of the day readying two armored vehicles that were kept in the basement garage of the palace.

Meanwhile, Manigat had determined to push his advantage. That afternoon, a major reshuffling of officers was announced. Among other dramatic changes, Colonel Prosper Avril, who had been a close aide to Jean-Claude Duvalier and remained a highly influential officer, was transferred to a minor post supervising Haitian military attachés abroad. Manigat had made a point of humiliating the officers, evoking memories of Papa Doc.

That evening, soldiers of the Presidential Guard piled into the two armored cars, rumbled out through the palace gates, and headed north on Route Nationale 1. The departure of two armored vehicles from the palace with no authorization during a time of political conflict seemed to attract no official attention. Manigat, whether because he didn't trust the guardsmen or because he thought he had won, had not come to the palace.

When the armored cars reached Namphy's house, the guardsmen, finding the Dessalines troops still on guard, fired their cannons. "They ran like butterflies in the sugarcane," a guardsman told me later, laughing as he quoted the Creole saying. The armored cars pushed their way through the gate, and the sergeant in command clambered out and ran into the house. There he informed a startled and, by some accounts, frightened General Namphy that he, Namphy, was on his way back to the palace, and back to power. The imprisoned general, humiliated by Manigat, abandoned by his fellow officers, had fallen into a deep depression; when the guardsmen appeared, he did not believe them at first, suspecting a Manigat stratagem to send him into exile. His wife, it was reported, burst into tears. Finally, the guardsmen managed to convince their general that it was not a trap. They helped him into his combat uniform, then put him and his wife, daughter, and brother into an armored car for the triumphant ride back to the palace.

Around this time, Port-au-Prince residents, unaware that anything unusual was happening, were plunged into darkness—troops sent to the electric company had "pulled the plug" and with the blackout came a barrage of gunfire from the palace. Instantly, the streets emptied. Minutes later, the celebrating soldiers gathered in the courtyard to greet their still befuddled chief with gunfire and cannon bursts. It was only now, according to several participants, that guardsmen were sent to fetch Colonel Avril and various other senior officers. (The five or six guardsmen I spoke to insisted that they had acted on their own, and had not been manipulated—as many Haitians, including Manigat, believe—by Avril and other officers.)

The excited guardsmen continued firing, hoping to intimidate the Dessalines troops next door. By then, Haitians were convinced that a major battle was taking place. "Everyone was frantically calling all night," a woman told me later. "I tried to call a friend to find out what the hell was going on, but all the circuits were busy." At one o'clock in the morning, Haitians saw a grotesque image flicker to life on their television screens. There before them, surrounded by officers and troops, stood a furious and almost incoherent Henri Namphy, steel helmet askew on his head, machine gun in his hand, shouting Creole at the camera in his barking, stuttering voice.

"Haitian people, here is your general, General Namphy," he said. "You know how we love our Haitian Army . . . You know that General Namphy loves you, too, that he loves the country. What happened is what they didn't want . . . that the army and the people, the people and the army, are the same thing."

High above the city, in the Villa d'Accueil, on the Petionville road, Leslie Manigat, his wife, his daughter, and a number of close aides watched in silence as the general rambled on. After the broadcast ended, the president turned to his family and associates and said simply, "You must prepare yourselves for anything, for now all is lost." Soon two armored cars were roaring into the courtyard, and at the sight of them a unit of Dessalines troops stationed outside the villa turned and fled. The guardsmen climbed down, and a soldier brought out a megaphone and announced to the now unguarded building, "Manigat, come down!" The president responded by turning off the lights. The soldiers fired a cannon, and "the whole house shook." Finally, Manigat shouted, "All right, we will come down quietly." When the president emerged with his wife and aides, their hands above their heads, the guardsmen cursed them: "Band of pigs!" Then they lined up the twenty or so people and raised their guns. "I thought they were going to kill us all," Mme. Manigat said later. But they contented themselves with firing in the air. The president and his family were then taken to the airport. In a few hours, the former first family would be in Santo Domingo.

Meanwhile, Paul was on the telephone negotiating, first with Namphy, later with Avril. Avril offered him a deal: If Colonel Paul agreed to support Namphy's new government, he could keep his command. Paul accepted— apparently persuaded not only by Avril's appeal to military solidarity but also by the noise of the automatic rifles and cannons of the Presidential Guard. For all the shooting that night, there was only one casualty: A soldier shot himself in the leg. ("Against unarmed civilians," Manigat said later, "the army is strong. But . . . in its military function the army is extraordinarily weak.")

The next morning, Colonel Paul stood beside Namphy as the general informed Haitians that Manigat had been trying to make of the military "a docile instrument of his personal power," as a first step on "an irreversible path toward dictatorship in its most brutal form." Manigat, in other words, had tried to become Duvalier; Haitians should be grateful that this time their brave soldiers had been able to prevent it. The general proceeded to dissolve the legislature and name himself president. But it was his appearance a few hours earlier that Haitians remembered—when, with a steel helmet on his head, Henri Namphy had waved his Uzi, and shouted at them "Now the army will rule—with this!"

Namphy II had begun.

THE HENRI NAMPHY who had returned to the palace was a very different man from the gruff but genial officer who had greeted journalists after the fall of Duvalier. Bitter and angry and paranoid, he would brook no challenge to his power. "To understand anything about Namphy Deux, you have to realize that he had never been respected in the army," a former Duvalier official told me. "That is the main reason Duvalier made him chief of staff. The officers would say, 'You know, Namphy's brain is burned out by alcohol. At two in the afternoon he's in civilian clothes. Friday to Monday he's drunk.'" Thanks to Manigat (who remarked in Santo Domingo that the general was "mentally ill"), the other officers' contempt for Namphy had been thrown into high relief: A puppet president had humiliated their commander, and not one of the officers had so much as raised his voice. Back in the palace, and marveling at his resurrection, the drunken, sickly general came to attribute it to nothing less than an act of God.

It was out of his isolation that Namphy made an alliance with Mayor Franck Romain. Like Papa Doc before him, Namphy had been set atop a fractious, plot-ridden military; like Papa Doc, Namphy tried to counterbalance the officers—in his case with Romain's Macoutes. Speaking at the palace on July 8, the general formally welcomed the Duvalierists back into official national politics. He declared that the 1987 constitution, which remained hugely popular, "introduces foreign elements into our history and traditions." It would be set aside; he, Namphy, would give the nation a new charter, one that would "take account of the Haitian reality."

In early July, Lafontant Joseph, an internationally known human-rights activist, was found murdered in his car; he had been beaten, and stabbed numerous times, and one of his ears had been severed. In the weeks that followed, Namphy's "Haitian reality" became increasingly clear: Churches were strafed and burned, priests were beaten and intimidated, and corpses were left on the streets each morning. In early August, a group of bishops issued a statement that detailed a numbing list of shootings, burnings, assaults, and other "atrocities," and bluntly concluded that "no one can live peacefully in such a state of insecurity."

In September, a group of prominent "democratic leaders" met to announce "Constitution Day." They asked Haitians to observe the appointed day, September 11, by wearing white—as they had in March, 1987, when 1 million Haitians turned out to ratify the constitution that Namphy had now abolished. Then the white had symbolized "yes"; now it was to "signify our formal willingness to stand by this constitution and to defend it."

On September 8, General Namphy visited City Hall, the stronghold of his friend Franck Romain, and gave an angry speech. "He was raving, his mouth wide open, talking so fast he was spitting, ranting against the Communists and the church, totally out of control," a frightened witness told me. The over-wrought general took the occasion to offer his "solemn warning to the dema-gogues, so that they don't try to come between the army and the people." Eventually, Mayor Romain took the president's arm and led him away.

On the morning of Constitution Day, a Sunday, the pews at St. Jean Bosco Church, near Port-au-Prince's La Saline slum, were a sea of white. A thousand or more people had squeezed into the nave to worship with the fiery and controversial Père Jean-Bertrand Aristide, the most outspoken of Haiti's liberation priests. (Only the Sunday before, Aristide had narrowly escaped the latest of several assassination attempts when a man waiting to receive communion was found to be concealing a .38-calibre revolver.)

Minutes after the service began, as the priest raised the chalice above his head, a rain of stones hammered against the side of the building. Through the windows in the back doors, which had been chained shut, worshippers could make out a crowd of men smashing the windshields of cars parked outside. As the people exchanged glances and began to move about nerv-ously, Aristide's young assistants called for calm, and began to lead the con-gregation in a song, urging them to raise their fists in triumph.

AS THE CONGREGATION stood with arms high, the doors burst open, and two dozen howling men stormed in, spraying the crowd with gunfire and swinging machetes, clubs, and knives. On their faces was a look "of crazed fury, worse than any animal," according to a woman in the congregation. The packed nave became a shrieking, deafening chaos: In panic, the people fled from the rear doors, crushing themselves into a surging mass near the altar as the bellowing attackers waded forward, slashing about them with their machetes and clubs and firing their pistols. "Right in front of me, I saw them stab a pregnant woman in the stomach," the woman told me. "I saw them stab a man to death, and shoot several people point blank. A man grabbed me and tried to use me as a shield as he pushed toward the door. I had to hit him, and finally pulled free. Then I felt a hand grabbing me, and I looked and saw one of them raising a machete over his head. For a second, I thought I was dead. But I pulled away with all my might, and left him standing there with the back of my dress in his hand."

Crying, screaming people were clogging the doorways, trampling one another. (A band of worshippers had instantly formed a circle around Père Aristide, and managed to hustle him out through the sacristy door.) "People were clawing at the doors, hiding behind the altar, diving under the pews, anywhere," the woman said. The bloody bedlam lasted for perhaps five minutes—"It seemed to go on forever," she said—during which more than seventy people were wounded, and at least thirteen, perhaps as many as twenty, were killed. In the courtyard, men stoned or clubbed those trying to escape, while others leisurely set about pouring gasoline around the bodies and torching the building. Père Aristide's church was soon engulfed in flames; only after it had been gutted and the roof had collapsed, in a great, crackling groan, did a fire truck arrive. "As I walked by the barracks," the woman said—there is a large military compound a few yards away—"I saw the soldiers leaning against the wall and peering out. They had watched it all."

Nor did the soldiers act when the gang of attackers moved past them down the Avenue Jean-Jacques Dessalines, the capital's main street, assaulting anyone they found wearing white (including some churchgoers who were unlucky enough to be wearing white choir robes). Within minutes, as the attackers went on to strafe and silence Radio Soleil and another radio station, then sack the party headquarters of two leading politicians—both of which lay in full view of the National Palace—the streets of the capital were deserted.

The next day, six people presented themselves at Radio Métropole. Soon astonished Haitians were treated to a peculiar "post-game interview," as the authors of the massacre offered their personal accounts of how they had carried it off. "I was at the head of the gang," one boasted. "What you saw yesterday was child's play," said another. "Whatever parish lets Father Aristide lead a mass, there will be a pile of cadavers attending. . . . We have good cutting weapons that can slice open backs and cut off heads." Making no effort to conceal their identities, the gang members later appeared on Télé Nationale, the state-owned station, to offer their accounts. To a question about the pregnant woman one replied matter-of-factly, "She shouldn't have been in our way." (The next day, they stormed into the city hospital's maternity ward, hoping to finish her off. They moved from bed to bed, lifting up the gown of each woman to look for stab wounds, but they left disappointed; the victim had been moved.) Mayor Romain, whose city hall employees had been recognized among the attackers, also took to the radio, advising the citizenry that it was Père Aristide who should be blamed, for "preaching violence." "He who sows the wind reaps the whirlwind," Romain intoned.

As had been intended, fear settled over the city; even Papa Doc had never put his Macoutes on the air to give Haitians public accounts of their massacres. Among the Presidential Guardsmen there was disgust as well. One respected soldier, Sergeant Frantz Patrick Beauchard, had arrived at St. Jean

Bosco near the end of the attack, fearing that his girlfriend had been in the congregation. "I saw the church in flames, the people running, and the guys chasing after them, stabbing them," he told me. "It was a shock to see people lying dead with Bibles in their hands."

BEAUCHARD WAS THE LEADER of a group of about thirty guardsmen who for some time had been discussing mounting a coup against Namphy. Ever since they brought the general back to the palace, they had been disgruntled, for they had not received the money or the attention they thought they deserved from the president who owed them everything. Instead, Namphy had spurned the army and come to rely on Frank Romain and his Macoutes who had traditionally been the soldiers' rivals and watchdogs, and had now taken on that function once again. "Several times, 'attachés' drew their guns on soldiers in the street," a guardsman told me angrily.

"It was after St. Jean Bosco that we decided things must change," a sergeant told me. "Everybody knew that Franck Romain's people did it. And Romain came to the palace every day." It was clear from a number of soldiers I talked to that the attack shamed them—that after that Sunday, as one young man put it, "a soldier could no longer walk with his head held high."

The coup was set for the following Saturday, September 17th. On Friday, Romain informed Namphy that a plot was under way, and the general asked his ally, along with a loyal officer, to investigate. Early on Saturday, Romain arrived at the palace, armed, with several of his men. By that time, Namphy had a list of thirty names. ("He sent men to dig thirty holes at Fort Dimanche," a private told me.) Leaving an officer and some of Romain's men to begin arresting and interrogating those on the list, the general and the mayor went off to attend a vodou ceremony in a slum south of the city.

In midafternoon, the officer and Romain's men began arresting soldiers. "The commandant and the attaché handcuffed one of the soldiers, and five others started shooting in the air," a guardsman told me. "The commandant and the attaché ran. I ran to get my gun. In the dormitory, a captain was on the floor trying to rip off his officer's stripes; when he saw me, he ran, jumping over a wall." As Haitians outside the palace, hearing the heavy firing, raced in panic to get off the streets, the soldiers brought out armored cars and trained their guns on Namphy's office, where the general, the mayor, and a number of armed attachés had holed up. Speaking through a megaphone, a soldier announced that Namphy had five minutes to surrender. A few rounds were fired down into the courtyard, causing a great deal of confusion and allowing Romain to make his escape.

The soldiers gave Namphy a second ultimatum. When he failed to respond, the soldiers, having taken care to turn their megaphone toward the Dessalines Barracks and warn their rivals—"This has nothing to do with you—it is our affair," began firing. Taking up his megaphone, Namphy offered to negotiate, but the soldiers told him it was too late and went on shooting. Some of their comrades were meanwhile tracking down Private First Class Délinois Sonthonax, the soldier who had provided Namphy with the names of the plotters. Discovered cowering in the shower, Private Sonthonax begged for a chance, according to a soldier who found him. "We said, 'No chance for you!' and we each gave him a *coup de Galil*. He took at least 250 rounds."

At last, General Namphy surrendered, and three soldiers, one of them armed with a heavy machine gun, brought him out of the palace, along with his wife and daughter. As they shoved him toward an armored car, he became sick and asked for his medicine. Then he appealed to the soldiers. "Whatever you want I'll give you," he said, "but let me stay here as a citizen of my country. Don't exile me."

"We told him, 'No, after what you've done you're no longer a citizen of this country!'" a soldier reported. After taking his wife's and daughter's purses, the soldiers pushed the general and his family into the armored car and sent them to the airport. In a few hours, General Namphy was occupying the same suite in the same Santo Domingo hotel that had accommodated the fallen Leslie Manigat three months before.

The rebels were now faced with the question of how to fill the empty presidential chair; many of the thirty original plotters, tipped off earlier that Namphy was on to them, had fled the palace grounds—including Sergeant Beauchard, the man who was meant to take the reins of power. The plan had been, Beauchard told me later, for him to hold power until the senior Supreme Court justice could be installed as a provisional president, responsible for leading the country toward "free and honest and rapid elections, according to the constitution Namphy shredded."

But when the time came Beauchard wasn't there. And Faustin Miradieu, the young private who was designated to find Beauchard, happened to be a supporter of Colonel Jean-Claude Paul, who, along with Prosper Avril (now a general) and several other officers, had by this time come to the palace in response to a frantic call from Namphy.

In the president's office, a number of soldiers were arguing about who should be given power. At this point, Private Miradieu led Colonel Paul into the room. As a sergeant later described the scene, "Faustin took Paul's hand, put him in the chair, and said, 'Jean-Claude Paul, you are president.'" General Avril, who had been observing the discussion; immediately agreed, and sat down to write the speech President Paul would shortly deliver to the nation. But then Captain Joseph-Frank Timothée, the man who had led the group that brought down Namphy, strode into the office, carrying his heavy machine gun. When he saw Paul seated in the president's chair, Timothée exploded. "No!" he said. "Paul is impossible," and he reminded the soldiers of their problems with Paul's attachés. The young soldiers continued to argue heatedly until, as one described it, "Timothée grabbed Paul by the collar and said, 'Get out!'"

A bizarre scene ensued in which the excited soldiers offered the presidency to one man after another—Lieutenant Luce Elie, Lieutenant Zamor—and each refused. "We weren't of a class to do it," a private told me. They didn't think they had enough education. Then someone was sent to fetch Sergeant Joseph Hebreux, a medic, who was distinguished from his colleagues by his high-school degree. After he was found—hiding under a bed in the infirmary—Sergeant Hebreux was offered the presidency, and he, too, refused, bursting into tears.

Finally, Timothée turned to Avril and said, "Get in there. *Take power!*"

As the luckless Beauchard later put it, a bit wistfully, "Power was there, floating in the air, and Avril only had to seize it."

"AH, *L'INTELLIGENT AVRIL,*" no less a judge of men than Papa Doc had famously remarked of his young aide-de-camp from the little town of Thomazeau, east of Port-au-Prince. And, indeed, Prosper Avril was to be a fixture in the palace for two decades, becoming even more essential to the young Duvalier than he had been to the old, taking his place not only as the dominant officer of the Presidential Guard but also as Jean-Claude's closest military confidant (the able officer who kept an office in the National Bank, and who was sophisticated enough to take numerous trips to Switzerland and elsewhere to see to the young dictator's "investments") and, finally, as the key figure behind the scenes during the Namphy regimes. Indeed, for most Haitians "behind the scenes" had been the defining characteristic of Prosper Avril; they would tap their temples and smile knowingly when his name was mentioned. Though he might not appear on television to address the nation, they would say, it was Avril who wrote the speeches. And, of course, however quiet his role in the palace, the young man from the provinces had made sure that his services were richly rewarded: Avril's home above the city—a spectacular mansion, every orange and rose brick of which was supposedly imported from Italy (along with the craftsmen who built it)—was famous throughout the country. Now the intelligent Avril had become president, and during the next hours and days Haitians would be able to see the fifty-year-old officer justify Papa Doc's comment.

Among the soldiers there was still dissatisfaction; they would not be content to wander back to their barracks empty-handed. So, in the chaos of that room, the new president modestly suggested—or perhaps helped the soldiers suggest—that it would be only fair for one of them to rule alongside him. And thus, in the early-morning hours, when frightened Haitians saw the inevitable gathering of soldiers appear on their television screens, they were startled to see an unfamiliar face. It was that of the tearful twenty-seven-year-old high-school graduate Sergeant Hebreux (with whom, as it happened, Avril was well acquainted, since Avril's wife worked in the same palace infirmary as the young man). Surrounded by enlisted men in helmets, the young Sergeant read out a statement prepared for him by the helpful General Avril, explaining that "the little soldiers," in deposing Namphy, had aimed at nothing more than "to restore honor to the army" and had therefore installed as Haiti's new president "one of the most honest officers in the army." Only then, after demonstrating to the Haitian people that he had come forward at the urgings of the "little soldiers," did Avril address the nation that he now proposed to "save" from "anarchy and chaos."

A charming man who had been trained by the United States Marines at Quantico and by the Navy at its intelligence school in Anacostia, who spoke English competently, and who, one diplomat observed during the next days, was "very worldly," Avril wasted no time in telephoning and then meeting with Ambassador McKinley. To the ambassador—who for the past three months (when the Americans' former client General Namphy seemed to have been transformed before their horrified eyes into another Papa Doc) had had reason to regret his embassy's cold treatment of Leslie Manigat— this meeting must have seemed too good to be true. It wasn't long before the embassy was reporting the new president's "hopes for a transition to civilian rule." Soon, too, it became clear that reports that Colonel Paul was to become the army's commander-in-chief (an unfortunate choice, in the American view) had been mistaken.

BUT THIS HAD BEEN a "little soldiers' coup," and though Avril very shortly had the aspect of a man riding a tiger, he actually managed to ride it very much in his chosen direction. For the soldiers, most of them uneducated peasants earning a few dollars a month, living in squalor, and enduring the contempt of their officers, the time for their own *déchoukaj*—their own chance to uproot—had at last arrived. In the capital and all around the country, angry enlisted men turned on their astonished officers. President Avril sat back to watch as one after another of his former colleagues was delivered, handcuffed and bound, to the army headquarters and left there, to the cheers of an excited crowd. In short order, virtually the entire upper tier of the military—comprising almost all of Avril's major rivals—had been swept way. Meanwhile, the home of Mayor Franck Romain, who had taken asylum in the Dominican Embassy, was sacked, and in front of the ruins of St. Jean Bosco many of the men who had been foolish enough to reveal themselves as the authors of the massacre were brought forward and burned alive.

President Avril busied himself behind the scenes. The day after the coup, the thirty original plotters called on him and demanded that he appoint Ser- geant Beauchard his interior minister. Avril, remarking gently that the Sergeant "was not competent to manage the politics of such a job," appointed him president of the National Gaming Commission instead—a post that had little to do with reform but offered toothsome opportunities for self-enrich- ment. After the soldiers presented Avril with a list of "Nineteen Points" that they had prepared to guide them after the coup—among which were "rein- state the constitution in its integrity," "organize free and honest elections within a year" "eliminate corruption," "eliminate paramilitary forces," and (no doubt bringing a smile to Avril's face) "forbid the military to run the country"—the avuncular president wisely created for the men an "Office of Suggestion" within the palace where they would be free to develop their plans.

Less than two weeks after taking power, Avril presented the Haitians with a stunning *coup de théâtre*. Jean-Claude Paul, the man whose reaction all Haitians had awaited with trepidation, had accepted retirement. Following a frank talk with the highly persuasive new president (who happened to be an old classmate from the Academy), Colonel Paul quietly left his stronghold and returned to his lovely home in Fermathe, high above Port-au-Prince. (A month later, after eating a bowl of soup, he collapsed and died. Accusations that he had been poisoned were never proved.) Hours after Paul left the Dessalines Barracks, Presidential Guardsmen stormed a safe house that he had established for the Macoutes, arrested a number of his "attachés," and confiscated a large store of weapons.

Meanwhile, General Avril was embarking on a political offensive. At the palace, he held a highly publicized series of "dialogues," in which he and the ever-present Sergeant Hebreux met with representatives of all sectors of Haiti's political world: popular leaders, unionists, and politicians of all stripes, including the leaders of the Communist Party. Avril vowed to put Franck Romain on trial; to close the dreaded Fort Dimanche; and to "definitively install democracy in Haiti." Along with this pledge, however, the general carefully noted his country's "pressing call to the international community to furnish financial aid . . . without which we will not be able to reach that point."

Within a few weeks, Haiti and the United States had signed an agreement under which the Americans would provide "financial assistance" to help the Haitians fight drug trafficking. A high-profile anti-narcotics campaign followed, and soon the Haitian government was presenting the Americans with more than three thousand pounds of captured cocaine, and the Americans were praising the new government for the "seriousness with which it considers the problem of illegal drugs in Haiti." A month later, the United States made about $30 million available to the Avril government.

In mid-October, when a month of highly publicized "uprootings" had left the top ranks of the army depleted, General Avril moved adroitly to rein in the renegade Haitian Army. No sooner were rumors of a coup plan circulating than it was announced that certain "plotters" had been arrested and jailed—none other than Sergeant Beauchard and the other "little soldiers" who had carried Prosper Avril to power a month before. "He said we were Communists and were planning a coup," Beauchard told me later. "It wasn't true. Avril just gave seventy dollars each to forty guys in the Guard to crush us." Avril made sure that his own men—especially the troops of the armored-car unit—were well rewarded. The Dessalines troops and the Léopards watched jealously as the longtime presidential guardsman consolidated his position.

During the winter and early spring, General Avril played a complicated cat-and-mouse game with the opposition: He held a televised "democratic forum" to discuss the question of elections; he imprisoned two prominent politicians on charges that they were planning terrorist acts; he saw to the appointment of a new Electoral Council but offered no clue to when elections might be held. Before long, as the economy continued to deteriorate, strike calls began.

In late March, the day after a senior State Department official paid a visit to the general, Avril fired four officers for alleged involvement in drug trafficking. During the early hours of April 2, a contingent of Léopards showed up at the general's mansion and took him prisoner. Several hours later, when the Léopards were transporting the handcuffed president to the airport for the flight to exile, they found their way blocked by the armored vehicles of the Presidential Guard, under the command of the dauntless Sergeant Hebreux. After a tense confrontation, General Avril was released, and the coup leader, Colonel Himler Rébu, of the Léopards, was taken hostage in his turn.

A week of confused intra-army warfare ensued, in which the capital remained under a nighttime curfew, stores were shuttered, and soldiers from opposed army units—rebellious Léopards and Dessalines Battalion troops who had joined them, and loyalist Presidential Guards—blocked roads, occupied airports, and, by turns, seized radio and television stations to declare their intentions to the Haitian people. Finally, the Presidential Guards launched a tremendous battle against the Dessalines troops, in their barracks, next to the palace. All over the capital, the noise of shelling and machine-gun fire was deafening, and scattered reports claimed huge losses of life. But by the time the guardsmen, in their armored cars, had forced their way into the Dessalines Barracks—only to find them half deserted—no more than six soldiers had died. (A few days later, the Haitians learned that their wise president had taken care to use "training rounds"—blanks—for nearly all his bombardment.) With the Dessalines men in flight and the Léopards demoralized, Avril grasped the opportunity to dissolve both units, and assigned most of their troops to isolated posts around the country. By that stroke he dismantled the divided, rivalrous "Duvalierized" army. Now his own Presidential Guard reigned unchallenged.

RECEIVING ME IN HIS OFFICE in the National Palace at the end of August, Avril stood at attention beside an immaculate desk, shoulders back, head held high, a very slight smile on his face. From the beginning to the end of our interview, he could have been playing the role of a competent, clever American-trained Third World military man, burdened with a distasteful job but determined to see it through: He would clean up the country, see it right, install true democracy at last; he didn't underestimate the difficulty of the job nor did he find the challenge insuperable.

The General spoke to me appreciatively of his American training at Quantico and at Anacostia and of his desire to "restructure" the Haitian Army. "The army has been neglected for thirty years," he told me. Then: "Wait, I'll show you," and with that he suddenly rose from his chair and left the room. In a moment he returned, with a sheaf of photographs in his hand. "Look, look at the work we have to do," he said, flipping through the pictures of military posts around the country, some of them barely more than huts. "This is the situation we find ourselves in. This is why we ask for aid. Look, here's the post at Abricot. How can such a force assure democracy? We need at least $9 million to fix up these posts."

For Avril, confronted with an American visitor, all questions turned on drugs and foreign aid. About the insecurity in the streets he said, "A good deal of this comes from the terrible struggle we are waging against drug trafficking. Last week, we captured five hundred kilos of cocaine. Many times when there are bodies in the streets it is these drug dealers settling scores with one another."

And the charges that Tontons Macoutes, cashiered soldiers, even some Presidential Guards, were preying on the citizenry at night?

"No, no, that is finished. We have carried out a number of searches to recover the Macoutes' weapons. We've published requests in the newspapers for people who know of Macoutes with weapons to let us know, and we send soldiers to get them." As for the "climate of insecurity," the General shook his head, smiling condescendingly. "You know, in any city of 1 million people there is violence," he said. "Here they say there is 'a climate of insecurity.' In New York, every day there are scores of cases in any hospital like these." (An American diplomat had made much the same point: If there were robberies and killings, it had less to do with "any grand design of Avril's than with the collapse of the police state"; that is, it was a good sign.)

"Things are starting to move now," the general told me. "American aid is starting to arrive. The World Bank money is starting to arrive. We are starting to do what we must: put the people to work, restructure the armed forces, better equip the police, so they can remedy the 'climate of insecurity.'" When I mentioned the constitutional provision that the police be separated from the army and placed under the Justice Ministry, the General looked at me with a wistful expression. "Well, of course we would like to do that," he said. "But it takes money."

What did the general think about the claims that he himself had stolen money—that he had served as Jean-Claude Duvalier's "bag man" on his trips to Switzerland and elsewhere, and that his enormous house and others like it were no small cause of the governmental poverty he was pointing to?

The general was indignant. "There was an American law firm here, investigating," he said. "They went through all the documents, from the National Bank, the Ministry of Finance—everything. They never found the name of Prosper Avril."

Perhaps this only proved that Prosper Avril was more intelligent than the others? The general smiled, acknowledging the compliment. "Ah, my friend," he said. "*That* intelligent it is not possible to be." He went on to say, "Right now, our job is clear: to assure a good start for our democracy, to arrange truly democratic elections, elections where the people choose a president."

IN SEPTEMBER, Avril's Electoral Council announced a complex schedule that would begin with local elections in January, continue with legislative elections in July and August, and conclude with presidential elections in October and November—more than two years after General Avril came to power. The schedule provoked criticism from candidates and popular leaders alike. Why, with the country's economy worsening daily, its coffers almost empty, and its currency collapsing, not to mention the "climate of insecurity" that left bodies in the streets every morning—why was such a long delay necessary before Avril's " irreversible democracy" could be installed? Unless, that is, the general intended to stay in power?

When I had raised with Avril the question of postponed elections, he had looked at me in mock horror. "But I cannot do that!" he said. "The council is *independent*. I cannot interfere in its decisions—and neither, for that matter, can the candidates." Besides, he said, it had been partly the lack of preparedness that had doomed the elections of November 1987. "To have elections when the country is in a state of revolution is just not possible," he said. "Even without the violence, there were no ballots, no polling places. It was a mess." This time, he added, things would he done right.

In August, the American government renewed Haiti's food aid—a $10 million shipment of wheat. "The most immediate thing we restored is the government's respectability," a senior diplomat told me. "You have to understand," he said, "that Avril—Avril is a politician, as Namphy never was. And we believe he's sincere when he says he wants to move the country toward elections. The only alternative, after all, is some sort of crackdown, and he just isn't the type for that."

After the council's schedule was announced, the pace of strikes and demonstrations increased. On October 31st, a coalition of twenty-three groups announced a month-long program of marches, strikes, and demonstrations to protest against the Avril regime and the "climate of insecurity" still prevailing in the country. On November 1st, soldiers arrested three prominent coalition leaders: Evans Paul, the head of the mass organization KID; Jean-Auguste Mesyeux, a leader of the union federation CATH; and Étienne Marineau, a former sergeant in the Presidential Guard who had been one of the "little soldiers" in the coup that brought Avril to power.

The night after the arrests, Major Léopold Clerjeune, head of the Anti-Gang Service—a division of what had been Jean-Claude Duvalier's political police—appeared on Télé Nationale and read a statement accusing the three men of having concocted a "terrorist" plot aimed at assassinating General Avril and "all the officers and noncommissioned officers of the Armed Forces of Haiti." While he spoke, the camera panned off to his side to show the three men, standing mutely by. Evans Paul's boyish face was a swollen mass, and his shirt was drenched in blood; Mesyeux's face was also badly bruised, and his head was clumsily wrapped in bandages; one of Marineau's eyes was swollen shut. "Right after their arrest, the soldiers beat them about the head, trunk, genitals, and feet with iron bars," Dr. Louis Roy, a surgeon who was permitted to visit them in the National Penitentiary, told me. "Marineau was bleeding from his right ear and his right eye. I would guess he had a cranial fracture. He was in very bad shape, as was Evans Paul."

The sight of the three startled many Haitians. It was true that killings in the night had increased, but such a public display of brutality did not seem Avril's style. Now an ever-larger segment of the political spectrum began denouncing the regime demanding its early departure. "We cannot have elections in these conditions. The people are united against elections now," said Dr. Roy, who is the head of the Association for the Defense of the Constitution. Hubert de Ronceray, the leader of a major coalition of centrist parties, put the matter bluntly: "We demand the departure of Avril because we know he is not seriously organizing elections. He is making fun of everyone."

As the second anniversary of the November 29th massacres approached, the only major figure who was still publicly declaring his readiness to participate in Avril's electoral process was Marc Bazin, who had come to be referred to as the "American candidate." "Yes, there is a 'climate of insecurity,'" he told me. "But will you tell me how not having elections will remedy that?" Bazin, in language that seemed especially crafted to soothe suspicious Duvalierists, was now urging "a recognition of 'Haitian realities.'"

But, as so often in Haiti, history seems to be repeating itself. Bazin's rivals accuse him of courting the officers; they say his strategy is to position himself as the only viable candidate in an election boycotted by the other leaders. ("Bazin is trying to pull a January 17th move," Dr. Roy said, referring to Leslie Manigat's ascension in a largely boycotted vote.) In any case, if the government remains deeply unpopular—and this seems likely in view of the steadily worsening economy, exacerbated by an I.M.F. "austerity" plan that has raised food prices—only a figure highly critical of the military rulers can be expected to win a free election. And the officers are unlikely to let that happen, as the massacres of November 29th show. And the more unpopular and controversial Prosper Avril becomes, the more repressive his regime is likely to become; the more repressive his regime, the less likely it is that Prosper Avril, with his mansion and his investments, will be able to walk away from the palace and live peacefully and prosperously in his native land. If he were to attempt it, there might be inquiries, investigations, trials—even (and perhaps more likely) "uprootings," for there are no independent courts, no strong Justice Ministry, no respected legal code that he can count on to protect him. He might well face the choice that so many Haitian rulers before him have faced: the palace or exile.

This is what Haitians mean when they speak wryly of *le Fauteuil*—the Chair. Every Haitian of note seems to want the Chair, but once he has taken his place in it the Chair imprisons him and transforms him. The mumbling country doctor becomes a ferocious monster, the stuttering general becomes a drunken Caligula. For, once in the Chair, the Haitian ruler—"provisional" or permanent, king or general—finds himself with no choice but to fight to keep it. It was in this fight, in his determination to endure, that François Duvalier revealed his genius, by fashioning a repressive system that persists to this day. "All these candidates and their pronouncements are a joke," one of his followers told me proudly not long ago. "Duvalier still rules this land. He will rule it for fifty years."

There is much truth in this, and not only in the Macoutes still haunting the neighborhoods, the Duvalierists still plotting in their big houses. The dictator's rule is strongest in the Haitian mind. He bequeathed to Haiti a more powerful, more corrosive version of its traditional politics of paranoia: The general in the palace sees plots everywhere, and feels compelled to crush them; the people outside can understand their leader only as a dictator, potential if not real. Along with the new paranoia, Papa Doc left his people a political desert: From a land virtually devoid of institutions and parties, a land whose politics seemed doomed to act out a recurring drama of conflict and conquest and terror—politics as bloody opera—the dictator had swept away even the players, the actors who had traditionally fought for power.

It is only this last that has begun to change. The strongest of the parties that sprang up after Jean-Claude have not vanished; they have become more established. Haitians have grown used to seeing the faces of their leaders on television, to hearing their voices on radio. At long last, the politicians have begun forming coalitions, to join together rather than split apart. For the first time since 1957, Haiti has an established opposition. It is just possible to hope that these new groupings are the fragile beginnings of those institutions the country so desperately needs if it is to arrest the human and political decay. But, even if they survive, they are only the beginnings.[3]

LATE ONE NIGHT LAST AUGUST, I was driving on Haiti's main road from Gonaïves to the capital when a thunderstorm swept in from the Caribbean. Within moments, a bridge was flooded. As I sat in my jeep in the darkness, waiting in a long line of stranded trucks, I turned on the radio, to find Marc Bazin being interviewed. Bazin, a well-educated, thoughtful man, articulate in several languages, graceful and charming, the highest product of Haiti's elite, was eloquent as he welcomed the current move toward political coalition. This was absolutely vital, he said, "to help the country emerge from the current crisis."

Suddenly, through the rain lashing the jeep's windows, I became aware of dark shapes outside, moving silently along the road. Looking more closely, I realized that I was sitting in the midst of a village; on either side of the road, scores of mud huts extended back into the trees. Now the rain had come, and—as would happen many times every year, hundreds of times in every lifetime—the villagers' homes had instantly been flooded, and the entire village had been forced from sleep out into the rain. With each flash of lightning, I could see them all, hundreds of them, standing mutely on either side of the road, thigh-deep in water. On the radio, Bazin's low voice droned on, smoothly, gracefully, forming its perfect sentences, continuing a brilliant analysis of Haiti's political crisis. When it rains in Haiti, the country's one highway is immediately impassable. When it rains in Haiti, the people have no shelter.

The New Yorker, December 11, 1989

II.

The Saddest Story

"This is the saddest story I have ever heard."
—Ford Madox Ford, *The Good Soldier*

AUSTRIA

HUNGARY

Lake
Balaton

Danube River

THE BALKANS
circa 1991-92

LJUBLJANA

SLOVENIA

ZAGREB

Sava

CROATIA

Eastern
Slavonia

ROMANIA

Vukovar

Vojvodina

River

The

Omarska

Bihać

Krajina

Banja Luka

BOSNIA

Bjijelina

Tuzla

Zvornik

Kravica

Potocari

Drina River

BELGRADE

Bratunac

Srebrenica

Knin

Podravanja

SARAJEVO

Zepa

SERBIA

Split

Pale

Gorażde

Drina
River

MONTENEGRO

PRISTINA

Adriatic

Dubrovnik

Sea

Račak

Kosovo

Stankovic

SKOPJE

ITALY

MACEDONIA

60°

20° 10° 0° 10°

FIN

NOR SWD

RUSSIA

IRE

DEN

50°

UK

GER

POL

BEL

UKRAINE

FRANCE

ROM

40°

SPAIN

ITALY

GRE

20°

30°

N

ALBANIA

GREECE

0   50 mi

0   50 km

How Not to Stop a War

I.

DURING THE SWELTERING DAYS of July 1995, any citizen of our civilized land could have pressed a button on a remote control and idly gazed, for an instant or an hour, into the jaws of a contemporary Hell. Taking shape upon the little screen, in that concurrent universe dubbed "real time," was a motley, seemingly endless caravan, bus after battered bus rolling to a stop and disgorging scores of exhausted, disheveled people. Stumbling down the stairs, bumping one against the other, the tens of thousands of Muslim refugees bent under the weight of bursting suitcases and battered trunks and unruly cloth bundles that now held their sole belongings. In their eyes, one could make out fear and a dulled shock, an inability to comprehend how they, who hours before had slept in houses and driven cars and worked in fields, had so abruptly been recast as homeless beggars.

In the former Yugoslavia, where in four years of war millions had been "ethnically cleansed," such eyes had long since grown familiar. And yet something set apart this particular sea of the uprooted: every last one was a woman or child. The men of Srebrenica had somehow disappeared.

Videotaped images, though, persist: in the footage shot the day before, the men can be seen among the roiling mob, together with their women and children, pushing up against the fence of the United Nations compound, pleading for protection from the conquering Serbs. Though two years before, foreign leaders had guaranteed the protection of Srebrenica's people and property by christening it a "safe area," the Serbs had needed but a few days to seize the town, and now the heavily armed Serbian warriors shouldered contemptuously aside the disarmed Dutch "blue helmets" of the UN and strode among their Muslim captives, menacing them with unblinking stares.

The night before, as the exhausted people tried to rest, the Serbs, drunk with triumph, walked among them. They pulled men away from their sobbing wives for "interrogation," and moments later gunshots told the women they would not see their husbands again. As they grew drunker, the Serbs dragged away for their pleasure young girls and boys, ten, eleven, twelve years old. Finally they no longer bothered to carry off their victims but simply fell upon them and did as they pleased amid hundreds of terrified people packed together in an abandoned factory: "Two took her legs and raised them up in the air, while the third began raping her. Four of them were taking turns on her. People were silent, no one moved. She was screaming and yelling and begging them to stop. They put a rag into her mouth and then we just heard silent sobs. . . ."[1]

By dawn the people of Srebrenica had become hysterical with fear, and the UN compound and its environs had become a vast, chaotic refugee camp of the terrified, with tens of thousands of desperate people moving about in waves of screaming and pleading and shouting.

Suddenly, quiet began spreading out from the edge of the crowd, and heads turned to see a stout, bull-necked general march forward, trailed by an entourage of officers and television cameras. Elated by his victory, General Ratko Mladic puffed out his barrel chest. "Please be patient!" he shouted. "Those who want to leave can leave. There is no need to be frightened. You'll be taken to a safe place." As his men passed out chocolates to the children, Mladic bent to pat the head of a frightened young boy—a telegenic image that was to circle the globe.

When the buses began to pull up, a "blue helmet" stepped forward and told Mladic timidly that he must speak to the Dutch commander before any refugees could be taken. The general smiled patronizingly. "I am in charge here," he said. "I'll decide what happens."

To the crowd, and to the world, Mladic proclaimed, "No one will be harmed. You have nothing to fear. You will all be evacuated." Yet when hundreds, thousands of families began to rush toward the buses, stumbling under the weight of their baggage, Mladic bellowed, "All men should go back! Only women can go to the buses."

Video images of tearful parting now, as the Serbs, weapons raised, stepped forward to pull fathers and sons and brothers from the desperate clutches of their women. "Follow the line!" the soldiers shouted.[2] And finally, casting pleading looks back over their shoulders, the women and children began to board.[3]

One by one the buses set out on their nightmare voyages, passing through darkened villages where Serb civilians shouted angry threats and attacked with a clatter of stones. In one town, "three soldiers came onto the bus and told us to give them the youngest child . . . so they could slit its throat."[4] Usually, though, the soldiers were content to rob and to rape, dragging out women of their choice, who wept and pleaded and did not return.

As the darkness faded, the women could begin to make out ghostly corpses taking shape by the roadside, and they forced themselves to stare at the bloody remains to see if their husbands or sons were among them. Near dawn they began to pass crowds of Muslim prisoners. "I saw about 2,000 of our men. . . . They had their hands tied above their heads. . . . The [Serbs] were standing around them with their guns at the ready."[5]

A couple thousand of these men the Serbs packed aboard trucks and unloaded at a school, where they forced them into a sweltering gymnasium that was so inhumanly crowded many had no choice but to sit for hours in one another's laps. Others the Serbs dumped out on an athletic field and pushed to their knees, prodding them with their rifles throughout the day as the men knelt frozen beneath the blazing sun. Still others they held imprisoned in buses and trucks, ordering them to sit for hour upon hour with their bodies bent fully forward and their heads held between their knees.

In each place General Mladic appeared, urging the men to "be patient," for "a prisoner exchange" was being worked out. And at last the Serbs announced that the negotiations had been completed and the Muslims would be driven to freedom.

Yet the men of Srebrenica were blindfolded before they were packed aboard the trucks, which rumbled only a short distance before they came to a stop and the men ordered to jump out:

> I saw grass underneath the blindfold. [My cousin] Haris took my hand. He said, "They're going to execute us." . . . I heard gunfire. . . . Haris was hit and fell towards me, and I fell with him. I heard moaning from people who were just about to die, and suddenly Haris's body went limp.
>
> I heard the [Serbs] talking. They sounded young. . . . Someone was ordering them to finish us off. . . . [T]he next . . . prisoners . . . were executed about twenty meters away. . . . I heard all the bullets whizzing by and thought I would be hit. . . . I also heard a bulldozer working in the background and became horrified. My worst nightmare was that I would be buried alive.
>
> I kept hearing people gasping, asking for water so they wouldn't die thirsty. . . . I lay on the ground with no shirt on all day; it was extremely hot, and ants were eating me alive. . . . Soon many of my body parts fell asleep. . . . [I blacked out and when] I woke up, [it] was night and I saw light beams from a bulldozer's headlights. I still heard the same noises . . . —trucks driving up, people getting out, and gunshots. I also remember distinctly an older voice calling, "Don't kill us, we didn't do anything to you," followed by gunfire. Later, I heard . . . someone saying, "No more left; it's late. . . . Leave some guards here and we'll take the bodies away tomorrow." . . . [N]o one wanted to stay. . . . They said, "They're all dead anyway," and then left.
>
> . . . When I finally decided to get up, I couldn't; my whole body was numb.

When at last he managed to get to his feet and pull off his blindfold he found himself gazing at a moonlit "sea of corpses." Though the meadow was broader and longer than a football field, the thousands of cadavers so thoroughly obscured every bit of ground that when he tried to flee "without stepping on the dead . . . [it] was impossible, so I tried at least not to step on the chests and torsos, but [only] onto arms and hands."[6]

Though neither the murderers nor their victims knew it, their images would twice more be committed to film.[7] As the men of Srebrenica stood before their executioners, a United States satellite high above had snapped a photograph, and in coming days, when an American pilot flew his spy plane over the same site, he would take another—of freshly covered plots of earth.[8]

II.

Back in Washington, the president was behind the White House, practicing his putting. As Bill Clinton crouched over his private putting green, Sandy Berger, his deputy adviser for national security affairs, and Nancy Soderberg, number three on the National Security Council staff, approached hesitantly. They had news from Srebrenica, Berger announced, and with that he began to tell the president tales of terror and murder. He did not get far. As Bob Woodward tells it:

> "This can't continue," Clinton said, blowing up into one of his celebrated rages. "We have to seize control of this." Where were the new ideas?
>
> Berger reminded him that [adviser for national security affairs Anthony] Lake was trying to develop an "endgame strategy."
>
> "I'm getting creamed!" Clinton said, unleashing his frustration, spewing forth profanity. He was putting, and he did not look up at Berger or Soderberg as he stroked the balls one after the other to the hole. They kicked the balls back to him to putt again. Soderberg felt almost as if she had fallen into Clinton's mind, and they were witnessing the interior monologue of his anxiety. He was in an impossible position, he said. He needed to do something.[9]

What is striking here is not Clinton's "forty-five-minute diatribe"—no follower of his career is unfamiliar with these—but that shortly after this particular eruption, his administration did indeed begin to "do something." If one had to identify a point where the half-hearted diplomatic initiatives and hollow threats and straddling of options finally coalesced into a purposeful American policy toward the Balkans, it would be here, after the fall of Srebrenica and the bloodbath that followed.

Scarcely three weeks later, on August 4, 1995, the Croats, having received a discreet "green light" from the Americans, launched a lightning attack on the Krajina, the Serb-inhabited region of Croatia that had been conquered by Serbia early in the war. In barely four days, the Croatian military, which had been rearmed with the help of Iran and other Middle Eastern states and had been trained by retired, high-ranking American officers, reconquered the entire region, and expelled the Serbs, many of whose families had lived there for centuries. The Croats—and the Bosnian Muslims as well, who, thanks to the efforts of American diplomats, were now fighting with the Croats in a loose coalition—swiftly began to retake territory from the Serbs. The tide of war had begun to turn.

On August 28, Serb artillerymen fired a mortar shell into a Sarajevo market, killing thirty-seven people. Clinton immediately pressed NATO to launch its fighter-bombers. More than two weeks of relentless bombing, together with the Serb and Croat victories of that summer—and the territorial and "demographic" changes (read: ethnic cleansing) that went along with them—helped to make possible the peace accord that was concluded some three months later at Dayton, Ohio, and the dispatch of twenty thousand American troops to enforce it.

Though President Clinton vowed to Congress and to the American people that the troops would leave Bosnia within a year, in Bosnia they remain, as does an obvious question: What led Clinton, after four and a half years of savage fighting—and unspeakable brutalities that left perhaps two hundred thousand dead and 3 million as refugees—at last to plunge the United States into direct involvement in the Yugoslav wars? True, Bob Dole—Clinton's likely opponent in the 1996 election—and other senators were bringing strong pressure to bear on the president, having voted on July 26, 1995, soon after the massacre at Srebrenica, to force him to lift the arms embargo on Bosnia. More important, the French and British were threatening to withdraw their peacekeeping contingents, which would force Clinton to fulfill his promise to send American troops to support what was sure to be a messy and bloody operation—and which meant that, just as the 1996 election was looming into view, American troops, one way or another, would be going to Bosnia.[10]

Plainly, though, Clinton, in his furious exhortation to "seize control of this," had in mind something more than sidestepping Dole or his European allies. Days after the fall of Srebrenica, during a meeting on Anthony Lake's plan for the "endgame" in Bosnia, the president declared that his administration's current Bosnia policy was "doing enormous damage to the United States and to our standing in the world. We look weak." And then: "Our position is unsustainable; it's killing the U.S. position of strength in the world."[11]

Bosnia "killing the U.S. position of strength in the world"? Could Clinton seriously believe this of an immiserated country of 3 million whose security, American officials had insisted for four years, seemed to touch no American national interest? During the Yugoslav war's first eighteen months, George H. W. Bush and his advisers had maintained a disciplined standoffishness ("We got no dog in this fight," as Secretary of State James Baker put it), which they held to even in the face of the uproar that followed televised pictures of emaciated Bosnians staring out from behind the barbed wire of concentration camps. As for Clinton, though he had announced his sympathy for the plight of the Bosnian Muslims in the 1992 campaign, in office he proved no more willing than Bush to risk American lives to help them.

Somehow Bosnia had now become not only one of America's national interests but a preeminent one—a "symbol of U.S. foreign policy," as Lake pronounced it. How and when did such a metamorphosis take place? After all, the Realpolitik fears about the war spreading—that Yugoslavia's breakup might, through heightened violence and repression in Kosovo, draw in Albania and Macedonia, and then Greece and Turkey, thereby pitting two countries of NATO's southern flank against one another—had not been realized.

Yet Clinton apparently believed he was pointing to an equally tangible threat. If during the Cold War human rights had never had much more than a decorative part in American foreign policy—they were the "idealist" concern par excellence—the prolonged killing in Bosnia, and the "international community's" powerlessness to stop it, had shown how, in the post–Cold War world, highly visible and widespread violations of human rights could threaten the prestige and thus the power of both the United States and international institutions. When soldiers of a small European power methodically murder great numbers of unarmed people virtually in front of the world's television cameras, and American leaders appear to do little more than look on and wring their hands, this will inevitably come to make the United States "look weak." And when American officials and their counterparts in Paris and London and Bonn spend their time exchanging nasty public criticisms, this will eventually make the Western alliance—the storied North Atlantic Treaty Organization that had emerged victorious from the Cold War only a half-dozen years before—look impotent and irrelevant.

By mid-1995, untrammeled mass murder in Europe had made these risks plain: If left unaddressed, the bloodshed might well undermine NATO; further weaken the United Nations and other international institutions at the very time they were struggling to define their true post–Cold War purposes; and eventually erode the international order that the United States, as the new, uncontested hegemon, appeared determined to bolster and maintain. "The Yugoslav war," writes James Gow in *Triumph of the Lack of Will,*

> moved from being an important question for European stability and security and a test of the then CSCE's brand new Conflict Prevention Centre, to being a test of the future of EU Common Foreign and Security Policy; from that it moved to being a test of UN diplomacy and UN peacekeeping; from that, it became a test of European, Transatlantic and East-West relations and post–Cold War cooperative security; and finally, it became a test of NATO credibility and with that of international and particularly American credibility. . . . [D]espite the commitments that went with these tests, for four years international diplomacy struggled to end the war.[12]

What happened in Yugoslavia was not unforeseen; few "crises" have been as accurately predicted. But if American leaders saw the wars in the former

Yugoslavia emerging on the horizon, they proved unable to understand their significance. Early on, when the threat might well have been averted at relatively low cost, the experienced men in charge of American policy made profound misjudgments that can only be ascribed to their own shaky grasp of reality as the United States passed, almost imperceptibly, into the unfamiliar seas of the post–Cold War world.

III.

In early 1989, in a tiny, smoky office on the seventh floor of the State Department, two old "Yugo hands" swapped stories about their Belgrade years. The office, and the smoke, belonged to Lawrence Eagleburger, President Bush's asthmatic deputy secretary of state designate, who was sneaking a cigarette. His visitor, Warren Zimmermann, a longtime foreign service officer whom the Senate had just confirmed as George H. W. Bush's ambassador to Yugoslavia, had come seeking advice from a man who had held the same post in the late 1970s and whom Zimmermann respected as "one of the foremost American experts on the Balkans."

Amid the smoke in that cramped space, the two men labored over a seemingly straightforward question: What were the United States' interests in Yugoslavia? By the time they had finished talking, they had begun to sketch out an answer:

> Eagleburger and I agreed that in my introductory calls [in Belgrade and the republics] . . . I would deliver a new message[:] I would say that Yugoslavia and the Balkans remained important to U.S. interests, but that Yugoslavia no longer enjoyed its former geopolitical significance. . . . It was no longer unique, since both Poland and Hungary now had more open political and economic systems. Its failures in the human rights area . . . now loomed larger.[13]

On their face the words seem unexceptionable. For American policy, Yugoslavia was almost wholly a creature of the Cold War. Since 1948, when Tito broke with Stalin and sought the soft embrace of the United States— which, Zimmermann says, in something of an exaggeration, "backed [him] in an extraordinary act of enlightened statesmanship"—the partnership had suited both parties: the Yugoslavs closed off the Adriatic and Mediterranean to the Soviets, shielded Greece and Italy, and generally helped secure NATO's southern flank. In return, Tito benefited from an unstated, "grey-area" Western security guarantee, received a steady supply of American planes and other weapons, and enjoyed full access to Western loans and credits—largesse that allowed Yugoslavia's leaders to give their country's fragile "third-way" socialist economy a facade of prosperity.

Now that the Cold War was drawing to a close, why should Yugoslavia remain a "pampered child of American and Western diplomacy"? But though Zimmermann and Eagleburger apparently believed they had devised the core of a fresh policy, they were plainly mistaken. True, "Yugoslavia no longer enjoyed its former geopolitical significance," but any new approach had to begin by answering the question: What was the country's significance now, and why? Lacking answers, Eagleburger and Zimmermann relied on premises that were rooted in the past, in the Cold War itself, proclaiming, in effect, that "if Yugoslavia's significance to the United States has heretofore been great, owing to the flourishing of the Cold War, then its significance must now be slight, owing to the Cold War's collapse." Such circular reasoning produced a rich example, in the words of then NSC aide Robert Hutchings, "of applying yesterday's strategic logic to tomorrow's problems."

From "this flawed premise," as Hutchings says, "flawed policies ensued."[14] Since Yugoslavia had abruptly become a country of relative insignificance to the United States, its looming political problems appeared impossible to resolve; or rather, the means that appeared necessary to "manage" the Yugoslav crisis—especially the threat, or even the use, of military force— American leaders took to be wholly disproportionate to the United States' diminished interest in the country.

Thus, in the recollections of many officials, one senses an underlying feeling of powerlessness. Even in Zimmermann's fine memoir, in which the ambassador describes the fascinating personalities and intricate plottings of Milosevic, Tudjman, Karadzic, and the rest (he opens his book by announcing that "this is a story with villains—villains guilty of destroying the multi-ethnic state of Yugoslavia"), one senses here and there a pungent fatalism. The bloodshed, however long anticipated, comes inexorably on, and no one, it seems—particularly no American official, even one as energetic, resourceful, and dedicated as Zimmermann—is able in the end to do much beyond look on in sad fascination.

This feeling of distracted powerlessness, it is only fair to note, was much more the rule than the exception among American officials. In 1990 and 1991, when vigorous, early diplomacy should have been brought to bear, the "principals" had their hands full preparing and directing the Gulf War; then, having triumphed in the Gulf with an ease none had anticipated, they had little interest in gambling the victory's political rewards by undertaking what appeared certain to be a much more risky engagement in a country that seemed plainly to have outlived its importance. As a result of this attitude, writes Hutchings, mid-level officials found that any initiative they suggested to their superiors "was dismissed out of hand at the highest levels of the State Department and especially the Pentagon as being pointless unless we were prepared to see the project through to its potential worst-case conclusion." And of course "worst-case" had now become, by definition, a non-starter.

Wielding disproportionate influence among "the principals" were the two old "Yugo hands," Eagleburger and Brent Scowcroft, Bush's adviser for national security affairs, who had served as air attaché in Belgrade during the early 1960s. Their influence, one NSC staff member told me, was almost entirely negative. . . . Their information on and familiarity with Yugoslavia was quite out of date, and yet because they had a sense of the place and thought they knew what was going on there, they felt they could rely on their instincts and ignore the reporting coming out of the country.

One old "Yugo hand," however, got things precisely right. We can be grateful to Zimmermann for having made the pilgrimage to Princeton so he can offer the reader these striking words from George F. Kennan, who served as United States ambassador to Yugoslavia from 1961 to 1963:

> Today, with the Cold War ending, people think Yugoslavia isn't in a position to do any damage. I think they're wrong. . . . I think events in Yugoslavia are going to turn violent and to confront the Western countries, especially the United States, with one of their biggest foreign policy problems of the next few years.

As so often in Kennan's long career, he was playing the part of the prophet in the wilderness. For he was speaking during the summer of 1989, at a time when the Yugoslav war was two years off, far away enough for American policymakers to have made use of their country's wealth and diplomatic resources to avert it—if they had thought it important to try.

BY THE EARLY 1980S, Yugoslavia's leaders, finding they owed $20 billion in borrowed money that they did not have, were forced to adopt an austerity plan that cut imports (and notably consumer goods) to the bone, left one in five Yugoslavs unemployed, and eventually pushed inflation beyond the 25,000 percent mark. For a society that since World War II had taken its growing prosperity for granted, the political effects were devastating: "More than a decade of austerity and declining living standards corroded the social fabric and the rights and securities that individuals and families had come to rely on," as Susan Woodward writes in *Balkan Tragedy*. "Normal political conflicts . . . became constitutional conflicts and then a crisis of the state itself among politicians who were unwilling to compromise."[15]

It was against this tattered economic background that Ambassador Zimmermann's "villains" brought to bear their racial schemes, manipulating and exacerbating the people's growing insecurity with nationalist slogans of hatred that were expertly disseminated over an all-powerful state television and radio. The Americans, whose aid program was by the late 1980s quite small but whose wealth might have allowed them to exert substantial influence, had decided, Zimmermann writes, to rely on "one of the few admirable figures in a landscape of monsters and midgets"—Prime Minister Ante Markovic. A modernizing businessman, Markovic dreamed of making Yugoslavia "a Western democratic country with a capitalist system." But he could do little without money. "Four billion dollars," he tells Zimmermann brightly, "would be a good start to help a reform that's going further than anything in Eastern Europe."

> Swallowing hard, I told him I'd report his request to Washington. I knew what the answer would be. U.S. policy in Eastern Europe was heavily focused on Poland and Hungary, countries that were moving on the reform path faster than Yugoslavia and without the baggage of divisive nationalism. Yugoslavia would be seen as a poor risk and therefore a low priority.

In a more sensible world, American officials might have seen in "divisive nationalism" a threat to be averted with aid rather than a disqualification for receiving it. David Gompert, then the NSC's senior director for Europe and Eurasia, manages to make the foolishness of this reasoning even more obvious:

> If Washington was pessimistic by late 1990, it was not paralyzed. The United States declared its sympathy for the teetering Yugoslav federal government of Ante Markovic, who was committed to democracy, a civil society, and a market economy. But the prime minister wanted debt relief and a public signal of unreserved American political backing—commitments that seemed unwarranted in view of his government's apparent terminal condition.[16]

It is hard to take much solace from the fact that Washington was "not paralyzed" when its actions were admittedly limited to declaring "sympathy" for a leader to whom it refused financial or political help, because of his regime's "apparent terminal condition."

Next to European policymakers, however, the Americans seem vigorous. By late summer 1990 NSC staff members had begun cabling the Europeans in an attempt to convince them to agree to consider the Yugoslav crisis at an upcoming meeting of NATO or the CSCE. To this sensible request the Americans received replies that were, says Hutchings, then NSC director of European affairs, "shockingly irresponsible." They ranged from expressions of mild interest on the part of the Austrians and Hungarians, to condescending admonitions not to "overreact" from the English and Germans, to blunt accusations, from the French, that the Americans (as usual) were "over dramatizing" the situation. If the Americans were showing themselves unwilling to do what it would have taken to confront the Yugoslav problem, the Europeans had yet to admit that a problem even existed.

In September 1990 the CIA produced a lengthy "National Intelligence Estimate" that declared flatly, according to an unnamed official quoted in the *New York Times*, that "the Yugoslav experiment has failed, that the country will break up," and that "this is likely to be accompanied by ethnic violence and unrest which could lead to civil war."[17] As Hutchings writes,

No one in the policy community disagreed with the main thrust of these judgments. . . . Yet the estimate had little impact, for it was so unrelievedly deterministic that it suggested *no possible avenue for American policy* that might avert or at least contain the violence attending Yugoslavia's seemingly inevitable disintegration. [Emphasis added]

From the U.S. Embassy in Belgrade, the message was much the same: Zimmermann was reporting that "no breakup of Yugoslavia could happen peacefully. . . . The shattering of Yugoslavia would surely lead to extreme violence, perhaps even war."

From this, American officials drew the conclusion that the only possible policy was to push for some form of "unity"—and they continued doing so long after it was obvious that the federation was doomed. Yet one can certainly conceive of another "possible avenue for American policy." "In retrospect," as Robert Hutchings said in an interview, "we would have been better to assume disintegration and focus all our efforts on what could we do to assure the process . . . was peaceful and orderly."[18] That is, had the United States accepted a breakup as inevitable early on, it might have made use of its unchallenged power and prestige to maintain peace—to assert that whatever the Yugoslav republics did, America's own interests would not permit a shooting war to break out in Europe.

To take such a course, Bush officials would have had, first of all, to recognize the real potential danger of the Yugoslav crisis, and to understand that preventing a long, bloody European war *was* America's prime interest. They would have had to seriously explore solutions—the possibility, for example, of redrawing borders to "reduce the number of national minorities in every republic" (as the Dutch government suggested in July 1991).[19] Most important, in order to support such active diplomacy, they would have had to have the will not to rule out, and even to threaten—even, indeed, to use—military force.

For the Bush administration, however, the last point would emerge, early on, as the "deal-breaker."

IV.

On June 21, 1991, a mere four days before the Slovenes and the Croats were to declare their independence, Secretary of State James A. Baker III swept into Belgrade. "He decided," says Zimmermann, "to throw himself personally into a last-ditch effort to head off the violence that we all expected as an aftermath to the destruction of Yugoslavia." And throw himself in he did, for the next eleven hours "shuttling"—as Baker described it—from one "huge, cavernous meeting room decorated with artwork from its own ethnic tradition" to another, meeting with the heads of each republic.[20] His American aides were dazzled by his performance: Hutchings, one of the note-takers at the meetings, describes how Baker "tried heroically": He was "disciplined, focused, persistent, and blunt." His press aide, Margaret Tutwiler, recalls Baker's "unique way of speaking, very straightforwardly and very frankly."[21] As for Zimmermann, "I had rarely, if ever, heard a secretary of state make a more skillful or reasonable presentation."

For his Yugoslav interlocutors, who had reached the tense climax of a protracted battle over their country's future, the impression left by these few whirlwind hours of American diplomacy appears to have been somewhat different. Momir Bulatovic, the Montenegrin leader, recalls that when he sat down with Baker, the secretary

> was confused about how to start the conversation with me, until they brought him his briefing book. . . . I peeked into it and there were just two lines [about Montenegro]:
> —the smallest republic in Yugoslavia.
> —a possible fifth vote for Mesic.[22]

Stipe Mesic, a Croat who had been scheduled to take his turn as head of the revolving presidency, had been blocked by Serbia, thus paralyzing the federation's executive. The Americans hoped to work a "mini-compromise" whereby Serbia would allow Mesic to take office in return for the Croats' and Slovenes' promise not to take "unilateral action" and secede. As Bulatovic notes, however, the American idea was too little, too late: "Baker said if we didn't vote for Mesic, there would be a great crisis and war would start. I agreed with him that war would start, but I didn't expect Mesic's election would stop it."

If Baker seemed puzzled by the identity of the Montenegrin president, he had no doubt about that of his main antagonist, Slobodan Milosevic: "Like most toughs," Baker recalls, "I knew he respected power. I decided not to pull any punches with him." Under no circumstance, the secretary lectured Milosevic sternly, "would the international community tolerate the use of force." And what precisely did the secretary mean by this? He meant, Baker hastened to make clear, that any use of force would be met with "ostracism by the international community."

As Zimmermann, Hutchings, and the others in the room well knew, and as Zimmermann writes, Milosevic was a "ruthless leader who might have been impressed by real military power but not by diplomatic overtures." Yet in his "last ditch effort to head off the violence," Baker not only refrained from making any explicit threats but went out of his way to make it plain that the country he represented—the superpower whose military only months before had destroyed the Iraqi army in a matter of days—had already ruled out any use of force. David Gompert concedes that "not even Baker the poker player could disguise the fact that the warning to the Serbs was not backed by the threat of force"—as if the secretary had attempted somehow to bluff Milosevic, or at least leave him wondering. But by then the American position was quite clear, as Zimmermann says:

At no point before the actual declarations of independence by Slovenia and Croatia did Washington threaten force against either republic, against Serbia, or against the Yugoslavia army.

Indeed, Baker's approach "had been crafted at the State Department and the NSC. The Defense Department was not yet playing a role—another indication that force options were simply not on the radar screen."[23] According to Gompert, Milosevic drew his own conclusion long before Baker's "last ditch effort."

> . . . Since the Bush administration was not prepared to take military action, it chose not to issue any explicit warnings, *even though nothing less would have changed Serbian policy*. Milosevic could see by 1990 that he was safe to ignore American pressure, since no concrete threats, much less actions, accompanied Washington's stern *démarches*. [Emphasis added]

No one can prove that "concrete threats" or even "actions" (and one can conceive of many, short of all-out war) could have prevented the conflicts to come. Nor can one say with certainty whether much could have been achieved without resort to real force. What is indisputable is that no effective diplomacy was conceivable at this point—before any real blood had been shed—without at least the possibility of a stronger hand. "Such force was not considered," Zimmermann claims, because

> the West was a prisoner of what could be called "the paradox of prevention." In the Yugoslav case, as in many other international situations, it is nearly impossible to mobilize governments to take risks for prevention, since it is impossible to prove that the events which are to be prevented will, in the absence of prevention, occur.

But in what sense was the West, and the United States in particular, really "a prisoner" of this paradox—particularly since no evidence exists that either the president or any other principals recognized that there was at least a need to "take risks for prevention" in the first place?

Having drawn the line at ostracism, Baker urged each republic's leader to take "no unilateral action" and to refrain from using violence to maintain national unity—the standard American position, which by now had neither timeliness nor clarity to recommend it. The problem was obvious, as Hutchings says: Slovenia was about to secede, which would lead to Croatia's secession; and the United States, by "warning equally against unilateral declarations of independence and [against] the use of force to hold the federation together . . . seemed to be sanctioning the latter [by the Serbs] if the Slovenes and the Croats resorted to the former."

Baker's plane departed the Belgrade airport, carrying an exhausted secretary brooding on how he found this whole Yugoslav matter (as he later wrote to his president) "downright depressing. Frankly, I think it's easier to deal with Shamir and Assad than it is to try to affect Milosevic and Tudjman." Exactly four days later, on June 25, 1991, the Slovenes and the Croats declared independence, just as they had planned, leaving Baker feeling personally affronted and "stung by his lack of influence."[24] And the Serbian generals of the Yugoslav National Army, after fighting a farcical ten-day "phony war" in Slovenia—a republic for which, because it had few Serbs, they cared little—sent their tanks and soldiers to invade and bloodily dismember Croatia. And all the while the generals believed, they claimed, that they were "only doing what Mr. Baker told them."[25]

V.

For Croatia, that autumn of 1991 became the time of the great sieges. Serb artillerymen and infantry encircled the beautiful Danubian city of Vukovar—the strategic gateway to much of Croatia—and shelled it for eighty days. Such bombardment of civilians would become the Serbs' trademark. ("Shoot at slow intervals until I order you to stop," Mladic told his gunners above Sarajevo. "Target Muslim neighborhoods—not many Serbs live there. Shell them until they're on the edge of madness."[26]) By the time of Vukovar's surrender in November 1991, the city would come to be known as "the Croatian Stalingrad"—both for the heroic resistance put up by its outnumbered and outgunned defenders and for the overwhelming destruction it suffered. After the city's surrender, Serb troops marched into its hospital, brought out several hundred wounded men and women, and executed them, burying them in one of the war's first mass graves.

As the world watched the Serbs methodically reduce Vukovar, another siege began on the Adriatic, that of the ancient walled city of Dubrovnik. Though the destruction and loss of life here could not compare to Vukovar, the Serbs had dared attack with gunboats and artillery a world cultural landmark (as certified by UNESCO), and this occasioned fierce outrage, particularly among Europeans. General John Galvin, at the time the Supreme Allied Commander, Europe (SACEUR), had prepared contingency plans that envisioned sending the fleet into the Adriatic and, as he told me, "just sweeping those [Serb] vessels out of there, and taking care of the artillery as well."[27]

In the Pentagon, meanwhile, American military planners were working on possible interventions in Vukovar and Dubrovnik. In particular, the long line of tanks and other armor moving into Croatia from Serbia—it stretched twenty miles—would have been especially vulnerable to American air attack. Colonel Karl Lowe, a U.S. Army military planner, was assigned to work on Yugoslavia at the time.

> First of all, the Yugoslav navy was quite small, in comparison to the United States Navy and the power it could bring to the scene in very short order. They couldn't contend with that kind of overwhelming power.

Similarly, the forces of the Serbian army in the vicinity of Vukovar could not have withstood air attack by the United States, particularly if those air attacks had been very concentrated and very concerted for a number of days, so you home in on the command and control apparatus . . .

Of course, to saturate that area with air power at that time would probably not even have been necessary had we sent a forceful demonstration. . . . That is: send the navy into the Adriatic, send ground forces from Central Europe down [toward] southeastern Europe and redispose air forces to simply fly over the area in a very forceful signal that we plan to act if they didn't back off.

Why should "a very forceful signal" have any effect? "Remember," said Lowe, "this is three months after Desert Storm. Everybody in the world looks at Desert Storm and says, 'This is a miracle.' One of the largest armies in the world has suddenly been destroyed in the course of no more than ninety days. . . ."[28]

Colonel Lowe is not alone in believing that the Gulf victory should have proved an enormous boon to American diplomacy, enabling the country to maintain world order without repeatedly resorting to force. President Bush himself declared that

because of what's happened we won't have to use U.S. forces around the world. I think when we say something that is objectively correct—like don't take over a neighbor or you're going to bear some responsibility—people are going to listen. Because I think out of all this will be a new-found—let's put it this way: a reestablished credibility for the United States of America.[29]

In the event, however, when it came to preventing or stopping the Balkan war, George H. W. Bush was unwilling to make use of the "reestablished credibility" he had brought to the country he led, either by intimating that vigorous American action would be taken if the Serbs did not desist or even by speaking out forcefully.

President Tudjman, desperate to save the city of Dubrovnik, pleaded with the United States to send the Sixth Fleet into the Adriatic to warn off the Serb gunboats, an objective that General Galvin, the commander of NATO, told me the Fleet "could have achieved . . . , I believe, at very little or no cost." Even if the ships took no action, a simple "sail-by" might warn the Serbs off. To Eagleburger, however, "might" was the key word:

They "might" have gotten the message. They might also *not* have gotten the message, and then we would be faced with the question of what to do next.[30]

This is a particularly clear example of a distinctive and rather odd way of thinking that one begins to find in U.S. policy in the Balkans, and elsewhere in the post–Cold War world. Call it "self-deterrence." Since in the case of any given forceful action, one cannot be sure the Serbs will be deterred; and since, if one takes an action and they are not deterred, one must take another action to see that they are (for not to do so would destroy America's credibility)—any given action, if one can't be absolutely certain of its success, holds within it the clear risk of unlimited and uncontrolled involvement. It is as if, having taken a single small step, the United States will inevitably lose all control of its policy. As Wayne Bert writes in *The Reluctant Superpower*, Eagleburger's statement is remarkable,

> given the ease with which any kind of hostile intent in moving the fleet could have been denied. Thus, Bush administration officials were not only unwilling to commit force to the conflict, but they were also very careful to avoid specific threats of force, and to go *out of their way to avoid leaving the impression that a threat was intended.* [Emphasis added]

Dangling at the end of this faulty chain of reasoning, we find a strange paradox, as Bert points out:

> Eagleburger seemingly had no misgivings about the value of American credibility unless some overt threat was made for which there was no follow-through. *Complete inaction, in his view, did not compromise U.S. credibility.* [Emphasis added][31]

Although only months before, President Bush had declared the so-called Vietnam Syndrome "buried once and for all" beneath the sands of the Persian Gulf, we see here its mirror image raising itself slowly from the dead. One finds precisely the same obsession with "credibility," but now it translates itself into a fear of entanglement. For, once committed, the United States *must* fight to the end; the notion that any initiative could be abandoned rather than followed relentlessly forward to its conclusion is dismissed, for it is assumed that such a retreat must be grievously harmful to the nation's prestige—more harmful, a priori, than carrying on with a policy that is plainly misguided or foolish or contrary to the nation's interests (as was the case in Vietnam). Any initiative commits prestige and credibility, and, once they are committed, control is effectively abandoned: There can be no turning back. The result, in the case of this new Vietnam Syndrome, is that nothing short of full-scale commitment can even be contemplated.

Under this line of thinking, the Yugoslav war could go on, worsen, attain levels of savagery not seen in Europe for half a century, and all the while the United States—if only it had the self-control to sit by and do nothing—need have no fear of compromising itself. The slightest sign of intervention, even the slightest intimation that the Americans had "not ruled out" the use of force (a relatively mild diplomatic warning), would send the country down that slippery road to full, uncontrolled involvement—which, says Baker the politician, "the American people would never have supported. . . . After all, the United States had fought three wars in this century in Europe—two hot ones and one cold one. And three was quite enough. . . ."

From the question of the mildest of threats we skip directly to the use of ground troops—the only use of force Baker mentions—and then to that ultimate stone wall: the well-known recalcitrance of the American people. It would take four more years of war, hundreds of thousands of dead, and the advent of a new and relatively inexperienced American president to drive home the point that it was inaction itself that was doing "enormous damage to the United States and to [its] standing in the world."

As it happened, that point in the autumn of 1991—the autumn of the sieges—was probably the last chance for the United States to halt the war in Croatia at relatively low cost, and thereby to prevent the outbreak of the much more savage war in Bosnia in March 1992.

Following Baker's eleven-hour effort in Belgrade, and his "personal affront" at the refusal of Milosevic and the other leaders he saw to accept his recommendations, the Americans had passed the responsibility for dealing with the former Yugoslavia to the Europeans, who, in a misplaced, post–Maastricht Treaty burst of enthusiasm, were more than happy to receive it. ("This is the Hour of Europe!" Foreign Minister Jacques Poos of Luxembourg exulted, in words that, in the poisonous irony they would shortly acquire, are destined to be forever linked in diplomatic history with the name of the man who had uttered them.) By handing the problem to the European Community, which had no collective defense arm to speak of—instead of to NATO, which, in its post–Cold War incarnation, should have been more than pleased to take on what was supposedly just the kind of contingency it supposedly now existed to confront—the Americans had ensured that no forceful action could be threatened. For the Europeans, at least collectively, had no real weapons to brandish.

Traveling across the continent from conference table to conference table, the Europeans were treated with contempt. In an attitude that would quickly become familiar, the combatants came to view the diplomats as merely instruments to gain the odd advantage: a means to play for time here, to prepare a defense there. When faced with the Europeans and their diplomatic *démarches*, the Serbs in particular could barely disguise their derision and disregard. Tim Judah, in his comprehensive study of the Serbs, quotes a transcript of a telephone conversation between Milosevic and Radovan Karadzic, leader of the supposedly independent Bosnian Serbs, leaked to the Yugoslav press in September 1991, when Milosevic was still claiming with a straight face to the Europeans that he and the Yugoslav National Army had nothing to do with the nascent Bosnia war:

MILOSEVIC: Go to [General] Uzelac [Yugoslav Army commander at Banja Luka], he'll tell you everything. If you have any problems, telephone me.

KARADZIC: I've got problems down in Kupres. Some Serbs there are rather disobedient.
MILOSEVIC: We can deal with that. Just call Uzelac. Don't worry, you'll have everything. We are the strongest.
KARADZIC: Yes, yes.
MILOSEVIC: Don't worry. As long as there is the army no one can touch us. . . .
KARADZIC: That's good. . . . But what's going on with the bombing in—
MILOSEVIC: Today is not a good day for the air force. The European Community is in session.[32]

At this point, in the middle of major Serb offensives in Croatia, the only regard Milosevic shows for European concerns is to keep his air force on the ground when the European Community is meeting. Soon, after he has conquered what he wants of Croatia, he will elicit the help of European and United Nations diplomats to reach a convenient cease-fire protecting his gains. Having sent thousands of his now available troops into the keeping of his protégé Karadzic, Milosevic will be free to use them to turn on the Bosnians.

Had the Americans, on the other hand, taken the sort of action Colonel Lowe describes, much evidence suggests that, while all fighting might not have ended, its scope could have been radically reduced. Even as the Yugoslav National Army was crushing the Croat defenders of Vukovar, the Serbs were so concerned about the possibility of outside intervention that Milosevic turned down an army plan to attack the Croatian capital of Zagreb itself, fearing, as a top aide put it, that "if we chose all-out war with Croatia, they'd call on Germany, Austria, Hungary, and God knows who. We don't have allies like that."[33] And, as Colonel Lowe points out, Milosevic had his own weaknesses:

> Politically, in Belgrade there was another disadvantage in that Milosevic had [had] almost continuous demonstrations between March and July calling for his ouster by various factions. [The Serbian public] were of a mixed view [about the war]. . . . So if you matched the political dynamics and the military dynamics at that time against the overall international situation where the United States had just been victorious against a very formidable army—much more formidable, I think, than the Serbian armed forces—then that was the time to act.

Such action would have carried with it no guarantees—as Eagleburger would have been the first to point out. It would probably have succeeded only in limiting the conflict. At most, it would have laid the foundation for a vigorous diplomatic initiative (of the very sort the Europeans were finding it impossible to mount).

By now, President Bush was hearing this message from leaders in Eastern Europe, who were becoming increasingly worried about the uncontrolled flames consuming their neighbor. As Hutchings describes it, Prime Minister Jozsef Antall of Hungary presented a strong case to Bush in October 1991:

> When Antall met with the president at the White House . . . , his focus was almost entirely on Yugoslavia, where Serbian forces were launching brutal assaults on Croatian towns and villages. . . . Antall got to the nub of the matter, as he had in two or three recent telephone calls to Bush: Serbia had to be confronted with the credible threat of force, and only a U.S.-led NATO effort could do the job, as the European Community was not up to it. This was wise counsel, but U.S. policy had become more inert than Antall knew since Secretary Baker's ill-fated visit to Belgrade in June.

The credible threat of force was a necessity for effective diplomacy. The fall of 1991, because of the conjunction of military and political factors Colonel Lowe cites, presented the perfect opportunity to develop an active policy. And yet it was precisely this kind of creative approach that was foreclosed by the Americans' refusal to consider any use of, or indeed even the mildest threat of, military force. Which leaves one to ask whether such an initiative would truly have been more destructive of American credibility than sitting by and doing nothing at all.

When General Galvin of NATO Supreme Allied Command contacted Washington and inquired about his plan for Dubrovnik, he received a predictable answer:

> I called Colin [Powell] and asked what was happening and he just said, "It's not on." I asked why and he said, "There's just no support for getting into this thing. Nobody wants to do it. It's just not gonna happen. . . ."

On November 18, Vukovar fell, and the world watched one of the first of the war's massacres: the murder of the wounded in the city hospital. The Europeans would now transform their diplomatic failure into something worse: "sympathy." The Germans insisted on recognizing the independence of Croatia and Slovenia, an empty diplomatic gesture that, with no military guarantee behind it, would finish the Federation and doom Bosnia to certain war. Certainly the Americans were aware of how ill-advised and harmful this step was; if they had been willing to exert strong pressure on their number-one ally, they might well have been able to prevent recognition. But as Zimmermann says, "I don't think there was a strong American push, and I think the reason was that Baker had been burned by his visit to Belgrade and felt that this was a can of worms and something that probably we should stay out of."[34] American officials thus did no more than look on in mounting horror, grateful, one presumes, that as Secretary of State James Baker had declared on his return from his frustrating visit to Belgrade, "We got no dog in this fight."

In the months to come, that position would become more and more difficult to hold. During the early days of August 1992, pictures appeared of a sort not seen in Europe since the 1940s: pictures of emaciated men staring dully out from behind barbed wire. That was when the world learned of a place called Omarska.

New York Review of Books, November 20, 1997

The Cleansing: A Televised Genocide

I.

TO THE HUNDREDS OF MILLIONS who first beheld them on their television screens that August day in 1992, the faces staring out from behind barbed wire seemed powerfully familiar.[11] Sunken-cheeked, hollow-eyed, their skulls shaved, their bodies wasted and frail, they did not seem men at all but living archetypes, their faces stylized masks of tragedy. One had thought such faces consigned to the century's horde of images: emaciated figures of the 1940s shuffling about in filthy, striped uniforms, bulldozers pushing into dark ditches masses of lank white bodies. Yet a mere half century later here came these gaunt beings, clinging to life in Omarska and Trnopolje and the other camps run by Serbs in northern Bosnia and now displayed before the eyes of the world like fantastic, rediscovered beasts.

The Germans, creators of millions of such living dead, had christened them *Muselmänner*—Musulmen: Muslims. At Auschwitz, wrote Primo Levi,

> the *Muselmänner*, the drowned, form the backbone of the camp, an anonymous mass . . . of non-men who march and labor in silence, the divine spark dead in them. . . . One hesitates to call them living: one hesitates to call their death death, in the face of which they have no fear, as they are too tired to understand.[2]

In Omarska as in Auschwitz the masters created these walking corpses from healthy men by employing simple methods: withhold all but the barest nourishment, forcing the prisoners' bodies to waste away; impose upon them a ceaseless terror, subjecting them to unremitting physical cruelty; immerse them in degradation and death and decay, destroying all hope and obliterating the will to live.

"We won't waste our bullets on them," a guard at Omarska, which the Serbs set up in a former open-pit iron mine, told a United Nations representative in mid-1992. "They have no roof. There is sun and rain, cold nights, and beatings two times a day. We give them no food and no water. They will starve like animals."[3]

On August 5, 1992, Ed Vulliamy of *The Guardian*, the first newspaper-man admitted into Omarska, stood in the camp's "canteen" and watched, stupefied, as thirty emaciated men stumbled out into the yard, squinting at the sunlight:

> . . . A group of prisoners . . . have just emerged from a door in the side of a large rust-colored metal shed. [T]hey run in single file across the court-yard. . . . Above them in an observation post is the watchful eye, hidden behind reflective sunglasses, of a beefy guard who follows their weary can-ter with the barrel of his heavy machine gun.
>
> Their . . . heads [are] newly shaven, their clothes baggy over their skele-tal bodies. Some are barely able to move. In the canteen, . . . they line up in obedient and submissive silence and collect . . . a meager, watery por-tion of beans. . . .[4]

They are given precisely three minutes to run from the shed, wait for the food and gulp it down, and run back to the shed. "Whoever didn't make it would get beaten or killed," a prisoner identified only as Mirsad told Helsinki Watch investigators. "The stew we were given was boiling hot . . . so we all had 'inside burns.' The inside of my mouth was peeling."[5]

Vulliamy and his colleagues stand and gaze at the creatures struggling to wolf down the rations:

> . . . [T]he bones of their elbows and wrists protrude like pieces of jagged stone from the pencil-thin stalks to which their arms have been reduced. Their skin is putrefied, the complexions . . . have corroded. [They] are alive but decomposed, debased, degraded, and utterly subservient, and yet they fix their huge hollow eyes on us with [what] looks like blades of knives.

It is an extraordinary confrontation, this mutual stare: Vulliamy and his colleagues are reporting from inside a working concentration camp. All the while, though, Serb guards in combat fatigues, cradling AK-47s and bearing great military knives sheathed at their hips, trudge heavily about the room, their eyes glaring above their beards.

Vulliamy moves forward to speak to a "young man, emaciated, sunken-eyed and attacking his watery bean stew like a famished dog, his spindly hands shaking," but the fellow stops him: "I do not want to tell any lies," he says, "but I cannot tell the truth." It is an eloquent comment: most of these *Muselmänner* prove "too terrified to talk, bowing their heads and excusing themselves by casting a glance at the pacing soldiers, or else they just stare, opaque, spiritless, and terrified."

The reporters ask to see the hospital and receive a curt refusal. Nor may they look inside that white building—the White House, the prisoners call it—or the great "rust-colored shed" from which the men had come, squinting at the August sun.

Later, survivors describe the shed as "a vast human hen coop, in which thousands of men were crammed for twenty-four hours a day . . . , living in their own filth and, in many cases, dying from asphyxiation." So tightly were prisoners packed together in the stifling, airless heat, "Sakib R." tells Vulliamy, that lying down was impossible and some lost consciousness standing up, collapsing one against another.

> I [counted] seven hundred that I could actually see [around me]. A lot of people went mad . . . : when they went insane, shuddering and screaming, they were taken out and shot.

Though guards at Omarska and other camps shot many prisoners, this was by no means the preferred method. If Auschwitz's killing tended to be mechanized and bureaucratized, Omarska's was emotional and personal, for it depended on the simple, intimate act of beating. "They beat us with clubs, bats, hoses, rifle butts," one survivor told a Helsinki Watch interviewer. "Their favorite was a thick rubber hose with metal on both ends." They beat us, said another, "with braided cable wires" and with pipes "filled with lead."

Next to the automatic rifle, next even to the knife (which was freely used at Omarska), the club or the pipe is exhausting, time-consuming, inefficient. Yet the guards made it productive. A female prisoner identified only as "J" told Helsinki Watch investigators:

> We saw corpses piled one on top of another. . . . The bodies eventually were gathered with a forklift and put onto trucks—usually two large trucks and a third, smaller truck. The trucks first would unload containers of food, and then the bodies would be loaded [on]. . . . This happened almost every day—sometimes there [were] . . . twenty or thirty—but usually there were more. Most of the deaths occurred as a result of beatings.[6]

One survivor interviewed by United Nations investigators estimated that "on many occasions, twenty to forty prisoners were killed at night by 'knife, hammer, and burning.' He stated that he had witnessed the killing of one prisoner by seven guards who poured petrol on him, set him on fire, and struck him upon the head with a hammer." All prisoners were beaten, but, according to the UN investigators, guards in all the camps meted out especially savage treatment "to intellectuals, politicians, police, and the wealthy."[7] When four guards summoned the president of the local Croatian Democratic Union, Silvije Saric, along with Professor Puskar from nearby Prijedor, for "interrogation," the female prisoner testified,

I heard beating and yelling. . . . At times it sounded as if wood were being shattered, but those were bones that were being broken.

. . . When they opened the door . . . , they started yelling at us, "Ustasa slut, see what we do to them!" . . . I saw two piles of blood and flesh in the corner. The two men were so horribly beaten that they no longer had the form of human beings.[8]

Apart from obvious differences in scale and ambition, it is the Serbs' reliance on this laborious kind of murder that most strikingly distinguishes the workings of their camps from those of the German death factories. At many of the latter, healthy arrivals would work as slaves until they were reduced to *Muselmänner*; death came when camp bureaucrats judged them no longer fit to provide any useful service to the Reich. The gas chambers—routinized, intentionally impersonal means of killing—had evolved partly out of a concern for the effect that committing mass murder would have on troops, even on men specially trained to do it. As Raul Hilberg observed,

The Germans employed the phrase *Seelenbelastung* ("burdening of the soul") with reference to machine-gun fire . . . directed at men, women, and children in prepared ditches. After all, the men that were firing these weapons were themselves fathers. How could they do this day after day? It was then that the technicians developed a gas van designed to lessen the suffering of the perpetrator.[9]

Even within the camps themselves, SS officers worried that violence and sadism would demoralize and corrupt their elite troops. "The SS leaders," Wolfgang Sofsky writes,

were indifferent to the suffering of the victims, but not to the morale of their men. Their attention was aroused . . . by the sadistic excesses of individual tormenters. As a countermeasure, camp brothels were set up, and the task of punishment was delegated to specially selected prisoners. The leadership also transferred certain thugs whose behavior had become intolerable.[10]

At Omarska such men would have been cherished; the out-and-out passion with which a guard administered beatings and devised tortures could greatly bolster his prestige. Acts of flamboyant violence, publicly performed, made some men celebrities of sadism. In his memoir *The Tenth Circle of Hell*, Rezak Hukanovic—a Muslim who was a journalist in Prijedor before he was taken to Omarska—describes how guards responded when a prisoner rejected the order to strip and stood immobile amid the cowering naked inmates:

The guard . . . fired several shots in the air. The man stood stubbornly in place without making the slightest movement. While bluish smoke still rose from the rifle barrel, the guard struck the clothed man in the middle of the head with the rifle butt, once and then again, until the man fell. Then the guard . . . moved his hand to his belt. A knife flashed in his hand, a long army knife.

He bent down, grabbing hold of the poor guy's hair. . . . Another guard joined in, continuously cursing. He, too, had a flashing knife in his hand. . . . The guards [used] them to tear away the man's clothes. After only a few seconds, they stood up, their own clothes covered with blood. . . .

. . . The poor man stood up a little, or rather tried to, letting out excruciating screams. He was covered with blood. One guard took a water hose from a nearby hydrant and directed a strong jet at [him]. A mixture of blood and water flowed down his . . . gaunt, naked body as he bent down repeatedly, like a wounded Cyclops . . . ; his cries were of someone driven to insanity by pain. And then Djemo and everyone else saw clearly what had happened: the guards had cut off the man's sexual organ and half of his behind.[11]

Hukanovic's memoir (in which he writes about himself in the third person as Djemo) and the testimony of other former prisoners overflow with such horror. Reading them, one feels enervated, and also bewildered: What accounts for such unquenchable blood-lust? This is a large subject; but part of the answer may have to do with the elaborate ideology that stands behind Serb objectives in the war. In order to achieve a "Greater Serbia," which will at last bring together all Serbs in one land, they feel they must "cleanse" what is "their" land of outsiders. Founding—or rather reestablishing—"Greater Serbia" is critical not only because it satisfies an ancient historical claim but because Serbs must *protect themselves from the "genocide" others even now are planning for them.*

In this thinking, such genocide has already begun—in Croatia, in Kosovo, in Bosnia itself: anywhere Serbs live but lack political dominance. As many writers point out, such ideas of vulnerability and betrayal can be traced far back in Serbia's past, and President Slobodan Milosevic, with his control of state radio and television, exploited them brilliantly, building popular hatred by instilling and reinforcing in Serbs a visceral fear and paranoia.

Administering a beating is a deeply personal affirmation of power: with your own hands you seize your enemy—supposedly a mortally threatening enemy, now rendered passive and powerless—and slowly, methodically reduce him from human to nonhuman. Each night at Omarska and other camps, guards called prisoners out by name and enacted this atrocity. Some of their enemies they beat to death, dumping their corpses on the tarmac for the forklift driver to find the next morning. Others they beat until the victim still barely clung to life; if he did not die, the guards would wait a week or so and beat him again.

For the Serbs it was a repeated exercise in triumph, in confronting and vanquishing an accumulated paranoia. As Hukanovic makes clear in his account of the first time his name was called, this torture is exceedingly, undeniably intimate, not simply because force is administered by hand but also because it comes very often from someone you know:

> "In front of me," the [bearded, red-faced] guard ordered, pointing to the White House. . . . He ranted and raved, cursing and occasionally pounding Djemo on the back with his truncheon. . . .
>
> . . . The next second, something heavy was let loose from above, from the sky, and knocked Djemo over the head. He fell.
>
> . . . Half conscious, sensing that he had to fight to survive, he wiped the blood from his eyes and forehead and raised his head. He saw four creatures, completely drunk, like a pack of starving wolves, with clubs in their hands and unadorned hatred in their eyes. Among them was the frenzied leader, Zoran Zigic, the infamous Ziga. . . . He was said to have killed over two hundred people, including many children, in the "cleansing" operations around Prijedor. . . . Scrawny and long-legged, with a big black scar on his face, Ziga seemed like an ancient devil come to visit a time as cruel as his own. . . .
>
> "Now then, let me show you how Ziga does it," he said, ordering Djemo to kneel down in the corner by the radiator, "on all fours, just like a dog." The maniac grinned. Djemo knelt down and leaned forward on his hands, feeling humiliated and as helpless as a newborn. . . .

Zigic began hitting Hukanovic on his back and head with a club that had a metal ball on the end. Hukanovic curled up trying to protect his head. Zigic kept hitting him, steadily, methodically, cursing all the while.

> The drops of blood on the tiles under Djemo's head [became] denser and denser until they formed a thick, dark red puddle. Ziga kept at it; he stopped only every now and then . . . to fan himself, waving his shirt tail in front of his contorted face.
>
> At some point, a man in fatigues appeared. . . . It was Saponja, a member of the famous Bosna-montaza soccer club from Prijedor; Djemo had once known him quite well. . . . "Well, well, my old pal Djemo. While I was fighting . . . , you were pouring down the cold ones in Prijedor." He kicked Djemo right in the face with his combat boot. Then he kicked him again in the chest, so badly that Djemo felt like his ribs had been shattered . . . Ziga laughed like a maniac . . . and started hitting Djemo again with his weird club. . . .
>
> Djemo received another, even stronger kick to the face. He clutched himself in pain, bent a little to one side, and collapsed, his head sinking

into the now-sizable pool of blood beneath him. Ziga grabbed him by the hair . . . and looked into Djemo's completely disfigured face: "Get up, you scum. . . ."

Then Ziga and the other guards forced Djemo to smear his bloody face in a filthy puddle of water.

"The boys have been eating strawberries and got themselves a little red," said Zigic, laughing like a madman. . . . Another prisoner, Slavko Eci-movic, . . . was kneeling, all curled up, by the radiator. When he lifted his head, where his face should have been was nothing but the bloody, spongy tissue under the skin that had just been ripped off.

Instead of eyes, two hollow sockets were filled with black, coagulated blood. "You'll all end up like this, you and your families," Ziga said. "We killed his father and mother. And his wife. We'll get his kids. And yours, we'll kill you all." And with a wide swing of his leg, he kicked Djemo right in the face. . . .

II.

Confronted by the televised faces behind barbed wire, Bush administration officials reacted instinctively: they denied knowing anything about the camps. Or rather, they first said they knew and then, next day, said they didn't.

On August 3, 1992, the day after Roy Gutman's first, highly graphic story on Omarska appeared in *Newsday*, the State Department deputy spokesman, Richard Boucher, faced reporters and announced that administration officials had not only been aware "that the Serbian forces are maintaining what they call detention centers" but that "abuses and torture and killings [were] taking place." Angry questions followed: If President Bush had known of these camps, why had he not publicly denounced them? Why had he not insisted the prisoners be released, or that the camps open their doors to the Red Cross? Why, finally, had he not at least *revealed* that the camps existed?

The next morning Thomas Niles, assistant secretary of state for European affairs, took his seat before the House Foreign Affairs Committee and told congressmen that "we don't have, thus far, substantiated information that would confirm the existence of these camps." Less than twenty-four hours before, Bush officials said they had known of the horrors at Omarska; now they were unable to say the camps existed.

Why this high-level Keystone Kops routine, particularly from an administration that prided itself on its cool, professional management of foreign affairs? The answer is not hard to find. The reporters' discovery of Omarska and the other camps, and the outrage their dispatches and videotape provoked, did not pose, for Bush, a problem of foreign policy but rather one of politics. For though Secretary of State James Baker had claimed that the administration did not act forcefully in the Balkans because "the American people would never . . . support it," the matter was not so simple. As Baker well knew, polls could fluctuate wildly: At various times during the Bosnia conflict, lurid television pictures provoked "spikes" in the fever chart of popular concern, and, if Americans still wouldn't support dispatching ground troops, they were not shy about demanding their government do *something*. The Bush people, having concluded nearly two years before that taking strong action posed unacceptable risks,[12] now feared that popular outrage, momentarily fueled by just this sort of "telegenic" but (in their view) ephemeral atrocity, might drag them toward such involvement; or else, popular sentiment would penalize them politically (with a presidential election barely three months away) for "doing nothing."

State Department officials, who approved Boucher's original announcement that the government had known of the camps, had wildly misjudged the response. In declaring that they had known, an unnamed official told Warren P. Strobel, author of *Late-Breaking Foreign Policy*, the intent had been "to move the ball forward one step, and the [news] reports moved it forward two steps." Two steps was clearly too much; so Niles was ordered up to Congress to try to move the ball back one, an absurd notion under the circumstances. "We kind of waffled around a little bit," acknowledged Lawrence Eagleburger, then acting secretary of state, in an interview with Strobel. "All of us were being a little bit careful . . . because of this issue of whether or not it was going to push us into something that we thought was dangerous."[13]

The pictures from the camps thus confronted Bush officials with the challenge not of how to deal with the reemergence of concentration camps in Europe but rather how to withstand the political pressures arising from the televised images of them. Concentration camps a half-century after the Nazis would have been bad enough, but *pictures* of the emaciated, tortured prisoners: this was the sort of thing that might stir the lethargic and fickle American public.

On August 6, the day pictures of the emaciated prisoners taken by Independent Television News (ITN) network were broadcast in the United States and around the world, President Bush finally called for international observers to be granted access to the camps and, for good measure, he asked that the United Nations authorize that "all necessary means" be used to deliver humanitarian supplies to Bosnia. Even as the president, faced with pictures of men in concentration camps, talked of the UN and food shipments, Governor Bill Clinton, now the Democratic presidential candidate, was demanding that the administration push NATO to send fighter bombers to save Bosnians from "deliberate and systematic extermination based on their ethnic origin." The next day, facing a barrage of questions at Kennebunkport, President Bush was defiant:

I don't care what the political pressures are. Before one soldier . . . is committed to battle, I'm going to know how that person gets out of there. And we are not going to get bogged down into some guerrilla warfare. We lived through that once.

As Eagleburger later put it, "Vietnam never goes away,"[14] and obviously this was dramatically the case for George Bush. The president plainly believed that any American involvement in Bosnia, even one undertaken to eliminate concentration camps, must inevitably lead to "a quagmire."

Thus, according to former ambassador to Yugoslavia Warren Zimmermann, when the possibility of an "air operation" to rescue victims of the camps was raised within the embattled administration that August, and Baker and the national security adviser, Brent Scowcroft, showed serious interest in it, "there was no sign . . . that the President ever did, and nothing was done." Indeed, as Zimmermann tells it, when officials discussed any change in Bush's passive policy, the ghost of Vietnam could be felt hovering in the room:

> The "lesson" drawn from Vietnam was that even a minimum injection of American forces could swell inexorably into a major commitment and produce a quagmire. The second objection . . . was the view that had prevailed during the successful prosecution of the Gulf War: there should be no U.S. military intervention unless the objectives were clear, the means applied to [them] would bring certain victory, there was an "exit strategy" (the earlier the better). . . . Pervading all these reasons was an almost obsessive fear of American casualties . . .[15]

In effect, requiring that the "means applied" always "bring certain victory" would likely preclude even minimal intervention. Arnold Kanter, a former high Bush administration official, put the matter squarely: Pentagon officers "clearly understand that if intervention options entail very large force requirements, it often has the practical political effect of virtually ruling out military intervention." As George H. W. Bush, "the foreign policy President," knew, and as Bill Clinton would soon discover, such an ideology, taken as faith by a Vietnam-haunted officer corps, has the effect in the end of severely limiting a president's freedom of *diplomatic* action. If the State Department "tends to be more willing . . . to threaten, deploy, and employ military forces," as Kanter says, this is because diplomats view "the threat and use of force as a key instrument of U.S. foreign policy. . . ."[16]

In late September, as the debate set off by the concentration camp pictures raged, Chairman of the Joint Chiefs General Colin Powell summoned to his office a *New York Times* reporter and gave a remarkable interview, which the *Times* ran on its front page under the headline "Powell Delivers a Resounding No On Using Limited Force In Bosnia." Powell declared:

> As soon as [politicians] tell me it is limited, it means they do not care whether you achieve a result or not. As soon as they tell me "surgical," I head for the bunker.

Insisting he did not believe the military must apply "overwhelming force in every situation," the general said leaders must "begin with a clear understanding of what political objective is being achieved," then determine whether the objective is "to win or do something else."

> Preferably, it is to win because it shows you have made a commitment to decisive results. . . . The key is to get decisive results to accomplish the mission.[17]

The simplicity is deceptive: For Powell the opposite of "to win" is not "to lose" but rather to fail to achieve "decisive results." If a military action does not prove "decisive," it has failed. And if a proposed mission cannot be virtually guaranteed to produce such results, it should not be attempted.

One might think the responsibility for determining what such "results" should be would properly fall not to Powell but someone "above his pay grade." If the president, having decided that he could define success as something less than what military officers deem to be "decisive results," chooses to employ "limited force" to strike, say, the rail lines or roads leading to Omarska—or to destroy the Drina River bridges in order to cripple the Bosnian Serb supply system—then this decision belongs to him, not to senior officers.

And so it comes as no surprise that the State Department spokesman's first response to the faces from Omarska had been the forthright one. Of course the American government had known about the Serbian camps, long before the pictures and stories had come out. The only question was exactly when. As John Fox, a regional official official in the State Department's policy planning office at the time, told *ABC News*, "The U.S. government had in its possession credible and verified reports of the existence of the camps, Serbian-run camps in Bosnia and elsewhere, as of June, certainly July, 1992, well ahead of media revelations."[18] I myself later received, as part of a declassified package of documents, a highly redacted Defense Intelligence Agency cable from the summer of 1992—the precise date, like much else, was blacked out—that included a "a list of prisons in Bosnian territory," with information listed for each camp under the rubrics "Location," "Number of Prisoners," and "Number Liquidated." The "Number Liquidated" column included three entries of more than a thousand, one of more than two thousand, and one of more than three thousand. By the summer of 1992, in other words, U.S. intelligence officers knew in quite precise terms that the Serbs were murdering thousands of people in prison camps and had "liquidated" more than ten thousand in five camps alone.

However much they knew, Bush officials said nothing to the American public of the killing and the torture; for the outrage that would greet such news was predictable. And the administration, now as before, was determined to do nothing at all.

As it happened, though, the public revelations of the camps in August 1992, and the political controversy that followed, were mirrored within the government by a quieter struggle: over the meanings, and implications, of genocide.

III.

In early April 1992, little more than a week after officers of the newly christened Bosnian Serb Army launched their campaign of limited conquest in Bosnia, officials in Washington began receiving reports of atrocities, among them mass executions, beatings, mutilations, and rape. Jon Western, then working at the State Department on human rights in Bosnia, recalls that

> many of these atrocities looked an awful lot like what we had heard and read about during World War II—the Balkans historically produce a lot of disinformation—and we were trained to look at them critically and decipher what was real. But as reports continued to come in . . . , it became apparent that they weren't just propaganda.
>
> In fact, we were getting reports from a number of sources: eyewitnesses who had been incarcerated in concentration camps begin filtering out in summer 1992 and began giving accounts of atrocities that we could cross-reference with those from other eyewitnesses. . . .[19]

As the Serbs prosecuted their "lightning campaign"—the Bosnian Serb Army of eighty thousand men, which had come fully equipped from the Yugoslav National Army, conquered 60 percent of Bosnian territory in scarcely six weeks—State Department officials compiled testimony of increasingly shocking and gruesome atrocities. Jon Western recalls that children were "systematically raped":

> There was one account that affected me: a young girl was raped repeatedly by Serb paramilitary units. Her parents were restrained behind a fence and she was raped repeatedly and they left her in a pool of blood and over the course of a couple of days she finally died, and her parents were not able to tend to her; they were restrained behind a fence. When we first heard this story, it seemed very hard to believe but we heard it from a number of eyewitnesses . . . and it became apparent there was validity to it.

Western and his colleagues were struck not only by the cruelty of these abuses but by their *systematic* nature; they very rapidly came to understand that though the Serb soldiers and, especially, the "paramilitary" troops responsible for "mopping up" were committing wildly sadistic acts of brutality, often under the influence of alcohol, their officers were making rational, systematic use of terror as a method of war. Rather than a regrettable but unavoidable concomitant of combat, rapes and mass executions and mutilations were here an essential part of it.

The Serbs fought not only to conquer territory but to "clear" it of all traces of their Muslim or Croat enemies; or, as the notorious Serb phrase has it, to "ethnically cleanse" what they believed to be "their" land. Of course making use of terror in such a way is probably as old—and as widespread—as warfare itself:

> Houses and whole villages reduced to ashes, unarmed and innocent populations massacred *en masse*, incredible acts of violence, pillage and brutality of every kind—such were the means which were employed by the Serbo-Montenegrin soldiery, with a view to the entire transformation of the ethnic character of regions inhabited exclusively by Albanians.

This account is drawn from the Carnegie Endowment's *Report of the International Commission to Inquire into the Cause and Conduct of the Balkan Wars*, published in 1914.[20] Substitute the word "Muslims" for "Albanians" and the sentence could have been composed in spring or summer of 1992. Not only was the technique of "ethnic cleansing" identical, its purpose—"the entire transformation of the ethnic character of regions"—was clear to all.

The motive force driving Serbs to fight to achieve a "Greater Serbia"—or "all Serbs in one country"—depends however on a fortuitous conjunction of factors: a set of powerful historical legends combined in a cherished nationalist myth, the advent of the economic hardship and uncertainty brought on by the end of the Cold War, and the rise of an ambitious, talented, and ruthless politician.

On the nationalist myth, in particular, Tim Judah writes powerfully, briefly describing the Battle of Kosovo of 1389, and discussing its transformation into the founding epic of the Serbian "exile." The story he tells does much to explain both the Serb obsession with the treachery of outsiders and their quasi-religious faith in the eventual founding, or rather reestablishment, of the Serbian state. It was at Kosovo that King Lazar and his Serb knights rode boldly out to take the field against the Turks under Sultan Murad and defend Europe against the infidel. The Serbs lost this battle—although, as Judah shows, the evidence for this is ambiguous, as it is for much of the story. In any case, they later came to blame the defeat on the (probably imaginary) treachery of Vuk Brankovic, one of Lazar's favorite knights. As Petar Petrovic-Njegos, prince-bishop of Montenegro, wrote in his 1847 epic, *The Mountain Wreath*:

Our Serbia chiefs, most miserable cowards,
The Serbian stock did heinously betray.
Thou, Brankovic, of stock despicable,
Should one serve so his fatherland,
Thus much is honesty esteem'd.

Judah argues that the "myth of treachery was needed as a way to explain the fall of the medieval state, and it has powerful seeds of self-replications contained within it," seeds which have sprouted into an obsession with betrayal. With "monotonous regularity" during the 1991–1995 war, as Judah notes, "losses were always put down to secret deals—and treachery."

In the last supper the night before the battle, Brankovic plays Judas to Lazar's Christ; in causing the Serbs to lose the battle, and thus their country, to the Turks, Brankovic's betrayal made way for the crucifixion of the Serb homeland itself. But Lazar's "idea that it is better to fight honourably and die than to live as slaves" not only "provided for Serbs an explanation for their oppression by the Ottomans,"

> it also identified the whole nation with the central guiding *raison d'être* of Christianity: resurrection. In other words Lazar opted for the empire of heaven, that is to say truth and justice, so that the state would one day be resurrected. An earthly kingdom was rejected in favor of nobler ideals—victimhood and sacrifice—and this choice is to be compared with the temptations of Christ.

As Jesus would be resurrected so Lazar would be: and so, as well, would Serbia. This becomes a holy certainty, premised on the Serbs' heroism and their sacrifice in losing to the Turks. "That is what people mean when they talk about the Serbs as a 'heavenly people,'" Zarko Korac, a psychology professor at Belgrade University, tells Judah.

> In this way the Serbs identify themselves with the Jews. As victims, yes, but also with the idea of "sacred soil." The Jews said, "Next year in Jerusalem," and after 2000 years they recreated their state. The message is: "We are victims, but we are going to survive."

Milosevic himself exploits this powerful ideological, primordial view of history as a motivating force; but he has not let it limit his tactical flexibility. Judah rightly emphasizes that Milosevic plainly did not always believe armed conquest and ethnic cleansing central to carrying out his project in Bosnia. Well before the Bosnians declared independence and war broke out in the spring of 1992, Milosevic tried hard to woo Bosnia into remaining in what was left of the Federation—which, of course, with Slovenia and Croatia having seceded (and the Serbs of the Krajina now "liberated" from Croatia and loosely tied to Serbia), was now politically dominated by the Serbs.

The Bosnians referred to Milosevic's planned state derisively as "Serboslavia" and it is no wonder they wanted no part of it; but the Serb leader's tenacious attempts to persuade the Bosnians not to follow the Slovenians and Croatians in seceding show him to be much more a ruthless political tactician than an ideologue, a distinction he would confirm by his behavior four years later when he abandoned to the "ethnic cleansing" of the Croatian army the very Krajina Serbs his National Army made such a show of "liberating" in 1991.

In the event, though, and not surprisingly, Bosnia would not be wooed. Although its inexperienced leader, Alija Itzetbegovic, understood the danger of declaring independence—his nascent state, a third of whose people were Serb, might instantly collapse in war—his desperate proposals (offered jointly with the Macedonian president) to make of Yugoslavia a loose confederation were hardly of interest to Serbia, Croatia, or Slovenia. Slovenia, a small, prosperous republic with few Serbs and therefore of no real importance to Milosevic, was determined to secede, and once the Slovenes departed, the Croats were bound to follow.

After both republics seceded in June 1991, the Bosnians were left with a stark choice: either passively sink into a reconfigured Yugoslavia dominated by Milosevic and the Serbs, or declare independence and pray that the world would recognize the new country and somehow protect it from the onslaught to come. Itzetbegovic chose the latter, imploring the "international community" to recognize his new country and to send United Nations monitors to patrol its territory and prevent the war he knew was coming. After the Bosnians voted for independence in a referendum in February 1992—the Bosnian Serbs boycotted—the "international community" in early April recognized Bosnia as a sovereign state, and gave it a seat at the United Nations. But recognizing independent Bosnia was one thing; sending troops—even lightly armed "monitors"—to protect it was quite another. Not that there weren't proposals: According to John Fox, then serving on the State Department's Policy Planning Staff,

> The French came to the [Bush] administration at very senior levels . . . once in the early phase of Belgrade's attack on Croatia, and at least once well before the military campaign against Bosnia, and they made a proposal to join with the United States, and other willing states, to put preventive peace-keepers on the ground across Bosnia—to support the legitimate elected government of Bosnia, to stabilize and prevent the outbreak of conflict, and to see Bosnia through that transition process to becoming a new independent state.[21]

One might consider the proposal to dispatch peacekeeping troops as either a relatively inexpensive way to prevent what seemed an inevitable and possibly horrendous war, or as a risky initiative that would involve Americans in a situation that didn't have a clear "exit strategy." The Policy Planning Staff, according to Fox, had urged that the Americans join the French, but "that proposal was not accepted." The result, he says, was that "the French never got a very clear answer."

Itzetbegovic would be given no "peacekeepers"; but after all he had international recognition. The Serbs were not impressed. "Milosevic couldn't care less if Bosnia was recognized," a laughing Dr. Karadzic later told a television interviewer. "He said, 'Caligula proclaimed his horse a senator, but the horse never took his seat. Itzetbegovic may get recognition, but he'll never have a state.'" Karadzic, the self-proclaimed leader of the Bosnian Serbs, now declared, in a famous speech during the waning days of the integral Bosnian parliament in Sarajevo, "I warn you, you'll drag Bosnia down to hell. You Muslims aren't ready for war—you'll face extinction."[22]

He was right. By the time Cyrus Vance, the United Nations negotiator, concluded the ceasefire in Croatia on January 2, 1992, thousands of Serb troops were heading for Bosnia in their tanks and armored personnel carriers. On May 5, all soldiers and officers of the Yugoslav National Army (JNA) who came from Bosnia were taken out of the main force, complete with their equipment, and officially christened a "Bosnian Serb Army" of more than eighty thousand fully trained men. Over the objections of the Bosnian government in Sarajevo, the Serb forces took up strategic positions around the country, clearly preparing for war. Jerko Doko, then Bosnia's minister of defense, later explained in testimony at The Hague that

> this could be seen by the deployment of units; the control of roads by the JNA; the relocation of artillery on hilltops around all the major cities of Bosnia-Herzegovina; their collaboration with extremist forces of the [Bosnian Serbian Democratic Party], arming them and assisting the arming of them.

But Belgrade retained control. "We promised to pay all their costs," said Borislav Jovic, then a close aide of Milosevic's. It was not, he said, as if the Bosnian Serbs had their own state budget to draw on. "They couldn't even pay their officers." Doko remembers the National Army commander, General Blagoje Adzic, visiting troops near Banja Luka and Tuzla toward the end of March 1992 in order to check their preparedness for the coming combat operations in Bosnia-Herzegovina.

As for the Bosnians, they were, as Karadzic said, unprepared for war. "Before the fighting," David Rieff writes in his bitter essay, *Slaughterhouse*, "Alija Itzetbegovic insisted there could be no war because one side—his own—would not fight. To have imagined that carnage could have been averted for this reason was only one of the many culpably naïve assumptions the Bosnian presidency made."[23]

The Serb leaders, on the other hand, could not have been more prepared. During the last few years a group of selected senior officers had secretly developed a military strategy to guide what was to be the "Bosnia Serb Army" in its campaign to seize control of most of Bosnia. The objectives were based on ideological claims of Serb vulnerability, Serb suffering, and Serb destiny that virtually every Serb who read a newspaper, listened to the radio, or watched television would by now know by heart. The center of the ideology remained, as it had for six centuries, the redemption of the fourteenth century defeat at Kosovo. In 1889, on the 500th anniversary of the battle, Serbia's foreign minister declared that the Serbs had "continued the battle in the sixteenth, seventeenth, and eighteenth centuries when they tried to recover their freedom through countless uprisings." As Judah notes, Milosevic himself would make use of this occasion a century later to invoke "Lazar's ghost" to come to the Serbs' aid.

IV.

By this time, Milosevic was making use of an ideological program, drawn up by Serbian intellectuals, which came to be called "the Memorandum," a kind of quasi-sociological rendition of the Lazar legend. In September 1986, extracts from this document, which was drafted by sixteen eminent economists, scientists, and historians in the Serbian Academy of Arts and Sciences at the suggestion of the prominent novelist and nationalist Dobrica Cosic, had been leaked to the Belgrade press, and (in Judah's phrase) shook "the whole of Yugoslavia" with "a political earthquake."

In the key section entitled "Position of Serbia and the Serbian People," the writers launch a vigorous, bitter attack on what they call the "Weak Serbia, strong Yugoslavia" policy implicit in the "injustices" of Tito's 1974 constitution. This document, it was said, in effect "divided Serbia in three," by making Vojvodina and Kosovo autonomous provinces: though part of Serbia's territory, they both retained a right to their own votes in national government institutions.

The increasing exodus of Serbs from the province of Kosovo—which, as Judah shows, had amounted only to a *relative* decrease of population with respect to the Albanians—the writers repeatedly describe as "the genocide in Kosovo." According to the memorandum, this shift in population in Kosovo—which resulted from "a physical, moral and psychological reign of terror"—together with the economic and legal "hardships" all Serbs suffer daily, "are not only threatening the Serbian people but also the stability of Yugoslavia as a whole." In the Federation's "general process of disintegration," the academicians wrote, the Serbs "have been hit hardest," and in fact the country's difficulties are "directed towards the total breaking up of the national unity among the Serbian people." Observing that 24 percent of all Serbs live outside the Serbian Republic and more than 40 percent outside of so-called "inner Serbia," the writers declare:

A nation which after a long and bloody struggle regained its own state, which fought for and achieved a civil democracy, and which in the last two wars lost 2.5 million of its members, has lived to see the day when a Party committee of apparatchiks decrees that . . . it alone is not allowed to have its own state. A worse historical defeat in peacetime cannot be imagined.[24]

The roots of Milosevic's and Karadzic's ideological campaigns are all here: the near-hysterical sense of historical grievance and betrayal, the resentment over Serbia's "inferior political position," the heightened rhetoric about the "genocide" of the Serbs—a term that is used to describe the exile of Serbs from their rightful lands but that evokes darker suspicions of the true intentions of Serbia's betrayers. To combat these injustices Serbs are obliged to seize their fate in their own hands and achieve the long-awaited resurrection of King Lazar: "the territorial unity of the Serbian people." They must act not only to ensure their survival but to lay claim at last to an ancient birthright: "the establishment," as the Memorandum says, "of the full national integrity of the Serbian people, *regardless of which republic or province it inhabits*, is its historic and democratic right."

Dominating the newspapers, television, and radio from the late 1980s onward, Milosevic and the other purveyors of this ideology brilliantly exploited the insecurities and fears of a people caught in a maelstrom of economic decline and political change. In the Serbian press all Muslims became "Islamic fundamentalists," all Croats "Ustase." Well before the actual breakup of Yugoslavia—as Norman Cigar writes in his *Genocide in Bosnia*— "influential figures in Serbia had begun to shape a stereotypical image of Muslims as alien, inferior, and a threat to all that the Serbs held dear."

Such propaganda, fed incessantly to a people who in many cases had been prepared for it by their own cherished historical myths, served to transform neighbors into "the other"—outsiders, aliens. And Milosevic did not find it difficult, in the bewildering world of nascent popular politics, to portray a relatively new phenomenon for Yugoslavs—the legitimate political opponent—as a mortal threat. By "isolating the entire Muslim community," writes Cigar, such propaganda would ensure that "any steps . . . taken against Muslims in pursuit of Belgrade's political goals would acquire legitimacy and popular support."[25]

Such "steps" were even then being prepared. During the late 1980s a small group of officers (among them, then Colonel Ratko Mladic) who called themselves the "military line" had begun meeting secretly with members of Serbia's secret police. By 1990, or perhaps a bit earlier—the timing here is a matter of controversy—the officers had drafted what they called the "RAM plan," which set out schemes for the military conquest of "Serb lands" in Croatia and Bosnia. The plan was called RAM, or "FRAME"—it is not known what the individual letters stand for—because it makes clear the boundaries, or frame, within which the new Serbian-dominated lands will be established. As Jerko Doko, the former Bosnian minister of defense, described it in his Hague testimony:

> The substance of the plan was to create a greater Serbia. That RAM was to follow the lines of Virovitica, Karlovac, Karlobag, which we saw confirmed in reality later on with the decision on the withdrawal of the JNA, the Yugoslav People's Army, from Slovenia and partly from Croatia to those positions.[26]

In their plan, the officers described how artillery, ammunition, and other military equipment would be stored in strategic locations in Croatia and then in Bosnia, and how, with the help of the Secret Police, local Serbian activists would be armed and trained, thereby creating "shadow" police forces and paramilitary units in the towns of the Croatian Krajina and throughout Bosnia. And, as early as July 1990, this is precisely what the army began to do. In the area of Foca, according to Doko,

> The JNA had distributed among the Serb voluntary units about 51,000 pieces of firearms and [among] SDS members, about 23,000. . . . [The Army] also gave them armored vehicles, about 400 heavy artillery pieces, 800 mortars. . . .

The leaders of the Bosnian Serb Army would be able to depend upon this "parallel power structure" of dedicated, often fanatical, and now well-armed men to support their troops as they carried out their campaign to conquer Bosnia. For "to conquer" here does not mean simply to subdue. In Bosnia, people of different religions tended to be well mixed together; many cities in the Drina Valley, for example, adjacent to the border of Serbia itself, contained large numbers of Muslims.

The officers confronted, then, both a demographic and a strategic challenge. They were determined to create a new state whose contiguous territory bordered the Serbian motherland—and which held most of the "liberated" Serbs. "The fact that Muslims are the majority," Karadzic said, "makes no difference. They won't decide our fate. That is our right." Serb lands were Serb lands, regardless of who happened to live there.

And thus came into use "ethnic cleansing"—an ancient and brutally effective technique of war christened by the Serbs with a modern, hygienic name. In city after city, town after town, in the spring and summer of 1992, the Bosnian Serb Army and its commandos and paramilitary units launched their attacks in precisely the same pattern. It was clear that these operations of conquest and cleansing were minutely, and centrally, planned. According to Vladimir Srebov, a former Serbian Democratic Party leader who read the "RAM Plan," the officers stipulated a vast program of ethnic cleansing the aim of which "was to destroy Bosnia economically and completely exterminate the Muslim people." As Srebov later told an interviewer:

The plan . . . envisaged a division of Bosnia into two spheres of interest, leading to the creation of a Greater Serbia and a Greater Croatia. The Muslims were to be subjected to a final solution: more than 50 percent of them were to be killed, a smaller part was to be converted to Orthodoxy, while an even smaller . . . part—people with money—were to be allowed to buy their lives and leave, probably, through Serbia, for Turkey. The aim was to cleanse Bosnia-Herzegovina completely of the Muslim nation.[27]

This plan was not fully accomplished, although it is astonishing to think that it might have been. With some exceptions, when the Serbs launched their campaign on March 27, 1992, they chose as their first objective to seize those parts of Bosnia closest to Serbia and to the (now Serb-occupied) Krajina, regardless of who lived there. Though Serbs made up slightly less than a third of Bosnians, within six weeks they controlled 60 percent of the country. Though they would later increase their gains, occupying, at their strongest, some 70 percent of Bosnia's territory, and though the fighting and shelling and skirmishing would go on, the frontlines would not change dramatically during the next three years of war.

When the Serb gunners began shelling cities and towns in Bosnia, the pattern of "cleansing" emerged immediately. Army units would form a perimeter around a town, setting up roadblocks. Messages were sent, inviting all Serb residents to depart. Then the artillerymen would begin their work, shelling the town with heavy and light guns. If defenders fired back, the Serb bombardment might last many days, destroying the town and killing most of those in it; if there was no resistance, the heavy guns might stop in a day or two. Once the town was considered sufficiently "softened up," the paramilitary shock troops would storm in.

Like the guards at Omarska and other camps—which they visited when they could in order to take part in torturing prisoners—the paramilitary troops had one responsibility: to administer terror. Many bore on their person all the iconography of World War II "Chetnik" nationalists: bandoliers across their chests and huge combat knives on their belts; fur hats with symbols of skull and crossbones; black flags, also with skull and crossbones; and the full beard, which, as Ivo Banac says, "in the peasant culture of Serbia is a sign of mourning; somebody dies, one does not shave. This was something that happened in times of war. . . ."[28]

Often the paramilitary troops would arrive at a newly conquered town with lists of influential residents who were to be executed; just as often they simply shot, or stabbed, or mutilated, or raped any resident they managed to find. These killers, many of whom were criminals who had been released from prison to "reform themselves" at the front, were attracted to the job by their virulent nationalist beliefs, by simple sadism, and by greed. Looting Muslim houses made many of them rich.

Many of the sadistic, high-living, and colorful paramilitary leaders soon became celebrities in Serbia. Zeljko Raznatovic, for example, known as

Arkan—everyone knew his Serb Volunteer Guard, by far the strongest and best armed of the paramilitaries, as Arkan's Tigers—was a famous criminal, a bank robber by profession who was thought to be wanted in a number of European countries, in several of which he had been imprisoned and escaped. Judah speculates that Arkan's legendary prison escapes owed much to his longstanding contacts with agents of an espionage network run out of the Yugoslav Secretariat for Internal Affairs, for whom he reputedly worked as an assassin abroad. (His day job was running a pastry shop.) Arkan went on to marry a Serbian pop singer in a huge wedding, and to become a member of the Yugoslav parliament.

Despite their flamboyance and seeming independence, Arkan's Tigers and the other paramilitaries—Vojislav Seslj's Chetniks; the White Eagles; the Yellow Ants (the name a testament to their prowess at looting)—were creatures of the Serbian state. As Milos Vasic, an expert on the Yugoslav military, writes, "They were all organized with the consent of Milosevic's secret police and armed, commanded, and controlled by its officers."[29]

Though it is unclear how specifically the officers described actual tactics in the RAM Plan, the similarity of atrocities committed in town after town lends credence to Beverly Allen's assertion, in *Rape Warfare*, that they debated in detail the most effective means of terror. Allen quotes one document, "a variation of the RAM Plan, written by the army's special services, including . . . experts in psychological warfare," that offers a chilling sociological rationale for the tactics of ethnic cleansing:

> Our analysis of the behavior of the Muslim communities demonstrates that the morale, will, and bellicose nature of their groups can be undermined only *if we aim our action at the point where the religious and social structure is most fragile. We refer to the women, especially adolescents, and to the children.* Decisive intervention on these social figures would spread confusion . . . , thus causing first of all fear and then panic, leading to a probable retreat from the territories involved in war activity.[30]

This is why Vasic calls the paramilitaries the "psychological weapon in ethnic cleansing." The men knew that they must be brutal enough, and inventive enough in their cruelty, that stories of their terror would quickly spread and in the next village, "No one would wait for them to come." Vasic estimates that the paramilitaries consisted on average of "80 percent common criminals and 20 percent fanatical nationalists."

From the well-documented stories of a great many cities and towns and villages, dating back to the cleansing of the Krajina of Croats during 1991 and 1992, one can extract a rough standard operating procedure for the "ethnic cleansing" that would follow:

1. **Concentration.** Surround the area to be cleansed, and after warning the resident Serbs—often they are urged to leave or are at least told to

mark their houses with white flags—intimidate the target population with artillery fire and arbitrary executions, and then bring them out into the streets.

2. **Decapitation.** Execute political leaders and those capable of taking their places: lawyers, judges, public officials, writers, and professors.

3. **Separation.** Divide women, children, and old men from men of "fighting age"—sixteen years to sixty years old.

4. **Evacuation.** Transport women, children, and old men to the border, expelling them into a neighboring territory or country.

5. **Liquidation.** Execute "fighting age" men, and dispose of their bodies.

Though these five steps are too schematic to do justice to the Serbs' minute planning—for each town, each village, each situation was different and dealt with differently—they comprise the main elements of the program that worked for the Serbs from 1991 to 1995. This is how Serb troops, both regular army and security forces, working closely with their savage paramilitary protégés, managed in mere weeks to "cleanse" the 70 percent of Bosnian territory they conquered.

Percentages of Bosnians actually killed varied widely, depending partly, it seems, on the strategic value of the target. In Brcko, for example, which commands the critical and vulnerable "Posavina Corridor" linking the two wings of Bosnian Serb territory, Serb troops herded perhaps three thousand Bosnians into an abandoned warehouse, tortured them, and put them to death. At least some U.S. intelligence officials must have strong memories of Brcko, for according to one account,

> They have photographs of trucks going into Brcko with bodies standing upright, and pictures of trucks coming out of Brcko carrying bodies lying horizontally, stacked like cordwood. . . .[31]

What cannot be overemphasized, however, was the planned rationality of this project, the mark of brutality routinized:

> Though many people *were* "indiscriminately" killed, tortured, beaten, and threatened, the process was anything but random. The first objective was to force the Muslim populations to flee their home towns and create an ethnically pure Serb territory. A certain amount of immediate, "demonstrative atrocity" was therefore deemed necessary. The more random and indiscriminate the terror and violence, the easier this goal would be achieved.

Imposition of terror, the more "indiscriminate" the better, bred fear; fear breeds flight. Some, however, would not be encouraged to flee:

> The second objective was to minimize possible future Muslim resistance. To the Yugoslav military, steeped in the Titoist tradition of territorial

defense and people's war, every man was a potential fighter. Thus, men of military age were singled out for particularly brutal treatment. In Viseg-rad, one observer witnessed a paramilitary gunman announcing, "The women and children will be left alone . . ." As for the Muslim men, he ran his finger across his throat.[32]

José Maria Mendiluce, an official of the United Nations High Commission on Refugees, who happened to pass through Zvornik on April 9, 1992, was watching the paramilitaries "mopping up" the town, when he suddenly realized that "the Belgrade media had been writing about how there was a plot to kill all Serbs in Zvornik. . . . This maneuver always precedes the killing of Muslims." Michael Sells, who includes this quotation in his book, *The Bridge Betrayed*, remarks that

> The national mythology, hatred, and unfounded charges of actual genocide in Kosovo and imminent genocide in Bosnia had shaped into a code: the charge of genocide became a signal to begin genocide.[33]

Army gunners—some of them positioned across the Drina in Serbia itself—targeted Zvornik and drove its few, lightly armed defenders out in a matter of hours. Then Vojislav Seslj and his Chetniks moved in. Mendiluce watched as the soldiers and the paramilitaries did their work:

> I saw lorries full of corpses. Soldiers were dumping dead women, children, and old people onto lorries. I saw four or five lorries full of corpses. On one bend, my jeep skidded on the blood.[34]

United Nations investigators say Seslj briefed his Chetniks in a local hotel, reading out a list of the names of local Muslims who were to be killed. "Milosevic was in total control," Seslj later told an interviewer, "and the operation was planned . . . in Belgrade."

> The Bosnian Serbs did take part. But the best combat units came from Serbia. These were special police commandos called Red Berets. They're from the Secret Service of Serbia. My forces took part, as did others. We planned the operation very carefully, and everything went exactly according to plan.[35]

According to the United Nations, some two thousand people from Zvornik remain unaccounted for. The remaining Muslims—47,000 of them—were expelled, many of them forced onto the roads with only what they wore. Zvornik, which had a thriving community of Muslims for half a millennium, now has none.

Sometimes the cleansing was carried out more gradually. Early in 1992, members of a small paramilitary group seized control of Prijedor's television transmitter, thus ensuring that the town received only programs from Belgrade—programs which, UN investigators wrote, "insinuated that non-Serbs wanted war and threatened the Serbs." Soon Yugoslav National Army troops, fresh from the Croatia war, began arriving in the Prijedor area. The army officers demanded that Prijedor's leaders permit their troops to take up positions around the city, from which they could control all roads to and from the district.

> It was an ultimatum. The legitimate authorities were invited for a guided sightseeing tour of two Croatian villages . . . which had been destroyed and left uninhabited. The message was that if the ultimatum was not [accepted], the fate of Prijedor would be the same. . . . The ultimatum was accepted.[36]

With Bosnian Serb troops guarding all roads, Prijedor was isolated. The Serbs closed down the bus service. They required that people have permits even to visit nearby villages. They imposed a curfew. Telephones were often not working.

On April 30, in a swift, well-executed *coup d'état*, local Serbs seized control of Prijedor itself. According to the United Nations investigators, the Serbs had been preparing to seize power for at least six months, arming themselves with weapons secretly supplied by the army and developing their own clandestine "parallel" administrations, including a "shadow" police force with its own secret service.

Non-Serbs now began to lose their jobs. Policemen and public officials were the first to be dismissed, but the purge went on until even many manual workers had been fired. The "shadow" administrations already long prepared by the Serbs simply took over the empty offices.

The new Serb policemen, often accompanied by paramilitaries, began to pay visits throughout Prijedor, pounding on the doors of all non-Serbs who held licenses to own firearms and demanding they turn them in.

> . . . The non-Serbs in reality [had become] outlaws. At times, non-Serbs were instructed to wear white armbands to identify themselves.

Finally, near the end of May, the local press—newspapers, radio, and television—began to broadcast a more hysterical version of Belgrade's propaganda, claiming that dangerous Muslim extremists were hiding around and within Prijedor, preparing to seize the town and commit genocide against the Serbs.

By now it had become quite clear what this accusation heralded. Those few Muslims and Croats who still had weapons decided to move first. As the UN investigators describe it:

> On 30 May 1992, a group of probably less than 150 armed non-Serbs had made their way to the Old Town in Prijedor to regain control of the

town. . . . They were defeated, and the Old Town was razed. In the central parts of Prijedor . . . , all non-Serbs were forced to leave their houses as Serbian military, paramilitary, police and civilians advanced street by street with tanks and lighter arms. The non-Serbs had been instructed over the radio to hang a white piece of cloth on their home to signal surrender.

According to the UN Report, "Hundreds, possibly thousands were killed . . . frequently after maltreatment." Those who survived were divided into two groups: women, children, and the very old were often simply expelled; as for the men, thousands were sent to Keraterm and Omarska, the two nearest concentration camps. Although the fighting on May 30 began a general exodus of non-Serbs—the Muslim population dropped from nearly 50,000 in 1991 to barely 6,000 in 1993—it quickly became clear that the Serbs were targeting for actual deportation the elite of the city: political leaders, judges, policemen, academics and intellectuals, officials who had worked in the public administration, important business people, and artists. And, after the burning of the old town, any "other important traces of Muslim and Croatian culture and religion—mosques and Catholic churches included—were destroyed."

On the morning of May 30, 1992, two heavily armed soldiers came to his door and summoned him and, within hours, Rezak Hukanovic, a forty-three-year-old father of two, broadcaster, journalist, and poet, found himself packed into a bus with scores of other frightened men, bent over, his head between his knees, peering out of the corner of his eye at the tongues of flame rising from the Old City of Prijedor. He was on his way to Omarska.

V.

In Washington, intelligence analysts were watching. "The initial Serb offensive moved an awful lot of people out of where they were living," said Jon Western, who was analyzing Bosnian war crimes at the State Department, "and we knew these people were not simply disappearing. Where were they being taken?"

Officials would soon discover the answer; by late June or early July, little more than a month after Rezak Hukanovic boarded the bus at Prijedor, Western and his colleagues had learned of the camps:

> We had information about the concentration camps, we were compiling that information and trying to get a more accurate picture but it was clear we knew. . . . To the extent that we could pinpoint and say that there was a camp here or here, we did that.[37]

The information was passed forward to Secretary of State James Baker and to senior officials at the Pentagon and the White House. It met with silence. Western was not surprised; when it came to information about war crimes in Bosnia, he said, the offices of senior officials were "generally a black box. We would send things up and nothing would come back. The only time we would get a response was when the press covered a particular event."

When the inevitable press disclosures came, in early August, the timing could not have been worse for the Bush administration. Throughout the summer influential voices demanding that something should be done to halt the carnage in Bosnia had been growing louder and President Bush, fighting desperately to win re-election, had been struggling to defend his government's own passivity.

For their part the Bosnian Serbs, seeing the dramatic increase of pressure on Bush to intervene, were quick to realize their blunder. In permitting Western journalists to see the camps, Karadzic apparently thought they could be duped into believing conditions were not so bad as the growing rumors seemed to suggest: in *Seasons in Hell*, Ed Vulliamy tells of later learning from a survivor who had been imprisoned at Omarska during the journalists' visit that "only the fittest" of prisoners had been displayed. (It is also remotely possible, as Judah suggests, that Karadzic did not allow himself to learn how dreadful conditions in the camps were.)

In any event, the Serbs quickly moved to close the most notorious camps. President Bush's denunciations and demands that the camps be opened to international inspectors no doubt helped quickly shut the doors of Omarska and some others; had Bush chosen to reveal the camps and spoken out when he and his officials had first learned of them the result would have surely been the same—except a great many prisoners might still be alive.

Closing the camps did not put an end to the controversy over the atrocities in Bosnia. "They kept saying the war would 'burn itself out,'" a State Department official told me. "I actually sat in a meeting where people suggested that what would be needed for the war to 'burn itself out' would be around 20,000 dead." On August 18, however, Senate investigators released a detailed report concluding that already in the first four weeks of the war 35,000 people, almost all Muslim victims of ethnic cleansing, had been killed.

Many press and television commentators, human rights representatives, members of Congress, leaders of Muslim and Jewish advocacy groups, and others now brought pressure to bear on the Bush administration to declare that what was taking place in Bosnia constituted "genocide." A number of administration officials, particularly lower- and mid-level foreign service officers with responsibility for Bosnia, also began to promote this cause within the State Department, believing, as Paul Williams, then a lawyer at the Office of European and Canadian Affairs, put it, that "if the United States identifies what is occurring in Bosnia as genocide, then it ups the ante, it creates a moral obligation as well as a legal obligation to take action."[38]

"Genocide," a word coined in 1944 by the scholar Raphael Lemkin, was meant to denote not simply murdering an entire people—the object of the law was to prevent the crime, not simply to define legally the extent of a massacre—but, in Lemkin's description, "a coordinated plan of different actions aiming at the destructions of different foundations of the life of national groups, with the aim of annihilating the groups themselves." The "actions" Lemkin lists as constituting genocide—"disintegration of the polit- ical and social institutions, of culture, language, national feelings, religion, and the economic existence of national groups, and the destruction of the personal security, liberty, health, dignity, and even the lives of the individuals belonging to such groups"[39]—read like a step-by-step description ethnic cleansing.

Lemkin's definition had laid the foundation for the United Nations' Con- vention on the Prevention and Punishment of the Crime of Genocide (1948), and it was according to the terms of this treaty that a growing num- ber of State Department officials were pressuring their government to define what was happening in Bosnia. The treaty calls on its signers to undertake "to prevent and to punish" crimes of genocide. But a simple declaration would not necessarily be of "operational importance," as a colleague told State Department official Richard Johnson, since individual war crimes "are easier to prove than genocide."

But that was exactly the point: To call ethnic cleansing by its proper name would be a powerful political act. As Johnson points out in his essay "The Pinstripe Approach to Genocide,"[40] a determination of genocide "would undermine the credibility of Western policies that rely on . . . peace talks to reach a 'voluntary settlement' between 'warring factions'—who would now be defined as the perpetrators and victims of genocide." And if the adminis- tration had officially identified what was happening as genocide, Paul Williams says, it would have created "a moral imperative. Genocide is a term that is recognized by the American people. It means something, both to the American people and under international law."

In the wake of the concentration camp controversy, George Bush and his senior officials recognized that a determination of genocide would multiply the pressure to act forcefully in Bosnia—and that was clearly the last thing they wanted. Having denounced the camps, Bush officials promised to sub- mit information on war crimes in Bosnia to the United Nations War Crimes Commission—and then assigned a single foreign service officer to the task. The secretary of state, meantime, requested a determination from the Office of Legal Advisor of whether or not what was going on in Bosnia constituted genocide, and was told, according to Williams, that "it appeared to be a simple question: if the atrocities which are occurring in Bosnia continue, this amounts to genocide."

With Governor Clinton strongly denouncing Bush's inaction—declaring, in what must have been an irritating echo of Bush's warning to Saddam Hus- sein, that "the legitimacy of ethnic cleansing cannot stand"—General Colin Powell once again went on the offensive. On October 10, three weeks before the election, General Powell published his own essay on the *New York*

Times's opinion page, in which he offered a strong endorsement of his beleaguered commander-in-chief and asserted that "Americans know they are getting a hell of a return on their defense investment."

> The reason for our success is that in every instance we have carefully matched the use of military force to our political objectives. President Bush, more than any other recent President, understands the proper use of military force. In every instance, he has made sure that the objective was clear and that we knew what we were getting into.

Though Powell doesn't mention Vietnam, it is evident his own demons lurk just beneath the surface:

> [Y]ou bet I get nervous when so-called experts suggest that all we need is a little surgical bombing or a limited attack. When the desired result isn't obtained, a new set of experts then comes forward with talk of a little escalation. History has not been kind to this approach.[41]

One way or another U.S. military officers would use this tactic of not so subtly brandishing Vietnam in front of policymakers and then the public to undermine nearly every proposal for action that the United States might take to influence the evolving conflict in Bosnia.[42] "The Pentagon's tactic," Warren Zimmermann says, "was never to say no, simply to raise objections which made proposals seem unworkable." And though it is true the officers "never got very good answers to [their] incessant questioning of what was the precise military objective and what political end would be served by achieving it[,] . . . it is also true that Bosnia proved the United States incapable of managing a complex war requiring a limited use of force for limited objectives." Zimmermann, America's "last ambassador to Yugoslavia," left the State Department; four of the young Foreign Service officers who were fighting for a change in Bosnia policy resigned in protest.

As for the demands that the administration do something about the horror—demands that had risen to a crescendo after the emaciated faces from Bosnia appeared on American television screens—Bush officials devised a novel solution. They would indeed do something, even going so far as to send American troops; but their mission would be to tend to a different population of emaciated beings on a different continent. In deciding to dispatch troops to feed starving Africans in Somalia, Eagleburger conceded, "We knew the costs weren't so great and there were some potential benefits." As for General Powell, he was said to have predicated his support for Somalia's "Operation Restore Hope" on one condition—that the United States "would attempt no such mission in Bosnia."[43]

New York Review of Books, December 4, 1997

Toward a Policy of Gesture:
The Safe Areas

I.

DURING THE SUMMER OF 1992, Arkansas governor and Democratic presidential challenger Bill Clinton was barnstorming the country and denouncing President Bush for failing to stop the horror in Bosnia. Late that July, Clinton demanded the United Nations tighten economic sanctions on "the renegade regime of Slobodan Milosevic," grant European and American warships the power to search vessels that might be carrying contraband to Serbia, and authorize Western warplanes to strike "against those who are attacking the relief effort." A week later, after the networks had broadcast pictures of emaciated Muslims and Croats imprisoned in Serb concentration camps, Clinton declared that the United Nations, supported by the United States, must do "whatever it takes to stop the slaughter of civilians and we may have to use military force. I would begin with air power against the Serbs."[1]

White House spokesman Marlin Fitzwater countered with condescension: Clinton's was "the kind of reckless approach that indicates he better do more homework on foreign policy," said Fitzwater. "It's clear he's unaware of the political complications in Yugoslavia."[2] It was equally clear that he was aware of the political implications in America. The Arkansas governor had found the perfect opening to attack the "foreign policy president" for inaction in the face of a moral drama that voters saw enacted each evening on their television screens. Americans may not have wanted their leaders to send troops to stop the killing, but they wanted them to do *something*. Not only did Bush officials stand defiantly aloof, they defended their inaction in the harshest terms. "I have said this 38,000 times," said acting Secretary of State Lawrence Eagleburger, "and I have to say this to the people of this country as well."

This tragedy is not something that can be settled from outside, and it's about damn well time that everybody understood that. Until the Bosnians,

Serbs, and Croats decide to stop killing each other, there is nothing the outside world can do about it.[3]

The secretary spoke seven weeks after reporters filmed concentration
camp prisoners. During the six months since the war began, the Serbs had
seized nearly three-quarters of Bosnia's territory and "cleansed" tens of thousands of Muslim civilians—murdering, during the first month alone, more
than twenty thousand, according to a detailed Senate investigation. To
describe the war, in the fall of 1992, as "Bosnians, Serbs, and Croats . . .
killing each other" was almost criminally misleading, as Eagleburger had to
have known.[4]

Even as George Bush and his top officials had favored standing back from
the conflict—and waiting for it "to burn itself out"—a public sporadically
outraged by bloody images had from time to time forced them to take some
action, producing a tangle of contradictory policies. In May 1992, after the
Serbs launched a mortar shell into a group of Sarajevans waiting in line for
bread and other supplies, Americans' disgust at the scenes of dismembered
and maimed civilians led Bush to support imposing economic sanctions.
The United Nations resolution, however, included no provision to board
and inspect ships.

In September 1991, as the war raged in Croatia, Bush had supported
imposing a United Nations arms embargo on the former Yugoslavia, an
action that appeared "even-handed" but which in practice—because the
Yugoslav National Army had at its disposal immense stocks of tanks, artillery
pieces, and warplanes, and controlled an advanced weapons industry—overwhelmingly favored the Serbs. After the Europeans and Americans recognized Bosnia in April 1992, they stipulated that the embargo would apply to
the new state. "The intent was not to try to keep the Bosnian Muslims from
winning their war," Secretary Eagleburger explained. "It was, in fact, to try to
keep anybody from putting more weapons into the place . . . than were
already there."[5] Yet the embargo's most important, and quite foreseeable,
effect was to cripple the Bosnians, who had many men willing to fight but
few weapons, in their effort to defend themselves against the heavily armed
Serbs.

By the time Governor Clinton began denouncing these policies, many
mid-level and junior officials had already turned against them. "He was stealing our lines," said John Fox of the State Department's Policy Planning
Office.

We'd been writing this for months to our superiors: allow the Bosnians to
defend themselves, take out the Serbs' heavy weapons shelling civilians in
Sarajevo and other Bosnian communities, use force to get the humanitarian assistance convoys through. [Clinton's words] were raising hopes
within the department that perhaps there would be sufficient pressure to
bring about a change, if not before the election then after.[6]

The rhetoric already represented a change: Unlike Bush officials with their fatuously "evenhanded" descriptions, candidate Bill Clinton took obvious satisfaction in denouncing "the renegade regime of Slobodan Milosevic." Members of Clinton's campaign made plain that their sympathies were with the Bosnian Muslims, and even before the inauguration vice president–elect Al Gore and other key officials had begun meeting with Bosnian representatives. When president-elect Clinton declared that "the legitimacy of ethnic cleansing cannot stand," it seemed a clear pledge that President Clinton would bring the great power of the United States to bear on the task of achieving justice in the Balkans.

"Justice," of course, was the crucial word, for it was becoming clear that in Bosnia securing justice was not at all the same as seeking peace; on the contrary. "Although many outside intervenors (or would-be intervenors) pursued both peace and justice in the former Yugoslavia," as Jean E. Manas wrote,

> they rarely faced up to the fact that, at any level of specificity, the two ideals are in tension: the pursuit of justice entails the prolongation of hostilities, whereas the pursuit of peace requires resigning oneself to some injustices.[7]

President Clinton had taken on this dilemma: He desired to stand for justice; he had pledged to do so. But he would find, before very long, that acting to achieve it would entail grave sacrifice. To restore justice to Bosnia—which meant restoring Muslim land and homes to those who rightly owned them, so that ethnic cleansing "would not stand"—Bill Clinton would have to be willing to undertake a vigorous diplomatic intervention, and dispatch at least some troops, and this would require that he deploy all his great political skills to persuade Americans to support him.

He had no stomach for it; it was not, in the end, his war. If to Governor Clinton, Bosnia had been a useful bloody flag to wave at President Bush during the campaign, what use was such a conflict now that the campaign was over? If to candidate Clinton it had represented an opportunity, to President Clinton it had become only a risk—and it was that risk that Clinton's political advisers came to emphasize. "Noninvolvement in Bosnia," political consultant Dick Morris later wrote, "had been a central element in my advice."

> "You don't want to be Lyndon Johnson," I had said early on, "sacrificing your potential for doing good on the domestic front by a destructive, never-ending foreign involvement. It's the Democrats' disease to take the same compassion that motivates their domestic policies and let it lure them into heroic but ill-considered foreign wars."

This was reasoning Bill Clinton could understand, particularly since, as Morris claimed, the new president "had no special vision of his foreign policy. He reacted, more or less reluctantly, to global concerns when they intruded so deeply into America's politics that he had to do something."[8]

Shortly after Clinton took office, Richard Holbrooke paid a visit to the White House to have lunch with his old friend Anthony Lake, now the president's national security adviser. Though Holbrooke remained a private citizen (he had been encouraged to expect that the president would nominate him to become ambassador to Japan), he had a deep interest in Bosnia, had made his own "fact-finding" trip there, and now "felt obliged, almost compelled, to offer some unsolicited thoughts" on the war to the new administration. As he lunched with Lake in his West Wing office, Holbrooke "urged him to press for a greater American effort to stop the accelerating catastrophe. . . ."

> [Lake] protested, arguing that while people were still dying in large numbers, "you don't know how many more people would now be dead if it were not for our efforts." I replied that this was true but irrelevant.[9]

The pathos in this exchange is striking. Lake had served with Holbrooke in Vietnam when they were both young foreign service officers; he was well-known within the foreign policy community for having resigned from Henry Kissinger's staff in 1971 in protest over the United States' so-called "incursion" into Cambodia. Such resignations on principle have not been usual in American diplomatic history, at least not until Bosnia.[10] Lake had based the brave words he had written for Clinton during the campaign on a simple belief that the Bosnian war must be stopped because of the horrors it was visiting on unarmed people and because the Serbs' gruesome strategy of ethnic cleansing had inflicted terrible wrongs that must be set right. To make good on those words, however, President Clinton would have to become involved in a foreign war that Americans cared little about and that might put at risk his much-promoted plans to reinvigorate the country's economy and reform its health care.

By the time Richard Holbrooke came to lunch in the White House, Lake the idealist seems already to have discovered that any policy his president might approve would fall far short of the words he had written for the candidate. Kissinger himself, in words that must have been painful for his one-time protégé to read, summarized the result unflinchingly. President Clinton, wrote the former secretary of state,

> committed his administration to acting on an aggressive, forceful policy of reversing Serbian seizures of land, of protecting Bosnia as a multi-ethnic society. And, from the beginning, he never adopted the level of force necessary to achieve these large aims. From the beginning, he proposed objectives that were totally incompatible with the means proposed for achieving those objectives. These commitments to higher moral principles unmatched by higher use of force led to a gradual emasculation of the

people we were supposed to be protecting. . . . We drifted into a pattern of behavior in which we were not willing to stop the war by force. But we were also not willing to accept a peace plan that could stop it by diplomacy. Thus, we inflamed the situation without providing the means for dealing with that inflammation.[11]

One can't know how clearly Lake might have seen this injurious and reprehensible scenario taking shape before him. As a man who had publicly resigned over principle during another war two decades before, he surely cannot have been happy about it. Nor can he have been pleased to hear Holbrooke, a colleague and rival who came to see him, free of the burdens of office, hector him about what he, Lake, already knew—and to do it, as Holbrooke himself recalls, with such harsh accuracy:

> Even if, as Tony claimed, the situation was better than if the Bush Administration were still in office, it still fell far short of what it should be, and of what the world had been led to expect by Governor Clinton's campaign rhetoric, which Tony was once so proud of having written. Agitated, Tony said he was doing his best and asked me to be patient. The meeting ended coolly and inconclusively.

Clinton had made promises, of course, courted the members of a constituency; this part of foreign affairs he well understood. In the early weeks of his new administration, Clinton would set out to placate that constituency. When the latest attempt to achieve "peace"—as opposed to delivering justice—was set before the new administration in the form of the Vance-Owen plan—an intricate and ingenious proposal to divide Bosnia into ten ethnically controlled "cantons" (three each for the Serbs, Croats, and Muslims, with Sarajevo shared as the capital)—Clinton officials did not squarely reject the plan but spoke of it with an offhanded contempt that left no doubt of their belief that they could fashion something better. Cyrus Vance, the former secretary of state, and David Owen, the former British foreign secretary, arrived in Washington on February 1, 1993, to brief Secretary of State Warren Christopher, and it soon became "painfully apparent," Owen recalls, "that the secretary of state knew very little about the detail of our plan."

> Particularly surprising, in view of the administration's public criticism, was that he had not been briefed on all the human rights provisions and safeguards that we had built in with the express purpose of reversing ethnic cleansing. . . . Warren Christopher appeared as if he had not had time to read even a short, factual information sheet on what was the essence of our plan. I was baffled as to how Christopher could come so badly briefed to meet his old boss, Cy, who was under virulent public attack over a plan his critics claimed favored ethnic cleansing.[12]

The next day's *New York Times*, under the headline "US Declines to Back Peace Plan as Balkan Talks Shift to UN," commented that Christopher was "setting the stage for a possible confrontation between the mediators and the Clinton Administration," noting that at a lunch with UN Secretary General Boutros Boutros-Ghali, Christopher had expressed his "ambivalence" about the plan.

It was the first dramatic example of what James Gow, in *Triumph of the Lack of Will*, describes as the Clinton administration's tendency on Bosnia "to pronounce on principle, prevaricate in practice and preempt the policies and plans of others."[13] Having done so much to preempt Vance-Owen, Warren Christopher now went up to Capitol Hill and pronounced on principle:

> This conflict may be far from our shores, but it is certainly not distant from our concerns. We cannot afford to ignore it.
>
> The events in the former Yugoslavia raise the question whether a state may address the rights of its minorities by eradicating them to achieve ethnic purity. Bold tyrants and fearful minorities are watching to see whether ethnic cleansing is a policy the world will tolerate. If we hope to promote the spread of freedom, if we hope to encourage the emergence of peaceful ethnic democracies, our answer must be a resounding no.

No American official, and certainly none so powerful, had stated the moral questions raised by Bosnia so bluntly and answered them so eloquently. Clinton's secretary of state did not stop there, however, but went on to describe explicitly what he called the United States' "direct strategic concerns" in Bosnia:

> The continuing destruction of a new United Nations member challenges the principle that internationally recognized borders should not be altered by force. In addition, this conflict itself has no natural borders. It threatens to spill over into new regions, such as Kosovo and Macedonia. It could then become a greater Balkan war like those that preceded World War I. Broader hostilities could touch additional nations such as Greece and Turkey and Albania. . . .[14]

Coming directly from the secretary of state, this was a declaration of fundamental American interest and one would be justified in expecting strong and dynamic action to follow. Behind the words, however, something different was going on among the newly installed officials of the Clinton administration. John Fox, who had stayed on at the State Department, watched closely as his new bosses undertook to study the Bosnia problem and place alternatives before the president.

> This was February '93: After an extensive policy review, in which a lot of very good middle-force options were raised—options between a Vietnam

scenario and a wring-your-hands scenario—the middle options were cut out, and cabinet-level officials came forward, and gave very tough rhetoric. Essentially, the people who wanted to do something got the rhetoric, but the people who didn't want to do anything got the policy.

So after declaring that what's going on in Bosnia is a vital interest of the United States they then lay out options that everybody knows aren't going to work. Very early on, a number of us saw pretty clearly that there would be little if anything done to follow through on the campaign pledges.[15]

But Bill Clinton was no longer making campaign promises. As his administration lurched from crisis to crisis, stumbling first into a fiasco involving gays in the military that set Clinton officials against Chairman of the Joint Chiefs, General Colin Powell, it became clear that Bosnia was the least of the president's concerns. According to Dick Morris,

The incessant TV coverage of scenes of depravity in Bosnia prompted him to remark, "They keep trying to force me to get America into a war."[16]

"They" were the reporters, the columnists, the television journalists. But Clinton was president now, and beyond the appearances there lay a real world he had to confront. And in that terrible winter of 1993 the Bosnian Serbs, unimpressed with the new president's preference for domestic policy, readied their artillery and their tanks and began a vicious attack on the captive towns of eastern Bosnia, just beyond the Drina from Serbia.

II.

Srebrenica had once been the richest inland city in the Balkans, a cosmopolitan mining town—its very name meant "silver" ("Argentaria" under the Romans)—bustling with German engineers and Ragusan metal traders and Franciscan friars.[17] But by early 1993, when Serb gunners in the hills above began to rain down shells with great intensity, Srebrenica had become a vast refugee camp, swarming with starving people and stinking of human excrement. Encircled by an iron band of Serb artillery and armor, overrun by refugees from surrounding towns that the Serbs had lately "cleansed," Srebrenica held many times the number of people it had before the war; tens of thousands of men, women, and children, many of them living in the streets, found themselves prisoners, with no access to the fields and markets that might have begun to feed the town. The result, as United Nations officials put it bluntly in a February 1993 report, was "there is no food such as we know it."

They have not had real food for months. They are surviving on the chaff from wheat and roots from trees. Every day people are dying of hunger and exhaustion.[18]

In the garbage-strewn, shell-pocked streets of Srebrenica, gaunt, bleak-eyed men and women gathered daily, poking and prodding impatiently at masses of sickly green grass plastered together with wheat chaff that were burning and sizzling fitfully on the fires. "It was a horrific place," said Louis Gentile, a United Nations relief worker who during the Serb offensive went in search of refugees from the besieged villages around the city.

> I drove south and the people walking along the road in the snow were completely emaciated. I particularly recall one woman who was walking with two children, and they looked like living skeletons; and when we stopped to talk to them, they couldn't respond because they were so hungry their minds had stopped working.
>
> We gave them some biscuits and said, "Wait for us right here, by the side of the road." And we drove further south and we encountered fighting and other [refugees] walking along in similar circumstances. When we came back to pick up the woman and her children we found only footprints leading off in the snow. They'd immediately gone off to eat the biscuits, and they'd just disappeared. To this day I can't forget those people, the faces of those kids.[19]

And yet the starving and shelling marked Srebrenica's triumph, for while other towns had fallen quickly to the Serb onslaught, the men of Srebrenica had fought back and by their heroism had won for their city a grim siege.

As far back as early 1991, Serbs and Muslims in Srebrenica had begun to arm themselves. The unceasing propaganda from Belgrade, particularly during the war in Croatia in the summer and fall of 1991, when the Muslims were painted as "Turk" foreigners who must be destroyed, had proved highly effective in instilling fear and paranoia. In Srebrenica, Muslims and Serbs grew suspicious, fearful, and embittered.

In August 1991, while the war raged in Croatia, the Srebrenica region had its first armed confrontation when Serb soldiers came to take possession of local draft records. Local Muslim officials refused to give them up; Serb nationalists demanded they comply. Chuck Sudetic, whose book *Blood and Vengeance* is a rich, personal account of how the forces of historical memory, propaganda, and suspicion produced a bloody rhythm of attack and retribution in Srebrenica and its surrounding villages, describes what happened next:

> Muslim police officers sided with the Muslim mob; Serb police officers sided with the Serb mob; and the Yugoslav army rushed in reinforcements. The two mobs exchanged curses and threats. They pointed guns at one another and fired into the air. The army commanders backed down before a riot broke out. . . .
>
> From that day on, Muslim and Serb peasants began standing guard around Kravica and the other villages near Srebrenica. . . . Men from both

communities left their jobs in Sarajevo, Serbia, and abroad to return home to take up arms and defend their families and protect their homes. Serbs were afraid to drive their cars through Muslim villages.[20]

Four days after the confrontation over the draft records, four Muslims drove through the predominantly Serb town of Kravica waving an Islamic green flag; the car was sprayed with bullets, and two of the passengers were killed. From his headquarters in Pale, Radovan Karadzic declared that no Muslim police would be allowed into Kravica to investigate.

Soon after the Serb military campaign began late in March 1992, Srebrenica residents learned of the mass killings and rapes; in nearby Zvornik the main Serb paramilitaries, Arkan's Tigers and Seslj's Chetniks, had been particularly brutal, murdering hundreds of people. Within a week, as Sudetic tells it, Serb army tanks were rumbling through Srebrenica and the nearby town of Bratunac, and members of Arkan's gang had begun abducting and killing local Muslims suspected of organizing their own militia.

> One day a pharmacist disappeared. The next day, a police detective. Then a factory foreman. The former police chief. . . . The Serbian Democratic Party's leaders had set up a drumhead court in the school. . . .The pharmacist was found to have sent bandages and other medical supplies to Muslims in the hills; he was sentenced to death. The police chief and factory foreman had shown up on a video taken of the mob outside the town hall when the army came looking for the draft records; they were sentenced to death.

In April 1992 the Serbs turned seriously to Srebrenica, which was not only an immensely rich prize, with its bauxite mines and tourist industry and factories, but a strategic necessity, for it stood squarely in the Drina Valley bordering Serbia. Though three in four of Srebrenica's citizens were Muslims, the Serbs believed that in order to establish a contiguous and workable "Greater Serbia" they had to conquer and cleanse the town. On April 17, the local judge and Serb leader Goran Zekic demanded that Srebrenica's Muslims turn in all their weapons by the following morning. The Muslims knew well the meaning of such an ultimatum—they had seen it handed down in Bijeljina, in Zvornik, in Visegrad, and in all these places it had been followed by terror. Instead of waiting for the Serb paramilitaries to seize control and commit the tortures, rapes, and murders deemed necessary to "cleanse" Srebrenica in its turn, thousands of Muslims packed their cars or boarded buses and fled their homes.

Soon notorious Zeljko Raznatovic—better known as Arkan—and his heavily armed paramilitary Tigers swaggered into Srebrenica and, together with the local Serbs, looted Muslim houses and shops. For the Serbs, Srebrenica had gone well: Arkan's carefully cultivated reputation for unlimited cruelty had led the Muslims of Srebrenica to "cleanse" themselves. Or so it seemed.

In fact, however, not every Muslim had fled Srebrenica: several hundred men had taken what guns they had and hidden in the woods. From there they watched as Arkan and his Tigers joined their former neighbors in looting their homes. From their forest hiding place, the Muslims watched and debated strategy. Months before, their leader, Naser Oric, had been ordered by Muslim officials in Sarajevo to prepare for just this moment. Short, powerfully built, with closely cropped dark hair and beard, Oric was a twenty-five-year-old body builder, former bar bouncer, and member of the Yugoslav special military police; indeed, Oric's martial skills were such that, though he was a Bosnian Muslim—his grandfather had been a member of the hated Ustase—he had been appointed a bodyguard to Milosevic himself. In the plans he devised to defend Srebrenica, he proved cunning and ruthless.

Two days after the Serbs seized the town, Oric and his poorly armed Muslims swept down from the forest and stunned the Serbs with a full-bore attack that left many wounded and several dead. Through early May Oric led his Muslims on a series of audacious raids against Zekic's local Serb militiamen, who were backed by paramilitaries and by Bosnian Serb Army gunners who shelled the Muslims from positions in the hills above the city. On May 8, a Muslim college student in Srebrenica managed to shoot Zekic in the head as the Serb leader drove by in his car. (For good measure, the young killer then attempted to toss a grenade through the window and managed to blow himself up.) For Srebrenica's Serbs, the brazen assassination of their leader proved too much; they murdered all the Muslim men they could find, then broke and fled, leaving the town under Oric's control.

The next day Red Beret troops from the Interior Ministry poured across the bridge from Serbia and burned nearby Muslim villages, executing any man they could get their hands on. In Bratunac, a few miles from Srebrenica, soldiers patrolled streets with megaphones, ordering Muslims from their homes. Thousands were herded into a soccer stadium. Women and children were loaded aboard buses and trucks and expelled. Seven hundred and fifty men were marched down Bratunac's main street and packed into a school gymnasium. Serb soldiers called the *hodza*, or Muslim holy man, to the front of the gymnasium, there they forced him to shimmy up a climbing rope, poured beer over his head, and then beat him with clubs and iron bars, demanding he make the sign of the Orthodox cross. After beating him nearly to death, the Serbs stabbed him in the back of the neck and shot him in the head. Then they began to beat the Muslim men; in three days they killed more than 350 and dumped the bodies in the Drina.

After this orgy of killing, the cycle of "blood and vengeance"—*kad tad*, goes the saying; "sooner or later"—was well advanced. Muslim and Serb knew they could expect no mercy from the other. In seizing control of Srebrenica, Naser Oric and his ragtag Muslim fighters achieved a triumph. From the hills above, however, and from every side, Serb guns stared down and before long Srebrenica's triumphant people began to starve.

III.

Throughout the late spring and summer Naser Oric and his commanders methodically built up their forces, launching raids to seize weapons and ammunition, which enabled them to recruit and train more soldiers and carry out more ambitious attacks. Indeed, as Honig and Both point out, this was "just about the only case in Bosnia where the much-vaunted Yugoslav territorial defense system was successfully applied by the Bosnians."[21] Oric's forces put into effect Tito's plan to resist invasion, relying not only on classic techniques of guerrilla warfare—lightning-fast small group attacks, sabotage, and assassination—but also on the belief that all men, uniformed or not, are real or potential fighters.

During the summer and fall, Oric's men attacked and ambushed without warning, taking, as Sudetic writes, "only a handful of prisoners and rarely [making] any distinction between combatants and civilians." By fall, they had killed several hundred Serb soldiers and civilians and had vastly increased the size of the Srebrenica pocket. Oric's forces had now swelled with bitter refugees from Bratunac and other towns, and all knew well that, if defeated, the best they could expect from the Serbs was a quick death. Indeed, the Muslim commander had discovered his greatest weapon:

> Oric could now count on a force that struck the fear of God into the Serb peasants . . . : a horde of Muslim refugees, men and women, young and old, who were driven by hunger . . . and, in many cases, a thirst for revenge. Thousands strong, these people would lurk behind the first wave of attacking soldiers and run amok when the defenses around Serb villages collapsed. Some . . . used pistols to do the killing; others used knives, bats, and hatchets. But most . . . had nothing but their bare hands and the empty rucksacks and suitcases they strapped onto their backs. They came to be known as *torbari*, the bag people. And they were beyond Oric's control.

The climactic battle in Oric's campaign came on January 7, 1993, Orthodox Christmas, when Oric's fighters swept down on the Serb town of Kravica. Serb women had worked for days preparing suckling pigs, fresh bread, pickled tomatoes, and peppers—an intoxicating feast to the starving *torbari* of Srebrenica. Oric had also been working for days, preparing the attack:

> After dark on Christmas Eve, some three thousand Muslim troops assembled on the slushy hilltops around Kravica. Behind them lurked a host of *torbari* who lit campfires to warm themselves. At dawn they started clattering pots and pans. "*Allahu ekber!* God is great!" the men shouted. The women shrieked. Shooting began. The Serb men in Kravica scrambled into their trenches. . . .

The Serbs were vastly outnumbered; the Muslims, many in white uniforms that blended with the snow, seemed to come from every direction. By mid-afternoon, thirty Serbs had died, and the front line had collapsed. Serbs ran into the town center, screaming for everyone to flee. Sudetic, in his account of the battle of Podravanja three months before, describes *torbari* assault:

> The Serb fighters left behind men and women who had been wounded and killed. . . .Then the *torbari* rushed in. Muslim men shot the wounded. They fired their guns into the bodies of the Serb dead, plunged knives into their stomachs and chests. They smashed their heads with axes and clubs, and they burned the bodies inside buildings. Oric's men grabbed half a dozen prisoners; one, a fighter from Serbia who had relatives in Podravanja, was beaten to death, and the others emerged bruised and battered when they were exchanged a month later.

In Kravica that Christmas Day the starving *torbari* found a paradise to plunder:

> The first of the *torbari* to arrive in Kravica found entire Christmas dinners that had been waiting to be eaten by Serb men who had gone off to fight that morning, thinking they would be back by noon. Three Muslim soldiers barged into one home and stood there as if paralyzed at the sight of the pastries and the jelly, the bottles of brandy, and the roast pork on the stove. They laughed and shouted and plunged into a cake. The ashes of burning houses . . . fell like snow on the hillside. The pigs ran wild. Sheep were butchered and roasted on the spit or herded back to Srebrenica with the cows and oxen. The dead lay unburied, and within days the pigs, dogs, and wild animals had begun to tear away at the bodies.

That day, though he didn't know it, Naser Oric had reached the summit of his power. He had broadened the area of Muslim control to 350 square miles around Srebrenica. Within the town, he had declared martial law and stood as all-powerful commander. (Another Muslim militia leader who tried to supplant him was arrested and murdered.)

A week after his Christmas victory at Kravica, Oric and his fighters attacked Skelani and tried to seize and destroy its steel-girdered bridge over the Drina. One of his men machine-gunned women and children as they fled in panic toward the Serbian side.

Throughout Serbia, people were outraged by the Muslim leader's brazen attack. Immediately General Ratko Mladic sent his tanks and artillery over the bridge and drove Oric's men back. They would retreat for ten days. Before they were able to stop and hold their ground, they were within ten miles of Srebrenica. And Mladic's real offensive had yet to begin.

IV.

In the White House that winter, President Clinton followed General Mladic's grim and steady progress in his morning briefings, watching as the Serb tanks and artillery pushed the lightly armed Muslims closer and closer to Srebrenica, seizing village after village until the Serbs stood on the outskirts of the city and began to rain down shells. Mladic's technique, as David Rieff describes it in *Slaughterhouse,* "combined the standard Yugoslav National Army (and Warsaw Pact) military doctrine—which can be summarized as never sending a man where a bullet can go first—with the Bosnian Serb predilection for targeting hospitals, water treatment plants, and refugee centers in order to produce the maximum amount of terror in the population."[22]

To produce such terror was not difficult; without shelter or defense, the refugees who had fled the surrounding towns and now slept in Srebrenica's streets were easy targets. During one horrible hour late in the siege, Serb shells killed sixty-four people and wounded more than a hundred. Many were children, as Louis Gentile, the UN official, described in a cable to his headquarters in New York:

> Fourteen dead bodies were found in the school yard. Body parts and human flesh clung to the schoolyard fence. The ground was literally soaked with blood. One child, about six years of age, had been decapitated. I saw two ox-carts covered with bodies. . . . I will never be able to convey the horror.[23]

Only weeks before the Serb offensive began, Bill Clinton had declared in his inaugural address that he would use military force if "the will and conscience of the international community is defied." That defiance now confronted him daily, particularly after Tony Birtley, a reporter working for *ABC News,* slipped into Srebrenica aboard a Bosnian helicopter with a small video camera. It was Birtley's reports smuggled out of the seige, as Warren P. Strobel says in *Late-Breaking Foreign Policy,* that for the first time showed the world "the medieval conditions in the city itself—people dressed in rags and living in the streets, children drinking sewer water."[24]

Srebrenica brought Clinton face to face with the contradiction between his idealistic rhetoric supporting the Bosnians and his pragmatic reluctance to commit his new administration to a complicated war. The horrible images of suffering, together with his own high-minded words, had pushed him to the verge of taking action. Finally, the Bosnians forced his hand: on February 12, officials in Sarajevo announced they would refuse any further shipments of aid to Sarajevo while aid to Srebrenica was cut off by the Serbs. The intent of this seemingly perverse decision was to force the Western nations, and particularly the as yet untried Clinton, finally to take strong action against the Serbs.

In fact, the Bosnians' announcement represented only their latest attempt to make use of the only lever they had that might force the West to act. In launching a program in June 1992 to deliver food to Bosnia under supervision of United Nations "blue helmets," the Western countries had intended to reduce the political pressures to do something to stop the slaughter—which would have meant, in effect, intervening militarily against the Serbs. The Bosnians now hoped to turn that strategy on its head. By showing the world that the food was not getting through, and that the result was "ethnic cleansing by starvation," they sought to force the Western nations to take stronger action, and preferably to use military force. The Sarajevo government was attempting to make use of Srebrenica and the other enclaves as—in the words of one United Nations official—"pressure points on the international community for firmer action."

> The longer that aid convoys were unable to reach them, the greater the pressure on the [UN] mandate. When convoys did succeed, calls for firmer action were unwarranted.

When aid convoys were blocked, however, the Western powers were placed in the position of watching as Bosnians starved. The United Nations official went further, arguing that the Bosnians actually timed their military offensives to coincide with successful aid deliveries. For example, he says, in November 1992,

> Two weeks after the first successful delivery, Muslims launched an offensive toward Bratunac. Thus the integrity of [the UN] was undermined, further convoys were impossible, and the pressure for firmer action [by the U.S. and other nations] resumed.[25]

In other words, the Sarajevo leaders sought to give the impression that UN aid helped their commanders carry out attacks. When Muslim military offensives followed closely after food shipments, this not only cast doubt on the UN's cherished "impartiality," weakening the organization's legitimacy as the principal Western instrument to deal with the Bosnian war. It also led Serbs to block future shipments, causing more starvation and misery and once again increasing the pressure on the West to intervene.

After the first months of the war, when their main goal had been to build up their forces by capturing weapons and sacking neighboring villagers' crops, Oric and his officers fought for two strategic objectives. First, they sought to conquer and cleanse territory that would eventually join together the isolated eastern enclaves—especially Zepa and Cerska—and form one larger, more powerful Muslim stronghold. This Oric's men achieved, battling through to Zepa in September 1992 and reaching Cerska after the Christmas victory at Kravica. They would hold this vast tract of territory for barely a month, however, before Mladic's armored forces sent Oric's infantry reeling back.

Oric's second objective was to force Mladic to thin his forces on other fronts and thereby to leave the Serbs, who were well armed but undermanned (and thus labored under precisely the opposite disadvantage of the numerous but poorly equipped Muslims), vulnerable to Bosnian government attacks elsewhere. Oric's campaigns of December and January, for example, helped draw Serb troops away from a major Muslim offensive that briefly succeeded in cutting the critical "Posavina corridor," which linked Serbia itself with Serb conquests in western Bosnia and the Serb-occupied Krajina.

Whatever the military rationales for Oric's operations, however, it is incontestable that the Bosnians were struggling to make use of the misery of the enclaves to force action by the United Nations and Western countries. Those working to deliver aid—and especially the officers and soldiers from France, Britain, and a number of other countries who formed part of the United Nations Protection Force (known as UNPROFOR) charged with protecting them—tended to see these Bosnian efforts as Machiavellian, or evil. The Bosnians, however, were simply trying to make use of the only weapon the peculiar and hypocritical international involvement in their country seemed to offer them. For though many of the individual aid workers performed great acts of heroism in Bosnia, the mission itself was built on a fatal contradiction: "The crux of the matter," as Wayne Bert writes it in *The Reluctant Superpower*, "was that the UN's primary mission was to get peace, making concerns with justice secondary."[26]

This of course was Clinton's dilemma: He had promised justice, but fulfilling that promise meant devoting major diplomatic attention and likely some military forces, spending political capital that risked undermining the domestic reforms he had come to Washington to make. In addition, a strong effort in Bosnia would force Clinton to confront both the United Nations and two major allies, the British and the French, who had officers and soldiers on the ground and had thereby committed themselves to "the UN's primary mission" of "getting peace." Indeed, this "mission" now belonged to France and Britain and the other Western allies; they had shaped it, designed it, and carried it out; but the dirty little secret was that the mission was animated by the determination to avoid increased involvement in Bosnia, especially any military intervention. It "was disingenuous of United Nations officials," as David Rieff writes, "to pretend that they were the only disinterested parties in the Bosnian tragedy."

> In reality, UN peacekeepers had been carrying out a very specific and well-thought-out political agenda from the beginning. Its premise was simple. The United Nations saw not just full-scale intervention in support of the Bosnians but any increased military activity, whether it was NATO air strikes or lifting the one-sided arms embargo against the Bosnian government, as putting at risk everything it had been trying to accomplish. . . .

And just what were United Nations officials, and, behind them, the Western nations, trying to accomplish? Rieff observes that the criterion of success was neither moral—"UN officials felt they had no business judging the rights and wrongs of the conflict"—nor political: "Although the Bosnian government was an internationally recognized state and the Bosnian Serb 'republic' an illegitimate rebellion, the United Nations felt compelled to deal with them equally, as 'the parties,' or 'the warring factions.'"

> Rather, the UN wanted to get the aid through and facilitate a peace. . . . The terms of the peace were, from the standpoint of UNPROFOR, almost irrelevant. It did not have to be a just peace, or even a peace that could be maintained. All that the United Nations required was that "the parties" agree to it.

If "peace" is the single goal, and its terms "almost irrelevant," we have in fact moved as far away from "justice" as we are likely to get, and the peculiar result was that the United Nations, for all its pretensions to "impartiality" between "the parties," had forced itself by its own interests to favor one side—the side that happened to be winning. Rieff sketches out this logic in a bitter and elegant passage:

> If the purpose of a mission is to stop a war, and one side, having won, appears ready to settle, while the other side, feeling its cause to be just but having turned out to be the loser, is determined to fight on, then those running this mission are likely to find that most of the time their interests coincide with those of the victors. They and the victors want peace. The vanquished, possessed of the notion that they have right on their side, refuse to accept their defeat. Given these convergences, it is only a small step to the victors and the international organization understanding that, when all is said and done, they share the same goal.[27]

That goal, of course, was forcing a Muslim surrender and a settlement on Serb terms—for what else could a settlement be if it was "negotiated" while the Serbs held more than 70 percent of Bosnian territory? "It might not be an ideal outcome," writes Rieff, "but at least people would stop getting killed." Such was the institutional interest of the United Nations, and such as well were the interests of the British and the French who stood behind it.

Now, however, a new and powerful player entered the game. The very fact that the Bosnians entertained high hopes for Bill Clinton, that they drew encouragement from his rhetoric, itself had a powerful effect. Why accept the ethnic partitions set out in the Vance-Owen plan while the leader of the Free World was declaring that "ethnic cleansing cannot stand"? Among the many bitter words one finds in David Owen's memoirs, none are more bitter than those directed at Clinton officials for their "encouragement" of the

Bosnians. In December 1992, even before the new administration took office, as Clinton transition officials let their muted criticisms and unattributed "ambivalences" about Vance-Owen seep into the press, Lord Owen landed in Sarajevo and, standing behind the forest of microphones on the tarmac, warned Bosnians, "Don't, don't, don't live under this dream that the West is going to come in and sort this problem out. Don't dream dreams. . . ."

UN officials were even more explicit. "If anything emboldens the Muslim government to fight on, it's things like this," said Yasushi Akashi, the UN secretary general's special representative, after senior United States officials opened a new embassy in Sarajevo in spring 1994. "They can point to that and say, 'See, the Americans are with us.' We can only hope that the failure of NATO to come to their aid around Gorazde will convince them the U.S. cavalry isn't around the corner."

Clinton's rhetoric did have serious effects in Bosnia; insofar as he used it as a substitute for meaningful action the policy of his administration was not only more duplicitous but in many ways more damaging than George H. W. Bush's had been. Bush by his inaction had missed any chance to use American power to prevent or limit the war; but he had never promised the U.S. cavalry might be on the way. Clinton had promised strong action—had vowed America would help—and when confronted with the need to deliver that help had offered only words. Those words did more than disappoint—they instilled hope which Bosnians paid for with blood.

By mid-February 1993, General Ratko Mladic's offensive had left the isolated eastern towns of Srebrenica and Cserska jammed with refugees. Mladic now blocked the aid convoys (which in any event had never succeeded in feeding the city) and those emaciated people—those who weren't killed by Mladic's shellfire—began to starve. Clinton, who had boldly declared that "ethnic cleansing cannot stand," was about to witness with the rest of the television-watching world the cleansing-by-hunger of tens of thousands of people.

In late February Clinton finally responded, offering a novel solution: American C-130 "Hercules" transport planes would drop food and medical supplies into Bosnia by air. The flights were carried out under the United Nations humanitarian mandate, having been conceived, as James Gow bluntly puts it, "by the U.S. in place of preparedness to make a stronger commitment by involving the deployment of its own troops."

By late March, only weeks after his secretary of state had delivered to Congress his eloquent affirmation of the moral and strategic importance of Bosnia, Clinton in his rhetoric was taking a leaf from Lawrence Eagleburger's book:

> The hatred between all three groups . . . is almost unbelievable. It's almost terrifying, and it's centuries old. That really is a problem from hell. And I think the United States is doing all we can to try to deal with that problem.

Clinton had begun to "climb down." Soon his secretary of state, in a chilling echo of British Prime Minister Neville Chamberlain's description of the pre-war dispute over the soon-to-be dismembered Czechoslovakia as "a quarrel in a foreign country between people of whom we know nothing," would be describing the war in Bosnia as "a humanitarian crisis a long way from home, in the middle of another continent."

The Clinton administration now began to flirt with the hitherto despised Vance-Owen plan to divide Bosnia into nine ethnically based provinces—and indeed Mladic was doubtless now attacking vigorously in the east of Bosnia partly because Vance-Owen envisaged granting this territory to the Muslims, and the Serb general was determined to preempt any such move by creating an irreversible "fact on the ground." In February 1993, the only obstacle lying between him and creating that fact was the presence of tens of thousands of starving people and a force of lightly armed Muslims.

V.

On February 28, four C-130 Hercules transport planes lumbered off the runway at a military airbase at Frankfurt and turned their noses south. A short while later, in the sky 10,000 feet above Cerska, about thirteen miles northwest of Srebrenica, American airmen pushed out heavily loaded pallets, and watched white parachutes flutter down against the black sky and disappear among the snow-covered mountains. The Americans executed the operation perfectly; the pallets plummeted into the snow precisely on target. Their good work, however, meant nothing; for by the time the food and medicine crashed through the leafless branches, the Serbs had overrun Cerska and were hard at work looting and burning houses and dispatching wounded Muslims. Those Muslims who were not now lying dead in the snow had long since fled.

Even as the Serbs took what they could find and burned what was left, Bosnians trudged through the bitter cold night, a great wave of refugees perhaps ten thousand strong, bundled in blankets and rags, grimly shuffling south toward Konjevic Polje, a hamlet that lay about ten miles north of Srebrenica. Many of these dull-eyed people had made such a grim trek before; ten months earlier they had been "cleansed" during the Serbs' brutal occupation of Zvornik, some twenty-five miles from Srebrenica. They were the lucky ones: the Serbs had murdered as many as 2,000 people. Now the cleansed of Zvornik were fleeing once again, a stream of hollow-eyed refugees flooding the Srebrenica "pocket."

From Srebrenica and other villages and towns, the ham radio operators who provided the eastern enclaves' only link to the outside world were filling the airwaves with detailed reports of mass killings, of Serb soldiers cutting the throats of women and children. Sadako Ogata, the UN High Commissioner for Refugees, sent a summary of these accounts in an urgent letter to Secretary General Boutros Boutros-Ghali. "If only 10 percent of the information is true," wrote Ogata, "we are witnessing a massacre in the enclaves without being able to do anything about it." Ogata then made a startling proposal: the United Nations must move to evacuate the Muslims from the Srebrenica enclave. In the past the UN had always opposed such evacuations. If carried out, Ogata's proposal would put the UN in the position of helping the Serbs cleanse the area of Muslims.

In New York, members of the Security Council ordered Boutros-Ghali to "take immediate steps to increase UNPROFOR's presence in Eastern Bosnia." On March 5, General Philippe Morillon, the white-haired, charismatic French officer who commanded UN forces in Bosnia, traveled to Konjevic Polje, then to Cerska itself to investigate the reports of atrocities. Reporters spoke to him as he climbed into his helicopter at Tuzla. "As a soldier, I, unfortunately, have the knack of smelling death," Morillon said dramatically. "I didn't smell it." The United Nations, he announced, would not evacuate the Srebrenica pocket after all. At the last moment, the Serbs had refused to permit any Muslims to leave unless the United Nations would replace them with ten thousand Serb civilians from towns under Bosnian control. And it was not only the Serbs who had prevented the desperate Muslims from leaving, as Sudetic writes:

> The Muslim commanders had also blocked the planned exodus, arguing that it would "undermine the morale" of Srebrenica's defenders and lead to the town's surrender; in other words, Naser Oric did not want to be deprived of the *torbari* who had once been his sword and were now his shield, and Alija Izetbegovic did not want to have the UN helping the Serbs remove the Muslim majority population from territory that the UN's own . . . Vance-Owen peace plan had earmarked to remain predominantly Muslim.

To the reporters assembled at the Tuzla airfield, General Morillon urged a sober, skeptical attitude. "I did not see any trace of massacres," said the general. "That's very important because we have to calm the fears there. . . . Srebrenica is in no danger."

Within a few hours, however, reporters would have something more credible to rely on than General Morillon's nose. Simon Mardel, a doctor working for the World Health Organization, had left Morillon's party at Konjevic Polje and hiked to Srebrenica. By ham radio, he reported that between twenty and thirty refugees were dying every day from pneumonia and other illnesses. For months, he said, Muslim doctors had been operating without anesthetics. Refugees were sleeping everywhere on Srebrenica's slushy streets and subsisting on roots and grass and buds. As for the airdropped supplies, the strongest people—officers, soldiers, members of work brigades responsible for digging trenches—took what they wanted, pilfering sacks of flour and grain and hiding them for their families. The weakest—the sick, the wounded, the homeless refugees—got nothing.

Eventually, Naser Oric abandoned any effort to organize distribution of the food and simply declared that it would be "everyone for himself." As Sudetic describes it,

> The mountainsides above Srebrenica now flickered with the flames of a legion of torches each night as desperate people streamed through the forest to the drop areas. Few of the newly arriving refugees . . . , many of them widows with children, . . . had the energy to make the journey and fight for food. . . . Men were killing one another in the forests to get at the flour. Falling pallets, which were as big as refrigerators and smashed into the ground at about eighty-five miles an hour, had crushed to death people who risked waiting inside the landing zones to improve their chances. . . . The Americans responded to the chaos by . . . dropping tens of thousands of individual meals in brown plastic wrappers that fell to the earth like vacuum-packed manna from heaven.

By now Mladic's troops were furiously shelling Konjevic Polje, broadening the stream of refugees flooding Srebrenica. General Morillon began to fear that Mladic was about to seize the entire enclave, which would not only create a humanitarian disaster but would likely scuttle the Vance-Owen peace talks. At that point, and despite the ambivalence of the United States, those talks were still "the only game in town."

On March 11, after consulting with his government in Paris and receiving permission from the Serbs to cross their lines, General Philippe Morillon set out for Srebrenica.

VI.

In the White House, members of Clinton's Principals Committee debated what policy the administration should adopt toward Bosnia. Progress was slow. Senior officials strongly differed on what to do, and in such a situation the president must make a clear and forceful decision, lest conflicting interests of the various departments, and the government's natural inertia, frustrate any desire he might have to act. Clinton, though, possessed both the vague impulse to do good and a strong apprehension that, if he actually did anything to fulfill the desire, he might fall into a trap from which he would be unable to extricate himself. Had not Lyndon Johnson, the master politician, been destroyed by a distant, useless war?

The Principals, meanwhile, increasingly left specific proposals behind and launched into abstract debates over America's role in the world. General Colin Powell, chairman of the Joint Chiefs of Staff and the sole holdover from the Bush administration, remarked in his memoirs that "it wasn't policy-making. It was group therapy—an existential debate over what is the role of America, etc." With all the disdain of a hardened professional forced to endure the pretensions of a group of amateurs, General Powell traced the poverty of the discussion directly to a political source:

> [T]he discussions [meandered] like a graduate student bull session or the think-tank seminars in which many of my new colleagues had spent the last twelve years while their party was out of power.

For his part, Powell did an eloquent job of confirming and reinforcing the president's doubts. The spectre of Vietnam haunted him more than it did Clinton, for he had been there, and he had derived from his command a grim determination to fight what he saw as the frivolity and irresponsibility of men like the young president who now sat across from him: "Those of us who were captains and majors in Vietnam," the general wrote in his memoirs, "will never let the politicians do this to us again." For those who favored military intervention for strongly idealistic reasons—and whom he clearly believed remained willfully ignorant of the burdens and responsibilities with which military professionals must contend—Powell reserved a withering contempt:

> The debate exploded at one session when Madeleine Albright . . . asked me in frustration, "What's the point of having this superb military that you're always talking about if we can't use it?" I thought I would have an aneurysm. American GIs were not toy soldiers to be moved around on some sort of global game board.[28]

Powell stood out as an immensely popular, uniquely independent figure. To overrule him on a matter of military judgment would have been politically perilous for any president. To a president who had sidestepped military service during the Vietnam war and who was regarded by significant numbers of Americans as a draft dodger; who had been publicly humiliated in an early, controversial struggle with the chairman over the so-called "gays in the military" issue—to President Bill Clinton, General Powell represented a powerful force that he was loath to challenge.

While Clinton and his advisers met and talked, and met and talked, officials in Christopher's State Department had been working away at their Bosnia "policy review," and hints began to appear in the press of a new, tougher plan, called "lift and strike." Under this proposal, the United Nations would lift the arms embargo on the Bosnians, allowing them to acquire heavy weapons, and NATO would strike at the Serbs with its warplanes to protect the Bosnians while, freshly armed, they learned the skills to "defend themselves." The plan had many virtues, though the most striking seemed designed to placate political constituencies at home rather than alter the military situation in Bosnia.

Lifting the arms embargo, for example, had become a popular idea, particularly among congressmen, and for good reason: of all the West's perverse and repugnant policies on Bosnia, the arms embargo had come to seem the most blatantly and incomprehensibly unfair. Under what rationale could the international community prevent a member state of the United Nations from defending itself—which was, after all, its explicit right under Article 51 of the UN Charter? To even the least informed voter, this seemed clearly wrong, and giving Bosnians "the means to defend themselves" not only seemed clearly right, it had a reassuringly American, pull-yourself-up-by-your-bootstraps sound to it. As for the "strike" part of "lift and strike," protecting Bosnians with NATO fighters and bombers until they could absorb their new weapons and use them to fight for themselves sounded like the sort of low-cost, middle-of-the-road help Americans should be willing to supply. Air power, after all, had not only proved spectacularly potent during the Gulf War, it had seemed hygienic, "surgical," and, even for the dashing Americans in the cockpits, safe.

If "lift and strike" had political virtues, however, its value as a practical policy was doubtful. For insofar as the purpose was to turn the tide of the war without deploying troops, "lift and strike" was based on logistical and geographic ignorance. As David Rieff wrote,

> To the question of how the weapons were going to be gotten into Sarajevo or Tuzla, supporters of this approach at best tended to respond vaguely. When pressed, they would concede that some outside force would have to bring in the arms the Bosnians needed. And yet, if one took them at their word, what they were calling for was military intervention in the strictest sense.[29]

Military officers and civilian Pentagon officials helpfully bolstered this point by estimating that to open a "land corridor" from Split to Sarajevo to deliver the weapons would require at least 100,000 troops. "Lift and strike's" main appeal—that it could be labeled an intervention to help the Bosnians without requiring a real intervention—began to evaporate.

That, however, turned out to be its strength. For "lift and strike" shimmered like a mirage just long enough for Warren Christopher to gather it up, place it in his briefcase, and take it to Europe, where he traveled from capital to capital supposedly trying to persuade the allied leaders to sign on and support it. Europeans, however, had an obvious problem with "lift and strike," which Christopher and other Clinton officials well understood: they had—the words would soon become a veritable mantra—"troops on the ground." What would happen to their blue-helmeted officers and soldiers now delivering food and medicine if the United Nations were to relinquish its "impartiality" and support not only lifting the arms embargo but, in effect, launching air strikes against Serb artillery and armor?

Of course, the Europeans' argument would have been more convincing if more aid were actually getting through—especially to, say, Srebrenica, which since the war began had received only a single convoy. For their part, the

Bosnians repeatedly declared that they would prefer that the humanitarian troops leave their country if this were deemed necessary for them to receive the benefits of "lift and strike," but it was a sad fact that in such matters the Bosnians' opinion did not by any means come first.

Christopher's trip to Europe was not successful—at least not in persuading the Europeans to accept the American policy. In another sense, though, it was a brilliant achievement, for it provided President Clinton with an effective alibi for his own inaction: If the president had not moved to lift the arms embargo against the Bosnians or to ready airstrikes against the Serbs, this was because the Europeans had troops on the ground, and, try as he might, he could not bring them around to accept his proposals.

For their part, the Europeans, on matters of great importance to their senior ally, were not accustomed to this sort of "honest consultation." They expected the Americans, in matters of true import, to lead, not to ask. For this and other reasons, his European hosts did not find the secretary's presentation persuasive: "I had the feeling, when he came to Brussels," said Willy Claes, at the time the Belgian Foreign Minister, "that he had felt very clearly that there was not a possibility to convince the Europeans." On his return, Christopher himself would be heard to remark on "what a loser this policy is."[30]

Given the choice of whether to back "lift and strike" or not, the Europeans would rather not. Real problems confronted them, of course: they feared shipping in more arms would inflame the war (which was, of course, the point of the policy in the first place); they feared that Milosevic, seeing his Bosnian Serb proxy's gains ready to evaporate, might bring his army to intervene; they feared that, having advanced so close to "peace"—on the Serbs' terms, yes, but that was a sad fact of life—arming the Bosnians would propel the war in precisely the opposite direction. In the end, however, it was British and French and Spanish troops that were on the ground and if the Americans weren't willing to insist—in effect, to threaten to breach NATO itself—the Europeans certainly could not take the proposal seriously.

By the time Christopher had returned from his disastrous May tour, Clinton's own doubts had grown. If the Americans insisted on intensifying the violence of the war by supplying the Bosnians with weapons, the Europeans warned, they could find themselves forced to withdraw their peacekeeping troops. And this, as they knew, the Americans would seek to avoid at all costs; for President Clinton, as the leader of NATO, had given his solemn pledge that if his allies withdrew from Bosnia—sure to be a dangerous and bloody operation—he would dispatch tens of thousands of American ground troops to support them. However much the president may have wished that "lift and strike" would "solve the problem from 20,000 feet," as the European negotiator David Owen derisively put it, Clinton could not impose the policy without also muddying the feet of some twenty-five thousand American troops in Bosnia—the very step "lift and strike" had been designed to avoid. The president was checkmated.

It was then that there emerged this curious fact: "lift and strike" was more effective as a dead policy than a live one. Clinton desired to act in Bosnia but the Europeans would not cooperate; thus the president was stymied. During the continuing diplomatic squabbling over the Vance-Owen plan, the imposition of a no-fly zone, the tightening of sanctions, "lift and strike" would stand forth as the single grand idea that Bill Clinton had put forward to fulfill his promise to save Bosnia—if only the Europeans, who, of course, had troops on the ground, would let him. Indeed, as James Gow points out,

> No sooner had the UK and France implicitly acknowledged that U.S. pressure would be irresistible and that "lift and strike," along with the withdrawal of UNPROFOR, would be inevitable, than the U.S. in September placed a six-month moratorium on its call to lift the embargo.
>
> Ironically, the Clinton Administration, having ebbed and flowed in arguments with the Allies on the arms embargo question, pulled back from the brink when finally forced to confront the real implications of withdrawal, lift and strike. . . .[31]

Bill Clinton had managed to shape the perfect policy: a rhetorical policy, one consisting solely of words. It brought moral credit; it carried no risk. As the president remarked in April, "The U.S. should always seek an opportunity to stand up against—at least speak out against inhumanity." These verbs—to stand up against and to speak out against—Clinton blends together in a single sentence as if they were one and the same; in fact they are very different. For Bill Clinton, as the Bosnians were slowly discovering, speaking out against inhumanity often seemed a means to avoid standing up against it.

Could he have stood up against it? After all, Colin Powell and his own military opposed him, the Europeans were skeptical and reluctant, and, most important, the problem had grown much more complicated since the first days of the war during the Bush administration. And yet, despite the accepted mythology, a majority of Americans tended to support taking strong action in Bosnia—if, that is, it was coordinated with the United States' allies. "The power of the President is considerable," as Wayne Bert writes,

> and a determined president who was willing to take responsibility for Bosnia policy might well have forged a coalition that could have surmounted the many obstacles and used force to get a satisfactory settlement. More than one European agreed with a diplomat who said that the President "should stop asking them their own opinion on what he plans to do and start telling them instead what he plans to go ahead with, preferably with their support."[32]

Such an approach was inconceivable for Clinton, for he had no commitment to making the sacrifices it would have taken to stop the war; rather, as

Gow says, he took a "stand on principle against 'ethnic cleansing' without being prepared to do what was necessary to stop it."

Rhetoric, as Lord Owen observed, creates illusions; it makes people "dream dreams." And leading people to dream those dreams, and act on them, was in retrospect Clinton's greatest failure. His rhetoric, however, was soon trumped by a proudly independent Algerian-born Frenchman who, by the force of his own personality, helped impose on the Bosnians the supreme rhetorical policy of the entire war.

VII.

On March 10, 1993, the Commander of the United Nations Protection Force in Bosnia, General Philippe Morillon, climbed into his armored car at Tuzla and set off for the imprisoned city of Srebrenica. Under his command were a column of white United Nations trucks and jeeps, loaded with food and medicines. Though he had received assurance from General Mladic personally that his supplies would be permitted to enter the city, Serb commanders halted the convoy: No food would be allowed into Srebrenica. After hours of discussion, Morillon finally decided to leave the convoy behind and enter the city himself. Though he was permitted to proceed with an armored vehicle, and one truck loaded with medicine and sugar, he was directed toward a treacherous mountain road that, as the Serbs knew, had been mined. As the tiny caravan crossed the frontline into Muslim territory, the truck hit a mine; it had to be left behind.

It was already dark when General Morillon drove slowly in his white car through the Dante-esque main avenue of Srebrenica. Refugees in rags filled the streets. Everywhere fires smoked and sputtered. The last trees having long since been cut down, refugees burned plastic bottles and garbage, filling the streets, already stinking of unwashed bodies and urine and excrement, with noxious fumes.

The next morning Morillon rose and met with Naser Oric and his commanders, along with several civilian leaders, to discuss the future of the enclave. Morillon urged the Muslims to avoid provoking the Serb soldiers who surrounded them. He would try, said the general, to negotiate a ceasefire, seek to arrange with the Serbs to let some aid convoys into the town. And then he suggested a broader, long-term strategy: Srebrenica, said the general, might become a demilitarized zone.

Naser Oric and his commanders were not pleased with the suggestion, for it seemed to raise more questions than it answered—most obviously, who would protect the town from the Serbs if the Muslims gave up their weapons? Could they really depend on the United Nations to protect them? But the situation of Srebrenica had become too dire; when Oric's men radioed Bosnian political leaders in Sarajevo to ask them about Morillon's proposal, they were told, according to a participant in the meeting quoted by Honig and Both, "Sarajevo supported it because there was nothing else."

There was, however, General Morillon. Since his arrival, Srebrenica had been quiet; the incessant shelling and firing had stopped. Even as Morillon was discussing the town's future, a radio operator in Sarajevo's Presidency Building was sending Oric a coded message from Srebrenica's exiled mayor, Murat Efendic: "Whatever happens, prevent Morillon from leaving Srebrenica until he provides security for the people there," Efendic said. "Do it in a civilized way. Use women and children."

Oric did precisely that. Women went house to house, bringing out into the streets hundreds of mothers and children. They sat and put together crude posters—"Don't Abandon Us!" "If You Leave, They Will Kill Us!" "We Are Hungry! Give Us Bread!"—and by the time General Morillon returned to his car that afternoon, it had been surrounded by a roiling ocean of shouting and crying women and children, some of whom were sitting down in front of its wheels. Morillon stood on the hood and addressed the women, assuring them that he would not abandon their town. Though he was eloquent in his appeal, the woman refused to budge. He asked Oric to help clear the way, but the military leader sadly admitted that confronted with such a problem he was powerless.

Finally Morillon went off to sleep and, at two o'clock in the morning, slipped quietly out of town on foot, to wait in Potocari, two miles away, for his driver to meet him. Unfortunately for him the women, who had deployed themselves in eight-hour shifts, were watching, and they blocked his car once more. He was forced to abandon it. By the time the general walked sheepishly back into town the crowd of women and children had grown larger than before.

Now General Morillon abruptly changed tactics. Soon the women and children filling the square would look up to the balcony of the post office to see the handsome general with the penetrating gaze standing at attention, brandishing in one hand the blue flag of the United Nations. He gazed down at the women, the flag flapping in the wind. "You are now under the protection of the UN forces," the general declared dramatically to the people of Srebrenica. "I will never abandon you."

It was a startling and unexpected turn of events and, for UN officials, not a particularly agreeable one. Morillon had essentially made use of his own captivity to place a United Nations shield over the town. And he had done this wholly on his own authority, as an act of grandiloquent inspiration. The next day, when Oric and the other commanders told Morillon he would be permitted to leave, the general refused. Only working from within the miserable, vulnerable pocket of Srebrenica, he now believed, would he be able to negotiate the delivery of aid, the evacuation of refugees, and, finally, a cease-fire and the demilitarization of the enclave.

The Serbs, outraged, declared that they would permit food convoys to enter Srebrenica only after the general left the enclave—hardly a believable promise since they had permitted only one convoy through during the entire siege. Meantime the Serbs shelled and bombarded the villages around Srebrenica, seizing one after another, making their way steadily closer to the town itself. Naser Oric, seeing that Srebrenica must soon fall, approached Morillon and asked if it could be made an "open town" and taken under the protection of the UN forces. Morillon laid down his conditions, as quoted by Honig and Both:

> My intention is that except for some [civilian police] . . . , all men who wish to stay here must give weapons to my command post here in Sre-brenica. Those who want to continue to fight must go to the hills. . . .

Unfortunately, the Serbs, unimpressed with Morillon's proposal to disarm the Muslims and determined now to seize the town, continued to advance. On March 19, the Serbs finally permitted an aid convoy to enter Srebrenica. The trucks were mobbed by desperate people. As soon as the food and med-icine had been unloaded, seven hundred women and children fought their way aboard. Although the temperature was far below freezing, they waited all night aboard the trucks; several woman and children suffocated; others froze to death. When they arrived in Tuzla, their condition shocked the doctors waiting to receive them.

> The refugees were hungry, cold, and dirty and were surrounded by a sick-ening stench. Their wounds had been neglected and amputations had to be performed immediately as gangrene was eating away at people's bodies.

On March 26, Morillon met with Milosevic and Mladic in Belgrade and obtained a ceasefire along with the Serb general's pledge to allow food con-voys into Srebrenica and, for the first time, evacuate those who wished to leave. Again, when the white trucks arrived desperate refugees virtually rioted in their attempts to force their way on; on the first convoy, twenty-four hundred people jammed into space meant to transport seven hundred. Younger women fought and sometimes severely injured their elders; some women threw their infants into the arms of anyone on the trucks willing to take them in a desperate attempt to save their lives. Doctors in Tuzla found the trucks covered with blood and vomit, and after the refugees poured out, invariably several corpses would be left behind, usually those of children.

It was clear to all, of course, that the United Nations was now doing Gen-eral Mladic's job. He expansively urged that three hundred trucks should be sent in daily to empty the town more rapidly. By this point, however, "the Bosnian government was getting worried and opposed further evacuations," as Honig and Both write.

> It wanted Srebrenica to become a safe haven, protected by UN forces. If the evacuations from Srebrenica continued at this rate, there would soon be no substantial civilian population left. Without civilians whose lives were directly under threat, the pressure on the United Nations to deploy peacekeepers in Srebrenica would subside.[33]

The same day, Muslim soldiers in Tuzla blocked a convoy filled with Muslim refugees, threatening to send the desperate people back to Srebrenica. "The convoy is not allowed to come in," said one Muslim officer. "We are ready to sacrifice these people." Although the people were eventually allowed into Tuzla, the positions of the Serbs and the Muslims were now completely reversed. The Serbs, who had blocked all access to Srebrenica, now permitted the UN to evacuate as many people as it could. The Bosnians, who had demanded that the way be opened to food convoys and the evacuation of refugees, now blocked all efforts to evacuate their people from Srebrenica.

Realizing that the Bosnians were now preventing the United Nations from, in effect, cleansing more Muslims from Srebrenica, General Mladic now determined to seize the city. His artillery and tanks launched a vicious attack, capturing one by one the villages encircling it and sending survivors scurrying for town. Deeply alarmed, General Morillon set off once more. (He had developed what his superiors and some of his staff considered an unhealthy obsession with Srebrenica.) But the Serbs turned his convoy back; when Morillon tried to pass through Zvornik with only two vehicles, he found himself surrounded by a crowd of infuriated Serb women. In a hellish echo of his experience in his beloved Srebrenica, the women shrieked, beat on his vehicle, and scrawled "Morillon Hitler" and other obscenities on his white United Nations car. To make Morillon's humiliation complete, he had to be rescued from the mob of screaming women by Mladic's chief of staff, who to reach him flew in a helicopter that violated the United Nations' own no-fly zone.

On April 12 Serb gunners launched two artillery bombardments on Srebrenica that killed fifty-six people and wounded many more. During the next three days, the Serb attacks grew steadily more ferocious. One by one the Muslims ran out of ammunition. Srebrenica, it was clear, had only hours left to live. Thinking of Bratunac and Kravica and all the other massacres and counter-massacres, the men of Srebrenica knew what fate to expect.

On April 16, as Russian and American envoys sat in Belgrade struggling to convince Slobodan Milosevic to "use his influence" with General Mladic and Dr. Karadzic to halt the Srebrenica offensive, United Nations negotiator David Owen was having an ominous telephone conversation with the president of Serbia:

I had rarely heard Milosevic so exasperated, but also so worried: he feared that if the Bosnian Serb troops entered Srebrenica there would be a bloodbath because of the tremendous bad blood that existed between the two armies. The Bosnian Serbs held the young Muslim commander in Srebrenica, Naser Oric, responsible for a massacre near Bratunac in December 1992 in which many Serb civilians had been killed. Milosevic believed it would be a great mistake for the Bosnian Serbs to take Srebrenica and promised to tell Karadzic so.[34]

Owen writes as if he took Milosevic's "worries" and "fears" at face value; it is, as is often the case, hard to know what the former British foreign secretary was really thinking. As for Milosevic, he was both a celebrated liar and a leader who, certainly in the spring of 1993, retained decisive influence over the Bosnian Serb Army—which until scarcely a year before, after all, had been simply a part of the Yugoslav National Army under his command. The idea that Milosevic found himself "exasperated" by General Mladic's launching an offensive a few miles from the border of Serbia itself is difficult to believe. The words Dr. Owen so scrupulously records admit of another, more plausible explanation: In case Mladic did seize the enclave, and his men went on to murder a great many people—for the very reasons Milosevic suggests—the Serb president wanted an alibi. He had tried to stop it, he had done his best for the forces of good; but Mladic, alas, proved uncontrollable.

As Milosevic chatted with Owen, General Mladic's men broke through the Muslim lines and surged toward the town. An unnamed eyewitness, quoted by Honig and Both, describes these last moments of the siege:

> We were sitting in the basement and shells were exploding every five seconds. . . .I went on to the balcony but immediately a machine-gun salvo hit the wall next to me. I went back to the basement. We could hear the shooting come closer and we thought we were going to be killed. Then suddenly I heard outgoing shells—a different sound. Either the Serbs had entered, or it was us!

He runs upstairs, finds a window, and cautiously surveys the main street.

> I saw more than a hundred men running up the hill towards the Serbs and I heard shouts: "Naser! Naser!" Later I heard that Naser Oric and two groups of 150 men had pushed back the Serbs 500 metres that day. . . .The artillery man who had fired the shells . . . told me they had kept fifty shells for a critical moment.

But this was not all. In Belgrade the Russian and American envoys had been hard at work. So had the diplomats in the United Nations Security Council laboring in far-off New York.

> Two hours after Naser pushed back the Serbs, there [came a radio] announcement that Srebrenica had been declared a safe area. We all jumped into the air and fell into each other's arms, crying and laughing at the same time. We had been saved.[35]

After so many months of siege, they still had faith. Had they already forgotten the words of General Morillon: "I will never abandon you."? True, he had been gallant, Morillon, but he was soon gone. Now, from New York, the diplomats and politicians of many nations gazed on Srebrenica, imagined the horror that might come when the Serbs overran the town and moved to protect it—but only with words. They looked on the doomed town of Srebrenica—and on its eastern neighbors Gorazde, Tuzla, Zepa, and also the "pocket" of Bihac—and christened them with the golden words: "safe areas."

To "oppose any aggression" on the new safe areas, according to the official French estimate, 40,000 peacekeeping troops would be required. (The United Nations Secretary General later reduced that number to 37,000 soldiers.) And yet few nations, after having uttered the magic words "safe areas" and raised their hands proudly to vote, proved willing to risk their troops. To "oppose any aggression" from the forces of General Ratko Mladic, Srebrenica would be provided not with tens of thousands of troops but with 140 lightly armed Canadians. A year later the Canadians were relieved by 570 Dutchmen. The other five designated enclaves and, eventually, Sarajevo, would be offered little more. In the end, in place of the Secretary General's 37,000 soldiers protecting the enclaves, no more than a few thousand soldiers could be scraped up, a number that could do little to "protect" anyone. "Without secure logistics lines and a large UN presence the isolated enclaves in eastern Bosnia would be indefensible," writes James Gow.

> They would therefore be no more than symbolically "safe" at the same time as they were hostages to fortune. This placed the UN on the hook. . . . First, the Security Council had made a commitment to protecting these areas; secondly, UNPROFOR was unable genuinely to deter attacks purely by a presence in the "safe areas"; thirdly, deterrence relied on the threat of using close air support to defend the troops, or possible air strikes, in response to bombardment of the areas; and fourthly, *the threat of using air power was neutralized by the vulnerability of the troops on the ground in those areas.* . . .(Emphasis added)[36]

In other words, the vulnerability to attack of the UN troops themselves meant that the threat of using aerial bombardment to protect the enclaves was in fact an empty one. As with the monitors outside the weapons' dumps in Sarajevo, United Nations troops would now serve mainly as potential hostages.

And just what were these "safe areas" that this handful of men were meant to "guard"? A United Nations relief officer gave this description:

> Violence, black-market activities, prostitution, theft are becoming the only activities of the population. Tensions are mounting between the majority refugee population and minority local population. As always the women, children, and elderly are most at risk. The enclave must now be recognized for what it is, namely a closed refugee camp of 50,000 persons without adequate facilities for more than about 15,000.[37]

"Safe havens" consisted of little more than words on scraps of official paper. If the powerful nations of the world were not prepared to add flesh to those words—to exercise their will and their power and somehow make them real—then they stood above that teeming, vulnerable refuge camp as little more than a cruel and cynical fiction.

New York Review of Books, December 18, 1997

Explosion in the Marketplace

I.

EARLY ONE UNSEASONABLY mild afternoon in February 1994, Sarajevans shed their heavy coats and hats and poured out into streets and markets, allowing themselves to forget, in the bright warming sun, that from artillery bunkers and snipers' nests dug into hills and mountains above the city, hunters stared down, tracking their prey. But the people of Sarajevo were not permitted to forget. As we cruised the city's streets in a small armored car, climbing, under a trembling, light-filled sky toward the Spanish Fort, signs fell abruptly into place: a sudden chaos of horns and screams and screeching tires; a blue van tearing by with one eye peering out from a shattered face, and, racing in its wake, a battered white Yugo with a smeared red handprint emblazoned on its door.

We turned and forced our way back, struggling to trace the source of this grim caravan. When a policeman bade us stop, we clambered out and trotted down cluttered streets, dodging and stumbling through jumbles of honking vehicles until we entered once more the tiny square where, the day before, we had edged our way through boisterous crowds, chatting with vendors behind bare wood tables that held the besieged city's paltry wares: handfuls of leeks and potatoes, plastic combs in garish pink and green, scatterings of loose nuts and bolts, a blackened bit of banana, a monkey wrench half-rusted, glinting fitfully in the beneficent sun.

Twenty-four hours later the Markela—the marketplace—stood precisely so, when, at 12:37 on February 5, 1994, a 120-millimeter mortar shell plunged earthward in an impossibly perfect trajectory, plummeted within view of the somber gray façade of the Catholic cathedral and by the windows of gray apartment buildings, passed through the market's ramshackle metal roof and erupted, its five pounds of high explosive spewing out red-hot shrapnel and sending corrugated metal shards slicing through the crowd; in an eye-blink a thick forest of chattering, gossiping, bartering people had been cut down.

Now, turning into the tiny square, we found not infernal smoke or darkness but, amid a terrible clarity, clumps of dark bundles strewn about the asphalt, and, between them, spreading slowly amid shards of charred metal and blackened vegetables and bits of plastic, puddles of slick, dark liquid.

We stepped gingerly forward, letting pass two men dragging a limp, softly moaning figure. Before us men moved from bundle to bundle, crouching, pressing fingers to a throat, pausing, pushing back an eyelid, staring. I left the curb, feeling my throat constrict as I passed into a cloud of invisible and nauseating cordite. Slipping and stumbling against a car, I looked down and saw my boot soles already shiny and slick.

A big man danced quickly by me, hoisting the video camera on his shoulder, and close at his back came sound, craning his silver boom forward over the cameraman's head so that the two together appeared like some great rapacious bird. I placed my hand on the sound man's back and followed step by careful step,[1] and we three passed through the bloody topography, tracing our way slowly past torsos and parts of torsos, past arms and hands and bits of limbs and unidentifiable hunks of flesh, all mixed with blackened metal and smashed vegetables and, here and there, a long splinter of wooden table. At the center of it all, a man in a dark overcoat lay on his back, fully intact, face perfectly gray, eyes perfectly empty, staring blankly up at the perfect sky.

I gripped my pen and notebook and looked about me, somewhat bewildered. Here and there I recognized, or thought I did, vendors I had chatted with the day before; some artilleryman on one of those mountainsides had made objects of them now, exhibits for us and for the evening news. I tried to tally the corpses, matching limbs to trunks, heads to limbs, counting, counting; but it was impossible. In the back of the market, three blank-faced men worked with black-gloved hands behind a decrepit truck, crouching, lifting, heaving. As I approached I realized they were trying to match up parts of bodies on long pieces of corrugated metal; by now the truckbed was half full and its tires and undercarriage were thick with gore.

Turning back I saw a big, mustached man weeping, his hands raised and grasping the air as he struggled to reach a blood-soaked bundle of cloth and flesh on the ground; two smaller men held him, murmuring softly to him, working to push him back. As the mustached face, red and distorted and full of fury, rose above the shoulders of those imprisoning him, I realized that I had chatted with him the day before, that he had been selling . . . . . . what? Yes, lentils, that was it, lentils and potatoes, and his wife, now eviscerated at his feet, had stood at his side. Now he lifted his great head, stared upward, and, raising a fist, began to shout. Along with several others, I followed his gaze and picked out the glinting specks in the bright blue sky: the planes of NATO, patrolling over the "safe area" of Sarajevo.

Amid the human wreckage of this sun-filled square, what could the phrase possibly mean? Since United Nations diplomats had coined it the previous spring, no one had quite known. Now, amid the stench of cordite in Sarajevo's

Markela, the world had at last been offered the hint of a definition: "safe area" meant very little. It was a pretense—a policy of gesture, made solely of words.

Now large glass lenses—more and more of them bobbing and glinting as ever more cameramen pushed their way into the tiny square—would make those words flesh. A few hundred miles away Germans and French would press a button on a remote control and confront overwhelming gore; across the ocean Americans, with (presumably) more delicate sensibilities, would be permitted to see much less, but enough blood would remain for many of these citizens to pose a heartfelt if ephemeral question: Why is nothing being done about this?

Though the Serbs had shelled Sarajevo for nearly two years; though they had destroyed the National Library, burning hundreds of thousands of books, and had methodically reduced to ruins many of the city's other cultural treasures; though they had cut off electricity and water, forcing Sarajevans to place themselves in snipers' telescopic sights as they chopped down every tree in every park in search of firewood and stood in line filling plastic bottles at outdoor water spigots—though the Serbs had killed and wounded thousands of Sarajevans from their bunkers in the hills and from their snipers' nests in the burned out high-rise buildings that lined "sniper's alley," after two years of siege only "an event" like the "Marketplace Massacre" had a chance of engaging the fickle attention of the world. The day before, the Serbs had launched three shells into the Dobrinja neighborhood, killing ten Sarajevans as they waited for food; twelve days before, two Serb shells had blown apart six children as they sledded in the filthy snow. How many days of such steady, methodical killing would be needed to match the marketplace's toll? Six? Seven? And yet such daily work, however deadly, didn't matter, for depending on the news in New York or London or Paris, it did not rise to the level of "massacre."

I stood in the morgue across the road from Kosevo Hospital. Compared to the bloodslick ground of the Markela, compared even to the hospital entrance—a hellhole with shattered figures dead and dying in the hallways and a doctor, face brightly flushed, furious, screaming at us ("Get out, get out, I said. Let us do our work!")—compared to that, it was quiet here, peaceful. I found myself alone for the first time that day. Alone with those who had suddenly become the most important actors in the Bosnia drama. It was they who had forced reluctant politicians and diplomats to come together—even now in Washington and Brussels and Paris they were gathering for urgent talks—and they who in the next few days would change the direction of the war. And yet they had done nothing more than thousands of Sarajevans before them: stood in a particular place at a particular time and, all unknowingly, found a sudden and unforeseen death.

I took out my notebook, drew a deep breath, and began to count. It was easier now, all had been properly arranged, what limbs and parts remained had been matched up by people well practiced in such things. Twenty-one, twenty-two, twenty-three . . . Yes, this was a big story, perhaps the biggest of the war. Thirty-one, thirty-two . . . Yes, a huge story. . . .

II.

"Many had ice in their ears."

"What? Excuse me?"

"Ice. They had ice in their ears," said Dr. Radovan Karadzic, psychiatrist, poet, businessman, leader of the Bosnian Serbs, as he prepared to take another bite of stew. "You know, the Muslims—they took bodies from the morgue and they put them there, in the market. Even when they shell themselves like this, no one shell kills that many. So they went to the morgue. . . . "

I was—and not for the first time during our lunch—left speechless. Dr. Karadzic, clearly a very intelligent man, had mastered the fine art of constructing and delivering with great sincerity utterances that seemed so distant from demonstrable reality that he left no common ground on which to contradict him. *Ice in their ears?* Muslim intelligence officers stealing into the morgue to snatch corpses, secreting them in cars, setting off a bomb in the marketplace, and in the smoke and confusion leaving the frozen corpses strewn about the asphalt: It seemed an absurd idea. My memories of the gore of the Markela, only two days before, were precise and vivid. And yet I found myself thinking of the man in the overcoat lying on his back, staring upward, open-eyed. His face was peculiarly gray. Strange he bore no evident wounds. . . . Ice in his ears? No. No, of course not.

Dr. Karadzic watched me, lightly smiled, took a bite of stew, and chewed heartily. He was a hearty man, enormous, wide as the side of a barn and standing six foot four. In fact, he appeared taller than that, and this is clearly owing to the trademark hair. The hair is huge and sweeping and all-encompassing. It seems to be emerging from everywhere, head, forehead, ears, nose, in a kind of riot of power and fertility. And indeed, though he lived in Sarajevo thirty years, took his psychiatric degree at the university, and practiced in Kosevo Hospital, when he wasn't studying medicine and dabbling in poetry for a year in New York; though he recited and sang his poetry in the cafés and bars of that most cosmopolitan of cities, the Bosnian capital, Radovan Karadzic was in fact a man of the mountains, from a small and rough Montenegrin village.

"He has a sense of grandiosity, like many mountain people—look at the Scots, say," said Dr. Ismet Ceric, the chief of psychiatry at Kosevo Hospital who had largely trained Karadzic and had been his close friend for twenty-five years. "People from the mountains—Milosevic is Montenegrin too, you know, both his parents come from there—these mountain people come down here fresh and strong, and they see city people as soft and corrupt."

In many ways, that theme—fresh, pure, hardy people descending from the mountains and from the countryside to take their revenge on the soft, corrupt cosmopolitans of the cities—had marked the conflict from the beginning. During the 1950s and '60s, the traditional Muslim gentry, deracinated by Tito's land reforms, had migrated to the cities, particularly

Sarajevo, where they joined an already well-established secular Muslim intelligentsia. As Ed Vulliamy writes in *Seasons in Hell*,

> When Bosnians (usually Muslims, nowadays) tell you that all three people lived together without regard to ethnic groups, they are by and large telling the truth. But . . . while the towns and cities were nonchalant arenas for the practice of multi-ethnic Bosnia, everyday life in the countryside was one in which Muslims, Serbs and Croats were more insular. The Second World War in Bosnia had been driven by undercurrents of civil war and in the villages, peasants who had fought on all sides, and in particular the Serbs, made sure to keep their weapons. For them, the war had not yet ended; it was a question of waiting for the right moment to recommence it.[2]

Later, during the 1960s and '70s, many Serbs also moved to the cities, drawn by jobs in Tito's factories; but many remained ill at ease and distrustful there. To these Serbs, those of the countryside and those who had taken uneasy root in the cities, the bloodbath carried out by the Croat fascist forces, the *Ustashe*, in the early 1940s remained very fresh, for almost all of them had lost family members in it. All Serbs could recite stories of the Croat-run concentration camp at Jasenovac, on the Bosnian border, where a hundred thousand or more Serbs were murdered; all could tell of massacres of Serbs like the one at Omarska (now become notorious as the site of the Serb-run concentration camp) and all could instruct a visitor by relating an anecdote about Ante Pavelic, Croatia's Nazi-puppet dictator (as told here by the Italian war correspondent and novelist Curzio Malaparte):

> . . . I gazed at a wicker basket on [Pavelic's] desk. The lid was raised and the basket seemed to be filled with mussels, or shelled oysters—as they are occasionally displayed in the windows of Fortnum and Mason in Piccadilly in London. [Italian minister Raffaele] Casertano looked at me and winked, "Would you like a nice oyster stew?"
> "Are they Dalmatian oysters?" I asked.
> Ante Pavelic removed the lid from the basket and revealed the mussels, that slimy and jelly-like mass, and he said smiling, with that tired good-natured smile of his, "It is a present from my loyal Ustashis. Forty pounds of human eyes."[3]

Many Serbs were well prepared for Belgrade's inescapable and incessant propaganda that marked President Franjo Tudjman and his Croats as a reborn Ustashes eager to recommence the work of massacre and annihilation of Serbs, and portrayed the Muslims both as the Croats' eager henchmen and as "Turks" determined to create an exclusivist "Islamic Republic" in the heart of Europe. And that deeply instilled suspicion and fear is partly why—when thousands of Sarajevans marched for peace in the first days of

April 1992, moving in a great river through the city toward the Holiday Inn, that impossibly ugly yellow box of a building where Dr. Karadzic had installed Serbian Democratic Party offices, and Dr. Karadzic's bodyguards climbed to the roof and began firing into the crowd, killing six people— that is why sixty thousand Serbs fled the city, almost all of them relatively recent arrivals who had come to enjoy the riches the city offered but still distrusted its sophisticated ways.

Some of these Serbs would enlist in the Bosnian Serb Army and take their places on the mountainsides, living in the tiny log cabins with their tiny wisps of cooking smoke that marked each artillery emplacement, and spending their days gazing, over the barrel of a cannon, at the beautiful city that had once welcomed them.

Radovan Karadzic, a well-traveled man who had broad and cosmopolitan interests, among them a devotion to American poetry, would seem to have little in common with such men. True, he had been born in 1945 into the violent postwar world of peasant Montenegro; his father had fought as a Chetnik, a Serbian nationalist guerrilla, and served time in Tito's prisons. During our conversation, the war Karadzic presided over from his Pale office and the slaughters of a half-century before often blended together.

"The Serbs did not invent ethnic cleansing," he told me, several times. "The Croats did, in World War II. When Tudjman and Izetbegovic formed a [Croat-Muslim] alliance, all Serbs were frightened to death that the same would happen as during the war, when hundreds of thousands of innocent Serbs were slaughtered."

This was true, at least in part: Karadzic well understood, as Goebbels did, that any effective propaganda must have within it a kernel of truth. But memories were only the beginning, necessary but not sufficient. Nationalist leaders like Milosevic, Tudjman, and Karadzic, as former U.S. ambassador to Yugoslavia Warren Zimmermann pointed out, could only "turn many normal people toward extremism by playing on their historic fears through the baleful medium of television, a matchless technological tool in the hands of dictators."

> The nationalist media sought to terrify by evoking mass murderers of a bygone time. The Croatian press described Serbs as "Cetniks." . . . For the Serbian press Croatians were "Ustase" (and later, Muslims became "Turks"). People who think they're under ethnic threat tend to seek refuge in their ethnic group. Thus did the media's terror campaign establish ethnic solidarity on the basis of an enemy to be both hated and feared.[4]

At the time Karadzic and I spoke, in early February 1994, the so-called historic Croat-Muslim alliance which had "frightened all the Serbs to death" had largely collapsed; Bosnian Croats and Muslims had fought one another bitterly in Mostar, Vitez, and elsewhere. Croat troops had seized Bosnians who had battled at their sides against the Serbs and had forced them, together with Muslims "cleansed" from west Mostar, Capljina, Stolae, and other villages, into concentration camps whose brutality rivaled that of Omarska. In September 1993, Ed Vulliamy visited prisoners kept underground at the Croatian camp at Dretelj:

> Their huge burning eyes, cropped heads and shriveled, sickly torsos emerged only as one became accustomed to the darkness: hundreds of men, some of them gaunt and horribly thin, crammed like factory farm beasts into the stinking, putrid spaces of two large underground storage hangars built into the hillside. . . . This infernal tunnel had been their hideous home for ten weeks now. . . .
>
> At the back of the hangars, the walls were pockmarked with bullet-holes. . . . Prisoners talked about Croatian guards coming up to the hangar doors after drinking sessions and singing as they fired into their quarters. . . . Estimates of the number of dead on these occasions ranged from three to ten.[5]

However much Karadzic insisted on the continuity of today's conflict with that of the early 1940s, he never seemed convincing, or to have convinced himself. For Karadzic's entire life had followed the opposite path: He had escaped from the past, fleeing the dark insular country for the cosmopolitan light of Sarajevo. Izeta Bajramovic, who ran a corner sweet shop, described the young Karadzic to a *Los Angeles Times* reporter as an awkward kid with a messy head of hair who used to hang around waiting for free pieces of baklava. "He was skinny, hairy and shy, very, very shy," she recalled. "I used to feel sorry for him. He was provincial, a typical peasant lost in the big city."

Many recall that he wore every day the same dirty white sweater, made from the wool of his native village, and that even then, his big head of hair set him apart. "He had a hillbilly kind of haircut, very fashionable in his village," recalled Mohamed Dedajic, the neighborhood barber. "When I tried to make a suggestion, he'd say, 'No, no, I like long hair.'"[6]

Perhaps he thought his Byronic locks appropriate to a great poet, for if one theme arises again and again in conversations about the younger Karadzic it is the breadth of his ambition, his single-minded determination to achieve greatness. "He told me he was the great poet of Serbian history," said Dr. Ceric, "I told him, 'I know ten here in Sarajevo who are better than you and maybe seven hundred in Belgrade.' He hardly reacted. He said, 'Well, I have three books out already and soon [my reputation] is going to go: boom!'"

"But it was the same with his psychiatry," said Ceric. "He was good, but not excellent. He had many ideas but to be excellent you must follow one way, have one thought. He had many other interests—soccer, poetry, business—that took too much of his time."

Karadzic married a psychoanalyst, the daughter of an old and well-to-do Serb family. Among his poet friends, his bride was not popular; they thought her unattractive and domineering, and they assumed he married her so that, as one man told me, "the peasant could get some money." Soon he was appointed official psychiatrist to the Sarajevo soccer team, a prominent and desirable position, but unfortunately his pep talks on the psychology of confidence and winning seemed to bring the young players little success. Meantime his face and hair became familiar to Sarajevans as he doggedly read his poems on television and radio and at the cafés. Still, however much he had tried, as Ceric told me, "His reputation among his colleagues remained relatively low."

One can see a traditional plot taking shape here: ambitious and idealistic country boy arrives in the glittering city, struggles desperately to make good, but succeeds only in earning the laughter and contempt of the cosmopolitan intellectuals he longs to impress; and so he climbs back up the mountainside, rejoins the "clean and pure" fellow peasants, and takes his revenge. It is a convenient story, particularly when one glances at the façades of Karadzic's old apartment house—his name remains on the bell—and of Kosevo Hospital, and notes the pockmarks from shells launched by the guns of Karadzic's men, emplaced just below his Pale chalet-office where we spoke. Several Sarajevans told me how the psychiatrist-poet, during a reading, had been laughed and jeered off the stage, how he had fled cursing and red-faced and resentful; but none could say where the event had taken place, or when. In his memoir, *The Tenth Circle of Hell*, Rezak Hukanovic writes of the planning for the Serb concentration camps:

> And where on earth was the poisonous game conceived? In the head of that bloodthirsty lyricist, the mad psychiatrist from Sarajevo, Radovan Karadzic. Years before, clearly spelling out the evil to come, he had written: "Take no pity let's go/ kill that scum down in the city."[7]

But the poem, written in 1971 and entitled "Let's Go Down to the Town and Kill Some Scum," seems clearly to have been an attempt to capture the feelings of Yugoslav peasants and was understood as such at the time. To read into it a secret program for wholesale extermination on the part of the author, a kind of *Mein Kampf* in verse, is to assume an intent for which there is little evidence. As Dr. Ceric told me, echoing many who knew Karadzic well,

> Radovan had a cosmopolitan approach to problems. You never felt he was a Serb, never. You never felt he was a religious man. I remain quite sure to this day that he is absolutely atheistic. A lot of his friends were Muslims. He was, in fact, a very typical man of this multicultural environment.

His neighborhood was fully integrated; Serbs, Croats, and Muslims occupied apartments in his building; Alija Izetbegovic, who was to be independent Bosnia's first president, lived around the corner. A Muslim stood as godfather to Karadzic's son. Even as his guns destroyed it—two days, indeed, after a shell had killed sixty-eight people who were shopping in the sunshine of the public marketplace—Dr. Karadzic spoke warmly of his city. "I liked very much living in Sarajevo," he told me. "It was very pleasant there. Culturally, the city looked more toward the West. At that time too, before the war, even Muslims felt more Serb than Muslim. Of course, that is what they are: Serbs who became Muslim under the Turks. Many of them identified themselves only as Yugoslavs, because religion was much less important than national unity."

Then came 1989, and Milosevic's fiery speech at the field of Kosovo, virtually threatening war; and the rise in Croatia and in Bosnia of nationalist parties under Tudjman and Izetbegovic. Radovan Karadzic, ever ambitious, ever searching for a means to achieve greatness, saw his chance and entered politics. One can gauge the depth of his nationalism by the fact that he first joined the Green Party. Only later did he transfer his loyalties to the Initiative for a Serbian Democratic Party, which Milosevic had started as a Bosnian vehicle to advance his program to achieve a Greater Serbia: "All Serbs in one nation." The embryonic party consisted of little more than a collection of bullies and thugs, and Karadzic, standing out as a well-known and cultured man, rose quickly. In July 1990, his new colleagues chose Dr. Radovan Karadzic, psychiatrist, poet, fledgling politician, to lead the now-official Serbian Democratic Party.

It was, as Dr. Ceric told me, echoing a comment I heard a dozen times, "a very big surprise." But though his Sarajevo acquaintances expressed bewilderment at "what happened to Radovan when the war started," by now the logic of his transformation takes on a certain clarity. If one constant in his life was great ambition, a fierce and unremitting conviction that he was in some way destined for greatness, another was a relative disregard for the means by which he would achieve it. A great doctor, an innovative psychiatrist, a celebrated poet: By 1990, none of these paths had yet carried him to triumph. Though he had not lost faith, he was impatient, unwilling to wait for the recognition of his genius. He recognized that politics in the era of Yugoslavia's dissolution might offer him instant greatness; and that untrammeled ambition, unencumbered as it was by any true principle—for Karadzic ideology resulted from ambition, it did not cause it—could not help but make him attractive to a great political manipulator like Milosevic. As Marko Vesovic, a well-known Montenegrin writer who has known Karadzic since 1963, told *Time* magazine:

> In poetry and in life, Karadzic was a person without personality. He was like clay, without personality, without character, who could be molded. . . . The man of clay was [Milosevic's] ideal student. He did what he was told.[8]

Dr. Ceric, himself a Muslim, who was bewildered by Karadzic's abrupt conversion to nationalism, demanded that his close friend and protégé give him a reason for it.

I asked him, "What is the problem—what is the political problem that you are trying to solve?"

He said, "There is only one problem: Alija [Izetbegovic] wants to organize an Islamic Republic here. . . ."

I said, "This is completely stupid, because even if Alija did want to organize such a thing a majority of Muslims don't want it and wouldn't accept it. I mean, even now, after we've lost 200,000 people, the majority by far wouldn't accept an Islamic Republic."

Could Karadzic have somehow made himself believe what he said? "He may well have forced himself to believe," Dr. Ceric told me. "Radovan had some mechanism for falsification of reality, there is no question about it. No doubt now he believes he's right. But when he lies in bed at night, he's neurotic, he has many neurotic symptoms because of what has happened in this country."

Anyone who has spoken to Dr. Karadzic will recognize this "mechanism for falsification of reality" as his most distinctive quality. When I inquired of him, over our plates of beef stew, in his small office with an Orthodox crucifix on one wall and color-coded maps showing diplomatic plans for slicing up Bosnia on the other, about the siege of Sarajevo, the siege that people around the world had been watching in transfixed horror for almost two years, the leader of the Bosnian Serbs replied that there was no siege—that, in fact, those artillery pieces and mortars had been dug into the mountainside to keep the Muslim hordes from breaking out of the city and attacking the Serbs. As always with Karadzic, the words seemed so distant from reality that one had trouble mustering arguments to challenge him.

I asked him about the shelling of the National Library, whose broken, cluttered ruins I had visited a few days before, picking through the odd charred scraps of paper, the pitiful remains of hundreds of thousands of irreplaceable books and manuscripts. How could he, a man of learning and culture, a poet himself, have countenanced his gunners lobbing shell after shell into the great building, destroying it in a day in a great conflagration that left his adopted city canopied in a cloud of priceless ash? Dr. Karadzic could only shake his head sadly, stare gravely into my eyes, and declare that of course the Muslims had destroyed this building themselves: "It was a Christian building, you know, from the Austro-Hungarian period, and so the Muslims hated it. Only Christian books were burned, you know. The others they removed."

And so it was with the shells that had reduced the world-renowned Institute of Oriental Culture to a burned carcass; so it was with the mortar round that had plunged into a crowd waiting outside a bakery in a downtown street and killed sixteen people in the telegenic horror of the Breadline Massacre of May 27, 1992, which forced the Western countries to impose the first set of sanctions against the Serbs; so it was with the two shells that had killed six sledding children twelve days before the Markela, and the three shells that had killed ten Sarajevans and wounded eighteen in Dobrinja on February 4.

In each case, Dr. Karadzic told me, the Muslims, "trying to gain the sympathy of the world," had "shelled themselves."

There was a certain brilliance to his blank and impenetrable sincerity. I actually found myself wondering, as a young blond waitress cleared the dishes from Karadzic's desk, whether he could possibly believe anything he was saying. "Mechanism for falsification of reality"—that was Dr. Ceric's term. And yet this seemed insane: Karadzic visited his troops as they sat in their hillside bunkers, shaking their hands and clapping them on the back as they smoked their cigarettes and cooked their soup. In a BBC film about Karadzic, the leader of the Serbs smiles as he sights down a cannon barrel and then offers a Russian visitor, the nationalist writer Eduard Limonov, the chance to fire off a shell into Karadzic's former city. Limonov graciously accepts.[9]

I thought of Karadzic's bodyguards, who had been lounging about the lobby as I waited for the Great Man. The guards appeared to have been chosen in large part for their beauty and they were clearly conscious of it as they sauntered about, laughing and preening, some wearing combat fatigues, others distinctive purple jumpsuits, all with 9-millimeter automatic pistols belted tightly at their hips; they ignored me while watching me closely. Who could this be, granted an interview with the Big Man, the man who shelled the Turks?

And yet it was clear that the consistent and inarguable preposterousness of Karadzic's answers held within it an importance far beyond any press conference or interview, reaching into the complex diplomatic struggle of the war itself. He was in the business of creating excuses—excuses, however absurd, that let the world allow the war to go on. What he said admitted of no answer. Ice in their ears? How could I respond? I was there, the bodies were real, you can't be serious. And Dr. Karadzic would look me in the eye and answer in that reasonable tone: Yes, but did you check their ears? You didn't? So how can you be sure?

III.

I am finally lost,
I am glowing like a cigarette
On a neurotic's lip:
While they look for me everywhere
I wait in the ambush of dawn.

—from "A Morning Hand Grenade" (1983),
by Radovan Karadzic[10]

Two days before, four hours after the mortar shell plummeted through the corrugated tin of the marketplace, I had sat in the cluttered ABC News Sarajevo office and watched television. Sarajevo TV was airing its video of the massacre virtually unedited and I watched again each torso and limb float past me on the screen as the announcer's voice intoned: Nura Odzak, Mladen Klacar, Ahmed Foco, Sakib Bulbul, Alija Huko. . . . Disjunctive, disorienting somehow, to watch the bundles that had had no names now being supplied them, in an effort to return the objects to the world of the human.

Someone switched to Great Britain's *Sky News* just in time for us to hear the young woman reading the news announce that Dr. Radovan Karadzic had reacted with outrage to accusations that the Serbs had bombed the marketplace, had demanded the charge be withdrawn, and had vowed that, until it was, his soldiers would block all food deliveries into the city. This was a grave threat indeed—not because it might bring Sarajevo's malnourished citizens to the point of starvation, although it might, but because if the Serbs did not permit Western troops to make "humanitarian deliveries" to Bosnia's besieged people, Western leaders—having said again and again that NATO warplanes could not bomb Serb artillery because they had "troops on the ground" vulnerable to Serb retribution—would have difficulty explaining exactly what their suddenly idle troops were doing in Bosnia beyond providing the Western leaders an excuse for refraining from taking strong action to stop the war that, it had long since become clear, they greatly preferred not to take.

Indeed, in Washington, where President Clinton was even now meeting with his senior advisers, a process of reevaluation had already begun, for one of those advisers—we learned from the *Sky News* reader—had hastened to let it be known that "sentiment" was growing that NATO planes should in fact bomb the Serbs. Meantime the president himself had denounced the slaughter—and demanded the United Nations "urgently investigate" who was to blame. Having delivered herself of that bit of news, the newsreader looked into the camera and with practiced gravity delivered her closing line: "There is no report yet," she said, "on who could be the author of this terrible crime."

The absurdity of this statement seemed so palpable that I started, then looked around the room, speechless, to see others' reactions. No one flinched; they were used to it. Nor would they have been surprised to learn that at that very moment a Canadian major assigned to the United Nations forces was crouching in the northeast corner of the marketplace, hard at work examining the "splash pattern" left by the shrapnel in order to determine whence the shell had come. In fact, the Canadian major was working on no less than the third of the afternoon's "crater analyses," a French lieutenant having conducted the first at two o'clock, and a French captain a second an hour later. As it happened—and not surprisingly with what was a rather inexact science—results differed markedly: While the French lieutenant concluded that the shell had followed a northerly course, and thus either Serb or Muslim gunners could theoretically have launched it, and the Canadian major arrived, by a slightly different path, at largely the same conclusion, the French captain found that the round had followed an easterly path—which would have put the mortar and its crew behind Muslim lines.[11]

To an innocent eye, the entire exercise appeared bewildering. Sarajevo lay in a valley surrounded by mountains from which for nearly two years Serb artillery pieces—including a great number of 120-millimeter mortars—had day after day rained down shells. During twenty-two months, Serb gunners and snipers had launched hundreds of thousands of shells and bullets and had killed perhaps ten thousand Sarajevans. Yet when a shell happened to kill a large number of people, United Nations officials, acting in the full flower of their "neutral" appreciation of the interests of Serbs and Muslims, felt obliged to treat the explosive's source as "undetermined." As much as anything did, this decision demonstrated the symbiosis that had developed between the Serbs, who were winning the war and thus bringing Bosnia "peace," and the United Nations forces, who remained loyal only to the neutrality they must maintain in order to keep feeding the victims.

Karadzic with his apparently absurd statements had in fact read the situation with great brilliance. As Peter Maass well describes in his memoir *Love Thy Neighbor*, the Serb leader succeeded in creating doubt where there should have been none because people wanted to doubt.

I knew that the things Karadzic said were lies, and that these lies were being broadcast worldwide, every day, several times a day, and they were being taken seriously. I am not saying that his lies were accepted as the truth, but I sense they were obscuring the truth, causing outsiders to stay on the sidelines, and this of course was a great triumph for Karadzic.[12]

If Karadzic could not prove that the Bosnians were "shelling themselves," he did not need to; he needed only to present the idea and, once presented, to harp on it, again and again. As Maass writes,

He needed, for example, to make everyone question whether the Bosnians were bombing themselves, and in fact everyone did wonder about that, because each time a lot of Bosnians were killed by a mortar in Sarajevo, Western governments asked the UN soldiers for a "crater analysis." . . . The incoming direction of the shell could be determined, but not the precise position from which it was fired. If Karadzic denied responsibility, and if the United Nations could not prove scientifically that the Serbs were responsible, then we should hold off on punishing them, right? Right. Thankfully, we have not always been so circumspect, and did not demand, during World War II, that Winston Churchill provide proof that the bombs exploding in London were German rather than British.

IV.

By late afternoon Saturday, after workers in Sarajevo's morgues had assembled corpses as best they could, the Sarajevo anchorman was able to announce that sixty-eight people had died in the Markela—a horrendous number, yes, but a fraction of those who had died since the United Nations Security Council had declared Sarajevo a "safe area" eight months before.

These sixty-eight Sarajevans, however, had perished together in a bloody holocaust whose immediate aftermath television cameras were able to capture. As with the Breadline Massacre in May 1992, or the revelation of Omarska and Trnopolje and other Serb-run concentration camps three months later, the pictures framed by a tiny screen helped overcome for an instant the world's power to ignore what was happening in Bosnia. Western leaders, caught in a paralysis they had begun to find increasingly embarrassing, now felt the eyes of the world turned briefly but intensely upon them.

As it happened, for some Clinton officials the shell had struck the marketplace at a propitious time. For almost a year, as the Americans had been largely passive, these so-called "hardliners" had become increasingly unhappy. Vice President Al Gore, national security adviser Anthony Lake, and UN Representative Madeleine Albright, among others, had long lobbied for a more assertive policy. By the time of the Market Massacre, the "hardliners" had acquired powerful allies in the new French government of Jacques Chirac. On January 21, 1994, Foreign Minister Alain Juppé had met with Secretary of State Christopher in Paris and demanded that the Americans take a more assertive part in Bosnia. The day before the massacre, Christopher wrote Lake that he was "acutely uncomfortable with the passive position we are now in and believe that now is the time to undertake a new initiative."[13]

Had the shell never struck the Markela, no one can say how long it might have been before the Americans moved to a more assertive policy, or indeed if they ever would have. As it was, the brutal images helped France push for aggressive action; without them "it would have taken weeks or months," as Michael McCurry, Christopher's spokesman, conceded. "The impact of the marketplace bombing . . . was to force there to be a response much quicker than the U.S. government" could normally produce.[14]

That response was a decision, taken with the French, to deliver an ultimatum to the Serbs: if they did not within ten days move their heavy weapons to sites outside an "exclusion zone"—in effect, a demilitarized zone—twenty kilometers from the center of Sarajevo, NATO fighter planes would attack the artillery emplacements and destroy them. This unprecedented ultimatum was to have unexpectedly far-reaching effects, not only for Sarajevo itself but for all of Bosnia—and for the thousands of men of Srebrenica.

V.

A few evenings after the shell landed in the marketplace, as Western foreign ministers prepared to meet at NATO headquarters in Brussels and the commander of the United Nations Protection Forces in Sarajevo, Lt. General Sir Michael Rose, labored to bring about a cease-fire—and thus, he hoped, avoid retaliatory NATO air strikes—I sat with three young Serb acquaintances in a living room in Pale, the capital of "Republica Srpska"—the unrecognized and unofficial "Serbian Republic" of Bosnia—and watched a two-hour television "special" on the bombing. TV Pale—an institution cobbled together largely out of stolen BBC equipment—had outdone itself. In a predominantly pink studio, an anchorman sauntered back and forth, Phil Donohue style, interviewing a panel of experts, several of them military officers who had brought with them drawings, charts, and graphs.

An artillery officer, his chest festooned with medals and ribbons, tapped a wooden pointer here and there on a diagram of the marketplace on which figures of the dead and wounded had been outlined in heavy black ink. "Those closest to the impact—here, here, and here—would have absorbed most of the shrapnel," he explained. "No mortar, therefore, could have done such damage." A scientific type wearing a black suit then displayed a chart on which seven or eight trajectories had been drawn and demonstrated, pointing with his pencil, how it was impossible that a mortar could have landed in that square—which was, after all, tiny (100 feet by 164 feet) and sheltered on two sides by seven-and eight-story buildings. And even had it been a mortar it must have come—here a map and a new chart were brought out—from a Muslim position. And in any case—we then saw a videotape of the Breadline Massacre in 1992 and several more charts—everyone knew the Muslims had done such things many times before.[15]

My Serb friends, sitting on the carpet beside me and nodding eagerly, were fully convinced, which did not surprise me. They were, however, not alone. The day after the bombing, David Owen, the European Union negotiator, had met with Dr. Karadzic in Zvornik to get him to agree to "a separate political and military peace agreement involving Sarajevo district." Lord Owen found Dr. Karadzic "very angry" about, among other things, reports that he would be presented with an "ultimatum."

> It was the emotive word used by the Germans before the bombing of Belgrade in 1941. Karadzic was vehement in denying that his forces had fired a mortar bomb into the marketplace and claimed that it had been done by the Muslims.

As for Lord Owen, he was sympathetic:

> Having now been exposed for eighteen months to the three parties' claims and counter-claims I was capable of believing that any of them could have been responsible.[16]

Though he doesn't say so in his book, Lord Owen had by this time become much more than "capable" of believing either side might have fired the shell. Owen, as he drove to meet Karadzic, had heard a radio interview with General Rose in which the UNPROFOR commander gave "the impression that the possibility that the bomb had not been fired by the Serbs had not even crossed his mind." As Owen told journalists Laura Silber and Allan Little,

I thought to myself "Blimey, he better be told a few things," and I made a quick phone call to the Ministry of Defense. . . . I hope the message got across.[17]

Clearly it did. For while the diplomats were drafting their ultimatum General Rose was working intensely to negotiate a cease-fire. For him NATO bombing would be a disaster. It was General Rose who commanded the "troops on the ground" and, he knew that from the moment the first NATO warplane dropped the first bomb, these troops would be transformed in the eyes of the Serbs from peacekeepers to warriors. As he explained it in a later interview,

When you deploy a peacekeeping force, you are excluding the war-fighting option. You're putting small groups of lightly armed people throughout the entire length and breadth of a land, delivering humanitarian aid, permanently exposed, permanently at risk—and, of course, from that basis, you would not possibly go and fight a war.

And therefore the option is there to go and fight a war, but you don't do it after you've deployed a peacekeeping force. You do it before; or you withdraw that force. . . . You cannot mix the two functions. The more force you use, the less receptive people are to your presence. Our mission is to sustain the people of this country. If the Bosnian Serbs withdrew their consent to our presence, we would have to leave. [18]

Even as the Western ministers in Brussels argued over the wording of their ultimatum, General Rose waited at the Sarajevo airport for Serb and Bosnian officers. But though the Serbs arrived, the Bosnians did not. The Serbs hoped the agreement Rose offered would allow them to avoid NATO bombing while saving face; but for that they needed Rose to force the Muslims to make concessions as well. Izetbegovic and his colleagues, on the other hand, hoped the marketplace bombing and the world sympathy that followed it would bring them what they had struggled for since the beginning of the war: the active military support of the West. They did not intend to let General Rose deprive them of it.

In a fury, General Rose—a dynamic and celebrated officer who had commanded Britain's elite commando unit, the Strategic Air Services—set out for the president's offices, where Izetbegovic was being interviewed by CNN. The general stalked in, and threatened, according to General Jovan Divjak, deputy commander of the Bosnian army, who was present, to "inform the international public . . . that we [the Bosnians] would be responsible for the continuation of the conflict, and that the Serb side had agreed to negotiate and that we had refused."[19]

At this point, according to senior UNPROFOR officers present, the general took out an envelope, showed it to Divjak and Izetbegovic, and said, "I have an allegation here" about the marketplace bombing. Apparently it was the second crater analysis—the one by the French captain, which implicated the Muslims. Aghast, President Izetbegovic apologized to Rose and immediately sent General Divjak and the other members of the delegation to the airport. Very shortly thereafter they agreed on a cease-fire.

As it happened, rumors that the Muslims had carried out the Marketplace Massacre were already widespread. As usual, Dr. Karadzic's determined hectoring had borne fruit. And it wasn't only Karadzic. Tanjug, the Yugoslav press agency, published a report datelined February 8 asserting that the shell was launched from "1 to 1.5 km. inside the territory under Muslim control" and attributing the story to "highly reliable and confidential sources within UNPROFOR" headquarters.[20] For General Rose and for other United Nations officers, the interests of the protection force were clearly paramount.

VI.

As darkness fell over Sarajevo on February 21, 1994, Serb tanks and cannons and mortars began moving slowly down off the mountainsides. Many of these heavy weapons were on their way to "collection areas" that were to be established in Serb-held territory and "monitored" by French, Russian, and Ukrainian peacekeepers. General Ratko Mladic and Dr. Radovan Karadzic, confronted by the threat of bombing by the warplanes of the West, had backed down. For President Izetbegovic and his Bosnian Muslims, it should have been a triumph.

It was not. For ten days the Serbs had stood defiant, ignoring the ultimatum, until British Prime Minister John Major—General Rose's true boss—had flown to Moscow and sought the intervention of Russian President Boris Yeltsin. With Major at his side, Yeltsin had angrily denounced the West's attempt to intervene in the Balkans without Russia's consent—the West had issued their ultimatum through NATO, not the United Nations, thus avoiding a possible Russian veto. Yeltsin then sent a message to Dr. Karadzic, offering to send Russian peacekeepers to protect Serb neighborhoods and to watch over Serb weapons.

As Russians rumbled into Sarajevo aboard their armored personnel carriers, Serbs cheered. Russians, their traditional allies, would defend them from the hordes of Bosnian infantry seeking to break through the lines at Sarajevo. In effect, UN peacekeeping troops themselves would help the Serbs partition Sarajevo, a goal Dr. Karadzic had sought since early in the war ("It can be like Beirut," he told me), when it had become clear that conquering the city would be impossible. Finally, the prospect of NATO warplanes swooping down to bomb and strafe Serb artillery positions—which a week before had seemed so real—had become more improbable than ever. How could NATO pilots drop their bombs while Russian soldiers patrolled Serb neighborhoods? Even more important, how could they bomb while small groups of lightly armed French and Ukrainian and Russian troops patrolled weapons "collection areas" on Serb territory, in constant risk of being taken hostage by angry Serb soldiers?

Dr. Karadzic, denounced by the world as the killer of the Markela, had brilliantly played on the divisions of the West—the newly aggressive French and Americans, the ever reluctant British, the resentful Russians—to turn what could have been a disaster into a triumph. He had emerged from the Marketplace Massacre stronger than before. President Izetbegovic, having seen the Western military support the Muslims had so long sought almost within his grasp, now found himself frustrated and humiliated, and trapped within a Sarajevo that was even less likely now to see those silver planes do anything more than circle overhead. In the end, the Marketplace Massacre crisis had imposed on Sarajevo many of the contradictions that for almost a year had plagued Srebrenica and the other so-called "safe areas" of eastern Bosnia.

VII.

On May 22, 1995, fifteen months after Bosnian Serbs had withdrawn their tanks and cannons and mortars from the mountains and ridges above the city, heavily armed Serb soldiers in camouflage uniforms forced their way into a United Nations "weapons collection point" and, strolling like leisurely weekend shoppers among the artillery pieces and armored vehicles, picking out from the tempting array two cannons. Laughing off the protests of humiliated French UN "blue helmets" charged with "monitoring" the weapons, the Serbs hitched them up to their trucks and drove out of the gate.

The following day, Serb troops visited other "collection points" and made off with more weapons. On the day after that, General Ratko Mladic ordered his rearmed and repositioned artillerymen to unleash on Sarajevo a merciless barrage, and they complied by battering the city with nearly three thousand shells. Some were fired from cannons and mortars they hadn't even bothered to remove from the charge of the "blue helmets"; the Serb troops took pleasure in destroying the city shell by shell from under the noses of those who were meant to protect it.

On May 24, Lieutenant General Rupert Smith, the unusually imaginative and strong-willed British officer who in February had succeeded General Rose as commander of United Nations ground troops in Bosnia, announced another, more pointed ultimatum. If the Serbs did not cease firing on Sarajevo, NATO fighter planes would attack them the following day. And when the Serbs, as was their custom, contemptuously ignored the United Nations order, General Smith startled General Mladic and much of the rest of the world by doing what everyone least expected: He sent NATO planes to attack.

Nor did he send them to drop a bomb or two on some isolated mortar or tank—the kind of timid and vaguely risible "pinprick" response that the hapless General Rose, on the few occasions he found himself unable to avoid ordering air attacks, had favored. To the intense annoyance and embarrassment of General Mladic, General Smith had the temerity to send his NATO fighter planes swooping down at 4:20 in the afternoon to bomb two ammunition bunkers near the Serbs' so-called "capital" of Pale, right in self-declared Serb President Radovan Karadzic's backyard.

The furious General Mladic immediately got on the radio and ordered his soldiers, perched as they were on the hills and ridges surrounding all six of the United Nations–designated "safe areas"—Bihac, Gorazde, Tuzla, Zepa, Srebrenica, and Sarajevo itself—to unleash their guns on the towns, and this, with the exception of Zepa, they promptly did. They pounded the Srebrenica city center with half a dozen well-placed rounds and lofted into Tuzla a mortar shell that exploded among a crowd of young people who were hanging out on a cobblestone street in front of a popular pizza joint, killing seventy-five teenagers (whose shattered remains went unobserved by any television camera).

General Smith didn't hesitate: At half past ten the following morning, he sent NATO warplanes back to Pale to bomb the remaining six bunkers in the depot. And, with that, General Mladic ordered his Bosnian Serb soldiers to take a step anticipated by virtually all the international leaders involved in Bosnia—UN special envoy Yasushi Akashi; his military commander, French General Bernard Janvier; President Bill Clinton and the leaders of Great Britain, France, and other allied powers, as well as General Smith himself. Mladic ordered his soldiers to surround the outgunned and outnumbered United Nations troops and take them hostage. Within hours people around the world were turning on their television sets to see the soldiers of France, Britain, and various other proud Western countries chained to hangars, ammunition depots, bridges, and other strategic targets that NATO might be tempted to bomb. "It is not us who will carry out the executions," one of Dr. Karadzic's advisers warned reporters, "but NATO."

As Tim Judah pointed out, this vivid display was in large part a well-planned, camera-ready propaganda exercise:

> In fact many of the prisoners had been chained up only during the filming. One was teased later as he drank beer with his guards who said that he had caught a suntan while being forced to pose. The propaganda value of such clips was obvious—its commercial value was even greater. Dragan Bozanic, the political editor of TV-Pale, had sold the film in an auction to the international news agencies with offices in Pale.[21]

Not for the first time Bosnia had become a hall of mirrors. For despite the teasing over suntans Bosnian Serb soldiers had indeed taken prisoner some 374 United Nations troops, and even as his men drank beer and laughed with the "blue helmets" General Ratko Mladic was loudly vowing to execute them if General Smith again sent his planes to attack.

This "UN hostage crisis," as the press inevitably christened it, was surely the most anticipated and long-awaited crisis in the history of the war, for its politically intimidating specter had dominated the imaginations of Western policymakers since their troops had arrived, under United Nations aegis, without adequate arms and without a clearly defined mission, to begin accompanying "humanitarian shipments" in late 1992.

Now, Smith was determined to call Mladic's bluff and, by so doing, to destroy the "air strike–hostage" cycle that was paralyzing Western policy in Bosnia. Smith proposed, as he put it, to "break the machine." The UN general's attempt to do so brought clearly into the open the tangle of public posturing and private reluctance and fear that lay at the heart of Western policy in Bosnia.

Less than three months before, during the first weekend in March, Dr. Karadzic and the unusual group of intellectual-politicians who were his political colleagues (including Vice President Nikola Koljevic, the ardent Shakespeare scholar, and Biljana Plavsic, the biologist who delighted in seeing her image painted on Serbian tanks), together with the camouflage-garbed General Mladic and his highest staff and intelligence officers, had welcomed to the resort hotel on the snowy heights of Mount Jahorina their counterparts and longtime sponsors from Belgrade for two days of serious discussion. Despite the beauty of their surroundings—it was down Jahorina's steep slopes that, a mere decade before, the greatest skiers had plunged, battling among themselves, as the world watched, for Olympic medals—Serb leaders from both sides of the Drina found themselves in a less than triumphant mood.

When, three years before, on March 27, 1992, the officers of the national Yugoslav Peoples Army had launched their intricate, minutely planned campaign to dismember Bosnia, the Serbs had counted on a short, intense, and successful war—and indeed they had managed, during six weeks of bombarding undefended cities and towns with tanks and heavy artillery, to seize and occupy nearly 70 percent of Bosnian territory. By the end of May 1992 they had conquered all but Bihac, Sarajevo, and the eastern enclaves of Tuzla, Cerska, Zepa, and Srenbrenica. They turned now to "cleansing" their conquered territory and by the end of the year nearly half the country's population—2 million people—had become refugees, many of them herded into the enclaves. Triumphant in their lightning victory, the Serbs had assumed that there would be plenty of time later for dealing with the enclaves themselves.

So instead of crushing the thoroughly unprepared and defenseless Bosnian government, as leaders of the Western alliance powers had clearly expected they would, the Serbs, in order to accomplish their ideological goal of ethnic cleansing, had left aside two prime strategic tasks: conquering the enclaves and forcing the Bosnian leaders to sue for peace. The delay, and the spectacular killings and tortures and rapes that were an integral part of the

Serbs' vast ethnic cleansing campaign, had forced reluctant Western leaders to respond. The result was a stalemate that no one had expected, as Chuck Sudetic explains:

> All of [General Mladic's] earlier efforts to force an end to the war had failed because intervention by the UN and NATO, however meager, had forced him to fold his hand. His bombardment of Sarajevo had failed to bring Muslim leaders to their knees, largely thanks to the UN military and refugee mission. The Muslims were still hanging on to Srebrenica and Zepa thanks to General Morillon and the UN. The attack on Gorazde had been stymied by NATO.[22]

The Bosnian Serbs could not afford to be stymied. Their chief sponsor, Slobodan Milosevic, who was desperate to persuade Western leaders to lift the economic sanctions that had crippled his economy, had grown furious with the intransigence of his one-time protégés. Flouting Milosevic's will, the Bosnian Serbs had rejected the Vance-Owen and the so-called Contact Group plans, both of them diplomatic proposals to end the war through partition along ethnic lines. Milosevic had in turn imposed restrictions on the Bosnian Serbs, significantly reducing the amount of weapons and supplies that made their way across the Drina.

More important, the Bosnian Serbs had long been aware that, though they far outstripped the Bosnian army in military equipment and training, they lacked the manpower to fight an extended war. As Serb soldiers, forced into the thankless task of guarding an enormously extended and vulnerable frontline, began to desert and to ignore their draft call-ups, strongly motivated Bosnians—many of them refugees or orphans—filled the ranks of the Bosnian government's army; and that growing army was gradually becoming a more effective and well-organized fighting force. Most important, the Bosnians, slowly, surreptitiously, but, to their antagonists, very obviously, had begun to find ways to acquire the weapons they so desperately needed.

VIII.

Beginning in the spring of 1994, heavy, unmarked cargo planes descended nightly from the black sky over Zagreb airport and taxied slowly to outlying hangars, where uniformed men silently awaited them. The Croatian soldiers ran forward, threw open the planes' heavy doors, and began unloading their precious cargos: crates of assault rifles, rocket launchers, grenades, ammunition. After they had put aside a third or more of the equipment—the Croatian army's customary fee for playing middleman—the soldiers hoisted what crates remained into heavy trucks, and the convoy set off for Bosnia, the final destination of a journey that had begun far to the east, in the vast and largely American-stocked arms warehouses of the Islamic Republic of Iran.

The secret airlift, which by mid-1994 had grown into a highly organized operation that carried tons of arms from Turkey and Saudi Arabia as well as Iran, had been built on the Washington Agreement of March 1, 1994, between the Bosnian Muslims and Croats, thus far the sole American diplomatic triumph of the war. Just ten days after the Serbs withdrew their heavy weapons from the precincts of Sarajevo, the Americans announced in Washington that thanks to months of patient cajoling and threatening by Special Envoy Charles Redman and U.S. ambassador to Croatia Peter Galbraith, Bosnian Muslims and Croats had come together at the White House and signed an agreement to end their war and establish a federation. The Washington Agreement not only put an end to a particularly savage and bloody war between Croats and Muslims and suggested a foundation for a workable Bosnian state, it made it possible for the Bosnian Muslims, despite the official arms embargo on all parties, to receive through Croatia a "secret" but much greater supply of weapons from the nations, most of them Muslim, that had long wished to send them.

There remained, of course, the matter of the arms embargo itself: Shipping arms to any of the belligerents of the Balkans violated international law. During the last week of April, Croatian president Franjo Tudjman inquired of Ambassador Galbraith what his government's "view would be" if Croatia resumed transshipment of weapons to Bosnia. The ambassador, well aware of the Europeans' sensitivities, passed the inquiry back to Washington. On April 27, President Clinton, Anthony Lake, and Strobe Talbott, deputy secretary of state, conferred aboard Air Force One—they were returning from the funeral of Richard M. Nixon—and the president decided to instruct his envoy to inform President Tudjman that, on the matter of the arms shipments, he had received . . . "no instructions." Having delivered this message but apparently uncertain whether the Croatian leader had caught the verbal wink, Ambassador Galbraith took it upon himself to advise Tudjman that he should "focus not only on what I had said yesterday, but what I had not said."

Two years later, testifying before senators of the Select Committee on Intelligence, Deputy Secretary Talbott explained the subtle diplomatic considerations implicit in the "no instructions" instructions:

> If we had said yes to the Croatians—that is, if we had explicitly, affirmatively approved the transshipment it would have put us in the position of actively and unilaterally supporting a violation of the arms embargo. The public disclosure of such a posture would have caused severe strains with our allies who had troops on the ground. . . . It would have triggered the precipitous withdrawal of UNPROFOR and that in turn would have required a substantial U.S. troop deployment as part of a potentially very dangerous and costly NATO extraction effort.
>   . . . If we had explicitly disapproved of the transshipments . . . we would have exacerbated the already desperate military situation of the Bosnians and very likely doomed the Federation of Moslems and Croats.[23]

The new policy was kept so secret that not only did Ambassador Galbraith make no written record of it, he neglected to inform his CIA station chief—who, noticing planeloads of weapons passing through Zagreb airport, suspected the ambassador was running a covert operation, and so informed his CIA bosses at Langley. No one had told them of the policy either; and their suspicions that the administration was running a White House–based, Iran-contra style "off-the-books" covert action were confirmed by their eavesdropping on the region. Specifically, the CIA overheard the Bosnians discussing an idea they had suggested to Assistant Secretary of State Richard Holbrooke whereby the Turks, Pakistanis, and Saudis would replace the Iranians as their main arms suppliers. The talk about this proposal—which Lake ultimately rejected, fearing it would anger the Europeans—finally brought Director of Central Intelligence James Woolsey complaining to the White House, whereupon Lake, who actually had initiated the policy in the first place, ordered a formal investigation by the president's Intelligence Oversight Board. In the absurd climax of this Keystone Kops routine, the board found Clinton officials guilty of "excessive secrecy."[24]

Some officials within the administration clearly wanted to go further in supporting the Croats. As the senators of the Select Committee on Intelligence later wrote in their report, a few months after Galbraith had given "the green light" to Tudjman (this was Ambassador Redman's term) the Director of Strategic Plans and Policy for the Joint Chiefs of Staff—though the senators do not name him, it was in fact General Wesley Clark, a native Arkansan who had attended Oxford with Clinton—flew to Sarajevo to meet with Bosnian leaders, including President Izetbegovic, and United Nations officers. In these meetings, General Clark

> moved seamlessly from exploring the implications of a unilateral lifting of the embargo to the question of whether one could rely upon the clandestine flow of embargo-breaking arms and thus avoid UNPROFOR's departure. . . . [The general] expressed a willingness to encourage greater third-party arms flows in violation of the UN arms embargo and/or to engage directly in covert embargo-busting.[25]

Thousands of tons of small arms and other light equipment were by now passing through the pipeline from Iran to Croatia, considerably fattening the Croatian as well as the Bosnian arsenals. In November 1994, Gojko Susak, the hard-line Croatian Defense Minister, wrote to Deputy Defense Secretary John Deutsch and asked if the Americans might provide his army with trainers and equipment. According to Ed Vulliamy, who has seen copies of these letters, "Mr. Deutsch replied explaining that the embargo prevented such direct involvement, but that it could be organized through a private consultancy."[26]

That very month the Croats, under a license from the U.S. State Department, signed a contract with Military Professional Resources Incorporated

(MPRI), an Alexandria, Virginia, consulting firm made up of retired high-ranking American officers. By January 1995 fifteen former officers—including General Carl Vuono, a former chairman of the Joint Chiefs of Staffs and an expert on artillery warfare—had begun training Croatian officers at the Petar Zrinjski Military Academy in Zagreb.

When the story surfaced in the press, General Ed Soyster, who had served for three years as director of the Defense Intelligence Agency and was now a Military Professional Resources vice president, repeatedly denied that MPRI's officers were providing the Croats with military intelligence or intelligence contacts, or even training them in military tactics. "To do so," he said, would "violate the international embargo against military equipment or services reaching Croatia."[27] Whatever the officers were teaching in Zagreb, however, the American training, as well as the increased flow of arms the Croats were receiving, clearly gave President Tudjman new confidence in his army. In February, in an ominous sign for the Serbs, he demanded that the 12,000 UN "blue helmets," who for three years had separated the two armies in Serb-occupied Kajina, be withdrawn.

During the second week of February 1995, American F-18 fighters reportedly accompanied a C-130 transport plane as it flew through Bosnian airspace to the eastern enclave of Tuzla, where it secretly dropped, by parachute, crates of communication gear, radar equipment, and, according to some accounts, anti-tank weapons. Though the Bosnians were still in desperate need of tanks and other heavy weapons, the communication equipment was vital, as Honig and Both note, in enabling "the Bosnian Army to coordinate offensive operations between larger units."[28]

By the spring of 1995, then, the Americans had finally come, however secretly, off the fence. Despite the maps that appeared every day in the world's newspapers testifying to Serb domination of Bosnia, the Muslims and Croats were growing steadily stronger. General Ratko Mladic, as he and his officers gazed worriedly at this new alliance from their perch on Mount Jahorina that March, must have known that his Serbs were running out of time.

IX.

A few miles down from the mountain, in battered Sarajevo—its concrete high-rises blackened and pockmarked, with wisps of dirty plastic trailing from shattered windows; its cratered streets glittering with broken glass—General Rupert Smith of the United Nations Protection Force consulted his staff officers, studied his maps and his daily reports, and came to much the same conclusion: General Mladic, with time running against him, must move to end the war during the coming summer of 1995. As Chuck Sudetic writes, the Serbs' strategy would be obvious: "to return to their original war aims."

> The first goal was to create hardship in Sarajevo in a bid to convince Muslim leaders that further resistance was futile; the second was to overrun the

Srebrenica, Zepa, Gorazde and Bihac safe areas in order to make possible the eventual merger of the Serb-held land in Bosnia with Serbia.[29]

But to accomplish this, Sudetic writes, the Serbs "had to first neutralize the UN and NATO." General Mladic—a gruff, bearish man whose blue eyes and savage manner had made him something of a sex symbol among many Serb women—now faced the same task that confronted his antagonist, the handsome parachute officer General Rupert Smith: He had to "break the machine."

The game had begun. For months Smith had been waiting for just this moment, outlining to every United Nations dignitary or allied official who passed through Sarajevo his "thesis"—here summarized by Honig and Both—that "the international community" must allow him

> to bomb targets other than "smoking guns" and "escalate to success," or, if they were not prepared to do so, "the machine would break." In the latter case, air power would lose its deterrent effect on the Serbs and, if the international community wanted UNPROFOR to continue to function, it would be forced to create another, better machine with a broader range of capabilities and more secure bases for the UN troops in Bosnia.[30]

Smith's strategy, at its heart, was a political one, aimed less at the Serbs than at the Western powers themselves, and therein lay both its brilliance and—as it turned out—its weakness. The agreement on "safe areas" may have helped to prevent a massacre in 1993 but increasingly, as Serbs shelled the enclosures and Muslim troops used them as bases for raids, they had become zones of conflict. For the UN troops, on the other hand, the safe areas had in effect become "reservations" from which the Serbs, when they attacked, could seize Western hostages. Designating these areas "safe" had been a political, not a military act; the real audience was not the Serbs—they could see that the troops the West had supplied were inadequate to defend them—but the people in the West, particularly Americans, who applauded what they saw as their leaders' strong assertion of will.

How then to transform the safe areas from a political pretense to a military reality? Smith's "thesis" implied two strategic phases: The first, which he called "escalating to success," he had begun by aggressively launching air strikes—air strikes, what is more, directed at Pale itself—in the full knowledge that the Serbs would respond by taking hostages. He proposed now to press on with more air strikes—ignoring the hostages and calling Mladic's bluff, in effect gambling that the Serbs would not risk harming the "blue helmets," perhaps the one action certain to bring down on them a powerful Western response.

However much he may have wanted to pursue this course, however, Smith fully expected a different outcome. Since the Serbs could bring strong political pressure on Western governments by televising pictures of captive

British and French soldiers, he understood that his first strategy demanded a steadfastness and political courage that no Western leader was likely to possess. And who could say what would happen if Mladic, against all rational calculation, actually began to execute the hostages?

When Western leaders failed to "escalate to success," however (and General Smith understood they probably would fail), he would have succeeded in proving—irrefutably, once and for all—that the United Nations' mission in Bosnia, now evolving, rapidly and haphazardly, into "peace enforcement," was in its present form unworkable. In Smith's terms, the public reluctance of Western leaders to "escalate to success" would prove that the "machine was broken." And when they had no alternative but to accept this, Smith and his superior, General Janvier, would be ready with an alternative: another, indisputably workable "machine."

And so it happened that on May 24, just as General Smith was announcing his ultimatum in Sarajevo, his commanding officer was presenting to the ambassadors of the Security Council in New York the alternative to "escalating to success"—what he and Smith had called, when they had met with Secretary General Boutros Boutros-Ghali in Paris ten days before, "measures to enhance UNPROFOR's effectiveness and security." These measures entailed, in the words of Honig and Both,

> making UN personnel less vulnerable through redeployment. Janvier and Smith proposed concentrating their troops in central Bosnia by withdrawing their most vulnerable personnel from the weapons collection point in Bosnian Serb territory . . . and by greatly reducing the UN presence in the safe areas. It was better to have just a few observers and forward air controllers in the enclaves who could call in air power when the safe areas were violated. This kind of presence . . . would counteract the main political weakness affecting the resolve of governments to use force: the vulnerability of UNPROFOR to hostage-taking by the Bosnian Serbs.

Smith's strategy to redeploy the United Nations troops was not only militarily and logically unassailable; it implicitly identified the true source of Western leaders' weakness and confusion in Bosnia: their lack of will. By in effect removing UN troops to "safe areas" of their own, Smith would dramatically reduce the risk of harm to them and thereby the risk of political damage to the leaders who had sent them. He would thereby free Western leaders to make use of their fighter bombers to attack the Serbs—and finally to add to their hobbled, halting diplomacy the critical ingredient of real military power. As General Janvier discovered to his chagrin, however, amid the tumult of angry voices assailing him from all sides of the Security Council, he and General Smith had failed to anticipate one small detail.

UN Representative Madeleine Albright embodied the deep contradiction of U.S. policy. Perhaps the key figure in creating the "safe areas" fiction in the first place—which she had touted as a strong response to Serb attacks on

Srebrenica and other Bosnian enclaves but which in the end had done much
to prevent the bombing she so often demanded—Mrs. Albright now accused
General Janvier of wanting to "dump the safe areas."[31] Created as a symbol
of strength, the safe areas were still seen, by Mrs. Albright and other politicians, as precisely that.

According to Honig and Both, "Albright told Janvier that while the status
quo was untenable and a more effective and robust UNPROFOR required,
she could not accept a withdrawal from the safe areas. . . ." She refused to see
that such a withdrawal had become the only politically workable way to
make such "effective and robust" action possible. She could not give up the
fiction of the safe areas for a reason that General Smith, with all his political
acumen, had not anticipated: if their creation had been politically inspired,
they had now become a symbol that could be made real only through an act
of political courage. Albright must have understood, and certainly President
Clinton would have, that withdrawing most "blue helmets" from the safe
areas would be very difficult to explain to suspicious congressmen and commentators in the press, and even more difficult to justify as the "robust" policy the administration had for so long, and without risk, been advocating.

When European political leaders began to intimate they might take the
extreme step of withdrawing their forces from Bosnia altogether, thus making possible the bombing the United States had so long demanded, Mrs.
Albright "changed her tune"; for in that case the administration would be
forced to send to Bosnia tens of thousands of troops and many of them
would likely die.

> Although Mrs. Albright [now] stopped calling for further air strikes, she
> still lamely insisted that the UN Secretary General should consider the
> cost of backing down in the face of the Bosnian Serbs.[32]

The vehemence of Ambassador Albright's reaction to General Janvier's
presentation was rivaled only by that of Ambassador Niek Biegman of Holland, several hundred of whose troops now "protected" Srebrenica. Other
ambassadors, who understood the logic of General Smith's redeployment
plan but had always opposed the "robust action" that would result from it,
were glad to let the American and the Dutchman do the talking for them.

While the ambassadors argued and berated Janvier behind the closed
doors of the Security Council, General Smith twice sent his planes into Pale
to drop their bombs. He watched patiently as the Serbs collected their
hostages, and waited for word from his commander in New York. On May
29, four days after he had launched the first air strike, General Smith
received his answer from Janvier, in the form of directive 2/95:

> The execution of the mandate is secondary to the security of UN person-
> nel. The intention being to avoid loss of life defending positions for their
> own sake and unnecessary vulnerability to hostage-taking.

In other words, Janvier wrote Smith four days later, "We must definitely avoid any action which may degenerate into confrontation, further escalation of tension and the potential use of air power."

General Janvier had failed. He had hoped to return from New York with permission to supply the eastern enclaves with his helicopters; to create, with his troops, a "ground corridor" into Sarajevo; and to strike with his warplanes at command headquarters, communications centers, bridges, and other strategic targets deep within Bosnian Serb territory. He returned from New York beaten, utterly without hope. His political betters had given him nothing with which to alter his basic predicament or to confront his current dilemma: the 324 men, half of them his countrymen, who remained in Serb hands.

Two days later, the French general traveled secretly to the formerly Muslim and now thoroughly "cleansed" city of Zvornik. He entered the Hotel Vidakovac, and sat down and faced Commanding General Ratko Mladic of the Republika Srpska, who listened patiently to his supplicant's appeals, on behalf of the hostages, to military honor and international reputation, and then placed before him a defiantly blunt document:

1. The Army of Republika Srpska will no longer use force to threaten the life and safety of members of UNPROFOR.
2. UNPROFOR commits to no longer make use of any force which leads to the use of air strikes against targets and territory of Republika Srpska.
3. The signing of this agreement will lead immediately to the freeing of all prisoners of war.

General Janvier did not sign; he didn't need to. By their refusal to act, the diplomats in New York had gone a long way toward accepting the agreement for him. A few days later, after Janvier brought the document back to UN headquarters, Special Envoy Yasushi Akashi announced that henceforth Janvier's men would strictly follow "peacekeeping principles"—that is, they would launch no further air strikes.

Within three days the Serbs freed half the hostages; within two weeks they had freed them all. As the fifteen thousand men of Srebrenica were very soon to discover, it was General Mladic who had broken the machine.

New York Review of Books,
February 5 and February 19, 1998

The Great Betrayal

I.

ON JULY 11, 1995, the Bosnian Serbs' beloved commander, General Ratko Mladic, had swaggered into Srebrenica, stalked past the ruined post office (from whose balcony two years before French General Morillon had dramatically promised Muslims that the UN "will never abandon you"), then turned to the camera:

> Here we are in Srebrenica on July 11, 1995. On the eve of yet another great Serbian holiday, we present this city to the Serbian people as a gift. Finally, after the rebellion of the Dahijas, the time has come to take revenge on the Turks of this region.

As his viewers would know, the "rebellion of the Dahijas" was a Serb uprising that the Turks had indeed suppressed with great brutality—in 1804.

In his talk of revenge General Mladic might better have reminded his audience of the great Muslim counter-offensive of May 1992, when Naser Oric led a daring attack to recapture Srebrenica from Serb paramilitaries who had seized and "cleansed" it. He might also have recalled Oric's audacious raids on Serb villages and towns: His murderous attack on Podravanja, for example, during which his *torbari*—the "bag people," emaciated Muslim refugees from Bratunac and other "cleansed" towns who followed the assaulting soldiers—dispatched the wounded with clubs and axes; or the infamous assault on Kravica, on Orthodox Christmas in January 1993, when Oric's men swept down out of the swirling snow, killed at least thirty Serbs, and drove off the entire population before seizing a great booty of Christmas food and drink and burning Kravica's houses to the ground.

For General Mladic that Christmas attack was too much, and his troops, armed with tanks and heavy artillery, began pushing Naser's lightly armed fighters back until, in April 1993, they had retreated, along with a flood of refugees, into Srebrenica itself. Only the United Nations and the Western powers that stood behind it had stopped General Mladic from seizing the town. Instead, Srebrenica became a "safe area," demilitarized—the Muslims in the town were ordered to hand over to the UN what few heavy weapons they had—and "protected" by a handful of Canadian, and later Dutch, United Nations "blue helmets." On the hills around the town, meantime, more than a thousand of General Mladic's Serbs manned their guns, watching and waiting.

Until two months before, Naser Oric, twenty-seven years old, heavily muscled, dark-bearded, clothed head to foot in camouflage fatigues, had ruled the enclave. Oric's men controlled the black market that kept alive Srebrenica's slowly starving people; they smuggled cigarettes and fuel from the Ukrainian "blue helmets" in Zepa, a day-long trek away, and profited from the huge food and fuel price increases brought on by the periodic embargoes imposed by the Serbs encircling the enclave and by the influx of perhaps 35,000 refugees into what had once been a prosperous little town of 8,000 souls. In February 1994, the uncrowned king of ravaged Srebrenica entertained a *Washington Post* reporter:

> Naser Oric's war trophies don't line the wall of his comfortable apartment—one of the few with electricity in this besieged Muslim enclave stuck in the forbidding mountains of eastern Bosnia. They're on a video-cassette tape: burned Serb houses and headless Serb men, their bodies crumpled in a pathetic heap.
> "We had to use cold weapons that night," Oric explains as scenes of dead men sliced by knives roll over his twenty-one-inch Sony.[1]

Though UN "blue helmets" had set up their "observation posts" between Muslim and Serb lines nearly a year before, Oric had still managed to lead his men on occasional nighttime raids, creeping past the UN posts, through gaps in the Serb encirclement, and then attacking and plundering Serb villages and farms. This not only infuriated the Serbs, who blamed the UN troops for failing to contain Oric and his men—and who retaliated by blocking fuel and equipment deliveries to the "blue helmets"—it angered the UN as well. Oric's Muslims, on the other hand, distrusted the UN soldiers—could they really depend upon these few hundred lightly armed foreigners? And the Muslims deeply resented it when in January 1995, as a second Dutch battalion was relieving the first, the Dutch allowed the Serbs to take advantage by moving their guns forward.

Naser Oric was furious, for he had warned the Dutch that the Serbs would try to advance, and at just this point. The Muslim commander of the sector forbade UN troops to set foot in his zone; when the Dutch came anyway, he seized a hundred as hostages and held them for four days.

As the town's food reserves ran out, tension between Oric's Muslims and the Dutch officers meant to protect them grew. According to Chuck Sudetic, "Dutch troops with night-vision goggles reported seeing Muslim soldiers sneak through the perimeter around Srebrenica and open fire on Dutch observation posts . . . to make it seem that the Serbs were attacking them."

Such incidents, if they happened, would not be surprising. The Muslims believed their survival depended on forcing the UN troops to abandon their treasured "neutrality" and support them against the Serbs. UN officials, however, saw Srebrenica's Muslim leaders as corrupt and dangerous *provocateurs.* "From Yasushi Akashi on down," Sudetic writes,

> UN military and refugee-relief personnel had by now had enough of Naser Oric. Akashi personally viewed the senior Muslim commanders in Srebrenica as criminal gang leaders, pimps and black marketeers.[2]

However accurate this appraisal, and however much it was shared by Muslim political and military leaders in Sarajevo—many of whom resented Oric's independence and arrogance—it was nonetheless true that he was a leader and that he had made his men into fighters who had managed, with virtually no outside help, to take back and then defend their town. "I am a man of action," Oric had declared to the *Washington Post* reporter. "I like adventure. As long as I am in Srebrenica, it will never be Serb. We will protect the hearths of our people. We will never be Palestinians."

But on March 21, 1995, Muslim military commanders sent an order to Oric and his lieutenants: They were to proceed to a mountain known as Orlov Kamen, or "Eagle Rock," and wait; and wait they did, for almost two weeks before a helicopter dropped out of the sky, plucked them from the frozen mountainside, and flew them off to Tuzla for "consultations and training." Naser Oric, the celebrated leader of Srebrenica, would not return.

II.

In the wake of Oric's mysterious and ominous departure, Srebrenica's malnourished people subsisted on little more than rumors: Sarajevo's commanders, it was said, had summoned Oric to help them plan a new offensive, a great onslaught that would at last liberate Srebrenica. No, Bosnian president Alija Izetbegovic and Bosnian Serb leader Radovan Karadzic had finally fashioned a secret deal, whereby the Muslims would trade away Srebrenica, Zepa, and Gorazde, the three eastern enclaves, in exchange for the Serb suburbs of divided Sarajevo. Yes, that must be it: Oric's military skills would no longer be needed; soon luxurious cars and buses would come for Srebrenica's bedraggled defenders and carry them to glittering Sarajevo, in whose suburbs each man would now be offered for his family a choice of fine apartments or houses. . . .

Many, of course, had long speculated about such a deal; Srebrenica's people could read a map as well as anyone. They knew that Srebrenica—heroic Srebrenica, whose men had fought off the "cleansing" of the notorious paramilitary leader Arkan and his Tigers and had pinned down for three years more than a thousand Serb troops—Srebrenica simply made no sense in the logic of peace, in the logic of settlement: in the logic of the map. The town stood ten miles from the Serbian border, dominating the Drina Valley, the "soft underbelly" of Serbia. Cyrus Vance and David Owen's diplomatic plan of 1993, which called for an integrated Bosnia divided into ten carefully drawn provinces, placed Srebrenica in the Muslim-dominated canton of Tuzla. The Contact Group map, introduced in 1994 and named for the "contact group" of diplomats from the United States, Great Britain, France, Germany, and Russia who were directly negotiating with the former Yugoslavs, also allotted Srebrenica to the Muslims. But since this plan set out what was in fact an ethnic division of Bosnia (with 51 percent of the land going to the Bosnians and Croats, 49 percent to the Serbs), Srebrenica and the other enclaves would have remained isolated and no doubt heavily armed islands in a sea of hostile territory. The implication was clear: If Srebrenica were to remain Muslim, Serbia itself could never be fully secure. Until Srebrenica and the other eastern enclaves changed hands—courtesy either of the diplomats or the generals—Slobodan Milosevic's goal of securing "Greater Serbia" would elude him, and the war would grind on.

Even as the Srebrenicans spent April and May of 1995 gossiping about a deal, President Milosevic sat in his hunting lodge near Belgrade working to negotiate it. At his side was Robert Frasure, a U.S. deputy assistant secretary of state and now President Clinton's special envoy for Bosnia. For more than six months, the French, British, and Russians had been pushing to revise the Contact Group map, intending to pressure the Bosnians to exchange Srebrenica and the other enclaves for the predominantly Serb suburbs of Sarajevo and thereby add, to a plan that built on the violent ethnic partition of Bosnia that had already been accomplished, provisions for wholesale "diplomatic" ethnic cleansing that would complete the job.[3] But Clinton officials, who from the start had loudly supported the rights of the Bosnians to justice and had advocated air strikes and other "robust action" against the Serbs— while steadfastly declining, as the Europeans never tired of pointing out, to put "troops on the ground"—had only lately shown signs of going along.

For by May 1995, British leaders had told the Americans that a majority of Prime Minister John Major's cabinet favored a withdrawal of their troops—now about 5,500—before the following winter. The French, who had contributed about 5,000 troops, had let it be known that, failing a stronger commitment by the Americans, they would follow suit. For American officials, already in the shadow of the 1996 presidential campaign, this came as a shock. Withdrawing UN troops would be difficult and bloody, and the Americans had pledged to support the operation with at least 20,000 soldiers. Thus far, President Clinton's role in the war had been largely rhetorical. Now, one way or another, rhetoric must give way to commitment.

So in May 1995 the Americans sent Ambassador Frasure to Belgrade, where Milosevic eagerly waited to deal. Not only had sanctions destroyed Serbia's economy, Milosevic could see that the Bosnian Serb leaders—men

he had created, like Radovan Karadzic, but who now in their arrogance presumed to ignore his directives—had been blinded to the fact that they had
reached the limits of their power. Thanks to American diplomacy, the Bosnians and Croats had formed a loose confederation. Iranian weapons were
flowing through Zagreb to the Bosnians—and also to the Croats, who kept
most of the heavy weapons for themselves. Retired American generals were
advising the much strengthened Croatian army—which on May 1, in Operation Flash, had stormed Serb-occupied western Slavonia and expelled more
than 12,000 Serbs. From the outset, the Bosnian Serbs, with many fewer
men to draw on, had known they must win the war quickly; but thanks in
part to the United Nations and its "humanitarian aid," the Muslims had
managed to hold on. Now, each day that went by, the Serbs grew weaker and
their enemies stronger. And, as Milosevic had made ominously clear by sitting on his hands while the Croats seized western Slavonia, whatever his pretensions to have fathered "Greater Serbia" he would not risk his power by
moving to rescue his erstwhile protégés in Pale.

Ambassador Frasure was in Belgrade to work out what was meant to be,
in outline, a simple deal: Milosevic would recognize Bosnia as an independent nation and in exchange the United Nations would suspend sanctions
on Serbia. Implied in the arrangement were "territorial adjustments" that
seemed to show how far the Americans had come in admitting a hard reality:
Since the Bosnians lacked the military strength to win and hold the territory
that would be needed to build a permanent connection between central
Bosnia and the eastern enclaves, and since the Western nations—and particularly the Americans—showed no willingness to take on such a task, any
negotiated end to the war would have to include trading the enclaves to the
Serbs. As early as the summer of 1993, Bosnian prime minister Haris Sila-
jdzic had "indicated" that if the Serbs traded the Serb-held suburbs of Sarajevo for the enclaves, "he would be prepared to go to Srebrenica and explain
to the people that they had to leave."[4]

The following spring the Serbs agreed in principle to such an arrangement. In January 1995, according to Richard Holbrooke, assistant secretary
of state for European affairs, President Alija Izetbegovic told him that, "in
the context of a larger settlement" and to achieve an undivided Sarajevo, he
was ready to give the Serbs Srebrenica and the other enclaves. "He said they
weren't his people," Holbrooke told me in an interview. "He didn't care
about it."

Unfortunately, even if the Bosnians and the Serbs, as well as Western leaders, privately acknowledged that in any deal Srebrenica would go to the
Serbs, no one was prepared to endorse openly that territorial swap. Such a
move, after all, would be seen as "rewarding ethnic cleansing" and giving in
to aggression, something President Clinton and his senior officials had
vowed never to do. And as long as President Clinton was unwilling to
endorse such a proposal, the Bosnians could be expected to hold out for a
better deal. For as far back as the presidential campaign of 1992, a pattern

had emerged: Clinton would speak out strongly for a "principled" course in Bosnia, according to which "ethnic cleansing will not stand"; the Bosnians would stiffen their resolve and their diplomatic position, anticipating substantial U.S. help; and the Americans, having given vent to a blast of strong idealistic rhetoric, would do little or nothing at all. "Among the Contact Group countries," Richard Holbrooke told me,

> the U.S. had the strongest moral position but the least involvement, which made our moral position hypocritical. In May 1995, when I suggested bombing the Serbs after they had taken UN troops hostage, a British official looked at me calmly for a moment and said, "Well, that's all very well, but they aren't your men, are they?"

Two-and-a-half years after coming to power, Clinton officials were still vacillating between, on the one hand, relying on diplomacy fashioned largely out of rhetoric and, on the other, taking action. Administration officials had pressed the United Nations to declare Srebrenica and four other besieged towns and cities "safe areas" but had stood by while the secretary general begged the world for, and ultimately failed to secure, adequate troops to defend them. Now, when they finally set out determined to make progress in settling the war through diplomacy, Clinton officials still found themselves confined within a rhetorical prison of their own making. As one official described the American representative's position within the Contact Group negotiations,

> In discussion, [Ambassador Charles] Redman accepted the possibility of the Zepa and Srebrenica enclaves being swapped for territory elsewhere, such as around Sarajevo. However, he was adamant that the Group could not put forward such a proposal, as they would be faced with public outcry.

In what remained a bitterly divided administration Redman belonged to the so-called "pragmatic group" while Vice President Al Gore and Ambassador Madeleine Albright led the "hard-liners," vigorously opposing "any move that appeased, as they saw it, Serb aggression." Honig and Both describe the American predicament this way:

> Having publicly made a clear distinction between aggressors (the Serbs) and victims (the Bosnians) from the moment they took office, they had stuck to this line ever since. Their credibility would be in doubt and their reputations damaged if they were now to give public approval to a territorial swap involving the eastern enclaves.[5]

To put the matter rather less cynically, and perhaps more accurately, one might say that however much Gore, Albright, and the Clinton administration's other "hard-liners" may have detested "appeasement" of the Serbs—

and there is little reason to doubt their sincerity—they failed the Bosnians miserably because they were unable, or unwilling, to persuade the president to put forward a workable policy based on their convictions.

Such a policy, in the end, could not have had as its foundation—as Clinton's did—the refusal to employ American troops or otherwise to commit vital American resources. It would not do simply to point to polls suggesting Americans' wariness of deep involvement in the Balkans; if Clinton was truly determined to achieve "justice" in Bosnia, to somehow reverse the ethnic cleansing, he would have to provide some means to accomplish it, rather than simply block peace proposals as "unjust" and thus unacceptable to his own proudly proclaimed ideals. "Hard choices needed to be made on Bosnia policy" from the time Clinton took office, Wayne Bert writes in *The Reluctant Superpower*, "but Clinton was not willing to choose. His instincts were to intervene and help stymie the Serb military actions in Bosnia, but there was a price to be paid for that and the president was not convinced that the intervention was worth the price." The burden of the administration "hardliners" was to persuade the president that he should pay the price; their sin was not that they were unwilling to compromise their "hard-line" reputations by appeasing the Serbs but that they were unable when it mattered to accomplish what was necessary to help the Bosnians.

As for the Europeans, all their talk of "humanitarian missions" and "troops on the ground," in the end had done much to prolong the war, and so prolonged their own reluctant involvement in it. From the beginning, as Bert writes, the "European allies had fundamentally misconstrued the war and what should be done about it."

> Limited intervention may help end a war if the intervenor takes sides and tilts the balance in a way that allows one side to win. Impartial intervention may end a war if the outside power takes complete control of the situation and imposes a peace settlement that all respect. The first type of intervention is limited but not impartial, the second is impartial but not limited. The Europeans tried to carry out both a limited and an impartial intervention, and it did not work.[6]

Now the suddenly material prospect of French and British troops carrying out a fighting retreat, with thousands of American troops supporting them—images of bodybags sent back to the United States, containing Americans killed for no other reason than to cover a humiliating failure—had begun to concentrate the Americans' minds. On May 18, 1995, Ambassador Frasure placed some documents in his briefcase, shook Milosevic's hand, and flew back to Washington. The Serbian dictator and the American diplomat had reached a deal.

It would be short-lived. It is true that in return for lifting sanctions and promising to adopt a constitution that went some way toward recognizing the Bosnian Serbs' "autonomy," Milosevic had agreed to recognize Bosnia and cut off military supplies and fuel shipments to the Bosnian Serbs until they accepted the Contact Group map. But "hard-line" Clinton officials feared that by agreeing to suspend sanctions (which only UN Secretary General Boutros-Ghali could then reimpose) they had left themselves no leverage over the Serb leader. The deal would thus seem a gift to Milosevic. Secretary of State Christopher could not support it. Ambassador Albright, the most prominent of the "hard-liners," reportedly threatened to resign.

Again, the political strictures were real and, for Clinton, self-generated; having long spoken eloquently of the legitimacy of the Muslim cause, having chosen to support justice for the "ethnically cleansed" Bosnians rather than peace "at any price," the president now found it difficult to adopt wholesale a policy of Realpolitik. But the practical problem was real as well: Having "dealt with the devil" and come to an arrangement, how would the Americans enforce it if Milosevic proved unwilling, or unable, to deliver—if, for example, Dr. Karadzic, Milosevic's own Frankenstein monster, were to defy his creator on this as he and his self-appointed "representatives" had earlier on the Vance-Owen plan?

The Clinton administration sent Frasure back to Belgrade with a proposal that would in effect allow the Americans to reimpose sanctions at their own discretion. Such a proposal had little chance of being accepted; in retrospect, with the sounds of shelling growing louder from Sarajevo to Srebrenica, Frasure's agreement doubtless had been the last hope for a diplomatic solution to the "problem" of the enclaves.

Though he and Frasure went on talking, by the end of May, Milosevic had concluded that the Americans would sign no deal. Having failed in his attempt to secure his increasingly precarious military gains by political means, Milosevic now "unleashed" General Ratko Mladic and his Bosnian Serbs.

III.

During the last week of May, Mladic's soldiers helped themselves to the tanks and cannons and mortars in the UN "Weapons Collections Points" and began bombarding Sarajevo. General Rupert Smith responded by directing NATO planes to bomb an arms depot near Pale. General Mladic countered by ordering his troops to take hostage more than 300 UN soldiers. On June 1, Serb troops staged an ambush within Srebrenica, killing thirteen civilians. On June 2, Serb rocket forces launched a surface-to-air missile at an American F-16 fighter patrolling the no-fly zone, destroying it and stranding its pilot, Scott O'Grady, behind Serb lines. (A marine commando force rescued him six days later). On June 3, seventy-five Serb paramilitaries stormed and seized the United Nations' southernmost observation post in Srebrenica, OP Echo, and shelled an armored personnel carrier, wounding two "blue helmets." The Dutch commander's frantic pleas to UN headquarters to send NATO fighter planes to bomb and strafe the Serb attackers were denied.

Six days later, with UN hostages still in Serb hands, General Bernard Janvier of France, the UN Force Commander in Bosnia, sat in a meeting room in the Croatian coastal city of Split opposite General Smith and Yasushi Akashi, Secretary General Boutros Boutros-Ghali's Special Representative, and delivered a grim appraisal. "We are no longer able to use air power," the general declared, "because of the obvious reason that our soldiers are on the ground. Whether we want it or not, the Serbs are controlling the situation."

It was June 9, five days after Janvier had traveled, hat in hand, to Zvornik in order to see General Ratko Mladic, the man who held 324 of his troops prisoner. "We were the supplicants," a close aide later said. "Janvier proposed the meeting. Janvier proposed the deal." The French officer signed no paper but instead pocketed the blunt document Mladic had prepared for his inspection and brought it back to UN headquarters.[7] Of course, the lack of a signature proves nothing, as Richard Holbrooke pointed out to me:

> There's no documentary evidence but [a deal] makes perfect sense. However it's simply not provable. Beyond the question of whether or not Janvier came to an understanding with Mladic is whether he did so at the direction of the Elysée. . . . It could well be that rather than Chirac someone within the Elysée bureaucracy instructed him to make the arrangement. Whatever actually happened between Janvier and Mladic, and between Janvier and the Elysée, you can only say there is a strong circumstantial chain.

To that chain Akashi's announcement, made on June 9 after the critical meeting with Generals Janvier and Smith, that henceforth the United Nations forces would abide by "strict peacekeeping principles," would seem to add the final link: The hostages would be released, the fighter planes would likely not return.[8] Whatever means were henceforth to be employed to protect Srebrenica from a Serb attack—to keep it a "safe area"—they were very unlikely to involve NATO warplanes. The principle seems to have been established, whether formally or not, that the Bosnian Serbs could prevent NATO air attacks, the only means of defending the enclaves from a Serb attack, by threatening the "blue helmets."

And General Smith, at least, according to the minutes of the meeting, was certain the Serbs would soon attack. "I remain convinced that the Serbs want to conclude [the war] this year and will take every risk to accomplish this," he said. "As long as [Milosevic's] sanctions remain on the Drina, [the Serbs] risk getting weaker every week relative to their enemy." The Serbs' determination to conclude the war would lead, Smith went on, "to a further squeezing of Sarajevo or an attack in the eastern enclaves, creating a crisis that short of air attacks we will have great difficulty responding to."

General Janvier's analysis was quite different. "The Serbs need two things," he explained to Smith and Akashi,

. . . international recognition, and a softening of the blockade on the Drina. I hope that these conditions will be met quickly, given the urgent situation. I think the Serbs are aware of how favorable the [political] situation is to them—I don't think they want to go to an extreme crisis. On the contrary, they want to modify their behavior, be good interlocutors. It is for this that we must speak to them—not negotiate, but to show them how important it is to have a normal attitude.

"I agree that they do not want a crisis," General Smith replied sarcastically. "They want to neutralize the UN and NATO . . . as they fight the Muslims." General Smith asked about the coming Rapid Reaction Force, an armored French-British contingent then being assembled to support UNPROFOR—or to assist in its withdrawal. "Are we going to use them to fight? If not I am not sure I want them—they will just be more mouths to feed, and create expectations that I cannot meet." And then, he said,

If we are not prepared to fight, we will always be stared down by the [Bosnian Serb Army]. We are already over the "Mogadishu line"; the Serbs do not view us as peacekeepers.

It was no use; General Janvier, Smith's commander, would have none of it. "I insist," he declared, "that we will never have the possibility of combat, of imposing our will on the Serbs." When Smith persisted, noting that he could "easily see a situation arising where we will be forced to request air power," Janvier was dismissive:

It is just for this that we must establish contact with the Serbs, to show, explain to them that there are just some things that they cannot do. . . . Once again, the Serbs are in a very favorable political position and that is something they will not want to compromise. The external political situation is such that the Serbs will come to understand the benefits of cooperation. Unless there is a major provocation by the [Bosnian Army], the Serbs will not act.

Within days, American intelligence officers at the National Security Agency found themselves listening to an interesting series of telephone conversations between General Ratko Mladic and General Momiclo Perisic, chief of staff of the Yugoslav Army. The two generals were planning a large joint offensive that would involve more than 10,000 troops, some 3,000 of them from the Yugoslav Army, thirty or so tanks, and many artillery pieces. From June 17, the two men spoke almost daily; and the transcripts of their conversations, according to one writer who claims to have seen them, show clearly "that the initiative for this military operation came from Belgrade."[9] In coming days, General Mladic traveled frequently to the Serbian capital, for that is where he and General Perisic planned the conquest of the "safe area" of Srebrenica.[10]

During the nights of late June and early July, Serb soldiers drove truckloads of fuel, weapons, and ammunition, as well as armored vehicles and tanks, across the Drina bridges into Bosnia. Mithad Salihovic, at the time a scout for the Bosnian Army's 28th Division, told a television interviewer,

> On June 21, from the direction of Belgrade via Sabac, Loznica, and Ljubovija, a paramilitary force run by Zeljko Raznatovic, nicknamed Arkan, crossed into the territory. About 4,000 of them assembled in Bratunac and they were then sent to different areas around the enclave.[11]

General Cees Nicolai, a Dutch brigadier who served as General Smith's deputy in Sarajevo, also remembers seeing reports that Arkan's Tigers had been sighted around the enclave. "Srebrenica was on their wish list," General Nicolai told *Newsday*, noting that the Tigers "always showed up at places where something was about to happen."[12]

As one NATO officer wrote in his daily report, he and other military observers well understood what the Tigers' sudden appearance around Srebrenica—swollen as it was with refugees—might portend:

> Any attempt to clear the enclave would probably be manpower intensive and require commitment as well as other less salubrious qualities. The Bosnian Serb Army soldiers are not showing these qualities so a unit like the Arkan Brigade would be necessary.[13]

All the signs were there. But who had an eye to see them, or a true interest in seeing? General Smith did, but Yasushi Akashi had told him clearly that he must defer to General Janvier, and the Frenchman believed fervently that the Serbs, if left unchallenged, would "come to understand the benefits of cooperation." As for the Americans, having failed to come to terms with Milosevic, they had begun fashioning a new diplomatic approach, which, according to a White House aide, "emphasized the need for defensibility of federal territory. It had to be compact, coherent and defensible," priorities that would not encourage American officials to comb intelligence intercepts looking for threats to Srebrenica—or, for that matter, to regret the disappearance altogether, one way or another, of "the eastern enclaves problem."

So even as American intelligence officers listened to Generals Mladic and Perisic plan their next move, American diplomats had decided, according to Sandy Vershbow, who was in charge of Bosnia policy at the National Security Council, that Srebrenica's future "seemed pretty gloomy. We were already then considering that some kind of swap for at least the smaller of the eastern enclaves for more territory would be wise." In fact the Americans had gone beyond "considering" and "were discreetly suggesting that

[Srebrenica] should be exchanged for territory elsewhere," which told the players involved that in the American government "far from reversing ethnic cleansing a decision had been made that more was needed."

Finally, the Bosnian leaders themselves, in the frank words of army commander General Rasim Delic, tended to see Srebrenica and the other enclaves as "an additional burden for the Bosnian army and government."[14] The Bosnians of Sarajevo had a good many more important things to worry about.

IV.

By early June 1995, Sarajevo, the once-beautiful city nestled in its bowl of pine-covered mountains, was suffering once more under a ferocious siege. From their bunkers on the mountainsides, Serb gunners had been shelling Butimir airport, effectively preventing, for more than two months, food and other humanitarian aid from reaching Sarajevo's people and sending prices soaring for what little food could still be found in the markets. The Serbs then cut off the water mains, forcing people to subsist on intermittent deliveries of water by Bosnian Army tanker trucks. They severed electric lines, even managing to destroy a cable Muslims had laid in a tunnel running under Butimir airport. Finally, Serb gunners poured shells down onto the ruined buildings, and when people ventured out onto the debris-littered streets, Serb snipers shot them down.

As General Smith had prophesied, General Mladic, in his eagerness to conclude the war that summer, was moving first to "squeeze" Sarajevo and pressure its leaders. And though the Bosnian government forces had grown considerably stronger than they had been a year before, the soldiers in Sarajevo still found themselves outgunned. Encircling the capital were seven brigades of well-trained, well-equipped soldiers—perhaps twelve thousand men—dug into more than two hundred reinforced bunkers and armed with at least three hundred large cannons and other artillery pieces. Facing them, the Bosnians could put in the field only their First Corps, consisting of twenty-five thousand men of whom perhaps fourteen thousand were available and only half of those properly armed, which had at its disposal a mere thirty artillery pieces and five tanks, three of them obsolescent. "In the face of such superiority," General Jovan Divjak, number two commander in the Bosnian army, explained to an interviewer on June 2,

> the Bosnian government army has no chance of an equal playing field. . . .
> To break out, we would need considerably greater resources and sophisticated armaments. . . . The balance of force is today such that the Army in the Sarajevo zone cannot advance without considerable reinforcements, but then nor can the Karadzic forces. So we're in a stalemate situation for the time being.[15]

By June, however, the stalemate was becoming untenable. Sarajevo had literally begun to starve. And, as Divjak and other Bosnian commanders well knew, worse would soon come. The NATO air strikes General Smith had ordered May 25 and 26 on an ammunition depot near Pale had hurt the Serbs and, according to Divjak, "set back all plans for fifteen to thirty days until they can get new supplies from the Serbian military"—which in effect would mean "a breathing space for the Bosnian Army."

On June 15, the Bosnians launched a full-scale attack north of Sarajevo. The ostensible objective was to "break out" of the siege, as President Alija Izetbegovic explained to his people in a blunt televised statement:

> There is nothing left in the city, no electricity, no water, no gas, no food, no medicines. . . . The world hasn't done anything to prevent it. . . . In a situation like this, our army has been given orders to prevent the further strangulation of the city.

Given the realities on the ground, the Bosnians' goals were equally likely to have been political: namely, by escalating the fighting, to push Western leaders to intervene and force the Serbs at least to open the airport so vital food shipments could be delivered.

For the residents of Sarajevo, the first days of the fighting were terrifying. "Sarajevo rocked and heaved with explosions," as Barbara Demick writes in *Logavina Street*, her study of one Sarajevo neighborhood in wartime. "Air raid sirens wailed incessantly."

> Quite literally, the entire city was smack in the middle of warring armies—cowering underneath a furious volley of mortar shells, rocket-propelled grenades flying across the hills. For three days, the noise was appalling. Then it stopped suddenly. . . . The offensive had failed.
>
> As always, the revenge was pitiless. The Bosnian Serbs let loose immediately on the water lines, the hospitals. In Kosevo [Hospital], a hepatitis patient was decapitated in his hospital bed by a mortar shell. The man's headless corpse lay undisturbed for hours because the doctors were too busy with the injured to move him. In the last two weeks of June, 66 civilians were killed in Sarajevo and more than 300 were wounded.[16]

At the height of the fighting, on June 17, Yasushi Akashi traveled to Belgrade to pay a call on Slobodan Milosevic. The diplomat, as he cabled in his report to New York, found Milosevic "somewhat tense and less self-confident than usual" and showing

> considerable concern about the strength of the Bosnian government offensive. . . . [He] expressed doubt that the Bosnian government would respond, in the absence of aid deliveries, to my appeal for a ceasefire. . . .

He stressed that both sides were weary of war and must stop fighting. I replied that the government would not have had an excuse for the offensive if Serbs had allowed aid to enter Sarajevo.

That the Bosnians, besieged in their capital, needed "an excuse" to try to break the siege exemplifies the thinking of the United Nations envoy: In the eyes of the "peacekeeper," any move to initiate hostilities, even if only an attempt to return to the status quo ante, must be wrong, for it violates "peace."

As he told Milosevic, Akashi believed Serb moves to seize back the weapons that had been collected by the UN resulted from "stupidity" rather than from a quite predictable determination to force the Bosnians to conclude the war:

> The stupidity of the Serbs in refusing to return heavy weapons to weapon collection points, and their attack on a populated part of Tuzla, had also contributed to the need for two air strikes on Pale. I emphasized that the Bosnian government was very confident now, somewhat disdainful of the UN, and very skilled at exploiting any Serb overreaction. It was therefore essential that the Serbs cooperate in supplying our forces and delivering aid. "Absolutely," replied Milosevic.

At this very moment General Mladic was assuring General Janvier, who was calling on him in Pale, that his soldiers would let convoys pass through their lines to resupply UN troops in Srebrenica and the other enclaves. Both promises were worthless. In fact, Srebrenica would remain cut off, its Dutch troops subsisting on combat rations, and Sarajevo would go on enduring its slow and agonizing strangulation.

Having blithely assured Akashi that aid deliveries would be resumed, the Serb president had another point to impress on the UN envoy:

> Milosevic stated that the most important initial step was to stop the government offensive and to avoid further air strikes. . . . Both Milosevic and [Serbian Foreign Minister Vladislav] Jovanovic referred to Bosnian abuse of safe areas, and reminded us that NATO aircraft had only attacked Serbs. Milosevic stated that, "if it is impossible for NATO to react against the Muslims due to U.S. pressure, then that is a good reason not to use air strikes against the Serbs, as the air strikes are ruining the position of the United Nations."

Milosevic not only knew that Akashi personally objected to air strikes, he also knew what was to come in Srebrenica. Speaking man-to-man, Milosevic showed himself willing to be understanding of Akashi's predicament: Of course, properly speaking, the UN official's "neutrality" would compel him to send NATO planes to strike against the Muslims in Srebrenica, as General

Smith had struck against the Serbs in Pale, but politics—no?—prevented Akashi from taking such a step.

Nonetheless, if political realities meant that Akashi couldn't send NATO planes to "punish" the Muslims, then the least he could do was to refrain from striking at the Serbs—particularly, Milosevic seemed to be implying, when the time came for Serbs to move against the safe areas. And Milosevic casually let it slip that "he had been advised by President Chirac of President Clinton's agreement that air strikes should not occur if unacceptable to Chirac."

Akashi records this revelation without comment and thus it is hard not to think that he already knows of, or in any event, has heard about, such an understanding—one, it should be noted, that White House spokesmen later vigorously denied existed. What the truth of the statement might be, particularly given Milosevic's fame as a liar, is harder to know. According to some reports, attributed to sources in the French government, President Chirac had "lengthy telephone conversations" with Milosevic—on June 3 (the day Serbs seized a southern observation post in Srebrenica); June 9 (the day Janvier met with Akashi and Smith in Split); and June 11—after which the Serbs released their (mostly French) hostages.

Sometime around the middle of June, even as the Americans were listening in on Generals Mladic and Perisic discussing Srebrenica, French intelligence officers also learned of the coming offensive. "This information was given to General Janvier . . . only in his capacity as a French military officer, not in his role as Supreme Commander of the UN forces."[17] According to this reconstruction, Janvier knew an attack was coming and understood that his government did not believe NATO should act forcefully to prevent its succeeding.

By his casual comment to Akashi, Milosevic seems to be suggesting that the Americans were effectively neutralized—and that he, President Milosevic, know it. American belligerence would no longer serve as an excuse. Air strikes, when it came to protecting Srebrenica's Muslims, were out of the question. The following day, after the Serbs released the last hostages, a high Serb official claimed publicly, in a statement from Pale, that the UN soldiers were freed because the Serbs had reached a deal with the UN not to undertake air strikes. In Moscow, Boris Yeltsin announced that President Chirac had told him NATO would undertake no further air strikes in Bosnia.

Within a day Serb military jets were violating the no-fly zone over Bosnia and Serb antiaircraft radar was "locking on" NATO fighters. NATO officers requested permission to attack the Serb airfield at Banja Luka and some surface-to-air missiles. Akashi, declaring that "such disproportionate action would immediately affect any ongoing diplomatic process and precipitate reprisal attacks against United Nations personnel," rejected the request. NATO officers demanded to know if the UN envoy had made a deal with the Serbs. Akashi denied it, insisting the hostages' release was "unconditional."

NATO commanders, however, were not stupid; they resented what they saw as the diplomat's irresponsibly risking their pilots, using sophisticated warplanes as nothing more than impotent "noisemakers in the skies." The officers reduced the number of patrols over Bosnia. In the future, if United Nations troops needed support from the air it was unlikely to be immediately available; the Dutch "blue helmets" in Srebrenica, for example, might be forced to wait four hours or more for NATO fighter planes.

Just before Bosnian troops launched their Sarajevo offensive in mid-June, the Bosnian officers in Srebrenica, like commanders throughout the country, had received secret orders to support the capital by staging attacks from the enclave and pinning down as many Serb troops as possible. On the morning of June 26, Muslim soldiers set out from Srebrenica before dawn, crept by the United Nations observation posts and through Serb lines, then marched about three miles to Visnjica. Villagers, awakened by the sound of automatic-weapons fire, fled their homes in terror and disappeared into the forest. From there they watched Muslim soldiers plunder their houses, drive off the livestock, and carry off the crops and anything else of value before setting fire to the houses. When a handful of Serbs launched a counterattack, the Muslims killed one soldier and wounded three civilians before retreating to Srebrenica. Within the space of a few minutes at least thirteen of Visnjica's families had become refugees.

By now Arkan's paramilitaries had been in the area for nearly a week; Serb soldiers had been driving tanks and artillery pieces in increasing numbers over the Drina bridges; General Mladic and General Perisic and their aides had been meeting and planning in Belgrade. Two days before, Mladic had written to United Nations officials and warned bluntly that

> These attacks against the territories controlled by [the Bosnian Serb] Army . . . brutally violate the status of [the] Safe Area of Srebrenica. . . . I strongly protest and warn you that we will not tolerate such cases in future.

Two days later, with Visnjica's burned houses still smoldering, the Serbs summoned foreign journalists. "We lived so well here," Savo Madzarevic, who had just watched his house burn, lamented to an American reporter. "We had two beds and a table. Now we will have to become refugees somewhere." When asked why the Muslims had attacked his village, the man paused. "I suppose," he said finally, "it is because we are Serbs."

The Bosnian Serb Army spokesman gathered journalists together to issue an angry statement:

> The Muslim soldiers who carried out this attack crossed lines patrolled by Dutch UN troops whose job it is to prevent just this kind of action. We therefore conclude that the UN forces are aligning themselves with the Muslim army.[18]

General Mladic had his men and equipment in place; he had "neutralized" the United Nations as a combative force; and now he had his *casus belli*. A Serb soldier, one of those who had driven off the Srebrenica raiders, listened to a reporter's question about the United Nations forces and gave a stark answer:

> It doesn't do any good to obey the rules of the UN. . . . Maybe it's time for the peacekeepers to go home. . . . There's a war going on here, and each side has to do what it has to do.

V.

Just after three o'clock on the morning of July 6, Dutch peacekeepers in the UN base at Potocari, a couple of miles north of Srebrenica, were awakened by the distinctive whistle, shriek, and explosion of rockets: six passed directly over the UN base. Two hours later, just before dawn, a flash lit the sky and then an explosion rocked Observation Post Foxtrot in the southeast of the safe area; two young Dutch soldiers manning the tower threw themselves to the plywood floor, felt the soil shower over their backs. Seconds later, another mortar shell landed, making their ears ring. One soldier fumbled for the radio. Then they clambered down the ladder behind the sandbags of the bunker.

In the pre-dawn gloom, the two young Dutchmen were half-asleep and disoriented; but they knew the shells had come from the Serb side. They had no idea what this meant, for from the start the peacekeepers had found themselves in an anomalous, confusing position, one that reflected all the ambiguity of the "safe areas" policy itself. As David Rohde writes in *Endgame*:

> On the one hand, . . . the Dutch were supposed to be neutral UN peacekeepers. They wore bright blue UN helmets, berets or baseball caps. Nearly every inch of the observation post's fifty-by-thirty-yard compound of prefabricated containers, canvas tents and sandbag bunkers was UN white. OP Foxtrot could be spotted—and shelled—from miles away. As far as . . . [the] Dutch were concerned, OP Foxtrot was a great white albatross, not a defensive position.
>
> But [the Dutch] peacekeepers were also expected to take sides if necessary and "deter" attacks by the Bosnian Serbs. Muslim soldiers had grudgingly turned over this and a half dozen other strategic hills to the UN when Srebrenica became a safe area. . . . But with few weapons, blue helmets and white vehicles, the Dutch were a meager fighting force. Both confused and discouraged by their contradictory mission, . . . Srebrenica's Dutch peacekeepers had spent most of the last five months hoping nothing would happen.[19]

From the day that the United Nations declared Srebrenica and the other enclaves "safe areas," contradictions dominated: General Mladic had demanded that the Bosnians surrender unconditionally. When they refused, the general ordered his men to maintain the siege, and though the Bosnians had relinquished two old tanks and some mortars and other artillery to the UN, the "blue helmets" found themselves manning a frontline between two armies still at war.

Though Secretary General Boutros-Ghali had determined that the safe areas would require at least 37,000 peacekeepers, he could persuade the nations of the world to contribute no more than 7,600, of which a mere few hundred—first 150 Canadians, then just under 600 Dutchmen—had been stationed in Srebrenica. Like the Canadians, the Dutch were forced to depend on the Serbs to let their supply convoys pass, and this, for more than two months, the Serbs had largely refused to do. By July, the Dutch had run very low on fuel and ammunition and had exhausted their supplies of fresh food; they were carrying equipment by mule and living on wretched combat rations. And since the Serbs had not permitted a number of soldiers who had departed on leave to return, the battalion, at 429 members, of whom scarcely half were actually soldiers, was seriously under strength.

Now the Serbs let it be known that they would not permit the Ukrainians, who were scheduled to relieve the weary and frustrated Dutch, into the enclave. The Dutch thus felt themselves condemned to remain imprisoned in the isolated city—which in July's heat stank almost unbearably of piled-up excrement and the body odor of 35,000 unwashed refugees, while the emaciated and vaguely repellent Srebrenicans combed through the Dutch garbage. So they spent their days staring back at the Serb gunners in the hills, recording the number of firing "incidents" in their notebooks, and trying to ignore the contemptuous gazes of the Muslim infantrymen, dug into a network of trenches just behind the observation posts and determined to force the Dutch to stay right where they were.

Now, in the midst of this meaningless and increasingly disagreeable assignment, the Serbs had suddenly turned their artillery on them. The two Dutch soldiers knew full well that a direct hit, which had to come sooner or later, would kill everyone in the observation post. Supposedly in such a situation their commander could call in NATO fighter planes to provide "close air support"—to strike at "smoking guns," which meant only those artillery and tanks that had been firing at them—but after the hostage-taking fiasco in May, the soldiers knew the UN commanders were more than reluctant to do so. The Dutch were in a precarious position.

And yet, why were the Serbs shelling them? The day before, on July 5, a long-range cannon had suddenly appeared on a hill a mile off; a pickup had sped by pulling a Serb antiaircraft gun, heading south; a hundred Serb soldiers passed in the distance, walking east. Apprised of these bewildering movements, the Dutch commanders told their troops not to worry—which meant, the soldiers knew, that the officers themselves had no idea what the movements were about.

Reading signs lay at the war's heart. What did it mean, the movement of a tank, a mortar, a battalion of troops? What story did these signs unwittingly disclose? Or was it a tale meant to deceive? During the five-day conquest of Srebrenica, the Serbs would move their tanks and guns and troops according to a delicate and bewildering choreography that, while seemingly without pattern, had been meticulously planned in Belgrade. The Serbs played on the divisions between the Dutch and the Bosnians and exploited the UN commander's deep aversion to ordering NATO planes to attack. A carefully designed series of movements allowed Muslims and United Nations officers and Western diplomats to convince themselves, at least for a time, that whatever the Serbs were up to, they had no intention of conquering the safe area. Generals Mladic and Perisic made it possible for their enemies to believe what they desired to believe, and by the time they could no longer avoid accepting what was truly happening, the Serbs had seized Srebrenica without a fight.

"The attack was typical of Serb military operations," write Honig and Both.

> They unfolded as if in slow motion. In their opening phases, attacks were marked by periods of intense shelling. Often these artillery barrages would not lead to anything more. They would just stop. Or, sometimes, there would be a pause, before another hail of artillery was released. The Serb military worked hard at making their bombardments appear random, so it was difficult to predict whether a particular bout of shelling was the prelude to a full offensive.[20]

Throughout the morning of July 6, Serb gunners pummeled Muslim trenches just behind the Dutch observation post; the Muslims fired back with their AK-47 assault rifles and launched a few mortar rounds.

At one o'clock, the Dutch soldiers were rocked by a tremendous explosion; the watchtower above shook; sand poured down on their heads from the sandbags that formed the bunker's walls. A Serb tank—a World War II-era T-34—was firing directly at the UN post. The commander of the OP's seven-man crew radioed headquarters, demanding NATO fighter planes be called in to protect them. Four hours later, the local commander informed the seven men that he had asked for the planes. More hours passed, shells kept coming, and when night fell the fighters still had not arrived.

The request for "close air support," like four similar requests that week, had been denied. When Lieutenant Colonel Ton Karremans, the Dutch "blue helmet" commander, reached Dutch Brigadier General Cees Nicolai, the chief of staff for UNPROFOR in Sarajevo, Nicolai explained that the new European envoy, Carl Bildt, would soon arrive in Belgrade to take up negotiations where Frasure had left off; a "military incident" now could destroy that effort. Nicolai also reminded Karremans of General Smith's May air strikes, out of which arose the explicit directive 2/95: "The execution of the mandate [was] secondary to the security of UN personnel." Since air strikes clearly risked the Serbs' taking UN personnel hostage, General Janvier simply could not permit them.

And how serious could this attack on a single observation post be? The answer seems obvious. For if Americans and perhaps Germans had been listening in on Generals Mladic and Perisic discussing a Srebrenica operation; if General Nicolai himself had seen dispatches reporting that Arkan and his Tigers had entered the area; if the Bosnians and doubtless the Americans knew that arms had been passing over the Drina bridges in great numbers— if all this was known, how could the UN officers and the Bosnians as well not have concluded that General Mladic was set on conquering Srebrenica?

Perhaps they failed to see what was happening: perhaps, as that truism of intelligence has it, "background noise" obscured the "real" signals. Perhaps some did not want to see it. The Americans, now at work on a new policy emphasizing "the defensibility of federal territory"—that is, a simplified map, which hardly could have provided for a Muslim Srebrenica—had no particular interest in ferreting out from their intelligence the conclusion that the Serbs had determined to seize Srebrenica. General Janvier had no interest in reaching such a conclusion either, for an assault on Srebrenica would leave him not only unarmed and impotent but exposed to the world as a gullible fool. Finally, the Bosnians, hunkered down in their trenches, did not want to believe that Mladic was finally sending his soldiers in to seize their town, for if this were true they knew that—in the absence of their great leader Naser Oric—they would be forced to place their lives in the hands of a few lightly armed and vaguely hostile United Nations troops, and nothing they had seen convinced them that the "blue helmets" were worthy of such trust.

The Serbs' genius was to recognize these fears and self-deceptions and to play upon them. Though they had the military strength to overwhelm the town with a sudden attack—after all, they had had artillery positions virtually encircling it for more than two years—such a strategy would have conveyed unmistakably to the Muslims, the UN leaders, and the world the Serbs' true intent, and possibly provoked a strong response. In any case this would have been contrary to the Serbs' accustomed methods, as Honig and Both observe:

> After gaining new ground the Serbs would invariably pause. . . . A pause enabled them to gauge the world's reaction. Also, it tended to make the attack appear like a limited or isolated incident—a moment of pique that would not continue. This usually succeeded in taking the sting out of any intended tough response.

At Srebrenica, then, the Serbs brought forward their tanks and artillery, slowly, cautiously, and only from the south. They thereby telegraphed a plausible explanation for their actions to those on the other side; for running through the southern part of the enclave was an important supply road upon which sat a bauxite mine that happened to belong to Rasko Dukic, an intimate of Radovan Karadzic who gave a great deal of money to the Serb leader's political party. By advancing slowly on that road, the Serbs offered an explanation for their movements: They were going to seize the road and finally get President Karadzic's well-to-do friend his mine back. With this obvious explanation available, all those who desired to avoid concluding the worst were free to do so.

On Saturday, July 8, the Serbs began shelling the observation post again, placing several rounds within the compound itself and destroying at least one of its walls. The young Dutch soldiers, crouching within the cramped bunker, tracking the deafening impact of each shell, and waiting for the one they would never hear, begged their commander once more for fighter planes; once more none came. After one shell, they smelled the observation post burning; in a panic, they radioed their commander and demanded that they be allowed to evacuate the post.

As the Dutch loaded their equipment into their armored personnel carrier, the soldier in the watchtower spotted a Serb tank scarcely one hundred yards away, its turret slowly turning, its gunbarrel swinging toward them. The Dutch fled back into the bunker. No shell came, however; instead, a party of twenty heavily armed Serb soldiers strode up to the observation post. Some of the men, according to Rohde, wore the black uniforms of Arkan's Tigers; others the camouflage of the Drina Wolves.

Outnumbered, lightly armed, placed squarely in the sights of the tank's cannon, the Dutch had no choice but to allow the Serbs inside. Many of the Serb soldiers were not unfriendly, but they methodically rifled through every bit of UN equipment and stole anything of use or value. They even demanded that the Dutch relinquish their personal weapons, which they readily did, and give up their helmets and uniforms, which the Dutch officer managed to persuade the Serbs to let them keep.

Finally, the Serb commander, admitting *sotto voce* that he was beginning to have difficulty controlling his men, advised the Dutch to depart. Did the "blue helmets" wish to go to Bratunac, the Serb town north of Srebrenica: In effect, he was inviting the Dutch to become hostages. No, replied the Dutch officer. Given the choice, he and his men would return to Srebrenica.

Between the observation post and UN headquarters, however, the Muslims crouched in their trenches, and they watched in growing fury what they saw as a cowardly retreat. By retreating from land the Muslims had won with their blood, the Dutch would force them to fall back from their trench line or risk being flanked and crushed by the advancing Serbs—which was why, since the Serbs had seized an earlier observation post in the same area on June 3, Muslim officers had repeatedly vowed to kill any "blue helmet" who fled an observation post. Such threats meant, as Rohde says, that "many of the Dutch were already more frightened of the Muslims they were supposed to be protecting than of the Serbs who surrounded the enclave."

As the white armored personnel carrier of the Dutch contingent rumbled slowly down the dirt road, the driver saw a number of Muslims, led by a middle-aged man with a rifle, building a barricade of trees and branches. The Dutch radioed for instructions. Their commander, fearing the Muslims would now take his soldiers hostage, ordered them to advance through the barrier. As the big, white vehicle ground slowly over the tree trunks the Dutch huddled inside heard the dull explosion of a grenade; the soldier in the top hatch collapsed on top of them, blood pouring from his temple. He died before they could get him back to base.

Later that day, when Serb soldiers took over a second observation post in the south, the "blue helmets" elected to go with the Serbs to Bratunac—to become, that is, Serb hostages. The Muslims had developed a clear strategy to force the "blue helmets" to defend them by imprisoning the Dutch in their observation posts, if necessary, so that they would be forced to become involved in any Serb assault on the enclave and thus would have no choice but to call in air strikes to defend themselves, if not the Muslims. But one of the Muslims had now killed a popular Dutch soldier. The strategy had backfired.

That evening, Lieutenant Colonel Ton Karremans, the Dutch commander, reported to his superiors in Sarajevo and Zagreb that the Serb attacks on his observation posts "must be regarded as part of an attempt to take possession of the Jadar Valley," the southern edge of the safe area. "The fact that there are no attacks on the rest of the enclave perimeter reinforces this view." Only the night before, however, Karremans had written that he did not anticipate the "seizure" of the observation posts. Only "in the long term" did the Serbs stand a chance of "neutralizing" the Muslims. In the short term, he had predicted, "due to a shortage of infantry, the [Serbs] will not be able to seize the enclave."

Although he had sent thousands more men over the Bajina Basta Bridge, General Mladic had held them back from Srebrenica, both to disguise his immediate intentions and to keep them in reserve for the operation's "second phase." So far, perhaps two thousand fresh troops had gathered around Srebrenica: Arkan's Tigers, Drina Wolves, mercenaries and irregulars from Greece, Germany, and Russia, as well as members of Milosevic's feared paramilitary police, who had had a central part in the brutal "cleansing" of Zvornik in the first weeks of the war. By now a total of perhaps four thousand Serbs had mustered close around Srebrenica—which was, as Chuck Sudetic has pointed out, "far fewer than the number a prudent commander would throw into a battle against five thousand men, the number of Muslims estimated to have guns in the 'safe area.'"[21] Mladic's aims were clearly limited; certainly he could not be planning to take Srebrenica itself.

Still, the Muslims were worried. Friday night, July 7, the Serbs had bombarded Srebrenica with 275 shells, forcing the people to spend the night in basements or any other shelter they could find. The day before, Ramiz

Becirovic, the Muslim military commander—a cautious middle-aged man with none of Naser Oric's bravado or charisma—had demanded that the United Nations commander allow the Muslims to take back their two tanks and their few other heavy weapons; Karremans, judging such a step premature, had refused. Now Karremans offered to let the Muslims have the arms, and Becirovic refused: He wanted to make it clear that it was the responsibility of the "blue helmets" to defend Srebrenica. "We don't want to take the weapons," he said. "Why don't you call for air strikes?"

When the Muslims had asked the same question after the attack on July 6, a Dutch liaison officer had lied, claiming that "no NATO aircraft were available." Repeating this hardly believable rationale would not do, particularly after Sunday, July 9, when the Serbs seized three more observation posts in the south. Serb gunners also shelled an enormous refugee center built by the Swedes, and set on fire a number of houses in Pusmulici, a village two miles south of Srebrenica. Muslim refugees were flooding north into Srebrenica. Serb tanks were slowly moving north. Muslim military leaders were beginning to panic.

Becirovic ordered his men to show restraint in the face of the Serb attack; he feared if the Muslims fired back, particularly with one or two of the artillery pieces they had hidden from the "blue helmets," they would in effect be providing the United Nations troops an excuse to abandon them. Militarily, the Bosnians of Srenbrenica had grown weaker during their years languishing in the safe area. They lacked fuel and shells for their two old tanks, they were low on ammunition, and many of their fighters had no working weapons. Some carried only a pistol or a single grenade, others knives or clubs. Becirovic believed that if Mladic had launched a cleverly camouflaged but all-out attempt to seize the enclave, the Muslims' only hope was to force United Nations officials—and Western leaders—to protect Srebrenica, as they had pledged to do. After making such a pledge, how could they let Srebrenica fall?

On Sunday, July 9, the Muslim commander buttonholed the Dutch liaison officer and told him angrily that the UN troops' response to the Serbs had been "shameful." Once again, he demanded to know where the NATO fighter planes were. What, he asked, were the "blue helmets" planning to do to prevent "a total massacre"? The liaison officer drew himself up. The Dutch, he said coldly, would "do the job their way." By evening, Mladic's soldiers were within a mile and a half of Srebrenica.

Karremans himself worried that NATO air strikes might put his men in danger. The Serbs had made sure that their Dutch hostages had telephoned their senior officers from Bratunac: The Serbs had put them up in a hotel and were treating them well. Karremans knew, however, that after the first NATO plane dropped the first bomb, in Mladic's eyes his Dutch "guests" would become allies of the Muslims and his prisoners of war, to be made use of as he liked. For the Dutch still in the field, meanwhile, Mladic had already employed less subtle arguments. David Rohde sets out the sequence:

The six rockets fired over the main Dutch compound when the attack began at 3 a.m. Thursday [July 6] appear to have made an impression on Karremans. The Soviet-made rockets make an ear-shattering noise before they pulverize whatever they hit. Between six and forty-two rockets can be fired in a volley, which means an acre of territory—the size of one of the Dutch compounds—can be incinerated in fifteen seconds. Since the attack began on July 6, whenever a Dutch vehicle left the UN compounds in Srebrenica and Potocari, shells would follow. Houses outside the main UN base at Potocari had also been pummeled by Serb gunners. The attempt to intimidate the Dutch was working.[22]

Because of the contradictions of UN policies in Srebrenica, Karremans was burdened with a seemingly insoluble practical problem: Although the United Nations was supposed to protect its "blue helmets" with NATO fighters providing "close air support"—which meant striking only guns and tanks that had themselves shelled the Dutch—the Serbs might well respond to air strikes by unleashing an enormous barrage on UN headquarters, killing scores, perhaps hundreds, of his men. Unless NATO warplanes destroyed much of the Serb artillery in one huge strike, Karremans clearly risked Dutch lives. Although NATO commanders were entirely willing to send their planes on such large-scale air strikes—the Americans had been pushing for them for months—General Janvier deeply opposed them. General Smith, who was ready to support them, was away on vacation; in any event, he was Janvier's subordinate and, as Akashi had made clear when the three men met in Split, would be treated as such.

Back in The Hague, meantime, Dutch government officials were deeply worried. According to Honig and Both, on Sunday, July 9, Defense Minister Joris Voorhoeve complained to Terry Dornbush, the American ambassador, that his men were "outnumbered" and "surrounded" and that Srebrenica was "indefensible." When an American representative at NATO headquarters in Brussels demanded that the alliance's planes be sent to strike the Serbs, the Dutch ambassador denounced the proposal as "counterproductive" and "dangerous."

By Sunday night, July 9, Dutch officers in Srebrenica and Potocari and UNPROFOR commanders in Sarajevo and Zagreb could no longer deny that General Mladic might well intend to seize Srebrenica. Some still found it impossible to believe. One of those not yet convinced happened to be General Janvier. To General Janvier, it seemed incomprehensible that Mladic would take the enclave at the very time negotiations were beginning in Belgrade.

General Janvier and Yasushi Akashi now sent to General Mladic what they called "a warning": they informed the Serb commander that the next morning Dutch soldiers would arrange their white armored personnel carriers in "blocking positions" on the road south of town. If General Mladic's men dared fire on them, General Janvier would have no choice but to order

NATO planes in to conduct "close air support" against the offending tank or cannon. Though General Janvier had mentioned certain (unspecified) "grave consequences" that would come of flouting this warning, when General Nicolai began to read the letter over the telephone to Mladic's deputy, General Zdravko Tolimir, his Serb interlocutor angrily interrupted:

What are you talking about? There are no Serbs in the enclave. General, you should not blindly trust Muslim propaganda.

The Dutch soldiers, for their part, did not much care for the idea of creating "a blocking force." When these orders were handed down, one sergeant recalled,

Everybody got a fright. You could easily get killed in such an operation. As far as I knew, we had not been sent to Srebrenica to defend the enclave, but rather as some kind of spruced-up observers.[23]

These strikingly blithe attitudes—"you could easily get killed in such an operation"—reflect perfectly the ambivalence and moral cowardice Western leaders had for four years displayed in their dealings with Bosnia and the former Yugoslavia. If the Dutch did in fact behave less like soldiers than "some kind of spruced-up observers," then this role had been set down for them at least two years before, when the empty "safe areas" idea had been proclaimed to the world. With the refugees fleeing wildly all around them and the Serb shells raining down on the town they were charged to protect, the Dutch officers and soldiers now found themselves enacting a sort of *mise-en-abîme*, a precise miniature duplication and repetition of that larger four-year-long plot.

Very early on Monday, July 10, the Serb gunners began a ferocious artillery attack on Srebrenica. Driving to take up their "blocking positions," one Dutch squad in a white armored personnel carrier was nearly hit by a mortar round and driven off the road. By nine the Dutch radioed once more for close air support; they were told their target list needed to be updated. When the planes finally arrived, at 10:30 a.m., they circled, patrolled, did nothing. Back in Zagreb, General Janvier had withheld permission to attack.

Aware of the firepower circling in the sky overhead, the Serbs now ignored the UN vehicles, concentrating their fire elsewhere. As the weather deteriorated, the shelling died down. The NATO planes returned to their Italian bases. In The Hague, Defense Minister Voorhoeve "told the Americans . . . that he believed that the situation was 'stabilizing' and he would only favor close air support if the Serbs resumed their attack. He opposed 'retaliation for retaliation's sake.'"

By now Srebrenica's market square was packed with thousands of refugees, many of them sitting on their bundles and bags, watching the smoke from their burning houses fill the southern sky. At noon General

Mladic's gunners began lobbing shells into the square, killing at least six instantly and sending the panicked crowd running in every direction. At dusk, about eighty heavily armed soldiers appeared, coming around the sharp, high turn at the southern entrance of the safe area. The Muslims, they knew, could see them perfectly, and they let themselves be seen. The Serbs stood at the gates of Srebrenica. "Looking down from the hairpin turn," Sudetic writes, the Serbs "could see the bedlam in the streets below."

> Families had fled their houses. . . . They carried with them suitcases, duffel bags, rucksacks, and their children. They pushed the lame and the aged in wheelbarrows. Some had cattle and horses and sheep. The wave of refugees burst through the gates of Camp Bravo and people poured in seeking protection from the shelling.[24]

The Dutch, horrified, urged the refugees to head north, to Potocari—precisely what the Serbs wanted, for they wanted to concentrate all civilians. But as Srebrenica's people ran up the street in terror, armed Muslims blocked their path. Becirovic knew—as Naser Oric had known in 1993, when Mladic offered the Muslims "free passage" out of the besieged town—that if the people of Srebrenica were evacuated the United Nations would have no incentive to take action. His soldiers would not permit Srebrenica's people, four in five of whom were refugees from elsewhere, to abandon it.

The Dutch commander meantime had faxed Zagreb an updated list of forty targets for "pinprick" air strikes. In his operations conference room in Zagreb General Janvier gathered the officers of his Crisis Action Team. The Serbs had breached the Dutch "blocking line" and all officers present now agreed that "pinprick" air attacks must be launched—all, that is, except one: General Janvier himself. Though Serb troops had entered the southern part of the town and had attempted, by shelling crowds of refugees, to herd the civilian population north, Janvier still refused to believe General Mladic intended to take Srebrenica. Even now, he observed, the Serbs seemed to be slowing their advance.

Janvier wanted more opinions. He directed his officers to telephone The Hague, Sarajevo, and the NATO base in Italy. At 8:15 p.m., according to unnamed Dutch officers, Janvier received a call from Paris, which he reportedly took "in another room, accompanied only by French officers," and after which he argued even more vehemently that Mladic could not be intending to seize Srebrenica.[25] Less than an hour later, Janvier spoke to Akashi and then made an attempt to get through to General Mladic himself. When he returned, he announced to his aides that though Mladic had not been available, he had just now spoken to Mladic's deputy, General Tolimir—the man who the day before had denied that Serbs had entered the enclave—and that Tolimir had confessed to him in some embarrassment that "renegade militias" were mounting the attack on Srebrenica. The Serbs, he said, would need time to get these renegades under control. (In fact, Janvier was forced to talk to Mladic's deputy because the Serb commander happened to be at the Yugoslav Army's Tara command center, just across the Drina in Serbia, with General Perisic at his side, personally directing the "renegade" operation.[26]) By now, night was falling. The targets would be too difficult to pick out. The planes returned to Italy.

At nine o'clock in the evening a Dutch hostage in Bratunac radioed his fellows in Srebrenica and conveyed an ultimatum from his Serb captors: The Dutch had forty-eight hours to evacuate the enclave. The clock would start running at 6 a.m. Three hours later Dutch commanders told their troops that the UN had countered that the Serbs had forty-eight hours to withdraw from the enclave and "failure to do so will result in large-scale air attacks."

It wasn't true. Someone in the tortuous UNPROFOR chain of command—Rohde says it was Janvier's deputy, General Nicolai—was confused. Janvier had approved only "close air support"—"pinprick" strikes, on any tank or gun that opened fire on United Nations troops. To General Nicolai's inaccurate message Colonel Karremans added a twist of his own: He announced to a midnight gathering of angry and skeptical Muslim military and political leaders that "between forty and fifty planes will be arriving over Srebrenica by 6 a.m. tomorrow. There will be a massive air strike." According to Rohde, the exhausted Dutch officer then approached a large map:

> "This area," Karremans said, pointing at the wide swath of territory now held by the Serbs south of Srebrenica, "will be a zone of death in the morning. NATO planes will destroy everything that moves."

The Muslims, deeply mistrustful, had no choice but to accept this promise. Earlier that evening, Srebrenica's mayor had managed to contact Alija Izetbegovic by radio. The mayor pleaded with his president for help. Izetbegovic told him he could do nothing for Srebrenica. Neither the Bosnian military commander nor the local commander in Tuzla would order an attack to support the town. Srebrenica's survival, President Izetbegovic told him bluntly, was now in the hands of the United Nations.

Before dawn, on the morning of Tuesday, July 11, Ramiz Becirovic shifted his forces westward, away from the front lines—away from any plausible defensive position—out of Karremans's "zone of death." Everyone watched the skies. Srebrenica had no other defense. All depended on the planes.

They did not come. While the Dutch and the Muslims strained their ears, desperate to hear the planes approach, Janvier and his officers sat in their control center, waiting to hear from the Dutch. Finally, Dutch officers radioed Tuzla, the sector headquarters:

> At 08.00, Dutchbat queried the lack of air support. But Sector North East was unable to pass on the query quickly. The person responsible for air support was not present and the secure fax machine was not working properly. . . . The message got stuck.

The drama had become farce. At eleven the Serbs attacked, moving quickly forward and lobbing artillery shells into the crowd of several thousand terrified refugees who had gathered outside the Dutch compound. Honig and Both quote a Dutch private:

> I do not know how many dead there were. It was a terrible sight. Most of us had never seen anything like it. While we were trying like mad to get the wounded to safety, we expected the next mortar attack. We should have been in the bunker.

About this time, in Zagreb, Yasushi Akashi, the UN envoy, spoke by telephone to Slobodan Milosevic in Belgrade. As a later "Chronology of Events" cable described it,

> AKASHI DESCRIBED TO MILOSEVIC DIFFERENCE BETWEEN CLOSE-AIR SUPPORT AND BATTLEFIELD AIR INTERDICTION (AIR STRIKES); MILOSEVIC REPLIES THAT TO MLADIC THERE WILL BE NO PERCEIVED DIFFERENCE AND UN FORCES IN SREBRENICA AREA RISK BEING TARGETED BY [SERBS]

As the Dutch brought trucks around to carry the wounded to Potocari, terrified people mobbed the vehicles, hanging desperately from the roofs, the doors, even the mirrors.

Finally, just after noon, having refused five official requests, General Bernard Janvier of France granted permission for NATO planes to strike at "any forces attacking the blocking UNPROFOR position" and "heavy weapons . . . shelling UN positions." By now, however, the first "package" of warplanes had been forced to return to base to refuel.

On a hill overlooking the burning town, a stocky, barrel-chested Serb officer in combat fatigues watched the planes depart. The officer, codenamed "Red," picked up a radio. "Down there," he told another officer as he looked over burning Srebrenica with its panicked crowds, "are our worst enemies. Are they fighting amongst themselves?"

"I don't think so," came the reply. "They're just scared to death."

Now "Red" was speaking to "Ruma." "Move ahead slowly and cautiously," he ordered the officer. "And good luck."

"Okay, see you down there."

The Serbs launched the final assault. They poured mortar rounds and artillery shells down on the town, herding the terrified mass of people toward the north. Muslim troops had already evacuated their lines, in the vain hope of a huge air strike. After more than three years there would be no great battle for Srebrenica. The Muslims were in full retreat.

It was 4:04 p.m. when Ruma radioed Red and asked him to mark his location. "Set a house on fire or a barn or some hay for them to see where you are."[27] The Serb troops, ecstatic with their easy victory, demanded to see their legendary leader, General Ratko Mladic, conquerer of Srebrenica.

Now the desperate Muslim officers, forced finally to admit that the UN soldiers really were going to let the "safe area" fall to the Serbs, hastily met and made a decision. As the enormous crowds of refugees pushed northward along the road, paying no heed to the wounded and the dying, they could see the Muslim men of Srebrenica climbing the hillside beside the road, heading west. Everywhere husbands bade goodbye to wives, fathers to children, sons to mothers. Srebrenica's men would not wait for the Serbs; they would take their chances in the forest.

As they gathered in their thousands up on the hill near Susnjara they watched the Serbs methodically reduce and conquer Srebrenica. One Muslim observer said:

> Tanks were firing. . . . We just sat and watched while houses were pummeled one by one. Then we saw a column of tanks, armored personnel carriers and different kinds of vehicles . . . about one mile from Srebrenica. . . . We could see the Cetniks shelling all the villages in the vicinity. They used the kind of shells that explode into fire. . . . The Cetniks were shelling exactly where the most people were concentrated. When I was sitting and looking at what they were doing to us, I started to cry and I said to myself that we would never survive this.

As he watched the smoke rise over Srebrenica, this man—the Human Rights Watch interviewers identify him only as J. N.—found himself gazing up at a wondrous and grotesque sight:

> These NATO planes circled two or three times around Srebrenica and then they dropped a couple of bombs. . . . I am sure none of them hit their targets. Even while the planes were dropping the bombs, [the Serbs] were still firing their tanks at the towns and villages. . . . After [the planes] left, the Cetniks began to bombard us harder than ever.[28]

The belated air strike did apparently destroy one tank. From Bratunac one of the captured Dutch officers telephoned a message to his fellows: If air strikes were not halted immediately the Serbs would not only shell the refugees and the Dutch compound directly, they would kill their Dutch hostages.

Without delay, or consultation with anyone in the NATO or United Nations chain of command, Dutch Defense Minister Voorhoeve telephoned the NATO base in Italy and ordered, "Stop, stop, stop!" Akashi and Janvier agreed. Flights over Srebrenica were suspended. Akashi, cabling the news of the fall of Srebrenica at 4:30 p.m. on July 11, emphasized in the same dispatch that "any withdrawal of the Netherlands battalion must be carried out through negotiation as the members are in some areas already interspersed with Serb forces."

The Dutch battalion's early evacuation was far and away the prime concern of the Dutch government and of United Nations officials. As the Serbs methodically and efficiently launched the second stage of the operation—as thousands of fresh Serb troops arrived in Potocari, many of them equipped with handcuffs and other police gear, or leading specially trained German shepherds; as they concentrated all refugees inside or around the Dutch compound at Potocari; as General Mladic announced to the crowd that "no one will be harmed" and then delivered sixty buses to begin evacuations; and then, as the Serbs, under the eyes of the Dutch, began separating all the remaining men from their families—throughout this entire, highly organized process, the officials of the United Nations would show once more that notwithstanding their duty to the 45,000 Muslims of Srebrenica, they in fact had only one real interest: the safety of the four hundred or so Dutch soldiers. As for the Dutch, unarmed, humiliated, they would serve in effect as the servants of the Serbs; they were outnumbered, powerless: What choice did they have?

"Everybody was afraid," said Hasan Nuhanovic, a Bosnian Muslim who had worked for the Dutch as an interpreter. He had begged the Dutch to place his family—father, mother, brother—on the list of UN dependents, and though they could have done so, they had refused.

> Everyone was afraid. The Dutch were afraid. We were afraid, but . . .
> I think we had much more reason to be afraid than the Dutch. As far as I
> know, the Dutch all returned home safely.

Nuhanovic never saw his family again.

During the next several days, the Serbs staged an operation of great efficiency. Only days before, the commander of Western military observers in Tuzla had concluded in a confidential report that the Serbs would never seize Srebrenica since "liquidation of a registered population of this size would be impossible." General Mladic's Serbs were about to prove him wrong.

PLUNGING FORWARD into pitch-black night, their faces lashed by unseen branches, Srebrenica's fleeing Muslims stumbled forward one against another. Fearing that the 15,000 men would disperse and scatter in the darkness, their commanders had linked many together with white string, one man's belt loop to the belt loop of the next, and then the next, until they formed an endless column snaking for mile after mile over eastern Bosnia's darkened mountains and through her wooded, mist-shrouded valleys. Fleeing into darkness, they shuffled blindly up and over Bosnia's black hills.

Though they had fled the fallen city, leaving their wives and daughters and fathers to the mercy of Serb conquerors, Srebrenica's 15,000 men well knew that they had not escaped. If Serb troops did not bother to follow, they did not need to: They knew the Muslims had undertaken a desperate attempt to reach Bosnian government-held territory forty miles away, knew the trails they must take, the roads they must cross. Gazing up at the hills above the city in the early morning gloom of July 12, the Serbs had watched the ten-mile-long column wend its way slowly out of the far reaches of the enclave and, after taking a few shots and picking off one or two of them, had taken up bullhorns. "We know you are going to try and pass through with your column!" they shouted. "Better for you to go to Potocari and leave with the buses!"[29]

However much they might have wanted, in their hunger and exhaustion, to believe these sweet words, however much they might have wanted to trust the Serbs to send them peacefully back to government-controlled land, the Muslims knew, as Bosnian prime minister Hasan Muratovic later put it, "what Serbs did before."

> Wherever they captured people, they either detained or killed all males from 18 to 55. It has never happened that the men of that age arrived across the front-line.[30]

Srebrenica's men understood as well that they were "special cases," that years of massacre and retribution meant that they could expect no quarter after the countless raids against nearby Serb villages. And so Srebrenica's 15,000 ignored the Serbs' siren song and set out in their long column, with fewer than one in three bearing some kind of weapon, and those, Srebrenica's soldiers, concentrated near the column's head.

The sun rose and with it July's baking heat as, two by two, they crossed a mine field and then trudged single file into a silent forest; and there, just after noon, machine-gun bullets ripped the silence, sending down on the screaming, bolting men a green blizzard of leaves and branches and scattering about the rough trail scores of bloodied bodies. The firing might have gone on for minutes but probably only seconds, and when the unseen Serb gunners halted their fusillade as abruptly as they had begun, surviving Muslims rose from the earth one by one and came together to gather on their coats the moaning wounded, and stagger on through the green woods.

AROUND MID-AFTERNOON ON JULY 12—about the time, back in conquered Srebrenica, that Serb soldiers, drawing back on the reins of their rearing horses or grasping tightly the leashes of their barking German shepherds, were herding together Muslim women and children and older men, under the gaze of the Dutch "blue helmets," and preparing for the arrival of General Mladic and his entourage of officers—Bosnian Army intelligence officers monitoring Serb radio communications intercepted a stark exchange:

> —We have found a place where civilians are concentrated. . . .
> —Please shell that place.[31]

Suddenly the forest exploded in red and yellow flashes. Everywhere earth erupted from the forest floor, mortar rounds sending up great clods of soil along with red-hot shrapnel; bullets raked the column of fleeing men; rocket-propelled grenades blasted bushes and trees so men thrown facedown hugging the earth were buried by leaves and branches and crushed beneath uprooted trunks.

The column broke into pieces; men became disoriented, fled into the forest in confusion:

> Almost immediately we began to hear detonations up ahead. . . . [A]fter about 700 or 800 meters, we came to an area where there were a lot of dead and wounded. My wife's brother was among the dead. . . .
>
> As we approached a creek we were elated because we thought we would be able to drink some water. But then we saw all the dead bodies, and I couldn't even think about taking a drink. . . . The bodies were lying all over the place like little pieces of wood.[32]

The men reached the heights of a ridge and from there they gazed down a long steep slope and saw the road they must cross—and on it green, armored vehicles and antiaircraft guns and tanks, placed along the roadside at twenty-meter intervals. Among the camouflaged armor of the Serbs there stood as well two prizes of war: a jeep and an armored personnel carrier painted bright white and emblazoned with the black "UN" of the United Nations Protection Force.

Among the tanks and cars Serb soldiers stood about, some cradling their weapons and smoking, others gazing casually up at the heavily forested slope. A wizened man in a dirty T-shirt stepped forward, raised his emaciated arms, and cupped his hands about his mouth: "Come here! I am here!" he shouts, squinting up at the hillside, and from off-camera—for this moment is preserved, thanks to the Serb cameraman General Mladic could not resist bringing along to memorialize his victory[33]—we hear a soldier order gruffly, "Tell them who you are with!"

> "I am with Ramo!"
> "Screw Ramo. Tell them you are with Serbs!"
> "With the Serbs!"
> "That's it, say with the Serbs . . . with Serbs, freely. 'Nermin, come down, I am here with the Serbs. . . .'"

We hear now a great explosion and see a column of smoke rising from the tree-covered hillside, and the camera returns to the skinny, sickly man shouting and we hear a second soldier's voice:

> "Say: all of you!"
> "All of you, come! Oo-oooh, Nermin. Come here freely, I am with the Serbs! Come all of you. . . ."

Soldiers in camouflage now step forward and begin to shout: "Come on, guys, come out! Come out with your hands up!" "Come on, guys, come out freely, guys!" And then: "There they are, you see? Tape that." And the camera wheels and among the green trees one can just make out here and there fleeing men, some of them running through open meadows and melting into silhouettes before vanishing into clouds of bright midsummer green.

From up on that ridge exhausted Muslims leaning against tree trunks, or squatting next to the wounded, gaze back down the slope toward the road, where a soldier wearing a UN blue helmet raises a megaphone to his lips. A strange metallic voice reverberates through the hills and valleys:

"Surrender! Surrender! No one will touch you! The UN will provide security for you to leave freely! Surrender! Surrender! . . ."

As night fell, thousands of Muslims, weakened by malnourishment and extreme thirst, deprived of sleep, and now beset by inescapable, bizarrely amplified voices incessantly luring them on—Surrender! Surrender!—succumbed to terror and paranoia.

The psyches of the men ruptured. Muslims mistook other Muslims for Serb infiltrators. They threw hand grenades and fired their automatics at one another.
. . . The soldiers' silhouettes huddled together and meandered through shadows. . . . The men here were strangers to one another. . . . Distrust spread like an infection. One Muslim soldier in a camouflage uniform let rip a spray of bullets and threw a hand grenade at a group of Muslim men; another man shot a bazooka and killed ten of his comrades.[34]

Men shouted and screamed hysterically and had to be gagged and bound. One placed the muzzle of a pistol in his mouth and squeezed the trigger. Another pressed a hand grenade to his neck and pulled the pin, decapitating himself and badly wounding several men around him.

From the road below the Serbs listened. From their armored turrets a few gunners opened fire, peppering the tree line with antiaircraft shells and mortar rounds that blanketed the dark treetops in a canopy of choking gray smoke. Most cradled their guns and leaned casually against their armored vehicles, gazing up at the dark ridgeline, smoking, waiting. Off-camera we hear voices—"Come on, surrender. Hurry up!"—and here and there Serb soldiers pass through the frame hustling the frightened men forward, prodding them with their rifles and making them stumble. "Come up, come. Come freely," a soldier says, pushing ahead of him four terrified men who are virtually dragging a wounded comrade. "Go, go, don't be afraid. We don't eat people."

Meanwhile, a few miles away, in the "cleansed" Serb town of Bratunac, local men—many of them refugees from villages Srebrenica's Muslims had raided and burned years before—hurried from house to house, excitedly summoning their fellows. "Come on," they said, "Grab your gun and come down to the soccer field. . . ."

On the tape of events near the road is a striking image, flickering into focus so briefly one can easily miss it. As a few Serb soldiers lie back in the grass, laughing, checking their pistols, the camera moves beyond them for a moment, and there in the middle distance stands a circle of Serb troops, pointing their rifles downward; and for a second, through the spaces between them, we glimpse unarmed men kneeling on the grass, their hands clasped on their heads. There may be one hundred, or two; perhaps more. They are dirty, exhausted; their faces are very pale. For that trembling instant one or two look directly at the man with the camera—directly at us. The Serb soldiers level their guns, loom up around them. The faces vanish. The tape goes black.

New York Review of Books, March 26, 1998

To the Killing Fields

I.

NEAR THE LOVELY NORTH PORTICO of the White House, on a mild and breezy evening in mid-June 1995, the president and first lady danced alone. In the background, musicians of the U.S. Marine Band played. Moments before, President Jacques Chirac and Mrs. Chirac of France had said their goodbyes. As Bill and Hillary Clinton danced, the president's foreign policy advisers—Warren Christopher, Madeleine Albright, Samuel Berger, and Richard Holbrooke—stood together looking on, for the night was warm and clear and beautiful and the White House, Holbrooke later recalled, "exuded all its special magic."

However seductive these romantic trappings, Holbrooke found himself preoccupied with other things. "I looked at Christopher, concerned that we would lose the moment," a moment Holbrooke had anxiously awaited since early that morning, when the "pre-brief"—a normally placid, pro forma meeting during which the president's aides and advisers prepare him for a session with a foreign leader—had "degenerated into an angry and contentious discussion." The anger and contention stemmed from the unfolding catastrophe in Bosnia. "The presentation given by members of the National Security Council staff," writes Holbrooke,

> was, in my view, misleading as to the situation, and especially the nature of American "automaticity" in assisting a UN withdrawal. When I started to offer a contrary view, the President, obviously disturbed that he was receiving contradictory information before [seeing] an important visitor, cut me off sharply.

Afterward, in the car on the way to the French embassy, where President Chirac expected Holbrooke and Christopher for lunch, the younger man expressed his "astonishment at what had just happened." Christopher, who, according to Holbrooke, had been "much sobered by the meeting," agreed that they must speak to the president as soon as they could.

And so we arrive at that magical night, the Chiracs having just departed after a pleasant dinner, the music playing, the First Couple tracing their solitary course across the White House dance floor. Finally the Clintons break, turn, stroll over to the North Portico. Holbrooke seizes his chance.

> "I hate to ruin a wonderful evening, Mr. President," I began, "but we should clarify something. . . . Under existing NATO plans, the United States is already committed to sending troops to Bosnia if the UN decides to withdraw. I'm afraid that we may not have that much flexibility left."
>
> The President looked at me with surprise. "What do you mean?" he asked. "I'll decide the troop issue if and when the time comes."
>
> There was silence for a moment. "Mr. President," I said, "NATO has already approved the withdrawal plan. . . . It has a high degree of automaticity built into it, especially since we have committed ourselves publicly to assisting NATO troops if the UN decides to withdraw."
>
> The President looked at Christopher. "Is this true?" he said. "Yes, it appears to be," Christopher said tersely. "I suggest that we talk about it again tomorrow," the President said grimly, and walked off without another word, holding Hillary's hand.[1]

To the gruesome tableaux the word "Bosnia" then conjured up in citizens' minds—artillery gunners bombarding unprotected civilians; emaciated prisoners staring from behind barbed wire; militiamen raping, mutilating, and slaughtering unarmed people—one is forced to add another, quieter and yet perhaps more chilling: of men thousands of miles from the battlefields who wear expensive suits and eat fine food and hold in their hands the power to stop the war but who lack, after two and a half years, a fundamental understanding of their commitments and responsibilities.

The morning after President Chirac dined with the Clintons, his troops in Sarajevo were forced to stand by and watch as Serb artillerymen beat back a desperate Muslim offensive by bombarding the city in an attack as savage as the war's opening months more than three years before. "In a new twist," wrote Tom Gjelten, the correspondent for National Public Radio,

> Serb gunners attached 500-pound bombs to makeshift rockets and directed them at sites where they could do maximum damage. On June 28, one such rocket blasted into the Sarajevo radio and television building, . . . killing a Bosnian policeman, wounding dozens of journalists, and demolishing the offices of foreign news crews. A half hour after the television center was hit, another rocket crashed into an apartment building across the street, wiping out three floors.
>
> A reporter for *Oslobodjenje*, Sara Jevols, visited the bombed apartment house.

One of the tenants, Josip Grbic, took us to the upper floors. . . .

"This flat in front of us," he said, "belonged to our neighbor Slavko. We don't know whether he's alive or not. Here is his shirt, you see. We know he came back from the battlefront yesterday. I'm very much afraid that he is lying under all this rubble." Slavko's body was found later.

A blonde lady, weeping, told us she was worried as well about Hamed Zivgovic, the father of two little boys who had been hurt and taken to the hospital. "Hamed was supposed to come back from the frontline yesterday," she said, "but we don't know if he did. We hope not." Hamid's body was also found later.[2]

Hundreds of civilians died in Sarajevo that June and July, blown apart by mortar shells, shot down in the street by snipers, or buried under the rubble of their homes. Meanwhile, in a revival of a routine they had performed regularly for more than two years, President Clinton demanded NATO send its warplanes to bomb and strafe the Serbs; President Chirac, Prime Minister John Major, and other Western leaders refused. In the end, the West did nothing.

By now Chirac and his colleagues, who had concluded that exposing their troops to artillery gunners, snipers, and hostage-takers did little more than pose a constant political risk to their governments, had begun speaking more insistently about bringing them home, and doing so before the coming winter. To be certain of completing this complicated and dangerous assignment before the snow came, NATO troops would have to begin "extraction" by late summer, less than two months hence.

As it happened, military planners at the Pentagon and at NATO headquarters in Brussels had during 1994 spent many months composing "OpPlan 40–104," a highly classified document of fifteen hundred pages that covered, according to Holbrooke, "every aspect of NATO's role in supporting a UN withdrawal, from bridge building to body bags." On June 8, 1995, after President Clinton and his senior officials had created an embarrassing controversy by making conflicting statements about American commitments to the Europeans in Bosnia, Holbrooke asked Pentagon officials to brief him on OpPlan 40–104, and Lieutenant General Howell Estes, the chief American planner, appeared at the secretary's office to describe what he called Operation Determined Effort. Holbrooke, by his account, listened in some amazement:

It was bold and dangerous. . . . It used twenty thousand American troops, some of whom were assigned to carry out a risky nighttime U.S. heliborne extraction of UN troops from isolated enclaves, an operation likely to produce casualties. As soon as General Estes finished, . . . I rushed to Christopher's office and insisted that he and his inner team get the same briefing immediately. When he heard it, Christopher was equally amazed.

The amazement of Clinton's foreign policy "principals" was, unfortunately, only beginning. "When OpPlan 40–104 came to the attention of senior officials," as Holbrooke somewhat delicately put it, "there was some confusion as to its status." President Clinton, though he had publicly vowed to support with American troops a withdrawal of the 25,000 UN peacekeepers from Bosnia, had never formally approved, or read, or even been "briefed on," NATO's actual plan. But the NATO Council in Brussels, which includes representatives from all alliance countries, including the United States, *had* approved it, and thus, notes Holbrooke, under NATO procedures the plan had been formally adopted. While no one could force the president of the United States to dispatch American troops, if Clinton declined to follow through on his pledge, "the United States," Holbrooke writes, "would be flouting, in its first test, the NATO process it had created. The resulting recriminations could mean the end of NATO as an effective military alliance, as the British and French had already said to us privately."

That Holbrooke felt especially sensitive to the implications of American Bosnia policy for the alliance was not surprising, for at the time he was charged with pushing through the national security bureaucracy President Clinton's policy of expanding NATO into Eastern Europe, a supremely delicate political operation that would not be helped by a failure of the United States to carry through on commitments it had made, whether or not its leaders were aware it had made them.

Holbrooke speaks of "complicated Cold War procedures," but of course the NATO Council was not an independent body. Americans held dominant power in its halls, and would have been able to alter, reshape, or even block the evacuation plan had they so wished. It needn't have been approved in the form it was. Even if, at the time "OpPlan 40–104" was devised, it had seemed unlikely it would ever be put into practice—indeed, even if, as seems possible, U.S. officers had purposely drafted a plan so risky that their civilian masters would resist putting it into practice—the document should never have been approved before senior American civilian officials had understood and passed on it. At the very time the American government was in effect pledging to commit twenty thousand troops to undertake a perilous mission in a war zone, no official of any rank in the Clinton administration appeared to have been paying much attention.

As Holbrooke notes, from the moment Clinton pledged publicly that American forces would support the allies if they chose to withdraw, the president had opened the possibility of a stark choice: either fulfill the promise or abandon the NATO alliance in its present form. That Bill Clinton didn't grasp this, that many of his own advisers did not seem to appreciate it, that the president had to have it explained to him on that evening of June 14—all of this, given the stakes for Bosnia and the United States, bespeaks a startling degree of confusion and ineptitude. When one considers that from Bill Clinton's first inauguration the *sine qua non* of his policy toward Bosnia had always been his refusal to send American ground troops, it is astonishing that

he was unaware that he had irrevocably committed himself, in some circumstances, to do just that. More important, his ignorance of the implications of
his pledge in effect poisoned his administration's policy toward the Balkan
war, for it meant that the president himself was unable to see clearly the terrain bounded on one side by his refusal to send troops and on the other by
his resulting need to keep the European peacekeepers there. Nor could he
have been able to grasp the larger implications of the Bosnia "endgame." As
Holbrooke writes,

> It was not an overstatement to say that America's post–World War II secu-
> rity role in Europe was at stake. Clearly, we had to find a policy that
> avoided a UN withdrawal. That meant a greater U.S. involvement.

In a war fraught with reversals and ironies, we have reached perhaps the
greatest of them all; for here Bill Clinton, Arkansas governor, comes squarely
face to face with George H. W. Bush, foreign policy president. It was President Bush who largely ignored the ample signs of Yugoslavia's collapse; it was
President Bush who after the Serbs attacked the Slovenes in July 1991, and
despite changes enacted only seven months before that had explicitly made
such "crisis management" part of the alliance's mission, chose to "hand off"
the conflict to the Europeans—but to the militarily toothless European
Union, not NATO; it was Bush who during late summer and fall of 1991
turned aside suggestions that American warplanes and ships attack Serb gunners shelling Dubrovnik and Vukovar; and it was Bush who in early 1992
turned aside a French suggestion that peacekeepers should be sent to Bosnia
to prevent war from breaking out.

Had President Bush made a different decision in any or all of these cases,
he might have succeeded in greatly circumscribing, or even preventing altogether, the Bosnian war. But Bush and his advisers had maintained the consistent and admirably unhypocritical position summarized in Secretary
James A. Baker's homely expression: "We got no dog in this fight."

Three years and hundreds of thousands of dead later, George Bush's successor had been forced to realize that something *was* at stake in Bosnia: the
Atlantic alliance. Now few could deny that four years of savage war allowed
to rage unchecked on the European continent had at last, and by a circuitous
route, reached the point of threatening the institutions—military, political,
financial—that since World War II had linked Europe and America. The
Americans did indeed have a dog in this fight.

If Holbrooke's normally impeccable reasoning seems somewhat paradoxi-
cal—"Clearly, we had to find a policy that avoided a UN withdrawal. That
meant a greater U.S. involvement"—this is because Clinton's abrupt com-
prehension had indeed turned matters upside-down. If Holbrooke's explanation to Clinton did indeed "ruin a beautiful evening," sending the president
stalking off with his wife, it was perhaps because Clinton, with an election
looming, had instantly grasped the political import of what Holbrooke had

said. Until a moment before, Bill Clinton had believed that the choice facing him on what surely was his administration's potentially most serious and politically damaging foreign policy issue was whether or not to dispatch American troops. In view of the tangled situation on the ground, the strong resistance of U.S. military officers, and, above all, the skepticism Americans expressed in their responses to polltakers, Clinton's answer, at least until after the election, and however bad things in Bosnia become, would have continued to be "no." But that secure and comforting world had suddenly collapsed, and Clinton had now to accept that the choice facing him was very different: between sending American troops to "implement a failure" or sending them to end a war.

II.

During the days after President Chirac's visit, senior officials of the Clinton administration gathered to undertake a Bosnia "policy review." Anthony Lake invited officials from the various departments, including State, Defense, and the CIA, to meetings to discuss an "endgame" approach that would take the Americans beyond "daily crisis management" to "planning strategically." Lake did not, however, invite Richard Holbrooke. "Disturbed by this exclusion," writes Holbrooke,

> I consulted Vernon Jordan, one of the wisest men in Washington and a close friend of the President. . . . I told Jordan that I was considering departure [from government] before the end of the summer. If Bosnia policy was going to be formulated without my involvement, then there was little reason to stay.[3]

Holbrooke's exile was short; Vernon Jordan had a word with the secretary of state and with the president and, Holbrooke writes, "the situation eased." Thus was the assistant secretary of state for European and Canadian affairs permitted to take part in the dreary business of "policy planning," in which bureaucracies grind out papers, "principals" meet and debate them, and those who leave the meetings disgruntled telephone a favored reporter and "leak" their concerns onto the pages of the country's leading newspapers.

Under the guise of this patient exercise, however, Lake, who as national security advisor was supposed to play the "honest broker" mediating between departments and ensuring that the president received an unbiased view, had determined that matters would take a different course. According to Bob Woodward (who is clearly following Lake's account), in late June 1995, and before passing on the recommendations from other departments, Lake gave the president his own paper, detailing what he called an "Endgame Strategy" that included a set of "carrots and sticks" to force all sides to the negotiating table:

Lake proposed that Clinton send him as a secret emissary to the allies so he could explain that Clinton had made firm and final decisions on the future course of U.S. policy on Bosnia. The foundation [of the proposal] would be an assertion that the United States would implement this new, long-term policy by itself, outside the umbrella of the United Nations and NATO, if necessary.

After two years of largely blaming the Europeans for the failure of the "lift and strike" strategy, President Clinton would boldly declare his readiness to strike out on his own. But in what cause? The plan, according to Woodward,

> included massive bombing of the Serbs if they did not cooperate and agree to peace negotiations. It also put pressure on the Bosnian Muslims by say-ing the United States would lift the arms embargo as the Muslims wanted, but if the Muslims did not negotiate, the United States would leave the region, effectively abandoning them. This was called "Lift and Leave."

It made for a dizzying journey, this rush down the road from defender of the "ethnically cleansed" Bosnian Muslims to single-minded and fiercely dis-interested enforcer of negotiations. It is unclear what precisely the terms of such negotiations might have been, what place "justice"—the return of cap-tured and "cleansed" territory—would have in them; but for the Bosnians, the signs were not good. For to insist on justice was to follow the costly and difficult and messy way to a settlement; it was Bill Clinton's insistence on justice, together with his reluctance to bear those difficulties, that had always been the central contradiction in his position. Now, in the blink of an eye, all this had changed. Now nothing must stand in the way of talks, talks that must at last bring the conflict to an end. Though he threatened "massive bombing" of the Serbs, the president had not changed his position on dis-patching ground troops. Instead, confronted with the threat of the UN sol-diers' departure and the dispatch of U.S. troops that (it was finally understood) must follow, all the squeamishness about "ratifying ethnic cleansing" had vanished; so as well had all the talk of "rewarding the aggres-sors"—a phrase with which Clinton officials had habitually tarred European peace plans from Vance-Owen onward. The president's rhetoric now placed him squarely among the peacemakers:

> "I want to get the diplomatic process back on track," Clinton said, adding that he felt stuck because under the UN agreements the United States and the other allies were prohibited from talking to the [Bosnian] Serbs, who were the aggressors. "We need to get them back to the table."

The Serbs' thoughts, however, were by now far from Washington and its "policy review" and far as well from the peace table. On June 21, a Bosnian

Muslim military scout had observed Zeljko Raznatovic, the celebrated criminal and militia commander popularly known as Arkan, leading thousands of his famously savage "Tigers" across the Drina and into Bratunac. All that night and those that followed, Serb soldiers drove tanks and armored vehicles, as well as truckloads of fuel and ammunition, across the Drina bridges. The signs of the imminent attack on Srebrenica were seemingly impossible to miss, and indeed they were not missed. The nations of the West, however, having grown accustomed to their impotence, chose to interpret the signs as they liked, and the Serbs, having for four years taken the psychological measure of the Western leaders, designed their attack especially to let the Americans and the British and the French and the Dutch think what they preferred.

And so on July 13, when—as everyone could see on television—General Mladic and his men finished loading the women and children on buses and expelling them from Srebrenica but kept the men back "for interrogation," the officials running the most powerful nation on earth were able to look on from the White House and, however improbably, tell themselves that their knowledge was limited.

On July 13, as General Mladic and his soldiers finished "cleansing" Srebrenica of its women and children, Jacques Chirac, according to Woodward, called Bill Clinton:

> Chirac was full of moral indignation. This was like World War II. The Serbs were separating the men and taking them off to camps. "We must do something."
> "Yes," Clinton said, "we must act."
> Chirac had a breathtaking suggestion. They ought to go in with French ground forces and American helicopters to recapture the city.

In Woodward's account, Clinton was "clearly stunned" by this outlandish suggestion. Holbrooke, however, gives a more plausible version; Chirac's proposal, he writes, "had already been discussed through official French channels, and run into fierce opposition not only from the British and the Pentagon, but from Chirac's own generals." Such opposition might be overcome, but the former cavalryman and new French president would need Clinton's support. It was not to come. Clinton, surrounded by aides and officials listening in on the conversation, "made it clear," according to Woodward, "that he didn't consider [Chirac's proposal] practical and wouldn't go along."

Clinton put down the telephone, looked at the faces of the men around him and, according to Woodward, addressed a young naval officer who had come into the office to set up the telephone.

"What do you think we should do on Bosnia?" Clinton asked.

"I don't know, Mr. President," the dumbfounded aide replied.[4]

As the president spoke, on a soccer field in the Serb town of Bratunac, Bosnian, Serb soldiers and militiamen were lining up the men of Srebrenica.

III.

Only later, years after he recorded the interview with CNN's *World Report*, can one see subtle signs of Richard Holbrooke's discomfort and unease. It was July 16, 1995, and even as the bloody catastrophe of Srebrenica was playing itself out four thousand miles to the east, the assistant secretary managed to answer Jeanne Meserve's questions with precision and aplomb. Yet look more closely at the videotape, study it frame by frame, and you will see that this Sunday afternoon finds Holbrooke pale, unsettled, distracted; and though CNN's producers had announced for that afternoon a typically self-regarding theme focused on the future—"The Bosnia Quagmire: How close is the United States to being pulled into the mess in Bosnia?"—it is hard not to suspect that their guest was preoccupied with an all-too-painful present.

As he sat answering the reporter's questions that Sunday afternoon, Holbrooke tells us in his memoirs,

> precise details of what was happening [in Srebrenica] were not known . . . , but there was no question that something truly horrible was going on.

An odd construction, that sentence, defining what was known only by what was not: Five days after the Serbs swept into Srebrenica, Holbrooke and other officials, men and women perched on the heights of the United States national security bureaucracy and benefiting from all of its vast powers of perception (satellites gazing down from space; spy planes snapping photographs from the upper atmosphere; unmanned "drone" planes relaying "real-time" video images; diplomats and attachés "in-country" working their informants for secrets and rumors and gossip)—five days later, these officials had no "precise details" of Serb actions in this one tiny place in eastern Bosnia but were able nonetheless to harbor the certainty that "something truly horrible was going on"?

How could they have been so certain? Doubtless the lack of "precise details" was meant partly to serve as something of a hedge against accusations of guilt through inaction. (Given *real* knowledge, so the implication goes, something might have been done.) But what after all could that "something truly horrible" have been? Did Richard Holbrooke and his colleagues really require "precise details" to answer that question? And in what would such details have consisted? Would Bosnian government minister Hasan Muratovic's explicit warning of July 13 qualify, when he told U.S. ambassador John Menzies in Sarajevo that Serb soldiers had gathered more than a thousand Muslim prisoners in a soccer stadium in Bratunac? How about Bosnian foreign minister Mohammed Sacirbey's detailed description, in a telephone call to UN representative Madeleine Albright the same day, of how the Serbs were committing atrocities around Srebrenica? Or a similar statement Sacirbey made, also on July 13, to his British opposite number,

Foreign Secretary Malcolm Rifkind, during an emergency meeting in London (and sent by cable to the State Department), that he

> had just spoke[n] with President Izetbegovic and had received "alarming news" about the refugees from Srebrenica. Large numbers of refugees were now being moved out of the enclave in buses and trucks unescorted by UNPROFOR troops. Many were being taken "off the main track" and "all sorts of atrocities" were being committed.

If Sacirbey's statement was not precise enough, it is hard not to suspect that the still-classified photo reconnaissance and cable traffic contained more details, for it is clear that American satellites and spy planes were taking many relevant photographs. The only question is who in the intelligence bureaucracy actually examined them and what they did with them and when. It is also clear that Bosnian Muslim intelligence officers were listening in on Bosnian Serb Army communications and likely passing on at least some of what they heard to the Americans, who in any event were likely listening in as well. "If it ain't scrambled, we're listening to it," as an American military intelligence officer said.

What "precise details" might these professional listeners have heard? The next evening, July 14, the Bosnians certainly heard Drina Corps commander General Radivoj Krstic order a major whose soldiers had surrounded a two-mile-long column of fleeing Muslims near a village called Glodzanje, "You must kill everyone. We don't need anyone alive." The Bosnian intelligence officers would have heard Major General Zivanovic of the Drina Corps tell one of his officers that the Muslims "must surrender with all their weapons," and that, after they did so, he should "shell the group with all your weapons and destroy it." When an officer identified only by the codename "Hawk" reported that he had found fifty Muslims in the forest and that "we must kill them," he is ordered by another officer, codenamed "Montenegro," to "do it slowly. We don't need any surprises. Surround them, and kill them slowly."[5]

We can count the foregoing, certainly, as a number of "precise details." Short of an exhaustive investigation, it is hard to know for sure when U.S. intelligence officers might have had this information; where and at what level of the security bureaucracy those officers might have found themselves; and finally, and most important, how quickly they passed the intelligence up the line to their superiors and how quickly these latter gave it over to their political masters.

And yet in the end, after one sets out the story of the killings in Srebrenica—the atrocity fated to be labeled "Europe's worst massacre since World War II"—that story does not derive from a scandal about information, about who knew what when. The massacre at Srebrenica, as Holbrooke himself implies, was a culmination, marking with stark barbarities committed on the people of a UN-guaranteed "safe area" the end of a long and terribly logical series of tawdry, cowardly decisions by the nations of the West.

From the Bosnia war's inception in April 1992, indiscriminate killing, rape, torture, and massacre had formed the essence of "ethnic cleansing," that war's signal technique, and U.S. intelligence had had "precise details" of this certainly by that summer and probably much earlier. A partly declassified Defense Intelligence Agency cable, for example, offers "a list of prisons in Bosnian territory, with the number of prisoners as of July 1992." The information is arranged in tabular form, under the rubrics "Location," "Number of Prisoners," and "Number Liquidated." U.S. intelligence officers, who presumably compiled in July or early August of 1992—the date, like much else, is blacked out by the government censor—lists the "Number Liquidated" at Zvornik's "Bratsvo" Stadium as more than two thousand; at three other prisons the number liquidated exceeded one thousand.

In "Brcko-Luka" the U.S. intelligence officers list the "Number Liquidated" as more than three thousand. "During the late spring and early summer of 1992, Charles Lane and Thom Shanker reported, "Some three thousand Muslims in the northern town of Brcko were herded by Serb troops into an abandoned warehouse, tortured, and put to death." As it happened, they go on, American intelligence officers were monitoring events in the town virtually in "real time."

A U.S. intelligence satellite orbiting over the former Yugoslavia photographed part of the slaughter. "They have photos of trucks going into Brcko with bodies standing upright, and pictures of trucks coming out of Brcko carrying bodies lying horizontally, stacked like cordwood," an investigator working outside the U.S. government who has seen the pictures told us. . . . The photographs of the bloodbath in Brcko remain unpublished to this day.[6]

It is difficult, then, to ascribe the Western response to Srebrenica to lack of "precise details," for the Western leaders acted as they had been accustomed to act for the past three years. The degree to which details might have been lacking was a convenience, an excuse for inaction, not an explanation. And for Holbrooke, who had loudly made known his disgust with the weak Western policy as early as 1992, when as a private citizen he had undertaken a "fact-finding" trip to the region, the final indignity, before he would be freed (by, in part, the horror of the massacre in Srebrenica itself) to launch into a virtuoso diplomatic performance, will be bearing the burden of "managing" the catastrophe of Srebrenica, part of which required him to sit in CNN's studio as a man keeping a horrible secret. One can not see inside his head; still, it is hard not to believe that his glances this way and that, his blinking, his frequent adverting to the CNN coffee mug, derived in large part from the effort of insisting on an ambiguity that by then was no ambiguity at all.

What might Holbrooke have been thinking about that "something truly horrible" that was taking place four thousand miles away? "Precise details" aside, of course, anyone who knew anything of the war's history had to know what the fall of Srebrenica would mean. For Holbrooke, the name Bratunac, where a well-remembered massacre of Serbs had taken place in 1993, would have had a special resonance, a resonance not so immediately evident to CNN's Sarajevo correspondent, who now, this Sunday two years later, as Holbrooke waited his turn to be interviewed, reported from an already-darkened Sarajevo that

> . . . perhaps as many as four thousand men were taken to an area [sic] called Bratunac which is just outside the Srebrenica enclave. Their precise conditions and whereabouts [are] not known.

Not to worry, however: officials of the International Red Cross had appealed to Serb leaders for permission to visit the refugees and, according to the CNN man, "In Sarajevo there's hope and expectation that that permission will come through."

Listening to these words Holbrooke sat silent and glum. A moment later he would also gamely insist on the need to "get access to the twenty thousand Bosnian men who are now apparently missing. . . ." But what can have been passing through his mind when he heard talk of Red Cross officials visiting the men at Bratunac? Whatever the lack of "precise details," the odds seemed very good that at this point, five days after General Mladic strode triumphantly into Srebrenica, Richard Holbrooke knew that any such visit by Red Cross officials to the "as many as four thousand men" in Bratunac would produce a very one-sided conversation.

In the five days since the enclave fell, Holbrooke writes in *To End a War*, he had

> spent long hours unsuccessfully trying to find a way to stop the tragedy in Srebrenica. . . . My recommendation—to use airpower against the Bosnian Serbs in other parts of the country, as well as Srebrenica—had been rejected by the Western European nations that had troops at risk in Bosnia, and by the Pentagon. . . .

Here again an oddly constructed sentence—would it not be more natural for an American official to speak of his recommendation as rejected "by the Pentagon, and by the Western European nations," not the other way around?—alerts the reader that a seemingly simple point is not quite so simple. Holbrooke's "recommendation," however vehemently argued, never had a chance of success. The power to order air strikes was constrained by the notorious "dual key" arrangement, according to which either United Nations officials or NATO leaders had the power to block a proposed attack. After they had refused to allow air strikes that might have stopped the Serbs at Srebrenica's gates—a refusal Holbrooke strongly implies might derive from "a deal" the UN Protection Force commander, French General

Bernard Janvier, had concluded with General Mladic a month before—would it have been at all likely that United Nations officials and Western leaders would approve them now, after the enclave had already fallen, and after the Dutch soldiers had been effectively taken hostage? As Holbrooke later wrote,

> The first line of resistance to any action was the Dutch government, which refused to allow air strikes until all its soldiers were out of Bosnia. . . . The Serbs knew this, and held the bulk of the Dutch forces captive in the UN compound at the nearby village of Potocari until they had finished their dirty work at Srebrenica.[7]

The "bulk of the Dutch forces" were indeed trapped in Potocari, having been carried there by a vast, chaotic wave of refugees who, fleeing the invading Serbs, clung frantically to the hatches and the mirrors of the armored personnel carriers—a Dutch report would later note the soft, repeated "bangs" that told the Dutch inside that "refugees (dead and/or alive) were [being] run over" beneath the treads.[8] But it is also true that a number of Dutch troops found themselves distributed about a few square miles of land upon which the Serbs had constructed, immediately after the fall of the enclave, a makeshift but highly organized, highly efficient killing machine. Although they had got wind of a handful of executions the Serbs had begun carrying out in and around the UN compound in Potocari, the Dutch troops only slowly began to suspect the horror of the larger story, and thus the reader of the *Report Based on the Debriefing on Srebrenica*, drawn from interviews conducted with them—after an unconscionable six-week-long delay—by Dutch Ministry of Defense officials, occasionally finds himself overcome by a very strange feeling, as if he were reading an account of a complex and unsettling landscape written by a man who is nearly blind but doesn't know it.

Fifty-nine Dutch troops, who had been seized as the Serb soldiers gradually "rolled up" one UN "observation post" after another, found themselves hostages of the Serbs, which meant that they stayed in a hotel and spent their time drinking beer and chatting with their families in Holland. As the report notes, the hotel happened to be in Bratunac. Something, in fact, had happened in Bratunac, a town conveniently located a few miles north of Potocari that seems to have served as a kind of "switching station" for General Mladic's complicated killing system. According to the Dutch report,

> On 14 July, there were a number of buses in Bratunac containing male refugees sitting with their heads between their knees and giving the impression that they were very frightened. There was a great deal of shooting in Bratunac, for example, from the direction of the so-called stadium (a football pitch surrounded by a fence).[9]

The Dutch soldiers, the report goes on, "did not, however, find any victims"—a rather misleading locution, managing to suggest as it does that the soldiers searched for victims, when they apparently did not, and that there were none, when there certainly were.

What had happened on that football field? After the Bosnian minister Hasan Muratovic told the American ambassador, John Menzies, on July 13 that Serbs had gathered hundreds of Muslim prisoners there, U.S. officials, according to one report, "obtained . . . a photo . . . of the stadium [which] did not bear out the assertion. No further search was undertaken."[10] If true, and in view of the further "precise details" we now have, this is a horrible admission; for it seems to confirm that the American government had the power not only to check these reports using photographs but to do it instantly—a charge which is, and remains, much disputed—while apparently showing how a minor mistake of timing not only can undermine that power but also reverse it, leading the Americans to believe that all their technological prowess had "disproved" an allegation that happened to be true.

By now, of course, we have other "precise details" that Richard Holbrooke and his colleagues then lacked; for Bratunac and other villages and towns in the area we have the estimates of the dead and, in many cases, the accounts of survivors. In the end, however, such "precise details," if they do not contradict the fact that "something horrible" was going on, are quite limited in what they really let us *know*. They do not let us know, for example, how the story of what happened in Bratunac that July really began more than two years before, after Nasir Oric led Srebrenica's Muslims on the notorious "Christmas attack" on the village of Kravica. Those Serbs who survived, now homeless, penniless, unable even to bury their mutilated dead, made their way through the snow to Bratunac. It was there, in 1996, that Chuck Sudetic interviewed Mihailo Eric, one of those survivors:

"After the Christmas attack, when the people from Kravica were refugees in Bratunac, the menfolk were bitter, weren't they?"

"They were angry. . . ."

"What did they say?"

"Revenge. . . . They said, 'Kad tad. Kad tad, sooner or later our five minutes will come.'"

". . . And the opportunity finally came."

"Yes."

"Vengeance?"

"Yes, blood vengeance."

"Did they come for you?" [He nodded.] "They were excited?"

"Yes. Yes."

"What did they say?"

"They said, 'Grab your gun, and come down to the soccer field.'"

The soccer field at Bratunac, that is, whence the Dutch hostages heard "a great deal of shooting." Much of that firing was done by men like Mihailo Eric. As it happens, though, Mihailo himself, a war hero, a man who had been gravely wounded, shot through the forehead earlier in the fighting, refused to take part. As he told Sudetic,

> "It's one thing to kill someone in battle, and it's something else to kill prisoners, men who've surrendered and have no guns."
> "And have their hands tied?"
> "Yes."

Mihailo's attitude was unusual; had it not been, the war would have been fought very differently. During Sudetic's interview, he and Mihailo were interrupted:

> The door behind me swung open. A man with a construction worker's beer belly stumbled in. He had a ruddy complexion, light eyes, and light hair. It was Mihailo's father, Zoran; he had been a member of an "obligatory work brigade" called to Bratunac on the day the killings began. We stood up. . . . The father sat down in Mihailo's chair, and Mihailo stood behind him, leaning against a wall.
> "Was it honorable to kill them all?" I asked the father.
> "Absolutely," he said. "It was a fair fight."
> Mihailo stared at me from behind him with a forlorn look in his eye.
> "Absolutely," the older man said again, and he turned to the woman: "Get some more brandy."

In Bratunac, in Kravica, one suspects that the father's view would be the accepted one. For him, Mladic's victory over Srebrenica offered an opportunity, a chance to end the cycle of attack and retribution. Having finally conquered the enclave, would one hand back to the Muslim leaders seven thousand men of military age so they could then, or at some point in the future, rejoin the fight—the fight, that is, to regain the homes they had just lost? What, after all, had losing his home done to Zoran Eric and the other survivors of the Muslim attack on Kravica?

No, the moment had to be seized, for future survival's sake; and even Mihailo, though he stood aloof from the killing, freely admitted to Sudetic that he understood the feelings that lay behind it:

> "And they killed all of them, everyone they could?"
> "Yes."
> "And the Muslims in the column who escaped across the road? They held them up . . . as long as they could so that they could get some men together and have one more crack at them, didn't they?"
> "They came around looking for volunteers."

"Did guys from Kravica go?"

"They wanted to kill as many of them as they could."

"So they could never come back? So there would not be enough military-age men left to fight their way back?"

"Never," Mihailo said.[11]

IV.

Emerging out of the early-morning darkness of July 22, 1995—eleven days after the fall of Srebrenica—a long caravan of white jeeps and trucks and white armored personnel carriers rumbled past ranks of cheering soldiers and politicians and dignitaries assembled at UN headquarters in Zagreb. Grinning beneath their blue helmets, the 430 Dutch soldiers and officers of the 13th Air Mobile Battalion passed before Netherlands Defense Minister Joris Voorhoeve, before Royal Army Commander General Hans Couzy, and, finally, before His Majesty, Crown Prince of the Netherlands Willem Alexander.

Later, as the sun rose, a forty-two-piece brass band would play some Glenn Miller arrangements for the troops. At makeshift outdoor bars, beer flowed freely. In the trailer-like "containers" that served as barracks, pornographic videos played. Soon drunken Dutch soldiers linked arms and began kicking their legs high in a tottering, raucous chorus line.

The next day, during a press conference with Defense Minister Voorhoeve and seventeen handpicked Dutch peacekeepers, Colonel Ton Karremans would praise Ratko Mladic for his military skills, while noting that the general was "a commander, not a gentleman." Among the things the Dutch had learned in Srebrenica, said Karremans, was that "the parties in Bosnia cannot be divided into 'the good guys' and 'the bad guys.'" Mladic had taken Srebrenica with "an excellently planned military operation" during which, Karremans conceded, his Dutch "blue helmet" battalion "was cleverly outmaneuvered by the Bosnian Serbian Army." The commander's clever feints, his disguising of his true motives, his final relentless assault—it had been, said Karremans, managed "in a very neat way by the Serbs . . . almost like a game of Pac-Man."

After the Serbs had taken the town, the Dutch had witnessed at least one execution and seen evidence of a handful of other killings within Potocari itself. Dutch hostages in Bratunac, meanwhile, began to hear from their proud Serb captors about the work the latter were doing every day. The Serbs, said Johan Bos, a Dutch sergeant, "bragged about how they had murdered people and raped women. . . ."

They seemed pleased with themselves in a sort of professional, low-key way. I believed what they said, because they looked and behaved as if they were more than capable of doing what they claimed. Each had an Alsatian dog, a gun, handcuffs, and a terrifying-looking knife with a blade about nine inches long.[12]

Other Dutch soldiers had heard shots, seen here and there bodies of murdered men—on the football field at Nova Kasaba, for example, from which, during the night of July 13–14, some "blue helmets" had heard forty-five minutes of small-arms fire. Next morning, two Dutch soldiers saw hundreds of bodies, and others had later glimpsed "'clean-up teams' . . . wearing gloves . . . as well as tipper trucks and lorries carrying corpses."[13]

Colonel Karremans's men had thus seen considerable evidence of killing, but the Dutch were frightened, demoralized; the Serbs had seized much of their equipment while making hostages of more than 10 percent of their force. Not only had unit solidarity, under these conditions, simply evaporated, making efficient collection and evaluation of intelligence about the killings nearly impossible, but every acknowledgment of an execution, not to mention a massacre, forced the Dutch soldiers to confront their own impotence and failure.

The result was that, even as he spoke in Zagreb, the colonel still did not know the full extent of what had just unfolded around him—did not know the numbers of dead, the scale of the operation. If he had, he likely would have described General Mladic in rather different words. Still, Karremans spoke with unwitting accuracy: Although the Dutch grasped this reality only vaguely from their vantage as prisoners within it, they had just played a minor part in a brilliantly organized military performance.

At its center was not the conquest of a town but the virtuoso display of ethnic cleansing that followed: an especial irony given the fact that many Western intelligence officers had judged it unlikely that Mladic intended to conquer Srebrenica—for the very reason that the Serbs would not be able "to deal with the refugees."[14] They need not have worried. Within thirty hours, little more than a single day, Mladic's men had expelled to Muslim territory twenty-three thousand women and children; within five days they had murdered more than seven thousand men.

Mladic had, of course, a reservoir of hatred already at his disposal, stored in the minds and hearts of men like Zoran Eric. He had several thousand of his own crack troops, including the Drina Corps; an unknown number of troops from Serbia, including "red berets" from the Serbian Interior Ministry; paramilitary "Black Wolves"; a number of heavily armed paramilitary forces, including the Drina Wolves, the White Eagles, the Specialna Policia, and the two most notoriously brutal of the Serb paramilitaries: the Militia of Vojislav Seslj and the Tigers of Arkan. What Mladic managed to conceive and construct, during those weeks working with Serb Chief of Staff General Momicilo Perisic and his colleagues across the Drina,[15] was an evanescent, makeshift system of temporary death camps, fashioned on a foundation of meticulous logistics. He would build nothing of permanence; this time there would be no sweltering barracks full of emaciated prisoners for reporters to visit. No, buses and trucks and school gymnasiums would serve Mladic as his barracks; grain warehouses and meadows and football fields as his gas chambers.

By July 12, when General Mladic appeared before the wretched frantic refugees inundating the Dutch camp at Potocari—"It is going to be a *meza*" (a long, luscious feast), the general reportedly told his troops as he gazed at the Muslims. "There will be blood up to your knees"[16]—the Serbs had already constructed an elaborate system designed to capture the Muslim men and then to move them with great speed and effectiveness over the mountains and passes of the Drina valley. At the system's heart was transport: scores and scores of buses and trucks. The operation's success depended, the Serbs knew, on rapid movement of large numbers of people, and so they painstakingly assembled north of Srebrenica, near the town of Bijeljina, parking lots full of vehicles. Serb officers moved as well an unknown number of buses and trucks across the Drina bridges from Serbia itself, many of which had Federal Republic of Yugoslavia license plates. So critical was having at hand a sufficient number of vehicles, in fact, that it determined the timing of the Srebrenica assault. A Serb soldier told a Dutch peacekeeper

> that the military action could have been carried out a week earlier, but that they had waited until there was sufficient transport capacity (buses/trucks) to evacuate the refugees.[17]

As it happened, American pilots flying U2 spy planes noticed the burgeoning fleet of vehicles and photographed them, but intelligence officers who examined the evidence—in another demonstration that such information, stark and inarguable as it may seem, lies many assumptions away from actual knowledge—concluded that the buses and trucks were intended to move Serb soldiers.[18]

When he confronted the sea of tens of thousands of people around the Dutch headquarters at Potocari, and raised his voice and sought to calm their fears, General Ratko Mladic followed a script that he and his men would repeat countless times during the coming days. In front of a Serb cameraman, the general and his entourage handed out chocolates to children ("Give us candy," the malnourished children can be heard shouting. "Give candy for my brothers and sisters"), and then told the terrified people again and again, "Do not be afraid. Do not be frightened. No one will do you any harm." Then the conquering general motioned to the crowd to be quiet and shouted, "Please, be very patient."

> All of you who wish to stay here can do so. If you wish to leave, there will be enough busses and trucks provided. You will be transported to Kladanj.[19]

Kladanj is Muslim territory, from which the refugees could make their way to Tuzla. However, even as the Dutch were "negotiating" the terms of the evacuation—in a memorable moment, Mladic is caught on videotape telling a Dutch officer, "I am in charge here, I'll decide what happens. I have my plans, and I'm going to carry them out. It will be best for you if you cooperate"—a fleet of trucks and buses suddenly appeared. Says the Dutch report, "The battalion was surprised by the speed with which the [Serbs] commenced the evacuation of the refugees."

> In a surprisingly short space of time, the [Serbs] appeared to have large numbers of buses and trucks. Mladic ignored protests by the battalion commander. UNPROFOR's orders to Dutchbat were to offer as much protection as possible to the refugees and to provide optimal support in transferring the population to safer locations. . . . The battalion initially assumed that there would be one escort per bus. This was not permitted by Mladic.

Thus began a smaller and more intricate version of the diplomatic duplicity that had accompanied the entire war: Mladic made promises to placate the Dutch—and Western leaders—and then blithely broke them. No sooner had he broken his last promise than he would make another, and the Dutch, and the West, would pretend to believe him. They had no choice; the alternative was to take action of some sort, and this they would not do.

That very day, July 12, back in New York, Kofi Annan, the UN undersecretary general for peacekeeping operations, was "briefing" ambassadors from the "contact group" countries (the United States, Russia, Great Britain, France, and Germany), plus Italy, "on the situation around Srebrenica" and how it related to a resolution then being drafted. According to the U.S. mission's cable,

> ANNAN SAID THAT THE SECRETARIAT WAS CONCERNED THAT THE RESOLUTION RAISED UNREALISTIC EXPECTATIONS THAT A MILITARY RESPONSE TO THE BOSNIAN SERB ATTACK ON SREBRENICA WAS POSSIBLE. IN FACT, UNPROFOR HAD REPORTED THAT NO MILITARY RESPONSE WAS POSSIBLE.

And how had the Dutch officers come to this conclusion?

> ANNAN SAID THAT THE BOSNIAN SERBS NOW HELD 51 DUTCH TROOPS AND HAD THREATENED TO SHELL THE UN COMPOUND IN POTOCARI IF NATO AIR POWER WAS USED AGAINST THEM. THE SERBS HAD DEPLOYED A NUMBER OF HEAVY WEAPONS WITHIN SIGHT OF THE UN COMPOUND TO EMPHASIZE THEIR POINT.

And what did the Dutch officers, given this uncomfortable situation, propose to do?

UNPROFOR WAS CONCENTRATING ON PROTECTING THE
CIVILIAN POPULATION OF THE ENCLAVE AND ARRANGING
THEIR EVACUATION.

And how were the UN peacekeeping troops going about this?

THE DUTCH COMMANDER HAD HELD TWO "HOSTILE"
MEETINGS WITH GENERAL MLADIC WHO IS IN SREBRENICA.
DURING THEIR FIRST MEETING MLADIC SLAUGHTERED A
PIG IN FRONT OF THE DUTCH COMMANDER TO PROVE HIS
TOUGHNESS. THE SECOND MEETING, HOWEVER, WAS MORE
POSITIVE AND MLADIC AGREED TO THE EVACUATION OF
THE CIVILIAN POPULATION. . . .

That is, the general "agreed" to what he had planned to do anyway, and
the Dutch, perceiving themselves to be quite powerless, gratefully accepted
Mladic's promises of "safeguards."

Still, one obstacle remained to the efficient commencement of Mladic's
plan, and one could almost hear Annan's frustration seeping through the
stark lines of the cable, as he complained "that the [Bosnian government]
was blocking the evacuation. . . ."

Perhaps this uncooperative behavior had to do with what Foreign Minister Sacirbey had only that day told UN representative Albright and British
foreign secretary Rifkind—that the Serbs were committing atrocities and
"genocide" on the people of Srebrenica? Whatever the reason for the Bosnian
officials' reluctance to see their citizens evacuated from Srebrenica under
such conditions, Undersecretary Annan "asked if members of the contact
group could pressure them to cooperate."

General Mladic, meanwhile, was doing precisely that. Earlier that day, the
Serb commander had his third meeting with Colonel Karremans, during
which, as the Dutch officer later wrote, it finally "became clear that Mladic
was operating entirely according to a pre-planned scenario." Karremans com-
municated to Defense Minister Voorhoeve Mladic's most menacing intention—to separate the men from the women. To this Voorhoeve responded
that the Dutch troops should not "assist in any way with the ethnic cleansing
and the separation of men and women," then added that they should "see to
it that the forced evacuation takes place in as humane a way as possible."[20]

That incomprehensible ambiguity shows the fecklessness into which the
UN mission had collapsed. "There was," as Holbrooke later wrote, "no more
energy left in the international system," and the result, as the Dutch report
put it in typically bureaucratic language, was that "in order to prevent
excesses with regard to the transport, the battalion commander decided to
cooperate in the evacuation."

What these words meant was that as the crowds of people carrying their
babies and their suitcases and their makeshift bundles pushed forward in a

great tide toward the buses, then passed between a makeshift "cordon" of Dutch blue helmets, Serb troops stepped forward to pull the Muslim men roughly away. The women shouted, wept, reached out, their hands grasping as they turned on the steps of the buses. It was no use. Their sons, brothers, husbands were led off: many were quite old or disabled; some were in their early teens, for most of Srebrenica's military-aged men had already fled the enclave, hoping to fight their way through to Tuzla. Now the Serbs led off the men who had elected to remain, installing them in selected houses to await "interrogation."

On the Petrovic videotape we can see the signs of the UN officers' impotent concern. A Kenyan military observer, Major Joseph Kingori, has just visited one of the interrogation houses, and we can hear his agitation as he speaks to the Dutch troops:

> This is not good, crowding at one place. . . . Where are all the men being taken. . . .They are separated from each other? It's too crowded. This is not good. . . .

How aware were the exhausted peacekeepers of what was happening? At one point on the videotape, we see a tall sunburned Dutch soldier in shorts and hear the reporter's voice:

> *Reporter:* For Independent Television in Belgrade: What's going on today here?
> *UN soldier:* You know what's going on.
> *Reporter:* I just came here.
> *UN soldier:* You know . . .

The Dutch plan to "escort" the buses fell instantly apart. The Serbs would not let the Dutch troops aboard; when the Dutch tried to follow in their white jeeps, the Serbs confiscated the vehicles and detained the troops. The Muslim women, having suddenly lost their husbands and fathers and sons, and trembling with their fear of what the Serbs might now do, were subjected to night voyages of terror. They passed through darkened Serb towns where villagers greeted them with angry shouts and threats and clatters of stones. Here and there the buses were stopped and Serb troops charged aboard, demanded money, threatened to cut off the breasts of those who had none to give; at some of these stops younger women were pulled off and never seen again. Eric Stover gives one woman's account of what happened when a Serb militiaman came aboard her bus at a checkpoint during that nightmare drive:

> He was young and hard-faced. She smelled the intensely familiar odor of cigarettes, musty sweat, and faint sweetness of alcohol. . . . He spoke, and his words came out in a slur. Suddenly he pulled a long knife from his belt and held it up in the air. He was smiling, and his large hands, she now saw,

were swollen from the heat. Then, in one motion, he leaned over and pulled the blade across the throat of a baby sleeping in her mother's arms. Blood splattered against the windows and the back of the seat. Screams filled the bus. The man shouted something at the woman, and then with his left hand he pushed her head down. . . . "Drink it, you Muslim whore," he screamed again and again. "Drink it!"[21]

By now the dawn had come; in the rising light many of the women once again saw their husbands and their fathers and their sons. They saw them in groups of ten and twenty and by the hundred, gathered by the side of the road, their hands raised in the three-fingered Serbian salute, as the Serb soldiers stood about them, cradling their rifles. They saw them sitting in a field, hundreds of them, their hands clasped behind their necks, their heads bent between their knees, afraid to look at the Serb soldiers who stood around them. The Serbs made the women look.

They said to us, "See your army?" Kneeling in the grass were many men I knew. They had their hands behind their necks. I saw one of my sons among them. But I could say nothing to him. I do not know if he saw me.[22]

As the buses drove on, the women saw other men lying on the road and in the grass beside it, pools of blood beneath their gashed necks, and as they drove past, the women forced themselves to look closely to see if those bodies were those of their husbands and fathers and sons.

V.

In Ratko Mladic's great composition, these men lying bloodied by the side of the road were no more than the hint of an overture. The women of Srebrenica, frozen in terror by their own vulnerability, did not dare grasp fully what was happening around them; but they knew well how the war had been fought, heard clearly what the Serbs encircling Srebrenica had always threatened, and, most of all, were free of the disabling ambivalence and guilt that helped the Dutch—and their masters in The Hague and other Western capitals—deny what was fast becoming undeniable.

Reviewing Sacirbey's charges and those of other Bosnian officials, as well as the accounts of Muslim women arriving exhausted and near hysterical in Tuzla, and the testimony of Dutch soldiers in Zagreb and The Hague; reading radio "intercepts" of Bosnian Serb officers giving orders to their men and gazing at photographs taken by American reconnaissance satellites and U2 spy aircraft; comparing, finally, the accounts of survivors—one is confronted by a blizzard of signs. Now their meaning is obvious, indisputable. Then, the evidence trickled in bit by bit; its reliability seemed to vary; it was put in separate boxes for consideration and study. As the UN's Yasushi

Akashi put it in a cable to New York on July 13, "WE ARE BEGINNING TO DETECT A SHORTFALL IN . . . OUR DATABASE"—this "short-fall" being thousands of Muslim men.

"Precise details," as Richard Holbrooke says, were lacking; but details were not necessary. "After Srebrenica fell," as a senior American intelligence official told *Washington Post* reporters, "everybody said atrocities were going to happen." Officials at the highest level of the government would have had to make a decision that all efforts must be made to prevent these atrocities. American officials might have made public what (considerable) information they had and focused all their resources on learning more; senior American political figures might have spoken out vigorously to warn General Mladic and Dr. Radovan Karadzic and the other Bosnian Serbs in Pale that atrocities in Srebrenica would be met with . . . what?

There was, as Holbrooke, said "no more energy left in the international system." From the moment in 1991—when American prestige and power was at its height after the Gulf War—that President Bush made it clear that the United States, come what may, would take no military action in the former Yugoslavia, American policy had followed a slow and steady path leading to the destruction of its own credibility. Bill Clinton, for all his strong words in support of the Bosnian Muslims, vowed he would never send American troops to Bosnia, and though he urged that NATO send its warplanes to attack the Serbs, the European allies, who did have troops there, blocked him, producing an inescapable paralysis. The takeover of Srebrenica, the failure to defend it by air strikes, constituted only the most horrible last step into utter powerlessness, and now the West could offer nothing, threaten nothing—had become, for the Serbs, nothing at all.

And so as the Serb soldiers with the handcuffs and the Alsatian dogs began to hustle Muslim men in Potocari into buses, pushing them forward roughly with their rifles, in Belgrade the U.S. *chargé d'affaires*, Rudolf V. Perina, paid a hurried call on Slobodan Milosevic. The fall of Srebrenica, the American diplomat declared, was a serious blow to peace negotiations; if Milosevic wanted to demonstrate his own "credibility," he should immediately "cut off all military supplies" to Mladic and his Bosnian Serbs.

"We felt [Milosevic] could prevent things from happening," said an official whom the *Washington Post* identified as "involved in the frantic effort to forestall atrocities." "His ability as interlocutor was on the line."

It was as if all the shadow play of the last four years, which had reached a climax only the previous week with Milosevic claiming he knew nothing of Mladic's attack on Srebrenica—and that anyway the general would never dare seize the enclave—had never taken place: the powerless force themselves to hear only what they want to hear. In any event, if Mr. Perina, a distinguished and respected diplomat, had really expected much from Milosevic, he was immediately disappointed. Affecting to be "stung" by the American's statements, the Serb leader, the arsonist now become fireman, responded plaintively: "Why blame me?" he asked the American. "I have been unable to contact Mladic."[23]

However dubious Milosevic's claim, it is certainly true that at this moment, and for the next several days, General Mladic's hands were very full. Indeed, if one wanted to make sense of the great movements of men and trucks and buses, the complex assignment of military units and weaponry and various sorts of "specialized" equipment—earthmovers and bulldozers, notably—that figured in Mladic's master plan, one could do worse than to follow the movements of the master himself. For it was in Srebrenica that Ratko Mladic—born and marked by a brutal war against the Croats and Muslims in which the father of young Ratko (the name means "warlike") died fighting the Ustashe when the boy was only two—was determined to enjoy his fullest and most complete triumph. He had conquered the pitiful West, had overwhelmed his most intransigent opponents, and now he would obliterate his enemies from the face of the earth, and he would be there to see firsthand that the job was done as it should be. At each critical spot along the way, General Mladic, along with a certain "red sports car" that seemed to serve as a distinctive command vehicle, made a personal appearance.

Even as Mr. Perina pleaded with Milosevic in Belgrade, General Mladic was paying visits to the seventeen hundred or so men who had been torn from their families and who now squatted, terrified, under the eyes of heavily armed Serb guards and their Alsatian dogs in various buildings and factories around the UN base at Potocari. At about six o'clock, the general, bull-necked, gigantic-seeming in his camouflage uniform with sleeves rolled up to expose his thickly muscled forearms, strode into a house where some two hundred men were crammed together on the floor and addressed the prisoners, most of them old or infirm, in a booming voice:

> Neighbors, if you have never seen me before, I am Ratko Mladic. I am the commander of the Serbian army, and you see we are not afraid of the NATO pact. They bombed us, and we took Srebrenica. And where is your country now? What will you do? Will you stand beside Alija [Izetbegovic]? He has led you to ruin. . . .

When a Muslim prisoner interrupted, demanding to know why they had been separated from their families, Mladic abruptly changed tone, turned soothing. He was negotiating a prisoner exchange, the general said, no one should worry: "Not a hair on your heads will be touched."

As Serb soldiers loaded the Muslims aboard waiting buses, Mladic himself spoke to the drivers, ordering them to follow the red sports car. Just before the drivers leaned forward to pull the handles that closed the pneumatic doors, Mladic's men stepped aboard, to stand at the drivers' shoulders throughout the journey. For these Muslims, though, the journey would be very short: The buses pulled over only a few miles away, in Bratunac, rumbling to a stop before a warehouse that had been used to store cattle feed. The doors swished open, the Serbs gestured with their guns, and the Muslims clambered down the steps and into the dark cavernous hall, collapsing on the cold earth floor.

One after another the buses and trucks drew up, and soon the Muslims sat packed together, legs crossed painfully beneath them or drawn up to their chests. Those who dared looked at the Serbs—men in camouflage uniforms who brandished Kalashnikovs and wore on their hips long, ugly knives—and struggled to master their fear. That Mladic would be negotiating their exchange, after all, made perfect sense; were they not too old, too young, too sick to fight? Why should the Serbs harm them? For what reason?

Outside the Serb guards, whose uniforms bore no insignia, went abruptly silent. "Through the doors," in Sudetic's account,

> some of the men in the warehouse heard members of the Drina Wolves receiving orders from an officer.
> "The twelve of you here tonight have been given an order to carry out the task assigned you. Is that clear?"
> "Clear, sir," shouted the militiamen.
> The gunmen entered the warehouse with flashlights. A pool of light fell on one Muslim.
> "You! Outside."
> The man wound his way to the door, turned to the left and disappeared. . . .
> There were thuds, then screams, cries for help, and gurgles. Inside the building there were muffled groans.
> "Do you know him? Who was that?"
> . . . "He's my relative."
> "Shut up."
> . . . A flashlight shone through the door. . . . "You! You!"[24]

Throughout the night the men kept their heads down and prayed that they would not be the next to be caught in the beams of light. They had no choice but to listen to the unmistakable sounds:

> Prisoners seated near the front of the warehouse heard the cries, gasps, and groans. . . .The Serbs cursed as they tortured their prisoners: "Turk bastard." After a few minutes a Serb would mutter, "He's finished." The loud hiss of air and gurgle of blood rushing out of a man's throat was followed by the sound of feet kicking the ground. As prisoners' throats were slashed, their bodies went into seizures.

At one point, several men were led out to relieve themselves and one managed to steal a glimpse in the half-light of Drina Wolves at work:

Seven or eight Serb soldiers had formed two lines. A Muslim prisoner was walking between them. On the left, one of the Serbs had what looked like an iron crowbar in his hand. He pummeled the prisoner with it. The man crumpled to the ground. On the right, one of the Serbs had an ax, which he embedded in the Muslim's back. The prisoner's body twitched. Blood spattered across the pavement.[25]

Back in Potocari, Serb soldiers gathered up the bundles and suitcases and packages the men had left behind, heaped them into a great pile, and set them afire.

VI.

Pushing their emaciated and sweat-soaked bodies up and down the punishing hills and mountains of eastern Bosnia, fifteen thousand Muslims of Srebrenica staggered onward, dreaming of sanctuary. Soon, very soon, they would reach government-held Tuzla, having avoided capture in Srebrenica, having boldly fled the town to keep their freedom.

It was all illusion. After months without a real meal, days without sleep, suffering under unbearable thirst, they thought they saw in their delirium a portal open before them; but it was their own inability to see the bars of the cage. The facts of geography were stark: To escape the ten-square-mile zone around the Srebrenica pocket and make it to Tuzla, they must pass over one of two roads, and even now all along these roads Serb troops and militiamen manning antiaircraft guns and mortars and heavy machine guns waited patiently, smoking, pacing, joking. The Muslims would come to them; they had no choice. Encircled by an "iron ring," those who survived the shelling would come staggering and tripping like exhausted children to enfold themselves in the great strong arms of Ratko Mladic.

First, however, the pressure on the Muslims, who were already near disabled by lack of sleep and nourishment and by paralyzing fear, must be steadily, carefully increased. "During the trek, it quickly became clear," as David Rohde writes, "that the threat to the column was as much psychological as physical."

Shells abruptly whizzed overhead. Gunfire erupted with no warning. Corpses littered their route. A Serb mortar had landed ahead of them . . . and killed five men. A human stomach and intestines lay across the green grass just below the intact head and torso of a man in his twenties. . . . The image would slowly eat at their minds.[26]

Paranoia infected the Muslims: Serbs had infiltrated the column, spied on their movements, prepared an ambush. Soon the Serbs filled the sky with booming metallic voices, and many of the sleep-starved men began to break. As a doctor recalled:

A megaphone voice reverberated against the mountainside. The [Serbs] summoned us to surrender. Escape was impossible, they said. . . . The waiting tried our nerves to the utmost. Some people in the group began to hallucinate. Fear. Stress. Such people were a danger to their comrades: They shouted and screamed and could betray our position. . . . Some armed men completely panicked and opened fire randomly. They shot a few of their own men. We had to overpower them with force.[27]

Far from "betraying their position," these "hallucinating" men had come to perceive the horror of it: that the Serbs knew where they were, that they were playing with them. Their fellows' dogged determination to escape had become the true hallucination. During the evening of July 12, as their wives and daughters and mothers began their phantasmagorical journeys along these roads, hundreds of exhausted men lay in a great grassy clearing on a hillside. As Rohde tells it, just as a young man rose from the crowd to search for his father,

The hillside exploded. Screams filled his ears. He dove toward a cluster of trees. Other men piled on top of him. He hugged the ground. Mortars whistled overhead. . . .

All around . . . men sprinted down the hill, then up and across in a panic. Weapons and bags with food were dropped in the pandemonium. Men gasped or groaned where they had fallen. Those carrying stretchers threw the wounded to the ground and ran for the nearest cluster of trees or bushes. . . . Men running downhill tripped, fell, and tumbled head over heels for fifty yards, the ground was so steep. . . .

[The gunners] had a devastating position . . . , [with] a half-mile-wide clearing filled with people for targets. For the first twenty seconds, it was a question of how many rounds the Serbs could fire, not whether they would hit anyone.

The next five minutes were the cruelest. The men who found cover in the foliage were trapped. In a macabre technique . . . , the Serbs would estimate which clusters of trees were filled with the most men and then methodically saturate them with flak from the antiaircraft gun and mortar rounds. Bodies were found stacked on top of each other in the trees. The living pulled the dead on top of them and used corpses as sandbags.[28]

This ambush effectively severed perhaps half of the Muslim civilians' communications with their military and political leadership at the head of the column and drained them of hope. Or rather it forced them to reach the desperate conclusion that a step that had seemed insane and suicidal the day before—delivering themselves into the hands of the Serbs—had become their only choice. They were unarmed, without food, without water, desperately in need of sleep; before them, blocking their escape, stood their well-armed, well-rested enemies. If they forced themselves onward these soldiers would surely kill them. And if, in their thousands, they surrendered? Was there not the chance that someone would help them, that someone would intervene? However savage the Serbs might wish their retribution to be, the men of Srebrenica were too many. Simple numbers must afford them some protection.

So they debated among themselves, and then one by one, score by score, hundred by hundred, they came down, into the kindly hands of the Serbs, who welcomed them with the soothing words of Mladic's script, treated them with gentleness and patience. On the Petrovic video, we see them come down, a great straggling line of them: dirty, unshaven, skinny, their chests sunken, their fear making them crouch, hunch their shoulders, look up, terrified, ratlike. And then comes the voice of the unseen cameraman—"Where are your guns?"—and the slightly resentful, slightly resigned, exhausted reply, from a man later identified as Ramo Mustafic: "I wasn't carrying a gun. I'm a civilian."

"Are you afraid?"
"How can I not be afraid?"

In the background, a Serb gunner lobs a few antiaircraft shells into the trees on the hillside; gray cloudlets rise and float over the luminous July green. Ghostly figures are briefly silhouetted, staggering from copse to copse. We hear again the cameraman's voice, talking to the Serb troops:

"How many have come out so far?"
"It must be three to four thousand, for sure."

In the distance a group of men seated on the ground turn briefly toward the cameraman, squinting in the bright sunlight as they look past the Serbs cradling their assault rifles: We see them for just an instant before the tape goes black. This is the last glimpse anyone will ever have of these men.

VII.

By Thursday, July 13, two days after the fall of Srebrenica, General Mladic's invisible death camp had miraculously taken shape. Using scores of buses and trucks, his troops had expelled, in a matter of hours, 24,000 Muslim women and children. Using antiaircraft guns and tanks and mortars, his troops had killed perhaps 2,000 Muslim men as they struggled frantically to slip the bounds of his "iron ring."

In the hills the few survivors who had fought the urge to surrender dragged themselves onward toward Tuzla. Many helped the wounded along; some carried relatives on blankets, a man on each corner. Exhaustion hobbled the men as they tried to advance through the grim Beckettian landscape. "I remember," said Dr. Pilav later, that I was walking, that is, I felt my body walk, but only with a small part of my consciousness. While I was running, and vaguely conscious of it, I was also sleeping and had crazy, terrible dreams. At one point, I heard my own voice say, "Enough, when I get some money together, I will buy a car and never walk again, not an inch." The strange sound of my own voice woke me up.

As in a nightmare, macabre visions confronted the reeling men at every turn. Corpses, parts of corpses, the mutilated and wounded lay everywhere. When one of Sudetic's relatives reached the bottom of a hill, emerging from the impenetrable early-morning fog,

he heard a bleating sound, like the sound of a goat in pain. Aman knelt there in the grass. The skin of his face had been stripped away, leaving a crusty black pulp of coagulated blood and muscle. His lips had been cut away, and from the cavern of his mouth he bleated again. His index finger sliced across his throat.

Paja's steps slowed as he turned all the way around and looked back at that face. He stopped long enough for the man to climb to his feet. Another bleating cry. Another appeal to cut his throat. Paja moved on.[29]

Far ahead at the front of the column were the military and political leaders of Srebrenica and its strongest soldiers. Behind were most of the civilian men who, having been strafed and shelled, having seen their friends and relatives left in pieces on the trail, having been bombarded for hours with the inescapable electronically amplified appeals of the Serbs—"Come down! We will exchange you for our prisoners!" "Come down! We have your women and children!" "Come down! United Nations troops are here and they will protect you!"—had finally come down the hillside by the thousands. Those who had not been led gently off into the woods to have their throats slit were now kneeling fearfully in some part of Mladic's ephemeral death camp, built as it was of buses and warehouses and football fields and grassy meadows.

This is how the women had seen their husbands and sons from the buses. This is how the Dutch "blue helmets" had glimpsed the men as well: kneeling fearfully, their hands clasped behind their necks, at these "collection and interrogation points." And this is how, later that Thursday, an American reconnaissance satellite photographed them, showing perhaps six hundred people crowding the football field surrounded by their Serb guards.[30]

Of all the people whose eyes were trained on the captured Muslims that day and the next, only the Americans could have brought great power to bear. It would be good to say that American officials, knowing, in Richard Holbrooke's words, that "something truly horrible was going on"—were watching Mladic's activities closely. It would be good to know that they made at least some effort to cast a strong light on what was about to happen.

And yet for all Holbrooke's talk of bombing and the recalcitrant Dutch and the other damnable obstacles, one can find no evidence that American officials made any such effort. Even those "aerial photographs" that Madeline Albright brought so triumphantly before her colleagues at the UN Security Council were displayed more than three weeks after the fall of Srebrenica—long after the thousands were dead and buried—and in any event they do not appear to have resulted from any directed attempt to discover "real-time" atrocities. For after Bosnian foreign minister Sacirbey telephoned Albright about the killings and she in turn telephoned Samuel Berger, the deputy national security adviser, at the White House, Berger simply told her, according to the *Washington Post* and other accounts, to ask "the intelligence community" to "find corroborating evidence."

Albright did apparently make such a request the next day—even as the Serbs were beginning to undertake the large-scale killings at various points around Srebrenica—but officials in "the intelligence community" seem to have ignored her. "Several officials," according to the *Washington Post*, said that "the National Photographic Interpretation Center (NPIC), which has a special group assigned to analyze satellite and U-2 spy-plane imagery of Bosnia, was not assigned the task in mid-July of looking for atrocities or mass graves." Failing a congressional investigation of the incident one can only speculate that, as one official told the *Washington Post*, "It was not a military priority. A lot of this [atrocity] stuff is not looked at" when the imagery comes down. Intelligence officials are always more interested in directing the country's intelligence assets toward military priorities, in this case toward the ongoing battle for Zepa, a second "safe area" nearby that the Serbs were trying to capture. To have truly made a change in this priority the call would have had to come not from Albright, who, as UN ambassador, did not rank high in the eyes of officials at the Pentagon's National Reconnaissance Office, but from the White House itself—from, say, Sandy Berger, the man who suggested Albright make the call. Given the timing and what was already known, it seems fair to assume that when Berger suggested Albright call the NRO or the CIA, he might have been thinking that such "corroborating evidence" of atrocities might eventually be useful diplomatically in helping force the Serbs into a settlement. There is no reason to believe, however, that Berger or his colleagues would have sought such evidence immediately in order to save lives, for doing so might have pushed the Clinton administration into the deeper involvement it had always shunned.

And so the satellites passed overhead, stared down, and took their pictures, and not until weeks later did anyone bother to look at what they showed. The Muslim men knelt on the ground while, according to the account of a young man who survived, the Serbs passed through the crowd, beating people, "hitting them on the head with their rifles" and selecting some for "interrogation" in a small house.

They were being taken to this house one by one. . . . They were taking certain people and saying, "Don't worry, your time will come. There's no need to be afraid. You're just going in for interrogation," but nobody was coming out again.

Very quickly the intentions of the Serbs became difficult to deny, and the realization showed on the Muslims' faces.

They were pale and terrified. They knew what was awaiting them—I did too. They knew they were going to be killed. They were praying to be simply killed. I heard people whispering that they were hoping to be killed without being made to suffer.[31]

Halfway through the baking afternoon, however, a silver-haired, bull-like figure in camouflage strode to the front of the crowd, which now numbered perhaps two thousand, and cupped his hands to his mouth. "You are welcome here," shouted Ratko Mladic. "No one will harm you!"

You should have given yourselves up earlier. You shouldn't have tried to go through the woods.
    Look what your Alija has done to you. He destroyed you. You will be going to Bratunac and be spending the night there.

As he and his red command car visited each "interrogation and collection point" that afternoon and evening—and survivors have told of his speeches in virtually all of them—he gently rebuked the prisoners, established his godlike authority, then reassured them by offering a detail or two about their immediate futures. Mladic had crafted a psychological message that would keep alive what little hope the men may have had and thereby serve to ensure docile behavior. Hopelessness, after all, might bring desperation, and with it desperate acts. In this operation planning was extremely tight, deadlines unyielding; Mladic had no time for irritating little rebellions.
    Now two sixty-foot-long trucks pulled up, and Serb troops packed aboard several hundred prisoners, shoulder to shoulder. After a short drive, the trucks stopped, and for several hours the men struggled to stay conscious in the suffocating darkness. At last the doors swung open, flashlight beams shone in, and the prisoners knew at once that Mladic had spoken the truth: They saw before them the faces of Serbs from Bratunac. These Serbs, most in civilian clothing, spoke kindly to any Muslims they knew and invited them to come down from the truck for a talk; they then began savagely beating them, and after a time they dragged their bodies away and the cowering prisoners heard shots. The Serbs returned, and the flashlight beams flickered among the faces again, searching for more.

Though they didn't know it, a short while before General Mladic had made a second appearance before the surviving prisoners in the agricultural warehouse of Bratunac. By now, the Serbs with their knives and axes had killed an unknown number of men. General Mladic spoke to his officers and then supervised, hands on hips, as six buses pulled up to the warehouse and the troops loaded the surviving prisoners aboard.

Everywhere on the territory encircled by the "iron ring" that Mladic had built around Srebrenica there was great activity this night: Convoys of trucks and buses moved thousands according to precise timetables; officers consulted with one another, radioed orders, moved truckloads of men about. Drivers delivered earthmovers, bulldozers, heavy equipment of all sorts from site to site.

The Dutch troops, meanwhile, who had seen perhaps a thousand Muslim prisoners kneeling on the football field near Nova Kasaba, and whom Serb troops had now detained in the village "for their own safety," heard "continuous shots from hand-held weapons . . . coming from the direction of the football pitch . . . for three-quarters of an hour to one hour." The next morning, two Dutch UN soldiers "reported that they had seen between 500 and 700 bodies." However, as the writer of *Report Based on the Debriefing on Srebrenica* carefully adds, "two other members of [the Dutch batallion] who were in the same vehicle reported seeing only a few corpses." Presumably the need to clarify this ambiguity (and not their frantic concern to find a way out of Bosnia) is why the Dutch did not find this eyewitness account of a substantial massacre worth broadcasting to the outside world, or indeed even worth mentioning at their press conference in Zagreb more than a week later.

It took more than three weeks and the flight of an American U2 spy plane for the world to gain a hint of what happened at Nova Kasaba that night. The plane took a photograph revealing that the assembly of hundreds of Muslim men seen in the earlier satellite picture had been supplanted by three large plots of recently disturbed earth.

Late in July interviewers from Human Rights Watch discovered a man who hid in the high grass not far from the field at Nova Kasaba and witnessed what happened after Mladic left and several hundred men were trucked to Bratunac. The Serbs, he said,

picked out Muslims whom they either knew about or knew, interrogated them and made them dig pits. . . . During our first day, the Cetniks killed approximately 500 people. They would just line them up and shoot them into the pits. The approximately one hundred guys whom they interrogated and who had dug the mass graves then had to fill them in. At the end of the day, they were ordered to dig a pit for themselves and line up in front of it. . . . [T]hey were shot into the mass grave. . . .

At dawn, . . . [a] bulldozer arrived and dug up a pit . . . , and buried about 400 men alive. The men were encircled by Cetniks; whoever tried to escape was shot.[32]

The Nova Kasaba men never made it to Bratunac, Mladic's main switching point: They were regarded, perhaps, as "overflow" in the general's meticulous hydraulics. That night thousands of Muslim men moved along various roads to and from Bratunac and then to a school in Karakaj. Here Serb troops hustled the men into a gymnasium—"Quickly! Quickly!"—and forced them to remove their jackets, hats, shirts. When the room had grown so crowded that most of the sweltering men were sitting in their neighbor's laps, Mladic appeared in the front of the gymnasium. He gazed at the men but said nothing to them; instead he spoke with his officers, laughed, smiled, then left. The Muslims could hear the engines of trucks and buses as they pulled up to the schools.

The final stage had begun. Mladic would make no more calming speeches. Now the Serbs would direct every action to suggest inevitability: There was no more talk of exchanges or rescue. The Muslims were half stripped, their shoes and other belongings rudely taken. They were beaten, bloodied; forced to shout "Long live Serbia," to run down hallways, jump into trucks, follow orders without question, even those final orders leading to their own executions. For Mladic and his men, the Muslims had to be made to see that they had already entered into a dark, bloody landscape— had already stepped partly into the world of the dead. "We were ordered to run out into the corridor" of the school, one survivor recalled.

> We were running barefoot on a floor that was covered in blood. I saw about twenty corpses lying near the front door. . . . The Cetniks kept on yelling to load more and more people into the truck until it was crammed full. . . . They ordered everyone to sit, but we couldn't because it was so tightly packed. . . . The Cetniks started to shoot at people in order to make us sit down.

The running, the shouting, the beating—the objective of all of this, as Honig and Both observe, was "to instill the execution process with a sense of inexorable movement and speed. No one, including the executioners, was given an opportunity to question the process." Mladic had carefully planned the operation so the execution sites lay only a few minutes from the final "interrogation points"—they might better be called "pre-execution chambers"—and thus the final truck ride, during which the blindfolded men could no longer deny what was about to happen, gave them no time to react. Upon their arrival at the pre-selected sites, and for the same reason, "operations" began instantly:

> When the truck stopped, we immediately heard shooting outside; stones were bouncing off the [truck's] tarpaulin. The Cetniks told us to get out, five at a time. I was in the middle of the group, and the men in the front didn't want to get out. They were terrified, they started pulling back. But we had no choice, and when it was my turn to get out with five others, I

saw dead bodies everywhere. . . . A Cetnik said, "Come on [Turk], find some space." . . . They ordered us to lie down, and as I threw myself on the ground, I heard gunfire. I was hit in my right arm and three bullets went through the right side of my torso . . . The man next to me was moaning and one of the Cetniks ordered the others to check and see what bodies were still warm. "Put a bullet through all the heads, even if they're cold." Another Cetnik replied, "Fuck their mothers! They're all dead!" Only one Cetnik came over to the pile and shot the man next to me, and I felt stones hitting the upper part of my right arm. He continued his job until he was done. Later I heard a truck leave . . .

At the agricultural warehouse in Kravica, the Serbs were firing randomly into the tightly packed ranks of men. The men huddled together, falling on top of one another, trying desperately to dodge the bullets. "There was a lot of screaming, shouting, people were crying out for help," said Hakija Huseinovic, fifty-two.

Many were wounded. As I lay down, the right-hand side of my body got soaked in blood. I couldn't stand it any longer so I got up from the blood and pulled a dead body underneath me to lie on top of it. When dawn started breaking [my neighbor] Zulfo Salilovic got up to urinate and have a drink of water. I tugged at his coat and told him, "Stay down," and he said, "I can't hold it any longer." A machine-gun burst cut him in half and he fell down. I covered myself with two dead bodies and stayed underneath for twenty-four hours. . . . Afterwards, a truck and a mechanical shovel appeared. They started tearing down the side of the warehouse facing the road, then they started loading. They loaded until nightfall. The shovel came very close. I was thinking, "This is the end for me. All that fear has been in vain" . . . And then I heard someone say, "Park the shovel, wash the tarmac and cover the dead bodies with hay. It's enough for today."[33]

Another survivor packed aboard one of the trucks describes his first glimpse of the execution site under the blindfold:

We came near to what I saw through my right eye was a wooded area. They took us off the truck in twos and led us out to some kind of meadow. People started taking off blindfolds and yelling in fear because the meadow was littered with corpses. I was put in the front row, but I fell over to the left before the first shots were fired so that bodies fell on top of me. . . .

About an hour later, I looked up and saw dead bodies everywhere. They were bringing in more trucks with more people to be executed. After a bulldozer driver walked away, I crawled over dead bodies and into the forest.

Within Mladic's "iron ring" bodies were everywhere, covering the fields, the mountains and hillsides. In the moonlight another survivor rose slowly and fearfully; he was wounded, bloody, and cramped from hours lying motionless beneath his dead countrymen. Now he gazed in astonishment out upon a moonlit "ocean of corpses," so many of them in the vast meadow that try as he might he could not avoid stepping on them as he moved to escape.

The following day, as his troops were hard at work with bulldozers and diggers, and as special "clean-up teams" scoured the roads filling trucks with stray corpses,[34] General Mladic traveled to Belgrade to meet with Milosevic, the UN's Yasushi Akashi, Carl Bildt of the European Community, and General Rupert Smith. Though Mladic had already "cleansed" the greater part of the population, even as he met with the diplomats he still held perhaps a thousand Muslims imprisoned in various warehouses and storage depots in Bratunac. In his cable reporting to Kofi Annan in New York, Akashi expresses his pleasure that "despite their disagreement on several points, the meeting re-established dialogue between the two generals."

INFORMAL AGREEMENT WAS REACHED IN THE COURSE OF THE MEETING ON A NUMBER OF POINTS BETWEEN THE TWO GENERALS WHICH WILL, HOWEVER, HAVE TO BE CONFIRMED AT THEIR MEETING SCHEDULED FOR 19 JULY. IN VIEW OF THE HIGHLY SENSITIVE NATURE OF THE PRESENCE OF MLADIC AT THE MEETING, IT WAS AGREED BY ALL PARTICIPANTS THAT THIS FACT SHOULD NOT BE MENTIONED AT ALL IN PUBLIC.

In the meeting four days later General Mladic, according to the UN summary, was in a "chipper mood," which the note-taker attributed to the general's "success in pressing his attack on Zepa." (He would conquer it in a few days.) Mladic had retained, as insurance, most of his Dutch hostages. Indeed the agreement negotiated is telling in its almost total focus on the Dutch, who would be freed on July 21, and its failure to take up what Akashi had referred to as the "shortfall in our database": the seven thousand missing Muslim men. Failing to agree on whether to refer to these parties as detainees (as Smith wanted) or POWs (as Mladic insisted), the generals contented themselves with guaranteeing access to the Red Cross—after July 20.

The following day, the Dutch battalion departed for Zagreb. The release of Dutch troops, always the West's primary concern, reflected a blatant self-interest that the Muslims found maddening. Before the fall of the town, a Muslim artillery officer had written bitterly on a Dutch colleague's pad a simple equation: "30 Dutch equals 30,000 Muslims."

After their celebration, the Dutch soldiers were shipped home and given six weeks leave. Only after they returned was an investigation undertaken. The events at Srebrenica, however, had already had their effect. General

Mladic had constructed his death camp and made of the "safe area" of Srebrenica an enormous killing field, and he had done it beneath the very eyes of the West. Now he turned his sights on Bihac, threatening the Croats. He had overreached himself. Even as he sat in CNN's studio on July 16—the very day that Serb troops at the state farm of Pilica machine-gunned the final thousand or so Muslims who had been held at Bratunac—Richard Holbrooke must have known that he and the other "hard-liners" in the administration were about to win.

New York Review of Books,
April 13 and September 24, 1998

Operation Storm and
the Cold Peace

I.

STANDING AMONG their hulking war machines like statues in the dark, 200,000 Croat soldiers dropped their cigarettes, clambered into tanks and trucks and armored personnel carriers and, in a sudden ear-splitting eruption of grating gears, pushed forward into Serb-held Krajina. Thus began, before dawn on August 4, 1995, "Operation Storm." Within hours Croat commanders knew their code name had been well chosen; for everywhere Serb soldiers—40,000 of them, with 400 tanks—retreated, melting away as before a hurricane. Within little more than a day, the red-and-white checkerboard flag of Croatia was flying once more over the castle, high above the Krajina's "capital" of Knin.

Clogging highways, more than 150,000 Serbs crowded onto tractors or cars or horse-drawn carts in caravans twenty or thirty or forty miles long and moved over the border into Bosnia in one great chaotic exodus that was easily the largest single instance of "ethnic cleansing" of the Yugoslav war. Even as the caravans moved out of the Krajina, a triumphant President Franjo Tudjman of Croatia—who had publicly invited the Serbs to stay in their houses, assuring them their persons and property would be protected (if, that is, they had not been implicated in "war crimes")—said of the Serbs, many of whose families had farmed Krajina land for generations:

> They disappeared ignominiously, as if they had never populated this land. We urged them to stay, but they did not listen to us. Well then, *bon voyage!*[1]

As Tudjman spoke, Serb villages burned. In a cable to the State Department, a U.S. diplomat described his drive though Knin a week after "Operation Storm" began:

The terrain quickly became a surreal mixture of burned or burning homes, . . . burned cars, overturned tractors, . . . castoff clothing and blankets. . . . Near Knin, virtually all [houses] had suffered some damage. . . .

Croatian soldiers were ubiquitous. . . . Many were going house to house in mop-up operations. Others were resting, lounging, and drinking beer in the yards of the abandoned homes. . . .

. . . Throughout Knin's homes, food was on the tables, clothing was hanging on the lines, toys remained outside, and all of the ostensible signs of life remained, except for the presence of human beings.[2]

The flames the U.S. diplomat observed came not from combat, of which there had been little, but from the main political tactic of "Operation Storm." A week after the American diplomat had driven through Knin, investigators on a Helsinki Federation Fact-Finding Mission found

evidence of systematic destruction and looting of Serbian homes and community buildings by the Croatian Army (HV), Croatian Civil Police, civilians and "arson teams" . . . ; conflicting claims from Croatian authorities concerning civilian casualties, missing persons, and summary executions; allegations of . . . suspected mass gravesites. . . .[3]

Even as the investigators gathered their evidence in the Krajina, Croatian special operations troops were still hard at work there:

One arson team dressed in military camouflage was operating an antitank gun and firing tracer and incendiary rounds into homes in the Bulajusa area . . . ; in the Kistanje area, civilian dressed "officials" with maps were observed pointing at houses, later some buildings were observed to be burning. . . . [We also] saw a group of four soldiers moving in and around buildings along the two main streets. . . . [Later] smoke began pouring from behind buildings on the main street. . . .

During the four days of the main assault, a United Nations military observer told the Helsinki investigator, he had heard "small-arms fire . . . in Knin and the surrounding areas around the clock. In his estimation the firing . . . occurred in blocks seeming to indicate that [Croat soldiers] were moving building by building and 'cleaning' out the inhabitants." The Croats were also harassing the refugees, in some instances spraying the convoys with automatic weapons fire.

Barely four years before, in these very towns and villages, these Serbs— formed into militias and reinforced by the Yugoslav People's Army—had "cleansed" the land of their Croat neighbors by first shelling them for hours or days to "soften them up," and then sending in paramilitary shock troops to loot, torture, rape, and murder those who remained. Terror, frank and implacable, lay at the heart of Serb ethnic cleansing.

Though they killed many, the Croats in their counterattack now relied on a more subtle strategy. First, Croat troops shelled villages and towns, in order (as a Croatian colonel serving as an information officer helpfully explained) "specifically to create a disorganized, mass panic and exodus of Serbs." Then waves of assault troops surged into town and looted stores and houses, followed quickly by militiamen come to pick the carcass clean.

Those Serbs who had refused to join the caravans and dared peep out of their windows saw a hellish scene: burning houses, smashed storefronts, bodies lying in the streets, and everywhere "soldiers driving civilian vehicles without license plates loaded with goods from both houses and stores." Not surprisingly, as these Serbs told the Helsinki investigators, "when they saw the damage from the burning and looting . . . , the majority of [them] decided they want[ed] to leave." According to many reports, Serbs who still had not reached this decision were helped along by Croat troops, who surrounded the houses of those who, because they were old or infirm, had stayed behind, and burned the houses down, sometimes with the residents locked inside.

And so the great crescent of land known as the Krajina, the land where in the summer of 1991 the Yugoslav wars had truly begun, had not only been reconquered but cleansed of Serbs. Many of these families had lived there since the sixteenth century, when they had been invited by the Austrians, who offered them free land in exchange for their creating a military "borderland," or *krajina*, intended to protect the Christian West from the Ottoman Turks. The Krajina had stood for four hundred years and now, in four days, it had vanished. The Serbs, having lived four years under the rule of "Greater Serbia," were gone. And though Tudjman went on intimating that the Serbs might someday return, it was clear, as Marcus Tanner writes, that

> the departure of the Serbs from the Krajina was as final as the flight of the Greeks from Asia Minor in 1921, the Germans from Bohemia and Poland after the Second World War or the *pieds noirs* from Algeria in 1961. After demanding all, they had lost all.[4]

After four years of ruling what he considered two-thirds of a state, Tudjman had at last solved his so-called nationalities problem, "purifying" his land. Bedraggled Serbs, moving in a panicked flood over the border, would go where Slobodan Milosevic's Yugoslav government directed them—to Vojvodina, to the Sanzjak, to Kosovo, all regions in need of Serb "repopulating."

Tens of thousands of Serbs were still on the road, pushing forward slowly on their brutal exodus, and providing yet another spectacle of suffering for the world's television screens, when Madeleine Albright came before the United Nations Security Council and presented those "aerial intelligence" photographs of the massacre at Srebrenica three weeks before. According to Albright, the photographs, which showed, among other scenes, six hundred men under guard in a field one day and then, in the same field several days later, large plots of disturbed earth, were not discovered by American intelligence officers until the week before. Now the UN ambassadors were "startled," "shocked," and "appalled"—and immediately found themselves in a distinctly less sympathetic mood toward Serbs, wherever they were from and whatever homes they had lost.

On the other side of the world, senior American officials were closely following the Krajina exodus and expressing their regret. "We certainly didn't want this to happen, we didn't urge it," declared Secretary of State Warren Christopher, speaking from Hanoi, where he was overseeing the normalizing of relations with Vietnam. On the other hand, Christopher went on, "the facts may possibly give rise to a new strategic situation that may turn out to be to our advantage. . . . Maybe these circumstances, tragic as they are, will provide a new basis for a negotiated settlement. We're going to be working on it."

II.

Shortly before Croat soldiers and tanks and artillery surged into the Krajina, Peter Galbraith, U.S. ambassador in Zagreb, had visited President Tudjman in his grandiose office and handed him a formal message from the American government. "We are concerned," the diplomatic note said in part, "that you are preparing for an offensive in sector south and north." Reading this to reporters later, Tudjman laughed. "Obviously," he said, the Americans' "secret service didn't let them down."[5]

Tudjman was ridiculing the delicious hypocrisy of diplomacy. Of course the Americans were thoroughly aware of his plans; not only had Galbraith known for days that an attack was imminent but the retired U.S. generals who were actually retraining the Croat army could not have been unaware of preparations for the enormous operation. Tudjman was also making it clear that he understood that his American sponsors were not quite as firm, or as unified, as they tried to make him believe. As Richard Holbrooke later wrote in his memoir,

> The Croatian offensive proved to be a wedge issue that divided not only Americans and Europeans, but the top echelons of the American government itself. Most officials saw these military thrusts as simply another chapter in the dreary story of fighting and bloodshed in the region. They felt that the duty of our diplomacy was to put a stop to the fighting, regardless of what was happening on the ground.

That American diplomats should strive merely to "put a stop to the fighting," whatever its implications—whoever, that is, might be winning—would place American strategy firmly beside that of the United Nations or, more properly, the Western allies in NATO. If American leaders had adopted as their goal simply to stop the fighting as quickly as possible—a policy that could be translated as "peace at any price," and therefore "peace in place," and would naturally favor the heretofore victorious Serbs—they would also have lost any chance of creating a vigorous new policy, which was to be Holbrooke's brief. "For me," Holbrooke wrote,

> the success of the Croatian . . . offensive was a classic illustration of a fundamental fact: the shape of the diplomatic landscape will usually reflect the actual balance of forces on the ground.[6]

This is a fair summary of the Realpolitik vision that Holbrooke would carry forward into his negotiations: if a map that all sides would accept (given the careful application of American pressure) had to be the ultimate and necessary result of any negotiations, then a good part of that map must be written on the ground, in blood. If the settlement of Holbrooke and the NATO allies who agreed with him envisioned a roughly equal division of territory between the Bosnian Serbs, on the one hand, and the Bosnian Croats and Muslims on the other, and if the Serbs held almost 70 percent of the territory, as they had before the Croat invasion of the Krajina, then some means had to be found to reduce their holdings before negotiations could have any chance to succeed.

For some time Clinton officials had been doing much to provide Croatia and Bosnia with those means. A year before, they had brokered the Washington Agreement between Bosnians and Croats, which not only made it possible to ensure a greater flow of arms to the Bosnians through Croatia but served, by means of the generous helpings of heavy weapons the Croats appropriated for themselves, to bolster the Croatian Army as well. Tudjman, meanwhile, poured the hard currency that mostly came his way from tourism—foreigners lounging on Croatian beaches while just to the north the Croatian army fought its way forward—into further replenishing his arsenals, buying liberally from the bulging Cold War inventories of Eastern European states. Through his defense minister, Gojko Susak, he had appealed to Pentagon officials to supply him with direct military aid. Deputy Secretary of Defense John Deutsch, pointing to the UN-imposed arms embargo, had directed Susak to Military Professional Resources, Inc., the "private" firm in Alexandria, Virginia, that employed many retired officers from the upper levels of the U.S. Army, including its former chief of staff.

Although their American instructors were supposedly confining their work at the Petar Zrinski Military Academy near Zagreb to a "Democracy Transition Program"–"We are there only to re-orient the officers in accordance with democratic principles," General Ed Soyster, former director of the Defense Intelligence Agency, told a reporter for *Stern*—not a few observers noted that in its design Tudjman's "Operation Storm" seemed to bear striking resemblances to current American military doctrine, in particular the set of tactics known as AirLand Battle 2000, in the development of which MPRI's General Carl Vuono had happened to have a key part. "The group acting in Zagreb," a German-based U.S. Army officer told *Stern*, "is discussing . . . organization and engagement of the armed forces."[7] Moreover, as a writer in the Zagreb-based weekly *Globus* pointed out, the evidence was clear to see for anyone who examined the attack:

> The tactics of the Croatian army in the operation resembled the AirLand 2000 doctrine to a degree, particularly in the coordinated actions of the army and the [air force] as well as the systematic targeting of the enemy's command and communication posts. The Croats also preferred quick and powerful attacks. . . .[8]

However much the Croats might have drawn on American instruction to stage their attack, Holbrooke makes it clear that many active American officers in the Pentagon actually opposed it, as did many in the "intelligence community," believing that any Croat offensive was sure to draw in the regular Serb army of Slobodan Milosevic and thus widen the war.

In the event, Milosevic sat on his hands, as Tudjman had insisted he would; and now, after seizing the Krajina, the Croats pressed their advantage, joining with the Bosnians to push back the Serbs in northwestern Bosnia. Still Milosevic did nothing. Even so, according to Holbrooke, many officials back in Washington still argued that the Croats should desist. When one member of Holbrooke's team put forward this view to Tudjman during a lunch in Zagreb on August 17, Robert Frasure, the former special envoy, passed Holbrooke a note:

> Dick: We "hired" these guys [the Croats] to be our junkyard dogs because we were desperate. . . . This is no time to get squeamish about things. This is the first time the Serb wave has been reversed. That is essential for us to get stability, so we can get out.

"Stability" meant a more balanced map, which in turn meant Serb defeats. In an indication of how confused U.S. policy on Bosnia remained in the summer of 1995, Holbrooke notes that this view, that of the U.S. lead negotiator,

> was not accepted by most of our Washington colleagues, especially the military and the CIA, which still feared, and predicted, a military response from the regular Yugoslav Army.

In addressing the role of the U.S. military in making policy on Bosnia Holbrooke has pointed again and again to Vietnam, to the so-called "Vietmalia effect"—the way the loss in Vietnam, now reinforced by Somalia, haunted U.S. military officers. He quotes from the memoirs of Colin Powell, the officer who had done so much to restrain American policy in Bosnia early in the war, when the options were broader and the risks of intervention less grave. "Many of my generation," Powell had written,

> the career captains, majors, and lieutenant colonels seasoned in that war, vowed that when our turn came to call the shots, we would not quietly acquiesce in half-hearted warfare for half-baked reasons that the American people could not understand or support.[9]

When his successors were confronted with the question of whether to encourage the Croats to retake the Krajina, or, later, whether to support them and the Bosnians when they were fighting together to retake Serb-conquered land in Bosnia, or whether, finally, to send NATO warplanes to attack the Serbs, in each case many in the military and intelligence agencies were against taking action, arguing stubbornly that it would bring only a wider war. They refused to acknowledge that, as Holbrooke says,

> Bosnia was different, and so were our objectives. While we had to learn from Vietnam, we could not be imprisoned by it. Bosnia was not Vietnam, the Bosnian Serbs were not the Vietcong, and Belgrade was not Hanoi. The Bosnian Serbs, poorly trained bullies and criminals, would not stand up to . . . air strikes the way the seasoned and indoctrinated Vietcong and North Vietnamese had. And, as we had seen in the Krajina, Belgrade was not going to back the Bosnian Serbs up the way Hanoi had backed the Vietcong.

By the end of the summer of 1995 everyone in the American government and in the Serbs' mountain capital of Pale had finally learned that lesson.

III.

"History," writes Holbrooke, "is often made of seemingly disparate events whose true relationship to one another becomes apparent only after the fact." Nowhere can one see this better demonstrated than in the diplomatic and military struggles over the Balkans in July and August of 1995, when Clinton administration officials were finally deciding, after three years of war and hundreds of thousands of dead, that they had no choice but to act forcefully to end the fighting in Bosnia. As allied officials were meeting in London, General Mladic was already besieging Zepa, the "safe area" near Srebrenica. The allies abandoned Zepa, which Mladic promptly seized, and drew "a line in the sand" at Gorazde, the last "safe area" in the East. After murdering many of Zepa's men, including the Bosnian commander (whom he had invited to his headquarters on the pretext of discussing surrender), Mladic turned his sights on the Bihac pocket, thus directly threatening Croatia. This led Tudjman—who had now recognized the true worth of international guarantees—to prepare his own offensive.

Even as the Croats were getting ready to launch "Operation Storm," sixty-nine U.S. senators voted for Senator Robert Dole's resolution to lift the arms embargo on Bosnia—and thereby ensured the Republican from Kansas a veto-proof margin. With a presidential election coming soon, the Senate, in the person of Clinton's likely rival, was threatening to take Bosnia policy out of the hands of the president. "He was about to lose control of foreign policy on a fundamental issue," a Clinton adviser told reporter Elizabeth Drew:

> The passage of the Dole bill made the President and others more aware of the political danger, that Congress could do real damage to American foreign policy, and of the problems presented by Presidential politics—meaning Dole. The fall of Srebrenica sent ten to fifteen senators across the line. Britain and France set up the rapid reaction force. The administration knew it had to get back on the offensive.[10]

Clinton officials knew as well that many European leaders treated their newly formed "rapid reaction force," with its tanks and heavy artillery, less as a means to protect convoys of peacekeeping troops than as an instrument to cover their soldiers' early retreat from Bosnia. Even now President Jacques Chirac, whose election had added much forcefulness to French policy, was calling for aggressive action to retake Srebrenica and to reinforce Gorazde; failing that, he vowed to bring his men home: "We can't imagine that the UN force will remain only to observe," he declared, "and to be, in a way, accomplices in the situation. If that is the case, it is better to withdraw."

If the Europeans decided to withdraw their troops, however—and it seemed that Chirac, Major, and the others might well reach such a decision before the end of the summer—President Clinton would find himself obliged to send American troops to the Balkans to manage the dangerous, thankless job of extracting them. With the election approaching President Clinton was caught in a vise. Shortly after the Croats triumphed in the Krajina, producing 150,000 new victims of "ethnic cleansing," the president declared that he was "hopeful that Croatia's offensive will turn out to be something that will give us an avenue to a quick diplomatic solution." Bill Clinton had traveled a long way from intoning that "ethnic cleansing cannot stand." There would be no more talk about what would or would not stand, or what the United States would or would not do; one way or another he was determined to put an end to the war.

General Mladic, meantime, was helping him. By undertaking his vast bloodletting in Srebrenica, the general had not only shocked the world and deeply humiliated the leaders of the West. He had "solved" one of the "problems of the map." Even before Mladic conquered Srebrenica, said Sandy Vershbow, then in charge of Bosnia policy on the National Security Council staff, its future "seemed pretty gloomy. We were already then considering that some kind of swap for at least the smaller of the eastern enclaves for more territory would be wise."

Ethnic cleansing itself would now help ensure the Americans "a quick diplomatic solution": an agreement on territory providing that rather than draw the lines in Bosnia in a way that might make sense according to where the current populations actually lived—or what National Security Adviser Tony Lake called "a higgedly-piggedly way"—the Americans must instead "do what we could to have a territory that was as simplified as possible."[11] To "simplify their territory" had been—for different reasons, of course—the desire of the Serbs as well.

Thus when Lake met his old friend and rival Holbrooke in London on August 12 for a "hand-off meeting"—Lake had just briefed the Europeans on the Americans' new plan to end the war, and Holbrooke would now take over the actual negotiating—he had already included in the proposal he had shown the Europeans the suggestion that the Americans abandon any attempt to protect and hold Gorazde, the last of the eastern enclaves. The source of that suggestion was clear. "The Pentagon," Holbrooke writes, "insisted it would not defend enclaves and slivers of land if it were called upon later to implement a peace agreement." That such an abandonment, which, a month after the massacres at Srebrenica and Zepa, would have created another 40,000 Muslim refugees, could have been included in an initial American proposal is almost grotesque. Bosnian leaders would certainly have rejected this proposal out of hand, as Holbrooke promptly did.

Holbrooke's first negotiating trip to Sarajevo was interrupted by a horrible accident on the treacherous Mount Igman road, which he and his team had been forced to travel because General Mladic would not guarantee their safety on a flight into the capital. An armored personnel carrier tumbled off the road and down a hillside, and ammunition stored within exploded, killing three senior American officials, including Robert C. Frasure, who as special envoy had been the lead negotiator.[12] This accident, of which Holbrooke gives a horrific and moving account in his memoir, may well be considered one of his "seemingly disparate events," for it had the effect, he says, of "steeling" the will of senior American officials on Bosnia, leaving them determined to push for a solution. And given the evident confusion and disagreements that had paralyzed U.S. policy up to then, this in effect meant placing more power in Holbrooke's hands.

The last of those "seemingly disparate events," however, Holbrooke owed to the Serbs, who on August 28, 1995, lofted into Sarajevo's Marshal Tito Boulevard a number of 120-millimeter mortar shells. Landing once again within sight of the Markela, the shells dismembered thirty-seven Sarajevans. On that day alone, "five people in the immediate neighborhood were killed," according to Barbara Demick. Among them were

Merima Ziga, 42, a legal secretary . . . was feeling ill and left work to see a doctor. Heading down Marshal Tito at midday, she walked directly into the trajectory of an incoming 120-mm mortar shell and was killed instantly. . . .

Adnan Ibrahimagic, 17, was supposed to have left town the Friday before to join his mother in Vienna. He had balked at the last minute, declaring to the neighbors, "I can't live without Sarajevo." And so it was that on Monday, he went downtown with a friend to pick up a take-out lunch of Sarajevo's cevapcici at a shop across from the market hall. Adnan ended up featured in the most widely published photograph of the massacre, a poster boy for genocide.

The gruesome picture showed his skinny teen-age body, dead, slumped over a railing outside the cevapcici shop. His friend, 16-year-old Dario Glouhi, had both his legs amputated in an attempt by surgeons to save his life. He died anyway.[13]

Holbrooke, who had just arrived in Paris for talks with Bosnian leaders, instantly saw the implications of the mortar attack: "The brutal stupidity of the Bosnian Serbs had given us an unexpected last chance to do what should have been done three years earlier. I told [Strobe Talbott, at that moment acting secretary of state] to start NATO air strikes against the Bosnian Serbs—not minor retaliatory 'pinpricks,' but a serious and, if possible, sustained air campaign." It had been the key issue of the war, whether or not to initiate such a "sustained air campaign." Now the entire cacophony of officials with a voice in Bosnia—American, European, Bosnian, United Nations—could be heard. Holbrooke's account of the means by which hundreds of NATO warplanes were at last launched against the Bosnian Serbs, four years after the war's outset, is fascinating and provocative. "As our negotiations gathered momentum," Holbrooke writes,

> almost everyone came to believe that the bombing had been part of a master plan. But in fact in none of the discussions prior to our mission had we considered bombing as part of a negotiating strategy. Lake himself never mentioned it during his trip to Europe, and in private he had shown great ambivalence toward it. The military was more than skeptical; most were opposed . . .[14]

From the beginning, though, Strobe Talbott, now the deputy secretary of state and a close Clinton friend, had considered a strong military response "essential." The president, in turn, reached as he vacationed in Wyoming, passed word to "hit them hard."

For three years the issue of air strikes had been central in American disagreements with the UN and the Europeans over Bosnia; but, in another of Holbrooke's "seemingly disparate elements," UN Secretary General Boutros Boutros-Ghali, who could be expected to oppose all air strikes, happened to be in flight on a commercial aircraft and unreachable, and thus his then deputy, Kofi Annan, found himself in charge. Annan earned the administration's considerable gratitude when he "instructed the UN's civilian officials and military commanders to relinquish for a limited period of time their authority to veto air strikes in Bosnia." (Holbrooke has said that Annan "won the job [of UN secretary general] on that day.) Meanwhile, the one UN military commander who could have been counted on to block the bombing, General Bernard Janvier, happened to be absent from his command as well, and in this case "the key" passed to Lieutenant General Rupert Smith, who was not only a determined believer in bombing but an officer who had actually sent NATO planes to attack the Serbs three months before. General Smith moved quickly to clear remaining UN troops from exposed positions where Serbs might take them hostage—in particular, he succeeded in withdrawing the last of the British soldiers from Gorazde, without alerting Serb commanders. He also prepared an artillery attack to coincide with the air strikes in order to suppress Serb cannon and mortar fire. Though Holbrooke doesn't say so, Smith's actions were essential to making the bombing effective.

"It took an outrageous Bosnian Serb action to trigger Operation Deliberate Force," Holbrooke concludes, "but once launched it made a huge difference." This last is an understatement, for the NATO warplanes essentially redrew the map. During two weeks beginning at the end of August, NATO pilots flew 3,400 sorties, destroying Serb antiaircraft batteries, radar sites, ammunition depots, command bunkers, bridges. Meanwhile the Croats and Bosnians pressed their combined attacks in northwest Bosnia, conquering town after town. Indeed, NATO planes—mostly American, but including French, British, and Dutch, among others—had in effect become the Croatian and Bosnian air force, ensuring that those armies would succeed, in just over two weeks, in changing the balance of power in Bosnia. By the end of September—less than three months after Tudjman launched his "Operation Storm"—the Serbs had lost enough territory to bring their holdings from 70 percent to close to the 51 percent that had been envisaged in the Contact Group plan.

In mid-September, Washington officials had begun pressing, privately and publicly, for the Croats and Bosnians to halt their offensives. Ambassador Galbraith was ordered to deliver an official message to the Croatian defense minister urging the Croats to stop their tanks. But Holbrooke and his team, with their eyes always on the map, pressed the Croats and Bosnians to keep going. According to Holbrooke, intelligence "experts" in Washington (the quotation marks are his) had once again misread the situation on the ground, assuming that with each Croat and Bosnian victory on the battlefield Milosevic was coming closer to sending his regular Yugoslav Army to intervene—and thus the message coming out of Washington, as an unnamed official told the *New York Times*, was "quit while you're ahead."

Though administration officials went on making blunt public statements that they wanted the fighting halted, Holbrooke never received, he says, "a clear instruction" to that effect. Even as the bombs fell and the

Croats and Bosnians pushed back the Serbs, negotiations continued. On September 17, Holbrooke sat down with President Tudjman in Zagreb and told him frankly, by his account, that "the offensive had great value to the negotiations."

> It would be much easier to retain at the table what had been won on the battlefield than to get the Serbs to give up territory they had controlled for several years. I urged Tudjman to take Sanski Most, Prijedor, and Bosanski Novi—all important towns that had become worldwide symbols of ethnic cleansing. If they were captured before we opened negotiations on territory, they would remain under [Croat-Bosnian] Federation control—otherwise it would be difficult to regain them in a negotiation.

But a critical decision lay ahead. Even as the two men spoke, the road to Banja Luka lay open before the Croat armies: Banja Luka, the largest city in Bosnian Serbia—the heart of "Republika Srpska"—and the city where the Serbs had not only raped and tortured and murdered thousands of Muslims but had forced them to wear white armbands, like the yellow stars of the Jews. "Mr. President," Holbrooke told Tudjman, "I urge you to go as far as you can, but not to take Banja Luka." The reason? Capturing the city "would generate over two hundred thousand additional [Bosnian Serb] refugees," and, more tellingly, "the city was unquestionably within the Serb portion of Bosnia [and] the Federation would have to return it to the Serbs in any peace negotiation."

If one had to pick a moment where Bill Clinton and his officials—and where America, under their leadership—chose between supporting peace or supporting justice in the Balkans, it would be here, during this conversation between a senior American diplomat and President Franjo Tudjman of Croatia. For at this moment, very briefly, two roads lay open: One of those, the road *around* Banja Luka, which Richard Holbrooke dutifully urged on Tudjman, would leave in place Republika Srpska—Bosnian Serbia—and in doing so would make necessary a final map in which, as Holbrooke says, there would be a "Serb portion of Bosnia." This solution—the "51–49 percent solution"—was already "on the table," a product of negotiations conducted among the "Contact Group": the United States, the Europeans, and the Russians. It could well bring peace to Bosnia but little justice.

Another solution presented itself to Tudjman and Holbrooke as they sat in those Louis Quinze chairs in Croatia's Presidential Palace. This was to push forward to the conquest of Banja Luka and with it the destruction of Republika Srpska—the destruction of General Mladic, Radovan Karadzic, and the other sinister ideologists of ethnic cleansing—and the reconstruction of some sort of integral Bosnia. Shattered as it was by NATO bombs, ignored by its godfather, Slobodan Milosevic of Yugoslavia, the Serb Republic of Bosnia could not survive the loss of its largest city.

For the United States, the risks of such a course would have been great and the responsibility heavy—not just the hundreds of thousands of refugees that would have been created, or the possibility that Milosevic might finally have felt forced to engage his troops, but the greater involvement it would have demanded of America in the task and responsibility of building a new state. In the event, Holbrooke, as talented a diplomat as the United States had, pushed for what his president had demanded and what his instincts urged: the "quick diplomatic solution."

For Holbrooke, of course, the solution would not be quick but arduous and demanding, and the skills he showed at Wright-Patterson Air Force Base in Dayton, Ohio, would be rightly praised. As part of what emerged from Dayton, Holbrooke managed to include, on paper anyway, some of the benefits a conquest of Banja Luka might have brought. Mladic and Karadzic, or so it was agreed, would be sent to an international tribunal and tried and punished as war criminals. So would many other of the less well known villains of the war. And, above all, according to the agreement, the refugees would be allowed to return home, no matter what part of Bosnia they came from. Even if the agreement might seem to rest upon a quasi-partition, Muslims would still be, theoretically, able to return to their houses in the Serb entity, just as Serbs would be free to resettle in Federation lands.

Though Holbrooke inserted within the broad lineaments of a Dayton agreement that looked very much like ethnic partition this liberal vision of peace and justice, the vision remained inert. The American and other Western troops occupying the land proved unwilling to do much in the service of this part of Holbrooke's vision. Paying for the bit of justice imagined in Dayton would likely have cost casualties which the Western governments, worried about their people's support for the Bosnia venture, did not believe they could afford. When Holbrooke writes in a note that one of his critics had "confused the Dayton agreement with the way it has been implemented"[15] —as if these were two separate entities with two separate realities—one wonders whether he ever thinks back to that moment when the road to Banja Luka lay open to the armies that could have seized it and, had it been taken, might have brought to Bosnia a very different future from the grim "cold peace" that imposed itself that winter among the exhausted people of the Balkans.

IV.

In the bitter wind and cold of late December 1995, shortly before the coming of Orthodox Christmas, the Serb fathers of Sarajevo began trudging toward the graveyards. Passing through the gates, they traced their way slowly through the uneven rows of white wooden crosses and the mounds of black earth bordering the open graves until at last they halted, stared downward for a moment, and dropped to their knees, falling forward to kiss the white crosses that bore their sons' names.

They lit yellow candles and opened bottles of plum brandy, pouring libations to the dead. When burly men approached with picks and shovels the fathers tore off hunks of bread and all downed shots of brandy. Then a gravedigger planted his feet and swung his pick, anchoring the point in the frozen soil; the others pried free the rock-solid clods. They fought their way into the earth, until they felt steel scrape on wood. As they wrestled free the coffins, nails pulled loose and planks gave way, and through the earth-smeared wooden splinters a leg or hand or perhaps a discolored, still-familiar face confronted once more his father's eyes.

A father unrolled the dark wool blanket and tucked it gently about his son. He took up hammer and nails and mended as best he could the splintered wood, unrolled the plastic sheeting, wrapped it about the dirty box, and nailed it firm. All now hoisted to their shoulders the fallen son and bore him slowly through the rows of crosses to the cemetery gates.[16] Scores were already there, sliding earth-caked caskets into the backs of vans or pickup trucks, lashing them to the roofs of cars, or to the narrow beds of donkey carts.

The fallen sons were going home, to houses and apartments in Vogosca or Illijas or Hadzici or Ilidza or Grbavica, Sarajevo neighborhoods Serbs had dominated for centuries—and had held during almost three years of war, protected by the artillery implanted on the mountains behind and by the snipers hidden in the apartments above. But they would not stay long. For now, as many Serbs had bitterly predicted, it was the politicians who had lost these lands. The sons would leave with their families, who would not risk the indignities the Muslim enemy might wreak upon heroic dead.

Arriving home the fathers found wives and daughters and young sons working with hammers and chisels and crowbars: ripping from walls sinks and bathtubs and stoves, punching holes in plaster to extract pipe and insulation and wire, tearing away door and window frames, pulling down lengths of wooden molding. All this they dragged outside and loaded into car trunks or heaved into truck beds or lashed to a car's already overburdened roof. What they could not carry they smashed or burned, lest it fall into the hands of their enemies.

The Serbs were readying themselves for another great trek. With the seizure of western Slavonia and the reconquest of the Krajina, the Croats had expelled half a million Serbs, who were now condemned to endure the twilight life of powerless refugees in unwelcoming Serbia. Now, only weeks after presidents Milosevic and Tudjman and Izetbegovic had initialed an agreement in far-off Dayton, Ohio, the Muslim government had begun taking power in the Serb neighborhoods, reuniting Sarajevo for the first time since the spring of 1992. Under the Dayton agreement, Izetbegovic's government had pledged to treat all citizens with equal justice and respect, even those Serbs who for two and a half years had shelled and sniped at their new rulers, killing more than ten thousand civilians, including a thousand children. The

Serbs' "freedom will be respected," Richard Holbrooke declared. "They do not need to leave Sarajevo."[17]

Bosnian government spokesmen, however, had been mostly silent. During the years of shelling and sniping, the Serbs had interfered with supplies of food, blocked water mains, crippled electrical power; Serb gunners had targeted the National Museum and the National Library, and set off great conflagrations in which more than a million books, the precious manuscript history of Bosnia, had gone up in flames. During the first months of siege, meantime, Muslim underworld gangs, having come together as paramilitary units to reinforce a desperately held front line, had assassinated many Serbs who remained on the government side, often torturing them before flinging their corpses into an eighty-foot-deep crevasse known as the "Kazani pit."[18]

Holbrooke's confidence that Sarajevo's peoples could be reconciled, that Serbs could place their fate in the hands of "the federation" of Muslims and Croats who now ruled, was thus not widely shared. Not until two days after the American diplomat made his appeal did Muslim officials for the first time offer a grudging echo of reassurance: "Don't abandon your homes," a Sarajevo television announcer told Serbs. "The federation will guarantee your safety."[19]

By this time the great Serb exodus already covered miles and miles of snowy mountain roads above Sarajevo: cars bearing tables and chairs and bathtubs lashed to their roofs and hoods, with battered coffins protruding from their trunks; trucks filled with firewood and doors and windows; tractors pulling carts loaded with sinks and wire and lengths of pipe; old women pushing sleds with bundles of clothing and rolled-up rugs and small kitchen stoves lashed to the slats. And interspersed with this crawling, skidding, sliding procession, amid the wildly honking cars and trucks and tractors, thousands of men and women trudged slowly forward, bearing on their backs great sacks and bundles and herding before them amid the cars scores of goats and cows and pigs, who mooed and squealed in dumb terror.

When it moved at all, this chaotic caravan moved yard by yard and many turned to gaze back at their city under its great pall of black smoke—not the accustomed grey fog of smoke from shelling that for so long had formed a canopy over Muslim Sarajevo but greasy gasoline-fired smoke rising from their own homes. In their neighborhoods even now young Muslim toughs prowled with guns and knives and grenades, looting Serb houses and apartments, shopping for suitable new lodgings. Bearded Serb paramilitaries in camouflage uniforms, bandoliers across their chests and heavy military knives at their hips, toting AK-47s and cans of gasoline, darted through back streets, edging their way behind sniper shields and through apartment complexes, setting fires where they pleased. The Serbs of Sarajevo had smashed doors and windows into useless splinters, had shredded old sheets and towels and pounded into rubble furniture and appliances they could not carry— had destroyed their houses so no Muslim could benefit from what they had been forced to abandon. These bearded men were determined to burn what remained.

Behind locked doors Serbs too old or too sick to flee Sarajevo shivered from cold and fear; in the streets outside, Serb thugs prepared to burn them out. From their mountain capital in Pale, Serb leaders—so the rumor went—had handed down an order: no Serb, no matter how old or infirm, was to remain in Muslim-ruled Sarajevo. The foreign troops who had come to enforce the Dayton agreement did little. When Italian soldiers arrested arsonists and (as Dayton prescribed) handed them over to the few Serb policemen left in the city, the men were instantly released. Serb firemen had long since fled, and French soldiers failed to persuade those on the Muslim side even to enter Serb neighborhoods: Serb paramilitaries had thrown grenades at their trucks. Officers of IFOR—the "Implementing Force" of the Dayton agreement, commanded by an American, Admiral Leighton Smith—might have ordered troops to guard the firemen, or even to fight the fires themselves; they might, in a show of strength, have sent their troops in force to seize control of the streets and arrest and jail arsonists. Such vigorous action, however, risked "exceeding the mandate" of the mission; and this mandate, the officers now showed, they intended to treat very narrowly indeed. Thus sixty thousand heavily armed foreign troops—of whom no fewer than twenty thousand were American, dispatched by the father of Dayton, President Bill Clinton, and a very reluctant U.S. Congress—managed in their first days "in-country" to do little more than look on as parts of Sarajevo burned.

On the roads above the city, the Serbs pushed slowly on. Behind them, in the cold, clear air over Sarajevo, black smoke stood in plumes and from the battered buildings orange flames rose and shimmered. Peace had come to Bosnia.

New York Review of Books,
October 22, 1998

Coda: Endgame in Kosovo

April 7, 1999

I.

ACROSS THIS near-exhausted century, imagery recurs. The knock at the door, the forced march, the mass evacuation—expressions now impossible to hear without their attendant echoes:

PRISTINA—The Albanian districts of the city have been pretty much emptied of their residents by now. Almost every home has been broken into, not even looted but simply destroyed.

The streets are filled with the sound of heavy gunfire both day and night. . . . Everyone seems to be shooting. . . .

I just interviewed the doctors who saw the body of the slain human-rights lawyer Bayram Klimendi. They said they could not confirm how many times he'd been shot because his body showed "bad and deep signs of maltreatment"—torture. . . .

My friends in the outside world call and tell me to leave. God, I do want to get out of here. I can't stand it anymore. . . .

But now it seems we have no choice. The knock on the door we had long feared has finally come. My family and I have been ordered to leave.

There is no time to finish this report. We have to leave NOW. I don't know where. It seems I am about to join the ranks of the refugees I was writing about only a few days ago.

Pray for me. Goodbye.[1]

One can envision the scene even as these words were hastily written: looming in the doorway heavily armed Serbian Interior Ministry troops—automatic weapons, long knives, red berets, woolen masks covering their faces. Even as the correspondent and his family drag their suitcases out the door, the men prod them with the muzzles of their rifles, hustling them forward as they stumble out into the packed street, there to join a great river of frightened people trudging in silence toward the railway station. They arrive to find scenes of unmitigated chaos: jammed coaches, mobbed platforms, vast crowds waiting for hours in fields around the building. Babies cry, the old and the sick moan. Each family's story is much the same:

> Then they were herded into passenger cars and livestock cars. Their money and their documents were stolen. . . .
>
> Before the trains departed . . . , Serbian troops joked bitterly that refugees were being given free train trips to Macedonia in exchange for their homes and belongings. . . .
>
> Enver Vrajolli, 25, an economics student, said he saw what happened to a neighbor in his sixties who refused to leave his house. He was shot.
>
> "We had only one choice: to leave or be killed. We chose to go," said Vrajolli. . . . "As we were leaving, [the city] was empty. There were only military forces and police left."
>
> "It was very horrible," Gjylizare Babatinca, 32, said as she described how her family was forced out of a house Wednesday by masked Serbs with automatic rifles. . . . "We were forced into the train cars they use for animals. We were packed tightly together. . . . It was completely dark, and we did not know where we were going."

The historical resonances could not be stronger, of course, though here the victims themselves could hear the echoes: "You can't imagine what kind of silence there was as we walked through the streets of Pristina," one young woman said. "I thought Hitler's time was coming back, and we were going to some kind of Auschwitz."[2]

Such drawing of half-century-old parallels, of *the* parallel, derives in fact from a failure of memory. How much more comfortable to invoke Europe in the 1940s than Croatia and Bosnia in the 1990s, a mere four years ago. It is no accident that Serb forces—regular army soldiers, Interior Ministry specialists, and paramilitary marauders—were able to "cleanse" hundreds of thousands from Kosovo in a matter of days. For nearly a decade now, while presidents George Bush and Bill Clinton and other Western leaders watched—while we watched—Slobodan Milosevic of Serbia, his Bosnian Serb henchman Dr. Radovan Karadzic, General Ratko Mladic, and various army and paramilitary commanders had been developing these techniques, refining them, perfecting them.[3]

As of mid-2009, as the plot recurs in stories of refugees interviewed hard upon the Albanian and Macedonian borders—reinterpreted, that is, as "news"—we must struggle to remember that by now the stories could not be more familiar, and hence more predictable. Consider Selim Popei, for example, from the village of Bela Krusa, who on April 3 paused not far from the Albanian border to speak into the microphones and tell the world's television viewers how, at eight o'clock on March 25, the morning after the NATO planes started bombing, Serb army tanks came and surrounded his village; how the Serb special police caught two hundred of the fleeing villagers; how from those they separated out forty-six men. For his part, Selim was sent over with the women—an old man, he had now become a witness:

> They killed five of my children. The youngest was thirteen, the oldest was forty-five. The others were thirty-two, twenty-two and eighteen. They killed my brother's sons too. I was about twenty steps away when I saw it with my own eyes. We all saw it, the women too.

Then there is Jalai al-Din Sepulahu, another old man, who told how the Serbs found him and his friends cowering in a basement in their village of Krusa Emade:

> They collected all the people. They separated the women from the men. They told the women to leave. They put the men against the wall. And they killed the men. I don't know what else to say. My brother was killed, three of my cousins, and the son of one of them. They were all killed.

And finally Mehmet Krashnishi, who comes from Krusa Evolva, a tiny village next door. He appears younger than the others, even with the burns on his face and his hands wrapped in white bandages. Early on the morning after NATO warplanes dropped their first bombs, he said, Serb troops came to his village.

> They rounded up all the villagers. They separated men from women. To the women they said, "You may go to the border," and they put us men in two big rooms. They said, "Now NATO can save you," and then they started to shoot. And when they finished shooting us they covered us with straw and corn and set it on fire. We were one hundred and twelve people. I survived with one other man.

Mehmet, reenacting a narrative familiar from the massacres at Srebrenica, collapsed and played dead as soon as the Serbs began shooting. He was burned in the fire, he said, but when the Serbs left to fetch more fuel to finish burning the bodies he managed to flee.[4]

Why look to Auschwitz when Zvornik and Brcko and Srebrenica lie so much closer to hand?

II.

Endgame: we have finally stumbled into it, the confrontation the West has labored so long and so hard to avoid, the consequences of a politics of gesture. All the hesitations, hypocrisy, half-solutions, compromises, and wishful thinking on which Western, and above all American, policy have rested for nearly a decade—all stand revealed for what they are in the reality of those hundreds of thousands of people massed along the Macedonian and Albanian borders, deposited there with such efficiency by Slobodan Milosevic, the great peacemaker of Dayton. Under the pressure of such events, memories of high officials flicker, grow dim. Consider Lawrence Eagleburger, George H. W. Bush's former secretary of state and perhaps the most influential American official during the first months of Yugoslavia's implosion in 1991 and 1992, who wrote, on Day Twelve of the bombing:

> When the Yugoslav Federation began to break up . . . and the first signs of ethnic strife became apparent, the Bush Administration took a relatively hard look at what to do. We had no illusions about the fact that to have an effect would mean involving several hundred thousand ground troops, and for better or worse we decided that it was a swamp into which we did not want to walk. NATO may no longer feel it has that choice; if so, it is vital that those who make the decisions take as realistic a view as we did as to what intervention would entail.[5]

Almost impossible not to admire the artistry here, the rhetorical subterfuges so densely interwoven and blithely deployed—from preventative shilly-shallying ("a relatively hard look," "for better or worse"), to dubious and self-justifying opinion masked as inarguable conclusion ("would mean involving several hundred thousand ground troops"), to illogical severing of present difficulties from past mistakes ("NATO may no longer feel it has that choice"), to mendacious pomposity ("it is vital that those who make the decisions take as realistic a view as we did").

Of the half-dozen or so opportunities that "the international community" had to avert and then to halt the violence in the former Yugoslavia, at least two—and those with the lowest potential cost—came during the administration of Mr. Eagleburger's former boss, the "foreign policy president," George H. W. Bush. At least from September 1990, when the CIA issued a "National Intelligence Estimate" predicting that "the Yugoslav experiment has failed, that the country will break up" and that "this is likely to be accomplished by ethnic violence and unrest which could lead to civil war," Eagleburger and others knew the war was coming, and they undertook no serious diplomatic effort to prevent it. When on the very eve of Yugoslavia's break-up, in late June 1991, Secretary of State James A. Baker III's one-day "flying visit" to Belgrade failed to solve the problem, Baker returned to Washington, licked his wounds, and uttered the now-famous dictum: "We've got no dog in this fight." The wisdom of this homely judgment is now clear for all to judge.

By the fall of 1991, as the Serbs prosecuted bloody artillery sieges of Vukovar and Dubrovnik, the Europeans' diplomatic effort had clearly failed and President Tudjman of Croatia begged the Americans to send the Sixth Fleet on a "sail-by" of Dubrovnik. Washington declined, unsure what the Serbs' response would be. "They 'might' have gotten the message," said Eagleburger. "They might also not have gotten the message and then we would be faced with the question of what to do next." Missing from this calculus, of course, is any notion that the prosecution of a prodigiously brutal war in post–Cold War Europe might somehow be harmful to American interests—that inaction might hold within it its own severe risks. On this point Secretary Eagleburger, a former ambassador in Belgrade who had known Slobodan Milosevic there, was emphatic:

> I have said this 38,000 times. . . . This tragedy is not something that can be settled from outside and it's about damn well time that everybody understood that. Until the Bosnians, Serbs and Croats decide to stop killing each other, there is nothing the outside world can do about it.[6]

Eagleburger believed that the war must be left to "burn itself out." The war's continuance posed risk only to the people "killing each other"—itself a remarkably misleading characterization coming from a high American official, since by then no one could doubt that, though all sides had committed atrocities, the Serbs, who were using "ethnic cleansing" as their main technique of war, had committed the overwhelming number.

In late 1992, Secretary of State Lawrence Eagleburger chose to send Slobodan Milosevic the so-called "Christmas Warning," advising that "in the event of conflict in Kosovo caused by Serbian action, the United States will be prepared to employ military force against the Serbs in Kosovo and in Serbia proper." Bosnia and Croatia could burn and smolder for years, and did; Kosovo, bordered by Macedonia and Albania, was deemed to be the geopolitical limit—the "red line," as a Clinton official later called it. If Eagleburger or other Bush officials even suspected that their refusal to commit resources of any sort, political or military, to stop Milosevic in Croatia or Bosnia might lead him to doubt their determination to prevent him taking what action he pleased in Kosovo, they showed no sign of it.[7]

As for Bill Clinton, as candidate he had uttered bold words threatening the Serbs with bombing; as president he limited his boldness to scuttling the peace proposals then on the table, which he criticized as not "going far enough" in reversing the Serb war gains, and then blamed his failure to attack the Serbs from the air on the recalcitrance of the European allies. And so, beneath the great welter of diplomatic activity, the matter essentially rested until the summer of 1995, when the Serbs seized the "safe area" of Srebrenica.

In Srebrenica, no UN soldier died at Serb hands; seven thousand Bosnian men did. The collective savagery and humiliation of Srebrenica, the pressures of the coming U.S. presidential election and Clinton's belated realization that if the Europeans decided to withdraw their troops from Bosnia, he would be obliged to commit U.S. troops to help extract them—all of these, in late August 1995, led NATO to send its warplanes at last to bomb the Serbs. Three months later Slobodan Milosevic sat at the peace table in Dayton, Ohio.

III.

As had the Yugoslav wars, the Dayton peace sprang from the forehead of Slobodan Milosevic, the man who had built his power by inciting and exploiting Serb nationalism. Milosevic would now be the "acceptable"
representative of Dr. Radovan Karadzic and his Bosnian Serb associates; he
"brought them along," guaranteed their compliance. When the foreign
troops arrived in Bosnia to enforce the agreement, his intelligence services
provided information about the movements and intentions of Muslim and
Serb "terrorists"—an indispensable service for the American military especially, whose first priority, because of the lack of political support for the mission at home, was to avoid casualties.

As Milosevic could not have failed to see, this priority would make of
Dayton a "cold peace," an agreement that would put an end to the fighting
but would do little to reverse ethnic cleansing or in punish its most notorious practitioners. Clinton, in one of the more eloquent speeches of his presidency, had explained to Americans why he must send their sons or daughters
to Bosnia. Still, approval ratings stayed low; his audience remained unconvinced. Given such inescapable realities, American officials sadly concluded,
as they had in Haiti the year before, that the loss of even one soldier might
threaten the mission. (Who could forget Mogadishu or the perils of "mission
creep"?) Certainly they did not intend to risk American troops to capture
Karadzic or Mladic or to escort refugees back to their homes.

And so the peace of Dayton was a half-peace. The Bosnian people were
left with half a country, a quasi protectorate. Though at the start of each of
the first two years that American troops were stationed in Bosnia, President
Clinton had promised they would be home in twelve months, he did not
keep his promises, nor did he renew them. Clinton well knew that if American soldiers went home so would Europeans and that without either, the
cold Dayton peace would surely collapse.

Milosevic, meantime, saw the men he had created, Karadzic and Mladic,
marginalized, named as criminals, while he attained an importance to the
West none could have imagined even months before. At home, he confronted an economy destroyed by sanctions and war and a political world
that seemed to be closing tightly around him. Having bid a humiliating
goodbye to Slovenia when it declared its independence in 1991; having
fought a bloody war over the Croatian land of Krajina and then watched
Tudjman's tanks sweep through and cleanse it of its two hundred thousand
Serb residents; having seen the Dayton Accords make of the Republika Srpska an unworkable parastate built on stolen land and mass graves—having
watched all this from his darkened Belgrade palace now become the heart of
a shrunken, imploding Yugoslavia, was it not perfectly natural that Slobodan
Milosevic would return to the scene of his greatest triumph, the Serb holy
land of Kosovo?

IV.

Appropriate then that Kosovo should be the scene of the endgame, the confrontation that Slobodan Milosevic himself helped the West escape in Bosnia. For Kosovo was not only the Serb leader's political birthplace, where he had traveled in 1987 to declare to resentful Serbs that the Kosovar Albanians "shall no longer dare to beat you!"—Kosovo was also where George Bush had drawn the "red line" on Christmas Day 1992, recognizing implicitly that however many people "killed each other" in Bosnia and Croatia, only "conflict in Kosovo" would so severely threaten American interests as to compel the United States to "employ military force." Four months later, Clinton's secretary of state, Warren Christopher, was rather more explicit:

> We fear that if the Serbian influence extends into [Kosovo or Macedonia], it will bring into the fray other countries in the region—Albania, Greece, Turkey. . . . So the stakes for the United States are to prevent the broadening of that conflict to bring in our NATO allies, and to bring in vast sections of Europe, and perhaps, as happened before, broadening into a world war.[8]

One might have expected a matter of such magnitude to have occupied a central place on the peace table at Dayton; and yet, though the Americans, according to Richard Holbrooke, "repeatedly emphasized to Milosevic the need to restore the rights of Kosovo's Albanian Muslims," the accords ignored Kosovo. The Americans were in a hurry: they needed a Bosnia agreement, only Milosevic could deliver it to them, and he knew it. He would brook no diplomatic meddling in what was unquestionably "Serb land."

To say that at Dayton "the long-feared crisis in Kosovo was postponed, not avoided,"[9] as Holbrooke does, does not go far enough; for the fact that the peacemakers, in "solving" Bosnia, ignored Kosovo dealt a severe blow to the prestige of Dr. Ibrahim Rugova, then the nonviolent "leader" of the Albanian "shadow republic" there. Rugova, as Noel Malcolm writes,

> had spent four years telling his people, in effect, that they must be patient until the international community imposed a final settlement on ex-Yugoslavia, in which their interests would also be respected. But that settlement . . . left the Albanians of Kosovo exactly where they were.[10]

Very quickly Rugova would find his political primacy challenged by the leaders of the Kosovo Liberation Army, a guerrilla band that, driven by long-suppressed grievances, rose up throughout the country with startling speed. American officials described the KLA publicly, and until very recently, as "a terrorist organization."

Less than a year earlier Milosevic began responding, as was his custom, by sending his security forces and policemen to storm those villages where the guerrilla presence seemed strongest—and to massacre anyone they found. The techniques could not have been more familiar. This, however, was Kosovo, beyond the red line. Had not the United States vowed to respond to such "Serbian action" by employing "military force . . . against the Serbs in Kosovo and in Serbia proper"? It seemed, however, that the red line had begun to fade; Clinton officials now spoke not of warplanes and tanks but of "using every appropriate tool we have at our command" and making "the Serb economy . . . head further south."[11]

In May, Holbrooke managed to persuade Milosevic for the first time to meet with Rugova; afterward the Clinton administration brought him back to Washington, hoping to "increase his international prestige." It was a significant achievement—or would have been, had not American diplomacy already been overtaken by the reality on the ground, where Milosevic's men went on murdering civilians, sending tens of thousands fleeing into the mountains. Under these conditions the "terrorist" KLA had decisively seized the political initiative from the pacifist politician.

Throughout the summer of 1998, the Americans and their Western allies struggled to negotiate a Kosovo agreement but were confounded by Milosevic's intransigence and by his Russian allies' insistence that the matter should be handled under the auspices of the United Nations (where the Russians, increasingly concerned about the West's exclusion of them from Balkan diplomacy, could make use of their veto to protect their Serb allies). Only in October would Holbrooke manage to negotiate a "unilateral" deal with Milosevic in which the Serb leader recognized Kosovo as a legitimate "international" issue; agreed to permit an "air reconnaissance regime" over the territory; and pledged to admit to the territory two thousand "unarmed observers."

Perhaps it would have worked had they been armed peacekeepers, but this Holbrooke had not even proposed. Milosevic would have resisted an armed force, whatever it was called. More important, President Clinton, who would have had to contribute American troops to any such mission, felt himself too weakened by the impeachment scandal even to contemplate asking Congress or the public to approve it. Still, Holbrooke's October agreement saved many lives: For a time Milosevic's forces withdrew and tens of thousands of civilians came down from the mountains.

But as Milosevic's forces moved out, in many areas KLA fighters moved in. And on January 15, Serb Interior Ministry troops stormed the village of Račak. Even as the operation unfolded, according to leaks from American intelligence, a Serb deputy prime minister was ordering the Kosovo police commander to "go in heavy."[12] Arriving in Racak the following day, investigators from the Kosovo Verification Mission would find:

> 1 adult male shot in the groin. He appeared to have been shot while running away.
> 3 adult males shot in various parts of their body including their backs. . . .

1 adult male killed outside his house. The top of his head had been removed and was found approximately 15 feet away from his place of death. The wound appeared to have been caused by an axe. . . .

5 adult males shot through the head.

1 adult male shot outside his house with his head missing. . . .

1 adult male shot in head and decapitated. All the flesh was missing from the skull.

1 adult female shot in back. . . .[13]

And so on. The Serbs had "gone in heavy." Forty-five were dead.

V.

From the bloody village of Račak to the elegant castle of Rambouillet: Here in late February the French held a farcical gathering complete with all the trappings of a grand diplomatic conference: Secretary of State Albright and her staff, her Western counterparts, various guerrilla leaders of the KLA. The two most important seats, however, were empty. No high-ranking NATO military leader attended, and neither did Slobodan Milosevic. Western leaders made their demands: Milosevic must withdraw most of his troops from Kosovo, must accept 28,000 armed peacekeepers (4,000 of them American), and agree to a three-year transition to autonomy for Kosovo. If he did not accept by the end of the conference, the West would bomb Serbia. President Clinton vowed not to let the deadline pass, then did. Western leaders seemed surprised when Milosevic didn't give in. Finally, caught in their own ultimatum, they were forced to send their warplanes, and this time there were no Croatian tanks or Bosnian infantry to fight for them on the ground.

All the while, Slobodan Milosevic was preparing his vast operation. In a long career, this would be his masterpiece, cleansing the Serb homeland of its Albanian interlopers in a matter of weeks. This should, again, have come as no surprise; as late as February, George Tenet, the director of Central Intelligence, had predicted in public testimony that Milosevic would do precisely this.[14]

June 17, 1999

VI.

Madeline Albright, carried forward amid an ocean of cheering refugees in the Stankovic refugee camp, could hardly contain her excitement. "We have been victorious," the secretary of state shouted triumphantly to the roaring crowds, "and Milosevic has lost!" As she spoke, Slobodan Milosevic issued orders in Belgrade. Russian troops, with his happy connivance, marched into Pristina, embarrassing their supposed NATO allies. And more than 850,000 Kosovar Albanians languished in tent cities in Albania, Macedonia, and Montenegro.

"We have fought this war so the refugees can go home," Albright told them, showing a more persuasive grasp of theater than of logic: two and a half months before, few of the men, women, and children surrounding her had been refugees. President Clinton, addressing his countrymen on the eve of the war, had announced quite a different goal. "We act," he told Americans on March 24, "to protect thousands of innocent people in Kosovo from a mounting military offensive. . . . We act to prevent a wider war, to defuse a powder keg at the heart of Europe that has exploded twice before in this century with catastrophic results."

President Clinton's geography, and his history, were as uncertain as his secretary of state's logic, but his argument came through with admirable clarity: "By acting now, we are upholding our values," he said. "Ending this tragedy," he said, "is a moral imperative."

Fine words on which to launch a war, and it is against them that the Kosovo "victory" must now be judged. How does one prepare a moral balance sheet? Begin with brute facts: before, a small province torn by a low-level guerrilla uprising and a savage counterinsurgency staged to suppress it; tens of thousands of people homeless, perhaps two thousand dead.

And after? A land destroyed; countless houses and schools burned; nearly a million people stripped of their homes, their belongings, their identities, deported and displaced. And finally—critical spaces still blank on the balance sheet—scores, perhaps hundreds, raped; thousands, perhaps many thousands, dead.

Brute facts are not all, of course. That "moral imperative" can be extended, telescoped, as President Clinton recognized on March 24:

All the ingredients for a major war are there. Ancient grievances, struggling democracies and in the center of it all, a dictator in Serbia who has done nothing since the Cold War ended but start new wars and pour gasoline on the flames of ethnic and religious division.

Slobodan Milosevic, of course, rules still in Belgrade. As for his policy of sowing "ethnic and religious" division—which, unopposed, had produced a Croatia "cleansed" of Serbs and an ethnically partitioned Bosnia—the West was now forced to confront it:

All around Kosovo, there are other small countries, struggling with their own economic and political challenges, countries that could be overthrown by a large new wave of refugees from Kosovo.

And yet, during the weeks after the president spoke, that "large new wave" of refugees that the war was intended to forestall did indeed break on the shores of Albania and Macedonia, rendering increasingly unstable this "major faultline between Europe, Asia and the Middle East," and making likely a partitioned, or solely Albanian, Kosovo.

It was Milosevic's calculated savagery that produced the refugees; the blame must be laid at his feet. Not entirely, though: at Rambouillet American and Western diplomats practiced a statecraft that was ill-prepared, fumbling, and erratic, and no one can say what Kosovo might look like—and how many Kosovar Albanians might still be alive—had Secretary Albright not handed to the Serbs an arrogant ultimatum whose consequences she and her fellow diplomats had confidently predicted (a quick capitulation, or at the very least a rapid Milosevic retreat)—and which they got precisely wrong.

"We learned some of the same lessons in Bosnia just a few years ago," Mr. Clinton advised Americans as the bombs began to fall. "The world did not act early enough to stop that war either."

> And let's not forget what happened. Innocent people herded into concentration camps, children gunned down by snipers on their way to school, soccer fields and parks turned into cemeteries. A quarter of a million people killed. . . .
>
> At the time, many people believed nothing could be done to end the bloodshed in Bosnia. They said, "Well, that's just the way those people in the Balkans are."

Who were these "many people" who "believed nothing could be done"? President Clinton's first secretary of state, Warren Christopher, perhaps, who in May 1993 called to mind Neville Chamberlain in describing Bosnia as "a humanitarian crisis a long way from home, in the middle of another continent"? Or President Clinton himself, who, in explaining why "the United States is doing all we can to try to deal with that problem," had noted that in Bosnia "the hatred between all three groups is almost unbelievable. . . . It's almost terrifying. . . . That really is a problem from hell. . . ."

In the Clinton White House, nothing was more ephemeral than history. In Bosnia, as the president recalled it, "We and our allies joined with courageous Bosnians to stand up to the aggressors" and thereby learned that "in the Balkans, inaction in the face of brutality simply invites brutality. But firmness can stop armies and save lives."

In Bosnia, of course, such "firmness," in the form of aerial bombardment, came from a paralyzed America only after three years of genocidal war and the deaths of hundreds of thousands of people. In Kosovo, the firmness came in the same form; but it did not "stop armies," at least not for seventy-nine days, and it is a difficult argument to make that it saved lives—or at least that it saved Kosovar lives.

American lives of course it did save. Amid the carnage of Kosovo, and the more than 1,200 dead civilians in Serbia, not a single American airman or soldier, indeed not a single member of the Western alliance, died; not one suffered injuries. And here we reach the bleak underside of President Clinton's "moral imperative" as it was played out during those seventy-nine days of bombing. For Kosovo certainly comes as close as yet achieved to that grail which American leaders have been so long seeking: the politically cost-free war.

Call it the Athenian Problem: How can a democracy behave as a world power? How might its citizens—used to rousing themselves to an interest in world affairs only during wartime, and lethargically even then—be persuaded to send its sons to fight in battles far away, in places apparently unrelated to the country's defense? American leaders have found the political costs of such persuasion to be high and have shown over the decades a growing eagerness to avoid them—in cloaking the country's foreign policy in covert action, as Eisenhower did by using the CIA to overturn governments in Iran in 1953 and Guatemala in 1954; or by refusing to order full mobilization and otherwise seeking to minimize the political cost and reach of war, as Johnson did at the outset in Vietnam.

Technology, America's most cherished faith, has carried the country a long way since then, making the immaculate war possible, even as the need behind that goal, the reluctance of American leaders to risk their political capital to persuade the people of a war's necessity, has grown ever more pressing. "Americans are basically isolationist," Clinton told George Stephanopoulos in 1993, as a firefight raged in Mogadishu. "Right now the average American doesn't see our interest threatened to the point where we should sacrifice one American life."[15]

Faced with other priorities, President Clinton would do nothing to convince that "average American" otherwise, and when eighteen bodybags arrived from Mogadishu he hastened to arrange for U.S. troops' departure from Somalia. When the following year he sent American troops into Haiti he did it in a way calculated to avoid casualties—the Americans did nothing to disarm Haitian paramilitaries and took few risks of any kind—and the invading force suffered none. Haiti today remains arguably worse off than before.

It was in Kosovo that the moral calculus behind this evolution became unmistakable. During his triumphant press conference of June 10, 1999, Secretary of Defense William Cohen described marvels of technology—the fact that "of more than 23,000 bombs and missiles used, we have confirmed just twenty incidents of weapons going astray from their targets to cause collateral damage." But during that very long "briefing," which runs to nearly thirty printed pages, the secretary of defense and his generals said nothing of the Kosovars and what had happened to them. Rather: "We were able to operate," said General Shelton, the Chairman of the Joint Chiefs, "without losses in a very robust air defense system. . . ."

Without losses: a war without losses. And indeed why should one complain about Americans surviving—about a flawless war? But of course it wasn't flawless. Perhaps one day there will be a method to calculate how many Kosovars had to be displaced and how many had to die in order for the West to prosecute its "perfect" war. How many fewer might have died if the "campaign" had targeted—or had plausibly threatened to target—the men with guns who were killing and expelling the people America's president had vowed to protect? Such a war would have held risks for Americans; their countrymen would not have liked that. Leaders who speak of "moral imperatives," however, should expect to be held responsible for their words and for persuading their people that some causes, once embraced, are worth the risk.

New York Review of Books,
May 6, 1999, and July 15, 1999

III.

Marooned in the Cold War

A war fought in the name of high moral principle
finds no early end short of total domination.

—George F. Kennan[1]

Marooned in the Cold War

April 21, 1997

I.

THREE YEARS have passed since I stood in a tiny market in Sarajevo, notebook in hand, gazing through a chaos of smoke and running feet at the scores of dead heaped about the blood-slick earth. I tried but failed to count the corpses: The explosion of the mortar shell had sent long sheets of the market's ramshackle metal roof slicing through the boisterous crowd, instantly reducing what had been people to limbs and torsos and bits of tissue. Already, burly men had begun piling scraps of flesh and bone on these blackened sheets of steel, flinging them into the bed of an ancient dump truck. Nearby, an enormous fellow in a black overcoat wept bitterly over the twisted torso of a woman lying at his feet, while two smaller men struggled to hold him back; imprisoned in the bear hug, he turned his great head toward the sky, and as I watched the cords in his neck tense and his mouth gape, I realized that though my eyes were filled with carnage and my nose with the stench of cordite my ears could hear nothing. Following his stare, I gazed upward and, just as the enormous, hate-filled scream broke through my consciousness, I saw the silver planes tracing their way elegantly through the bright blue sky: American F-16s—the fighter planes of NATO, on patrol, guarding the besieged city of Sarajevo.

I had not meant to be at the market that sunny afternoon. I had planned instead to revisit a favorite landmark. A dozen years earlier—before television had made its streets as familiar to us as those of Saigon once had been—I had traveled to Sarajevo and found myself standing beside the tiny bridge where, seven decades before, nineteen-year-old Gavrilo Princip had raised his revolver, fired twice, and ushered in the modern world. Standing in his footsteps—quite literally, for the Yugoslav government had seen fit, for the benefit of posterity and the tourist industry, to sink impressions of the soles of the young man's shoes into the concrete sidewalk—I closed my eyes, blotted out the noise of the city around me, and tried to imagine what it had felt like to change the course of history with two squeezes of the finger.

Of course the young Bosnian Serb's intent in murdering the Austrian arch-duke had been nowhere near so grandiose. That he succeeded in over-turning history on such a scale proved only that the stability of that edifice had been greatly exaggerated. And for many, that revelation—of the shallow-ness of what men had come to call "modern civilization," soon to be proven in such bloody fashion on the Great War's battlefields—brought with it a good deal of pathos. On that sunny day in Sarajevo, eyes closed, I felt a wisp of that pathos, as the memory of some fragmented bit of eloquence floated through my mind; only after a good deal of searching did I find the words I had not quite been able to place: "The plunge of civilization into this abyss of blood and darkness," Henry James had written to a friend in 1914, "is a thing that so gives away the whole long age in which we have supposed the world to be, with whatever abatement, gradually bettering, that to have to take it all now for what the treacherous years were all the while really making for and meaning is too tragic for any words."[2]

Eight years have now passed since our own *annus mirabilis* of 1989: eight years since the Germans tore down with hammers and crowbars the wall that had severed their country, and the political tide set forth in the streets of Berlin and Prague and Budapest began its inexorable flow east, sweeping before it, two years later, the Soviet Union itself. A four-decade military con-frontation between the two most heavily armed nations in history, each able to obliterate in a matter of hours the surface of the planet, collapsed in danc-ing and celebration, without the movement of a single tank or a sole infantryman, without a shot fired or a drop of blood shed. After four decades of ominous black skies, who could have imagined the Cold War would offer escape through such a sunlit portal?

And yet have we truly managed to walk through that portal even now? What have these eight years been "really making for and meaning"? For James's words treated not only the agony of 1914 but the unforgiving charac-ter of history itself: The "treacherous years" care little for the construction put on them by men; they delight in their own grim ironies. And so at its very creation the vaunted "post–Cold War world" would plunge into its own "abyss of blood and darkness," gaping wide in peaceful Europe itself, and at the precise place where Princip and his revolver christened our century.

The wars in the former Yugoslavia—with their confusing narratives, their endlessly complicated maps, their faceless diplomats flying this way and that offering one more peace plan named for themselves—seem today very far off. Yet it was scarcely two years ago that the scenes from Europe, from modern Europe where the cars and the roads and the restaurants look much like our own, could be tuned in on any television set: Gunners man-ning modern artillery pounding ancient cities into rubble. Soldiers search-ing the ruins for survivors, raping the women and girls, massacring the men; or herding them into concentration camps, there to be abused, tor-tured, left to starve. We had seen nothing like it in Europe since the Second World War—or so it was often said. It would be more accurate to say simply that we had seen nothing like it. For, unlike the Second World War, unlike the Great War over which James so bitterly grieved, we no longer had to open the paper to follow the "plunge of civilization into this abyss of blood and darkness"—we had only to press a small button on the remote control and *see*. The gunners shelling, the children shrieking on the operating table, the battered faces of emaciated men staring dully out from behind barbed wire: We sat in our living rooms and watched all of them as they enacted the drama before our eyes, clearly, undeniably, day in and day out. And while we watched, 100,000 people died.

Who Is to Blame?

In the eschatology of the Cold War, the signs of the End of Time had always been clear: The trumpets would sound, the Wall would be pulled down, Europe would be whole and free. Now the beginning of the End of Time, so miraculously achieved, had loosed a fountain of blood in Europe—and the West, the all-powerful and triumphant West, could do no more than look on in horror and paralysis. For however complicated the story of the demise of the former Yugoslavia, history will likely prove itself relatively uninterested in the details and focus instead on what was sorely lacking on the part of the West during those years of war: the will to act. No doubt historians will find no small irony in the fact that the Western countries, during these years of impotent bickering, would blame their collective inertia on the need to preserve consensus in the very institution that had borne them unscathed through the "treacherous years" of the Cold War: the North Atlantic Treaty Organization.

NATO had, of course, been created in 1949 to bring together the nations of North America and Western Europe to oppose the Soviet Union; keeping the peace in Yugoslavia had never been part of its brief. Still, the fiasco in the Balkans could not help but severely tarnish the alliance's reputation. Not only had the televised barbarity in Europe forever undermined any claim NATO might have had to be protector of the "moral values" of the West, but by late 1994 "the most successful military alliance in history"—torn by conflicts and recriminations of a bitterness not seen since the Suez crisis of 1956—had come near to splitting apart. If Clinton administration officials were finally moved to take strong action in Bosnia, they did so in part because they had at last been forced to acknowledge that the war was no longer simply about an obscure country with little strategic value but was now also about the powerlessness of the West and the feebleness of its institutions, NATO first among them.

Whatever the future of the Dayton Accords, the wars in Yugoslavia had cast into strong relief an inevitable question: As the Cold War slipped further and further into the past, what exactly was the purpose of the Atlantic alliance? The Soviet Union had disappeared. And yet, even as West Germany absorbed the former East Germany to become the incipient economic powerhouse of the continent, several hundred thousand heavily armed American troops stood at the heart of its reconstituted territory; 100,000 remain today, manning their tanks and armored personnel carriers, guarding a border that no longer exists.

The "post–Cold War world" is a trope that has long since become a cliché, and like many clichés it bears more scrutiny than it customarily receives. For though it has not escaped notice that the United States now lacks a "doctrine" to guide its foreign policy, the vaunted "containment" policy having presumably been superseded, and though officials of the Clinton administration have struggled to create memorable phrases to characterize their presumably new approach to a presumably new world ("assertive multilateralism" was put forward—alas—during the Bosnia fiasco; "enlargement of market democracies" headed a more recent effort)—despite these rhetorical exercises, in broad outline America's policy toward the world remains a good deal more like that of the past four decades than different from it.

Preponderant Power

American national security planners remained determined to maintain "preponderant power" in the world—the phrase first appeared in 1950 in the central Cold War planning document known as NSC-68—and to do so by means of a grand strategy that still depends on the forward basing of American troops: 100,000 in the heart of Europe; 100,000 in Asia, divided between Korea and Japan; 25,000 in the Middle East; and a grand armada of 12 aircraft carriers.

The purpose of these forces is clear, as Pentagon planners declared bluntly in 1994: To "maintain the mechanisms for deterring potential competitors from even aspiring to a larger regional or global role." Although too polite to say so, they clearly had in mind as the most important "potential competitors" the Germans and the Japanese. In both countries, American troops, the successors of the original occupation forces, had traditionally served a "dual containment" role. While protecting Germany and Japan from "outside aggression" the Americans prevented both countries from rearming and thereby once again threatening their neighbors and undermining the regional security systems constructed after the Second World War.

A half dozen years after the collapse of the Soviet Union, the United States shows no sign of abandoning the remnants of this containment policy. On the contrary, American security officials have worked hard to "delink" the need for U.S. troops from the Soviet menace, and have pushed to the fore, among other supposed new threats, "rogue states" like North Korea, Iran, and Iraq. American forces thus remain abroad to maintain a post–Cold War hegemony independent of the defunct Soviet Union, and to support that hegemony the United States spends roughly $260 billion a year on armaments and troops—an amount that, though a good deal lower than the peaks of the Reagan years, easily exceeds that of the ten next most heavily armed nations combined. And henceforth American defense spending is almost certain to rise.

For now the other shoe has dropped, the second major event to mark the eight "treacherous years" since 1989: The North Atlantic Treaty Organization has announced its intention to march east. Last July, the leaders of the sixteen alliance countries met in Madrid and invited Poland, Hungary and the Czech Republic to join the very anti-Soviet organization that they had once, as Warsaw Pact members, manned the front line in confronting. Although the United States has never considered these nations vital to its national interest, it will now undertake to guarantee their security with its own armed forces, to regard an attack on them as an attack on itself, and to repel such an attack with all its powers, including nuclear weapons. And it will do so in the face of resentment and angry protests from Russian leaders, who, until this decision, had shown themselves to be extraordinarily cooperative in reaching a favorable and stable settlement with the West.

Who would have predicted that the jubilation of 1989 would lead to this? How can we begin to account for it? During her Senate confirmation hearings, Secretary of State Madeleine Albright declared that Americans "must be more than an audience, more even than actors; we must be the authors of the history of our age."[3] It was a dramatic statement of great ambition, phrased in the kind of exceptionalist language that has been so familiar in America's history—and oftentimes so damaging to a clear-eyed vision of what America's true resources and vital interests actually are. Looking at the current policies of America's leaders one suspects that, rather than plunging ahead to embrace a new, post–Cold War world, they find themselves marooned in the Cold War, pursuing an uncertain and empty hegemony, struggling to expand and justify a predominance the United States already possesses.

II.

On February 18, 1997, Madeleine Albright—self-proclaimed child of Munich, refugee from Nazism and Stalinism, and now America's first female secretary of state—leaned forward over the conference table of the North Atlantic Council's Great Hall in Brussels, gazed at the fifteen other foreign ministers gathered about her, and proclaimed the new world. "We have chosen as our common purpose to do for Europe's east what NATO did fifty years ago for Europe's west," the Czech-born secretary declared, "to integrate new democracies, eliminate old hatreds, provide confidence in economic recovery, and deter conflict."[4]

To "do for Europe's east what NATO did fifty years ago for Europe's west"? For a stateswoman who lets pass no opportunity to underline her personal connection to the great European tragedies of this century, the comparison seemed stunningly inapt. A half-century ago, Germany found itself in a state of utter devastation, its people clawing through ruins and brambles in search of scraps of food; France and Britain were financially and spiritually exhausted; and in the occupied states to the east, the soldiers of the Red Army crouched menacingly, the spearhead of a nation that had arisen triumphant from the war and saw before it now no power that could possibly oppose it.

Compare this dark world to the Eastern Europe of today. Poland, Hungary, and the Czech Republic enjoy democratic politics, however tenuously, and they are forcing their economies through various painful stages of transition to free market systems. The Soviet Union has shattered into a congeries of fifteen separate states and the once-terrible Red Army has achieved a state of almost complete disintegration: Desertions, lack of money, and plummeting morale have meant that, far from threatening Europe, Russia, as the world saw demonstrated most horribly during the Chechnya war, can no longer even invade itself.

If Albright's comparison seems foolish rhetoric, why then has the alliance determined to move east, with all the political and financial expense that that will entail? As with most such enormous government decisions, the interests that brought this one about are many and diverse, and reach back a number of years, to the half-decade before the collapse of the Soviet Union. During those years, Presidents Reagan and Bush had worked with President Gorbachev to push through a revolutionary series of arms control agreements that together established a new and much more stable security regime in central Europe. Among other things, the leaders agreed to reduce dramatically troops, heavy battle tanks, and other "conventional" weapons; to withdraw all intermediate-range nuclear missiles stationed on European soil; and to reduce nuclear artillery shells and other battlefield nuclear weapons.

These were historic agreements, and because they lessened traditional Soviet advantages in Europe, particularly the Red Army's superiority in troops and tanks, many of them were judged deeply favorable to the West. Because they focused on the most dynamic and threatening weapons, the agreements together helped put in place a new structure of security that made a surprise attack of any sort in central Europe almost impossible. Because of this "defense dominance"—the term is Michael Mandelbaum's, from his book *The Dawn of Peace in Europe*[5]—the leaders of either side would need many months to prepare an actual attack, and thus the chance of war breaking out was greatly reduced. As Mandelbaum points out, these agreements formed the basic structure of a new, mutually verifiable means of promoting stability and peace between what had been two hostile alliances.

Then came the revolutions of 1989. Gorbachev, who still had enormous military force at his fingertips, might have reacted quite differently; other Soviet leaders certainly would have. Instead, he chose to view the events in Eastern Europe as inevitable, and to work to ensure the peaceful disintegration of what had been the outer wall of the Soviet empire. President Bush in turn emphasized that further cooperation with the West would depend on the Soviets' measured response to events in the east. At the same time, Bush let the Soviets understand that in exchange for their cooperation in letting "the process," such as it was, go forward peacefully, the West would not take advantage of the uprisings to threaten Soviet borders—by, say, inviting the newly free nations of the east to join NATO.

For its first tumultuous year, the Clinton administration held generally to this policy. Soon, however, President Clinton began listening to the passionate appeals of Lech Walesa, Vaclav Havel, and other east European leaders, who demanded with increasing desperation to be admitted into the Western alliance. Not only had the Poles, Hungarians, Czechs and the others suffered greatly during the titanic wars of this century, subsisting under Nazi occupation during much of the Second World War and under Soviet hegemony after it, they had always seen themselves as culturally and historically part of the West: For many of the leading east European dissidents, "Europe" had been their rallying call. But having succeeded in miraculously tearing themselves from the Soviet grasp, the east European leaders were increasingly perplexed by their cherished "Europe's" ambivalent attitude toward them.

The expected ocean of financial aid had not arrived. Worse, the countries of the West, rather than welcoming them into the European Union—the glittering palace of capitalist trade and growth—had raised insuperable barriers to their entry. If the true goals of Western policy in eastern Europe were, as Secretary Albright maintained, "to integrate new democracies, eliminate old hatreds, provide confidence in economic recovery, and deter conflict," the best vehicle to achieve this was not NATO—which is, after all, a military alliance—but the EU, whose reason for being was the promotion of economic growth and stability through integration with western Europe.

The EU, however, was quietly moving in the other direction. The French, fearing the prospect of a Germany dominating the continent, had been willing to agree to German reunification only on condition that the Union's center of gravity remain firmly anchored in the West; and the Maastricht Treaty of 1991 had in effect enshrined this principle by establishing budgetary and financial conditions for entry that the east European countries could not possibly meet (and that would finish, ironically, by plunging much of western Europe into recession). The west European leaders were above all pragmatic; rather than force their farmers, say, to put their crops in competition with much cheaper east European produce, they would satisfy the east Europeans, via NATO, with an American nuclear guarantee.

Four years after the 1989 revolutions, the desperation of the Poles and their eastern neighbors was growing. Not for the first time in their history, "Europe" seemed to desire them much less than they desired it. If admission into the European Union was an unrealistic dream, at least for the near future, if NATO was all the "Europe" they might be offered, they would gladly grasp it. In so doing, they hoped they were taking in hand not only Madeleine Albright's bromides about promoting democracy and economic stability but a Western guarantee against eventual Russian revanchism.

The "Security Vacuum"

In Washington, they had influential allies. By late 1993, Henry Kissinger and Zbigniew Brzezinski, among others, had begun to criticize the Clinton administration for allowing a "security vacuum" to emerge in Eastern Europe. Within the administration, key members of the bureaucracy began to stake out positions. Senior military officers and civilian Pentagon officials generally opposed expanding NATO, fearing that the result would be to "dilute" the alliance and produce a kind of "NATO lite" in which guarantees to the newly admitted countries would be less reliable than those to existing members. Many in the State Department, including Strobe Talbott, then the president's special envoy to Russia, argued that expanding NATO would alienate the Russians with little compensating reward. Other senior officials, notably Undersecretary of State Lynn Davis, began to push hard for granting some sort of limited membership to the east European countries.

In the White House, meantime, President Clinton, who had been listening to German chancellor Helmut Kohl worry about securing his newly united country's eastern frontier, began to muse openly about the "security limbo" in Eastern Europe. Clinton's adviser on national security affairs, Anthony Lake, had been conducting a number of discussions with Brzezinski, who was strenuously promoting a "parallel track" strategy, which envisioned admitting the eastern European countries to NATO while placating the Russians with a separate diplomatic agreement. According to an extensive account by Michael Dobbs in the *Washington Post*, it was Brzezinski who eventually succeeded in convincing Lake to push this general approach.

Into this maelstrom of interests now intruded two events that embody the odd contingency of history. First, Clinton nominated his old friend Strobe Talbott to be deputy secretary of state, and Talbott found himself undergoing bruising Senate hearings during which prominent Republicans accused him, in effect, of being "soft" on Russia; the political implications for Clinton, who would be facing voters in two years, were obvious. Second, Talbott moved to bring Richard Holbrooke, then ambassador to Germany and an official notorious for his aggressiveness and ambition, back to Washington to become assistant secretary of state for European affairs. Holbrooke, as the *Post's* Dobbs put it, "made clear that he regarded the reshaping of Europe's security architecture as the modern-day equivalent of the 1919 Conference of Versailles, and that he was in charge."[6]

Holbrooke proceeded to push NATO expansion through the national security bureaucracy with his customary vigor and vehemence. According to Dobbs, when, at the first meeting of a key interagency group of military officers, diplomats, and other officials who had been brought together to "study" the question of expansion, Gen. Wesley Clark, an influential friend of Bill Clinton (and now the NATO commander in Europe), observed mildly that there remained "some issues we need to discuss," Holbrooke thundered back: "That sounds like insubordination to me. We need to settle this right now. Either you are on the president's program or you are not."[7]

To Holbrooke's powerful advocacy were now added the pressures of the coming presidential election: Promoting NATO expansion would not only shelter Bill Clinton from any Republican charge that he might be "soft on Russia," it would also help him in several key states of the Northeast and upper Midwest that had large populations of Americans of east European descent. During the campaign, Clinton would give only one foreign policy speech, traveling to heavily ethnic Chicago to declare dramatically that "the question is no longer whether NATO will take on new members, but when and how."

"Us" versus "Them"

What the president notably did not say was why—why the United States, eight years after the collapse of the Eastern bloc, six years after the disintegration of the Soviet Union, had determined to extend its military obligations to protect countries in eastern Europe that it had never viewed as vital to its national security. On this question, the rhetoric coming from the administration has been deeply confused, in part because different audiences—Europeans, east and west; Russians; Americans—are being addressed, and the messages required to placate them contradict one another.

To the American and European publics, for example—and in part to the Russians as well—Clinton officials have offered what might be called the "one Europe" rationale. As Secretary Albright put it in Moscow last May when she unveiled the Founding Act on Mutual Relations, Cooperation, and Security between NATO and the Russian Federation, the alliance's decision to extend a formerly hostile military alliance to the Russian border, far from threatening Russia's security, instead would produce "an undivided, democratic, and free Europe" and "anchor Russia within a European system." "This NATO," the secretary insisted, "is not directed against Russia." In this new world, "it is not us versus them or them versus us. We are all on the same side."

How all these countries—some within the alliance, some outside of it—could be "all on the same side" the secretary did not explain. As Henry Kissinger put it, Clinton officials "keep talking about the absence of dividing lines. With all due respect, this is nonsense. If you have an alliance, you have a dividing line." President Clinton himself, before he saw the light on expanding the alliance, warned darkly that to take such a step would be to "draw a new line through Europe just a little further east." Now, three years later, and against all logic, expanding the alliance has come to mean creating a "Europe whole and free."

Of course, if one looks beyond the rhetoric of public relations, and the eloquent appeals of east European leaders, and the strivings of ambitious bureaucrats, and the transitory demands of U.S. election campaigns—if one looks beyond all these, one finds that the plan to expand the alliance is indeed motivated by an "us versus them" premise, and, at its heart, by an exfoliating tree of assumptions about European history, Europe's probable future, and the inevitable behavior of powerful states, which is precisely why the Poles and the Czechs and the Hungarians have pleaded so tenaciously to be admitted. "If this request is rejected," writes Kissinger, "and the states bordering Germany are refused protection, Germany will sooner or later seek to achieve its security by national efforts, encountering on the way a Russia pursuing the same policy from its own side. A vacuum between Germany and Russia threatens not only NATO cohesion but the very existence of NATO as a meaningful institution. NATO cannot long survive if the borders it protects are not threatened while it refuses to protect the borders of adjoining countries that do feel threatened."[8]

Beyond all the talk about an undivided Europe, it is this sort of reasoning that one finds at the root of why the United States has now decided to guarantee the security of Eastern Europe. Such reasoning has a great ring of authority but is fraught with contradictions. Like many "realist" arguments, it pretends to set out timeless truths but instead is saturated with history. It broods about the grim past and the morbid future while ignoring almost entirely the possible present. It is not statesmanship. It is fatalism posing as realism.

A statesman might have proposed a different path. He might have insisted that the United States—by making use of its diplomatic weight—persuade the Europeans to "protect" and "stabilize" the states of Eastern Europe by integrating them firmly into their economic system, of which Germany forms the vigorous heart. He might have recognized that the security agreements of the late 1980s and early 1990s had strongly bolstered the stability of central Europe and seen that the key to preventing any so-called vacuum between Germany and Russia is to avoid taking a fateful and unnecessary military initiative sure to poison relations with the Russians at a time when their domestic politics are delicate in the extreme, hanging on the fragile health of one ailing man. He might have observed that the proposed expansion might push the so-called vacuum east, by drawing a new line gratuitously isolating Ukraine and the Baltics, in effect reducing them to the role of Russia's new "buffer states"—buffer states with very considerable ethnic Russian minorities that hold within them the true seeds of Russian revanchism, and which may find themselves pressed into demanding that NATO admit them, a move the Russians would be unable to countenance.

More broadly, the statesman might have asked himself whether the American people—whose leaders have not bothered to consult them on the matter—are committed to defending the countries of Eastern Europe:

whether Americans are willing to send their young people to fight in Poland, or to launch their nuclear weapons to defend it. And, if they are not, he might have wondered what effect building such an empty guarantee into the alliance would eventually have. He might have acknowledged that the United States should first of all look after its own principal interests, and that those interests are broader than so-called NATO cohesion for its own sake. They are a stable and increasingly self-reliant Europe, with a prosperous and secure Germany at its center, and an unthreatened and unthreatening Russia. Whatever else it may do, it is not at all clear that rushing to absorb Eastern Europe into the Western alliance at this time will advance those interests.

The evidence thus far strongly suggests the contrary. Not only has the unprecedented collaboration between Washington and Moscow come to an abrupt halt, but members of the Duma are now refusing to ratify the all-important START II agreement, which reduces both sides" nuclear arsenals by roughly two-thirds. And though Russian leaders, given the conditions of their army and economy, were scarcely in a position to block the entry of the east European countries, President Clinton, for reasons known only to him, felt bound to grant them extraordinary concessions in the Founding Act. Not only did he vow not to station foreign troops or nuclear weapons on the soil of the newly admitted countries, Clinton invited the Russians to share in making alliance decisions as a member of a new "Permanent Joint Council"—an astounding step that led Kissinger to remark acidly that "Russia seems to be achieving NATO participation before the new applicants."[9]

Whatever the impact of these concessions on American security, they point to a much larger question: What will the significance be for us, as Americans? The United States has come to a critical crossing point, and before the country can move ahead, its leaders and its citizens must reach agreement about the part their nation will now play in the world. Twice before during this century Americans have stood on such a precipice. Out of debates cluttered with ideological baggage emerged two very different views of the country's mission. What stayed close in outline, however, was the rhetoric, the jargon of American exceptionalism that can be traced back deep in the country's history. This fall, as the Senate debates the amended treaty and as American taxpayers learn how much they will be expected to pay to modernize the Polish and Hungarian and Czech militaries, this rhetoric will once again echo loudly through the land. Must not Americans be, as Secretary Albright said, "the authors of their age"?

Imbued as we are with such romantic notions it has become very difficult to recognize that the answer to Albright's question is plainly "no." Americans need not be the authors of their age. As in 1919, as in 1945, Americans have a choice to make, one that must be based on an informed discussion of interests and resources, not on a flurry of rhetoric. In a democracy, words should serve as instruments that the people apply to explain and promote interests, not empty slogans that saddle and imprison those that use them. In the words we see flowing already from the Clinton administration, we can make out the shape of the rhetoric to come, and it seems all too strangely familiar. Once again, we will be told that Americans, because they are Americans, must step boldly forward and bear the burden of leadership, for if they do not, who will? Is not America, after all, "the indispensable nation"?

III.

Although it is hard to know when America first became "indispensable," the notion clearly emerges from what historians call American exceptionalism: the idea of America as separate, godly, pure; a nation fundamentally unlike all others—America as, in the Puritan John Winthrop's famous phrase, "the city on a hill." This idea animates much of the best-known literature of early American diplomacy, from President Washington's admonition, in his Farewell Address, to avoid "entangling alliances" to John Quincy Adams's prescription that America should "not go abroad in search of monsters to destroy."

Throughout the nineteenth century, as the United States followed a vigorous program that would expand its continental territory by diplomacy, purchase, and war, the rhetoric of its foreign policy embodied independence, purity, and, with respect to the power politics of Old Europe, a proudly ignorant disgust. If already in 1796, George Washington could observe that the European countries had "a set of primary interests which to us have none or a very remote relation," Woodrow Wilson, exactly twelve decades later, could say bluntly that with the causes and issues of the First World War Americans "are not concerned. The obscure foundations from which its stupendous flood has burst forth we are not interested to search for or explore."

We see here the flowering of a sweet-smelling but noxious illusion: America as an island secure and strong behind its two broad oceans, its inexhaustible resources rendering it wealthy and virtuous, threatened only by the predations and corruptions of the Old World. However beautiful this myth, like most myths it has not served as a reliable guide to self-understanding—or to the clear action that can only follow from such understanding. In their drive to conquer their continent, Americans behaved much as other vigorous, young peoples have; their treatment of inconvenient obstacles—be they native peoples and Mexicans, or the competing demands of rival countries—was neither appreciably better nor worse than that of many others. As for the unscrupulous and looming Old World nations, it was not the broad deep ocean or Americans' inherent virtue that protected them but the benevolent power of Great Britain and its Royal Navy.

America entered what was to be its century—the bloodiest century in the history of mankind—in a kind of waking dream. To ward off the Realpolitiker scheming of European diplomats, it had become accustomed to presenting scraps of paper: If America was secure and isolated in its hemisphere, for example, this was owed to President Monroe's promulgation of his famous "doctrine" in 1823, warning that American lands, north and south, "are henceforth not to be considered as subjects for future colonization by any European powers." And that was that; no navy or army needed: Forceful words equal power. The delusion became early on an American habit.

Throughout the nineteenth century, Great Britain quietly supplied the shield behind which America prospered: Britain's all-powerful navy patrolled the seas, protecting transatlantic trade routes, and British diplomats labored, by shaping alliances that would prevent the emergence of any one hegemonic state, to maintain a balance of power on the European continent. Both of these traditional British policies were in fact crucial to the United States: not only in its need for secure trade routes but because it, no less than Great Britain, would inevitably be threatened by the emergence of an expansionist power dominating the continent. Americans, accustomed to viewing European diplomatic machinations with condescension, generally ignored this dependence. Only many years later, and after the shedding of much blood, would the point be driven home.

When in 1914 Gavrilo Princip set off Europe's second Thirty Years' War, in which tens of millions of people would eventually perish, it was inevitable that Americans would look on with mesmerized horror and revulsion, as if at a kind of barbaric spectacle that could not possibly concern them. The implications that seem so obvious now—that an aggressive Imperial Germany might succeed in ruling the continent and dominating the seas—did not seem at all apparent then.

It is one of the great ironies of American history that at the very moment this country's inescapable involvement in European affairs was about to become crystal clear it had at its head an idealistic man singularly unequipped to recognize this fact, or to explain it to his people. Woodrow Wilson aimed instead to reconstruct the world, to render it, as would become his great rallying cry, "safe for democracy." For this task purity and distance must be maintained; the hands of the United States must not be tainted, for how then could it serve as impartial creator of the new world order?

So, as the conflict wore on, and the states of Europe cast generation after generation of their young men into the bloody pit, President Wilson wasted any diplomatic influence the United States might have had by nattering on about "freedom of the seas," as if such a right were God-given and did not depend ultimately on military power and political influence. Only in April 1917, thanks to Germany's attacks on U.S. ships and revelations about its diplomatic conniving with Mexico, were Americans finally persuaded to enter the war, and by then it was very late: Not only had the main antagonists become so embittered that any reasonable settlement approximating Wilson's "peace without victory" would be near impossible but the Czar had been forced to abdicate and the Cold War had in effect begun. With moralistic flags flying, Wilson led his country into battle, and then, after the armistice, on to the Paris Peace Conference, sweeping into Europe on an avalanche of apocalyptic rhetoric. "We are seeking," declared the president, "permanent not temporary foundations for the peace of the world."

Wilson's encounter with the Old World is one of the great set pieces of modern history. "While we were dealing in momentous questions of land and sea," David Lloyd George, the British prime minister, later recounted, "he was soaring in clouds of serene rhetoric."[10] The victorious European nations had bled and died, had lost blood and treasure to an extent unknown in history; they wanted territory and they wanted revenge. Wilson meantime played the Jamesian ingénue, innocent and beguiling, taken in by the calculating predators of corrupted Europe. While the lands of the former Austro-Hungarian and Ottoman empires were parceled out, the American fulminated and protested but in the end showed himself to be, as John Maynard Keynes observed, singularly "incompetent [in] the agilities of the council chamber."[11] In the end, Wilson's inspirational talk of "national self-determination" would yield the independence of much of eastern Europe—an achievement for which he is still worshipped there—and the grandiose and idealistic League of Nations that his countrymen would in the end decline to join, thus dooming it to irrelevancy.

Moral Beauty and Foreign Policy Failure

Embodying in their purest form aspirations that resonate loudly through American history, Wilson's project was one of great moral beauty; but as foreign policy it was an abject failure. Whatever practical influence the United States might have had in inventing a new and durable world order—and its military and economic strength might have ensured it great influence indeed—was dissipated in an impractical program maladroitly managed. And of this failure, unfolding relentlessly like the pitiless mechanisms of a Greek tragedy, would be born the much greater carnage of the Second World War.

The unique circumstances of the Great War's end—the tumultuous revolution in Russia; the spiritual desolation of the Western democracies; the deep humiliation of a reeling and unstable Germany; and the creation of a group of weak and unprotected countries huddled between Germany and the Soviet Union—led by the mid-1930s to Kissinger's classic "security vacuum" in eastern Europe.

"My mindset is Munich," Madeleine Albright famously proclaimed, "most of my generation's is Vietnam. I saw what happened when a dictator was allowed to take over a piece of a country and the country went down the tubes. And I saw the opposite during the war when America joined the fight. For me, America is really, truly the indispensable nation."[12] Speaking in her native Prague, Albright drew the conclusion that has by now become synonymous with the word Munich: that to appease a dictator is to bring on war, that provocation must be met with strength.

Yet it was an odd argument to be making—particularly in Prague, and particularly by a professional academic who had fled not only the Nazis but the Communists. For whatever the celebrated cupidity of the Western powers at Munich, by 1938 the fate of eastern Europe had largely been determined: As George Kennan pointed out, the military and spiritual weakness of the West, and the overwhelming strength of the rising totalitarian powers, meant that the democracies would almost certainly be unable to defeat Hitler's Germany and Stalin's Soviet Union if the dictators joined together.[13] The West would eventually be forced to ally itself with one totalitarian power against the other. Apart from the moral catastrophe such a compact represented, one need only glance at a map to see how it effectively doomed "Wilson's children" to certain subjugation under either a German or a Soviet imperium.

Only one thing could save the independence of the eastern countries: an early and vigorous entry of America into the war. But the United States, having midwifed the creation of the new countries of the east, had withdrawn its military power and political influence from Europe as abruptly as it had brought them to bear, leaving the way clear for Munich. Now, as the German divisions swept over the continent, America once again proved standoffish, its people reluctant and unpersuaded; Roosevelt, though a much more practical man than Wilson, could judge well the country's mood. When America finally returned to Europe, thanks to the Japanese attack on Pearl Harbor in December 1941 and Hitler's precipitous declaration of war, it did so as an ally of the Soviet Union.

In Europe, America's sole obsession was to crush the Axis; its British allies, whose memories were longer and who understood that the war was not only about Germany but about the Soviet Union and the political shape of the postwar continent, were repeatedly frustrated in their efforts to persuade the Americans to open an early second front, either by attacking through the Balkans, or from Italy, or by driving more directly and rapidly toward Berlin itself—anything that might overtake the Red Army's steady march to envelope Eastern Europe. To the British pleas that the Western allies must move rapidly to take Prague or Vienna or Berlin before the Soviets did, "the Americans," in the words of historian Martin Walker, "point-blank refused, insisting that they would not take casualties for political reasons."[14]

There is something striking in this blank pigheadedness; for what was the war about if not politics? For the Americans, it had become a moral crusade, the defeat of Nazism as the ultimate evil; as for their new allies, the Soviets, they had been transformed, overnight, from anti-capitalist villains to heroic allies, reasonable men who could be dealt with reasonably after the war. If the triumphant Red Army managed to occupy eastern

Europe then surely moral principles inscribed on scraps of paper would persuade them to leave, or at least to behave like good democrats while they were there.

In the event, of course, the Soviets had their own ideas. As the First World War had led inexorably to the Second, so now the Second would lead to a different kind of conflict, one that would endure half a century and would impose on the combatants enormous expense—and on the peoples of eastern Europe, enormous suffering.

IV.

By late 1945, American troops had begun to demobilize and return home. With western Europe reeling from the effects of the war, the plot could easily have reprised that of the post–First World War years. But the men in charge of American policy were of a different cast; many had seen the errors of 1919 at close hand and were determined not to repeat them. Instead, with frank self-consciousness and startling abruptness, the United States would declare itself a true world power over the span of a few weeks in the spring of 1947.

Greece was under siege, its right-wing government near collapse from a domestic Communist insurgency; Turkey was also bending under Soviet pressure. In February 1947, the British ambassador, whose country's "sphere of influence" traditionally encompassed the eastern Mediterranean, informed the State Department that His Majesty's Government, itself teetering near bankruptcy, had determined to withdraw its troops from both Greece and Turkey—and to do so within six weeks. In Greece, this would clearly lead to an early Communist takeover.

"Under the circumstances," as Dean Acheson, then undersecretary of state, recalled, "there could be only one decision."[15] But if the decision was preordained the manner in which it was explained and justified was not. While granting substantial aid to Greece and Turkey clearly had historic implications—the United States for the first time would be taking on a broad peacetime role in European politics—President Truman could have couched the policy in the narrowest terms, as simply a move by the United States to come to the aid of two friendly governments struggling to survive amid the stresses of postwar turmoil. The decision need have created no precedent.

In the event, he did quite the opposite. On March 12, 1947, scarcely three weeks after the British ambassador's visit, President Truman went up to Capitol Hill and delivered to both houses of Congress a grand speech setting forth America's new role in the world:

> At the present moment in world history nearly every nation must choose between alternative ways of life. . . . One way of life is based upon the will of the majority, and is distinguished by free institutions, representative government, free elections. . . . The second way of life is based upon the will of the minority forcibly imposed upon the majority. It relies upon

terror and oppression, a controlled press and radio, fixed elections. . . . I believe it must be the policy of the United States to support free peoples who are resisting attempted subjugation by armed minorities or by outside pressures.

The need to respond to a limited crisis in the eastern Mediterranean had produced a sweeping American commitment to help threatened nations around the world. Amid the confluence of interests that produced this momentous result, two stand out. First was the felt need to offer a strong and unambiguous statement of policy in response to an increasingly aggressive Soviet Union. Almost exactly a year before, and only a few weeks after George Kennan had sent his celebrated "Long Telegram" from Moscow—on which, along with the same diplomat's later "X" article, the containment doctrine would be based—Winston Churchill had traveled to Fulton, Missouri, and declared that "an iron curtain had descended across the continent."

A few months after Churchill's speech, Truman had asked his special counsel, Clark Clifford, to put together a comprehensive analysis of the country's relationship with the Soviet Union. Clifford and his assistant, George Elsey, prepared for the president a lengthy document, titled "American Relations with the Soviet Union," in which they argued that Soviet leaders had set themselves "on a course of aggrandizement designed to lead to eventual world domination by the U.S.S.R." Among other things, they concluded, the United States "should support and assist all democratic countries which are in any way menaced and endangered by the U.S.S.R."

Amid the many phrases of the Clifford and Elsey report that would find their echo in the Truman Doctrine six months later, this is the most important, for it forms the kernel of what would become the most frequently quoted passage of the entire speech—what Clifford referred to as the credo: "I believe it must be the policy of the United States to support free peoples who are resisting attempted subjugation by armed minorities or by outside pressures." The rewriting is revealing: "democratic countries" becomes the more evocative "free peoples"; "menaced and endangered" is recast as the more heroic "resisting armed subjugation"; and the blunt "U.S.S.R." is broadened out to "armed minorities or outside pressures."

The report's hardnosed insistence that the United States must act aggressively abroad to strengthen its own security has been transformed into something quite different: a call to promote the nation's fundamental principles around the world. The frank pursuit of national interest has become the export of American morality, to make "the world safe for democracy."

The old reliable Wilsonian idealism had returned: refurbished, reanimated, but recognizably the same. When Secretary of State Marshall complained that the speech had "too much rhetoric," White House officials responded that this was needed to gain approval in the Senate. Two weeks before, the president had invited the leaders of Congress to the White House to discuss the situation, and Acheson had taken the floor to draw a lurid picture in which the fall of Greece would lead directly to the Soviet "penetration" of three continents. The congressmen, deeply impressed, urged the president to make this case publicly, for only thus would he have a hope of securing the necessary funds. Sen. Arthur Vandenberg, chairman of the Senate Foreign Affairs Committee, implored the president to "scare hell out of the American people."

But Truman's speech achieved its object not simply by means of scare tactics but by arguing for America's moral mission in the world. Underlying the words was the idea of an America free, democratic, and exemplary, a nation exercising, as Wilson had put it, "the infinite privilege of fulfilling her destiny and saving the world." What is fascinating about this annunciation of America's apotheosis as a world power is the seamless grafting of this familiar ideological messianism onto the felt necessities of national security (a combination that Wilson's idealistic League of Nations proposal conspicuously lacked). The budding national security establishment's insistence that the country launch a worldwide struggle against the Soviets was deftly couched in a positive call for the safeguarding and advancement of freedom. And those who crafted the moral terms in which the doctrine was set clearly understood them to be a crucial political tool in convincing the American people to set sail on a course that was, after all, unprecedented.

The Faustian Bargain

And yet, in bidding for political support by casting America's risk and responsibility in the broadest possible terms, Truman had forfeited the chance to define, as clearly and as narrowly as possible, the country's bedrock interests. In making the threat "clearer than truth," as Acheson later put it, he and his colleagues had handed the country, and the policymakers who would succeed them, a statement that suggested America's commitments lay everywhere and at all times.

Walter Lippmann, who during the war had famously defined proper statecraft as the "bringing into balance, with a comfortable surplus of power in reserve, the nation's commitments with the nation's power,"[16] criticized in Truman's speech the "vague global policy that sounds like the tocsin of an ideological crusade [that] has no limits. It cannot be controlled. Its effects cannot be predicted."[17]

In sounding this "tocsin of an ideological crusade," Truman had signed a Faustian bargain: He won overwhelming public support for placing the country in a role unanticipated in its history—that of a permanent player in the politics of Europe and much of the rest of the world—and in return he had put his country on record as the sovereign protector of all the world's "threatened peoples." Indeed, it is hard to imagine a doctrine that might do less to "bring into balance the nation's commitments with the nation's power." Far from serving as a realistic statement of the country's responsibilities, the Truman Doctrine constitutes, in the writer Theodore Draper's words, "the original codification of the Pax Americana illusion;" in many of their most important postwar foreign policy decisions—from Korea and Vietnam all the way up to the marine mission in Lebanon in 1982—American statesmen tended to "substitute" the doctrine "for any rational calculus of means and ends."[18]

Providing such a rational calculus, of course, is meant to be the obligation of statesmen, and that they failed to do so cannot be blamed solely on Truman's speech. In later hearings, both Acheson and Vandenberg stressed that in future crises the United States would "of course"—in Acheson's words— act "according to the circumstances of each specific case." Both made it clear that they saw America's policy as "limited containment," not some universal crusade.

But as soon became clear, this worthy intention concealed a paradox: To follow such a prudent course would require not only that the country's statesmen display seasoned judgment but that its politicians show themselves willing and able to lead and to shape public opinion, rather than flee before it. And, in the event, the same political reality that led the Truman administration to cast its doctrine in the broad terms it did too often led subsequent policymakers either to make imprudent decisions themselves, or to succumb to their fear of politicians who made powerful demagogic use of the grandiose role that Truman had set out for the United States.

Thus, the Truman Doctrine firmly anchored America's worldwide role in the realm of domestic politics; subsequent events, especially the traumatic "loss" of China, would show the deforming effect those politics could have on American foreign policy. Acheson himself, in attempting to develop as secretary of state a practical policy toward Communist China—in effect, an engagement with Mao—found himself repeatedly stymied by the domestic political implications of the Truman Doctrine; if he had thought the United States would be free to act "according to the circumstances of each specific case," he now discovered that he had helped shape a domestic political reality that did not provide for such diplomatic freedom. How could the administration pledge to fight Communists around the world one day and treat with them the next?

These implications would become painfully apparent in the early years of Vietnam, during which many prominent opponents of Presidents Kennedy and Johnson (notably Richard Nixon) brandished the "domino theory" to exclude the possibility of any retreat in Southeast Asia. Had Kennedy or Johnson backed down and South Vietnam fallen to the North, the Democrats could have expected to be blamed for opening the entire Pacific to communist penetration. This widely acknowledged political reality dominated decision making during the early years of what would be a disastrous policy. On a recently released recording of a 1964 telephone conversation with Georgia's Sen. Richard Russell, President Johnson can be heard wearily conceding that the thought of sending large numbers of young American boys to Vietnam "just sends chills up my spine" but that the constraints of domestic politics left him no choice in the matter: "They'd impeach a president, though, that would run out, wouldn't they?"[19]

V.

As Johnson had feared, Vietnam proved to be disastrous, the great crevasse cutting across the Cold War; into it disappeared not only his presidency and that of his successor but much of the motivating power of the old Cold War rhetoric. Newly assertive congressmen blocked the Ford administration's efforts to come to the aid of the collapsing South Vietnamese regime in 1975, and even managed to prevent Secretary of State Kissinger from intervening covertly against the Cubans and Soviets in Angola. Bitter military officers, who believed the United States would have prevailed in Vietnam had it not been for a lack of national commitment, offered a more subtle inhibition; it would be a decade, and a painful struggle over American intervention in Central America, before this sentiment was publicly codified in the Weinberger Doctrine, wherein Reagan's secretary of defense offered, for any proposed U.S. intervention abroad, a test of six points—among them, that the country enter into no hostilities unless "vital interests were at stake," unless it had a "reasonable assurance of the support of the American people and their representatives," and unless it could do so "wholeheartedly and with a clear intention of winning." To this would be appended the "Powell Corollary," which added to Weinberger's the strictures that intervention could be undertaken only with "overwhelming military force" and a clear "exit strategy." The Weinberger Doctrine, and its corollary—which, among other things, helped block any vigorous American action in Bosnia—were the natural children of the Vietnam Syndrome.

Ambitions and Weakness

For all their differences, both innovations in post-Vietnam American foreign policy—Jimmy Carter's human rights crusade and the Reagan Doctrine—were notable not only for their rhetorical dependence on the messianic strain but for the striking contrast between their grand ambitions and the weakness of the steps undertaken to achieve them. Carter did manage surprising successes, particularly in Latin America, with a campaign of rhetorical and economic pressure; but his human rights rhetoric also contributed to the administration's paralysis in the face of attacks on traditional American allies in Iran and Nicaragua. And President Reagan, for all his bluster about "rolling back Communism," actually dared to employ American troops only in minor skirmishes in Grenada and Libya, and in the short-lived fiasco in Lebanon.

It fell to that least imaginative of presidents, George H. W. Bush, to pro-claim the rise of the new world order. He did so not in Europe but on the sands of the Persian Gulf—beneath which, he declared, he had buried "the specter of Vietnam . . . forever." His assertion was contradicted not only by America's hurried exit from Iraq—leaving Saddam Hussein in power—but by the administration's prewar scrambling to build domestic support for launching the attack.

After rehearsing a variety of rationales—from the threat of Saddam armed with nuclear weapons to the prospect of Iraq in control of world oil supplies to Secretary of State James Baker's homely assertion that the confrontation was about "jobs, jobs, jobs"—President Bush settled on a familiar but ever more shopworn argument: The United States had a duty to lead the crusade of freedom against tyranny. The president repeatedly portrayed "the dictator, Saddam Hussein" (with whom the administration had had an extensive trad-ing and security relationship) as "worse than Hitler" and "Hitler revisited." Still, only very late in the day did the Senate finally sanction the attack, and then by a single vote; as for the people, they remained largely unconvinced—until, that is, the television pictures began to come in.

Television—and the new drama of the so-called CNN effect—by the late 1980s had begun to assert an odd pressure on U.S. foreign policy, contra-dicting, with the unblinking power of its images, America's waning asser-tions of moral hegemony. It is no accident that George Bush decided to intervene in Somalia, from which images of starving children began to flood American television screens only weeks after the pictures of emaciated men staring from behind barbed wire were aired from Bosnia's Omarska concen-tration camp. If Bush was unwilling to lay hold of the Yugoslav "tar baby," he would protect his moral mantle in a safer, simpler place. And he would do so with no public discussion, no debate in Congress; the lame duck George Bush, powerless and gray-faced as he prepared to leave the White House, simply appeared on Americans' television screens one fine day in December 1992 and announced that "sometimes America must act."

Bush left it to his hapless successor to discover that the situation was rather more complicated than that, that the hungry Somalis whom telegenic American soldiers got so much credit for feeding actually owed their hunger to a civil war. Even before the American Rangers plunged into a firefight that left eighteen of them dead, no one had managed to explain how American troops would be able to leave Somalia a better place than they had found it unless they pacified the country: Had they stormed the beach simply to deliver a few hot meals? And the failure to build political support for the intervention meant that a single horrible television picture of a dead American airman being dragged through the streets of Mogadishu was enough to destroy the entire mission. Clinton, finding himself attacked from all sides, hastened to withdraw. America's crusade to save starving Somalia, created by television images, would be destroyed by television images only a few months later.

VI.

Images of those corpses that surrounded me in the blood-soaked Sarajevo marketplace quickly took shape on American television screens as well— although the glittering NATO fighter aircraft, tracing their lazy arabesques in the sky overhead, were nowhere to be seen. The meaning of the silver planes, after all, was more ambiguous. The alliance had spent years doing little more than watching and patrolling, standing meekly aside as U.N. peace-keepers were ridiculed and humiliated. Looking back, the history seems to have followed a bitter and logical progression, as if all the while the diplomats had been steadily fading from view, losing substance so slowly that only now do we realize that they had always been little more than ghosts, with but power enough to hover over the battlefield and affix their seals, in law, on what the generals had accomplished in blood. Only after almost four years of the most savage "ethnic cleansing" did Western leaders give their pilots leave to fire. If American power proved necessary to achieve a truce, so too did the carnage that led up to it.

Bill Clinton, like George Bush fearing he might be trapped in a "quag-mire," took no action until the combatants had shed enough blood and con-quered enough territory to make the shaky Dayton Agreement possible. Fearing that pictures of the eighteen American servicemen killed in Somalia would damage him politically, Clinton shut down the mission and brought the troops home. Fearing pictures of Americans killed in Haiti might do the same, Clinton approved an occupation that focused almost obsessively on safeguarding the lives of American troops. And when the time came to send troops to monitor the cease-fire in Bosnia, Clinton made sure the Americans stayed mostly within their barracks while the war criminals who, under Day-ton, were to be arrested and judged, moved freely about.

Today, the great majority of them, including the most notorious and influential, remain at large, and as they flout the agreement they undermine its chances for success, making it daily less likely that American troops will be able to leave Bosnia next summer without consigning the country to war again. To be in a position strong enough that would allow him to order U.S. troops to move vigorously to enforce the accord, President Clinton would need to be willing to build political support at home, or at least to try to do so. This he has so far been unwilling to do. The political ironies here are many, for the debate on maintaining American troops in Bosnia that may come about owing to the administration's own cowardice may well coincide and become entangled with the debate over NATO expansion; and, given that two of the major tasks of the expanded alliance are meant to be "crisis management" and "peacekeeping," the timidity of the Clinton administra-tion and its allies in Bosnia will not bode well for the future—and may even dim the treaty's chances for ratification.

Throughout the post–Cold War years, American leaders have shown themselves fearful of political retribution from a suspicious public. They proved unwilling even to try to make a vigorous case to Americans that their country's interests were involved abroad: not in Haiti, not in Somalia, not even in the former Yugoslavia (a country which after all borders Italy, a member of the Western alliance). They appeared quite at a loss to argue why the United States might have an interest in preventing or stopping a brutal war in Europe itself. At one time they might have relied on the ideological consensus embodied in the Truman Doctrine, on its seamless blending of national security and moral mission; but the political struggles of the 1960s and early 1970s had left that consensus in shreds.

How then will the country's leaders ask Americans to give their solemn commitment to defend Poland and Hungary and the Czech Republic? And what can such a commitment possibly mean? Up to now, Clinton officials have said little about it. A true public debate might have brought us to the real reason why this policy is so deeply misguided: that despite the appeals of the east Europeans, despite the dire warnings of an imminent "security vac-uum" between Germany and Russia, the decision to expand NATO points our country, and Europe—west and east—toward the past and not toward the future. A half century ago, NATO's first secretary general, Lord Ismay, famously characterized the alliance's purpose as "keeping the Americans in, the Russians out, and the Germans down." Current American leaders, as they supposedly set out to construct a "new security structure for the West," seem to echo hauntingly all of these purposes.

First is the matter of keeping "the Russians out"—a goal Yeltsin character-ized as "squeezing Russia out of Europe." Such inflammatory words, obvi-ously, were meant both for Western ears and for those of angry representatives in the Duma. But that the Russians have "come around" and accepted expansion means little; for the question is not Russia's current weakness but the long-run effect of the policy. George Kennan, for one, declares that it "may be expected to inflame the nationalistic, anti-Western and militaristic tendencies in Russian opinion; to have an adverse effect on the development of Russian democracy; to restore the atmosphere of the Cold War to East-West relations, and to impel Russian foreign policy in directions decidedly not to our liking."[20] The least that can be said is that the effect will be dynamic and unpredictable, and the long-term influence on Russian politics is unlikely to be good.

For Russia's current leaders, the political vulnerabilities it exposes are obvious. "The West wants us to explain to our people that there is nothing to fear," Russian prime minister Viktor Chernomyrdin told two *Washington Post* reporters in Moscow. "How can we explain this? Nobody is going to listen to any explanations. Developments in Russia could take an omi-nous turn." Chernomyrdin was surprisingly frank about the "security implications," or lack of them: "I'm not afraid that Poland or Hungary or anyone else will be within NATO," he said. "It is not so dangerous for Rus-sia. The thing is I'm worried about Russia, what might happen in Russia, and nothing else." Ultranationalists like Vladimir Zhirinovsky, he said, "will accuse the president and the government of doing nothing to prevent this development . . . so we have to arm ourselves. The production facilities are there in brand new condition, they are waiting. This is how the employment problem will be resolved. . . . The tanks will be rolling out, and the planes. Do we need this?"[21]

A Larger Reality

Chernomyrdin's comments point up a larger reality: Russia now has politics—democratic politics, demagogic politics, politics that go beyond the Politburo. In finding himself forced to accept the West's policy, Boris Yeltsin will leave himself open to the criticisms of powerful figures who already attack him for his dependence on Western loans, for his weakness in facing Russia's former adversaries, for his inability to maintain Russia's storied power. The persistent refusal of Duma members to consider ratifying START II may well mean Russia will retain more than 20,000 nuclear weapons, enough to destroy the United States many times over. Who can argue that these weapons—palpable, ominous, and all too present—are less threatening to the United States than some "security vacuum" purportedly destined to open up between Germany and Russia sometime in the distant future?

In an essay vigorously arguing that the alliance must expand eastward, Peter Rodman, a noted "realist" and Kissinger protegé, suddenly bursts out: "Russia is a force of nature; all this is inevitable."[22] The frankness is refreshing. But while the NATO decision is not inevitable, in moving east the Western alliance may well set in train events and processes that are unstoppable. "If NATO expands eastward," as one Yeltsin aide put it, "Russia under any government will become a revisionist power striving to undermine the already fragile European order."

Which is to say, this move by the West may turn out to help produce the very "revanchist" Russia it professes to guard against. And, in that case, the famous pledge embodied in Chapter Five of the NATO Charter—that all alliance countries "treat an attack on any one of them as attack on all of them"—will come into clear focus. The United States will have formally taken on the defense of Eastern Europe, a region that lies thousands of miles from its shores and at the frontiers of Russia itself. Are Americans willing to challenge a resurgent Russia, "force of nature" that it is, in Poland, its historic back yard? Will they raise an army to take on the task? Are they really willing to bring to bear their nuclear weapons to shield the east? During the Cold War's closing years, after all, the nuclear umbrella over Germany itself was growing ever more frayed; if Americans are unwilling to sacrifice New York for Berlin, can anyone truly believe they would do so for Warsaw or Budapest or Prague?

In their coming struggle to convince the U.S. Senate and the American people, Clinton administration officials are unlikely to speak of the decision in these terms. Instead, they will echo Vaclav Havel, the Czech president, who declared that the alliance "is first and foremost an instrument of democracy intended to defend mutually held and created political and spiritual values."[23] Although these phrases would have perplexed Lord Ismay, who believed he was running a military alliance, they hold in them a kernel of truth, one that expansion will surely nurture.

For it is difficult not to conclude, particularly when one takes a hard look at the likelihood of Americans agreeing to fight Russians in (say) Poland, that the alliance is in fact being transformed. President Clinton's agreement to limit arms deployments in the eastern countries constitutes precisely what U.S. military officers so feared, the dilution of NATO: The security guarantee to the nations of eastern Europe will in fact mean less, probably much less, than it does to those of the west. Not only will the east Europeans have no alliance troops and no nuclear weapons on their soil but when they proudly take their seats for the first time in the great hall at Brussels, they will look across the historic table to see none other than their old friends, the Russians. What the Russians' power will be here is as yet uncertain, but clearly they believe it will be great, and they will push relentlessly to make it greater. This is indeed "a refined definition of the purpose, mission and identity of NATO," as Havel demands, but it is unlikely to be the one he had in mind.

Avoiding Reality

"The opportunity to make decisions about common defense," Havel writes, "should not be denied a priori to countries that have embraced and advanced Euro-American political cultural values. Some of the candidates for NATO membership have undergone pain for the sake of these values." Havel's appeal to values, his eagerness to remind the West what it owes his and the other east European countries, his desperation about being closed out of the "Europe" he so prizes: All of this is understandable.

That it is not for the first time—that east Europeans remember 1919 and 1945, that they brood over the Hungarian Revolution of 1956 and the Prague Spring of 1968 and all the other times they have called out to the West and received no reply—that for them all this remains part of living history, accounts for their desperate desire to be admitted into the alliance club. They want to see themselves affirmed at last as part of Europe. Already resentment over the West's refusal to admit them into its economic company has helped undermine many of those politicians who led the original anti-communist movements of the late 1980s, who waved as their standard the flag of Europe and what it stands for. In many places in eastern Europe, a grim nationalism, often championed by the Communist leaders of a few years back, now gains power in those Westerners' place.

These, however, are not problems a military alliance can solve. They are political, and the solution is to admit Eastern Europe into the politics and economy of Europe. To admit them to the European Union in a series of clearly predetermined steps would bolster their economies and stabilize their politics without threatening the Russians. This would be complicated and expensive and, because of the migration of inexpensive east European workers, politically controversial; but in the end these matters are details. At the heart of the problem is the simple reality that the so-called project of Europe never really included the countries to the east; that the Cold War allowed the West to avoid confronting the larger and more difficult question of Europe. Now that the Wall has been torn down, it is the United States that is doing the same thing: helping Europe avoid reality. In so doing, America is avoiding reality itself.

VII.

For the United States, at bottom, the decision to expand the alliance represents a failure of vision and a failure of strength; it is a policy of weakness and passivity. It derives not only from a lack of imagination but from an unwillingness to make and apply difficult decisions and a failure to attempt what would be a truly creative approach to the problem of Europe and its evolving relationship with the United States. When America's great senior statesmen speak darkly of Germany seeking "to achieve its security by national efforts," they are groping blindly with issues of the past, not seizing hold of and shaping the future.

The Second World War is a half-century gone, but American policies cling to it. U.S. troops protect the Europeans from the Germans, and the Germans from themselves. U.S. policy should look to a future that has at its center a more self-reliant Europe, a stronger "European pillar"—a Europe, that is, where Europeans themselves take on more of the burden of their own defense, and the defense of their former antagonists to the east. Institutions—the Western European Union, the European Security and Defense Identity, among others—already exist, though in pallid, embryonic form; what is needed to give them life is the will to make a broad philosophical shift within the alliance, and only the United States can initiate and sustain that.

The Europeans will never emerge from the shadow of the Americans until the Americans feel less ambivalent about withdrawing their shadow. And the Americans will never truly emerge from the Cold War until they come to a decision to do so. Such a decision does not imply isolationism (a misleading word that has never accurately described American attitudes); it implies reality.

As I write, the train is racing down the tracks toward the Senate debate. No one, it appears, can derail the expansion decision, though there has not even been a reliable public estimate of its costs. As for the policy's architects, they prefer to ignore the coming debate and behave as if the future were somehow predetermined. ("NATO's expansion is vital," intones

Richard Holbrooke, in near Biblical cadences, "and will be done.") Such mismanagement and fatalism may mean an ugly public skirmish, in which administration officials, having advanced their arguments for "a Europe whole and free" and the United States as the "indispensable nation" to provide it, will find themselves falling back on dark warnings that a decision has been made, and that a move by American senators to reject it would be "devastating" to the alliance. And so it might well be. It would be a great irony if the Poles and the Hungarians and the Czechs, in their desire to be sheltered within the warm embrace of the West, will have finished by weakening, perhaps fatally, the alliance itself.

In any event, the words of the senators are unlikely to be elevating. We will hear about democracy, about credibility, and perhaps, dark intimations about the Russians. Hard-line senators will denounce President Clinton for his concessions, warning that by welcoming the Russians into the alliance's halls, he has helped them achieve what they could not in half a century of struggle: subverting the Western alliance.

A true debate, held at the proper time, might have brought to the public the real weaknesses of expanding the alliance: that it promises to achieve political and economic goals in Eastern Europe that a military alliance cannot deliver; that it may unsettle Russia in ways impossible to prophesy; that it makes a pledge to defend the Eastern European countries which, in a real crisis, is unlikely to be kept; and that, in so confusing the real purposes and pledges of NATO, it will lead eventually to the "hollowing out" of the entire alliance.

But we have had no debate. America's leaders, persuaded that the country's citizens are ignorant of and uninterested in the world, hope to escape what might threaten to become a true debate—and, lurking behind it, the dire possibility that, having raised the subject of NATO expansion, Americans might begin to question the reason, eight years after the Cold War's supposed end, they are still being asked to pay for the alliance at all. What a final irony it would be if a hasty lunge toward NATO's expansion were to lead, finally, to its dissolution.

That would be more than ironic, of course; it would be tragic. America has a strong interest in a prosperous and stable Europe, which will buy American products and serve as a bulwark against disorder and instability. America's leaders, either when addressing Bosnia or NATO, have been as unwilling to make this case to the public as they are loath to debate the use of American troops abroad. Because of this, when presidents have decided to send troops they have found their freedom severely circumscribed, ensuring that if things go badly for American forces, they and their president will find little support at home—in turn encouraging administration officials to conclude that Americans simply refuse to support an activist foreign policy. The pitiable lack of debate over sending American troops to Somalia, and later to Haiti, showed what happens when a president moves to intervene abroad without any real discussion: The policies in both countries dangled from a slender thread, vulnerable to the least reversal, to the smallest number of American casualties.

That great matters of state are still handled in this fashion demonstrates once again how darkly the Cold War still looms over American policy. The National Security Act of 1947, which provided for the design of Cold War military and security bureaucracies, still governs how our foreign policy officials do business. Designed to oppose a powerful enemy in a perpetual, low-level conflict, this statute emphasized centralized decision making and secrecy. A responsible Congress would rewrite it for a new world, one where the threat is less immediate, secrecy is less important, and foreign affairs can be conducted more democratically, as the Founders intended. At the least, the United States needs a recrafted version of the War Powers Resolution of 1973, not mainly to limit the president's power but to ensure public debate—and, crucially, the clear rationale for policy that should emerge from it—as well as to force the president, Congress, and, most important, the people themselves, to assume responsibility for the most important decisions the nation can make.

Imagined Hegemony

As will become evident during the debate over NATO, an ideological vacuum lies at the heart of American foreign policy. The old Truman Doctrine consensus has passed; and despite sporadic attempts, officials have managed to put nothing in its place. In the coming months American officials will speak imploringly of "integrating new democracies" in Eastern Europe, of creating "a Europe whole and free" which can only be accomplished by America, "the indispensable nation." For Americans this sort of idealistic rhetoric—as Wilson sadly discovered—is not enough; to succeed it must be grafted—as Truman showed—to a clear and demonstrable threat to America's interests. Clinton officials have not managed to square this circle, and for a very good reason: Given their muddled thinking, it cannot be done.

In marching east with NATO, Washington seeks to maintain for the country an empty hegemony, one composed of remnant scraps of the Cold War world and rooted, as one Bush official put it, in "semi-permanent factors of power and geography," with a nod to newly ascendant "rogue nations" that America must be prepared to fight two at a time. It is not simply that such an imagined world hegemony is expensive and wasteful, pointing toward the past and not toward the future, but that it is unlikely, when it is finally brought clearly before the eyes of the American people, to engage their support.

To gain such support the country's leaders will need to explain the path they have chosen; they will need to convince Americans—at a time when their schools fail to educate their children; when their public pension and medical systems lack for funds; when their political institutions have lost the confidence of the people—why at such a time their country must preserve and even enlarge its role in the world, and how it can do so while bringing "into balance, with a comfortable surplus of power in reserve, the nation's commitments with the nation's power." If America's leaders cannot make this case, the soldiers sitting in their tanks in prosperous Germany will begin to appear, sooner rather than later, very absurd indeed.

The president, a man celebrated for his skills in persuading, has shown little interest in taking on such a task. For to do so would be to expend precious "political capital" that, he presumably believes, could be more profitably invested elsewhere. This is the definition of shortsightedness, as President Clinton may well discover yet again during the coming debate over NATO. Whatever the ultimate result of the "Faustian bargain" that President Truman signed on to in making his famous speech half a century ago, the difference in responsibility between him and the present occupant of his office is striking.

Eight years after the fall of the Berlin Wall America stands on the verge of great opportunity—not only to shape a policy for a new world but to tell its people frankly about that policy, and the reasons why it is right for the country. But no one is talking. Thus far, it has seemed far easier to call up the familiar smokescreen, to swoon over America as "the indispensable nation." And yet the "post–Cold War world," however one defines it, is only beginning. For Americans, ever able to recreate themselves, the question is whether they will be able to do so now—whether they will be able to walk through that sunlit portal offered them in 1989.

America possesses overwhelming power, and great prosperity. As we gaze outward, our world may seem on the whole placid and bright. But we remain marooned in the Cold War, encumbered with a policy that imposes upon the world a mindless hegemony, a predominance for its own sake; and we can only hope that we do not one day discover, with James, that despite the bright and blinding sunshine, it was a different reality the treacherous years were all the while really making for and meaning.

World Policy Journal, Fall 1997

IV.

Lost in the Forever War

We're an empire now, and when we act,
we create our own reality . . .

—A George W. Bush senior advisor, Summer, 2002

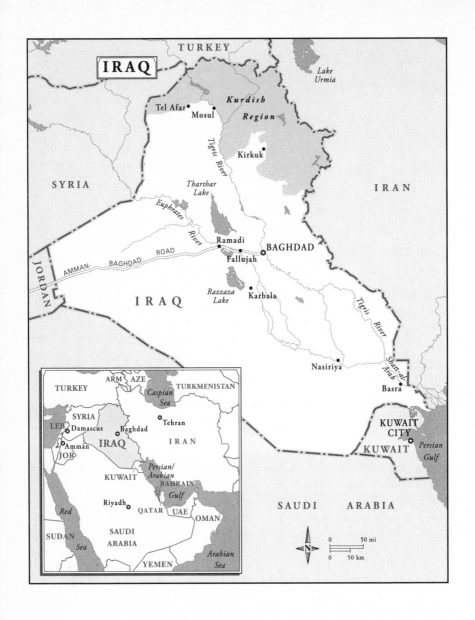

The Battlefield in the American Mind

October 16, 2001

IN AFGHANISTAN, the targets are running out. Such are the frustrations of the powerful; Joseph Conrad, writing of an African "heart of darkness" a century ago, well understood: "Once, I remember, we came upon a man-of-war anchored off the coast. There wasn't even a shed there, and she was shelling the bush. . . . In the empty immensity of earth, sky, water, there she was, incomprehensible, firing into a continent."

What "high-value targets" remained in the wasteland of Afghanistan, American warplanes have destroyed. The rabble of mullahs and seminarians known as the Taliban is fleeing the battered cities. To replace the Taliban with an enduring order, to build something where now there is nothing— that likely will require much greater power than America has shown itself to possess. To make America once again safe from terrorism certainly will.

For Americans, Conrad's "incomprehensible" looms near, for cruise missiles and laser-guided bombs will not protect them from terrorism nor shield them from the political challenge they face. The battleground of the new war is not Afghanistan but here, and in his very choice of weapons our enemy has left America at a grave disadvantage, one the country has not begun to grasp, let alone confront.

For at least a quarter-century American power has coexisted with American inconstancy and capriciousness. Alongside the triumphant Cold War narrative we have shaped for ourselves one can easily trace another story, one of bluster and flight and uneasy forgetting: the Bay of Pigs debacle of 1961; the panicked retreat from Saigon in 1975; the humiliation at the hands of the Iranian "students" in 1979; the wholesale flight from Beirut after the American Embassy and Marine barracks bombings in 1984; the abandonment of Mogadishu, Somalia, after the death of eighteen American servicemen in 1993—this last an event that led not only to the retreat of the USS *Harlan County* from Haiti, but to the American refusal to act to halt the Rwandan genocide the following year.

This litany points not to any lack of American courage but to a lack of political grounding that has haunted the country's foreign policy for a half-century. America's power has been technologically robust and politically fragile. Since Vietnam this paradox—the country's enormous power and the suspicion and impatience of its citizens when confronted with its use—has bedeviled American politicians, who with few exceptions have been unwilling to expend the political capital required to convince the country to act decisively when its interests are at stake. It is no wonder that the terrorist operatives of al Qaeda, whose true genius has been an ability to search out their victims' points of vulnerability, chose to attack America at its weakest point: its political psyche. With 18 deaths the world's only superpower was chased from Somalia; why should 5,000 not chase it from the Persian Gulf?

The nineteen men who changed the world on September 11 used as their primary weapon not box cutters or jet airliners but something more American and much more powerful: the television set. The box cutters and the planes were tools in constructing the great master image, the Spectacular; the television set was their delivery vehicle. In an instant, the Spectacular altered the terms of debate, creating a sense of pervasive and unprecedented vulnerability among Americans, a sense revivified by each new report of anthrax, each fresh incident of a deranged assailant on a plane or a Greyhound bus. And the Spectacular thereby transformed American foreign policy, heretofore a matter of disregard among most Americans, into a vital question of their own security, a matter of their own life and death.

HOWEVER ARDENTLY we stare at the blurry night-vision photographs from Kabul, the battlefield is here, in the American mind. The anthrax incidents, in bringing to the surface a latent hysteria, are more important skirmishes in this new war than anything that happens in the Afghan mountains. The Spectacular of September 11 prepared the battlefield; the blows that are sure to come will strike more effectively at the true target: Americans' commitment to the country's role in the world, and particularly the Persian Gulf.

"This is not aimed at our policies," Henry Kissinger said after the attacks. "This is aimed at our existence." That is precisely wrong. The "evildoers" who gave their lives on September 11 and those who sent them have precise objectives and a clear plan to achieve them.

They want to bring about a new order of purity and righteousness in the Islamic world and particularly in the moderate states of the gulf, where they see only wealth and corruption and autocracy, all of it held in place by the power of America, the inheritor of the old colonial order. They see American planes and ships not as symbols of freedom but as the mainstay of the corrupt order they seek to replace—the obstacle standing between the corruption and oppression of the present and the new Islamic order that lights the way to the future.

Gazing at this corrupt world, these men believe they have found its point of vulnerability in the American mind—in the fragile commitment of the American people to a permanent role in the gulf. Given recent history, their analysis is not at all unsound. In the triumphant aftermath of the Persian Gulf War, Saddam Hussein's taunt—that American society "cannot accept 10,000 dead in one battle"—seemed an empty boast. Ten years later, as he sits in power in Baghdad watching his adversary's son struggle with the consequences of an uncompleted war, the remark seems not quite so ridiculous. The first President Bush's refusal to go to Baghdad and remove Saddam Hussein—a decision in good part based on worries that Americans' satisfaction with an easy victory would turn to anxiety over a possible quagmire—meant that the threat from Iraq remained. In countering that threat by stationing American troops permanently in Saudi Arabia, the president traded one political risk for another. For it was the Saudi monarchy's acceptance of those troops that led to the permanent break with Osama bin Laden, their prodigal son, and brought his unforgiving wrath down upon them—and now upon us.

AMERICA HAD NO CHOICE but to respond militarily. Yet with each air strike, it condemns itself more vividly to the role that its enemies have chosen for it: the violent, blundering superpower dominating the gulf, its fragile allies cowering in its shadow.

Our enemies understand this: Their greatest strength is their clear conviction that this war is political and psychological. For this their weapon—terror—is precisely chosen and, in its impact, enormously powerful. Faced with the spectacular use of terrorism intended to weaken American resolve, American leaders have emitted a barrage of rhetoric about "attacks on freedom" and the fight between good and evil, demonstrating once again what has been a longstanding preference, in times of crisis abroad, for stock ideology over a clear and honest defense of our interests and our commitments. Deeply apprehensive about America's commitment to a vigorous and permanent role in the world, our presidents have habitually turned to ideology to rally the citizenry.

President Bush follows in this tradition as he calls on Americans to battle a vast, worldwide enemy—an enemy of apocalyptic proportions that "hates our freedoms"—by appealing to them as representatives of an indispensable nation: the city upon a hill. Unfortunately, as we know from the last quarter-century or more, political support thus purchased tends to be brittle and weak, having been built on emotion. In the days and hours following the next terrorist Spectacular, or the next, Americans may well begin to ask themselves why exactly they are being targeted and what exactly it is they are risking their lives for. Crusading against evildoers is likely by then to seem a less satisfying answer.

The American troops and warships in the gulf, the unpopularity of our presence there, the fragility of the regimes we support—these facts are not secrets, but among Americans they are not widely known. In the gulf, as in other places and at other times, America stands not for freedom but for stability. Its interest is in the unfettered flow of oil from the gulf to the industrialized world. Now, as in 1991, American policy makers will struggle to achieve this interest within the bounds of the forbearance of the American public. We should be aware that it is precisely that forbearance that the terrorists have begun to attack. That they have chosen a point of vulnerability is incontestable; that our leaders are prepared to defend against that political vulnerability—rooted in a longstanding refusal to speak honestly about the country's interests—even now is less clear.

The New York Times, October 16, 2001

Struggles of Democracy and Empire

October 8, 2002

A year after a tiny band of religious zealots managed with stunning audacity to mutilate the face of America, the world's sole superpower trembles on the threshold of a new imperial season. That America, despite its great power, "goes not abroad, in search of monsters to destroy," has been a cherished truism of our foreign policy, central to how Americans look at themselves and at their role in the world. Until yesterday John Quincy Adams's words could still be thought true. Tomorrow, if America invades and occupies Iraq, they no longer will be.

Behind the blizzard of claims and counterclaims of the last two months— about whether Iraq has nuclear weapons; about whether United Nations inspectors should be trusted to uncover them; about whether America should heed the views of allies or the international community at all—a more important and subtler drama is being played, about the character of American power and its proper role in the world. Or rather replayed, for we have seen its like before, in 1947 and, before that, in 1919. As on those occasions, America is struggling after the end of a great conflict to come to terms with what it means to be both democracy and empire. Call it the Athenian problem: How do the guardians of empire ensure support for its maintenance among the people?

As far back as January, President Bush began presenting the proposed Iraq campaign as a keystone of his war on terror, an essential battle in a carefully constructed ideological crusade that casts terrorists as "the heirs of all the murderous ideologies of the twentieth century"—the moral descendants of Communists, embodiments of evil who "hate our freedoms." By focusing relentlessly on this threat—and by remaining resolutely coy about a decision to go to war that seems to have been made a year ago—President Bush and his advisers have succeeded brilliantly in largely confining debate to the modalities of confronting the threat (inspections, diplomacy and so on) and thus forcing their opponents, political and diplomatic, to fight on their ground.

In promoting the Iraq expedition as a necessary response to an immediate terrorist threat, however, they have failed to prepare the American public for what looks to be a long and costly engagement in the Middle East. Much of the confusion surrounding the Iraq debate thus far is owed to the chasm between the justifications proffered and the more elaborate geopolitical enterprise motivating many in the Bush administration.

The first phase of the war on terror saw the overthrow of the Taliban in Afghanistan and the escape of the leaders of al Qaeda. The second sent American troops to the Philippines, Georgia and Yemen for counterinsurgency missions against parts of the Qaeda network. The third phase, now about to unfold in the Persian Gulf, envisions the remaking of the Middle East.

Behind the notion that an American intervention will make of Iraq "the first Arab democracy," as Deputy Defense Secretary Paul Wolfowitz put it, lies a project of great ambition. It envisions a post–Saddam Hussein Iraq—secular, middle-class, urbanized, rich with oil—that will replace the autocracy of Saudi Arabia as the key American ally in the Persian Gulf, allowing the withdrawal of United States troops from the kingdom. The presence of a victorious American Army in Iraq would then serve as a powerful boost to moderate elements in neighboring Iran, hastening that critical country's evolution away from the mullahs and toward a more moderate course. Such an evolution in Tehran would lead to a withdrawal of Iranian support for Hezbollah and other radical groups, thereby isolating Syria and reducing pressure on Israel. This undercutting of radicals on Israel's northern borders and within the West Bank and Gaza would spell the definitive end of Yasir Arafat and lead eventually to a favorable solution of the Arab-Israeli problem.

This is a vision of great sweep and imagination: comprehensive, prophetic, evangelical. In its ambitions it is wholly foreign to the modesty of containment, the ideology of a status-quo power that lay at the heart of American strategy for half a century. It means to remake the world, to offer to a political threat a political answer. It represents a great step on the road toward President Bush's ultimate vision of "freedom's triumph over all its age-old foes."

In its ambition and grandiosity there has been nothing like it in American foreign policy since the "rollback" ambitions of General Douglas MacArthur and his allies in the Republican Party a half-century ago. Perhaps most striking, this vision—drawn from an administration that has abhorred all talk of root causes and treats terror as a free-floating malignancy with no political history and no political goals—acknowledges that for the evil of terror to be defeated the entire region from which it springs must be made new.

The audacity of the crusade's ambitions is matched by the magnitude of its risks. Before September 11, the Islamist radicals had been on the run, their project flagging. They had turned their talents on the United States—the distant power that lay behind the thrones in Riyadh and Cairo—only after suffering defeat on the primary battlegrounds of Algeria and Egypt and Saudi Arabia. By invading and occupying Iraq and using it as a base to remake the region, the United States risks revitalizing the political project embodied by Osama bin Laden. It is not only that Islamic radicalism may gain new life and new converts but that moderate regimes will be threatened and will respond harshly, leading them not toward democracy but away from it, and that, finally, the force to which the United States remains most vulnerable—terror—will once again visit our shores. And this time, terror may come not just from a reanimated al Qaeda but from Hezbollah and other groups that heretofore saw the American threat as not quite so direct. To divide the world into good and evil, however effective that is as a means of building political support and however gratifying that may be to Americans who see their country as a "city upon a hill," risks broadening a war that would be better kept narrowly defined.

Grand projects have not been treated kindly in the Middle East. The shah of Iran, America's policeman in the Gulf, was swept away by revolution; to confront the new radical threat from Tehran, the United States found an unlikely successor, a secular dictator in Baghdad named Saddam Hussein. Supplanting him now will likely be the easiest part of the mission; building a new order, engineering a workable politics in a land beset by sectarian struggles and by the trauma of three decades of brutal dictatorship, will be much harder, demanding persistence, steadfastness, quantities of treasure and perhaps of blood. President Bush, hammering away at the threat posed by nuclear weapons that do not now exist, has been reluctant to speak of these costs. Thus far, he has abdicated his responsibility to build the political support he will need to shape the Iraq, and the Middle East, that will follow Saddam Hussein.

For America, the great risk of this new crusade is that the political will might be lacking to carry it out—that the public, unprepared for the imperial ambitions about to play out in the Middle East, will quickly lose heart if the project comes to grief; that after the inevitable setbacks and perhaps after further attacks at home, the occupation will grow unpopular and that even those in the administration whose vision is not so ambitious will want to cut and run, leaving ruin once more in America's wake.

Baghdad is not Mogadishu. It will not be enough, as after the bombing of the Marine barracks in Beirut in 1983, to declare victory, sail over the horizon and invade Grenada. The risks of a failed intervention in Iraq are more grave: weakening regimes friendly to the United States, kindling a broader Middle East war, bringing terror to American cities. In this sense, September 11 did change everything. The threats are closer now, more malignant; the world much smaller than the one John Quincy Adams knew. If America chooses in this dark season to go abroad in search of monsters to destroy, it had better well destroy them—and show the will to leave something lasting in their place.

New York Times, October 8, 2002

How Not to Win a War

August 28, 2003

W E SEE THE WORLD through the stories we tell, and until recently the story most Americans told themselves about the war in Iraq was a simple and dramatic narrative of imminent threat, daring triumph, and heroic liberation—a story neatly embodied in images of a dictator's toppling statue and a president in full flight gear swaggering across a carrier deck. Those pictures, once so bright and clear, have now faded, giving place to a second, darker story beneath: the story of an unfinished war, undertaken for murky reasons, that has left young Americans ruling indefinitely over people who do not welcome them and who are killing more and more of them each day. As long as Saddam Hussein remains at large, as long as the weapons our leaders said were threatening us are not found, and as long as Iraqis go on killing Americans, this second, darker story may come to blot out and finally to mock the memory of the first.

As the war's ending and, increasingly, its beginning grow more cloudy, Americans are confronted on their television screens with a violent present that day by day becomes more difficult to comprehend. That the attacks on American soldiers in Iraq "do not pose a strategic threat to the mission," in the words of the American proconsul L. Paul Bremer, is true but meaningless. The war in Iraq—in the streets of Baghdad no less than in the halls of Congress or in the stump speeches of the campaign trail—is in its essence political, not military. Like the terrorists who hijacked American airliners and flew them into American buildings, the fighters daily ambushing American troops are attacking not American military power but American will. And thanks to the way President Bush and his colleagues chose to build the case for war, and the errors they have made in prosecuting it, American will is an increasingly vulnerable target. In the end defeat or victory in Iraq will be judged not by who controls Baghdad but by whether the war has left Americans more secure than they were before it was undertaken. All the ringing presidential pronouncements of "Mission Accomplished!" will not change the reality: America could still lose this war.

LIKE THE STRIKES on the World Trade Center and the Pentagon, the attacks in Iraq—ambushes and assassinations of American troops; sabotage of Iraqi oil pipelines, water mains, electrical lines, and other critical infrastructure; suicide bombing of UN headquarters and other "soft" targets—are aimed not at defeating American forces directly but at creating a political spectacle that will impress, frighten, and persuade a number of audiences, among them the Iraqi people, the Arab world, and finally the American public. During a briefing on July 16, General John Abizaid, who succeeded General Tommy Franks as head of Central Command, described the authors of these attacks as

> . . . mid-level Ba'athist, Iraqi intelligence people, Special Security Organization people, Special Republican Guard people that have organized at the regional level in cellular structure and are conducting what I would describe as a classical guerrilla-type campaign against us. . . . We're seeing a cellular organization of six to eight people, armed with RPGs, machine guns, etc., attacking us at . . . times and places of their choosing. . . . There are some foreign fighters. . . . Remember in the early stages of capturing Baghdad, there were an awful lot of foreign fighters, and it's possible that . . . they've reformed and reorganized.[1]

The enemy in Iraq, in other words, is dynamic and changeable, a shadowy and loose group of forces made up of former officers and soldiers of the vast security and intelligence organs of the *ancien régime*; foreign-born jihadis, or ideological commandos, who have slipped into Iraq from Saudi Arabia, Syria, and other Islamic countries determined to confront and defeat the United States; and, perhaps increasingly, young, unemployed Iraqis, angry at the American occupation and the difficulties it has brought, eager to avenge a relative's death or a personal affront, or simply desperate to earn some easy money by hiring themselves out to attack Americans. We know little of this shadowy world, and depend for what we do know on military sources, named and unnamed, and inferences drawn from the pattern, character, and frequency of the attacks; but it is likely that the relative weight and influence of its various actors, and the alliances and rivalries among them, are in a constant state of flux, as are the opposition's political interests and the tactics it adopts to achieve them. On this, General Abizaid, in the same briefing, set out the salient point:

> War is a struggle of wills. You look at the Arab press; they say, "We drove the Americans out of Beirut, we drove them out of Somalia; . . . we'll drive them out of Baghdad."

To these names of the familiar symbols of a great power's defeat and withdrawal in the face of a determined irregular force—whether using suicide bombings (Beirut, 1983) or guerrilla warfare (Mogadishu, 1993)—General Abizaid might have added the name of Afghanistan. For the jihadis, in particular, Iraq presents the chance to do to the American empire in the Middle East what they believe they did a decade ago to the Soviet empire in Central Asia—to force on the occupier a long, bloody stalemate leading to retreat and, finally, to collapse.

By now it is clear that this campaign began long before the fall of Baghdad last April. As early as January, according to *Newsweek*, the Iraqi secret police issued an order instructing its forces to "do what's necessary after the fall of the Iraqi leadership to the American-British-Zionist Coalition forces," and setting out eleven steps, among them, "looting and burning all the government institutions that belong to our Directorates and other ones," and sowing chaos in the country by sabotaging power plants and assassinating imams and other public figures.[2]

It now seems likely that much of the looting and plundering that Secretary of Defense Rumsfeld dismissed as mere "untidiness," the inevitable concomitant of the coming of democracy, constituted the first stage of a carefully planned "war beyond the war." Secretary Rumsfeld's strategy of "going in light"—of conquering Iraq with a quick, highly focused attack employing a minimum of troops—left the Americans uniquely vulnerable to this kind of planned chaos and the widespread feeling of insecurity it fostered. As the military commentator Anthony Cordesman put it,

> The same strategy designed to deliver a carefully focused attack on the regime did not provide enough manpower to simultaneously occupy and secure the areas that the Coalition liberated . . . and deal with the wide range of local, regional, ethnic and religious divisions [the Coalition] encountered.[3]

The weeks of looting and disorder that followed not only continued the destruction of Iraq's infrastructure, preventing the Americans from supplying the country with electricity and other basic services. More important, the looting and mayhem destroyed American political authority even before it could be established; such political authority is rooted in the monopoly of legitimate violence, which the Americans, after standing by during weeks of chaos and insecurity, were never able to attain.

DURING THE LAST four months, the tactics of those opposing or defying the occupation have steadily evolved, as General Abizaid acknowledged, "getting more organized . . . learning . . . adapting to our tactics, techniques and procedures. . . . They're better coordinated . . . less amateurish . . . more sophisticated." As the tactics of the insurgents have changed—from the intensive looting and mayhem of the first weeks, to the hit-and-run small-arms attacks of late spring and early summer, to the more sophisticated use of radio-controlled and timed explosives of July and August, and finally to the suicide truck bombings of late summer—the American forces, adapting in their turn, have responded by launching a series of large-scale raids against opposition strongholds in the so-called "Sunni Triangle" of central Iraq. These raids netted a large haul of weapons and explosives and hundreds of prisoners; they also further alienated from the occupation many Iraqis who might have been disposed to welcome it, or at least to tolerate it.

This is the dynamic that various opponents of the occupation must try to sustain. By whatever means, they aim to produce in Iraq growing political anger and discontent and to focus that anger and discontent on the occupiers, thus alienating more and more Iraqis, who might join the anti-occupation forces, actively support them, or at least count themselves sympathetic to the cause. Since the numbers of the armed opposition, as Paul Bremer noted, are far too small to defeat the Americans militarily, their strategy relies on provoking the Americans to take actions that will create among Iraqis the broader support needed to sustain a guerrilla war.

By launching paramilitary attacks almost daily, the opponents hope to force the Americans to adopt increasingly aggressive and intrusive tactics that will further alienate a citizenry already frustrated by the failure to bring order to the country. By blowing up electrical pylons, sabotaging water mains, destroying oil pipelines, and staging attacks on the United Nations and other nongovernmental organizations, they hope to further degrade the quality of life of ordinary Iraqis, who are increasingly shocked and angered by the Americans' failure to provide basic services. By threatening and assassinating Iraqis who collaborate with the Americans, they hope to show Iraqis that the occupiers cannot protect them, further slowing the rate of reconstruction, deepening the country's bitter political divisions, and making the daunting task of building a stable politics friendly to America all the more difficult.

That Iraqis loyal to a security-obsessed totalitarian regime of three decades would seek to fight the Americans who have overthrown it is not surprising. Nor should it be surprising that jihadis from outside and inside Iraq should seize the opportunity to attack infidels occupying an Islamic country. What is surprising is the degree to which the Americans, through their own lack of attention to the critical political tasks of the war's aftermath, have in effect assisted their efforts. The civilian leadership of the Pentagon remains in thrall to fashionable concepts of war-fighting such as "Shock and Awe" and "Network-Centric Warfare," which emphasize information, speed, and the use of light forces, but which leave out, in the words of the military historian Kenneth W. Kagan, "the most important component of war," which is to provide "a reliable recipe for translating the destruction of the enemy's ability to continue to fight into the accomplishment of the political objectives of the conflict."[4]

The obligation to provide such a "reliable recipe" in Iraq falls in the end to U.S. political leaders, but they have largely abdicated this responsibility. Shortly before the war, the president, discarding many months of effort by the State Department, handed over control of occupation planning to Pentagon officials, who hastily constructed a plan based largely on optimistic assumptions about the warmth of the Iraqis' attitude toward the Americans, and about the ease with which new leaders could be imposed on the existing governing institutions. Many of these expectations, which were encouraged by favored Iraqi expatriates, dovetailed perfectly with the Pentagon's own reluctance to provide sufficient military police and dirty its hands with other distasteful "nation-building" tasks. When their assumptions proved unfounded, administration officials were excruciatingly slow to admit reality and make adjustments. These first weeks of the occupation, in which security in Baghdad collapsed, chaos ruled the streets, and the fledgling occupation authority daily issued conflicting statements and made promises it did not keep, were a fiasco. They proved an enormous boon to violent opponents, providing them, in the lawless streets of postwar Iraq, the political equivalent of a warm Petri dish in which to grow.[5]

As NEAR AS ONE CAN TELL, the Bush administration launched its war against Iraq for three broad reasons:

1. Weapons of Mass Destruction: To disarm Iraq of its alleged chemical and biological weapons and eliminate its nuclear program.
2. National Security: To remove Iraq as a threat to American dominance of the Persian gulf and to Israel, and make it America's central ally and base in the region, replacing an increasingly unstable and Islamicist Saudi Arabia, from which American troops could be withdrawn.[6]
3. Regional Transformation: To make Iraq an example of Arab democracy as the first step in "the transformation of the Middle East" which, in the words of National Security Adviser Condoleezza Rice, "is the only guarantee that it will no longer produce ideologies of hatred that lead men to fly airplanes into buildings in New York and Washington."[7]

Nearly six months after the war was launched, these three rationales for America's first preemptive war have been stood on their heads.

Different officials clearly lent different weight to these arguments, but we know, thanks to Deputy Secretary of Defense Paul Wolfowitz, that "bureaucratic reasons"—"because it was the one reason everyone could agree on"—at least in part led the administration to focus on the first.[8] More important, in the wake of September 11, the argument that Saddam might give weapons of mass destruction to terrorists who would attack the United States, or might use them to attack Persian Gulf nations and Israel, was clearly the most politically potent—the principal argument likely to convince the broad mass of Americans to support a preemptive war. (It was also the only argument that, as embodied in a number of United Nations resolutions, had some degree of international legitimacy.)

By now, however, the argument that Iraq threatened vital U.S. interests with weapons of mass destruction seems to have been disproved: No weapons have been found, and even if some are eventually uncovered it seems highly implausible that they could have posed an imminent threat.[9]

The collapse of the case for weapons of mass destruction and the revelations about how the administration relentlessly and recklessly exaggerated the evidence of the threat have left the occupation of Iraq with a singularly fragile foundation of public support.

That support is likely to be further eroded by the continuing violence and combat deaths in Iraq, for which the president did nothing to prepare the country. President Bush's approval ratings have declined steadily since his triumphant landing on the USS *Abraham Lincoln* last May and in some polls have now dipped below his pre–September 11 lows. With a lackluster economic record—he looks to be the first president since Herbert Hoover to see the total number of jobs decline during his term—President Bush has relied on his aggressive foreign policy and his claimed competence in national security to sustain his political strength. He has used the war on terror politically with great skill and ruthlessness and apparently plans to make it the heart of his reelection effort, scheduling the 2004 Republican convention in New York so as to recall the 9/11 anniversary.

All of this ensures that the Democratic candidates will make the war in Iraq—the exaggerations about weapons of mass destruction that led to it, the Americans who continue to die in a war advertised to the public as "a cakewalk," the billion dollars a week the country is paying for a war that has no visible conclusion—a central issue in the campaign. The controversy this July over "the sixteen words" in the president's State of the Union speech, which claimed falsely that Saddam Hussein had sought uranium oxide from Africa, and the damage this controversy did to the president's popularity, suggest that Bush, far from launching his reelection campaign energized by a triumphant war, may find Iraq to be a political albatross around his neck.

HOWEVER GOOD THIS NEWS may be for Democrats and their supporters, it is unlikely to be good for the Iraqis. The Bush administration has proved unwilling so far to provide the protection and resources necessary to rebuild the country. At the same time, the administration, holding to a policy that poisoned international relations before the war, is doggedly refusing to grant the modicum of authority to the United Nations that would be necessary to bring in anything more than a token number of troops from other countries, particularly from India, Pakistan, and Turkey. Whether in one month or three, this attitude may well change. Indeed, faced with the prospect of running for reelection on the record of an increasingly unpopular and inconclusive war, the administration, shielded by as many international forces as it can muster, may be tempted to take the equivalent of Senator George Aitken's long-ago advice about Vietnam: Declare victory and go home.

As one who argued strenuously against invading Iraq, I find this prospect particularly troubling to contemplate.[10] Having invaded and occupied Iraq, and unleashed a horde of political demons there, the United States faces a number of extremely difficult choices, one of the worst of which is precipitous withdrawal. Already Secretary Wolfowitz's notion that the invasion would "demonstrate especially to the Arab and Muslim world that there is a better way than the way of the terrorist" has acquired a grimly ironic cast.[11] For all its grandiose talk about establishing in Iraq "a shining example for the Arab world," the administration has so far not been willing to devote the necessary troops or resources to the task. The recent influx of jihadis hoping to take advantage of the chaos in Iraq in order to make of it "the new Afghanistan" suggests another possibility: that Iraq, far from becoming a symbol of the promise of democracy in the Middle East, may become afflicted with a low-level and prolonged nationalist war which the Islamists would use to attract recruits and build their movement politically, while they use terror and other guerrilla tactics to bleed and diminish the United States and weaken its position in the Middle East.

That, of course—like "the war after the war" itself—is a political project, not a military one. Not for the first time, the United States has shown itself to be a strange, hybrid creature, military giant and political dwarf. But Iraq is not Lebanon, from which the U.S. could sail away and invade Grenada; the stakes are much higher. "You can't just get up and walk away from Iraq like you did Lebanon," said Ghassan Salamé, the former Lebanese government minister and scholar, who was working for the UN headquarters in Baghdad when it was bombed. "No matter how bad it gets. If Iraq turns into anarchy, it's likely to spill into the rest of the Gulf. It would be a catastrophe."[12]

This is the national security argument, stood on its head: Saddam Hussein, it was said, with his weapons of mass destruction and his reckless ambitions, would inevitably acquire nuclear weapons and threaten both the established order in the Middle East and U.S. access to its oil supplies in the Persian Gulf. Since he posed a lingering threat to the United States, why not eliminate that threat now, when the American people, in the wake of the September 11 attacks, could be persuaded to support a preemptive war?

The irony, nearly six months after the United States launched this war, is that while Saddam Hussein has been unseated, the threat that Iraq posed to the Gulf has not been removed. Indeed, it may be that the United States, with its overwhelming military power, has succeeded only in transforming an eventual and speculative threat into a concrete and immediate one. Now the Bush administration finds itself trying to perform the tightrope walk of building a stable and friendly government beneath the shadow of escalating violence and a growing and inevitable nationalism—and it does so in the face of an impatient and bewildered public and an approaching election campaign. The administration began its Iraq venture with an air of absolute determination, taking a kind of grim pride in defying the United Nations and "doing what is right." America, and Iraq, will need a different kind of determination now—and a newfound honesty to go with it.

New York Review of Books, September 25, 2003

Delusions in Baghdad

November 19, 2003

I.

UTUMN IN BAGHDAD is cloudy and gray. Trapped in rush-hour traffic one October morning, without warning my car bucks up and back, like a horse whose reins had been brutally pulled. For a jolting instant the explosion registers only as the absence of sound, a silent blow to the stomach; and then a beat later, as hearing returns, a faint tinkling chorus: the store windows, all along busy Karrada Street, trembling together in their sashes. They were tinkling still when over the rooftops to the right came the immense eruption of oily black smoke.

Such dark plumes have become the beacons, the lighthouses, of contemporary Baghdad, and we rushed to follow, bumping over the center divider, vaulting the curb, screeching through the honking chaos of seventies-vintage American cars, trailing the blasting horns and screaming tires for two, three, four heart-pounding moments until, barely three blocks away, at one end of a pleasant residential square, behind a gaggle of blue-shirted Iraqi security men running in panic about the grass, shouting, waving their AK-47s, we came upon two towering conflagrations, rising perhaps a dozen feet in the air, and, perfectly outlined in the bright orange flames, like skeletons preserved in amber, the blackened frames of what moments before had been a van and a four-wheel drive.

Between the two great fires rose a smaller one, eight or nine feet high, enclosing a tangled, mass of metal. Pushing past the Iraqis, who shouted angrily, gesturing with their guns, I ran forward, toward the flames: The heat was intense. I saw slabs of smashed wall, hunks of rubble, glass, and sand scattered about, and behind it all an immense curtain of black smoke obscuring everything: the building, part of the International Red Cross compound, that stood there, the wall that had guarded it, the remains of the people who, four minutes before, had lived and worked there.

"Terrorism," as a U.S. Army lieutenant colonel had told me ruefully the week before, "is Grand Theater," and, as a mustached security man yanked me roughly by the arm, spinning me away from the flames, I saw that behind me the front rows had quickly filled: photographers with their long lenses, khaki vests, and shoulder bags struggled to push their way through the Iraqi security men, who, growing angrier, shouted and cursed, pushing them back. Swinging their AK-47s, they managed to form a ragged perimeter against what was now a jostling, roiling crowd, while camera crews in the vanguard surged forward.

Now a U.S. Army Humvee appeared; four American soldiers leaped out and plunged into the crowd, assault rifles raised, and began to scream, in what I had come to recognize as a characteristic form of address, "GET. THE FUCK. BACK! GET. THE FUCK. BACK!" Very young men in tan camouflage fatigues, armed, red-faced, flustered; facing them, the men and women of the world press, Baghdad division, assembled in their hundreds in less than a quarter of an hour: in the front row, those who, like me, had had the dumb luck to be in the neighborhood; behind them network crews who had received a quick tip from an embassy contact or an Iraqi stringer, or had simply heard or felt the explosion and pounded their way up to the hotel roof, scanning the horizon anxiously, locating the black beacon, and racing off to cover the story—or, as Lieutenant Colonel George Krivo put it bitterly, to "*make* the story. Here, media is the total message: I now have an understanding of McLuhan you wouldn't believe. Kill twenty people here? In front of that lens it's killing twenty thousand."

Behind the flames and the dark smoke, amid the shattered walls and twisted metal, a dozen people lay dead, many of whom had been unlucky enough to find themselves passing the front of the International Red Cross compound when, at half past eight in the morning, a man later claimed to be of Saudi nationality[1] drove an ambulance with Red Cross markings up to the security checkpoint and detonated what must have been several thousand pounds of explosives, collapsing forty feet of the protective wall and sending a huge sandbag barrier cascading forward. The Red Cross compound, with its security wall and sandbags and manned checkpoints, was a "hardened target"—as were, indeed, the three police stations that, within the next forty-five minutes, suicide bombers struck, in the Baghdad neighborhoods of al-Baya'a, al-Shaab, and al-Khadra.

In the rhetoric of security, all of these attacks failed dismally. "From what our indications are," Brigadier General Mark Hertling told Fox News that afternoon, "none of those bombers got close to the target." In the rhetoric of politics, however, the attacks were a brilliant *coup de théâtre*. In less than an hour, four men, by killing forty people, including one American soldier and twenty Iraqi police, had succeeded in dominating news coverage around the world, sending television crews rushing about Baghdad in pursuit of the latest plume of smoke and broadcasting the message, via television screens in a hundred countries, first and foremost the United States, that Baghdad, U.S. official pronouncements notwithstanding, remained a war zone.

Within a week, as members of the Red Cross left Iraq and many of the few remaining international organizations followed close behind, the attackers had set in motion, at the "highest levels" of the Bush administration, a "reevaluation" of American policy. Within two weeks, even as President Bush went on vowing publicly that the United States "would not be intimidated," he abruptly recalled L. Paul Bremer, the American administrator in Iraq, who rushed back to Washington so hurriedly he left the prime minister of Poland, one of America's few major allies in Iraq, waiting forlornly for an appointment that never came.

After two days of intensive consultations, administration officials unveiled a new policy. They decided to discard what had been a carefully planned, multiyear process that would gradually transform the authoritarian Iraqi state into a democracy—seven clearly defined steps intended to allow democratic parties, practices, and institutions to take root, develop, and grow, eventually leading to a new constitution written and ratified by the Iraqi people and, finally, a nationwide election and handover of power from American administrators to the elected Iraqi politicians it produced. The administration put in its place a hastily improvised rush to "return power to the Iraqis." In practice, this meant that in seven months the United States would hand over sovereignty to unelected Iraqis (presumably those on the American-appointed Governing Council, many of them former exiles, who had been pressing for such a rapid granting of power since before the war). Elections and a constitution would come later.[2] Despite President Bush's fervent protestations to the contrary, this was clearly a dramatic change in his policy of "bringing democracy to Iraq"—and, by extension, of making Iraq the first step in what he described as his "forward strategy of democracy in the Middle East."

IF VICTORY IN WAR is defined as accomplishing the political goals for which military means were originally brought to bear, then eight months after it invaded Iraq, the United States remains far from victory. If the political goal of the war in Iraq was to remove Saddam Hussein and his Baathist regime and establish in their place a stable, democratic government, then that goal, during the weeks I spent in Iraq in late October and early November, seemed to be growing ever more distant.

When I arrived in Baghdad, Iraqi insurgents were staging about fifteen attacks a day on American troops; by the time I left the number of daily attacks had more than doubled, to thirty-five a day. Though military leaders like General Ricardo Sanchez, the overall commander, have repeatedly denigrated the attacks on his troops as "strategically and operationally insignificant," those attacks led the CIA to conclude, in a report leaked in mid-November, that the "U.S.-led drive to rebuild the country as a democracy could collapse unless corrective actions are taken immediately."[3] The

United States fields by far the most powerful military in the world, spending more on defense than the rest of the world combined, and as I write a relative handful of armed insurgents, numbering in the tens of thousands or perhaps less, using the classic techniques of guerrilla warfare and suicide terrorism, are well on the way toward defeating it.

"What we have here," Lieutenant Colonel William Darley told me, "is basically a constabulary action. I mean, this is pretty much the Old West here. Peacekeeping. Where are the regiment-on-regiment, division-on-division engagements? We've seen almost nothing above the squad level. Basically this is not a real war." I heard this view, in various versions, expressed by American military men all over Iraq, from staff officers to combat commanders to lieutenants on the ground. Most of these men I found deeply impressive: well trained, well schooled, extremely competent. What joined them together, as the war grew steadily worse for American forces, was an inability, or perhaps a reluctance, to recognize what was happening in Iraq as a war.

"THERE'S A DEEP CULTURAL BIAS in the United States that if a military doesn't resemble ours, it's no good," the military strategist George Freidman of the private intelligence company Stratfor told me. "We have the strongest conventional forces in the world. So no one fights us conventionally. They fight us asymmetrically."

In Iraq, asymmetric warfare has meant a combination of guerrilla attacks on U.S. and other coalition forces and terrorist attacks on a variety of prominent nonmilitary targets, including hotels, embassies, and international organizations. Beginning late this spring, the guerrilla attacks were centered in Baghdad and the so-called "Sunni Triangle" north and west of the capital, but, since mid-autumn, they have increasingly spread to the north and, more slowly, the south of the country. Since late summer, highly effective terrorist attacks, including suicide bombings, have grown steadily more audacious and sophisticated, particularly in their use of the international press to multiply their political effect. In responding to both lines of attack, U.S. intelligence—critical in fighting any guerrilla war—has seemed poor or nonexistent.

The guerilla attacks have built on, and worsened, the American occupation's unpopularity among many Iraqis, capitalizing on, among other things, the U.S. military's failure to provide security during the early weeks of the occupation and the daily humiliations and occasional brutalities that come with the presence of an occupying army. The terrorist attacks have served to consolidate and then worsen the international isolation the Americans have labored under since the catastrophic diplomatic decisions that led up to the war and have succeeded in depriving the coalition of additional military forces and international help in rebuilding the country.

Terrorism is certainly, as the lieutenant colonel put it, Grand Theater. Or to put it a slightly different way, terrorism is a form of talk. To hear what is being said, one must look at the sequence of major bombings in Iraq over the last several months:

- August 7, Jordanian Embassy: A suicide car bomber kills nineteen people.
- August 19, United Nations Headquarters: A suicide truck bomber kills twenty-three, including the UN's chief envoy in Iraq.
- September 22, UN Headquarters: A suicide car bomber kills two and wounds nineteen.
- October 9, police station: A suicide car bomber kills ten.
- October 12, Baghdad Hotel: A suicide car bomber kills eight and wounds thirty-two.
- October 14, Turkish Embassy: A suicide car bomber kills two and wounds thirteen.
- October 27, Red Cross Headquarters and four police stations: Car bombers kill about forty and wound two hundred.
- November 12, Italian Carabinieri Headquarters, Nasariyah: A truck bomber kills thirty-one.

If one listens to what these attacks are saying—I list only the major ones—one can discern a rather methodical determination to sever, one by one, with patience, care, and precision, the fragile lines that still tie the occupation authority to the rest of the world. Suicide bombers struck at the countries that supported the Americans in the war (Jordan), that support the occupation with troops (Italy) or professed a willingness to do so (Turkey). They struck at the heart of an "international community" that could, with increased involvement, help give the occupation both legitimacy (the United Nations) and material help in rebuilding the country (the Red Cross). Finally they repeatedly struck at Iraqis collaborating with occupation authorities, whether as members of the American-selected Governing Council (several of whom lived in the Baghdad Hotel) or as policemen trained and paid by Americans.

By striking at the Jordanians, the bombers helped to ensure that no Arab country will contribute troops to support the occupation. By striking at the Turks, they helped force them to withdraw their controversial offer to send soldiers. By striking at the United Nations and the Red Cross, they not only forced the members of those two critical institutions to flee the country but led most other nongovernmental organizations, who would have been central to supplying expertise and resources to rebuilding Iraq, to leave as well. And by striking at the homes of several members of the Governing Council (wounding one member and, in a separate incident, assassinating another), they forced those officials to join the Americans behind their isolating wall of security, further separating them from Iraqis and underlining their utter political reliance on the Americans.

"Signs and symbols," the Italian security officer said. "Terrorism is nothing but signs and symbols." He looked at the sandbags and barbed wire, the rows of concrete Jersey barriers and armed guards that surrounded his embassy. "None of this will matter," he told me. "If they want to hit us, they will, and though they won't get to the building, it will still be a victory because it will kill people and make news. Terror," he said, "is quite predictable." What, I asked, did the signs and symbols mean? He spoke matter-of-factly: that anyone who helps the Americans will be a target; that the Americans cannot protect their allies and provide security to Iraqis; that the disorder is growing and that deciding to work with the Americans, who in their isolation are looking like a less-than dominant and in any event ephemeral presence, is not the most prudent of bets; that the war, whatever fine words President Bush may pronounce from his aircraft carrier, is not over. Terror, he said, has a logic of its own. Two weeks after we spoke a suicide bomber killed nineteen Italians at Nasariyah.

II.

Autumn in Baghdad is sunny and bright. Drive about the bustling city of tan, sundried brick and you will hear the noise of honking horns and see crowded markets, the streets overwhelmed by an enormous postwar expansion of traffic, the sidewalks cluttered with satellite disks and other new products flooding into the newly opened Iraqi market. During the last several months, however, a new city has taken root amid these busy streets and avenues, spreading rapidly as it superimposes itself over the old tan brick metropolis: a new grim city of concrete. It is constructed of twelve foot-high gray concrete barriers, endless roadblocks manned by squads of men with Kalashnikovs, walls of enormous steel-reinforced bags of earth and rubble and mile upon mile of coiled razor wire, and studded here and there with tanks rooted behind sandbags and watchful soldiers in combat fatigues. This city has a vaguely postmodern, apocalyptic feel, "a bit of Belfast here, a bit of Cyprus there, here and there a sprinkling of West Bank," as one network cameraman put it to me.

Many streets, including several of the grand ceremonial avenues of Saddam's capital, are now entirely lined with raw concrete a dozen feet high, giving the driver the impression of advancing down a stone tube. Behind these walls entire chunks of Baghdad have effectively vanished, notably the great park and building complex that had housed Saddam's Republican Palace and now comprises the so-called Green Zone—a four-and-a-half-square-mile concrete bunker that has at its heart the headquarters of the Coalition Provisional Authority (CPA).

To enter the palace you must secure, first, an appointment—hard to get, and made immeasurably harder by the fact that most members of the CPA are difficult or impossible to reach by telephone—and then make your way down several hundred yards of sidewalk lined with razor wire. Your journey will be broken by three checkpoints, two military (concrete cordons, sand-bags, machine guns) and one civilian. At two of these you present two iden-tifications and submit to full body searches, standing with your legs parted and arms extended and staring straight ahead, in a ritual I found myself repeating, on a busy day in Baghdad, a dozen times. Finally, after securing an identification badge, you wait for a military escort to drive you to the palace, where yet another series of checks and searches will be performed.

Inside Saddam's Republican Palace—his huge likeness in the central atrium is discreetly masked by a large blue cloth—you will find, amid the dark marble floors and sconces and chandeliers, a great many Americans striding purposefully about, some in uniform but many in casual civilian clothing: chinos, jeans, sport shirts. They look bright, crisp, self-assured, and extremely young; they look, in other words, like what they are: junior staffers from Washington—from the Capitol, the departments, and various agencies and think tanks. After all the combat fatigues on the city streets ("During my two weeks here," an oil industry contractor told me, "I've not seen one American who wasn't in uniform"), it is a bit of a shock to find this great horde of young American civilians secreted in Saddam's marble-lined hide-away, now become Baghdad's own Emerald City.

I spoke to one young expert from the Governance Department at some length about the Americans' "seven-point plan" to install democracy in Iraq, which was then stalled at point three: writing the constitution. (To summa-rize very crudely, the Shia, the majority on the Governing Council and in the country, were insisting that the writers of the constitution be chosen in a nationwide election; the others, fearing the Shia's numerical dominance, were pushing for the writers to be "selected" under various methods. This deadlock over the constitution is a precise reflection of the larger "gover-nance problem" in Iraq—beginning with Shia numerical dominance—that would need to be resolved if Iraq is ever to become a working democracy.) I found myself impressed with the young woman's knowledge and commit-ment. In general, the CPA members seem dedicated and well-meaning—they'd have to be, to come to Baghdad. They also seem entirely isolated, traveling twice daily by a military-driven bus within the bunkered com-pound from their places of work in the bunkered palace to their places of rest in the bunkered Rasheed Hotel.

Or rather they made that trip until October 26, when, just before six in the morning, a person or persons unknown towed a small blue two-wheeled trailer—to any observer (including, presumably, the soldier manning the checkpoint a couple hundred yards away), it looked like a generator, a com-mon sight in electricity-starved Iraq—up to the park across from which the Rasheed stood resplendent behind its impressive concrete barriers, quickly opened the trailer's doors, turned it around, directed it toward the hotel, and ran off, no doubt looking back to gaze in satisfaction a few moments later when a dozen or so converted French-made air-to-surface missiles whooshed out of their tubes and began peppering the rooms in which the Americans running the occupation slept, wounding seventeen people, killing one (a lieutenant colonel), and coming within a few yards of killing the visiting Paul L. Wolfowitz, United States deputy secretary of defense and mastermind of the Iraq war.

My friend in Governance was thrown from her bed and, finding her door jammed shut by the blast damage and taking "one look at the smoke coming from under that jammed door and realizing if I didn't get out of there I was going to die," she climbed out on the ledge and crept along it, ten floors up, to the room next door and the smoke-filled, chaotic hallway beyond. The Rasheed was evacuated and many of its former occupants found themselves sleeping on quickly assembled cots in Saddam's palace. As for my friend's "seven-point plan," two weeks later President Bush decided to abandon it. Instead of confronting the problem that had blocked the writing of a new Iraqi constitution—the question of how the fact of Shia numerical dominance, and other unresolved conflicts in the Iraqi state, would be integrated into a functioning Iraqi democracy—the president, faced with mounting attacks from Iraqis opposed to the new political dispensation he had declared himself committed to create, decided to abandon the effort.

SECURITY UNDERLIES everything in Iraq; it is the fault line running squarely beneath the occupation and the political world that will emerge from it. As I look back, perhaps my most frightening moment in the country came not at the Red Cross bombing, or an ambush on the highway between Fallujah and Ramadi where five civilians were killed, or at various other scenes of violence of one kind or another, but at a press conference the afternoon of the Rasheed attack, when General Martin E. Dempsey, the impressive commander of the First Infantry Division, characterized the rocket launcher—that cleverly disguised weapon that some unknown persons had used to pierce successfully the huge security perimeter around the Rasheed and thereby kill and wound, under the noses of tens of thousands of U.S. soldiers, the Americans who were supposedly running Iraq, and nearly kill the deputy secretary of defense—as "not very sophisticated . . . a science project, made in a garage with a welder, a battery, and a handful of wire." What frightened me was the possibility that General Dempsey—a sophisticated man who no doubt had read the literature on counterinsurgency and knew well "the lessons" of the British in Malaya and the French in Algeria and the Americans in Vietnam, but who, like almost every other impressive American commander in Iraq, had been trained to fight with, and against, larger armored formations—was aware of the condescension evident in his tone.

"The idea behind these stay-behind insurgent groups is that they're clandestine, they use what's *available*—an old drainpipe, whatever," said a private security officer working for an American television network who like many of the security professionals in Iraq, was a veteran of Britain's elite Special Air Service. "They don't need to be sophisticated, they need to be *effective*—and that device that hit the Rasheed was very effective." After General Dempsey's comments, Raymond Bonner, a *New York Times* reporter, made a somewhat broader point: "The good news is it was a science project put together in a garage. The bad news is it was a science project put together in a garage."

Ten days later, when a colleague, a strong advocate of the United States' invasion, declared to me with some impatience, "The United States will not lose. The United States has *absolute military superiority in Iraq!*,"[4] I remembered Bonner's comment. In view of the progress of the war against the U.S. coalition—the spreading activities of the opposition, the growing sophistication of their methods, the increasing numbers of Americans being killed—is the fact that the United States has "absolute military superiority" in Iraq good or bad news? All differences aside (and there are a great many differences), people commonly made the same point about Vietnam; but if it is true that "the United States had absolute military superiority in Vietnam," then what exactly do those words mean—and what do they tell us about those who utter them?

III.

Fall in Fallujah is dusty and bright. Here, on an average day in late October, insurgents attacked American soldiers eight times, twice the rate of a month before, according to General Chuck Swannack, commander of the 82nd Airborne Division. The method of choice was IEDs—"improvised explosive devices," in military parlance—planted, presumably, by FRLs, or "former regime loyalists." On the road leading into town, just emerging from the cloverleaf off the main highway, I saw the aftermath of one such attack. Late that afternoon, as an American armored convoy rumbled up the highway into the city, someone set off what the general described as

> a very sophisticated device, three barrels of flammable material rigged to a triggering mechanism, using a remote-controlled trigger. As our squad was clearing the cloverleaf, the individuals set off the device, killed a paratrooper, and then some individuals directed fire at us with AK-47s from the houses.

General Swannack's men dismounted, returned fire, stormed the houses, and arrested several civilians, leading them roughly away in flex cuffs. It was a typical day in Fallujah, with a typical score: one dead American soldier, two dead civilians, several civilians wounded, several arrested, with an indeterminate number of family members, neighbors, and friends of those killed, wounded, and arrested left furious at the Americans and nursing strong grievances, which tribal honor, an especially strong force in Fallujah, now demanded they personally avenge—by killing more Americans. As for the handful of "individuals" who had set off the device and opened fire on the

Americans, they managed—as they do in all but a few such ambushes—to get away clean.

As I write, 423 Americans have died in Iraq since the United States invaded in March and more than 2,300 have been wounded there, many grievously; and the rate at which Americans are being killed and wounded is increasing. But while these tolls are having a discernible effect on President Bush's popularity among Americans, the major goal of this kind of warfare is not only to kill and wound Americans but to increase Iraqi recruits, both active and passive, who will oppose the occupation; its major product, that is, is political. "The point," said General Swannack, "is to get the Americans to fire back and hopefully they'll get some Iraqi casualties out of that and they can publicize that."

After first estimating the guerrilla strength in and around Fallujah at 20,000, the general revised his figure: "Probably about a thousand people out there really want to attack us and kill us and another nineteen thousand or so really really don't like us." Such estimates vary wildly around Iraq, depending on whom you ask. General Sanchez recently put the total number of the opposition nationwide at five thousand. Whatever the numbers, the guerrillas' main business is to make them grow, particularly the number of strong sympathizers; and all evidence suggests that thus far they are succeeding.

SADDAM'S IRAQ was a national security state dominated by the interlocking intelligence services of the government and the elite security units of the army, all of it rooted in the enormous Baath Party, a highly elaborated structure that over a half-century spread and proliferated into every institution in the country and that had grown from what was originally a complex network of conspiratorial cells of three to seven members. Saddam's elite Republican Guard numbered 80,000; his even more select Special Republican Guard numbered 16,000; his Fedayeen Saddam, a paramilitary force—in effect, Saddam's brownshirts—numbered 40,000. The Mukhabarat and the various intelligence services, of which there were perhaps a dozen, numbered thousands more. All of these men were highly trained, well armed, and tested for their political loyalty. Few of them died in the war.

In May, in an astonishing decision that still has not been adequately explained, American administrator L. Paul Bremer vastly increased the number of willing Iraqi foot soldiers by abruptly dissolving the regular Iraqi army, which had been established by King Faisal I in 1921, and thereby sent out into bitter shame and unemployment 350,000 of those young Iraqis who were well trained, well armed, and deeply angry at the Americans. Add to these a million or so tons of weapons and munitions of all sorts, including rockets and missiles, readily available in more than a hundred mostly unguarded arms depots around the country, as well as vast amounts of money stockpiled during thirty-five years in power (notably on March 18, when Saddam sent three tractor trailers to the Central Bank and relieved it of more than a billion dollars in cash), and you have the makings of a well-manned, well-funded insurgency.

During the months since the fall of Baghdad in April, that insurgency has grown and evolved. Its methods have moved from assassinations of isolated U.S. soldiers, to attacks on convoys with small arms, to increasingly sophisticated and frequent ambushes of convoys with remote-controlled explosives and attacks on helicopters with rocket-propelled grenades and missiles. While there seems to be some regional coordination among groups, it is clear that the opposition is made up of many different organizations, some regionally based, some local; some are explicitly Saddamist, some more broadly Baathist, some Islamist, and some frankly anti-Saddam and nationalist. "I don't see a vision by these disparate groups of insurgents or partisans," said Ahmed S. Hashim, a professor at the Naval War College who has closely studied the opposition. "But at this stage they do not need one. They are making our stay uncomfortable; they have affected our calculus and are driving a wedge between us. What I know is the coalition is losing ground among Iraqis." Within and among these groupings a competitive politics now exists, an armed politics that will evolve and develop, depending on how successful they are in attacking the Americans and forcing them to adjust their policies and, eventually, to leave the country.

BY NOW MUCH evidence exists, including documents apparently prepared by Iraqi intelligence services, to suggest that this insurgency, at least in its broad outlines, was planned before the war and that the plan included looting, sabotage, and assassination of clerics.[5] Particularly damaging was the looting, in which government ministries and other public buildings, including museums, libraries, and universities, were thoroughly ransacked, down to the copper pipes and electrical wiring in the walls, and then burned, and the capital was given over to weeks of utter lawlessness while American soldiers stood by and watched. This was an enormously important political blow against the occupation, undermining any trust or faith Iraqis might have had in their new rulers and destroying any chance the occupiers had to establish their authority. Most of all, the looting created an overwhelming sense of insecurity and trepidation, a sense that the insurgents, with their bombings and attacks, have built on to convince many Iraqis that the Americans have not achieved full control and may well not stay long enough to attain it.

All of this is another way of saying that if security is the fault line running beneath development in Iraq, then politics is the fault line running beneath security. By now the failures in planning and execution that have dogged the occupation—the lack of military police, the refusal to provide security in the capital, the dissolution of the Iraqi army—are well known.[6] All have originated in Washington, many born of struggles between the leading departments of government, principally the State Department, the CIA, and the Pentagon, which the White House has never managed to resolve. (The most obvious product of these struggles was the president's decision, barely two months before the invasion, to discard the year of occupation planning by the State Department and shift control to the Pentagon, which proved itself wholly unprepared to take on the task.)

In Iraq, after the Big Bang of the American invasion, a new political universe is slowly being born. Part of this Iraqi political universe is called the Governing Council, and it does its work behind the concrete barriers of the Green Zone. Another part works at the level of nascent local government throughout the country. Still another works in the mosques of the south and among the Shiite religious establishment known as the Hawza. And yet another part—now a rather large and powerful part—is armed and clandestine and is making increasingly sophisticated and effective use of guerrilla warfare and terrorism, hoping to force the Americans from the country and claim its share of power. The Americans seek to define the armed claimants as illegitimate, as not part of the recognized universe at all. But in order to enforce that definition—to confine the game to the actors they regard as legitimate—the Americans must prove themselves able to make use of their power, both military and political, more effectively.

As I write, U.S. military forces in Iraq are conducting Operation Iron Hammer, striking with warplanes and artillery bases thought to be occupied by Iraqi insurgents. American television broadcasts are filled with dramatic footage of huge explosions illuminating the night sky. In Tikrit, Saddam's political base and a stronghold of the opposition, the Americans staged a military show of force, sending tanks and other armored vehicles rumbling through the main street. "They need to understand," Lieutenant Colonel Steve Russell told ABC News, "it's more than just Humvees we'll be using in these attacks."

The armed opposition in Iraq seems unlikely to be impressed. However many insurgents the Americans manage to kill in bombing runs and artillery barrages, the toll on civilians, in death and disruption, is also likely to be high, as will damage to the fragile sense of normalcy that Americans are struggling to achieve and the opposition forces are determined to destroy. Large-scale armored warfare looks and sounds impressive, inspiring overwhelming fear; but it is not discriminate, which makes it a blunt and ultimately self-defeating instrument to deploy against determined guerrillas. In general, the American military, the finest and most powerful in the world, is not organized and equipped to fight this war, and the part of it that is—the Special Forces—are almost entirely occupied in what seems a never-ending hunt for Saddam. For American leaders, and particularly President Bush, this has become the quest for the Holy Grail: Finding Saddam will be an enormous political boon. For the American military, this quest has the feel of a traditional kind of war not wholly suited to what they find in Iraq. "We are a hierarchy and we like to fight hierarchies," says military strategist John Arquilla. "We think if we cut off the head we can end this."

Whatever the political rewards of finding Saddam, they will not likely include putting a definitive end to the insurgency in Iraq.[7] "The Americans need to get out of their tanks, get out from behind their sunglasses," a British military officer, a veteran of Northern Ireland told me. "They need to get on the ground where they can get to know people and encourage them to tell them where the bad guys are." As I write, operations on the ground seem to be moving in the opposite direction. In any event it is difficult to impress an opponent with a military advance plainly meant to cover a political retreat.

President Bush's audacious project in Iraq was always going to be difficult, perhaps impossible, but without political steadfastness and resilience, it had no chance to succeed. This autumn in Baghdad, a ruthless insurgency, growing but still in its infancy, has managed to make the president retreat from his project, and has worked, with growing success, to divide Iraqis from the Americans who claim to govern them. These insurgents cannot win, but by seizing on Washington's mistakes and working relentlessly to widen the fault lines in occupied Iraq, they threaten to prevent what President Bush sent the U.S. military to achieve: a stable, democratic, and peaceful Iraq, at the heart of a stable and democratic Middle East.

New York Review of Books, December 18, 2003

Abu Ghraib: Hidden in Plain Sight

Free societies in the Middle East will be hopeful societies, which no longer feed resentments and breed violence for export. . . . The terrorists are fighting freedom with all their cunning and cruelty because freedom is their greatest fear—and they should be afraid, because freedom is on the march.

—President George W. Bush, Republican National Convention,
New York, September 2, 2004

It was discovered that freedom in this land is not ours. It is the freedom of the occupying soldiers in doing what they like . . . abusing women, children, men, and the old men and women whom they arrested randomly and without any guilt. No one can ask them what they are doing, because they are protected by their freedom. . . . No one can punish them, whether in our country or their country. They expressed the freedom of rape, the freedom of nudity and the freedom of humiliation.

—Sheik Mohammed Bashir, Friday prayers,
Um al-Oura, Baghdad, June 11, 2004[1]

September 9, 2004

THEY HAVE LONG SINCE taken their place in the gallery of branded images, as readily recognizable in much of the world as Marilyn struggling with her billowing dress or Michael dunking his basketball: Hooded Man, a dark-caped figure tottering on a box, supplicant arms outstretched, wires trailing from his fingers; and Leashed Man, face convulsed in humiliation above his leather collar, naked body twisted at the feet of the American female in camouflage pants who gazes down at him without expression, holding the leash casually in hand. The ubiquity of these images in much of the world suggests not only their potency but their usefulness and their adaptability. For the first of the many realities illuminated by the Global War on Terror—or the GWOT, as the authors of the latest Pentagon reports on Abu Ghraib designate it—is the indisputable fact that much of the world sees America rather differently from the way Americans see themselves.

Out of the interlocking scandals and controversies symbolized by Hooded Man and Leashed Man, the pyramids of naked bodies, the snarling dogs, and all the rest, and known to the world by the collective name of Abu Ghraib, one can extract two "master narratives," both dependent on the power and mutability of the images themselves. The first is that of President Bush, who presented the photographs as depicting "disgraceful conduct by a few American troops, who dishonored our country and disregarded our values"—behavior that, the president insisted, "does not represent America." And the aberrant, outlandish character of what the photographs show—the nudity, the sadism, the pornographic imagery—seemed to support this "few bad apples" argument, long the classic defense of states accused of torture.

The facts, however, almost from day one, did not: the Red Cross report, the army's own Taguba report, even the photographs themselves, some of which depicted military intelligence soldiers assisting in abuses they supposedly knew nothing about—all strongly suggested that the images were the brutal public face of behavior that involved many more people than the seven military police who were quickly charged.[2] The new reports not only decisively prove what was long known, widening the circle of direct blame for what happened at Abu Ghraib to nearly fifty people, including military intelligence soldiers and officers—although subsequent disclosures suggest the number is at least twice that. More important, the reports suggest how procedures that "violated established interrogation procedures and applicable laws" in fact had their genesis not in Iraq but in interrogation rooms in Afghanistan and Guantánamo Bay, Cuba—and ultimately in decisions made by high officials in Washington.

As General George R. Fay writes, in a section of his report that was classified and kept from the public,

> Policies and practices developed and approved for use on al Qaeda and Taliban detainees [in Afghanistan and Guantánamo] who were not afforded the protection of the Geneva Conventions, now applied to detainees who did fall under the Geneva Conventions' protections.[3]

According to General Fay, these "policies and practices" included, among others, "removing clothing, isolating people for long periods of time, using stress positions, exploiting fear of dogs and implementing sleep and light deprivation."

WHAT WE KNOW AS "the Abu Ghraib scandal" has in fact become an increasingly complex story about how Americans in Afghanistan and Cuba and Iraq came to commit acts, with the apparent approval of the highest officials, that clearly constitute torture. The images themselves, however, having helped force open the door to broader questions about how the Bush administration has treated prisoners in the War on Terror, are now helping as well to block that door; for the images, by virtue of their inherent grotesque power, strongly encourage the view that "acts of brutality and purposeless sadism," which clearly did occur, lay at the heart of Abu Ghraib. Even public officials charged with investigating the scandal—these are the fourth and fifth full reports on the matter, with at least four more to come—at the same time seek to contain it by promoting the view that Abu Ghraib in its essence was about individual misbehavior and sadism: "Animal House on the night shift," as former secretary of defense James Schlesinger characterized it, even as his own report showed in detail that it was a great deal more.[4]

The second "master narrative" of Abu Ghraib is that of the Muslim preacher Sheik Mohammed Bashir, quoted above, and many other Arabs and Muslims who point to the scandal's images as perfect symbols of the subjugation and degradation that the American occupiers have inflicted on Iraq and the rest of the Arab world. In this sense Hooded Man and Leashed Man fill a need, serving as powerful brand images advertising a preexisting product. Imagine, for a moment, an Islamic fundamentalist trying to build a transnational movement by arguing that today "nations are attacking Muslims like people attacking a plate of food," and by exhorting young Muslims to rise up and follow the Prophet's words:

And why should ye not fight in the cause of Allah and of those who, being weak, are ill-treated (and oppressed)?—women and children—whose cry is: "Oh Lord, rescue us from this town, whose people are oppressors; and raise for us from thee one who will help!"

For such an Islamic fundamentalist, quoting these words to give legitimacy to his call for jihad against the United States—as Osama bin Laden did in his famous 1998 fatwa "Jihad Against Jews and Crusaders"[5]—what better image of Arab ill-treatment and oppression could be devised than that of a naked Arab man lying at the feet of a short-haired American woman in camouflage garb, who stares immodestly at her Arab pet while holding him by the throat with a leash? Had bin Laden sought to create a powerful trademark image for his international product of global jihad, he could scarcely have done better hiring the cleverest advertising firm on Madison Avenue.

And not only are these photographs perfect masterpieces of propaganda; they have, to paraphrase Henry Kissinger, the considerable advantage of being true. Or, to put it another way: If Hooded Man and Leashed Man and the naked human pyramids and the rest shocked Americans because of their perverse undermining of the normal, they shocked Iraqis and other Arabs because the images seemed to confirm so vividly and precisely a reality that many had suspected and feared but had tried not to believe.

I.

I always knew the Americans would bring electricity back to Baghdad. I just never thought they'd be shooting it up my ass.

—Young Iraqi translator, Baghdad, November 2003

On first setting eyes on Hooded Man in April, I thought instantly of this joke, which I'd heard in a Baghdad street six months before. At that moment, the insurgency, wholly unanticipated by American officers on the ground and stubbornly denied by their political masters in Washington, had been gaining strength for months. Enormous suicide bombings had killed hundreds, had driven the United Nations, the Red Cross, and many other international organizations from the country, and had turned Baghdad into a city of stone, its public buildings and hotels and many of its roads encircled by massive concrete blast barriers and its American occupation government wholly inaccessible behind the barbed-wire and machine-gun nests of the grim fortress called the Green Zone.

The only Americans most Iraqis saw were the sunglasses-wearing machine-gunners atop the up-armored Humvees and Bradley fighting vehicles that barreled through traffic several times a day. These patrols were coming under increasingly frequent attack, usually from the ubiquitous "improvised explosive devices," or IEDs, which insurgents concealed in garbage cans or behind telephone poles. By November the number of attacks against Americans had doubled, to nearly forty a day. In May 2003, the month President Bush declared that "major combat" was over, forty-one Americans died in Iraq; in November, six months later, 110 died. And by and large, as was clear in Iraq at the time, and as these reports amply confirm, the American officers had very little idea who was killing their troops and had become increasingly desperate to find out. General Fay writes in his report that

> as the pace of operations picked up in late November–early December 2003, it became a common practice for maneuver elements to round up large quantities of Iraqi personnel [i.e., civilians] in the general vicinity of a specified target as a technique. Some operations were conducted at night. . . .[6]

Representatives of the Red Cross, who visited Abu Graib nearly thirty times in this period, offered a more vivid account of "cordon and capture":

> Arresting authorities entered houses usually after dark, breaking down doors, waking up residents roughly, yelling orders, forcing family members into one room under military guard while searching the rest of the house and further breaking doors, cabinets and other property. They arrested suspects, tying their hands in the back with flexi-cuffs, hooding them, and taking them away. Sometimes they arrested all adult males

present in a house, including elderly, handicapped or sick people. Treatment often included pushing people around, insulting, taking aim with rifles, punching and kicking and striking with rifles. Individuals were often led away in whatever they happened to be wearing at the time of arrest—sometimes in pyjamas or underwear. . . .[7]

IN THIS WAY the Americans arrested thousands of Iraqis—or, as Schlesinger puts it, "they reverted to rounding up any and all suspicious-looking persons—all too often including women and children. The flood of incoming detainees contrasted sharply with the trickle of released individuals."[8] Soon the population of the U.S. military's detention system approached ten thousand and very few Iraqis did not have some family member or friend who had gained intimate familiarity with American "cordon and capture." When Sheik Bashir complained to the Sunni faithful at the Um al-Oura mosque that Friday in June of the occupying soldiers "abusing women, children, men, and the old men and women whom they arrested randomly and without any guilt," he had no need to point to photographs. In Baghdad and Fallujah eight months before, I had heard the same bitter complaints, not only about the brutality of the tactics but about the obvious randomness of the arrests, which General Fay now confirms:

> SGT Jose Garcia, assigned to the Abu Ghraib Detainee Assessment Board, estimated that 85 to 90 percent of the detainees were of no intelligence value. . . . Large quantities of detainees with little or no intelligence value swelled Abu Ghraib's population and led to a variety of overcrowding difficulties. . . . Complicated and unresponsive release procedures ensured that these detainees stayed at Abu Ghraib—even though most had no value.[9]

Among the many disadvantages of these nighttime sweeps as a tactic for fighting an insurgency was that prisoners scooped up in this way soon flooded the system, inundating the very prisons where detainees were meant to be "exploited for actionable intelligence." And having filled Abu Ghraib largely with Iraqis of "no intelligence value"—whose families in most cases had no way to confirm where they were—the overwhelmed American command could not devise a way to get them out again, especially when faced with the strong opposition of those who had arrested them in the first place:

> Combat Commanders desired that no security detainee be released for fear that any and all detainees could be threats to coalition forces. . . . The [chief of intelligence, Fourth Infantry Division] informed [Major General] Fast that the Division Commander did not concur with the release of any detainees for fear that a bad one may be released along with the good ones.

Major General Fast, the senior intelligence officer in Iraq, described the attitude of the combat commanders as, "We wouldn't have detained them if we wanted them released." A sensible attitude, one might think, but as General Fay points out, the combat soldiers, in their zeal to apprehend Iraqis who might conceivably be supporting those shadowy figures attacking American troops, neglected to filter out those who clearly didn't belong in prison. The capturing soldiers

> failed to perform the proper procedures at the point-of-capture and beyond with respect to handling captured enemy prisoners of war and detainees (screening, tactical interrogation, capture cards, sworn statements, transportation, etc.). Failure of capturing units to follow these procedures contributed to facility overcrowding, an increased drain on scarce interrogator and linguist resources to sort out the valuable detainees from innocents who should have been released soon after capture, and ultimately, to *less actionable intelligence*. [My emphasis.][10]

THE SYSTEM was self-defeating and, not surprisingly, "interrogation operations in Abu Ghraib suffered from the effects of a broken detention operations system." Indeed, these reports are full of "broken systems" and "under-resourced" commands, from Abu Ghraib itself, a besieged, sweltering, stinking hell-hole under daily mortar attack that lacked interpreters, interrogators, guards, detainee uniforms, and just about everything else, including edible food, and that, at its height, was staggering under an impossible prisoner-to-guard ratio of 75 to 1, all the way up to the command staff of Lieutenant General Ricardo Sanchez, which lacked, among other vital resources, two thirds of its assigned officers. In Iraq, as the Schlesinger report puts it bluntly, "there was not only a failure to plan for a major insurgency, but also to quickly and adequately adapt to the insurgency that followed after major combat operations."[11] And though they don't say so explicitly, it is clear that the writers of these reports put much of the blame for this not on the commanders on the ground but on the political leadership in Washington, who, rather than pay the political cost of admitting the need for more troops—admitting, that is, that they had made mistakes in planning for the war and in selling it to the public—decided to "tough it out," at the expense of the men and women in the field and, ultimately, the Iraqis they had been sent to "liberate." All told, the reports offer a vivid and damning picture of a war that is understaffed, undersupplied, underresourced, and, above all, undermanned.

In this sense Abu Ghraib is at once a microcosm of the Iraq war in all its failures and the proverbial canary in the mineshaft, warning of what is to come. In fighting a guerrilla war, the essential weapon is not tanks or helicopters but intelligence, and the single essential tool to obtain it is reliable political support among the population. In such a war, arresting and imprisoning thousands of civilians in murkily defined "cordon and capture" raids is a blatantly self-defeating tactic, and an occupying army's resort to it means not only that the occupier lacks the political support necessary to find and destroy the insurgents but that it has been forced by the insurgents to adopt tactics that will further lessen that support and create still more insurgents. It is, in short, a strategy of desperation and, in the end, a strategy of weakness.

BY LATE SUMMER 2003—a time when Bush administration officials had expected to start "drawing down" American forces "in theater" until a stabilization force of no more than 30,000 Americans remained in Iraq—the U.S. military, even with 130,000 troops, was losing the initiative to an insurgency that seemed to have come out of nowhere and, after carrying out its increasingly bloody IED attacks and suicide bombings, regularly managed to disappear back into the same place. Officials in Washington were growing worried and impatient, and intelligence officers in Iraq were feeling the pressure.

In mid-August, a captain in military intelligence (MI) sent his colleagues an e-mail—recently shown to me—in which, clearly responding to an earlier request from interrogators, he sought to define "unlawful combatants," distinguishing them from "lawful combatants [who] receive protections of the Geneva Convention and gain combat immunity for their warlike acts." After promising to provide "an ROE"—rules of engagement—"that addresses the treatment of enemy combatants, specifically, unprivileged belligerents," the captain asks the interrogators for "input . . . concerning what their special interrogation knowledge base is and more importantly, what techniques would they feel would be effective techniques." Then, reminding the intelligence people to "provide Interrogation techniques 'wish list' by 17 AUG 03," the captain signs off this way:

> The gloves are coming off gentlemen regarding these detainees, Col Boltz has made it clear that we want these individuals broken. Casualties are mounting and we need to start gathering info to help protect our fellow soldiers from any further attacks. I thank you for your hard work and your dedication.
> MI ALWAYS OUT FRONT!

On August 31 Major General Geoffrey Miller, the commander of the U.S. detention camp in Guantánamo, would arrive, ordered to Iraq "to review current Iraqi Theater ability to rapidly exploit internees for actionable intelligence." He and his team would bring with them news and advice drawn from the American government's and the U.S. military's latest thinking on interrogation. For those at Abu Ghraib charged with "breaking" prisoners, help was on the way.

II.

In the case of Khalid Shaikh Mohammed, a high-level detainee who is believed to have helped plan the attacks of Sept. 11, 2001, CIA interrogators used graduated levels of force, including a technique known as "waterboarding," in which a prisoner is strapped down, forcibly pushed under water and made to believe he might drown.

—*The New York Times*, May 13, 2004[12]

In the matter of Americans' use of torture there are, to paraphrase Donald Rumsfeld, the things we know, the things we know we don't know, and the things we don't know we don't know. We know, for example, that much of the 9/11 Commission report's meticulous account of the unfolding of the World Trade Center plot comes from secret interrogations of Khalid Shaikh Mohammed and other "high value detainees." We know we don't know where he and his score or so fellows are being held—and neither, reportedly, does President Bush, who "informed the CIA that he did not want to know where they are"[13]—though it is likely that the CIA is holding them at a secret military base somewhere in Asia, perhaps in Afghanistan, Thailand, or even Jordan. We know we don't know specifically what "graduated levels of force" means, though we have a general idea:

After apprehending suspects, U.S. take-down teams—a mix of military special forces, FBI agents, CIA case officers and local allies—aim to disorient and intimidate them on the way to detention facilities.

According to Americans with direct knowledge and others who have witnessed the treatment, captives are "softened up" by MPs and U.S. Army Special Forces troops who beat them up and confine them in tiny rooms. The alleged terrorists are commonly blindfolded and thrown into walls, bound in painful positions, subjected to loud noises and deprived of sleep.[14]

We do know, finally, what "waterboarding" is, though it is not clear what version of this shock the Americans are applying. There is, for example, the version French policemen and soldiers used on prisoners during the Algerian War, as in this account from Bechir Boumaza, a thirty-one-year-old Algerian interrogated in Paris in 1958:

I was taken off the bar [on which he had been hung and subjected to electric shock] and my guards started their football again [beating and kicking him], perhaps for a quarter hour. Then they led me, still naked and blindfolded, into a neighboring room on the same floor. I heard: "We'll have to kill him, the bastard."

Then they laid me on a bench, flat on my stomach, head extending into the air, and tied my arms against my body with cords. Again the same question, which I refused to answer. By tilting the bench very slowly, they dipped my head into a basin filled with stinking liquid—dirty water and urine, probably. I was aware of the gurgling liquid reaching my mouth, then of a dull rumbling in my ears and a tingling sensation in my nose.

"You asked for a drink—take all you want."

The first time I did drink, trying to appease an insupportable thirst. I wanted to vomit immediately.

"He's puking, the bastard."

And my head was pushed back into the basin. . . .

From time to time one of them would sit on my back and bear down on my thighs. I could hear the water I threw up fall back into the basin. Then the torture would continue.[15]

The Latin American version, called *el submarino*, uses a wooden table, an oil drum filled with water, and a set of hooks linking the two, so that when the interrogators lift the table, the prisoner's head is submerged. Here is the account of Irina Martinez, an Argentine student activist, who was arrested at her parents' house in Buenos Aires in 1977, during the Dirty War:

She was immediately blindfolded. Her first torture session was in a basement full of soldiers, where she was stripped naked, tied, and beaten. "They slapped my face, pinched my breasts. 'You have to talk, this is your last opportunity, and this is your salvation.' And then they put me on a table. And I thought, 'Well, if they are going to kill me, I hope they kill me pretty soon.' They pushed my head underwater, so I could not breathe. They take you out, ask you things, they put you in, they take you out—so you cannot breathe all the time. 'Who did you receive this from? Who do you know?' Who can control anything when you cannot breathe? They pull you out, you try to grab for air, so they put you back in so you swallow water, and it is winter and you are very cold and very scared and they do that for a long time. Even if you are a good swimmer you cannot stand it anymore. . . ."[16]

Waterboarding, as those Americans who used the method on Khalid Shaikh Mohammed and other "high value detainees" surely know, is very effective in inducing fear; as a Uruguayan army interrogator put it, "There is something more terrifying than pain, and that is the inability to breathe." It is most effective, as these examples show, when combined with other techniques, including stress positions, sensory and sleep deprivation, and direct "physical coercion," or beatings.

WE DON'T KNOW precisely when the officers of the CIA began applying such "enhanced interrogation techniques," as the agency calls them, to their "high-value detainees," but we can see signs of the trend toward using these techniques very soon after the attacks of September 11, and also signs of strong interest in learning immediately the results of interrogation coming from high up in the security bureaucracies, including from the office of Secretary of Defense Rumsfeld. As early as October 2001, after the capture of John Walker Lindh in Afghanistan, a navy admiral told the intelligence officer interjrogating Lindh that "the secretary of defense's counsel has authorized him to 'take the gloves off' and ask whatever he wanted."[17]

Lindh's interrogators stripped the young American, who had been shot in the foot, taped him to a stretcher, propped it up against a shipping container in the cold open air of Afghanistan, and proceeded to interrogate him in marathon sessions that went on for days. According to documents that were leaked to a *Los Angeles Times* reporter, Lindh's responses during these interrogation sessions were cabled back to the Defense Department as often as every hour. During the coming months and years, as the United States gradually built a network of secret and semi-secret prisons in Bagram and Kandahar, Afghanistan; Guantánamo, Cuba; Qatar and Diego Garcia, as well as Abu Ghraib and Camp Cropper, Iraq, this direct attention from senior officials in Washington has remained constant. As Lieutenant Colonel Steven Jordan, the head of the Joint Intelligence and Debriefing Center at Abu Ghraib, told General Taguba in February 2004, "Sir, I was just told a couple times . . . that some of the reporting was getting read by Rumsfeld, folks out of Langley [CIA headquarters], some very senior folks."[18] For Jordan, that meant a lot of pressure to produce. It also meant that what went on at Abu Ghraib and other interrogation centers was very much the focus of the most senior officials in Washington.

III.

In an article in *The New York Review*,[19] I wrote about the case of an Iraqi man who had spent time in Abu Ghraib and had given a sworn statement, after his release, to investigators of the U.S. Army's Criminal Investigation Command. This statement had been leaked, along with those of twelve other detainees, to the *Washington Post*, which posted them on its Web site. Here now is General Fay's full account of what happened to the anonymous prisoner, and his analysis of who was responsible:

> In October 2003, DETAINEE-07, reported alleged multiple incidents of physical abuse while in Abu Ghraib. DETAINEE-07 was a [military intelligence] hold and considered of potentially high value. He was interrogated on 8, 21 and 29 October; 4 and 23 November and 5 December. DETAINEE-07's claims of physical abuse (hitting) started on his first day of arrival. He was left naked in his cell for extended periods, cuffed in his cell in stressful positions ("High cuffed"), left with a bag over his head for extended

periods, and denied bedding or blankets. DETAINEE-07 described being made to "bark like a dog, being forced to crawl on his stomach while MPs spit and urinated on him, and being struck causing unconsciousness."

On another occasion DETAINEE-07 was forced to lie down while MPs jumped onto his back and legs. He was beaten with a broom and a chemical light was broken and poured over his body. DETAINEE-04 witnessed the abuse with the chem-light. During this abuse a police stick was used to sodomize DETAINEE-07 and two female MPs were hitting him, throwing a ball at his penis, and taking photographs. This investigation surfaced no photographic evidence of the chemical light abuse or sodomy. DETAINEE-07 also alleged that CIVILIAN-17, MP Interpreter, Titan Corp., hit DETAINEE-07 once, cutting his ear to an extent that required stitches. He told SOLDIER-25, analyst, B/321 [Military Intelligence Brigade], about this hitting incident during an interrogation. SOLDIER-25 asked the MPs what had happened to the detainee's ear and was told he had fallen in his cell. SOLDIER-25 did not report the detainee's abuse. SOLDIER-25 claimed the detainee's allegation was made in the presence of CIVILIAN-21, Analyst/Interrogator, CACI [Corporation], which CIVILIAN-21 denied hearing this report. Two photos taken at 2200 hours, 1 November 2003, depict a detainee with stitches in his ear; however, we could not confirm the photo was DETAINEE-07.

Based on the details provided by the detainee and the close correlation to other known MP abuses, it is highly probable DETAINEE-07's allegations are true. SOLDIER-25 failed to report the detainee's allegation of abuse. His statements and available photographs do not point to direct [military intelligence] involvement. However, MI interest in this detainee, his placement in Tier 1A of the Hard Site, and initiation of the abuse once he arrived there, combine to create a circumstantial connection to MI (knowledge or implicit tasking of the MPs to "set conditions") which are difficult to ignore. MI should have been aware of what was being done to this detainee based on the frequency of interrogations and high interest in his intelligence value.[20]

What is interesting here is not simply that General Fay confirms the account of Detainee-07 but the strange Kabuki dance the general performs when he comes to the point of assigning responsibility. During a period of about two months, military police beat the detainee savagely into unconsciousness, ripped his ear, urinated on him, "high-cuffed" him to the bars of his cell for hours so that the skin of his hand split and oozed pus, and sodomized him with a police baton—to give only a brief summary of what, in the detainee's statement, is an exhaustive and exhausting catalog of imaginative and extremely disgusting tortures carried out over many days.[21] Now during this time, as General Fay meticulously confirms, military intelligence soldiers interrogated Detainee-07 on at least six occasions, as befits a prisoner judged of "potentially high value." General Fay, however, finds here only a "circumstantial connection to MI," concluding that the intelligence officers "should have been aware of what was being done to this detainee."

The problem here is that it is quite obvious from the report that military intelligence officers *were* "aware of what was being done to the detainee"— indeed, that they *ordered* it. Throughout the general's patient recounting of his forty-four "serious incidents"—his careful sifting of them into categories ("Nudity/Humiliation," "Assault," "Sexual Assault," "Use of Dogs," "The 'Hole,'" and "Other"), his determination to classify them according to responsibility ("MI," "MP," "MI/MP," or "UNK," for unknown), and his dogged effort to separate what he calls "violent/sexual abuse incidents" (which is to say those, generally speaking, committed by military police, which were not a matter of policy) from "misinterpretation/confusion incidents" (those committed by military intelligence soldiers, who, however, were "confused" about what was permitted at Abu Ghraib as a matter of policy)—throughout all this runs a tone of faintly hysterical absurdity. Throughout we see distinctions that are not distinctions at all, and that recall nothing so much as the darkest passages of *Catch-22*; for example, this passage, on "sleep adjustment":

> Sleep adjustment was brought with 519 [Military Intelligence Battalion] from Afghanistan. It is also a method used at GTMO [Guantánamo]. . . . At Abu Ghraib, however, the MPs were not trained, nor informed as to how they actually should do the sleep adjustment. The MPs were just told to keep a detainee awake for a time specified by the interrogator. The MPs used their own judgment as to how to keep them awake. Those techniques included taking the detainees out of their cells, stripping them and giving them cold showers. CPT Wood stated she did not know this was going on and thought the detainees were being kept awake by the MPs banging on the cell doors, yelling, and playing loud music.[22]

Abu Ghraib was a mess; training was deficient; the chain of command was dysfunctional. But that military intelligence soldiers would have had no idea what was being done to prisoners whom they spent hours and hours each day interrogating is simply not credible.

WHAT IS CREDIBLE, or at least comprehensible, is the subtle bureaucratic strategy that has been adopted in these reports, and which has been visible, indeed obvious, from the moment the story of Abu Ghraib broke. For at that moment, in late April 2004, a bureaucratic and political war erupted over torture and its implications, and over Abu Ghraib and how broad-reaching and damaging the scandal that bore its name was going to be. On one side were those within the administration, many of whom had opposed the use of "enhanced interrogation tactics" from the beginning, including many in the judge advocate generals' offices of the various military services and career lawyers in the Justice Department, who have been leaking a veritable flood of documents detailing legally questionable and politically damaging administration decisions about torture and interrogation. On the other side are those at the highest political levels of the Department of Defense, the Department of Justice, and the White House who have struggled, so far successfully, to keep Abu Ghraib from becoming what it early on threatened to be: a scandal that could bring down many senior officials in the Department of Defense, and perhaps the administration itself.

With no fear of a full, top-to-bottom investigation from a Congress that is firmly in Republican hands, administration officials, and particularly those at the Department of Defense, have managed to orchestrate a slowly unfolding series of inquiries, almost all of them carried out within the military by officers who by definition can only direct their gaze down the chain of command, not up it, and who are each empowered to examine only a limited and precisely defined number of links in the chain that connects the highest levels of the government to what happened on the ground in Abu Ghraib and elsewhere in the war on terror. Thus General Taguba investigated the military police; General Paul Mikolashek, as the army's inspector general, reported on detention procedures; General Fay on military intelligence, and so on.

Beyond the reports themselves, the key strategy of the defense is both to focus on the photographs and to isolate the acts they depict—which, if not the most serious, are those with the most political effect—from any inference that they might have resulted, either directly or indirectly, from policy. Thus the dogged effort to isolate these acts as "violence/sexual abuse incidents" that originated wholly in the minds of sadistic military police during the wee hours, and that, above all, had nothing whatever to do with what was done "to set the conditions" for interrogation—even though this division is quite artificial and many of the latter activities, as vividly demonstrated by the sufferings of Detainee-07, were conducted by precisely the same people and were equally, or more, disgusting, sadistic, and abusive.

Only against this background can one properly appreciate the opening paragraph of former secretary Schlesinger's report, five powerfully peculiar sentences, in which the bureaucratic priorities of this political containment effort have thoroughly corrupted the language:

> The events of October through December 2003 on the night shift of Tier 1 at Abu Ghraib prison were acts of brutality and purposeless sadism. We now know these abuses occurred at the hands of both military police and military intelligence personnel. The pictured abuses, unacceptable even in wartime, were not part of authorized interrogations nor were they even directed at intelligence targets. They represent deviant behavior and a failure of military leadership and discipline. However, we do know that some of the egregious abuses at Abu Ghraib which were not photographed did occur during interrogation sessions and that abuses during interrogation sessions occurred elsewhere.[23]

Mr. Schlesinger and his fellow commissioners begin by defining all the events at Abu Ghraib as "acts of brutality and purposeless sadism," though they admit, in the next sentence, that they in fact occurred "at the hands of both military police and military intelligence." The next sentence abruptly and arbitrarily narrows the subject from "the events . . . on the night shift" to "the pictured abuses"—that is, those in the photographs—which the writers say were not "even directed at intelligence targets." These "represent deviant behavior"—except for the fact, as they go on to concede in the fifth sentence (where perhaps counsel intervened), that "some of the egregious abuses . . . which were not photographed did occur during interrogation sessions." It is a strange tangle of self-contradictory and oddly qualified sentences which seems designed to allow Mr. Schlesinger and others in the administration to contend that their report proved decisively that the abuses at Abu Ghraib were nothing more than the photographs—an argument that in fact the report that follows decisively disproves.

The "celebrity abuses"—those known through the photographs—are segregated firmly within the realm of "acts of brutality and purposeless sadism," as Mr. Schlesinger calls them—"Animal House on the night shift"—and thereby sealed off entirely from the responsibility of policymakers. Even now seven hapless MPs are being prosecuted—two have already pleaded guilty—but only, in effect, for taking pictures; that is, only for those acts which can be said to have taken place outside the realm of interrogation or of acts "setting the conditions for interrogation." On the other hand, acts of brutality that can't be attributed entirely to sadistic military police, and which clearly involved military intelligence and the process of interrogation—those, that is, that risk implicating policymakers, who in the end are responsible for deciding what the interrogators can and cannot do—are ascribed in the reports to "misinterpretation/confusion" on the part of the intelligence people about what interrogation techniques could and could not be used at Abu Ghraib. These actions, after all, are where the political danger lies; for knowledge about "interrogation techniques" leads to knowledge about the official doctrine that allowed those techniques, doctrine leads to policy, and policy leads to power.

IV.

NIXON: Do you think we want to go this route now? Let it hang out?
DEAN: Well, it isn't really that.
HALDEMAN: It's a limited hang-out.
EHRLICHMAN: It's a modified, limited hang-out.

—The White House, March 22, 1973

The delicate bureaucratic construction now holding the Abu Ghraib scandal firmly in check rests ultimately on President Bush's controversial decision, on February 7, 2002, to withhold protection of the Geneva Convention both from al Qaeda and from Taliban fighters in Afghanistan. The decision rested on the argument, in the words of White House Counsel Alberto Gonzalez, that "the war against terrorism is a new kind of war," in fact, a "new paradigm [that] renders obsolete Geneva's strict limitations on questioning of enemy prisoners and renders quaint some of its provisions. . . ."[24] In a prefiguring of later bureaucratic wars, lawyers in the State Department and many in the military services fought against this decision, arguing, prophetically, that it "would undermine the United States military culture, which is based on a strict adherence to the law of war."[25]

For torture, this decision was Original Sin: It made legally possible the adoption of the various "enhanced interrogation techniques" that have been used at CIA secret prisons and at the U.S. military's prison at Guantánamo Bay. As it turns out, however, for the administration, Bush's decision was also Amazing Grace, because, by implying that the U.S. military must adhere to wholly different rules when interrogating, say, Taliban prisoners in Guantánamo, who do not enjoy Geneva Convention protection, and Iraqi insurgents at Abu Ghraib, who do, it makes it possible to argue that American interrogators, when applying the same techniques at Abu Ghraib that they had earlier used in Afghanistan or at Guantánamo, were in fact taking part not in "violent/sexual abuse incidents," like their sadistic military police colleagues, but instead in "misinterpretation/confusion incidents."

A central figure in all this is Major General Geoffrey Miller, who when last we saw him, in late August 2003, was on his way from Guantánamo, where he commanded the detention facility, to Abu Ghraib, where he had been ordered "to review current Iraqi Theater ability to rapidly exploit internees for actionable intelligence." General Miller's report, which remains secret but was made available to me, recommends, among other things, that those in charge of Abu Ghraib should "dedicate and train a detention guard force subordinate to [the Joint Interrogation and Debriefing Center] that sets conditions for the successful interrogation and exploitation of internees/detainees. This action," he adds, "is now in progress." The MPs, in other words, should be working for the interrogators and spending significant time "softening up" prisoners, by keeping them awake, "making sure this one has a bad night," etc.—doing, that is, precisely what the accused military police, no doubt self-servingly, claimed they were doing in at least some of those dreadful photographs.

Before he left Iraq, General Miller also "left behind a whole series of [Standard Operating Procedures] that could be used as a start point for [Abu Ghraib] interrogation operations." After returning to Guantánamo, the general dispatched to Iraq a follow-up team who, according to General Fay, brought with it the secretary of defense's letter of April 16, 2003, "outlining the techniques authorized for use with the GTMO detainees." Various parts of the bureaucracy, both inside and outside the Department of Defense, had been fighting over these interrogation techniques since the previous December. On December 2, 2002, Secretary Rumsfeld had approved, among other techniques, yelling at detainees, use of stress positions, use of isolation, deprivation of light and auditory stimuli, use of hoods, use of twenty-hour interrogation, removal of clothing, use of mild physical contact, and "use of detainees' individual phobias (such as fear of dogs) to induce stress."

SIX WEEKS LATER, reportedly after vigorous opposition from lawyers in the Department of the Navy, among others, Rumsfeld rescinded these instructions and convened a working group to recommend suitable methods for Guantánamo. Though the derivation of interrogation techniques eventually adopted for Iraq is Talmudic in its intricacy, and though the list of methods permitted changed at least three times during the critical fall of 2003, Fay makes it clear in his report that Lieutenant General Sanchez's command in Iraq "relied heavily on the series of SOPs [standard operating procedures] which MG G. Miller provided to develop not only the structure, but also the interrogation policies for detainee operations."[26] Other sources include, according to a classified section of Fay's report made available to me, the interrogation policy of the shadowy, elite unit Joint Task Force-121, which spent its time searching for "high value targets" in Iraq. "At some point," Fay says, the leading military intelligence battalion at Abu Ghraib "came to possess the JTF-121 interrogation policy" and the first set of interrogation rules used by this unit "were derived almost verbatim from JTF-121 policy," which

> included the use of stress positions during fear-up harsh interrogation approaches, as well as presence of military working dogs, yelling, loud music, and light control. The memo also included sleep management and isolation approaches.

On September 14, 2003, Lieutenant General Sanchez signed a policy that included elements of the JTF-121 procedures and elements drawn from General Miller's GTMO policy, including the use of dogs, stress positions, yelling, loud music, light control, and isolation, among other techniques.

The policy at Abu Ghraib would change at least twice more but what is critical here is Fay's point, included in a still-secret section of the report, that "policies and practices developed and approved for use on al Qaeda and Taliban detainees who were not afforded the protection of the Geneva Conventions, now applied to detainees who did fall under the Geneva Conventions' protections." Sanchez later tried to define, unilaterally, some of his detainees as "unlawful combatants"—and the e-mail I quoted earlier, sent in August 2003 by a captain in military intelligence, suggests that interrogators feeling the pressure to produce results were eager that this be done. But in fact, as Schlesinger points out, Sanchez had no authority to make such a determination.

This confusion over doctrine supposedly allowed some of the more gruesome practices that are so patiently set out in General Fay's report, including sensory deprivation, routine nudity and humiliation, "exploiting the Arab fear of dogs," and prolonged isolation of a particularly revolting kind:

DETAINEE-14 was detained in a totally darkened cell measuring about 2 meters long and less than a meter across, devoid of any window, latrine or water tap, or bedding. On the door the [Red Cross] delegates noticed the inscription "the Gollum," and a picture of the said character from the film trilogy "Lord of the Rings."

Detainee-14 was one of eight detainees to whom General Sanchez denied the Red Cross access.

The fact is that countless details in these reports give the lie to any supposed rigid division between the "violent/sexual acts incidents" and the "misinterpretation/confusion incidents," not only because in many cases military police really were setting "the conditions for the successful interrogation and exploitation of internees/detainees," as Major General Miller recommended they should, but because general practices, like the extensive use of nudity, "likely contributed," as General Fay wrote in his report, to "an escalating 'dehumanization' of the detainees and set the stage for additional and more severe abuses to occur."

There simply was no clear dividing line, no point where sadistic abuses became instances of "misinterpretation/confusion"—where, that is, an interrogator simply erred in applying a technique that, while permitted in Afghanistan or Guantánamo, constituted a violation in Iraq of the Geneva Conventions. How isolated could the so-called "Animal House on the night shift" abuses of the military police have been from military intelligence when, as we learn in the Fay report, one of the most notorious images, that of "several naked detainees stacked in a 'pyramid,'" served as a "screen saver" on one of the computers in the military intelligence office?

V.

JAMES HARDING (*FINANCIAL TIMES*): Mr. President, I want to return to the question of torture. What we've learned from these memos this week is that the Department of Justice lawyers and the Pentagon lawyers have essentially worked out a way that U.S. officials can torture detainees without running afoul of the law. So when you say you want the United States to adhere to international and U.S. laws, that's not very comforting. This is a moral question: Is torture ever justified?

PRESIDENT BUSH: Look, I'm going to say it one more time. . . . Maybe I can be more clear. The instructions went out to our people to adhere to law. That ought to comfort you. We're a nation of law. We adhere to laws. We have laws on the books. You might look at these laws, and that might provide comfort for you. And those were the instructions . . . from me to the government.

—News conference, Sea Island, Georgia, June 10, 2004

As I write, four months have passed since a series of bizarre photographs were broadcast on American television and entered the consciousness of the world. Seven military police, those "few bad apples," have been indicted and two have pled guilty. According to the military's latest account, reported in the *New York Times*, thirteen service members have been discharged, and fifty-four have suffered some form of "lesser disciplinary action," while fifty-seven others have been "referred to court-martial proceedings"—although it is impossible to know how many such "proceedings" will result in actual charges and trials, and it seems unlikely that any would before the election. What has been on trial thus far, however, is the acts depicted in the photographs and these acts, while no doubt constituting abuse, have been carefully insulated from any charge that they represent, or derived from, U.S. policy—a policy that permits torture. Thus far, in the United States at least, there has been relatively little discussion about torture and whether the agents of the U.S. government should be practicing it.

The twenty-seven military intelligence officers and soldiers implicated in General Fay's report, meanwhile, have so far escaped indictment. A number of them have claimed the equivalent of Fifth Amendment protection and military prosecutors have so far declined to bring cases against them. Until they do, or offer grants of immunity for their testimony, it will be difficult to prosecute successfully the remaining military policemen, who include those men and women accused of the most serious photographed crimes. On the other hand, at least some of the military intelligence officers may be in a position to implicate officials above them. Such a threat, however implicit, might be a powerful lever to dissuade the administration from prosecution, at least before the election.

As for Major General Geoffrey Miller, the former commander of GTMO, he is now in command of Abu Ghraib. It is unclear precisely who ordered Major General Miller to make his "assessment visit" to Abu Ghraib late last summer, and if it is true, as seems likely and as many believe, that these orders originated at the top levels of the Pentagon—perhaps even from the office of the county's leading "intelligence junkie," Donald Rumsfeld—then no proof of this has emerged. Nor, at this point, would such proof, or anything short of evidence linking Rumsfeld to what was shown in the photographs, make a decisive difference. The fact that the legal trail at Abu Ghraib has been directed toward the abuses that appear in the photographs means that the question of policy—of whether the United States should be torturing prisoners, of what the political and moral costs of this will finally be, and of what responsibility those who ultimately direct that policy really bear—has hardly been seriously debated, whether in Congress or anywhere else. Only now, more than four months after the photographs were broadcast to the world, and after eight prominent retired generals and admirals wrote to President Bush publicly demanding a truly independent and far-reaching investigation, has there been some small sign that the administration, perhaps finally pressed by a reluctant Republican Senate, might be forced to go beyond the piecemeal and dilatory efforts it has so far grudgingly made.

If that does happen, it will have been long in coming—and again, almost certainly, and critically for the administration, no results could be known until after the election. So far, officials of the Bush administration, who counted on the fact that the public, and much of the press, could be persuaded to focus on the photographs—the garish signboards of the scandal and not the scandal itself—have been proved right. This makes Abu Ghraib a peculiarly contemporary kind of scandal, with most of its plotlines exposed to view—but with few willing to follow them and fewer still to do much about them. As with other controversies over the Iraq war, the revelations have been made, the behavior exposed, but the moral will to act, or even to debate what action might be warranted, seems mostly lacking.

MEANTIME THE HOODED MAN has taken his place among the symbols calling forth, in some parts of the world, a certain image of the United States and what it stands for. Sheik Bashir, who said of the occupying soldiers that "no one can punish them, whether in our country or their country," has thus far been proved right. Only those at the lowest rung of the ladder have so far been punished and the matter of what was actually happening within the interrogation rooms of Abu Ghraib, not to mention in the secret detention centers of the CIA, has hardly been debated. The Iraqis know this, even if many Americans do not. Meanwhile the political damage to U.S. interests in the world has been very great. As the military strategist Anthony Cordesman put it,

> We need to understand that this image is going to be used for years to come. We are dealing with an ideological climate in which the extremists are the threat, not the moderates. And they are going to use these images for years to come, and they are going to couple them to images like Israeli treatment of the Palestinians and find ways of tying this to all their conspiracy theories and hostile images of the West. And the end result is that they will be tools for insurgents and extremists and terrorists.[27]

There is no weighing such ongoing damage against the intelligence that these techniques may have gained. How can such things as these be quantified? According to the Schlesinger report,

> There were five cases of detainee deaths as a result of abuse by U.S. personnel during interrogations. . . . There are 23 cases of detainee deaths still under investigation. . . .[28]

The words are blunt, though a writer less fond of euphemism might have put the matter even more plainly: "American interrogators have tortured at least five prisoners to death." And from what we know, Mr. Schlesinger's figures, if anything, substantially understate the case.

It has become a cliché of the Global War on Terror—the GWOT, as these reports style it—that at a certain point, if the United States betrays its fundamental principles in the cause of fighting terror, then "the terrorists will have won." The image of Hooded Man, now known the world over, raises a stark question: Is it possible that that moment of defeat could come and go, and we will never know it?

New York Review of Books, October 7, 2004

A Doctrine Left Behind

November 21, 2004

I T SEEMED SOMEHOW FITTING, and fittingly sad, that Colin Powell saw his resignation accepted as secretary of state on the day marines completed their conquest of Fallujah, ensuring that the televised snapshots of glory drawn from his long public career would be interspersed with videotape of American troops presiding over scenes of urban devastation in a far-off and intractable war.

As I watched images from Mr. Powell's life flicker past, and as the fruits of the American victory became clear—a ravaged city; an elusive enemy, most of whom had escaped; a countrywide counterattack in which insurgents seized parts of Mosul—I felt a ghostly echo of words I could not quite grasp. Two days later, watching an American general declare that in Fallujah our forces had "broken the back of the insurgency," I felt the sentences I'd struggled to recall suddenly take shape; I reached for Mr. Powell's memoir and found these bitter lines:

> Our senior officers knew the war was going badly. Yet they bowed to groupthink pressure and kept up pretenses. . . . Many of my generation, the career captains, majors, and lieutenant colonels seasoned in that war, vowed that when our turn came to call the shots, we would not quietly acquiesce in halfhearted warfare for half-baked reasons that the American people could not understand.[1]

Those plain words about Vietnam stand out with refreshing immediacy today, in this age of the destruction of the fact, when incontrovertible but unwelcome information is dismissed as partisan argument. What might the Colin Powell who wrote those words, or the younger officer in Vietnam who envisaged his future as a man who could never "quietly acquiesce," have said about our present war? What might "many of his generation"—who are indeed the men now commanding in Iraq—have said, had they not themselves quietly acquiesced?

412

They might have said that it is a deeply uncontroversial fact that the United States has from the beginning had too few troops in Iraq: too few to secure the capital or effectively monitor the borders or even police the handful of miles between Baghdad and its airport; too few to secure the arms dumps that litter the country; and too few to mount an offensive in one city without leaving others vulnerable.

They might have said that it is a deeply uncontroversial fact that the insurgency is spreading: when I arrived in Iraq thirteen months ago, the insurgents were mounting seventeen attacks a day; last week there were 150 a day. If the old rule of thumb about counterinsurgency warfare holds true—that the guerrilla wins by not losing and the government loses by not winning—then America is losing the Iraq war. The Iraqi insurgents have shown "outstanding resilience," as a marine intelligence report compiled after Fallujah put it, and "will continue to find refuge among sympathetic tribes and former regime members."

Finally, these imaginary officers who refused to "quietly acquiesce" might have said that it is a deeply uncontroversial fact that if indeed the war is going very badly, the fault belongs not with commanders in the field but with policymakers in Washington, who in conceiving and executing the war made a series of flagrant mistakes and then doggedly refused to acknowledge or correct them: the failure over many weeks to establish law and order in Baghdad and other cities; the failure to begin an effective reconstruction program, leaving many Iraqis without electricity, water and other basic supplies for months; and finally—according to James R. Schlesinger, a Republican and former secretary of defense, in his report on the abuses at Abu Ghraib prison—the failure not only "to plan for a major insurgency, but also to quickly and adequately adapt to the insurgency that followed after major combat operations."

It is a sad and familiar litany. But however widely these disasters are acknowledged, many Americans seem willing to treat them as if they were acts of God rather than the results of decisions that were made, and not made, by our officials—decisions that stem ultimately from a failure to coordinate the agencies and departments of American power.

This job falls, by statute and custom, to the national security adviser. And it is directly to that office that "the major interagency coordination problems between State and Defense and the striking ineffectiveness of the National Security Council" can be traced, in the words of Anthony Cordesman. Mr. Cordesman, a nonpartisan military analyst at the Center for Strategic and International Studies, is one of many professionals who trace the disasters in Iraq back to failure to resolve conflicts between major government departments, as well as to debilitating "ideological efforts to shape the nation-building effort and personnel deployed to Iraq."

After Condoleezza Rice's elevation as Mr. Powell's successor, so much of the commentary seemed focused on her "closeness" to the president that it might have seemed the height of indiscretion to point out that she has been something of a disaster in her present job—a fact widely acknowledged among foreign policy professionals.

No one can say how many lives could have been saved had the responsible officials asked the right questions. As it happens, those questions had been laid out with courage and clarity back in 1992, by the chairman of the Joint Chiefs of Staff at the time, Colin Powell. While the Powell Doctrine is generally thought simply to prescribe the setting of clear objectives and the use of overwhelming force to achieve them, it also sets out a series of questions that policymakers must ask and answer before committing American lives to war. They make sobering reading today:

> Is the political objective we seek to achieve important, clearly defined and understood? Have all other nonviolent policy means failed? Will military force achieve the objective? At what cost? Have the gains and risks been analyzed? How might the situation that we seek to alter, once it is altered by force, develop further and what might be the consequences?[2]

Faced with the war in Iraq, how might Mr. Powell have answered these questions? The main "political objective" the United States sought in Iraq, insofar as the president identified it, was to deprive Saddam Hussein of his weapons of mass destruction. These always ghostly objects have long since evaporated; and no matter how often administration officials repeat that the French, Germans, Russians, and the United Nations also judged that Mr. Hussein had weapons, this will not change the recalcitrant fact that these parties did not accept that they posed enough of a threat to support an immediate war.

Second, had "all other nonviolent means failed" to disarm Mr. Hussein? Though the president is still fond of declaring, as he did in this year's first presidential debate, that "Saddam Hussein had no intention of disarming," the rest of us have perhaps not entered too deeply into the post-factual age not to acknowledge what we now know: that in fact Saddam Hussein did disarm, and that the international inspectors on the scene, given time and sufficient diplomatic support, would eventually have confirmed this—just as David Kay, the administration's arms inspector, was able to do in the war's aftermath. As Mr. Kay allowed himself to say in a moment of near-suicidal honesty, in the matter of the weapons the Iraqis "were telling the truth." But it is in posing his last several questions that the younger Mr. Powell becomes a truly heartbreaking figure—the questions about "gains and risks" and about consequences. How do we evaluate these? We can speak of the 1,200 Americans dead and 9,000 wounded, or even of the thousands of Iraqis who have died. But what objective do we weigh them against?

And finally: "How might the situation that we seek to alter, once it is altered by force, develop further and what might be the consequences?" The question is unflinching, but there is little evidence that the administration Secretary Powell served ever made a serious attempt to answer it. What would such an attempt have looked like? We know the answer; for in 1992 the general himself offered us an example of the "logical process" he had in mind, analyzing why President George H. W. Bush did not order our forces to take Baghdad in 1991:

"We must assume that the political objective of such an order would have been capturing Saddam Hussein," he wrote. "What purpose would it have served? And would serving that purpose have been worth the many more casualties that would have occurred? Would it have been worth the inevitable follow-up: major occupation forces in Iraq for years to come and a very expensive and complex American proconsulship in Baghdad? Fortunately for America, reasonable people at the time thought not."[3]

These lines carry with them the whiff of far-off times, a lost world of pragmatism that pre-dated the religious trappings of the war on terrorism. Today, "the major occupation forces" Mr. Powell warned against are fighting a guerrilla war in a country on the Persian Gulf, through which half the industrial world's oil passes—a country far more strategically important than Vietnam.

Begun as an ideological crusade, the war has now settled into something bloody, murderous and crude, with no "exit strategy" in sight. The war's beginning, built on the threat of weapons that did not exist, and its ending, which flickered to life so temptingly on the flight deck of the aircraft carrier USS *Abraham Lincoln* eighteen months ago, have disappeared, leaving American troops fighting and dying in a kind of lost, existential desert of the present. We may not have yet reached Colin Powell's vision of "half-hearted warfare for half-baked reasons that the American people could not understand." But we are well on the way.

The New York Times, November 21, 2004

We Are All Torturers Now

January 6, 2005

A T LEAST SINCE **WATERGATE,** Americans have come to take for granted a certain story line of scandal, in which revelation is followed by investigation, adjudication and expiation. Together, Congress and the courts investigate high-level wrongdoing and place it in a carefully constructed narrative, in which crimes are charted, malfeasance is explicated and punishment is apportioned as the final step in the journey back to order, justice and propriety.

When Alberto Gonzales takes his seat before the Senate Judiciary Committee today for hearings to confirm whether he will become attorney general of the United States, Americans will bid farewell to that comforting story line. The senators are likely to give full legitimacy to a path that the Bush administration set the country on more than three years ago, a path that has transformed the United States from a country that condemned torture and forbade its use to one that practices torture routinely. Through a process of redefinition largely overseen by Mr. Gonzales himself, a practice that was once a clear and abhorrent violation of the law has become in effect the law of the land.

Shortly after the 9/11 attacks, Americans began torturing prisoners, and they have never really stopped. However much these words have about them the ring of accusation, they must by now be accepted as fact. From Red Cross reports, Maj. Gen. Antonio M. Taguba's inquiry, James R. Schlesinger's Pentagon-sanctioned commission and other government and independent investigations, we have in our possession hundreds of accounts of "cruel, inhuman and degrading" treatment—to use a phrase of the Red Cross—"tantamount to torture."[1]

So far as we know, American intelligence officers, determined after Sept. 11 to "take the gloves off," began by torturing Qaeda prisoners. They used a number of techniques: "waterboarding," in which a prisoner is stripped, shackled, and submerged in water until he begins to lose consciousness, and other forms of near suffocation; sleep and sensory deprivation; heat and light and dietary manipulation; and "stress positions."

Eventually, these practices "migrated," in the words of the Schlesinger report, to Abu Ghraib prison in Iraq, where for a time last spring the marvel of digital technology allowed Americans to see what their soldiers were doing to prisoners in their name.[2]

Though the revelations of Abu Ghraib transfixed Americans for a time, in the matter of torture not much changed. After those in Congress had offered condemnations and a few hearings distinguished by their lack of seriousness; after the administration had commenced the requisite half-dozen investigations, none of them empowered to touch those who devised the policies; and after the low-level soldiers were placed firmly on the road to punishment—after all this, the issue of torture slipped back beneath the surface. Every few weeks now, a word or two reaches us from that dark, subterranean place. Take, for example, this account, offered by an unnamed F.B.I. counterterrorism official reporting in August, more than three months after the Abu Ghraib images appeared, on what he saw during a visit to Guantánamo:

> On a couple of occasions, I entered interview rooms to find a detainee chained hand and foot in a fetal position to the floor, with no chair, food or water. Most times they had urinated or defecated on themselves, and had been left there for 18 to 24 hours or more . . . When I asked the M.P.s what was going on, I was told that interrogators from the day prior had ordered this treatment, and the detainee was not to be moved. On another occasion . . . the detainee was almost unconscious on the floor, with a pile of hair next to him. He had apparently been literally pulling his own hair out throughout the night.[3]

This is a fairly mild example when judged against the accounts of the "abuses" that have entered the public record. I put quotation marks around the word "abuses" because most of these acts—as the F.B.I. agent acknowledged ("the interrogators from the day prior had ordered this treatment")—were in fact procedures, which would not have been possible without policies that had been approved by administration officials.

In the next few days we are likely to hear how Mr. Gonzales recommended strongly, against the arguments of the secretary of state and military lawyers, that prisoners in Afghanistan be denied the protection of the Geneva Conventions. We are also likely to hear how, under Mr. Gonzales's urging, lawyers in the Department of Justice contrived—when confronted with the obstacle that the United States had undertaken, by treaty and statute, to make torture illegal—simply to redefine the word to mean procedures that would produce pain "of an intensity akin to that which accompanies serious physical injury such as death or organ failure."[4] By this act of verbal legerdemain, interrogation techniques like waterboarding that plainly constituted torture suddenly became something less than that.

But what we are unlikely to hear, given the balance of votes in the Senate, are many voices making the obvious argument that with this record, Mr. Gonzales is unfit to serve as attorney general. So let me make it: Mr. Gonzales is unfit because the slow river of litigation is certain to bring before the next attorney general a raft of torture cases that challenge the very policies that he personally helped devise and put into practice. He is unfit because, while the attorney general is charged with upholding the law, the documents show that as White House counsel, Mr. Gonzales, in the matter of torture, helped his client to concoct strategies to circumvent it. And he is unfit, finally, because he has rightly become the symbol of the United States' fateful departure from a body of settled international law and human rights practice for which the country claims to stand.

On the other hand, perhaps it is fitting that Mr. Gonzales be confirmed. The system of torture has, after all, survived its disclosure. We have entered a new era; the traditional story line in which scandal leads to investigation and investigation leads to punishment has been supplanted by something else. Wrongdoing is still exposed; we gaze at the photographs and read the documents, and then we listen to the president's spokesman "reiterate," as he did last week, "the president's determination that the United States never engage in torture." And there the story ends.

At present, our government, controlled largely by one party only intermittently harried by a timorous opposition, is unable to mete out punishment or change policy, let alone adequately investigate its own war crimes. And, as administration officials clearly expect, and senators of both parties well understand, most Americans—the Americans who will not read the reports, who will soon forget the photographs and who will be loath to dwell on a repellent subject—are generally content to take the president at his word.

But reality has a way of asserting itself. In the end, as Gen. Joseph P. Hoar pointed out this week, the administration's decision on the Geneva Conventions "puts all American servicemen and women at risk that are serving in combat regions." For General Hoar—a retired commander of American forces in the Middle East and one of a dozen prominent retired generals and admirals to oppose Mr. Gonzales[5]—torture has a way of undermining the forces using it, as it did with the French Army in Algeria.

The general's concerns are understandable. The war in Iraq and the war on terrorism are ultimately political in character. Victory depends in the end not on technology or on overwhelming force but on political persuasion. By using torture, the country relinquishes the very ideological advantage—the promotion of democracy, freedom and human rights—that the president has so persistently claimed is America's most powerful weapon in defeating Islamic extremism. One does not reach democracy, or freedom, through torture.

By using torture, we Americans transform ourselves into the very caricature our enemies have sought to make of us. True, that miserable man who pulled out his hair as he lay on the floor at Guantánamo may eventually tell his interrogators what he knows, or what they want to hear. But for America, torture is self-defeating; for a strong country it is in the end a strategy of weakness. After Mr. Gonzales is confirmed, the road back—to justice, order and propriety—will be very long. Torture will belong to us all.

New York Times, January 6, 2005

The Real Election

March 31, 2005

I.

The essence of any insurgency, and its most decisive battle space, is the psychological. [It's] armed theater: You have protagonists on the stage, but they're sending messages to wider audiences. Insurgency is about perceptions, beliefs, expectations, legitimacy, and will. Insurgency is not won by killing insurgents, not won by seizing territory; it's won by altering the psychological factors that are most relevant.[1]

JUST PAST DAWN on January 30, Iraq's Election Day—the fourth of the U.S. occupation's "turning points," after the fall of Baghdad, the capture of Saddam Hussein, and the "handover of sovereignty"—I stood at the muddy gates of Muthana Air Base outside Baghdad watching the sun rise, pink and full, into a white-streaked sky; then, feeling a sudden tremor beneath my feet, I started abruptly: The explosion was loud and, judging by the vibrations, not far off.

I turned to the U.S. Army captain who had been waiting with me next to Muthana's inner watchtower, and saw his lazy smile. He had been watching me.

"Mortar?"

"No, sir," Captain Vic Schairstein said. "That would be an IED"—an improvised explosive device. "That's the low pitch. We've taken so many mortar rounds by now you can tell by the pitch whether they're 60s, 82s, whatever. It's like an outfielder judging a pop fly by the sound of the bat."

My face, puffy from a sleepless night spent on a makeshift canvas cot tracking incessant small-arms fire and intermittent explosions, must have betrayed concern, for here the captain's smile broadened. "Don't worry, sir, it's early," he said. "They haven't had time to go to the mosque to get all jihaded up yet." Then, as my ride appeared—two armored BMWs rumbling slowly up the muddy track toward blast walls and barbed wire—and the captain helped me gather up my flak jacket and my helmet, he offered a final word for the day ahead. "Those VBIEDs"—"vee-bids," vehicle-borne improvised explosive devices, military-speak for car bombs—"have you ever noticed how they all tend to be white? I guess that's for purity. Anyway, you might keep that in mind."

The sun was turning orange now, the sky pale gray, and the gathering light on Baghdad's streets revealed no cars, pure white or otherwise. Driving slowly through the monumental avenues and great squares we saw . . . nothing: no cars, no people, no dogs. Nothing moved. It was as if every living thing had been felled by a sudden and lethal plague.

Until we noticed, wrapped about a distant bridge, a glittering necklace of barbed wire; within it a clutter of tan American armor and, among the Humvees and blast barriers and tank traps, a sudden burst of movement. What was happening? We slowed and squinted, and in a moment realized with a start that *we* were happening: The soldiers had seen us—four or five assault rifles were leveled at us and the big gun of one of the Humvees was swinging to. Arms flailed in the air; mouths opened and closed; they were shouting, though we could hear no words. A soldier sprinting forward, rifle pointed at us in his right hand, held up a clear signal with his left: We were not to move.

Three or four minutes passed; we were scrutinized through binoculars, telescopic sights. We kept our eyes forward and our hands visible and waited. Up ahead now, at the bridge checkpoint, I saw the soldier motion with his rifle: come forward—but slowly, slowly. We crept forward and then about two hundred yards from the checkpoint we were halted once more and with his rifle the soldier motioned the driver from the car.

Our Iraqi driver, who worked for the *New York Times*, glanced back at me. He was to have collected me at Muthana the night before but, in the gathering darkness and the imminent curfew, American soldiers had stopped him. "When I started to get out of the car they fired over my head," he told me. "The soldier ordered me to kneel on the ground and then to walk to him on my knees with my hands on my head. Then he rested his gun barrel here"—he touched his temple—"and said, 'They're going to search the car. If *anything* happens, the first thing I do is shoot you.'"

Slowly, carefully, our driver opened the door and stepped out; hands on head, he advanced slowly toward the bridge, a sleepwalker in the suddenly bright morning. Several guns were trained on him but most remained fixed on us. No one spoke. When he reached the soldiers he was roughly seized, his shirt pulled up, torso searched, credentials checked; then a full body search. Finally, guns raised, they motioned us out. Arms up, we inched forward; at last we in turn were seized, frisked, credentials checked; led finally into a small barbed-wire enclosure: wait here. The driver was sent back to the car, ordered to bring the vehicle forward—but slowly, slowly. We stood watching as the soldiers encircled the car, opened the hood, trunk, passed a mirror under the chassis, began dismantling the panels in the trunk . . .

ONTO THE DUSTY TAN CITY that was Baghdad, dotted with Saddam's grandiloquent Babylonian modernism—the minatory office towers, the ceremonial gates and looming monuments—had been superimposed, in the two years of occupation, an entirely new architecture: a harsh gray city of a distinctive high-brutalist style. Oceans of concrete had flowed into Baghdad, miles of barbed wire had been unwound around and through it, mountains of sand had been poured over it, and everywhere these most basic of elements had been gathered and shaped into the distinctive forms I saw before me. Lining the bridge, "Berliners": twelve- or fifteen-foot-high blast barriers of rough concrete named for the Berlin Wall that now marched by the hundreds and thousands along Baghdad's main streets and avenues, masking vast parts of the city from public view.

Blocking the bridge and surrounding the American armor were Jersey barriers: concrete half-walls that, arranged in the form of "chicanes," or tight S-curve-shaped obstacles, force vehicles to slow and stop. Tank traps: massive iron bars welded together in crisscross forms so that they resemble the jacks a giant child might play with, typically draped, as here, in flamboyant swirls of barbed wire. Hesco barriers: huge square canvas bags reinforced with steel and filled with dirt or cinderblocks, the giant's version of a sandbag, stacked in their scores and hundreds. Sandbagged bunkers. Steel watchtowers. Iron blast doors. X-ray machines. Magnetometers. Sniffer dogs. And the ubiquitous squads of men, some uniformed but more often not, armed with 9 mms and AK-47s and the clear willingness to fire first and ask questions afterward.

A year before the concrete elements of this new architecture had encircled the ministries, the public buildings, the military bases, and of course the hotels. Now, under the pressure of hundreds of suicide bombings and kidnappings, they had metastasized, acquiring extra layers and additional cordons, and moved in force into residential neighborhoods, surrounding the homes of government workers and politicians and businessmen and finally doctors and lawyers and anyone of any means or power, anyone who might conceivably, for reasons political or financial, be targeted for assassination or kidnapping.

So pervasively had this new rough concrete and steel world imposed itself that one evening in the well-to-do district of Mansour, my driver, bewildered by the proliferating roadblocks and checkpoints and chicanes, found himself unable to find a way out of a neighborhood he had known well for decades but that had now become something alien and unfamiliar, a kind of gray mirror-maze of security. In barely two years the capital on which Saddam had lavished such money and attention had been entirely recast, by architects at least as megalomaniacal: the insurgents and their suicide bombers, and the security experts, military and civilian, who took on the task of thwarting them. Together the bombers and their adversaries had built this city, one bomb at a time—hundreds of bombs since the occupation began, killing at least two thousand people.[2] And on Election Day it remained a work in progress.

The half-dozen checkpoints at which we were stopped, the barbed-wire pen in which I now stood—all of this was the insurgents' doing; for they had let it be known, in the couple of weeks before Election Day, that "150 car bombs and 250 suicide attackers are prepared to strike in coming days." Asked at a "Green Zone" news conference about these reports, which CNN had attributed to "intelligence sources" cited by "a top Iraqi police official,"[3] the interior minister of the interim government remarked that "the insurgents were trying to increase talks and rumors on the streets." Indeed, and they had succeeded; now the Americans were responding.

Fifteen months before, on the second day of what came to be known as the Ramadan Offensive, when insurgents in the space of forty-five minutes struck Red Cross headquarters and several police stations with suicide car bombs, I had an appointment with a top American intelligence officer. When I finally arrived at the meeting, a bit late and somewhat disheveled— I had happened to be near the Red Cross when the car bomber struck[4]—I remarked that such attacks were probably impossible to prevent. You're quite wrong in that, the officer had responded sharply:

> We could stop these things entirely if we were willing to do what was necessary. We could stop car bombers if we stopped all driving. But that would be inconsistent with another, overriding imperative—letting Iraqis live a reasonably normal life. That would prevent the return to normalcy that we need to have. Politically at least, we can't take those steps. Which means that in the end these things are not a military problem, they are a political problem. We could stop them but to do it, we would have to *shut the place down*.

On Election Day, the political imperatives were different. In the months before, the Americans had increased the number of U.S. troops in the country by 20,000 and had mounted a series of aggressive offensive operations against the insurgency that had reduced Fallujah to near rubble, had sent insurgents in other cities of the Sunni heartland underground, and had filled to capacity Abu Ghraib and the other military prisons in the country with suspected AIFs (or "anti-Iraqi forces," as the Americans now called the insurgents).[5]

At the checkpoint, as U.S. Army helicopters passed low overhead, the soldiers finished searching the car and brought us out from behind the barbed wire, searched us again more thoroughly, then let us put our bags back in the car and allowed us to depart. I asked the military's translator—his face covered by a brown knit ski mask, to prevent insurgents retaliating against him or his family—whether he would vote that day; he said nothing. "Speaking for this sector, sir," his sergeant put in quickly, "the polling sites are real secure. The question is whether people will come out of their houses and vote. If they want to, it's real secure." He gestured all around him. "No way a car bomb gets through this." On Election Day, there would be no "vehicle-borne improvised explosive devices" for there would be no vehicles. On Election Day the American military in Iraq had shut the place down.[6]

II.

And so, on Election Day, we walked. We had stopped at the bureau after the long drive across Baghdad—watched a leader of the Independent Electoral Commission of Iraq tell the Green Zone television cameras, "We plead with Iraqi citizens to take the risk, if they still consider it a risk, to perform their duty . . ."—and then, with the car useless, we set out on foot. We came out slowly, hesitantly into the mid-morning, a couple of security people walking ahead, passed through a checkpoint or two, then advanced down the middle of the nearly deserted main avenue. It was odd, after the armored cars and flak jackets and helmets, to be walking on the street: I felt unnaturally light, but also vulnerable, as if I had escaped from captivity and soon would be recaptured. The shift in point of view—from behind the walls of the barricaded hotel or the armored car to the strangely deserted streets—was jarring.

Three weeks after Election Day, in a newspaper report of a series of attacks on February 19, an image caught my eye:

> In a fifth suicide attack, a suicide bomber rode a bicycle into a tent full of mourners at a funeral in southwest Baghdad, killing at least three people and wounding 55. Afterward, from a high building nearby, it could be seen that parts of human bodies below had been gathered together in piles.[7]

What struck me about this was not the macabre innovation (the use of a bicycle on the Shiite holiday of Ashura, when cars would be suspect); nor the peculiar dimness of the bomber, who, unlike his four somewhat abler colleagues, managed to strike the wrong target. ("He was an idiot," a housewife wounded in the attack told a reporter. "It was a Sunni funeral, not a Shiite one.") It was rather the point of view, which offers the reader a picture of the aftermath "from a high building nearby" from which one can discern "parts of human bodies below . . . gathered together in piles." The image is striking, grotesque; but the point of view is lofty, aerial—distant.

Increasingly during the past year the newspaper reader and especially the television viewer has been looking at the great complicated tableau of occupied Iraq through a highly constricted lens, as if trying to examine an enormous history painting by squinting through a straw. For more than a year insurgents have targeted foreigners for assassination and especially for kidnapping—at last count, 189 "foreign nationals" had been kidnapped in Iraq, and thirty-three of them had been killed.[8] What began as acts of political terror, complete with televised pleas on the part of the victim and in a few cases televised beheadings, quickly devolved into a cash business, in which criminal gangs, spotting a foreigner, seize him or her as a "target of opportunity" and market their prize to insurgent groups, who televise pictures of their acquisition and can earn, when they like, a substantial amount of cash in exchange for release. "You must realize," a Jordanian security expert told me in Amman, "that as a foreigner the moment you enter Iraq now, you are transformed from human being into commodity—a commodity worth half a million to a million dollars."

As suicide bombers and kidnappers created the new concrete city, they have driven reporters off the streets, away from the restaurants and shops, away from "ordinary Iraqis," forcing them to sheath themselves in flak jackets and helmets, move in armored cars, and finally take refuge behind blast walls and barbed wire and armed guards in fortress-like hotels. Television reporters, politically the most important journalists on the ground—for they supply information, and above all images, to by far the largest number of people—are in practical terms the most vulnerable; their large "footprint"—the cameras and other equipment they carry, the crews they bring to carry it—makes them most conspicuous, and thus most restricted.

The correspondent you watch signing off his nightly report from the war zone with his name, network, and dateline "Baghdad" is usually speaking from the grounds or the roof of a fully guarded, barricaded hotel—a virtual high-rise bunker—and may not have ventured out of that hotel all day, having spent his time telephoning, reading the wires, and scrutinizing footage from Iraqi "stringers" who have been out on the street. When he does leave the hotel it will be in an armored car, surrounded by armed security guards, and very likely the destination will be a news conference or briefing or arranged interview in the vast American-ruled bunker known as the Green Zone. Sorties beyond Baghdad, or even to "hot" neighborhoods within the capital, can usually be undertaken only by "embedding" with American troops. It is a bizarre, dispiriting way to work, this practice of "hotel journalism,"[9] producing not only a highly constrained picture of the country and its politics but, on the part of the journalist, constant fear, anxiety, and ultimately intense frustration. "I am getting out of here, getting out soon," one network correspondent told me. When I asked why—for American foreign correspondents Iraq is, after all, the most important story going—he shrugged: "It's no longer honest work."

ALL OF THIS MADE Election Day, thanks to the massive security presence on the street, a day of liberation for the foreign press. Journalists were set free. We walked, and looked, flinching now and again at the sound of mortars; and pretty soon—by now it was mid-morning—we began to see people, first one or two here and there, and eventually a group of three blue-shirted policemen walking abreast, all holding up purple fingers. They were jolly, laughing, giddy in the near-deserted street. Above the din of a couple of U.S. Army Apache helicopters passing overhead, they gladly told us their votes:

one for Iyad Allawi, the present interim prime minister (whose face could be seen staring out from posters on many of the walls and concrete barriers around us, vowing "Strong Leadership, A Safe Country"); one for a list sympathetic to Muqtada al-Sadr, the young Shiite rebel (who, officially, was boycotting the vote), and one for List 169, the great Shiite coalition gathered together under the auspices of Grand Ayatollah Ali al-Sistani (whose face, though he supposedly favored no particular list, was similarly ubiquitous on the 169 posters).

A few hundred yards down the street we came upon a barrier manned by a handful of Iraqi policemen and plainclothes security men. A cop wearing a ski mask gave me my seventh or eighth body search of the day, checked our credentials, wrote something down, took our cell phones, and finally, after some low-voiced discussion among the police, waved us by the concrete barrier. We walked down a short path, turned into a small courtyard, and were startled to see revealed . . . The Spectacle.

Filling the few hundred or so square yards of the courtyard of this small neighborhood school were perhaps a couple of hundred Iraqis—old men in threadbare suits, women in traditional *abeyas*, young men in tracksuits and sweatshirts—gathered together in five or six lines, talking in low voices, flinching at the occasional explosion, looking about somewhat self-consciously, but all waiting patiently to vote. I hesitated a moment. After all the Election Day images of mass carnage that had filled our heads during the last week, conveyed in rumors and threats and grim questions at news conferences, this gathering of people—the sheer public *vulnerability* of them—seemed shocking. We plunged in among them.

Vox populi, or, in journalese, *vox pops*: man-on-the-street interviews in today's Iraq, a rare, almost unheard-of pleasure. Such journalistic toe-dippings are generally attempts, among other things, to find "the great quote"—the person who manages to articulate, in his or her own way, the broader narrative, the plotline already determined. Such exercises are thus simultaneously a matter of evidence gathering and of analytic confirmation. On this day we wanted answers to questions which had to do, at bottom, with why these Iraqis had risked their lives to come out to vote: our questions, that is, fit in with the central narrative about the war, and especially about why America had fought it, what had brought America to Iraq in the first place. Before us, after months of explosions and suicide bombings and dead soldiers and civilians, stood people who might seem the perfect symbols of liberation, who embodied the war's purpose in a single image: Iraqis waiting to express their voices in an exercise of democratic will. We needed now the image to speak.

FOR THE MOST PART, though, they didn't seem to want to cooperate. Why are you here, I asked a young man wearing a Ray's Pool Hall shirt. "Why?" He looked surprised. "To vote." But why, why did you come? "We are a normal people, an independent people. We want to be like other people, to vote. We need security, stability—that's all." He volunteered nothing about Saddam, about the war, the Americans, the occupation; when asked he seemed reluctant, like many of his neighbors in line, to discuss them.

A young woman, wearing a beautiful sea-green *abeya*, asked by a colleague about Saddam, grew annoyed. "No, this is not about Saddam. Forget Saddam. I am an engineer and I have no job. Neither does my husband." Then, a bit exasperated, "We want a *normal country*."

I looked behind her: On the low roof of the school building, a policeman stood watching with his AK-47. We asked an old man, wearing a checked *kaffiyeh* and a white beard, what he expected from the elections. He too seemed reluctant. "I already talked to the press," he grumbled. But what did he hope to accomplish by voting? He thought a moment. "Now we'll have good officials. Now we'll talk to them and they'll talk to us. Before they just hit you, beat you, punished you." He was eighty-three, had lived, he said, under eight governments. "The monarchy was the best. There was stability then."

Among these mostly middle-class people I heard this thought expressed again and again: the desperate need for security, for stability—for normalcy. Several, when I asked why they had come out to vote, looked at me with varying degrees of surprise or condescension and said, "So we will have a government. Look around, we need a government." Some, when I asked whom they'd voted for, refused, smiling: This is democracy—secret ballot.

Others, when asked several times, offered the names of candidates—but only the famous ones, those leaders of the main lists; for of course the "security situation"—the bombing, the kidnappings, the beheadings—had prevented any public campaign: there had been no rallies, no door-to-door canvassing for votes, no chance even to learn who was running. Indeed, many of the candidate lists were, in effect, secret. Only the names of the party leaders were widely known: Iyad Allawi, Abdel Aziz al-Hakim, Ibrahim Jaafari, and a few others, all of them among the exiles returning from London and Washington and Tehran, who had dominated the American-appointed governing bodies since the fall of Saddam.

It seemed like a country fair, this gathering, a kind of journalistic grand buffet: the beautiful women in their traditional dress, young men in T-shirts and sweatpants, old men in their *kaffiyehs*. We met engineers and builders and schoolteachers, an elegant former government minister, and "one of the last eight Jews in Baghdad." (This last man, who would give his name only as Samir, told me he could be certain of his exalted status because "I know all the other ones.") After the "hotel journalism" and all the fear, it was a delight to move among this crowd. And yet, as a political matter, these people did not offer the desired symbolic justifications, the capstone in the narrative building already under construction that day. What would be the verbal equivalent for the images that already were dominating the world's television screens: the lines of people, the purple fingers, the explosions in the background that made the voters flinch but not waver? We needed someone to say: Thank heaven Saddam has gone, thank heaven the Americans came, thank you for giving us democracy. And no one—at least here in this voting place in Baghdad—seemed to want to say it.

MY FAVORITE VOTER that morning was the former minister, Dr. Ahmed Dujaily—an elegant eighty-year-old engineer wearing a traditional *sidari* on his head and a beautifully tailored blue pinstriped suit—who had served as minister of agricultural reform in 1966 and 1967 ("the last brief time of good government") and who offered, after we complimented him on his suit ("Ah yes"—smiling, gazing down at himself—"I wear this for weddings, parties . . . elections also"), in a richly cadenced English bespeaking a fine English education, what I took to be the most enlightening dialogue of the day:

So, we began, for whom had he voted?

"In fact, I voted for List 169 . . ."—the so-called Sistani List.

That is the Shiite List? You are Shiite?

"Yes, I am Shiite but I am Iraqi before anything. Religion is for myself. This election is for Iraq."

And why are you voting?

"I feel I must give service to my country and I voted for these people, Abdel al-Hakim and Jaafari, because I trust them. . . ."

And how do you feel about Saddam? a colleague put in.

"Well . . . of course, I am happy the Saddam regime is abolished. He is not human, he is an animal. . . ."

Who abolished it?

"Who? Why, he did."

Well (trying another tack, and gesturing upward, at the buzzing Blackhawks), those helicopters, who are they?

"They are the Americans."

Yes, and are they good or bad?

"Good or bad?" A puzzled pause. "Not good or bad. They are the Americans."

No, no, what I wanted to ask . . .

He knew, of course, what we wanted to ask. He smiled and tried to be helpful. "Listen, we thank Americans for destroying the regime of Saddam but they did many things that were not required of the country. They made many, many mistakes here. I know what the Americans want." He smiled; he was matter-of-fact. "They want military bases. They want to dominate the new regime. They want the oil."

"Saddam was a criminal, a lot of people were killed. Now these others"—he gestured in the vague direction of the most recent explosion; he meant the insurgents—"they are bombing one place, another place. This doesn't help, this does nothing for the country." Then, a bit of history—from the 1920s but clearly relevant to him today: "When the British kicked out the Turks, the

Shia, you know, fought the British also. But the Sunnis stuck with the British, and the British took those who stuck with them and formed a government."

Now, clearly, it was the Sunnis who were fighting, and the Shiites who were "sticking with" the occupying power, this time the Americans. "But the elections should be carried forward, whether the Americans like the results or not," he said. "This is determined by the people. We want an independent country." As for the Americans, "when they came people were happy but they made many, many mistakes in the occupation. After all these mistakes, now they will not leave. They will have their military headquarters established in Iraq and when they leave I do not know. The bases, the oil . . . And of course"—he gestured at the voters, grinned, and, with a philosophical roll of his eyes, said—"they are using Iraq for propaganda for their own elections: 'Democracy and the Republicans.'"

III.

It was after one when we returned to the bureau to find the television pictures—scores of Iraqis in line, waving their purple fingers, smiling in incomparably powerful images of democracy—already making their way over the airwaves to greet the early risers in London, New York, and Washington. The voices over the images were enthusiastic, almost breathless, informing the viewer that officially 72 percent of Iraqis had turned out at the polls, a dramatic but mysterious number that within the hour would be transformed into "probably more than 80 percent"—mysterious because, as I realized after a moment, there was simply no way, physically, to have arrived at such a figure.

Television correspondents in Baquba and at other locations in the ravaged "Sunni Triangle" were reporting, with great excitement, heavy turnouts—"The Sunnis are voting, the Sunnis are voting"—another piece of news which seemed unlikely and turned out, sadly, to be as much wishful thinking as the turnout figures themselves. The numbers were withdrawn that evening—the spokesman for the Independent Electoral Commission of Iraq confessing that the 72 and 80 percent figures, repeated by on-air correspondents all day and run continuously as a crawl on CNN and other networks, had in fact been based on "estimated voter flow to the polls." But by that time they had done their work; the numbers, the breathless reports, all were needed to match the pictures that alone would determine that day's story.

A voice from the Muthana Air Base a few hours before floated into my mind. It belonged to Captain Aaron Kalloch, an operations officer, who at the end of a long interview, with both of us growing tired, had spoken about a suicide car bomb attack the week before, a high-profile attempt on the headquarters and, presumably, on the life of interim Prime Minister Iyad Allawi. "*Boom!* Remember that, the other day, that IED attack in Kindi Traffic Circle?" He leaned forward and nearly shouted, as he gave his mocking version of the television broadcaster: "*Boom!!* Headlines on CNN: Chaos in Baghdad! Prime minister nearly assassinated! *Boom!*"

He leaned back in his chair. "Well, was it? Was it 'chaos in Baghdad'? I mean, let's take a look at that attack for a moment. What happened? The guy didn't get close to Allawi's headquarters. Allawi wasn't even there. The guy slightly wounded two people. And the guy killed . . . *himself!* I mean, *he killed himself!* That *was it!* And that was the lead story of the day on CNN."

"I ask you, should it have been?" He paused and glared at me, then answered his own question. "*Nothing happened!* Allawi was perfectly safe. The guy killed *himself.* . . . Nothing happened—except that they scored an IO victory, and that stuff really pisses me off." IO was military-speak for "information operation"—an event intended to turn the vital political war at the heart of any insurgency in one's favor.

"The simple fact is that how things are perceived here is almost as important as how things actually are. And here IO is everything. Insurgency is relatively easy for the enemy because he's got his own personal international IO platform. . . ." He paused, waited.

And what is that?

"The U.S. media!" he said. He paused again. "The fact is, whoever wins the IO battle here, wins. And this thing tomorrow, this is *the* event. If Iraqis come out to the polls, if people vote . . . I mean, there will be violence but the question is how effective that violence will be. If the AIF"—anti-Iraqi forces—"come after this—and they will, they have to—and people do vote, then that is it. They are done, it's over. They may last one or two more years but they've lost. And they know it. And that's the IO. Whoever wins the IO battle here, wins."

AT THE POLLING PLACE I had admired the voters and their strangely complicated response to what it was they were doing. But I realized that "the IO" was not there but here before me now, on the television set, with the lines of voters and their smiles and purple fingers and the heavy breathing about "more than 80 percent" turnout. This was the IO. There was indeed violence, as Captain Kalloch had said—that day would see in fact nine suicide bombings and perhaps fifty dead and its 260 insurgent attacks were the highest number of any single day of the occupation.[10] But that violence would not interfere with the IO, for that was established by the images early that day, and the violence, however pervasive, would not get on television. And it would not get on television in part because Iraq was effectively *locked down*—the absence of vehicles meant explosions were limited to the size of a bomb that could be carried by a man on foot—and the mobility of journalists was severely restricted (we could see only as many polling places as we could reach on foot, in my case two) and in part because of well-thought-out "IO rules"—the most effective one being, in retrospect, that cameras, still and video, were admitted only into five predetermined and highly protected polling places.

I visited one of these in the afternoon, in the heavily Shia commercial neighborhood of Karrada, and found there a level of security far above that of the little school: One had to pass through cordons of U.S. military, Iraqi military, Iraqi police, and finally Electoral Commission security. Four layers of security; each checked credentials and identification and the first three performed searches. There would be no suicide bombing before the television cameras.

DURING THE MORE THAN two years since the Iraq war began Americans have seen on their television screens its four major turning points: the fall of Baghdad, the capture of Saddam Hussein, the "transfer of authority" to the interim Allawi government, and now the Iraq elections. Each has been highly successful as an example of the management of images—the toppling of Saddam's statue, the intrusive examination of the unkempt former dictator's mouth and beard, the handing of documents of sovereignty from coalition leader L. Paul Bremer to Iraqi leader Iyad Allawi, the voters happily waving their purple fingers—and each image has powerfully affirmed the broader story of what American leaders promised citizens the Iraq war would be. They promised a war of liberation to unseat a brutal dictator, rid him of his weapons of mass destruction, and free his imprisoned people, who would respond with gratitude and friendship, allowing American troops to return very quickly home.

With the exception of the failure to find WMDs, the images have fit so cleanly into the original narrative of the war that they could almost have been designed at the time the war was being planned. And because these images fit so closely with the story of what Americans were told the war would be, they have welcomed each of them with enthusiasm. Unfortunately, after the images faded, the events on the ground that followed refused to fit that original narrative. In this the January 30 election has been no exception.

As I write, two months have passed since Iraqis went to the polls and voted—58 percent of those who were registered, according to official figures, though likely fewer than half of those eligible.[11] No government has taken office, the national assembly elected in January still hasn't chosen a prime minister, and the interim administration of Iyad Allawi has long since entered a state of drift, with ministries frozen in place, unable to issue orders or carry out policies. And, as General John Abizaid, the commander of U.S. forces in the Middle East, told CNN on March 27, "the longer we have a delay in the formation of an Iraqi government, the more uncertainty there will be. The more uncertainty, the greater chance for escalated violence." Though as an "information" operation, the elections had been an enormous success—particularly in the United States, where the images reinvigorated the conviction, at least for a time, that the war made sense—as a political fact in Iraq the results of the election were much more mixed.

"The real problem is the story here can't be shown in images," said my friend, the television correspondent who, disgusted with "hotel journalism," had left Baghdad before the election. "You can't show the fear here with a television picture. You can't show the atmosphere of paranoia. The story escapes the images—the tools—that we have to tell it." On Election Day, for example, the images could show clearly the beautiful, intricate ballot, with its hundred and ten-odd parties and coalitions—but not the fact that there were really only three choices, each with enormous sources of money: the Kurdish list, with its funding from the Kurdish autonomous government, in the north; the Shiite list, with its image of Ayatollah Ali al-Sistani and its funding from the mosques in the south and the Iranians across the border; and the Allawi list, with its control of the interim government and its access to that government's money and television. On Election Day, Kurds voted for the Kurdish list, Shiites voted for the Shiite list, a relative handful (about 12 percent) voted for the Allawi list—and the Sunnis made their presence known by not voting at all. The election, in effect, was an ethnic census.

In the ideal vision of a post-Saddam Iraq, the people would have come out to bless the new political dispensation, in which the Shiites assume their rightful place as the majority party and the Kurds and especially the Sunnis, the erstwhile elite who throughout its modern history had ruled Iraq, take their place as proud, active, and politically vital minorities. This is not what happened on January 30. Shiites won a majority, but not enough under the peculiar rules imposed by the occupation to form a government. Kurds, turning out in enormous numbers for their single list, were overrepresented in the new assembly and gained, in effect, a veto over who would form the new government. And finally, little more than one in ten Iraqis came out and voted for Allawi, dashing American hopes that he could remain in power.

TELEVISION CAMERAS, which could only show what was before them in the polling places, could not show the day's critical actors, the Sunnis, who did not appear. The real story on Election Day was that the Sunnis didn't vote. If the election was to mark the point from which Iraqis would settle their differences through politics and not through violence, it failed; for those responsible for the insurgency—not only those planting suicide bombs but those running the organizations responsible for them and the leaders of the community that has shown itself sympathetic enough to the insurgents' cause to shelter them—did not take part. The political burden of the elections was to bring those who felt frightened or alienated by the new dispensation into the political process, so they could express their opposition through politics and not through violence; the task, that is, was to attract Sunnis to the polls and thereby to isolate the extremists. And in this, partly because of an electoral system that the Sunnis felt, with some reason, was unfairly stacked against them, the election failed.

The images could not show, finally, the peculiar system of government under which those elected are now struggling to function—a system in effect imposed by the American occupation in the interim constitution, known as the "transitional administrative law." That system demands, among other things, that the national assembly bring together two thirds of its votes to confirm a government, a requirement found in no other parliamentary system in the world. That requirement is an artifact of the larger conundrum of Iraqi politics: It was demanded by America's critical Iraqi ally, the Kurds, who are deeply ambivalent about their connection to and role in an Iraqi state dominated by Shiites, and it was supported by the Americans. In effect the two-thirds requirement, and the political impasse it has fostered, is a legacy of the Americans' reluctance to confront the logical implication of their war to unseat Saddam Hussein and his Sunni elite: that there will come to power in Iraq a government dominated by the Shia, powerfully influenced by Islamic law and favorably inclined toward the United States' foremost enemy in the region, the Islamic Republic of Iran.

New York Review of Books, April 28, 2005

The Secret Way to War

May 12, 2005

I.

IT WAS OCTOBER 16, 2002, and the United States Congress had just voted to authorize the president to go to war against Iraq. When George W. Bush came before members of his cabinet and Congress gathered in the East Room of the White House and addressed the American people, he was in a somber mood befitting a leader speaking frankly to free citizens about the gravest decision their country could make.

The 107th Congress, the president said, had just become "one of the few called by history to authorize military action to defend our country and the cause of peace." But, he hastened to add, no one should assume that war was inevitable. Though "Congress has now authorized the use of force," the president said emphatically, "I have not ordered the use of force. I hope the use of force will not become necessary." The president went on:

> Our goal is to fully and finally remove a real threat to world peace and to America. Hopefully this can be done peacefully. Hopefully we can do this without any military action. Yet, if Iraq is to avoid military action by the international community, it has the obligation to prove compliance with all the world's demands. It's the obligation of Iraq.

Iraq, the president said, still had the power to prevent war by "declaring and destroying all its weapons of mass destruction"—but if Iraq did not declare and destroy those weapons, the president warned, the United States would "go into battle, as a last resort."

It is safe to say that, at the time, it surprised almost no one when the Iraqis answered the president's demand by repeating their claim that in fact there were no weapons of mass destruction. As we now know, the Iraqis had in fact destroyed these weapons, probably years before George W. Bush's ultimatum: "The Iraqis"—in the words of chief U.S. weapons inspector David Kay—"were telling the truth."

As Americans watch their young men and women fighting in the third year of a bloody counterinsurgency war in Iraq—a war that has now killed more than 1,600 Americans and tens of thousands of Iraqis—they are left to ponder "the unanswered question" of what would have happened if the United Nations weapons inspectors had been allowed—as all the major powers except the United Kingdom had urged they should be—to complete their work. What would have happened if the UN weapons inspectors had been allowed to prove, before the United States went "into battle," what David Kay and his colleagues finally proved afterward?

THANKS TO A FORMERLY SECRET memorandum published by the London *Sunday Times* on May 1, 2005, during the run-up to the British elections, we now have a partial answer to that question. The memo, which records the minutes of a meeting of Prime Minister Tony Blair's senior foreign policy and security officials, shows that even as President Bush told Americans in October 2002 that he "hope[d] the use of force will not become necessary"—that such a decision depended on whether or not the Iraqis complied with his demands to rid themselves of their weapons of mass destruction—the president had in fact already definitively decided, at least three months before, to choose this "last resort" of going "into battle" with Iraq. Whatever the Iraqis chose to do or not do, the president's decision to go to war had long since been made.

On July 23, 2002, eight months before American and British forces invaded, senior British officials met with Prime Minister Tony Blair at 10 Downing Street to discuss Iraq. The gathering, similar to an American "principals meeting," brought together Geoffrey Hoon, the defense secretary; Jack Straw, the foreign secretary; Lord Goldsmith, the attorney general; John Scarlett, the head of the Joint Intelligence Committee, which advises the prime minister; Sir Richard Dearlove, also known as "C," the head of MI6 (the equivalent of the CIA); David Manning, the equivalent of the national security adviser; Admiral Sir Michael Boyce, the chief of the Defense Staff (or CDS) equivalent to the chairman of the Joint Chiefs; Jonathan Powell, Blair's chief of staff; Alastair Campbell, director of strategy (Blair's communications and political adviser); and Sally Morgan, director of government relations.

After John Scarlett began the meeting with a summary of intelligence on Iraq—notably, that "the regime was tough and based on extreme fear" and that thus the "only way to overthrow it was likely to be by massive military action," "C" offered a report on his visit to Washington, where he had conducted talks with George Tenet, his counterpart at the CIA, and other high officials. This passage is worth quoting in full:

C reported on his recent talks in Washington. There was a perceptible shift in attitude. Military action was now seen as inevitable. Bush wanted to remove Saddam, through military action, justified by the conjunction of terrorism and WMD. But the intelligence and facts were being fixed around the policy. The NSC had no patience with the UN route, and no enthusiasm for publishing material on the Iraqi regime's record. There was little discussion in Washington of the aftermath after military action.[1]

Seen from today's perspective this short paragraph is a strikingly clear template for the future, establishing these points:

1. By mid-July 2002, eight months before the war began, President Bush had decided to invade and occupy Iraq.
2. Bush had decided to "justify" the war "by the conjunction of terrorism and WMD."
3. Already "the intelligence and facts were being fixed around the policy."
4. Many at the top of the administration did not want to seek approval from the United Nations (going "the UN route").
5. Few in Washington seemed much interested in the aftermath of the war.

We have long known, thanks to Bob Woodward and others, that military planning for the Iraq war began as early as November 21, 2001, after the president ordered Secretary of Defense Donald Rumsfeld to look at "what it would take to protect America by removing Saddam Hussein if we have to," and that Secretary Rumsfeld and General Tommy Franks, who headed Central Command, were briefing American senior officials on the progress of military planning during the late spring and summer of 2002; indeed, a few days after the meeting in London leaks about specific plans for a possible Iraq war appeared on the front pages of the *New York Times* and the *Washington Post*.

WHAT THE DOWNING STREET MEMO confirms for the first time is that President Bush had decided, no later than July 2002, to "remove Saddam, through military action," that war with Iraq was "inevitable"—and that what remained was simply to establish and develop the modalities of justification; that is, to come up with a means of "justifying" the war and "fixing" the "intelligence and facts . . . around the policy." The great value of the discussion recounted in the memo, then, is to show, for the governments of both countries, a clear hierarchy of decision making. By July 2002 at the latest, war had been decided on; the question at issue now was how to justify it—how to "fix," as it were, what Blair will later call "the political context." Specifically, though by this point in July the president had decided to go to war, he had not yet decided to go to the United Nations and demand inspectors; indeed, as "C" points out, those on the National Security Council—the senior security officials of the U.S. government—"had no patience with the UN route, and no enthusiasm for publishing material on the Iraqi regime's record." This would later change, largely as a result of the political concerns of these very people gathered together at 10 Downing Street.

After Admiral Boyce offered a brief discussion of the war plans then on the table and the defense secretary said a word or two about timing—"the most likely timing in U.S. minds for military action to begin was January, with the timeline beginning 30 days before the U.S. congressional elections"—Foreign Secretary Jack Straw got to the heart of the matter: not whether or not to invade Iraq but how to justify such an invasion:

> The Foreign Secretary said he would discuss [the timing of the war] with Colin Powell this week. It seemed clear that Bush had made up his mind to take military action, even if the timing was not yet decided. But the case was thin. Saddam was not threatening his neighbors, and his WMD capability was less than that of Libya, North Korea or Iran.

Given that Saddam was not threatening to attack his neighbors and that his weapons of mass destruction program was less extensive than those of a number of other countries, how does one justify attacking? Foreign Secretary Straw had an idea:

> We should work up a plan for an ultimatum to Saddam to allow back in the UN weapons inspectors. This would also help with the legal justification for the use of force.

The British realized they needed "help with the legal justification for the use of force" because, as the attorney general pointed out, rather dryly, "the desire for regime change was not a legal base for military action." Which is to say, the simple desire to overthrow the leadership of a given sovereign country does not make it legal to invade that country; on the contrary. And, said the attorney general, of the "three possible legal bases: self defense, humanitarian intervention, or [United Nations Security Council] authorization," the first two "could not be the base in this case." In other words, Iraq was not attacking the United States or the United Kingdom, so the leaders could not claim to be acting in self defense; nor was Iraq's leadership in the process of committing genocide, so the United States and the United Kingdom could not claim to be invading for humanitarian reasons.[*][2] This left Security Council authorization as the only conceivable legal justification for war. But how to get it?

---

[*] The latter charge might have been given as a reason for intervention in 1988, for example, when the Iraqi regime was carrying out its Anfal campaign against the Kurds; at that time, though, the Reagan administration—comprising many of the same officials who would later lead the invasion of Iraq—was supporting Saddam in his war against Iran and kept largely silent. The second major killing campaign of the Saddam regime came in 1991, when Iraqi troops attacked Shiites in the south who had rebelled against the regime in the wake of Saddam's defeat in the Gulf War; the first Bush administration, despite President George H. W. Bush's having urged Iraqis to "rise up against the dictator, Saddam Hussein," and despite the presence of hundreds of thousands of American troops within miles of the killing, stood by and did nothing.

AT THIS POINT in the meeting Prime Minister Tony Blair weighed in. He had heard his foreign minister's suggestion about drafting an ultimatum demanding that Saddam let back in the United Nations inspectors. Such an ultimatum could be politically critical, said Blair—but only if the Iraqi leader turned it down:

> The Prime Minister said that it would make a big difference politically and legally if Saddam refused to allow in the UN inspectors. Regime change and WMD were linked in the sense that it was the regime that was producing the WMD. . . . If the political context were right, people would support regime change. The two key issues were whether the military plan worked and whether we had the political strategy to give the military plan the space to work.

Here the inspectors were introduced, but as a means to create the missing *casus belli*. If the UN could be made to agree on an ultimatum that Saddam accept inspectors, and if Saddam then refused to accept them, the Americans and the British would be well on their way to having a legal justification to go to war—the attorney general's third alternative of authorization by the UN Security Council.

Thus, the idea of UN inspectors was introduced not as a means to avoid war, as President Bush repeatedly assured Americans, but as a means to make war possible. War had been decided on; the problem under discussion here was how to make, in the prime minister's words, "the political context . . . right." The "political strategy"—at the center of which, as with the Americans, was weapons of mass destruction, for "it was the regime that was producing the WMD"—must be strong enough to give "the military plan the space to work." Which is to say, once the allies were victorious the war would justify itself. The demand that Iraq accept UN inspectors, especially if refused, could form the political bridge by which the allies could reach their goal: "regime change" through "military action."

But there was a problem: As the foreign secretary pointed out, "on the political strategy, there could be U.S./UK differences." While the British considered legal justification for going to war critical—they, unlike the Americans, were members of the International Criminal Court—the Americans did not. Mr. Straw suggested that given "U.S. resistance, we should explore discreetly the ultimatum." The defense secretary, Geoffrey Hoon, was more blunt, arguing

> that if the Prime Minister wanted UK military involvement, he would need to decide this early. He cautioned that many in the United States did not think it worth going down the ultimatum route. It would be important for the Prime Minister to set out the political context to Bush.

The key negotiation in view at this point, in other words, was not with Saddam over letting in the United Nations inspectors—both parties hoped he would refuse to admit them, and thus provide the justification for invading. The key negotiation would be between the Americans, who had shown "resistance" to the idea of involving the United Nations at all, and the British, who were more concerned than their American cousins about having some kind of legal fig leaf for attacking Iraq. Three weeks later, Foreign Secretary Straw arrived in the Hamptons to "discreetly explore the ultimatum" with Secretary of State Powell, perhaps the only senior American official who shared some of the British concerns. As Straw told the secretary, in Bob Woodward's account, "If you are really thinking about war and you want us Brits to be a player, we cannot be unless you go to the United Nations."[3]

II.

Britain's strong support for the "UN route" that most American officials so distrusted was critical in helping Powell in the bureaucratic battle over going to the United Nations. As late as August 26, Vice President Dick Cheney had appeared before a convention of the Veterans of Foreign Wars and publicly denounced "the UN route." Asserting that "simply stated, there is no doubt that Saddam Hussein now has weapons of mass destruction [and] there is no doubt that he is amassing them to use against our friends, against our allies, and against us," Cheney advanced the view that going to the United Nations would itself be dangerous:

A return of inspectors would provide no assurance whatsoever of his compliance with UN resolutions. On the contrary, there is great danger that it would provide false comfort that Saddam was somehow "back in the box."

Cheney, like other administration "hard-liners," feared "the UN route" not because it might fail but because it might succeed and thereby prevent a war that they were convinced had to be fought.

As Woodward recounts, it would finally take a personal visit by Blair on September 7 to persuade President Bush to go to the United Nations:

For Blair the immediate question was this: Would the United Nations be used? He was keenly aware that in Britain the question was, Does Blair believe in the UN? It was critical domestically for the prime minister to show his own Labour Party, a pacifist party at heart, opposed to war in principle, that he had gone the UN route. Public opinion in the UK favored trying to make international institutions work before resorting to force. Going through the UN would be a large and much-needed plus.[4]

The president now told Blair that he had decided "to go to the UN" and the prime minister, according to Woodward, "was relieved." After the session with Blair, Bush later recounts, he walked into a conference room and told the British officials gathered there that "your man has got *cojones*." ("And of course these Brits don't know what *cojones* are," Bush tells Woodward.) Henceforth this particular conference with Blair would be known, Bush declares, as "the *cojones* meeting."

That September the attempt to sell the war began in earnest, for, as White House Chief of Staff Andrew Card had told the *New York Times* in an unusually candid moment, "You don't roll out a new product in August." At the heart of the sales campaign was the United Nations. Thanks in substantial part to Blair's prodding, George W. Bush would come before the UN General Assembly on September 12 and, after denouncing the Iraqi regime, announce that "we will work with the UN Security Council for the necessary resolutions." The main phase of public diplomacy—giving the war a "political context," in Blair's phrase—had begun. Though "the UN route" would be styled as an attempt to avoid war, its essence, as the Downing Street memo makes clear, was a strategy to make the war possible, partly by making it politically palatable.

AS IT TURNED OUT, however—and as Cheney and others had feared—the "UN route" to war was by no means smooth, or direct.

Though Powell managed the considerable feat of securing unanimous approval for Security Council Resolution 1441, winning even Syria's support, the allies differed on the key question of whether or not the resolution gave United Nations approval for the use of force against Saddam, as the Americans contended it did, or whether a second resolution would be required, as the majority of the council, and even the British, conceded it would. Sir Jeremy Greenstock, the British ambassador to the UN, put this position bluntly on November 8, the day Resolution 1441 was passed:

> We heard loud and clear during the negotiations about "automaticity" and "hidden triggers"—the concerns that on a decision so crucial we should not rush into military action. . . . Let me be equally clear. . . . There is no "automaticity" in this Resolution. If there is a further Iraqi breach of its disarmament obligations, the matter will return to the Council for discussion as required. . . . We would expect the Security Council then to meet its responsibilities.

Vice President Cheney could have expected no worse. Having decided to travel down "the UN route," the Americans and British would now need a second resolution to gain the necessary approval to attack Iraq. Worse, Saddam frustrated British and American hopes, as articulated by Blair in the July 23 meeting, that he would simply refuse to admit the inspectors and thereby offer the allies an immediate *casus belli*. Instead, hundreds of inspectors entered Iraq, began to search, and found . . . nothing. January, which Defense Secretary Hoon had suggested was the "most likely timing in U.S. minds for military action to begin," came and went, and the inspectors went on searching.

On the Security Council, a majority—led by France, Germany, and Russia—would push for the inspections to run their course. President Jacques Chirac of France later put this argument succinctly in a television interview just as the war was about to begin:

> France is not pacifist. We are not anti-American either. We are not just going to use our veto to nag and annoy the United States. But we just feel that there is another option, another way, another more normal way, a less dramatic way than war, and that we have to go through that path. And we should pursue it until we've come [to] a dead end, but that isn't the case.[5]

Where would this "dead end" be found, however, and who would determine that it had been found? Would it be the French, or the Americans? The logical flaw that threatened the administration's policy now became clear. Had the inspectors found weapons, or had they been presented with them by Saddam Hussein, many who had supported the resolution would argue that the inspections regime it established had indeed begun to work—that by multilateral action the world was succeeding, peacefully, in "disarming Iraq." As long as the inspectors found no weapons, however, many would argue that the inspectors "must be given time to do their work"—until, in Chirac's words, they "came to a dead end." However that point might be determined, it is likely that, long before it was reached, the failure to find weapons would have undermined the administration's central argument for going to war—"the conjunction," as "C" had put it that morning the previous July, "of terrorism and WMD." And as we now know, the inspectors would never have found weapons of mass destruction.[6]

VICE PRESIDENT CHENEY had anticipated this problem, as he had explained frankly to Hans Blix, the chief UN weapons inspector, during an October 30 meeting in the White House. Cheney, according to Blix,

> stated the position that inspections, if they do not give results, cannot go on forever, and said the United States was "ready to discredit inspections in favor of disarmament." A pretty straight way, I thought, of saying that if we did not soon find the weapons of mass destruction that the United States was convinced Iraq possessed (though they did not know where), the United States would be ready to say that the inspectors were useless and embark on disarmament by other means.[7]

Indeed, the inspectors' failure to find any evidence of weapons came in the wake of a very large effort launched by the administration to put before the world evidence of Saddam's arsenal, an effort spearheaded by George W.

Bush's speech in Cincinnati on October 7, and followed by a series of increasingly lurid disclosures to the press that reached a crescendo with Colin Powell's multimedia presentation to the UN Security Council on February 5, 2003. Throughout the fall and winter, the administration had "rolled out the product," in Card's phrase, with great skill, making use of television, radio, and all the print press to get its message out about the imminent threat of Saddam's arsenal. ("Think of the press," as Joseph Goebbels had advised, "as a great keyboard on which the government can play.")

As the gap between administration rhetoric about enormous arsenals—"we know where they are," asserted Donald Rumsfeld—and the inspectors' empty hands grew wider, that gap, as Cheney had predicted, had the effect in many quarters of undermining the credibility of the United Nations process itself. The inspectors' failure to find weapons in Iraq was taken to discredit the worth of the inspections, rather than to cast doubt on the administration's contention that Saddam possessed large stockpiles of weapons of mass destruction.

Oddly enough, Saddam's only effective strategy to prevent war at this point might have been to reveal and yield up some weapons, thus demonstrating to the world that the inspections were working. As we now know, however, he had no weapons to yield up. As Blix remarks, "It occurred to me [on March 7] that the Iraqis would be in greater difficulty if . . . there truly *were* no weapons of which they could 'yield possession.'" The fact that, in Blix's words, "the UN and the world had succeeded in disarming Iraq without knowing it"—that the UN process had been successful—meant, in effect, that the inspectors would be discredited and the United States would go to war.

President Bush would do so, of course, having failed to get the "second resolution" so desired by his friend and ally, Tony Blair. Blair had predicted, that July morning on Downing Street, that the "two key issues were whether the military plan worked and whether we had the political strategy to give the military plan the space to work." He seems to have been proved right in this. In the end his political strategy only half worked: The Security Council's refusal to vote a second resolution approving the use of force left "the UN route" discussed that day incomplete, and Blair found himself forced to follow the United States without the protection of international approval. Had the military plan "worked"—had the war been short and decisive rather than long, bloody, and inconclusive—Blair would perhaps have escaped the political damage the war has caused him. A week after the Downing Street memo was published in the *Sunday Times*, Tony Blair was reelected, but his majority in Parliament was reduced, from 161 to 67. The Iraq war, and the damage it had done to his reputation for probity, was widely believed to have been a principal cause.

IN THE UNITED STATES, on the other hand, the Downing Street memorandum has attracted little attention. As I write, no American newspaper has published it and few writers have bothered to comment on it. The war continues, and Americans have grown weary of it; few seem much interested now in discussing how it began, and why their country came to fight a war in the cause of destroying weapons that turned out not to exist. For those who want answers, the Bush administration has followed a simple and heretofore largely successful policy: blame the intelligence agencies. Since "the intelligence and facts were being fixed around the policy" as early as July 2002 (as "C," the head of British intelligence, reported upon his return from Washington), it seems a matter of remarkable hubris, even for this administration, that its officials now explain their misjudgments in going to war by blaming them on "intelligence failures"—that is, on the intelligence that they themselves politicized. Still, for the most part, Congress has cooperated. Though the Senate Intelligence Committee investigated the failures of the CIA and other agencies before the war, a promised second report that was to take up the administration's political use of intelligence—which is, after all, the critical issue—was postponed until after the 2004 elections, then quietly abandoned.

In the end, the Downing Street memo, and Americans' lack of interest in what it shows, has to do with a certain attitude about facts, or rather about where the line should be drawn between facts and political opinion. It calls to mind an interesting observation that an unnamed "senior adviser" to President Bush made to a reporter last fall:

> The aide said that guys like me [i.e., reporters and commentators] were "in what we call the reality-based community," which he defined as people who "believe that solutions emerge from your judicious study of discernible reality." I nodded and murmured something about enlightenment principles and empiricism. He cut me off. "That's not the way the world really works anymore," he continued. "We're an empire now, and when we act, we create our own reality. And while you're studying that reality— judiciously, as you will—we'll act again, creating other new realities, which you can study too, and that's how things will sort out. We're history's actors . . . and you, all of you, will be left to just study what we do."[8]

Though this seems on its face to be a disquisition on religion and faith, it is of course an argument about power, and its influence on truth. Power, the argument runs, can shape truth: Power, in the end, can determine reality, or at least the reality that most people accept—a critical point, for the administration has been singularly effective in its recognition that what is most politically important is not what readers of the *New York Times* believe but what most Americans are willing to believe. The last century's most innovative authority on power and truth, Joseph Goebbels, made the same point but rather more directly:

> There was no point in seeking to convert the intellectuals. For intellectuals would never be converted and would anyway always yield to the stronger, and this will always be "the man in the street." Arguments must therefore

be crude, clear and forcible, and appeal to emotions and instincts, not the intellect. Truth was unimportant and entirely subordinate to tactics and psychology.[9]

I thought of this quotation when I first read the Downing Street memorandum; but I had first looked it up several months earlier, on December 14, 2004, after I had seen the images of the newly reelected President George W. Bush awarding the Medal of Freedom, the highest civilian honor the United States can bestow, to George Tenet, the former director of central intelligence; L. Paul Bremer, the former head of the Coalition Provisional Authority in Iraq; and General (ret.) Tommy Franks, the commander who had led American forces during the first phase of the Iraq war. Tenet, of course, would be known to history as the intelligence director who had failed to detect and prevent the attacks of September 11 and the man who had assured President Bush that the case for Saddam's possession of weapons of mass destruction was "a slam dunk." Franks had allowed the looting of Baghdad and had generally done little to prepare for what would come after the taking of Baghdad. ("There was little discussion in Washington," as "C" told the Prime Minister on July 23, "of the aftermath after military action.") Bremer had dissolved the Iraqi army and the Iraqi police and thereby created 400,000 or so available recruits for the insurgency. One might debate their ultimate responsibility for these grave errors, but it is difficult to argue that these officials merited the highest recognition the country could bestow.

Of course truth, as the master propagandist said, is "unimportant and entirely subordinate to tactics and psychology." He of course would have instantly grasped the psychological tactic embodied in that White House ceremony, which was one more effort to reassure Americans that the war the administration launched against Iraq has been a success and was worth fighting. That barely four Americans in ten are still willing to believe this suggests that as time goes on and the gap grows between what Americans see and what they are told, membership in the "reality-based community" may grow along with it. We will see. Still, for those interested in the question of how our leaders persuaded the country to become embroiled in a counterinsurgency war in Iraq, the Downing Street memorandum offers one more confirmation of the truth. For those, that is, who want to hear.

Taking Stock of the Forever War

September 11, 2005

I.

S ELDOM HAS AN IMAGE so clearly marked the turning of the world. One of man's mightiest structures collapses into an immense white blossom of churning, roiling dust, metamorphosing in fourteen seconds from hundred-story giant of the earth into towering white plume reaching to heaven. The demise of the World Trade Center gave us an image as newborn to the world of sight as the mushroom cloud must have appeared to those who first cast eyes on it. I recall vividly the seconds flowing by as I sat gaping at the screen, uncomprehending and unbelieving, while Peter Jennings's urbane, perfectly modulated voice murmured calmly on about flights being grounded, leaving unacknowledged and unexplained—*unconfirmed*—the incomprehensible scene unfolding in real time before our eyes. "Hang on there a second," the famously unflappable Jennings finally stammered—the South Tower had by now vanished into a boiling caldron of white smoke—"I just want to check one thing . . . because . . . we now have. . . . What do we have? We don't? . . ." Marveling later that "the most powerful image was the one I actually didn't notice while it was occurring," Jennings would say simply that "it was *beyond our imagination*."

Looking back from this moment, precisely four years later, it still seems almost inconceivable that ten men could have done that—could have *brought those towers down*. Could have *imagined* doing what was "beyond our imagination." When a few days later, the German composer Karlheinz Stockhausen remarked that this was "the greatest work of art in the history of the cosmos," I shared the anger his words called forth but couldn't help sensing their bit of truth: "What happened there—spiritually—this jump out of security, out of the everyday, out of life, that happens sometimes to a small extent in art, too."[1] No "to a small extent" here: However profoundly evil the art, the sheer immensity and inconceivability of the attack had forced Americans instantaneously to "jump out of security, out of the everyday, out of life" and had thrust them through a portal into a strange and terrifying new world, where the inconceivable, the unimaginable, had become brutally possible.

In the face of the unimaginable, small wonder that leaders would revert to the language of apocalypse, of crusade, of "moral clarity." Speaking at the National Cathedral just three days after the attacks, President Bush declared that while "Americans do not yet have the distance of history . . . our responsibility to history is already clear: to answer these attacks and *rid the world of evil.*" Astonishing words—imaginable, perhaps, only from an American president, leading a people given naturally in times of crisis to enlisting national power in the cause of universal redemption. "The enemy is not a single political regime or person or religion or ideology," declared the National Security Strategy of the United States of America for 2002. "The enemy is terrorism—premeditated, politically motivated violence perpetrated against innocents." Not Islamic terrorism or Middle Eastern terrorism or even terrorism directed against the United States: terrorism itself. "Declaring war on 'terror,'" as one military strategist later remarked to me, "is like declaring war on air power." It didn't matter; apocalypse, retribution, redemption were in the air, and the grandeur of the goal must be commensurate with the enormity of the crime. Within days of the attacks, President Bush had launched a "global war on terror."

Today marks four years of war. Four years after the attack on Pearl Harbor, U.S. troops ruled unchallenged in Japan and Germany. During those forty-eight months, Americans created an unmatched machine of war and decisively defeated two great enemies.

How are we to judge the global war on terror four years on? In this war, the president had warned, "Americans should not expect one battle but a lengthy campaign." We could expect no "surrender ceremony on a deck of a battleship," and indeed, apart from the president's abortive attempt on the USS *Abraham Lincoln* to declare victory in Iraq, there has been none. Failing such rituals of capitulation, by what "metric"—as the generals say—can we measure the progress of the global war on terror?

FOUR YEARS AFTER the collapse of the towers, evil is still with us and so is terrorism. Terrorists have staged spectacular attacks, killing thousands, in Tunisia, Bali, Mombasa, Riyadh, Istanbul, Casablanca, Jakarta, Madrid, Sharm el Sheik and London, to name only the best known. Last year, they mounted 651 "significant terrorist attacks," triple the year before and the highest since the State Department started gathering figures two decades ago. One hundred ninety-eight of these came in Iraq, Bush's "central front of the war on terror"—nine times the year before. And this does not include the hundreds of attacks on U.S. troops. It is in Iraq, which was to serve as the first step in the "democratization of the Middle East," that insurgents have taken terrorism to a new level, killing well over 4,000 people since April in Baghdad alone; in May, Iraq suffered 90 suicide bombings. Perhaps the "shining example of democracy" that the administration promised will someday come, but for now Iraq has become a grotesque advertisement for the power and efficacy of terror.

As for the "terrorist groups of global reach," al Qaeda, according to the president, has been severely wounded. "We've captured or killed two-thirds of their known leaders," he said last year. And yet however degraded al Qaeda's operational capacity, nearly every other month, it seems, Osama bin Laden or one of his henchmen appears on the world's television screens to expatiate on the ideology and strategy of global jihad and to urge followers on to more audacious and more lethal efforts. This, and the sheer number and breadth of terrorist attacks, suggest strongly that al Qaeda has now become al Qaedaism—that under the American and allied assault, what had been a relatively small, conspiratorial organization has mutated into a worldwide political movement, with thousands of followers eager to adopt its methods and advance its aims. Call it "viral al Qaeda," carried by strongly motivated next-generation followers who download from the Internet's virtual training camp a perfectly adequate trade-craft in terror. Nearly two years ago, Secretary of Defense Donald H. Rumsfeld, in a confidential memorandum, posed the central question about the war on terror: "Are we capturing, killing or deterring and dissuading more terrorists every day than the madrassas and the radical clerics are recruiting, training and deploying against us?"[2] The answer is clearly no. "We have taken a ball of quicksilver," says the counterinsurgency specialist John Arquilla, "and hit it with a hammer."

What has helped those little bits of quicksilver grow and flourish is, above all, the decision to invade and occupy Iraq, which has left the United States bogged down in a brutal, highly visible counterinsurgency war in the heart of the Arab world. Iraq has become a training ground that will temper and prepare the next generation of jihadist terrorists and a televised stage from which the struggle of radical Islam against the "crusader forces" can be broadcast throughout the Islamic world. "Islamic extremists are exploiting the Iraqi conflict to recruit new anti-U.S. jihadists," Porter J. Goss, director of the C.I.A., told the Senate in February. "These jihadists who survive will leave Iraq experienced in, and focused on, acts of urban terrorism. They represent a potential pool of contacts to build transnational terrorist cells, groups and networks in Saudi Arabia, Jordan and other countries."[3]

As the Iraq war grows increasingly unpopular in the United States— scarcely a third of Americans now approve of the president's handling of the war, and scarcely 4 in 10 think it was worth fighting—and as more and more American leaders demand that the administration "start figuring out how we get out of there" (in the words of Senator Chuck Hagel, a Republican), Americans confront a stark choice: whether to go on indefinitely fighting a politically self-destructive counterinsurgency war that keeps the jihadists increasingly well supplied with volunteers or to withdraw from a post–Saddam Hussein Iraq that remains chaotic and unstable and beset with civil strife and thereby hand al Qaeda and its allies a major victory in the war on terror's "central front."

Four years after we watched the towers fall, Americans have not succeeded in "ridding the world of evil." We have managed to show ourselves, our friends and most of all our enemies the limits of American power. Instead of fighting the real war that was thrust upon us on that incomprehensible morning four years ago, we stubbornly insisted on fighting a war of the imagination, an ideological struggle that we defined not by frankly appraising the real enemy before us but by focusing on the mirror of our own obsessions. And we have finished—as the escalating numbers of terrorist attacks, the grinding Iraq insurgency, the overstretched American military and the increasing political dissatisfaction at home show—by fighting precisely the kind of war they wanted us to fight.

II.

Facing what is beyond imagination, you find sense in the familiar. Standing before Congress on September 20, 2001, George W. Bush told Americans why they had been attacked. "They hate our freedoms," the president declared. "Our freedom of speech, our freedom to vote and assemble and disagree with each other." As for al Qaeda's fundamentalist religious mission:

> We are not deceived by their pretenses to piety. We have seen their kind before. They are the heirs of all the murderous ideologies of the twentieth century. By sacrificing human life to serve their radical visions—by abandoning every value except the will to power—they follow in the path of fascism, and Nazism, and totalitarianism. And they will follow that path all the way, to where it ends: in history's unmarked grave of discarded lies.[4]

Stirring words, and effective, for they domesticated the unthinkable in the categories of the accustomed. The terrorists are only the latest in a long line of "evildoers." Like the Nazis and the Communists before them, they are Americans' evil twins: tyrants to our free men, totalitarians to our democrats. The world, after a confusing decade, had once again split in two. However disorienting the horror of the attacks, the "war on terror" was simply a reprise of the Cold War. As Harry S. Truman christened the Cold War by explaining to Americans how, "at the present moment in world history, nearly every nation must choose between alternative ways of life," George W. Bush declared his global war on terror by insisting that "every nation, in every region, now has a decision to make. Either you are with us, or you are with the terrorists." The echo, as much administration rhetoric since has shown, was not coincidental. Terrorists, like Communists, despised America not because of what our country did but because of who we are. Hating "our values" and "our freedoms," the evildoers were depicted as deeply irrational and committed to a nihilistic philosophy of obliteration, reawakening for

Americans the sleeping image of the mushroom cloud. "This is not aimed at our policies," Henry Kissinger intoned. "This is aimed at our existence."

Such rhetoric not only fell easily on American ears. It provided a familiar context for a disoriented national-security bureaucracy that had been created to fight the Cold War and was left, at its ending, without clear purpose. "Washington policy and defense cultures still seek out cold-war models," as members of the Defense Science Board, a Defense Department task force commissioned to examine the war on terror, observed in a report last year. "With the surprise announcement of a new struggle, the U.S. government reflexively inclined toward cold-war-style responses to the new threat, without a thought or a care as to whether these were the best responses to a very different strategic situation."[5]

Al Qaeda was not the Nazis or the Soviet Communists. Al Qaeda controlled no state, fielded no regular army. It was a small, conspiratorial organization, dedicated to achieving its aims through guerrilla tactics, notably a kind of spectacular terrorism carried to a level of apocalyptic brutality that the world had not before seen. Mass killing was the necessary but not the primary aim, for the point of such terror was to mobilize recruits for a political cause—to move sympathizers to act—and to tempt the enemy into reacting in such a way as to make that mobilization easier. And however extreme and repugnant al Qaeda's methods, its revolutionary goals were by no means unusual within Islamist opposition groups throughout the Muslim world. "If there is one overarching goal they share," wrote the authors of the Defense Science Board report, "it is the overthrow of what Islamists call the 'apostate' regimes: the tyrannies of Egypt, Saudi Arabia, Pakistan, Jordan and the gulf states. . . . The United States finds itself in the strategically awkward—and potentially dangerous—situation of being the longstanding prop and alliance partner of these authoritarian regimes. Without the U.S., these regimes could not survive. Thus the U.S. has strongly taken sides in a desperate struggle that is both broadly cast for all Muslims and country-specific."[6]

The broad aim of the many-stranded Salafi movement, which includes the Muslim Brotherhood of Egypt and the Wahhabis of Saudi Arabia and of which al Qaeda is one extreme version, is to return Muslims to the ancient ways of pure Islam—of Islam as it was practiced by the Prophet Muhammad and his early followers in the seventh century. Standing between the more radical Salafi groups and their goal of a conservative Islamic revolution are the "apostate regimes," the "idolators" now ruling in Riyadh, Cairo, Amman, Islamabad and other Muslim capitals. All these authoritarian regimes oppress their people: on this point al Qaeda and those in the Bush administration who promote "democratization in the Arab world" agree. Many of the Salafists, however, see behind the "near enemies" ruling over them a "far enemy" in Washington, a superpower without whose financial and military support the Mubarak regime, the Saudi royal family and the other conservative autocracies of the Arab world would fall before their attacks. When the United States sent hundreds of thousands of American troops to Saudi Arabia after Saddam Hussein invaded Kuwait, al Qaeda seized on the perfect issue: The "far enemy" had actually come and occupied the Land of the Two Holy Places and done so at the shameful invitation of the "near enemy"—the corrupt Saudi dynasty. As bin Laden observed of the Saudis in his 1996 "Declaration of Jihad": "This situation is a curse put on them by Allah for not objecting to the oppressive and illegitimate behavior and measures of the ruling regime: ignoring the divine Shariah law; depriving people of their legitimate rights; allowing the Americans to occupy the Land of the Two Holy Places."

But how to "reestablish the greatness of this Ummah"—the Muslim people—"and to liberate its occupied sanctities"? On this bin Laden is practical and frank: because of "the imbalance of power between our armed forces and the enemy forces, a suitable means of fighting must be adopted, i.e., using fast-moving light forces that work under complete secrecy. In other words, to initiate a guerrilla warfare." Such warfare, depending on increasingly spectacular acts of terrorism, would be used to "prepare and instigate the Ummah . . . against the enemy."[7] The notion of "instigation," indeed, is critical, for the purpose of terror is not to destroy your enemy directly but rather to spur on your sleeping allies to enlightenment, to courage and to action. It is a kind of horrible advertisement, meant to show those millions of Muslims who sympathize with al Qaeda's view of American policy that something can be done to change it.

III.

Fundamentalist Islamic thought took aim at America's policies, not at its existence. Americans tend to be little interested in these policies or their history and thus see the various Middle East cataclysms of the last decades as sudden, unrelated explosions lighting up a murky and threatening landscape, reinforcing the sense that the 9/11 attacks were not only deadly and appalling but also irrational, incomprehensible: that they embodied pure evil. The central strand of American policy—unflinching support for the conservative Sunni regimes of the Persian Gulf—extends back sixty years, to a legendary meeting between Franklin D. Roosevelt and King Saud aboard an American cruiser in the Great Bitter Lake in Egypt. The American president and the Saudi king agreed there on a simple bond of interest: The Saudis, rulers over a sparsely populated but incalculably wealthy land, would see their power guaranteed against all threats, internal and external. In return, the United States could count on a stable supply of oil, developed and pumped by American companies. This policy stood virtually unthreatened for more than three decades.

The eruption of Iran's Islamic revolution in 1978 dealt a blow to this compact of interests and cast in relief its central contradictions. The shah, who owed his throne to a covert C.I.A. intervention that returned him to power in 1953, had been a key American ally in the gulf, and the Islamic revolution that swept him from power showed at work what was to become a familiar dynamic: "friendly" autocrats ruling over increasingly impatient and angry peoples who evidence resentment if not outright hostility toward the super-power ally, in whom they see the ultimate source of their own repression.

Iran's Islamic revolution delivered a body blow to the Middle East status quo not unlike that landed by the French Revolution on the European auto-cratic order two centuries before; it was ideologically aggressive, inherently expansionist and deeply threatening to its neighbors—in this case, to the United States' Sunni allies, many of whom had significant Shia minorities, and to Iraq, which, though long ruled by Sunnis, had a significant Shia majority. Ayatollah Khomeini's virulent and persistent calls for Saddam Hussein's overthrow, and the turmoil that had apparently weakened the Iranian armed forces, tempted Saddam Hussein to send his army to attack Iran in 1980. American policy makers looked on this with favor, seeing in the bloody Iran-Iraq war the force that would blunt the revolutionary threat to America's allies. Thus President Reagan sent his special envoy Donald Rumsfeld to Baghdad in 1983 to parlay with Hussein, and thus the administration sup-ported the dictator with billions of dollars of agricultural credits, supplied the Iraqis with hundreds of millions of dollars in advanced weaponry through Egypt and Saudi Arabia and provided Hussein's army with satellite intelli-gence that may have been used to direct chemical weapons against the massed infantry charges of Iranian suicide brigades.

The Iraqis fought the Iranians to a standstill but not before ripples from Iran's revolution threatened to overwhelm American allies, notably the Saudi dynasty, whose rule was challenged by radicals seizing control of the Grand Mosque in Mecca in November 1979, and the Egyptian autocracy, whose ruler, Anwar el-Sadat, was assassinated by Islamists as he presided over a mil-itary parade in October 1981. The Saudis managed to put down the revolt, killing hundreds. The Egyptians, under Hosni Mubarak, moved with ruth-less efficiency to suppress the Islamists, jailing and torturing thousands, among them Osama bin Laden's current deputy, Ayman al-Zawahiri. Merci-less repression by both autocracies' effective security services led thousands to flee abroad.

Many went to Afghanistan, which the Soviet Red Army occupied in 1979 to prop up its own tottering client, then under threat from Islamic insur-gents—mujahedeen, or "holy warriors," who were being armed by the United States. "It was July 3, 1979, that President Carter signed the first directive for secret aid to the opponents of the pro-Soviet regime in Kabul," Zbigniew Brzezinski, Carter's national security adviser, recalled in 1998. "And that very day, I wrote a note to the president in which I explained to him that in my opinion this aid was going to induce a Soviet military inter-vention." It was a strategy of provocation, for the gambit had the effect of "drawing the Russians into the Afghan trap. . . . The day that the Soviets offi-cially crossed the border, I wrote to President Carter: We now have the opportunity of giving to the U.S.S.R. its Vietnam War."[8]

If, to the Americans, supporting the Afghan mujahedeen seemed an excellent way to bleed the Soviet Union, to the Saudis and other Muslim regimes, supporting a "defensive jihad" to free occupied Muslim lands was a means to burnish their tarnished Islamic credentials while exporting a growing and dangerous resource (frustrated, radical young men) so they would indulge their taste for pious revolution far from home. Among the thousands of holy warriors making this journey was the wealthy young Saudi Osama bin Laden, who would set up the Afghan Services Bureau, a "helping organization" for Arab fighters that gathered names and contact information in a large database, which would eventually lend its name to an entirely new organization. Though the Afghan operation was wildly successful, as judged by its American creators—"What is most important to the history of the world?" Brzezinski said in 1998. "Some stirred-up Muslims or the liberation of Central Europe and the end of the Cold War?"—it had at least one unexpected result: It created a global jihad movement, led by veteran fighters who were convinced that they had defeated one superpower and could defeat another.

The present jihad took shape in the backwash of forgotten wars. After the Soviet Army withdrew in defeat, the United States lost interest in Afghanistan, leaving the mujahedeen forces to battle for the ruined country in an eight-year blood bath from which the Taliban finally emerged victorious. In the gulf, after eight years of fantastically bloody combat, Saddam Hussein forced the Iranians to sign a cease-fire, a "victory" that left his regime heavily armed, bloodied and bankrupt. To pay for his war, Hussein had borrowed tens of billions of dollars from the Saudis, Kuwaitis and other neighbors, and he now demanded that these debts be forgiven—he had incurred them, as he saw it, defending the lenders from Khomeini—and that oil prices be raised. The Kuwaitis' particularly aggressive refusal to do either led Hussein, apparently believing that the Americans would accept a *fait accompli*, to invade and annex the country.

The Iraqi Army flooding into Kuwait represented, to bin Laden, the classic opportunity. He rushed to see the Saudi leaders, proposing that he defend the kingdom with his battle-tested corps of veteran holy warriors. The Saudis listened patiently to the pious young man—his father, after all, had been one of the kingdom's richest men—but did not take him seriously. Within a week, King Fahd had agreed to the American proposal, carried by Dick Cheney, then the secretary of defense, to station American soldiers—"infidel armies"—in the Land of the Two Holy Places. This momentous decision led to bin Laden's final break with the Saudi dynasty.

The American presence, and the fatal decision to leave American forces stationed in Saudi Arabia as a trip-wire or deterrent even after Hussein had been defeated, provided bin Laden with a critical propaganda point, for it gave to his worldview, of a Muslim world under relentless attack, and its central argument, that the "unjust and renegade ruling regimes" of the Islamic world were in fact "enslaved by the United States," a concrete and vivid reality. The "near enemies" and their ruthless security services had proved resistant to direct assault, and the time had come to confront directly the one antagonist able to bring together all the jihadists in a single great battle: the "far enemy" across the sea.

IV.

The deaths of nearly 3,000 people, the thousands left behind to mourn them, the great plume hanging over Lower Manhattan carrying the stench of the vaporized buildings and their buried dead: Mass murder of the most abominable, cowardly kind appears to be so at the heart of what happened on this day four years ago that it seems beyond grotesque to remind ourselves that for the attackers those thousands of dead were only a means to an end. Not the least disgusting thing about terrorism is that it makes objects of human beings, makes use of them, exploits their deaths as a means to accomplish something else: to send a message, to force a concession, to advertise a cause. Though such cold instrumentality is not unknown in war—large-scale bombing of civilians, "terror bombing," as it used to be known, does much the same thing—terrorism's ruthless and intimate randomness seems especially appalling.

Terror is a way of talking. Those who employed it so unprecedentedly on 9/11 were seeking not just the large-scale killing of Americans but to achieve something by means of the large-scale killing of Americans. Not just large-scale, it should be added: spectacular.

The asymmetric weapons that the nineteen terrorists used on 9/11 were not only the knives and box cutters they brandished or the fuel-laden airliners they managed to commandeer but, above all, that most American of technological creations: the television set. On 9/11, the jihadists used this weapon with great determination and ruthlessness to attack the most powerful nation in the history of the world at its point of greatest vulnerability: at the level of spectacle. They did it by creating an image, to repeat Peter Jennings's words, "beyond our imagination."

The goal, first and foremost, was to diminish American prestige—showing that the superpower could be bloodied: that for all its power, its defeat was indeed conceivable. All the major attacks preceding 9/11 attributed at least in part to al Qaeda—the shooting down of U.S. Army helicopters in Mogadishu in 1993, the truck bombing of American military housing at Khobar in 1996, the car bombing of the American embassies in Nairobi and Dar es Salaam in 1998, the suicide bombing of the USS *Cole* in Aden in 2000—were aimed at the same goal: to destroy the aura of American power. Power, particularly imperial power, rests not on its use but on its credibility; U.S. power in the Middle East depends not on ships and missiles but on the certainty that the United States is invincible and stands behind its friends. The jihadis used terrorism to create a spectacle that would remove this certainty. They were by no means the first guerrilla group to adopt such a strategy. "History and our observation persuaded us," recalled Menachem Begin, the future Israeli prime minister who used terror with great success to drive the British out of Palestine during the mid-1940s, "that if we could succeed in destroying the government's prestige in Eretz Israel, the removal of its rule would follow automatically. Thenceforward, we gave no peace to this weak spot. Throughout all the years of our uprising, we hit at the British government's prestige, deliberately, tirelessly, unceasingly."[9] In its most spectacular act, in July 1946, the Irgun guerrilla forces led by Begin bombed the King David Hotel, killing ninety-one people, most of them civilians.

The 9/11 attacks were a call to persuade Muslims who might share bin Laden's broad view of American power to sympathize with, support or even join the jihad he had declared against the "far enemy." "Those young men," bin Laden said of the terrorists two months after the attacks, "said in deeds, in New York and Washington, speeches that overshadowed all other speeches made everywhere else in the world."

> The speeches are understood by both Arabs and non-Arabs—even by Chinese. . . . [I]n Holland, at one of the centers, the number of people who accepted Islam during the days that followed the operations were more than the people who accepted Islam in the last 11 years." To this, a sheik in a wheelchair shown in the videotape replies: "Hundreds of people used to doubt you, and few only would follow you until this huge event happened. Now hundreds of people are coming out to join you."[10]

Grotesque as it is to say, the spectacle of 9/11 was meant to serve, among other things, as an enormous recruiting poster.

But recruitment to what? We should return here to the lessons of Afghanistan, not only the obvious one of the defeat of a powerful Soviet Army by guerrilla forces but the more subtle one taught by the Americans, who by clever use of covert aid to the Afghan resistance tempted the Soviets to invade the country and thereby drew "the Russians into an Afghan trap." Bin Laden seems to have hoped to set in motion a similar strategy. According to a text attributed to Saif al-Adel, a former Egyptian Army colonel now generally identified as bin Laden's military chief, "the ultimate objective was to prompt" the United States "to come out of its hole" and take direct military action in an Islamic country. "What we had wished for actually happened. It was crowned by the announcement of Bush Jr. of his crusade against Islam and Muslims everywhere."[11] ("This is a new kind of evil," the president said five days after the attacks, "and we understand . . . this crusade, this war on terrorism, is going to take a while.")

The 9/11 attacks seem to have been intended at least in part to provoke an overwhelming American response: most likely an invasion of Afghanistan, which would lead the United States, like the Soviet Union before it, into an endless, costly, and politically fatal quagmire. Thus, two days before the attacks, Qaeda agents posing as television journalists taping an interview murdered Ahmed Shah Massoud, the charismatic leader of the Northern Alliance, with a bomb concealed in a video camera—apparently a preemptive strike intended to throw into confusion the United States' obvious ally in the coming invasion of Afghanistan.

For the jihadists, luring the Americans into Afghanistan would accomplish at least two things: by drawing the United States into a protracted guerrilla war in which the superpower would occupy a Muslim country and kill Muslim civilians—with the world media, including independent Arab networks like Al Jazeera, broadcasting the carnage—it would leave increasingly isolated those autocratic Muslim regimes that depended for their survival on American support. And by forcing the United States to prosecute a long, costly and inconclusive guerrilla war, it would severely test, and ultimately break, American will, leading to a collapse of American prestige and an eventual withdrawal—first, physically, from Afghanistan and then, politically, from the "apostate regimes" in Riyadh, Cairo and elsewhere in the Islamic world.

In his "Declaration of Jihad" in 1996, bin Laden focused on American political will as the United States' prime vulnerability, the enemy's "center of gravity" that his guerrilla war must target and destroy:

> The defense secretary of the crusading Americans had said that "the explosions at Riyadh and Al-Khobar had taught him one lesson: that is, not to withdraw when attacked by cowardly terrorists." We say to the defense secretary, Where was this false courage of yours when the explosion in Beirut took place in 1983?
>
> But your most disgraceful case was in Somalia. . . . When tens of your soldiers were killed in minor battles and one American pilot was dragged in the streets of Mogadishu, you left the area carrying disappointment, humiliation, defeat and your dead with you. . . . The extent of your impotence and weaknesses became very clear.[12]

In Afghanistan, bin Laden would be disappointed. The U.S. military initially sent in no heavy armor but instead restricted the American effort to aerial bombardment in support of several hundred Special Operations soldiers on the ground who helped lead the Northern Alliance forces in a rapid advance. Kabul and other cities quickly fell. America was caught in no Afghan quagmire, or at least not in the sort of protracted, highly televisual bloody mess bin Laden had envisioned. But bin Laden and his senior leadership, holed up in the mountain complex of Tora Bora, managed to survive the bombing and elude the Afghan forces that the Americans commissioned to capture them. During the next months and years, as the United States and its allies did great damage to al Qaeda's operational cadre, arresting or killing thousands of its veterans, its major leadership symbols survived intact, and those symbols, and their power to lead and to inspire, became al Qaeda's most important asset.

After Tora Bora, the Qaeda fighters who survived regrouped in neighboring countries. "We began to converge on Iran one after the other," Saif al-Adel recalled in a recent book by an Egyptian journalist. "We began to form some groups of fighters to return to Afghanistan to carry out well-prepared missions there." It is these men, along with the reconstituted Taliban, that 16,000 American soldiers are still fighting today.

Not all the fighters would return to Afghanistan. Other targets of opportunity loomed on the horizon of the possible. "Abu Mus'ab and his Jordanian and Palestinian comrades opted to go to Iraq," al-Adel recalled, for, he said, an "examination of the situation indicated that the Americans would inevitably make a mistake and invade Iraq sooner or later. Such an invasion would aim at overthrowing the regime. Therefore, we should play an important role in the confrontation and resistance."[13]

Abu Mus'ab is Abu Mus'ab al-Zarqawi—or A.M.Z. to the American troops who are pursuing him and his Qaeda in Mesopotamia forces all over the shattered landscape of occupied Iraq. The United States, as al Qaeda had hoped, had indeed come out of its hole.

V.

It was strangely beautiful, the aftermath of the explosion in Baghdad: two enormous fires, bright orange columns of flame rising perhaps twenty feet into the air, and clearly discernible in the midst of each a cage of glowing metal: what remained of two four-wheel-drive vehicles. Before the flames, two bodies lay amid a scattering of glass and sand; the car bomb had toppled the sandbags piled high to protect the building, collapsing the facade and crushing a dozen people. It was October 27, 2003, and I stood before what remained of the Baghdad office of the International Committee of the Red Cross. In the distance, I heard a second huge explosion, saw rising the great plume of oily smoke; within the next forty-five minutes, insurgents attacked four more times, bombing police stations throughout the capital, killing at least thirty-five. Simultaneity and spectacle: Qaeda trademarks. I was gazing at Zarqawi's handiwork.

Behind me, the press had gathered, a jostling crowd of aggressive, mostly young people bristling with lenses short and long, pushing against the line of young American soldiers, who, assault rifles leveled, were screaming at them to stay back. The scores of glittering lenses were a necessary part of the equation, transforming what in military terms would have been a minor engagement into a major defeat.

"What we have here is basically a constabulary action," an American lieutenant colonel told me a couple of days before in frustration and disgust. "Where are the regiment-on-regiment, division-on-division engagements? We've seen almost nothing above the squad level. Basically, this is not a real war."

It was not a war the Americans had been trained or equipped to fight. With fewer than 150,000 troops—and many fewer combat soldiers—they were trying to contain a full-blown insurgency in a country the size of

California. The elusive enemy—an evolving, loose coalition of a score or so groups, some of them ex-Baathists from Saddam Hussein's dozen or so security agencies, some former Iraqi military personnel, some professional Islamic insurgents like Zarqawi, some foreign volunteers from Saudi Arabia or Kuwait or Syria come to take the jihad to the Americans—attacked not with tanks or artillery or infantry assaults but with roadside bombs and suicide car bombers and kidnappings. Iraq, bin Laden declared, had become a "golden opportunity" to start a "third world war" against "the crusader-Zionist coalition."

Amid the barbed wire and blast walls and bomb debris of post-occupation Iraq, you could discern a clear strategy behind the insurgent violence. The insurgents had identified the Americans' points of vulnerability: their international isolation; their forced distance, as a foreign occupier, from Iraqis; and their increasing disorientation as they struggled to keep their footing on the fragile, shifting, roiling political ground of post-Saddam Iraq. And the insurgents hit at each of these vulnerabilities, as Begin had urged his followers to do, "deliberately, tirelessly, unceasingly."

When, during the summer of 2003, the Bush administration seemed to be reaching out to the United Nations for political help in Iraq, insurgents struck at U.N. headquarters in Baghdad, killing the talented envoy Sergio Vieira de Mello and twenty-one others and driving the United Nations from the country. When the Americans seemed to be trying to attract Arab forces to come to Iraq to help, the insurgents struck at the Jordanian Embassy, killing seventeen. When the Turks offered to send troops, the insurgents bombed the Turkish Embassy. When nongovernmental organizations seemed the only outsiders still working to ease the situation in Iraq, insurgents struck at the Red Cross, driving it and most other nongovernmental organizations from the country.

Insurgents in Iraq and jihadists abroad struck America's remaining allies. First they hit the Italians, car-bombing their base in Nasariyah in November 2003, killing twenty-eight. Then they struck the Spanish, bombing commuter trains in Madrid on March 11, 2004, killing 191. Finally they struck the British, bombing three London Underground trains and a double-decker bus this July, killing fifty-six. It is as if the insurgents, with cold and patient precision, were severing one by one the fragile lines that connected the American effort in Iraq to the rest of the world.

With car bombs and assassinations and commando attacks, insurgents have methodically set out to kill any Iraqi who might think of cooperating with the Americans, widening the crevasse between occupiers and occupied. They have struck at water lines and electricity substations and oil pipelines, interrupting the services that Iraqis depended on, particularly during the unbearably hot summers, keeping electrical service in Baghdad far below what it was under Saddam Hussein—often only a few hours a day this summer—and oil exports 300,000 barrels a day below their prewar peak (helping to double world oil prices). Building on the chaotic unbridled looting of the first weeks of American rule, the insurgents have worked to destroy any notion of security and to make clear that the landscape of apocalyptic destruction that is Baghdad, with its ubiquitous concrete blast walls and rolls of concertina wire and explosions and gunshots, should be laid at the feet of the American occupier, that unseen foreign power that purports to rule the country from behind concrete blast walls in the so-called Green Zone but dares to venture out only in tanks and armored cars.

> With . . . officials attempting to administrate from behind masses of barbed wire, in heavily defended buildings, and . . . living in pathetic seclusion in "security zones," one cannot escape the conclusion that the government . . . is a hunted organization with little hope of ever being able to cope with conditions in this country as they exist today.

However vividly these words fit contemporary Baghdad, they are in fact drawn from the report of the American consul general in Jerusalem in 1947, describing what Begin's guerrilla forces achieved in their war against the British.[14] "The very existence of an underground," as Begin remarked in his memoirs, "must, in the end, undermine the prestige of a colonial regime that lives by the legend of its omnipotence. Every attack which it fails to prevent is a blow to its standing."[15]

In Iraq, the insurgents have presided over a catastrophic collapse in confidence in the Americans and a concomitant fall in their power. It is difficult to think of a place in which terror has been deployed on such a scale: There have been suicide truck bombs, suicide tanker bombs, suicide police cars, suicide bombers on foot, suicide bombers posing as police officers, suicide bombers posing as soldiers, even suicide bombers on bicycles. While the American death toll climbs steadily toward 2,000, the number of Iraqi dead probably stands at ten times that and perhaps many more; no one knows. Conservative unofficial counts put the number of Iraqi dead in the war at somewhere between 25,000 and 30,000, in a country a tenth the size of the United States.

Civil wars, of course, are especially bloody, and a civil war is now being fought in Iraq. The country is slowly splitting apart along the lines where French and British negotiators stitched it together early in the last century out of three Ottoman provinces—Mosul, Baghdad and Basra—and it is doing so with the enthusiastic help of the Islamists, who are doing all they can to provoke a Shia-Sunni regionwide war.

The Kurds in the north, possessed of their own army and legislature, want to secure what they believe are their historic rights to the disputed city of Kirkuk, including its oil fields, and be quit of Iraq. The Shia in the south, now largely ruled by Islamic party militias trained by the Iranians and coming under the increasingly strict sway of the clerics on social matters, are evolving their oil-rich mini-state into a paler version of the Islamic republic next door. And in the center, the Baathist elite of Saddam Hussein's security services and army—tens of thousands of well-armed professional intelligence operatives and soldiers—have formed an alliance of convenience with Sunni Islamists, domestic and foreign, in order to assert their rights in a unitary Iraq. They are in effective control of many cities and towns, and they have the burdensome and humiliating presence of the foreign occupier to thank for the continuing success of their recruitment efforts. In a letter to bin Laden that was intercepted by American forces in January 2004, Zarqawi asked: "When the Americans disappear . . . what will become of our situation?"

As Zarqawi described in his letter and in subsequent broadcasts, his strategy in Iraq is to strike at the Shia—and thereby provoke a civil war. "A nation of heretics," the Shia "are the key element of change," he wrote. "If we manage to draw them onto the terrain of partisan war, it will be possible to tear the Sunnis away from their heedlessness, for they will feel the weight of the imminence of danger."[16] Again a strategy of provocation—which plays on an underlying reality: that Iraq sits on the critical sectarian fault line of the Middle East and that a conflict there gains powerful momentum from the involvement of neighboring states, with Iran strongly supporting the Shia and with Saudi Arabia, Kuwait, Jordan and Syria strongly sympathetic to the Sunnis. More and more, you can discern this outline in the chaos of the current war, with the Iranian-trained militias of the Shia Islamist parties that now control the Iraqi government battling Sunni Islamists, both Iraqi and foreign-born, and former Baathists.

IN THE MIDST OF IT ALL, increasingly irrelevant, are the Americans, who have the fanciest weapons but have never had sufficient troops, or political will, to assert effective control over the country. If political authority comes from achieving a monopoly on legitimate violence, then the Americans, from those early days when they sat in their tanks and watched over the wholesale looting of public institutions, never did achieve political authority in Iraq. They fussed over liberalizing the economy and writing constitutions and achieving democracy in the Middle East when in fact there was really only one question in Iraq, emerging again and again in each successive political struggle, most recently in the disastrously managed writing of the constitution: how to shape a new political dispensation in which the age-old majority Shia can take control from the minority Sunni and do it in a way that minimized violence and insecurity—do it in a way, that is, that the Sunnis would be willing to accept, however reluctantly, without resorting to armed resistance. This might have been accomplished with hundreds of thousands of troops, iron control and a clear sense of purpose. The Americans had none of these. Instead they relied first on a policy of faith and then on one of improvisation, driven in part by the advice of Iraqi exile "friends" who used the Americans for their own purposes. Some of the most strikingly ideological decisions, like abruptly firing and humiliating the entire Iraqi Army and purging from their jobs many hundreds of thousands of Baath Party members, seemed designed to alienate and antagonize a Sunni population already terrified of its security in the new Iraq. "You Americans," one

Sunni businessman said to me in Baghdad last February, shaking his head in wonder, "you have created your own enemies here."

The United States never used what authority it had to do more than pretend to control the gathering chaos, never managed to look clearly at the country and confront Iraq's underlying political dysfunction, of which the tyranny of Saddam Hussein was the product, not the cause. "The illusionists," Ambassador John Negroponte's people called their predecessors, the officials of the Coalition Provisional Authority under L. Paul Bremer III. Now, day by day, the illusion is slipping away, and with it what authority the Americans had in Iraq. What is coming to take its place looks increasingly like a failed state.

VI.

It is an oft-heard witticism in Washington that the Iraq war is over and that the Iranians won. And yet the irony seems misplaced. A truly democratic Iraq was always likely to be an Iraq led not only by Shia, who are the majority of Iraqis, but by those Shia parties that are the largest and best organized—the Supreme Council for the Islamic Revolution in Iraq and the Dawa Islamic Party—which happen to be those blessed by the religious authorities and nurtured in Iran. Nor would it be a surprise if a democratic Saudi Arabia turned out to be a fundamentalist Saudi Arabia and one much less friendly to the United States. Osama bin Laden knows this, and so do American officials. This is why the United States is "friendly" with "apostate regimes." Democratic outcomes do not always ensure friendly governments. Often the contrary is true. On this simple fact depends much of the history of American policy not only in the Middle East but also in Latin America and other parts of the world throughout the Cold War. Bush administration officials, for all their ideological fervor, did the country no favor by ignoring it.

In launching his new Cold War, George W. Bush chose a peculiarly ideological version of cold-war history. He opted not for containment, the cautious, status quo grand strategy usually attributed to the late George F. Kennan, but for rollback. Containment, by which the United States determinedly resisted Soviet attempts to expand its influence, would have meant a patient, methodical search for terrorists, discriminating between those groups that threaten the United States and those that do not, pursuing the former with determined, practical policies that would have drawn much from the military and law-enforcement cooperation of our allies and that would have included an effective program of nonproliferation to keep weapons of mass destruction out of terrorist hands. Rollback, on the other hand, meant something quite different; those advocating it during the 1950s considered containment immoral, for it recognized as the status quo communist hegemony in Eastern Europe and parts of Asia. They wanted instead to destroy communism entirely by "rolling back" Communists from territory they had gained, as Gen. Douglas MacArthur did briefly and, it turned out, catastrophically, in North Korea, and as President Eisenhower refused to do when he declined to support the Hungarian revolutionaries against the Soviet invasion in 1956.

The original advocates of rollback lost that struggle. In this new Cold War, the rollback advocates triumphed and adopted as the heart of their policy a high-stakes, metaphysical gamble to "democratize the Middle East" and thus put an end, once and for all, to terrorism. They relied on a "domino theory" in which the successful implantation of democracy in Iraq would lead to a "democratic revolution" across the region. The ambition of this idea is breathtaking; it depends on a conception of American power as virtually limitless and on an entirely fanciful vision of Iraqi politics, a kind of dogged political wish-fulfillment that no sober analysis could penetrate. Replacing any real willingness to consider whether a clear course existed between here and there, between an invasion and occupation of Iraq and a democratic Middle East, was, at bottom, the simple conviction that since the United States enjoyed a "preponderance of power" unseen in the world since the Roman Empire, and since its cause of democratic revolution was so incontrovertibly just, defeat was inconceivable. One detects here an echo of Vietnam: the inability to imagine that the all-powerful United States might lose.

American power, however, is not limitless. Armies can destroy and occupy, but it takes much more to build a lasting order, especially on the shifting sands of a violent political struggle: another Vietnam echo. Learning the lesson this time around may prove more costly, for dominoes can fall both ways. "Political engineering on this scale could easily go awry," Stephen D. Biddle, a U.S. Army War College analyst, wrote this past April in a shrewd analysis.

> If a democratic Iraq can catalyze reform elsewhere, so a failed Iraq could presumably export chaos to its neighbors. A regionwide Lebanon might well prove beyond our capacity to police, regardless of effort expended. And if so, then we will have replaced a region of police states with a region of warlords and chronic instability. This could easily prove to be an easier operating environment for terrorism than the police states it replaces.[17]

The sun is setting on American dreams in Iraq; what remains now to be worked out are the modalities of withdrawal, which depend on the powers of forbearance in the American body politic. But the dynamic has already been set in place. The United States is running out of troops. By the spring of 2006, nearly every active-duty combat unit is likely to have been deployed twice. The National Guard and Reserves, meanwhile, make up an unprecedented 40 percent of the force, and the Guard is in the "stage of meltdown," as General Barry McCaffrey, retired, recently told Congress. Within twenty-four months, "the wheels are coming off."[18] For all the apocalyptic importance President Bush and his administration ascribed to the Iraq war, they made virtually no move to expand the military, no decision to restore the draft. In the end, the president judged his tax cuts more important than his vision of a "democratic Middle East." The administration's relentless political style, integral to both its strength and its weakness, left it wholly unable to change course and to add more troops when they might have made a difference. That moment is long past; the widespread unpopularity of the occupation in Iraq and in the Islamic world is now critical to insurgent recruitment and makes it possible for a growing insurgent force numbering in the tens of thousands to conceal itself within the broader population.

Sold a war made urgent by the imminent threat of weapons of mass destruction in the hands of a dangerous dictator, Americans now see their sons and daughters fighting and dying in a war whose rationale has been lost even as its ending has receded into the indefinite future. A war promised to bring forth the Iraqi people bearing flowers and sweets in exchange for the beneficent gift of democracy has brought instead a kind of relentless terror that seems inexplicable and unending. A war that had a clear purpose and a certain end has now lost its reason and its finish. For Americans, the war has lost its narrative.

Of the many reasons that American leaders chose to invade and occupy Iraq—to democratize the Middle East; to remove an unpredictable dictator from a region vital to America's oil supply; to remove a threat from Israel, America's ally; to restore the prestige sullied on 9/11 with a tank-led procession of triumph down the avenues of a conquered capital; to seize the chance to overthrow a regime capable of building an arsenal of chemical and biological weapons—of all of these, it is remarkable that the Bush administration chose to persuade Americans and the world by offering the one reason that could be proved to be false. The failure to find the weapons of mass destruction, and the collapse of the rationale for the war, left terribly exposed precisely what bin Laden had targeted as the critical American vulnerability: the will to fight.

How that collapse, reflected in poll numbers, will be translated into policy is a more complicated question. One of 9/11's more obvious consequences was to restore to the Republicans the advantage in national security they surrendered with the Cold War's end; their ruthless exploitation of this advantage and the Democrats' compromising embrace of the Iraq war has in effect left the country, on this issue, without an opposition party. Republicans, who fear to face the voters shackled to a leader whose approval ratings have slid into the low forties, are the ones demanding answers on the war. The falling poll numbers, the approaching midterm elections and the desperate manpower straits of the military have set in motion a dynamic that could see gradual American withdrawals beginning in 2006, as Gen. George W. Casey Jr., the commander in Iraq, acknowledged publicly in July. Unless Iraq's political process, which has turned another downward spiral with Sunni negotiators' rejection of the constitution, can somehow be retrieved, American power in Iraq will go on deteriorating.

Two and a half years into the invasion, for U.S. policy in Iraq, the time of "the illusionists" has finally passed. Since the January elections, which Sunnis largely boycotted, American officials have worked hard to persuade

Sunni leaders to take part in the constitutional referendum and elections, hoping thereby to isolate the Baathist and Islamist extremists and drain strength from the insurgency. This effort comes very late, however, when Iraqi politics, and the forces pulling the country apart, have taken on a momentum that waning American power no longer seems able to stop. Even as the constitutional drama came to a climax last month, the president telephoned Abdul Aziz Hakim, the Shia cleric who leads the SCIRI party, appealing for concessions that might have tempted the Sunnis to agree to the draft; the Shia politician, faced with the American president's personal plea, did not hesitate to turn him down flat. Perhaps the best hope now for a gradual American withdrawal that would not worsen the war is to negotiate a regional solution, which might seek an end to Sunni infiltration from U.S. allies in exchange for Shia guarantees of the Sunni position in Iraq and a phased American departure.

For all the newfound realism in the second-term administration's foreign policy, in which we have seen a willingness finally to negotiate seriously with North Korea and Iran, the president seems nowhere close to considering such an idea in Iraq, insisting that there the choice is simple: The United States can either "stay the course" or "cut and run." "An immediate withdrawal of our troops in Iraq, or the broader Middle East, as some have called for," the president declared last month, "would only embolden the terrorists and create a staging ground to launch more attacks against America and free nations."[19] These words, familiar and tired, offering no solution beyond staying a course that seems to be leading nowhere, have ceased to move Americans weary of the rhetoric of terror. That does not mean, however, that they may not be entirely true.

VII.

We cannot know what future Osama bin Laden imagined when he sent off his nineteen suicide terrorists on their mission four years ago. He got much wrong; the U.S. military, light years ahead of the Red Army, would send no tank divisions to Afghanistan, and there has been no uprising in the Islamic world. One suspects, though, that if bin Laden had been told on that day that in a mere forty-eight months he would behold a world in which the United States, "the idol of the age," was bogged down in an endless guerrilla war fighting in a major Muslim country; a world in which its all-powerful army, with few allies and little sympathy, found itself overstretched and exhausted; in which its dispirited people were starting to demand from their increasingly unpopular leader a withdrawal without victory—one suspects that such a prophecy would have pleased him. He had struck at the American will, and his strategy, which relied in effect on the persistent reluctance of American leaders to speak frankly to their people about the costs and burdens of war and to expend the political capital that such frank talk would require, had proved largely correct.

He has suffered damage as well. Many of his closest collaborators have been killed or captured, his training camps destroyed, his sanctuary occupied. "What al Qaeda has lost," a senior Defense Department official said five months after the attacks, "again, it's lost its center of gravity. . . . The benefits of Afghanistan cannot be overestimated. Again, it was the one state sponsor they had." This analysis seems now a vision of the past. Al Qaeda was always a flexible, ghostly organization, a complex worldwide network made up of shifting alliances and marriages of convenience with other shadowy groups. Now al Qaeda's "center of gravity," such as it is, has gone elsewhere.

In December 2003, a remarkable document, "Jihadi Iraq: Hopes and Dangers," appeared on the Internet, setting out a fascinating vision of how to isolate the United States and pick off its allies one by one. The truly ripe fruit, concludes the author, is Spain:

> In order to force the Spanish government to withdraw from Iraq the resistance should deal painful blows to its forces . . . [and] make utmost use of the upcoming general election. . . . We think that the Spanish government could not tolerate more than two, maximum three blows, after which it will have to withdraw. . . .[20]

Three months later, on March 11, 2004—3/11, as it has come to be known—a cell of North African terrorists struck at the Atocha Train Station in Madrid. One hundred ninety-one people died—a horrific toll but nowhere near what it could have been had all of the bombs actually detonated, simultaneously, and in the station itself. Had the terrorists succeeded in bringing the roof of the station down, the casualties could have surpassed those of 9/11. In the event, they were quite sufficient to lead to the defeat of the Spanish government in elections several days later and the decision of its successor to withdraw its troops from Iraq.

What seems most notable about the Madrid attack, however—and the attack on Jewish and foreign sites in Casablanca on May 17, 2003, among others—is that the perpetrators were "home-grown" and not, strictly speaking, al Qaeda. "After 2001, when the U.S. destroyed the camps and housing and turned off the funding, bin Laden was left with little control," Marc Sageman, a psychiatrist and former C.I.A. case officer who has studied the structure of the network, has written. "The movement has now degenerated into something like the Internet. Spontaneous groups of friends, as in Madrid and Casablanca, who have few links to any central leadership, are generating sometimes very dangerous terrorist operations, notwithstanding their frequent errors and poor training."[21]

Under this view, al Qaeda, in the form we knew it, has been subsumed into the broader, more diffuse political world of radical Salafi politics. "The network is now self-organized from the bottom up and is very decentralized," Sageman wrote. "With local initiative and flexibility, it's very robust."

We have entered the era of the amateurs. Those who attacked the London Underground—whether or not they had any contact with al Qaeda— manufactured their crude bombs from common chemicals (including hydrogen peroxide, bleach and drain cleaner), making them in plastic food containers, toting them to Luton Station in coolers and detonating them with cellphone alarms. One click on the Internet and you can pull up a Web site offering a recipe—or, for that matter, one showing you how to make a suicide vest from commonly found items, including a video download demonstrating how to use the device: "There is a possibility that the two seats on his right and his left might not be hit with the shrapnel," the unseen narrator tells the viewer. Not to worry, however: "The explosion will surely kill the passengers in those seats."[22]

During the four years since the attacks of 9/11, while terrorism worldwide has flourished, we have seen no second attack on the United States. This may be owed to the damage done al Qaeda. Or perhaps planning and preparation for such an attack is going on now. When it comes to the United States itself, the terrorists have their own "second-novel problem"—how do you top the first production? More likely, though, the next attack, when it comes, will originate not in the minds of veteran Qaeda planners but from this new wave of amateurs: viral al Qaeda, political sympathizers who nourish themselves on Salafi rhetoric and bin Laden speeches and draw what training they require from their computer screens. Very little investment and preparation can bring huge rewards. The possibilities are endless, and terrifyingly simple: rucksacks containing crude homemade bombs left under tables in McDonald's—one, say, in Times Square and one on Wilshire Boulevard in Los Angeles, 3,000 miles away, exploded simultaneously by cellphone. The effort is small, the potential impact overwhelming.

Attacks staged by amateurs with little or no connection to terrorist networks, and thus no visible trail to follow, are nearly impossible to prevent, even for the United States, with all of its power. Indeed, perhaps what is most astonishing about these hard four years is that we have managed to show the world the limits of our power. In launching a war on Iraq that we have been unable to win, we have done the one thing a leader is supposed never to do: issue a command that is not followed. A withdrawal from Iraq, rapid or slow, with the Islamists still holding the field, will signal, as bin Laden anticipated, a failure of American will. Those who will view such a withdrawal as the critical first step in a broader retreat from the Middle East will surely be encouraged to go on the attack. That is, after all, what you do when your enemy retreats. In this new world, where what is necessary to go on the attack is not armies or training or even technology but desire and political will, we have ensured, by the way we have fought this forever war, that it is precisely these qualities our enemies have in large and growing supply.

New York Times Magazine, September 11, 2005

The War of the Imagination

Today, if we went into Iraq, like the president would like us to do, you know where you begin. You never know where you are going to end.

—George F. Kennan, September 26, 2002[1]

I ask you, sir, what is the American army doing inside Iraq? . . . Saddam's story has been finished for close to three years.

—President Mahmoud Ahmadinejad of Iran
to Mike Wallace on *Sixty Minutes*, August 13, 2006

November 16, 2006

IN THE RUINED CITY of Fallujah, its pale tan buildings pulverized by Marine artillery in the two great assaults of this long war (the aborted attack of March 2004 and then the bloody, triumphant *al-Fajr*—"The Dawn"—campaign of the following November), behind the lines of giant sandbags and concrete T-walls and barbed wire that surrounded the tiny beleaguered American outpost there, I sat in my body armor and Kevlar helmet and thought of George F. Kennan. Not the grand old man of American diplomacy, the ninety-eight-year-old Father of Containment who, listening to the war drums beat from a Washington nursing home in the fall of 2002, had uttered the prophetic words above. I was thinking of an earlier Kennan, the brilliant and ambitious young diplomat who during the late 1920s and 1930s had gazed out on the crumbling European order from Tallinn and Berlin and Prague and read the signs of the coming world conflict.

For there in the bunkered Civil-Military Operations Center (known as the C-Moc) in downtown Fallujah, where a few score Marines and a handful of civilians subsisted in a broken-down bunkered building without running water or fresh food, I met young Kennan's reincarnation in the person of a junior State Department official: a bright, aggressive young man who spent his twenty-hour days rumbling down the ruined streets in body armor and helmet with his reluctant marine escorts, meeting with local Iraqi officials, and writing tart cables back to Baghdad or Washington, telling his bosses the truth of what was happening on the ground, however reluctant they might be to hear it. This young diplomat was resourceful and brilliant and indefatigable, and as I watched him joking and arguing with the local sheikhs and politicos and technocrats—who were meeting, as they were forced to do, in the American bunker—I thought of the indomitable young Kennan of the interwar years, and of how, if the American effort in Iraq could ever be made to "work," only undaunted and farseeing young men like this one, his spiritual successor, could make it happen.

This was October 2005, on the eve of the nationwide referendum on Iraq's proposed constitution, and I had come to Fallujah, the heart of rebellious Anbar province, to see whether the Sunnis could gather the political strength to vote it down. In a provision originally insisted on by the Kurds, a provision that typified an American-designed political process that had been intended to unify the country but that instead had helped pull it inexorably apart, the proposed constitution could be rejected if, in three of Iraq's eighteen provinces, more than two in three Iraqis coming to the polls voted no. During the first post-Saddam election the previous January, the televised extravaganza of "waving purple fingers" which had become perhaps the most celebrated of the many promised "turning points" of this long war, the Sunnis had boycotted the polls. This time, after Herculean efforts of persuasion and negotiation by the American ambassador, most Sunnis were expected to vote. What would draw them, though—or such anyway was the common wisdom—was the chance not to affirm the constitution but to doom it, and the political process along with it.

And so as I sat after midnight on the eve of the vote, scribbling in my notebook in the dimly lit C-Moc bunker as the young diplomat explained to me the intricacies of the politics of the battered city, I was pleased to see him suddenly lean forward and, with quick glances to either side, offer me a confidence. "You know, tomorrow you are going to be surprised," he told me, speaking softly. "Everybody is going to be surprised. People here are not only going to vote. People here—a great many people here—are going to vote yes."

I WAS STUNNED. That the Sunnis would actually come out to support the constitution would be an astonishing turnabout and, for the American effort in Iraq, an enormously positive one; for it would mean that despite the escalating violence on the ground, especially here in Anbar, Iraq was in fact moving toward a rough political consensus. It would mean that beneath the bloody landscape of suicide bombings and assassinations and roadside bombs a common idea about politics and compromise was taking shape. It would mean that what had come to seem a misbegotten political process that charted and even worsened the growing divisions among Iraqis had actually become the avenue for bringing them together. It would mean there might be hope.

I took the young diplomat's words as an invaluable bit of inside wisdom from the American who knew this ground better than any other, and I kept them in mind a few hours later as I traveled from polling place to polling place in that city of rubble, listening as the Fallujans told me of their anger at the Americans and the "Iranians" (as they called the leading Shiite politicians) and of their hatred for the constitution that they believed was meant to divide and thus destroy Iraq. I pondered the diplomat's words that evening, when I realized that in a long day of interviews I'd not met a single Iraqi who would admit to voting for the constitution. And I thought of his words again several days later when it was confirmed that in Anbar province—where the most knowledgeable, experienced, indefatigable American had confided to me what he had plainly ardently believed, that on the critical vote on the constitution "a great many people would vote yes"—that in Anbar ninety-seven out of every one hundred Iraqis who voted had voted no. With all his contacts and commitment, with all his energy and brilliance, on the most basic and critical issue of politics on the ground he had been entirely, catastrophically wrong.

I.

"You know where you begin. You never know where you are going to end." The ninety-eight-year-old George F. Kennan, sitting in the Washington nursing home as the war came on, knew from eight decades of experience to focus first of all on the problem of what we know and what we don't know. You know, though you spend your endless, frustrating days speaking to Iraqis, lobbying them, arguing with them, that in a country torn by a brutal and complicated war those Iraqis perforce are drawn from a small and special subset of the population: Iraqis who are willing to risk their lives by meeting with and talking to Americans. Which is to say, very often, Iraqis who depend on the Americans not only for their livelihoods but for their survival. You know that the information these Iraqis draw on is similarly limited, and that what they convey is itself selected, to a greater or lesser extent, to please their interlocutor. But though you know that much of your information comes from a thin, inherently biased slice of Iraqi politics and Iraqi life, hundreds of conversations during those grueling twenty-hour days eventually lead you to think, must lead you to think, that you are coming to understand what's happening in this immensely complicated, violent place. You come to believe you know. And so often, even about the largest things, you do not know.

As this precious stream of flickering knowledge travels "up the chain" from those on the shell-pocked, dangerous ground collecting it to those in Washington offices ultimately making decisions based upon it, the problem of what we really know intensifies, acquiring a fierce complexity. Policymakers, peering second-, third-, fourth-hand into a twilight world, must learn a patient, humble skepticism. Or else, confronted with an ambiguous reality they do not like, they turn away, ignoring the shadowy, shifting landscape and forcing their eyes stubbornly toward their own ideological light. Unable to find clarity, they impose it. Consider, for example, these words of Donald H. Rumsfeld, speaking about the Iraq war on November 9, two days after the midterm elections and the day after President Bush fired him:

> It is very clear that the major combat operations were an enormous success. It's clear that in Phase Two of this, it has not been going well enough or fast enough.[2]

Such analyses are not uncommon from Pentagon civilians; thus Dov Zakheim, a former Rumsfeld aide, to a television interviewer later that evening:

> People will debate the second part, the second phase of what happened in Iraq. Very few are arguing that the military victory in the first phase was anything but an outright success.[3]

Three years and eight months after the Iraq war began, the secretary of defense and his allies see in Iraq not one war but two. One is the Real Iraq War—the "outright success" that only very few would deny, the war in which American forces were "greeted as liberators," according to the famous prediction of Dick Cheney which the vice president doggedly insists was in fact proved true: "true within the context of the battle against the Saddam Hussein regime and his forces. That went very quickly."[4] It is "within this context" that the former secretary of defense and the vice president see America's current war in Iraq as in fact comprising a brief, dramatic, and "enormously successful" war of a few weeks' duration leading to a decisive victory, and then . . . what? Well, whatever we are in now: a Phase Two, a "postwar phase," which has lasted three and a half years and continues. In the first, successful, Real Iraq War, 140 Americans died. In the postwar phase 2,700 Americans have died—and counting. What is happening now in Iraq is not in fact a war at all but a phase, a non-war, something unnamed, unconceptualized—unplanned.

ANYONE SEEKING to understand what has become the central conundrum of the Iraq war—how it is that so many highly accomplished, experienced, and intelligent officials came together to make such monumental, consequential, and, above all, obvious mistakes, mistakes that much of the government knew very well at the time were mistakes—must see beyond what seems to be a simple rhetoric of self-justification and follow it where it leads: Toward the War of Imagination that senior officials decided to fight in the spring and summer of 2002 and to whose image they clung long after reality had taken a sharply separate turn. In that War of Imagination victory was to be decisive, overwhelming, evincing a terrible power—enough to wipe out the disgrace of September 11 and remake the threatening world. In *State of Denial*, Bob Woodward recounts how Michael Gerson, at the time Bush's chief speechwriter, asked Henry Kissinger why he had supported the Iraq war:

> "Because Afghanistan wasn't enough," Kissinger answered. In the conflict with radical Islam, he said, they want to humiliate us. "And we need to humiliate them." The American response to 9/11 had essentially to be more than proportionate—on a larger scale than simply invading Afghanistan and overthrowing the Taliban. Something else was essential. The Iraq war was essential to send a larger message, "in order to make a point that we're not going to live in this world that they want for us."[5]

Though to anyone familiar with Kissinger's "realist" rhetoric of power and credibility his analysis will come as no surprise, Gerson, the deeply religious idealist who composed Bush's most soaring music about "ending tyranny" and "ridding the world of evil," seems mildly disappointed: Kissinger "viewed Iraq purely in the context of power politics. It was not idealism. He didn't seem to connect with Bush's goal of promoting democracy."

Gerson, of course, was author of what would come to be called the Bush Doctrine, a neoconservative paean to democracy that maintains that "the realistic interests of America would now be served by fidelity to American ideals, especially democracy." Others in the administration, however, plainly did "connect" with Kissinger's stark realism: Donald Rumsfeld, for example, whom Ron Suskind depicts, in *The One Percent Doctrine*, struggling with other officials in spring 2002 to cope with various terrifying warnings of impending attacks on the United States:

> All these reports helped fuel Rumsfeld's sense of futility as to America's ability to stop the spread of destructive weapons and keep them from terrorists. That futility was the fuel that drove the plans to invade Iraq . . . as soon as possible.
>
> Cheney's ideas about how "our reaction" would shape behavior—whatever the evidence showed—were expressed in an off-the-record meeting Rumsfeld had with NATO defense chiefs in Brussels on June 6. According to an outline for his speech, the secretary told those assembled that "absolute proof cannot be a precondition for action."
>
> The primary impetus for invading Iraq, according to those attending NSC briefings on the Gulf in this period, was to make an example of Hussein, to create a demonstration model to guide the behavior of anyone with the temerity to acquire destructive weapons or, in any way, flout the authority of the United States.[6]

In the great, multicolored braid of reasons and justifications leading to the Iraq war one might call this "the realist strand," and though the shape of the reasoning might seem to Gerson to stand as far from "democracy building" and "ending tyranny" as "power politics" does from "idealism," the distance is wholly illusory, dependent on an ideological clarity that was never present. In fact, the two chains of reasoning looped and intersected, leading inexorably to a common desire for a particular action—confronting Saddam Hussein and Iraq—that had been the subject of the administration's first National Security Council meeting, in January 2001, and that had been pushed to the fore again by Defense Department officials in the first "war cabinet" meeting after the September 11 attacks.

WOODWARD DESCRIBES a report commissioned by Paul Wolfowitz, then deputy secretary of defense, intended to produce "the kinds of ideas and strategy needed to deal with a crisis of the magnitude of 9/11." After the attacks, Wolfowitz talked to his friend Christopher DeMuth, president of the American Enterprise Institute, who gathered together a group of intellectuals and academics[7] for a series of discussions that came to be known as "Bletchley II" (after the World War II think tank of mathematicians and cryptographers set up at Bletchley Park). Out of these discussions, DeMuth drafted an influential report, entitled "Delta of Terrorism," which concluded that "the United States was in for a two-generation battle with radical Islam":

> "The general analysis was that Egypt and Saudi Arabia, where most of the hijackers came from, were the key, but the problems there are intractable. Iran is more important, where they were confident and successful in setting up a radical government." But Iran was similarly difficult to envision dealing with, [DeMuth] said.
>
> But Saddam Hussein was different, weaker, more vulnerable. DeMuth said they had concluded that "Baathism is an Arab form of fascism transplanted to Iraq." . . .
>
> "We concluded that a confrontation with Saddam was inevitable. He was a gathering threat—the most menacing, active and unavoidable threat. We agreed that Saddam would have to leave the scene before the problem would be addressed." That was the only way to transform the region.[8]

According to Woodward, this report had "a strong impact on President Bush, causing him to focus on the 'malignancy' of the Middle East"—and the need to act to excise it, beginning with an attack on Iraq that would not only serve, in its devastating rapidity and effectiveness, as a "demonstration model" to deter anyone thinking to threaten the United States but would begin a process of "democratic transformation" that would quickly spread throughout the region. The geopolitical thinking animating this "democratic domino theory" could be plainly discerned before the war, as I wrote five months before U.S. Army tanks crossed the border into Iraq:

> Behind the notion that an American intervention will make of Iraq "the first Arab democracy," as Deputy Defense Secretary Paul Wolfowitz put it, lies a project of great ambition. It envisions a post–Saddam Hussein Iraq—secular, middle-class, urbanized, rich with oil—that will replace the autocracy of Saudi Arabia as the key American ally in the Persian Gulf, allowing the withdrawal of United States troops from the kingdom. The presence of a victorious American Army in Iraq would then serve as a powerful boost to moderate elements in neighboring Iran, hastening that critical country's evolution away from the mullahs and toward a more moderate course. Such an evolution in Tehran would lead to a withdrawal of Iranian support for Hezbollah and other radical groups, thereby isolating Syria and reducing pressure on Israel. This undercutting of radicals on Israel's northern borders and within the West Bank and Gaza would spell the definitive end of Yasir Arafat and lead eventually to a favorable solution of the Arab-Israeli problem.
>
> This is a vision of great sweep and imagination: comprehensive, prophetic, evangelical. In its ambitions, it is wholly foreign to the modesty of containment, the ideology of a status-quo power that lay at the heart of American strategy for half a century. It means to remake the world, to offer to a political threat a political answer. It represents a great step on the road toward President Bush's ultimate vision of "freedom's triumph over all its age-old foes."[9]

It represented as well a breathtaking gamble, for if the victory in Iraq was to achieve what was expected—which is to say, "humiliate" the forces of radical Islam and reestablish American prestige and credibility; serve as a "demonstration model" to ward off attacks from any rogue state that might threaten the United States, either directly or by supplying weapons of mass destruction to terrorists; and transform the Middle East by sending a "democratic tsunami" cascading from Tehran to Gaza—if the Iraq war was to achieve this, victory must be rapid, decisive, overwhelming.

Only Donald Rumsfeld's transformed military—a light, quick, lean force with very few "boots on the ground" and dependent on overwhelming firepower directed precisely by high technology—could make this happen, or so he and his planners thought. Victory would be quick and awe-inspiring; in a few months the Americans, all but a handful of them, would be gone: Only the effect of the "demonstration model," and the cascading consequences in the neighboring states, would remain. The use of devastating military power would begin the process but once begun the transformation would roll forward, carried out by forces of the same thrilling "democratic revolution" that had erupted on the streets of Prague and Budapest and East Berlin more than a decade before, and indeed on the streets of Kabul the previous year. Here was an evangelical vision of geopolitical redemption.

II.

Thus the War of Imagination draped all the complications and contradictions of the history and politics of a war-torn, brutalized society in an ideologically driven vision of a perfect future. Small wonder that its creators, faced with grim reality, have been so loath to part with it. Since the first thrilling night of shock and awe, reported with breathless enthusiasm by the American television networks, the Iraq war has had at least two histories, that of the war itself and that of the American perception of it. As the months passed and the number of attacks in Iraq grew, the gap between those two histories opened wider and wider.[10] And finally, for most Americans, the War of Imagination—built of nationalistic excitement and ideological hubris and administration pronouncements about "spreading democracy" and "greetings with sweets and flowers," and then about "dead-enders" and "turning points," and finally about "staying the course" and refusing "to cut and run"—began, under the pressure of nearly three thousand American dead and perhaps a hundred thousand or more dead Iraqis, to give way to grim reality.

The midterm elections of November 7, 2006, mark the moment when the War of Imagination decisively gave way to the war on the ground and when officials throughout the American government, not least the president himself, were forced to recognize and acknowledge a reality that much of the American public had discerned months or years before. The ideological canopy now has lifted. The study groups are at their work. Americans have come to know what they do not know. If confronted with that simple question the smiling President Ahmadinejad of Iran put to Mike Wallace last August—"I ask you, sir, what is the American Army doing inside Iraq?"—how many Americans could offer a clear and convincing answer?

As the war drags on and alternatives fall away and American and Iraqi deaths mount, we seem to know less and less, certainly about "where we are going to end." Thus we arrive at our present therapeutic moment—the moment of "solutions," brought on by the recognition, three and a half years on, that we have no idea how to "end" Phase Two. This is now a matter for James A. Baker's Iraq Study Group and the military's "strategic review team" and the new Democratic committee chairmen who will offer, to a chastened president who admits he thought "we would do all right" in the elections, the "new ideas" he now professes to welcome.[11] However quickly the discussion now moves to the geopolitical hydraulics, to weighing partition against partial withdrawal against regional conferences and contact groups and all the rest, the truth is that none of these proposals, alone or in combination, will end the war anytime soon.

It bears noticing that Kennan himself, having predicted that we will never know where we are going to end in Iraq, lived to see disproved, before his death at the age of 101 last March, what even he, no innocent, had taken as a given: that "you know where you begin." For as the war's presumed ending—constructed from carefully crafted images of triumph, of dictators' statues cast down and presidents striding forcefully across aircraft carrier decks—has flickered and vanished, receding into the just-out-of-grasp future ("a decision for the next president," the pre-election President Bush had said), the war's beginning has likewise melted away, the original rationale obscured in a darkening welter of shifting intelligence, ideological controversy, and conflicting claims, all of it hemmed in now on all sides by the mounting dead.

III.

Out of this maelstrom, how does one fix now on "how we began" in Iraq? One might do worse than the National Security Presidential Directive entitled "Iraq: Goals, Objectives and Strategy," the top-secret statement of American purpose intended to guide all the departments and agencies of the government, signed by President George W. Bush on August 29, 2002:

> U.S. goal: Free Iraq in order to eliminate Iraqi weapons of mass destruction, their means of delivery and associated programs, to prevent Iraq from breaking out of containment and becoming a more dangerous threat to the region and beyond.
>
> End Iraqi threats to its neighbors, to stop the Iraqi government's tyrannizing of its own population, to cut Iraqi links to and sponsorship of international terrorism, to maintain Iraq's unity and territorial integrity. And liberate the Iraqi people from tyranny, and assist them in creating a society based on moderation, pluralism and democracy. . . .
>
> Objectives: To conduct policy in a fashion that minimizes the chance of a WMD attack against the United States, U.S. field forces, our allies and friends. To minimize the danger of regional instabilities. To deter Iran and Syria from helping Iraq. And to minimize disruption in international oil markets.[12]

This secret document is presumably the plainest, least ideological statement of what American officials thought the country they led would be trying to achieve in the coming war. The words have now a sad and antique air, as if scrawled on yellowed parchment and decipherable only by a historian skilled in the customs and peculiarities of a far-off time and place. What can we say now, as we look at the Iraq of November 2006, about these official goals and objectives of the Iraq war?

The famous weapons of mass destruction are gone, most of them probably fifteen years gone, and their absence has likely damaged the United States and its power—the power, deployed daily, that depends on the authority of words and pronouncements and not directly or solely on force of arms—more severely than their presence ever could have. While no doubt convinced that Iraq had at least some chemical and biological weapons, Bush administration officials, like the cop framing a guilty man, vastly exaggerated the evidence and in so doing—and even as they refused to allow UN inspectors to examine and weigh that evidence—they severely undermined the credibility of the United States and its intelligence agencies, and the support for the war and U.S. policy among Americans, among Muslims, and around the world.

The containment of Iraq, threatened only in the realm of policymakers' imaginations before the war, has been breached. The country's "threat to the region," with jihadis flowing from neighboring Sunni powers into Anbar and Baghdad and Iranian intelligence agents flowing into the Shia south, is growing daily, with the ultimate worst-case future, the confused and blackened landscape of a regional sectarian war, already standing clearly visible on the horizon as a possible consequence of an escalating conflict.

THOUGH SADDAM stands convicted of mass murder and condemned to death, and though an elected and ineffectual government deliberates within the Green Zone, it is hard to argue that the "tyrannizing" of the Iraqi population beyond its walls has not worsened. Every day on average a hundred or more Iraqis die from the violence of an increasingly complicated civil war. Sunnis attack Shia with bombs of every description—suicide bombers and car bombs and bicycle bombs and motorcycle bombs—and they maintain the pace of terror at an unprecedented, almost unimaginable rate. In the last six months alone Baghdad has endured 488 "terror-related bombings," an average of nearly three a day.[13]

Shia leaders respond with death squads, whose members, drawn from party militias and often allied with the Ministry of Interior and the Iraqi police, have by now tortured and assassinated thousands of Sunnis. As Iraqis do their shopping or say their prayers they are blown to pieces by suicide bombers. As they drive through the cities in broad daylight they are pulled from their cars by armed men at roadblocks who behead them or shoot them in the back of the neck. As they sit at home at night they are kidnapped by men in police or army uniforms who load them in the trunks of their cars and carry them off to secret places to be tortured and executed, their bound and headless bodies to be found during the following days in fields or dumps or by the roadside. These bodies, examined by United Nations officials in the Baghdad morgue,

> often bear signs of severe torture including acid-induced injuries and burns caused by chemical substances, missing skin, broken bones (back, hands and legs), missing eyes, missing teeth and wounds caused by power drills or nails.[14]

As Iraqis know well, the power drills and nails were a favorite of Saddam's torturers—though now, according to the United Nations special rapporteur on torture, "the situation is so bad many people say it is worse than it has been in the times of Saddam Hussein."[15] The level of carnage is difficult to comprehend. According to official figures published by the United Nations, which certainly understate the case, 6,599 Iraqis were murdered in July and August alone. Estimates of the number of Iraqi civilians killed during the war range from a conservative 52,000, by the Web site Iraq Body Count, to 655,000 by the Johns Hopkins School of Public Health, with the Iraqi Health Minister recently announcing a cumulative total of 150,000.[16]

As for the country's links to international terrorism, we might look to the official consensus of the American intelligence agencies issued in April 2006 that "the Iraq jihad is shaping a new generation of terrorist leaders and operatives" and that "the Iraq conflict has become the *cause célèbre* for jihadists, breeding a deep resentment of U.S. involvement in the Muslim world and cultivating supporters for the global jihadist movement."[17] The Bush administration's fears about Iraq's possible collaboration with terror groups, largely conjectural, have since Sadam's fall attained a terrible reality.

Iraq's "unity and territorial integrity," meantime, has become the central issue, as the war becomes increasingly sectarian, cities and regions are "ethnically cleansed," and the Shia have pushed through a law, in the face of bitter Sunni opposition, making possible the autonomy of the South, the culmination of a political process that, beginning with the first vote boycotted by Sunnis, has served to worsen sectarian conflict.

The central question of how power and resources should be divided in Iraq and what the country should look like, a question that was going to be settled peacefully by the nascent political institutions of the "first Arab democracy," has become the critical issue dividing Kurd from Sunni and Sunni from Shia, and also dividing the sectarian political coalitions themselves. Prime Minister Nuri al-Maliki, the leader of the "unity government," on whom President Bush has repeatedly called to "dismantle the militias," is in fact dependent for his own political survival on Moqtada al-Sadr, the creator and leader of the largest militia, the Mahdi Army. Indeed, the two most important militias are controlled by the two most powerful parties in parliament.

Increasingly the "unity government" itself, quarreling vituperatively within the Green Zone, serves as an impotent echo of the savage warfare raging beyond the walls. The partitioning of Iraq is now openly advocated by many—including such prominent American politicians as Senator Joseph Biden of Delaware, the incoming chairman of the Senate Foreign Relations Committee—desperate to find "a solution," however illusory, to the war, anything that will allow the Americans to withdraw, while avoiding any admission of defeat.

IV.

Kennan's problem of knowing "where you are going to end" begins, as he knew well, on the ground; but it does not end there. Information obtained by dedicated but deeply fallible humans travels from places like Fallujah by cable and e-mail and word of mouth into the vast four-mile-square bunker of the Green Zone, with its half-dozen concentric layers of concrete blast walls and sandbags and barbed wire, and from there to the great sprawling labyrinth of the Washington national security bureaucracy, up through the thousands of competing staffers in the layers of bureaus and agencies and eventually to the highly driven people at the tops of the organizational pyramids: The people who, it is said, "make the decisions." In the best managed of administrations there exists, between those on the ground who listen and learn and those in the offices who debate and decide, a great deal of bureaucratic "noise." And this, alas, as so many accounts of decision making on the war make all too clear, was not the best managed of administrations. Indeed, its top officials, talented and experienced as many of them were, seem to have willingly collaborated, for reasons of ego or ambition or ideological hubris, in making themselves collectively blind.

Consider, for example, this striking but typical discussion in the White House in April 2003 just as the Iraq occupation, the vital first step in President Bush's plan "to transform the Middle East," was getting underway. American forces are in Baghdad but the capital is engulfed by a wave of looting and disorder, with General Tommy Franks's troops standing by. The man in charge of the occupation, Lt. Gen. (ret.) Jay Garner, has just arrived "in-country." Secretary of State Colin Powell has come to the Oval Office to discuss the occupation with the president, who is joined by Condoleezza Rice, then his national security adviser. Powell began, according to Bob Woodward, by raising "the question of unity of command" in Iraq:

> There are two chains of command, Powell told the president. Garner reports to Rumsfeld and Franks reports to Rumsfeld.
> The president looked surprised.
> "That's not right," Rice said. "That's not right."
> Powell thought Rice could at times be pretty sure of herself, but he was pretty sure he was right. "Yes, it is," Powell insisted.
> "Wait a minute," Bush interrupted, taking Rice's side. "That doesn't sound right."
> Rice got up and went to her office to check. When she came back, Powell thought she looked a little sheepish. "That's right," she said.

What might Kennan, the consummate diplomatic professional, have thought of such a discussion between president, secretary of state, and national security adviser, had he lived to read of it? He would have grasped its implications instantly, as the president and his national security adviser apparently did not. Which leads to Powell's patient—too patient—explanation to the president:

> You have to understand that when you have two chains of command and you don't have a common superior in the theater, it means that every little half-assed fight they have out there, if they can't work it out, comes out to one place to be resolved. And that's in the Pentagon. Not in the NSC or the State Department, but in the Pentagon.[18]

The kernel of an answer to what is the most painful and intractable question about the Iraq war—how could U.S. officials repeatedly and consistently make such ill-advised and improbably stupid decisions, beginning with their lack of planning for "the postwar"—can be found in this little chamber play in the Oval Office, and in the fact that at least two thirds of the cast seem wholly incapable of comprehending the script. In Woodward's account, Rice, who was then the official responsible for coordinating the national security bureaucracies of the U.S. government, found what was being said "a rather theoretical discussion," somehow managing to miss the fact that she and the National Security Council she headed had been cut out of decision making on the Iraq war—and cut out, further, in favor of an official, Secretary of Defense Rumsfeld, who, if we are to believe Woodward, did not bother even to return her telephone calls.

The Iraq occupation would have all the weaknesses of two chains of command, weaknesses that would become all too apparent in a matter of days, when Lt. General Ricardo Sanchez, the junior three-star in the entire army, replaced General Franks and L. Paul Bremer replaced Garner, leaving the occupation in the hands of two officials who despised one another and hardly spoke. And both chains would end not in the White House but in the Pentagon, a vast bureaucracy not known for the delicate political touch that would be needed to carry out an occupation of this degree of complexity.

We hear again the patient explanation of Powell—whose fate in the Bush administration seems to have been to play the role of Cassandra, uttering grim prophecies destined to be ignored as reliably as they were to be proved true—letting Woodward (but this time not the president) know of his certainty that "the Pentagon wouldn't resolve the conflicts because Wolfowitz and Feith were running their own little games and had their own agenda to promote Chalabi."

THE NAME OF AHMAD CHALABI, the brilliant, charming, cunning impresario of the Iraqi exile community, evokes memories of disasters past and dreams dashed: the king to be who was, alas, never crowned. He is an irresistible character and has served as the off-screen villain in the telling of many an Iraq war melodrama, with particular attention to his part in helping to supply intelligence to various willing recipients within the U.S. government, bolstering the case that Iraq had significant stockpiles of weapons of mass destruction. In fact, however, Chalabi had a much more consequential role, that of the Pentagon's ruler-to-be, the solution to that vexing question of what to do about "the postwar."

Inherent in the War of Imagination were certain rather obvious contradictions: Donald Rumsfeld's dream of a "demonstration model" war of quick, overwhelming victory did not foresee an extended occupation—on the contrary, the defense secretary abjured, publicly and vociferously, any notion that his troops would be used for "nation-building." Rumsfeld's war envisioned rapid victory and rapid departure. Wolfowitz and the other Pentagon neoconservatives, on the other hand, imagined a "democratic transformation," a thoroughgoing social revolution that would take a Baath Party–run autocracy, complete with a Baathist-led army and vast domestic spying and security services, and transform it into a functioning democratic polity—without the participation of former Baathist officials.

How to resolve this contradiction? The answer, for the Pentagon, seems to have amounted to one word: Chalabi. "When it came to Iraq," James Risen writes in *State of War*,

> the Pentagon believed it had the silver bullet it needed to avoid messy nation building—a provisional government in exile, built around Chalabi, could be established and then brought in to Baghdad after the invasion.

This so-called "turnkey operation" seems to have appeared to be the perfect compromise plan: Chalabi was Shiite, as were most Iraqis, but he was also a secularist who had lived in the West for nearly fifty years and was close to many of the Pentagon civilians. Alas, Chalabi provoked strong opposition elsewhere in the government, particularly from powerful officials in the State Department and CIA, some of whom had worked with him for many years and distrusted him. In the end, it was the president himself who would put an end to the "Chalabi option," for, as it turned out, the confirmed idealist in the White House "was adamant that the United States not be seen as putting its thumb on the scales" of the nascent Iraqi democracy. Chalabi, for all his immense popularity in the Pentagon and in the vice president's office, would not be installed as president of Iraq.

Though "Bush's commitment to democracy was laudable," as Risen observes, his awkward intervention "was not really the answer to the question of postwar planning." He goes on:

> Once Bush quashed the Pentagon's plans, the administration failed to develop any acceptable alternative. . . . Instead, once the Pentagon realized the president wasn't going to let them install Chalabi, the Pentagon leadership did virtually nothing. After Chalabi, there was no Plan B.

An unnamed White House official describes to Risen the Laurel-and-Hardy consequences within the government of the president's attachment to the idea of democratic elections in Iraq:

> Part of the reason the planning for post-Saddam Iraq was so nonexistent was that the State Department had been saying if you invade, you have to plan for the postwar. And DOD said, no you don't. You can set up a provisional government in exile around Chalabi. DOD had a stupid plan, but they had a plan. But if you don't do that plan, and you don't make the Pentagon work with State to develop something else, then you go to war with no plan.[19]

V.

Anyone wanting to answer the question of "how we began" in Iraq has to confront the monumental fact that the United States, the most powerful country in the world, invaded Iraq with no particular and specific idea of what it was going to do there, and then must try to explain how this could have happened. In his account Woodward resists the lure of Chalabi but not the temptation of melodrama, instead choosing, with typically impeccable political timing, to place Donald Rumsfeld in the role of mustache-twirling villain, a choice that most of the country, in the wake of the elections and the secretary's instant fall from power, seems happy to embrace. And the secretary, truculent, arrogant, vain, has shown himself perfectly willing to play his part in this familiar Washington morality tale, setting himself up for the predictable fall by spending hours at the podium before fawning reporters and their television cameras during and after the invasion.

The Fall of Rumsfeld gives pace and drive to Woodward's narrative. No doubt this will please readers, who find themselves increasingly outraged at the almost unbelievable failures in planning and execution, rewarding them with a bracing wave of *schadenfreude* when the inevitable defenestration finally takes place—outside the frame of the book but wholly predictable from its storyline. Indeed, the fact of *State of Denial's* publication a month before the election, complete with the usual national television interviews and other attendant publicity, was not the least of the signs that the knives were out and glinting and that the secretary's days were numbered.

Irresistible as Rumsfeld is, however, the story of the Iraq war disaster springs less from his brow than from that of an inexperienced and rigidly self-assured president who managed to fashion, with the help of a powerful vice president, a strikingly disfigured process of governing. Woodward, much more interested in character and personal rivalry than government bureaus and hierarchies, refers to this process broadly as "the interagency," as in "Rice said the interagency was broken." He means the governing apparatus set up by the National Security Act of 1947, which gathered the government's major security officials—secretaries of state, defense, and treasury, attorney general, director of national intelligence, among others—into the National Security Council, and gave to the president a special assistant for national security affairs (commonly known as the national security adviser) and a staff to manage, coordinate, and control it. Through the National Security Council and the "deputies committee" and other subsidiary bodies linking the various government departments at lower levels, information and policy guidance are supposed to work their way up from bureaucracy to president, and his decisions to work their way down. Ron Suskind, who has been closely studying the inner workings of the Bush administration since his revealing piece about Karl Rove and John Dilulio in 2003 and his book on Paul O'Neill the following year,[20] observes that "the interagency" not only serves to convey information and decisions but also is intended to perform a more basic function:

> Sober due diligence, with an eye for the way previous administrations have thought through a standard array of challenges facing the United States, creates, in fact, a kind of check on executive power and prerogative.[21]

This is precisely what the president didn't want, particularly after September 11; deeply distrustful of the bureaucracy, desirous of quick, decisive action, impatient with bureaucrats and policy intellectuals, the president wanted to act. Suskind writes:

> For George W. Bush, there had been an evolution on such matters—from the early, pre-9/11 president, who had little grasp of foreign affairs and made few major decisions in that realm; to the post-9/11 president, who met America's foreign challenges with decisiveness born of a brand of preternatural, faith-based, self-generated certainty. The policy process, in fact, never changed much. Issues argued, often vociferously, at the level of deputies and principals rarely seemed to go upstream in their fullest form to the president's desk; and, if they did, it was often after Bush seemed to have already made up his mind based on what was so often cited as his "instinct" or "gut."[22]

Woodward tends to blame "the broken policy process" on the relative strength of personalities gathered around the cabinet table: the power and ruthlessness of Rumsfeld, the legendary "bureaucratic infighter"; the weakness of Rice, the very function and purpose of whose job, to let the president both benefit from and control the bureaucracy, was in effect eviscerated. Suskind, more convincingly, argues that Bush and Cheney constructed precisely the government they wanted: centralized, highly secretive, its clean, direct lines of decision unencumbered by information or consultation. "There was never any policy process to break, by Condi or anyone else," Richard Armitage, the former deputy secretary of state, remarks to Suskind. "There was never one from the start. Bush didn't want one, for whatever reason." Suskind suggests why in an acute analysis of personality and leadership:

Of the many reasons the president moved in this direction, the most telling may stem from George Bush's belief in his own certainty and, especially after 9/11, his need to protect the capacity to will such certainty in the face of daunting complexity. His view of right and wrong, and of righteous actions—such as attacking evil or spreading "God's gift" of democracy—were undercut by the kind of traditional, shades-of-gray analysis that has been a staple of most presidents' diets. This president's traditional day began with Bible reading at dawn, a workout, breakfast, and the briefings of foreign and domestic threats. . . . The hard, complex analysis, in this model, would often be a thin offering, passed through the filters of Cheney or Rice, or not presented at all.

. . . This granted certain unique advantages to Bush. With fewer people privy to actual decisions, tighter confidentiality could be preserved, reducing leaks. Swift decisions—either preempting detailed deliberation or ignoring it—could move immediately to implementation, speeding the pace of execution and emphasizing the hows rather than the more complex whys.

What Bush knew before, or during, a key decision remained largely a mystery. Only a tiny group—Cheney, Rice, Card, Rove, Tenet, Rumsfeld—could break this seal.[23]

To the rest of the government, of course, this "mystery" must have been excruciating to endure; Suskind describes how many of those in the "foreign policy establishment" found themselves "befuddled" by the way the traditional policy process was viewed not only as unproductive but "perilous." Information, that is, could slow decision making; indeed, when it had to do with a bold and risky venture like the Iraq war, information and discussion—an airing, say, of the precise obstacles facing a "democratic transition" conducted with a handful of troops—could paralyze it. If the sober consideration of history and facts stood in the way of bold action then it would be the history and the facts that would be discarded. The risk of doing nothing, the risk, that is, of the status quo, justified acting. Given the grim facts on the ground—the likelihood of a future terrorist attack from the "malignant" Middle East, the impossibility of entirely protecting the country from it—better to embrace the unknown. Better, that is, to act in the cause of "constructive instability"—a wonderfully evocative phrase, which, as Suskind writes, was

the term used by various senior officials in regard to Iraq—a term with roots in pre-9/11 ideas among neoconservatives about the need for a new, muscular, unbounded American posture; and outgrowths that swiftly took shape after the attacks made everything prior to 9/11 easily relegated to dusty history.

The past—along with old-style deliberations based on cause and effect or on agreed-upon precedents—didn't much matter; nor did those with knowledge of prevailing policy studies, of agreements between nations, or of long-standing arrangements defining the global landscape.

What mattered, by default, was the president's "instinct" to guide America across the fresh, post-9/11 terrain—a style of leadership that could be rendered within tiny, confidential circles.

America, unbound, was duly led by a president, unbound.[24]

It is that "duly led," of course, that is the question. Information, history, and all the other attributes of a deliberative policy may inhibit action but they do so by weighing and calculating risk. Dispensing with them has no consequences only if you accept the proposition that the Iraq war so clearly disproves: that bold action must always make us safer.

VI.

So there would be no President Chalabi. Unfortunately, the president, who thought of himself, Woodward says, "as the calcium in the backbone" of the U.S. government, having banned Chalabi's ascension, neither offered an alternative plan nor forced the government he led to agree on one. Nor did Secretary Rumsfeld, who knew only that he wanted a quick victory and a quick departure. To underline the point, soon after the U.S. invasion the secretary sent his special assistant, Larry DiRita, to the Kuwait City Hilton to brief the tiny, miserable, understaffed, and underfunded team led by the retired General Garner which was preparing to fly to a chaotic Baghdad to "take control of the transition." Here is DiRita's "Hilton Speech" as quoted by an army colonel, Paul Hughes:

> "We went into the Balkans and Bosnia and Kosovo and we're still in them. . . . We're probably going to wind up in Afghanistan for a long time because the Department of State can't do its job right. Because they keep screwing things up, the Department of Defense winds up being stuck at these places. We're not going to let this happen in Iraq."
>
> The reaction was generally, Whoa! Does this guy even realize that half the people in the room are from the State Department?
>
> DiRita went on, as Hughes recalled: "By the end of August we're going to have 25,000 to 30,000 troops left in Iraq."[25]

DiRita spoke these words as, a few hundred miles away, Baghdad and the other major cities of Iraq were taken up in a thoroughgoing riot of looting and pillage—of government ministries, universities and hospitals, power stations and factories—that would virtually destroy the country's infrastructure, and with it much of the respect Iraqis might have had for American competence. The uncontrolled violence engulfed Iraq's capital and major cities for weeks as American troops—140,000 or more—mainly sat on their tanks, looking on. If attaining true political authority depends on securing a monopoly on legitimate violence, then the Americans would never achieve it in Iraq. There were precious few troops to impose order, and hardly any military police. No one gave the order to arrest or shoot looters or otherwise take control of the streets. Official Pentagon intentions at this time seem to have been precisely what the secretary of defense's special assistant said they were: to have all but 25,000 or so of those troops out of Iraq in five months or less.

How then to secure the country, which was already in a state of escalating chaos? Most of the ministries had been looted and burned and what government there was consisted of the handful of Iraqi officials who Garner's small team had managed to coax into returning to work. In keeping with the general approach of quick victory, quick departure, Garner had briefed the president and his advisers before leaving Washington, emphasizing his plan to dismiss only the most senior and personally culpable Baathists from the government and also to make use of the Iraqi army to rebuild and, eventually, keep order.

Within weeks of that meeting in the Kuwait Hilton, L. Paul Bremer arrived in Baghdad, replacing Garner, who had been fired after less than a month in Iraq. On Bremer's first full day "in-country," in Woodward's telling, one of Garner's officials ran up to her now–lame duck boss and thrust a paper into his hand:

"Have you read this?" she asked.
"No," Garner replied. "I don't know what the hell you've got there."
"It's a de-Baathification policy," she said, handing him a two-page document.

The document was Bremer's "Coalition Provisional Authority Order Number 1—De-Baathification of Iraqi Society," an order to remove immediately from their posts all "full members" of the Baath Party. These were to be banned from working in any government job. In every ministry the top three levels of managers would be investigated for crimes.

"We can't do this," Garner said. He still envisioned what he had told Rumsfeld would be a "gentle de-Baathification"—eliminating only the number one Baathist and personnel directors in each ministry. "It's too deep," he added.

Garner headed immediately to Bremer's office, where the new occupation leader was just settling in, and on the way ran into the CIA chief of station, referred to here as Charlie.

"Have you read this?" Garner asked.
"That's why I'm over here," Charlie said.

"Let's go see Bremer." The two men got in to see the new administrator of Iraq around 1 PM. "Jerry, this is too deep," Garner said. "Give Charlie and me about an hour. We'll sit down with this. We'll do the pros and cons and then we'll get on the telephone with Rumsfeld and soften it a bit."

"Absolutely not," Bremer said. "Those are my instructions and I intend to execute them."

Garner, who will shortly be going home, sees he's making little headway and appeals to the CIA man, who "had been station chief in other Middle East countries," asking him what will happen if the order is issued.

> "If you put this out, you're going to drive between 30,000 and 50,000 Baathists underground before nightfall," Charlie said. . . . "You will put 50,000 people on the street, underground and mad at Americans." And these 50,000 were the most powerful, well-connected elites from all walks of life.
>
> "I told you," Bremer said, looking at Charlie. "I have my instructions and I have to implement this."[26]

The chain of command, as we know, goes through Rumsfeld, and Garner gets on the phone and appeals to the secretary of defense, who tells him that the matter is out of his hands:

> "This is not coming from this building," [Rumsfeld] replied. "That came from somewhere else."
>
> Garner presumed that meant the White House, NSC or Cheney. According to other participants, however, the de-Baathification order was purely a Pentagon creation. Telling Garner it came from somewhere else, though, had the advantage for Rumsfeld of ending the argument.[27]

SUCH TACTICS are presumably what mark Rumsfeld as a "skilled bureaucratic infighter," the description that has followed him through his career in government like a Homeric epithet. In fact, according to Bremer, he had received those orders at the Pentagon a few days before from Douglas Feith, Rumsfeld's undersecretary for policy. In Bremer's telling, Feith gave him the draft order, emphasizing "the political importance of the decree":

> We've got to show all the Iraqis that we're serious about building a New Iraq. And that means that Saddam's instruments of repression have no role in that new nation.[28]

The following day, Bremer's second in Iraq, the hapless Garner was handed another draft order. This was Order Number 2, disbanding the Iraqi ministries of Defense and Interior, the entire Iraqi military, and all of Saddam's bodyguard and special paramilitary organizations:

> Garner was stunned. The de-Baathification order was dumb, but this was a disaster. Garner had told the president and the whole National Security Council explicitly that they planned to use the Iraqi military—at least 200,000 to 300,000 troops—as the backbone of the corps to rebuild the country and provide security. And he'd been giving regular secure video reports to Rumsfeld and Washington on the plan.

An American colonel and a number of CIA officers had been meeting regularly with Iraqi officers in order to reconstitute the army. They had lists of soldiers, had promised emergency payments. "The former Iraqi military," according to Garner, "was making more and more overtures, just waiting to come back in some form." Again, Garner rushed off to see Bremer:

> "We have always made plans to bring the army back," he insisted. This new plan was just coming out of the blue, subverting months of work.
> "Well, the plans have changed," Bremer replied. "The thought is that we don't want the residuals of the old army. We want a new and fresh army."
> "Jerry, you can get rid of an army in a day, but it takes years to build one."

Again Bremer tells Garner that he has his orders. The discussion attains a certain unintended comedy when the proconsuls go on to discuss the Iraqi Ministry of the Interior, which Bremer has also announced he will abolish:

> "You can't get rid of the Ministry of the Interior," Garner said.
> "Why not?"
> "You just made a speech yesterday and told everybody how important the police force is."
> "It is important."
> "All the police are in the Ministry of the Interior," Garner said. "If you put this out, they'll all go home today."[29]

On hearing this bit of information, we are told, Bremer looked "surprised"—an expression similar, no doubt, to Rice's when she and the president learned from the secretary of state that the civilian occupation authority would not be reporting to the White House but to the Pentagon. Unfortunately, within the Pentagon there coexisted at least two visions of what the occupation of Iraq was to be: the quick victory, quick departure view of Rumsfeld, and the broader, ideologically driven democratic transformation of Iraqi society championed by the neoconservatives. The two views had uneasily intersected, for a time, in the alluring person of Ahmad Chalabi, who seemed to make both visions possible. With a Chalabi coronation taken off the table by President Bush, however, determined officials with a direct line to Bremer were transforming the Iraq adventure into a long-term, highly ambitious occupation. Presumably as Garner woke up on May 17, reflecting that "the United States now had at least 350,000 more enemies than it had the day before—the 50,000 Baathists [and] the 300,000 officially unemployed soldiers," he could take satisfaction in having managed, by his last-minute efforts, to persuade Bremer to "excise the Ministry of Interior from the draft so the police could stay."

VII.

One can make arguments for a "deep de-Baathification" of Iraq. One can make arguments also for dismantling the Iraqi army. It is hard, though, to make an argument that such steps did not stand in dramatic and irresolvable contradiction to the Pentagon's plan to withdraw all but 30,000 American troops from Iraq within a few months. With no Iraqi army, with all Baath Party members thrown out of the ministries and the agencies of government, with all of Saddam's formidable security forces summarily sacked—and with all of these forces transformed into sworn enemies of the American occupation—who precisely was going to keep order in Iraq? And who was going to build that "new and fresh army" that Bremer was talking about?

These questions loom so large and are so obvious that one feels that they must have some answer, even if an unconvincing one. The simple fact is that these two enormously significant steps—launching a "deep de-Baathification" of the government and dissolving the Iraqi army—together with Bremer's decision, taken also during his first days, to downgrade to that of a figurehead the status of the group of Iraqi politicians known as the Iraqi Governing Council, transformed what had been the Pentagon's plan for a quick victory and quick departure into a long-running and open-ended occupation that would perforce involve the establishment of a new Iraqi army.

The political implications within Iraq were incalculable, for the de-Baathification and the dissolution of the army both appeared to the Sunnis to be declarations of open warfare against them, convincing many that they would be judged not by standards of individual conduct but by the fact of their membership in a group—judged not according to what they had done but according to who they were. This in itself undermined what hope there was to create the sine qua non of a stable democracy: a loyal opposition, which is to say an opposition that believes enough in the fairness of the system that it will renounce violence.

It is unlikely that the Pentagon's vision of a rapid departure ever could have worked, Bremer or no Bremer. What is striking, however, is the way that the most momentous of decisions were taken in the most shockingly haphazard ways, with the power in the hands of a few Pentagon civilians who knew little of Iraq or the region, the expertise of the rest of the government almost wholly excluded, and the president and his highest officials looking on.

In the event, the Bush administration seems to have worked hard to turn Kennan's problem of knowing the facts on its head: The systemic failures in Iraq resulted in large part from an almost willful determination to cut off those in the government who knew anything from those who made the decisions. Woodward tells us, for example, that Stephen Hadley, then Rice's deputy and now her successor,

> first learned of the orders on de-Baathification and disbanding the military as Bremer announced them to Iraq and to the world. They hadn't been touched by the formal interagency process and as far as Hadley knew there was no imprimatur from the White House. Rice also had not been consulted. It hadn't come back to Washington or the NSC for a decision. . . .
>
> One NSC lawyer had been shown drafts of the policies to de-Baathify Iraq and disband the military—but that was only to give a legal opinion. The policymakers never saw the drafts, never had a chance to say whether they thought they were good ideas or even to point out that they were radical departures from what had earlier been planned and briefed to the president.[30]

AS FOR THE uniformed military, the men who were responsible for securing Iraq and whose job would thus be dramatically affected both by de-Baathification and by the dissolution of the Iraqi army, they were given no chance to speak on either question. Woodward writes:

> General Myers, the principal military adviser to Bush, Rumsfeld and the NSC, wasn't even consulted on the disbanding of the Iraqi military. It was presented as a fait accompli.
>
> "We're not going to just sit here and second-guess everything he does," Rumsfeld told Myers at one point, referring to Bremer's decisions.
>
> "I didn't get a vote on it," Myers told a colleague, "but I can see where Ambassador Bremer might have thought this is reasonable."

Since it is the cashiered Iraqi troops who, broke, angry, and humiliated ("Why do you Americans punish us, when we did not fight?" as one ex-soldier demanded of me that October), would within days be killing Myers's soldiers with sniper fire and the first improvised explosive devices, General Myers's forbearance might appear uncommonly generous.

This was the time, of course, when the civilians in the Pentagon had attained their greatest power and prestige. Rumsfeld's daily press conferences were broadcast live over the cable news channels, with an appreciative audience of journalists chortling at the secretary's jokes on national television. No one then seems to have questioned his "distrust of the interagency." Instead, Woodward writes, from April 2003 on, the constant drumbeat that Hadley heard coming out of the Pentagon had been "This is Don Rumsfeld's thing, and we're going to do the interagency in Baghdad. Let Jerry run it."[31]

"Jerry," it might be said at this point, seems a well-meaning man, but he had never run anything larger than the United States embassy in the Netherlands, where he served as ambassador. He spoke no Arabic and knew little of the Middle East and nothing of Iraq. He had had nothing to do with the meager and inadequate planning the Pentagon had done for "the postwar" and indeed had had only a few days' preparation before being flown to Baghdad. He apparently never saw the extensive plans the State Department had drawn up for the postwar period. And as would become evident as the occupation wore on and he became more independent of the Pentagon civilians, he had no particular qualifications to make and implement decisions of such magnitude, decisions that would certainly prolong the American occupation and would ultimately do much to doom it. For Rumsfeld, however, Bremer's supposed independence in Baghdad had its uses:

> Rumsfeld later said he would be surprised if Wolfowitz or Feith gave Bremer the de-Baathification and army orders. He said he did not recall an NSC meeting on the subject. Of Bremer, Rumsfeld said, "I talked to him only rarely . . ."[32]

It is impossible to believe, even in this administration, that Bremer decided on his own, on his second day in Baghdad, to dissolve the Iraqi army, and it is unlikely that Rumsfeld's own involvement in a matter of such magnitude would have slipped the defense secretary's mind. To the "skilled bureaucratic infighter," however, especially one with little or no oversight from president or Congress, what Woodward calls "the rubber-glove syndrome—the tendency not to leave his fingerprints on decisions"—can prove useful in avoiding responsibility for wreckage caused—for a time, anyway. It cannot, however, prevent the consequences on the ground and, in Iraq, it has not.

VIII.

Nearly four years into the Iraq war, as we enter the Time of Proposed Solutions, the consequences of those early decisions define the bloody landscape. By dismissing and humiliating the soldiers and officers of the Iraqi army our leaders, in effect, did much to recruit the insurgency. By bringing far too few troops to secure Saddam's enormous arms depots they armed it. By bringing too few to keep order they presided over the looting and overwhelming violence and social disintegration that provided the insurgency such fertile soil. By blithely purging tens of thousands of the country's Baathist elite, whatever their deeds, and by establishing a muscle-bound and inept American occupation without an "Iraqi face," they created an increasing resentment among Iraqis that fostered the insurgency and encouraged people to shelter it. And by providing too few troops to secure Iraq's borders they helped supply its forces with an unending number of Sunni Islamic extremists from neighboring states. It was the foreign Islamists' strategy above all to promote their jihadist cause by provoking a sectarian civil war in Iraq; by failing to prevent their attacks and to protect the Shia who became their targets, the U.S. leaders have allowed them to succeed.

To Americans now, the hour appears very late in Iraq. Deeply weary of a war that early on lost its reason for being, most Americans want nothing more than to be shown a way out. The president and his counselors, even in the weeks before the election, had begun redefining the idea of victory, dramatically downgrading the goals that were set out in the National Security Presidential Directive of August 2002. Thus Vice President Cheney, asked the week before the election about an "exit strategy" from Iraq, declared that "we're not looking for an exit strategy. We're looking for victory" but then went on to offer a rather modest definition:

> Victory will be the day when the Iraqis solve their political problems and are up and running with respect to their own government, and when they're able to provide for their own security.[33]

This was before Americans had gone to the polls and overwhelmingly condemned the administration's Iraq policies—with the result that, as one comedian put it, "On Tuesday night, in an ironic turnaround, Iraq brought regime change to the United States."[34] On the day after the election President Bush, stripped of his majorities in Congress, came forward to offer a still more modest definition: Victory would mean producing in Iraq "a government that can defend, govern and sustain itself."[35]

In fact, even these modest words have come to seem ambitious. As I write, Operation Together Forward, the joint effort by American and Iraqi forces to secure the city of Baghdad, has failed. The American commander in the capital, faced with a 26 percent increase in attacks during the operation, declared the results "disappointing," an on-the-record use of direct language that a year ago would have been inconceivable coming from a senior U.S. officer.

Operation Together Forward was not only to have demonstrated that the Iraqis were now "able to defend themselves," as the president said, but to have made it possible for "the unity government to make the difficult decisions necessary to unite the country." The operation was intended to blunt the power of Sunni insurgents and thus clear the way for Prime Minister Nuri al-Maliki to lend his support to disarming and eliminating the Shia militias that are responsible for much of the death-squad killing in Baghdad. Unfortunately, the militias—in particular, the Mahdi Army and the Badr Organization—remain a vital part of the unity government's political infrastructure. This inconvenient but fundamental political fact renders much of the Bush administration's rhetoric about its present strategy in Iraq almost nonsensical. The evident contradiction between policy and reality, and the angry reactions by al-Maliki to efforts by the U.S. military to rein in the militias by launching raids into Sadr City, have stirred rumors, in Baghdad and Washington, of a possible post-election coup d'état to replace Maliki with a "government of national salvation." It is hard to know what such a government, whether led by Ayad Allawi, a longtime Washington favorite who was briefly interim prime minister (and who derided the possibility of coming to power by a coup), or some other "strongman," might accomplish, or whether any gains in security could outweigh the political costs of conniving in the overthrow of a government that, however ineffectual it is, Iraqis elected. The establishment of that government stands ever more starkly as one of the few (if ambiguous) accomplishments remaining from the original program for Iraq.

To Americans the Iraq war seems to have entered its third and final act. Though the plans and ideas now will come apace, all of them directed toward answering a single, dominant question—How do we get out of Iraq?—none is likely to supply a means of departure that does not carry a very high cost. The present "sense of an ending" about Iraq has its roots more in American weariness and frustration than any real prospect of finding a "solution" or "exit strategy" that won't, in its consequences, be seen for what it is: a de facto acknowledgment of a failed and even catastrophic policy.

Only the week before the election, President Bush warned an interviewer about the consequences of an American defeat in Iraq:

> The terrorists . . . have clearly said they want a safe haven from which to launch attacks against America, a safe haven from which to topple moderate governments in the Middle East, a safe haven from which to spread their jihadist point of view, which is that there are no freedoms in the world; we will dictate to you how you think. . . . I can conceivably see a world in which radicals and extremists control oil. And they would say to the West: You either abandon Israel, for example, or we're going to run the price of oil up. Or withdraw. . . .[36]

A few days after the Republican defeat at the polls, the president's chief of staff, Josh Bolten, discussing the Iraqi government, put the matter in even starker terms:

> We need to treat them as a sovereign government. But we also need to give them the support they need to succeed because the alternative for the United States, I believe, is truly disastrous. . . . We could leave behind an Iraq that is a failed state, a haven for terrorism, a real threat to the United States and to the region. That's just not an acceptable outcome.[37]

We are well down the road toward this dark vision, a wave of threatening instability that stands as the precise opposite of the Bush administration's "democratic tsunami," the wave of liberalizing revolution that American power, through the invasion of Iraq, was to set loose throughout the Middle East. The chances of accomplishing such change within Iraq itself, let alone across the complicated landscape of the entire region, were always very small. Saddam Hussein and the autocracy he ruled were the product of a dysfunctional politics, not the cause of it. Reform of such a politics was always going to be a task of incalculable complexity. Faced with such complexity, and determined to have their war and their democratic revolution, the president and his counselors looked away. Confronted with great difficulties, their answer was to blind themselves to them and put their faith in ideology and hope—in the dream of a welcoming landscape, magically transformed. The evangelical vision may have made the sense of threat after September 11 easier to bear but it did not change the risks and the reality on the ground. The result is that the wave of change the president and his officials were so determined to set in course by unleashing American military power may well turn out to be precisely the wave of Islamic radicalism that they had hoped to prevent.

In the coming weeks we will hear much talk of "exit strategies" and "proposed solutions." All such "solutions," though, are certain to come with heavy political costs, costs the president may consider more difficult to bear than those of doggedly "staying the course" for the remainder of his term. George W. Bush, who ran for president vowing a "humble" foreign policy, could not have predicted this. Kennan said it in October 2002:

> Anyone who has ever studied the history of American diplomacy, especially military diplomacy, knows that you might start in a war with certain things on your mind as a purpose of what you are doing, but in the end, you found yourself fighting for entirely different things that you had never thought of before. In other words, war has a momentum of its own and it carries you away from all thoughtful intentions when you get into it.[38]

If we are indeed in the third act then it may well be that this final act will prove to be very long and very painful. You may or may not know where you begin. You never know where you are going to end.

New York Review of Books, December 21, 2006

Voices from the Black Sites

> We need to get to the bottom of what happened—and why—so we make sure it never happens again.
>
> —Senator Patrick Leahy, Chairman, Senate Judiciary Committee[1]

March 12, 2009

I.

WE THINK TIME and elections will cleanse our fallen world but they will not. Since last November, George W. Bush and his administration have seemed to be rushing away from us at accelerating speed, a dark comet hurtling toward the ends of the universe. The phrase "War on Terror"—the signal slogan of that administration, so cherished by the man who took pride in proclaiming that he was "a wartime president"—has acquired in its pronouncement a permanent pair of quotation marks, suggesting something questionable, something mildly embarrassing: something past. And yet the decisions that that president made, especially the monumental decisions taken after the attacks of September 11, 2001—decisions about rendition, surveillance, interrogation—lie strewn about us still, unclaimed and unburied, like corpses freshly dead.

How should we begin to talk about this? Perhaps with a story. Stories come to us newborn, announcing their intent: Once upon a time . . . In the beginning . . . From such signs we learn how to listen to what will come. Consider:

> I woke up, naked, strapped to a bed, in a very white room. The room measured approximately 4m x 4m. The room had three solid walls, with the fourth wall consisting of metal bars separating it from a larger room. I am not sure how long I remained in the bed. . . .

A man, unnamed, naked, strapped to a bed, and for the rest, the elemental facts of space and of time, nothing but whiteness.

The storyteller is very much a man of our time. Early on in the "War on Terror," in the spring of 2002, he entered the dark realm of "the disappeared"—and only four and a half years later, when he and thirteen other "high-value detainees" arrived at Guantánamo and told their stories in interviews with representatives of the International Committee of the Red Cross, did he emerge partly into the light.[2] Indeed, he is a famous man, though his fame has followed a certain path, peculiar to our modern age: jihadist, outlaw, terrorist, "disappeared." An international celebrity whose name, one of them anyway, is instantly recognizable. How many people have their lives described by the president of the United States in a nationally televised speech?

> Within months of September the 11th, 2001, we captured a man known as Abu Zubaydah. We believe that Zubaydah was a senior terrorist leader and a trusted associate of Osama bin Laden. . . . Zubaydah was severely wounded during the firefight that brought him into custody—and he survived only because of the medical care arranged by the CIA.[3]

A dramatic story: big news. Wounded in a firefight in Faisalabad, Pakistan, shot in the stomach, groin, and thigh after jumping from a roof in a desperate attempt to escape. Massive bleeding. Rushed to a military hospital in Lahore. A trauma surgeon at Johns Hopkins awakened by a late-night telephone call from the director of central intelligence and flown in great secrecy to the other side of the world. The wounded man barely escapes death, slowly stabilizes, is shipped secretly to a military base in Thailand. Thence to another base in Afghanistan. Or was it Afghanistan?

We don't know, not definitively. For from the moment of his dramatic capture, on March 28, 2002, the man known as Abu Zubaydah slipped from one clandestine world, that of al Qaeda officials gone to ground in the days after September 11, into another, a "hidden global internment network" intended for secret detention and interrogation and set up by the Central Intelligence Agency under authority granted directly by President George W. Bush in a "memorandum of understanding" signed on September 17, 2001.

This secret system included prisons on military bases around the world, from Thailand and Afghanistan to Morocco, Poland, and Romania—"at various times," reportedly, "sites in eight countries"—into which, at one time or another, more than one hundred prisoners . . . disappeared.[4] The secret internment network of "black sites" had its own air force and its own distinctive "transfer procedures," which were, according to the writers of the International Committee of the Red Cross (ICRC) report, "fairly standardised in most cases":

> The detainee would be photographed, both clothed and naked prior to and again after transfer. A body cavity check (rectal examination) would

be carried out and some detainees alleged that a suppository (the type and the effect of such suppositories was unknown by the detainees), was also administered at that moment.

The detainee would be made to wear a diaper and dressed in a track-suit. Earphones would be placed over his ears, through which music would sometimes be played. He would be blindfolded with at least a cloth tied around the head and black goggles. In addition, some detainees alleged that cotton wool was also taped over their eyes prior to the blind-fold and goggles being applied. . . .

The detainee would be shackled by [the] hands and feet and trans-ported to the airport by road and loaded onto a plane. He would usually be transported in a reclined sitting position with his hands shackled in front. The journey times . . . ranged from one hour to over twenty-four to thirty hours. The detainee was not allowed to go to the toilet and if neces-sary was obliged to urinate and defecate into the diaper.[5]

One works the imagination trying to picture what it was like in this otherworldly place: blackness in place of vision. Silence—or "sometimes" loud music—in place of sounds of life. Shackles, together with gloves, in place of the chance to reach, touch, feel. One senses metal on wrist and ankle, cotton against eyes, cloth across face, shit and piss against skin. On "some occasions detainees were transported lying flat on the floor of the plane . . . with their hands cuffed behind their backs," causing them "severe pain and discomfort," as they were moved from one unknown loca-tion to another.

For his part, Abu Zubaydah—thirty-one years old, born Zein al-Abedeen Mohammad Hassan, in Riyadh, Saudi Arabia, though coming of Palestinian stock, from the Gaza Strip

alleged that during one transfer operation the blindfold was tied very tightly resulting in wounds to his nose and ears. He does not know how long the transfer took but, prior to the transfer, he reported being told by his detaining authorities that he would be going on a journey that would last twenty-four to thirty hours.[6]

A long trip then: perhaps to Guantánamo? Or Morocco? Then back, apparently, to Thailand. Or was it Afghanistan? He thinks the latter but can't be sure. . . .

II.

All classified, compartmentalized, deeply, deeply secret. And yet what is "secret" exactly? In our recent politics, "secret" has become an oddly complex word. From whom was "the secret bombing of Cambodia" secret? Not from the Cambodians, surely. From whom was the existence of these "secret overseas facilities" secret? Not from the terrorists, surely. From Americans, presumably. On the other hand, as early as 2002, anyone interested could read on the front page of one of the country's leading newspapers:

U.S. Decries Abuse but Defends Interrogations:
"Stress and Duress" Tactics Used on Terrorism Suspects
Held in Secret Overseas Facilities

Deep inside the forbidden zone at the U.S.-occupied Bagram air base in Afghanistan, around the corner from the detention center and beyond the segregated clandestine military units, sits a cluster of metal shipping containers protected by a triple layer of concertina wire. The containers hold the most valuable prizes in the war on terrorism—captured al Qaeda operatives and Taliban commanders. . . .

"If you don't violate someone's human rights some of the time, you probably aren't doing your job," said one official who has supervised the capture and transfer of accused terrorists. "I don't think we want to be promoting a view of zero tolerance on this. That was the whole problem for a long time with the CIA. . . ."

This lengthy article, by Dana Priest and Barton Gellman, appeared in the *Washington Post* on December 26, 2002, only months after the capture of Abu Zubaydah. A similarly lengthy report followed a few months later on the front page of the *New York Times* ("Interrogations: Questioning Terror Suspects in a Dark and Surreal World").[7] The blithe, aggressive tone of the officials quoted—"We don't kick the [expletive] out of them. We send them to other countries so they can kick the [expletive] out of them"—bespeaks a very different political temper, one in which a prominent writer in a national newsmagazine could headline his weekly column "Time to Think About Torture," noting in his subtitle that in this "new world . . . survival might well require old techniques that seemed out of the question."[8]

So there are secrets and secrets. And when, on a bright sunny day in 2006, just before the fifth anniversary of the September 11 attacks, the president of the United States strode into the East Room of the White House and informed the high officials, dignitaries, and specially invited September 11 survivor families gathered in rows before him that the United States government had created a dark and secret universe to hold and interrogate captured terrorists—or, in President Bush's words, "an environment where they can be held secretly [and] questioned by experts"—he was not telling a secret but instead converting a known and well-reported fact into an officially confirmed truth:

In addition to the terrorists held at Guantánamo, a small number of suspected terrorist leaders and operatives captured during the war have been held and questioned outside the United States, in a separate program operated by the Central Intelligence Agency. . . . Many specifics of this program, including where these detainees have been held and the details of their confinement, cannot be divulged. . . .

We knew that Abu Zubaydah had more information that could save innocent lives, but he stopped talking. . . . And so the CIA used an alternative set of procedures. These procedures were designed to be safe, to comply with our laws, our Constitution, and our treaty obligations. The Department of Justice reviewed the authorized methods extensively and determined them to be lawful. I cannot describe the specific methods used—I think you understand why. . . .[9]

I was watching the live broadcast that day—September 6, 2006—and I remember the uncanny feeling that came over me as, having heard the president explain the virtues of this "alternative set of procedures," I watched him stare straight into the camera and with fierce concentration and exaggerated emphasis intone once more: "The United States does not torture. It's against our laws, and it's against our values. I have not authorized it—and I will not authorize it." He had convinced himself, I thought, of the truth of what he said.

This speech, though not much noticed at the time, will stand, I believe, as George W. Bush's most important: perhaps the only "historic" speech he ever gave. In telling his version of Abu Zubaydah's story, and versions of the stories of Khaled Shaik Mohammed and others, the president took hold of many things that were already known but not acknowledged and, by means of the alchemical power of the leader's voice, transformed them into acknowledged facts. He also, in his fervent defense of his government's "alternative set of procedures" and his equally fervent denials that they constituted "torture," set out before the country and the world the dark moral epic of the Bush administration, in the coils of whose contradictions we find ourselves entangled still. Later that month, Congress, facing the midterm elections, duly passed the president's Military Commissions Act of 2006, which, among other things, sought to shelter from prosecution those who had applied the "alternative set of procedures" and had done so, said the president, "in a thorough and professional way."

At the same time, perhaps unwittingly, President Bush made it possible that day for those on whom the "alternative set of procedures" were performed eventually to speak. Even as the president set out before the country his version of what had happened to Abu Zubaydah and the others and argued for its necessity, he announced that he would bring him and thirteen of his fellow "high-value detainees" out of the dark world of the disappeared and into the light. Or, rather, into the twilight: The fourteen would be transferred to Guantánamo, the main acknowledged offshore prison, where—"as soon as Congress acts to authorize the military commissions I have proposed"—they "can face justice." In the meantime, though, the fourteen would be "held in a high-security facility at Guantánamo" and the International Committee of the Red Cross would be "advised of their detention, and will have the opportunity to meet with them."

A few weeks later, from October 6 to 11 and then from December 4 to 14, 2006, officials of the International Committee of the Red Cross—among whose official and legally recognized duties it is to monitor compliance with the Geneva Conventions and to supervise treatment of prisoners of war—traveled to Guantánamo and began interviewing "each of these persons in private" in order to produce a report that would "provide a description of the treatment and material conditions of detention of the fourteen during the period they were held in the CIA detention program," periods ranging "from sixteen months to almost four and a half years."[10]

As the ICRC interviewers informed the detainees, their report was not intended to be released to the public but, "to the extent that each detainee agreed for it to be transmitted to the authorities," to be given in strictest secrecy to officials of the government agency that had been in charge of holding them—in this case the Central Intelligence Agency, to whose acting general counsel, John Rizzo, the report was sent on February 14, 2007. Indeed, though almost all of the information in the report has names attached, and though annexes contain extended narratives drawn from interviews with three of the detainees, whose names are used, we do find a number of times in the document variations of this formula: "One of the detainees who did not wish his name to be transmitted to the authorities alleged . . ."—suggesting that at least one and perhaps more than one of the fourteen, who are, after all, still "held in a high-security facility at Guantánamo," worried about repercussions that might come from what he had said.

In virtually all such cases, the allegations made are echoed by other, named detainees; indeed, since the detainees were kept "in continuous solitary confinement and incommunicado detention" throughout their time in "the black sites," and were kept strictly separated as well when they reached Guantánamo, the striking similarity in their stories, even down to small details, would seem to make fabrication extremely unlikely, if not impossible. "The ICRC wishes to underscore," as the writers tell us in the introduction, "that the consistency of the detailed allegations provided separately by each of the fourteen adds particular weight to the information provided below."[11]

The result is a document—labeled "confidential" and clearly intended only for the eyes of those senior American officials to whom the CIA's Mr. Rizzo would show it—that tells a certain kind of story, a narrative of what happened at "the black sites" and a detailed description, by those on whom they were practiced, of what the president of the United States described to Americans as an "alternative set of procedures." It is a document for its time, literally "impossible to put down," from its opening page—

Contents

—to its stark and unmistakable conclusion:

> The allegations of ill-treatment of the detainees indicate that, in many
> cases, the ill-treatment to which they were subjected while held in the CIA
> program, either singly or in combination, constituted torture. In addition,
> many other elements of the ill-treatment, either singly or in combination,
> constituted cruel, inhuman or degrading treatment.[12]

Such unflinching clarity, from the body legally charged with overseeing
compliance with the Geneva Conventions—in which the terms "torture"
and "cruel, inhuman, and degrading treatment" are accorded a strictly
defined legal meaning—could not be more significant, or indeed more welcome after years in which the president of the United States relied on the
power of his office either to redefine or to obfuscate what are relatively
simple words. "This debate is occurring," as President Bush told reporters in
the Rose Garden the week after he delivered his East Room speech,

> because of the Supreme Court's ruling that said that we must conduct our-
> selves under the Common Article III of the Geneva Convention. And that
> Common Article III says that, you know, there will be no outrages upon
> human dignity. It's like—it's very vague. What does that mean, "outrages
> upon human dignity"?[13]

In allowing Abu Zubaydah and the other thirteen "high-value detainees" to tell their own stories, this report manages to answer, with great power and authority, the president's question.

III.

We return to a man, Abu Zubaydah, a Palestinian who, in his thirty-one years, has lived a life shaped by conflicts on the edge of the American consciousness: the Gaza Strip, where his parents were born; Riyadh, Saudi Arabia, where he apparently first saw the light of day; Soviet-occupied Afghanistan, where he took part in the jihad against the Russians, perhaps with the help, directly or indirectly, of American dollars; then, post-Soviet Afghanistan, where he ran al Qaeda logistics and recruitment, directing aspiring jihadists to the various training camps, placing them in cells after they'd been trained. The man has been captured now: traced to a safe house in Faisalabad, gravely wounded by three shots from an AK-47. He is rushed to the Faisalabad hospital, then to the military hospital at Lahore. When he opens his eyes he finds at his bedside an American, John Kiriakou of the CIA:

> I asked him in Arabic what his name was. And he shook his head. And I asked him again in Arabic. And then he answered me in English. And he said that he would not speak to me in God's language. And then I said, "That's okay. We know who you are."
> And then he asked me to smother him with a pillow. And I said, "No, no. We have plans for you."[14]

Kiriakou and the "small group of CIA and FBI people who just kept 24/7 eyes on him" knew that in Abu Zubaydah they had "the biggest fish that we had caught. We knew he was full of information . . . and we wanted to get it." According to Kiriakou, on a table in the house where they found him "Abu Zubaydah and two other men were building a bomb. The soldering [iron] was still hot. And they had plans for a school on the table. . . ." The plans, Kiriakou told ABC News correspondent Brian Ross, were for the British school in Lahore. Their prisoner, they knew, was "very current. On top of the current threat information."

With the help of the American trauma surgeon, Abu Zubaydah's captors nursed him back to health. He was moved at least twice, first, reportedly, to Thailand; then, he believes, to Afghanistan, probably Bagram. In a safe house in Thailand the interrogation began:

> I woke up, naked, strapped to a bed, in a very white room. The room measured approximately [13 feet by 13 feet]. The room had three solid walls, with the fourth wall consisting of metal bars separating it from a larger room. I am not sure how long I remained in the bed. After some time, I think it was several days, but can't remember exactly, I was transferred to a

chair where I was kept, shackled by [the] hands and feet for what I think was the next two to three weeks. During this time I developed blisters on the underside of my legs due to the constant sitting. I was only allowed to get up from the chair to go [to] the toilet, which consisted of a bucket. Water for cleaning myself was provided in a plastic bottle.

I was given no solid food during the first two or three weeks, while sitting on the chair. I was only given Ensure [a nutrient supplement] and water to drink. At first the Ensure made me vomit, but this became less with time.

The cell and room were air-conditioned and were very cold. Very loud, shouting type music was constantly playing. It kept repeating about every fifteen minutes twenty-four hours a day. Sometimes the music stopped and was replaced by a loud hissing or crackling noise.

The guards were American, but wore masks to conceal their faces. My interrogators did not wear masks.

During this first two to three week period I was questioned for about one to two hours each day. American interrogators would come to the room and speak to me through the bars of the cell. During the questioning the music was switched off, but was then put back on again afterwards. I could not sleep at all for the first two to three weeks. If I started to fall asleep one of the guards would come and spray water in my face.[15]

A naked man chained in a small, very cold, very white room is for several days strapped to a bed, then for several weeks shackled to a chair, bathed unceasingly in white light, bombarded constantly with loud sound, deprived of food; and whenever, despite cold, light, noise, hunger, the hours and days force his eyelids down, cold water is sprayed in his face to force them up.

One can translate these procedures into terms of art: "Change of Scenery Down." "Removal of Clothing." "Use of Stress Positions." "Dietary Manipulation." "Environmental Manipulation." "Sleep Adjustment." "Isolation." "Sleep Deprivation." "Use of Noise to Induce Stress." All these terms and many others can be found, for example, in documents associated with the debate about interrogation and "counter-resistance" carried on by Pentagon and Justice Department officials beginning in 2002. Here, however, we find a different standard: The Working Group says, for example, that "Sleep Deprivation" is "not to exceed four days in succession," that "Dietary Manipulation" should include "no intended deprivation of food or water," that "removal of clothing," while "creating a feeling of helplessness and dependence," must be "monitored to ensure the environmental conditions are such that this technique does not injure the detainee."[16] Here we are in a different place.

But what place? Abu Zubaydah was not only the "biggest fish that we had caught" but the first big fish. According to Kiriakou, Zubaydah, as he recovered, had "wanted to talk about current events. He told us a couple of times that he had nothing personal against the United States. . . . He said that 9/11 was necessary. That although he didn't think that there would be such a massive loss of life, his view was that 9/11 was supposed to be a wake-up call to the United States."[17]

In those initial weeks of healing, before the white room and the chair and the light, Zubaydah seems to have talked freely with his captors, and during this time, according to news reports, FBI agents began to question him using "standard interview techniques," ensuring that he was bathed and his bandages changed, urging improved medical care, and trying to "convince him they knew details of his activities." (They showed him, for example, a "box of blank audiotapes which they said contained recordings of his phone conversations, but were actually empty.") According to this account, Abu Zubaydah, in the initial days before the white room, "began to provide intelligence insights into al Qaeda."[18]

Or did he? "How Good Is Abu Zubaydah's Information?" asked a *Newsweek* "Web exclusive" on April 27, 2002, less than a month after his capture. The extreme secrecy and isolation in which Abu Zubaydah was being held, at a location unknown to him and to all but a tiny handful of government officials, did not prevent his "information" being leaked from that unknown place directly into the American press—in the cause, apparently, of a bureaucratic struggle between the FBI and the CIA. Even Americans who were not following closely the battling leaks from Zubaydah's interrogation would have found their lives affected, whether they knew it or not, by what was happening in that faraway white room; for about the same time the Bush administration saw fit to issue two "domestic terrorism warnings," derived from Abu Zubaydah's "tips"—about "possible attacks on banks or financial institutions in the Northeastern United States" and possible "attacks on U.S. supermarkets and shopping malls." As *Newsweek* learned from a "senior U.S. official," presumably from the FBI—whose "standard interview techniques" had produced that information and the "domestic terrorism warnings" based on it—the prisoner was "providing detailed information for the 'fight against terrorism.'" At the same time, however, "U.S. intelligence sources"—presumably CIA—"wonder whether he's trying to mislead investigators or frighten the American public."[19]

For his part, John Kiriakou, the CIA man, told ABC News that in those early weeks Zubaydah was "willing to talk about philosophy, [but] he was unwilling to give us any actionable intelligence." The CIA officers had the "sweeping classified directive signed by Mr. Bush," giving them authority to "capture, detain and interrogate terrorism suspects," and Zubaydah was "a test case for an evolving new role, . . . in which the agency was to act as jailer and interrogator of terrorism suspects." Eventually a team from the CIA's Counterterrorism Center was "sent in from Langley" and the FBI interrogators were withdrawn.

> We had these trained interrogators who were sent to his location to use the enhanced techniques as necessary to get him to open up, and to report some threat information. . . . These enhanced techniques included

everything from what was called an attention shake, where you grab the person by their lapels and shake them, all the way up to the other end, which is waterboarding.[20]

They began, apparently, by shackling him to the chair, and applying light, noise, and water to keep him awake. After two or three weeks of this Abu Zubaydah, still naked and shackled, was allowed to lie on the bare floor and to "sleep a little." He was also given solid food—rice—for the first time. Eventually a doctor, a woman, came and examined him, and "asked why I was still naked." The next day he was "provided with orange clothes to wear." The following day, however, "guards came into my cell. They told me to stand up and raise my arms above my head. They then cut the clothes off of me so that I was again naked and put me back on the chair for several days. I tried to sleep on the chair, but was again kept awake by the guards spraying water in my face."[21]

What follows is a confusing period, in which harsh treatment alternated with more lenient. Zubaydah was mostly naked and cold, "sometimes with the air conditioning adjusted so that, one official said, Mr. Zubayah seemed to turn blue."[22] Sometimes clothing would be brought, then removed the next day. "When my interrogators had the impression that I was cooperating and providing the information they required, the clothes were given back to me. When they felt I was being less cooperative the clothes were again removed and I was again put back on the chair." At one point he was supplied with a mattress, at another he was "allowed some tissue paper to use when going to toilet on the bucket." A month passed with no questioning. "My cell was still very cold and the loud music no longer played but there was a constant loud hissing or crackling noise, which played twenty-four hours a day. I tried to block out the noise by putting tissue in my ears." Then, "about two and half or three months after I arrived in this place, the interrogation began again, but with more intensity than before."[23]

It is difficult to know whether these alterations in attitude and procedure were intended, meant to keep the detainee off-guard, or resulted from disputes about strategy among the interrogators, who were relying on a hastily assembled "alternative set of procedures" that had been improvised from various sources, including scientists and psychiatrists within the intelligence community, experts from other, "friendly" governments, and consultants who had worked with the U.S. military and now "reverse-engineered" the resistance training taught to American elite forces to help them withstand interrogation after capture. The forerunners of some of the theories being applied in these interrogations, involving sensory deprivation, disorientation, guilt and shame, so-called "learned helplessness," and the need to induce "the debility-dependence-dread state," can be found in CIA documents dating back nearly a half-century, such as this from a notorious "counterintelligence interrogation" manual of the early 1960s:

The circumstances of detention are arranged to enhance within the sub-ject his feelings of being cut off from the known and the reassuring, and of being plunged into the strange. . . . Control of the source's environ-ment permits the interrogator to determine his diet, sleep pattern and other fundamentals. Manipulating these into irregularities, so that the subject becomes disorientated, is very likely to create feelings of fear and helplessness.[24]

A later version of the same manual emphasizes the importance of guilt: "If the 'questioner' can intensify these guilt feelings, it will increase the subject's anxiety and his urge to cooperate as a means of escape." Isolation and sensory deprivation will "induce regression" and the "loss of those defenses most recently acquired by civilized man," while the imposition of "stress positions" that in effect force the subject "to harm himself" will produce a guilt leading to an irresistible desire to cooperate with his interrogators.

IV.

Two and a half months after Abu Zubaydah woke up strapped to a bed in the white room, the interrogation resumed "with more intensity than before":

Two black wooden boxes were brought into the room outside my cell. One was tall, slightly higher than me and narrow. Measuring perhaps in area [3½ by 2½ feet by 6½ feet high]. The other was shorter, perhaps only [3½ feet] in height. I was taken out of my cell and one of the interrogators wrapped a towel around my neck, they then used it to swing me around and smash me repeatedly against the hard walls of the room. I was also repeatedly slapped in the face. . . .

I was then put into the tall black box for what I think was about one and a half to two hours. The box was totally black on the inside as well as the outside. . . . They put a cloth or cover over the outside of the box to cut out the light and restrict my air supply. It was difficult to breathe. When I was let out of the box I saw that one of the walls of the room had been covered with plywood sheeting. From now on it was against this wall that I was then smashed with the towel around my neck. I think that the plywood was put there to provide some absorption of the impact of my body. The interrogators realized that smashing me against the hard wall would probably quickly result in physical injury.[25]

One is reminded here that Abu Zubaydah was not alone with his inter-rogators, that everyone in that white room—guards, interrogators, doctor—was in fact linked directly, and almost constantly, to senior intelli-gence officials on the other side of the world. "It wasn't up to individual interrogators to decide, 'Well, I'm gonna slap him. Or I'm going to shake him. Or I'm gonna make him stay up for forty-eight hours," said John Kiriakou.

> Each one of these steps . . . had to have the approval of the Deputy Director for Operations. So before you laid a hand on him, you had to send in the cable saying, "He's uncooperative. Request permission to do X." And that permission would come. . . . The cable traffic back and forth was extremely specific. And the bottom line was these were very unusual authorities that the agency got after 9/11. No one wanted to mess them up. No one wanted to get in trouble by going overboard. . . . No one wanted to be the guy who accidentally did lasting damage to a prisoner.[26]

Smashing against hard walls before Zubaydah enters the tall black coffin-like box; sudden appearance of plywood sheeting affixed to the wall for him to be smashed against when he emerges. Perhaps the deputy director of operations, pondering the matter in his Langley, Virginia, office, suggested the plywood?

Or perhaps it was someone higher up? Shortly after Abu Zubaydah was captured, according to ABC News, CIA officers "briefed high-level officials in the National Security Council's Principals Committee," including Vice President Dick Cheney, National Security Adviser Condoleezza Rice, and Attorney General John Ashcroft, who "then signed off on the [interrogation] plan." At the time, the spring and summer of 2002, the administration was devising what some referred to as a "golden shield" from the Justice Department—the legal rationale that was embodied in the infamous "torture memorandum," written by John Yoo and signed by Jay Bybee in August 2002, which claimed that for an "alternative procedure" to be considered torture, and thus illegal, it would have to cause pain of the sort "that would be associated with serious physical injury so severe that death, organ failure, or permanent damage resulting in a loss of significant body function will likely result." The "golden shield" presumably would protect CIA officers from prosecution. Still, Director of Central Intelligence George Tenet regularly brought directly to the attention of the highest officials of the government specific procedures to be used on specific detainees—"whether they would be slapped, pushed, deprived of sleep or subject to simulated drowning"—in order to seek reassurance that they were legal. According to the ABC News report, the briefings of principals were so detailed and frequent that "some of the interrogation sessions were almost choreographed." At one such meeting, John Ashcroft, then attorney general, reportedly demanded of his colleagues, "Why are we talking about this in the White House? History will not judge this kindly."[27]

We do not know if the plywood appeared in Zubaydah's white room thanks to orders from his interrogators, from their bosses at Langley, or perhaps from their superiors in the White House. We don't know the precise parts played by those responsible for "choreographing" the "alternative set of procedures." We do know from several reports that at a White House meeting in July 2002 top administration lawyers gave the CIA "the green light" to move to the "more aggressive techniques" that were applied to him, separately and in combination, during the following days:

> After the beating I was then placed in the small box. They placed a cloth or cover over the box to cut out all light and restrict my air supply. As it was not high enough even to sit upright, I had to crouch down. It was very difficult because of my wounds. The stress on my legs held in this position meant my wounds both in the leg and stomach became very painful. I think this occurred about three months after my last operation. It was always cold in the room, but when the cover was placed over the box it made it hot and sweaty inside. The wound on my leg began to open and started to bleed. I don't know how long I remained in the small box, I think I may have slept or maybe fainted.
>
> I was then dragged from the small box, unable to walk properly and put on what looked like a hospital bed, and strapped down very tightly with belts. A black cloth was then placed over my face and the interrogators used a mineral water bottle to pour water on the cloth so that I could not breathe. After a few minutes the cloth was removed and the bed was rotated into an upright position. The pressure of the straps on my wounds was very painful. I vomited. The bed was then again lowered to horizontal position and the same torture carried out again with the black cloth over my face and water poured on from a bottle. On this occasion my head was in a more backward, downwards position and the water was poured on for a longer time. I struggled against the straps, trying to breathe, but it was hopeless. I thought I was going to die. I lost control of my urine. Since then I still lose control of my urine when under stress.
>
> I was then placed again in the tall box. While I was inside the box loud music was played again and somebody kept banging repeatedly on the box from the outside. I tried to sit down on the floor, but because of the small space the bucket with urine tipped over and spilt over me. . . . I was then taken out and again a towel was wrapped around my neck and I was smashed into the wall with the plywood covering and repeatedly slapped in the face by the same two interrogators as before.
>
> I was then made to sit on the floor with a black hood over my head until the next session of torture began. The room was always kept very cold.
>
> This went on for approximately one week. During this time the whole procedure was repeated five times. On each occasion, apart from one, I was suffocated once or twice and was put in the vertical position on the bed in between. On one occasion the suffocation was repeated three times. I vomited each time I was put in the vertical position between the suffocation.

During that week I was not given any solid food. I was only given Ensure to drink. My head and beard were shaved everyday.

I collapsed and lost consciousness on several occasions. Eventually, the torture was stopped by the intervention of the doctor.

I was told during this period that I was one of the first to receive these interrogation techniques, so no rules applied. It felt like they were experimenting and trying out techniques to be used later on other people.[28]

V.

All evidence from the ICRC report suggests that Abu Zubaydah's informant was telling him the truth: He was the first, and, as such, a guinea pig. Some techniques are discarded. The coffin-like black boxes, for example, barely large enough to contain a man, one six feet tall and the other scarcely more than three feet, which seem to recall the sensory-deprivation tanks used in early CIA-sponsored experiments,[29] do not reappear. Neither does the "long-time sitting"—the weeks shackled to a chair—that Abu Zubaydah endured in his first few months.

Nudity, on the other hand, is a constant in the ICRC report, as are permanent shackling, the "cold cell," and the unceasing loud music or noise. Sometimes there is twenty-four-hour light, sometimes constant darkness. Beatings, also, and smashing against the walls seem to be favored procedures; often, the interrogators wear gloves.

In later interrogations new techniques emerge, of which "longtime standing" and the use of cold water are notable. Walid Bin Attash, a Yemeni national involved with planning the attacks on the U.S. embassies in East Africa in 1998 and on the USS *Cole* in 2000, was captured in Karachi on April 29, 2003:

On arrival at the place of detention in Afghanistan I was stripped naked. I remained naked for the next two weeks. I was put in a cell measuring approximately [3 1/2 by 6 1/2 feet]. I was kept in a standing position, feet flat on the floor, but with my arms above my head and fixed with handcuffs and a chain to a metal bar running across the width of the cell. The cell was dark with no light, artificial or natural.

During the first two weeks, I did not receive any food. I was only given Ensure and water to drink. A guard would come and hold the bottle for me while I drank. . . . The toilet consisted of a bucket in the cell. . . . I was not allowed to clean myself after using the bucket. Loud music was playing twenty-four hours each day throughout the three weeks I was there.[30]

This "forced standing," with arms shackled above the head, a favorite Soviet technique (known as the *stoika*) that seems to have become standard procedure after Abu Zubaydah, proved especially painful for Bin Attash, who had lost a leg fighting in Afghanistan:

508   STRIPPING BARE THE BODY

After some time being held in this position my stump began to hurt so I removed my artificial leg to relieve the pain. Of course my good leg then began to ache and soon started to give way so that I was left hanging with all my weight on my wrists. I shouted for help, but at first nobody came. Finally, after about one hour a guard came and my artificial leg was given back to me and I was again placed in the standing position with my hands above my head. After that the interrogators sometimes deliberately removed my artificial leg in order to add extra stress to the position. . . .[31]

By his account, Bin Attash was kept in this position for two weeks—"apart [from] two or three times when I was allowed to lie down." Though "the methods used were specifically designed not to leave marks," the cuffs eventually "cut into my wrists and made wounds. When this happened the doctor would be called." At a second location, where Bin Attash was again stripped naked and placed "in a standing position with my arms above my head and fixed with handcuffs and a chain to a metal ring in the ceiling," a doctor examined his lower leg every day—"using a tape measure for signs of swelling."

I do not remember for exactly how many days I was kept standing, but I think it was about ten days. . . . During the standing I was made to wear a diaper. However, on some occasions the diaper was not replaced and so I had to urinate and defecate over myself. I was washed down with cold water everyday.

Cold water was used on Bin Attash in combination with beatings and the use of a plastic collar, which seems to have been a refinement of the towel that had been looped around Abu Zubaydah's neck:

Every day for the first two weeks I was subjected to slaps to my face and punches to my body during interrogation. This was done by one interrogator wearing gloves. . . .

Also on a daily basis during the first two weeks a collar was looped around my neck and then used to slam me against the walls of the interrogation room. It was also placed around my neck when being taken out of my cell for interrogation and was used to lead me along the corridor. It was also used to slam me against the walls of the corridor during such movements.

Also on a daily basis during the first two weeks I was made to lie on a plastic sheet placed on the floor which would then be lifted at the edges. Cold water was then poured onto my body with buckets. . . . I would be kept wrapped inside the sheet with the cold water for several minutes. I would then be taken for interrogation. . . .[32]

Bin Attash notes that in the "second place of detention"—where he was put in the diaper—"they were rather more sophisticated than in Afghanistan because they had a hose-pipe with which to pour the water over me."

VI.

A clear method emerges from these accounts, based on forced nudity, isolation, bombardment with noise and light, deprivation of sleep and food, and repeated beatings and "smashings"—though from this basic model one can see the method evolve, from forced sitting to forced standing, for example, and acquire new elements, like immersion in cold water.

Khaled Shaik Mohammed, the key planner of the September 11 attacks who was captured in Rawalpindi on March 1, 2003—nine of the fourteen "high-value detainees" were apprehended in Pakistan—and who, after a two-day detention in Pakistan during which he alleges that a "CIA agent . . . punched him several times in the stomach, chest and face [and] . . . threw him on the floor and trod on his face," was sent to Afghanistan using the standard "transfer procedures." ("My eyes were covered with a cloth tied around my head and with a cloth bag pulled over it. A suppository was inserted into my rectum. I was not told what the suppository was for.") In Afghanistan, he was stripped and placed in a small cell, where he "was kept in a standing position with my hands cuffed and chained to a bar above my head. My feet were flat on the floor." After about an hour,

> I was taken to another room where I was made to stand on tiptoes for about two hours during questioning. Approximately thirteen persons were in the room. These included the head interrogator (a man) and two female interrogators, plus about ten muscle guys wearing masks. I think they were all Americans. From time to time one of the muscle guys would punch me in the chest and stomach.[33]

These "full-dress" interrogations—where the detainee stands naked, on tiptoe, amid a crowd of thirteen people, including "ten muscle guys wearing masks"—were periodically interrupted by the detainee's removal to a separate room for additional procedures:

> Here cold water from buckets was thrown onto me for about forty minutes. Not constantly as it took time to refill the buckets. After which I would be taken back to the interrogation room.
>   On one occasion during the interrogation I was offered water to drink, when I refused I was again taken to another room where I was made to lie [on] the floor with three persons holding me down. A tube was inserted into my anus and water poured inside. Afterwards I wanted to go to the

toilet as I had a feeling as if I had diarrhoea. No toilet access was provided until four hours later when I was given a bucket to use.

Whenever I was returned to my cell I was always kept in the standing position with my hands cuffed and chained to a bar above my head.[34]

After three days in what he believes was Afghanistan, Mohammed was again dressed in a tracksuit, blindfold, hood, and headphones, and shackled and placed aboard a plane "sitting, leaning back, with my hands and ankles shackled in a high chair." He quickly fell asleep—"the first proper sleep in over five days"—and remains unsure of how long the journey took. On arrival, however, he realized he had come a long way:

I could see at one point there was snow on the ground. Everybody was wearing black, with masks and army boots, like Planet-X people. I think the country was Poland. I think this because on one occasion a water bottle was brought to me without the label removed. It had [an] e-mail address ending in ".pl."[35]

He was stripped and put in a small cell "with cameras where I was later informed by an interrogator that I was monitored 24 hours a day by a doctor, psychologist and interrogator." He believes the cell was underground because one had to descend steps to reach it. Its walls were of wood and it measured about ten by thirteen feet.

It was in this place, according to Mohammed, that "the most intense interrogation occurred, led by three experienced CIA interrogators, all over sixty-five years old and all strong and well trained." They informed him that they had received the "green light from Washington" to give him "*a hard time.*" "They never used the word 'torture' and never referred to 'physical pressure,' only to '*a hard time.*' I was never threatened with death, in fact I was told that they would not allow me to die, but that I would be brought to the '*verge of death and back again.*'"

I was kept for one month in the cell in a standing position with my hands cuffed and shackled above my head and my feet cuffed and shackled to a point in the floor. Of course during this month I fell asleep on some occasions while still being held in this position. This resulted in all my weight being applied to the handcuffs around my wrist resulting in open and bleeding wounds. [Scars consistent with this allegation were visible on both wrists as well as on both ankles.] Both my feet became very swollen after one month of almost continual standing.[36]

For interrogation, Mohammed was taken to a different room. The sessions last for as long as eight hours and as short as four.

The number of people present varied greatly from one day to another. Other interrogators, including women, were also sometimes present. . . . A doctor was usually also present. If I was perceived not to be cooperating I would be put against a wall and punched and slapped in the body, head and face. A thick flexible plastic collar would also be placed around my neck so that it could then be held at the two ends by a guard who would use it to slam me repeatedly against the wall. The beatings were combined with the use of cold water, which was poured over me using a hose-pipe. The beatings and use of cold water occurred on a daily basis during the first month.[37]

Like Abu Zubaydah; like Abdelrahim Hussein Abdul Nashiri, a Saudi who was captured in Dubai in October 2002, Mohammed was also subjected to waterboarding, by his account on five occasions:

I would be strapped to a special bed, which could be rotated into a vertical position. A cloth would be placed over my face. Cold water from a bottle that had been kept in a fridge was then poured onto the cloth by one of the guards so that I could not breathe. . . . The cloth was then removed and the bed was put into a vertical position. The whole process was then repeated during about one hour. Injuries to my ankles and wrists also occurred during the waterboarding as I struggled in the panic of not being able to breathe. Female interrogators were also present . . . and a doctor was always present, standing out of sight behind the head of [the] bed, but I saw him when he came to fix a clip to my finger which was connected to a machine. I think it was to measure my pulse and oxygen content in my blood. So they could take me to [the] breaking point.[38]

As with Zubaydah, the harshest sessions of interrogation involved the "alternative set of procedures" used in sequence and in combination, one technique intensifying the effects of the others:

The beatings became worse and I had cold water directed at me from a hose-pipe by guards while I was still in my cell. The worst day was when I was beaten for about half an hour by one of the interrogators. My head was banged against the wall so hard that it started to bleed. Cold water was poured over my head. This was then repeated with other interrogators. Finally I was taken for a session of water boarding. The torture on that day was finally stopped by the intervention of the doctor. I was allowed to sleep for about one hour and then put back in my cell standing with my hands shackled above my head.[39]

Reading the ICRC report, one becomes eventually somewhat inured to the "alternative set of procedures" as they are described: The cold and repeated violence grows numbing. Against this background, the descriptions of daily life of the detainees in the black sites, in which interrogation seems merely a periodic heightening of consistently imposed brutality, become more striking. Here again is Mohammed:

> After each session of torture I was put into a cell where I was allowed to lie on the floor and could sleep for a few minutes. However, due to shackles on my ankles and wrists I was never able to sleep very well. . . .The toilet consisted of a bucket in the cell, which I could use on request [he was shackled standing, his hands affixed to the ceiling], but I was not allowed to clean myself after toilet during the first month. . . . During the first month I was not provided with any food apart from on two occasions as a reward for perceived cooperation. I was given Ensure to drink every four hours. If I refused to drink then my mouth was forced open by the guard and it was poured down my throat by force. . . . At the time of my arrest I weighed 78 kg. After one month in detention I weighed 60 kg.
>
> I wasn't given any clothes for the first month. Artificial light was on twenty-four hours a day, but I never saw sunlight.[40]

VII.

Q: Mr. President, . . . this is a moral question: Is torture ever justified?

PRESIDENT GEORGE W. BUSH: Look, I'm going to say it one more time. . . . Maybe I can be more clear. The instructions went out to our people to adhere to law. That ought to comfort you. We're a nation of law. We adhere to laws. We have laws on the books. You might look at these laws, and that might provide comfort for you.

—Sea Island, Georgia, June 10, 2004

Abu Zubaydah, Walid Bin Attash, Khaled Shaik Mohammed—these men almost certainly have blood on their hands, a great deal of blood. There is strong reason to believe that they had critical parts in planning and organizing terrorist operations that caused the deaths of thousands of people. So in all likelihood did the other twelve "high-value detainees" whose treatment while secretly confined by agents of the U.S. government is described with such gruesome particularity in the report of the International Committee of the Red Cross. From everything we know, many or all of these men deserve to be tried and punished—to be "brought to justice," as President Bush, in his speech to the American people on September 6, 2006, vowed they would be.

It seems unlikely that they will be brought to justice anytime soon. In mid-January, Susan J. Crawford, who had been appointed by the Bush administration to decide which Guantánamo detainees should be tried before military commissions, declined to refer to trial Mohammed al-Qahtani, who was to have been among the September 11 hijackers but who had been turned back by immigration officials at Orlando International Airport. After he was captured in Afghanistan in late 2002, Qahtani was imprisoned in Guantánamo and interrogated by Department of Defense intelligence officers. Crawford, a retired judge and former general counsel of the army, told the *Washington Post* that she had concluded that Qahtani's "treatment met the legal definition of torture."

> The techniques they used were all authorized, but the manner in which they applied them was overly aggressive and too persistent. . . .
>
> You think of torture, you think of some horrendous physical act done to an individual. This was not any one particular act; this was just a combination of things that had a medical impact on him, that hurt his health. It was abusive and uncalled for. And coercive. Clearly coercive.[41]

Qahtani's interrogation at Guantánamo, accounts of which have appeared in *Time* and the *Washington Post*, was intense and prolonged, stretching for fifty consecutive days beginning in the late fall of 2002, and led to his hospitalization on at least two occasions. Some of the techniques used, including longtime sitting in restraints, prolonged exposure to cold, loud music, and noise, and sleep deprivation, recall those described in the ICRC report. If the "coercive" and "abusive" interrogation of Qahtani makes trying him impossible, one may doubt that any of the fourteen "high-value detainees" whose accounts are given in this report will ever be tried and sentenced in an internationally recognized and sanctioned legal proceeding.

In the case of men who have committed great crimes, this seems to mark perhaps the most important and consequential sense in which "torture doesn't work." The use of torture deprives the society whose laws have been so egregiously violated of the possibility of rendering justice. Torture destroys justice. Torture in effect relinquishes this sacred right in exchange for speculative benefits whose value is, at the least, much disputed. John Kiriakou, the CIA officer who witnessed part of Zubaydah's interrogation, described to Brian Ross of ABC News what happened after Zubaydah was waterboarded:

> He resisted. He was able to withstand the water boarding for quite some time. And by that I mean probably 30, 35 seconds. . . . And a short time afterwards, in the next day or so, he told his interrogator that Allah had visited him in his cell during the night and told him to cooperate because his cooperation would make it easier on the other brothers who had been

captured. And from that day on he answered every question just like I'm
sitting here speaking to you. . . . The threat information that he provided
disrupted a number of attacks, maybe dozens of attacks.[42]

This claim, echoed by President Bush in his speech, is a matter of fierce
dispute. Bush's public version, indeed, was much more carefully circumscribed: among other things, that Zubaydah's information confirmed the
alias ("Muktar") of Khaled Shaik Mohammed, and thus helped lead to his
capture; that it helped lead, indirectly, to the capture of Ramzi bin al-Shibh,
a Yemeni who was another key figure in planning the September 11 attacks;
and that it "helped us stop another planned attack within the United States."
    At least some of this information, apparently, came during the early, non-
coercive interrogation led by FBI agents. Later, according to the reporter
Ron Suskind, Zubaydah

> named countless targets inside the United States to stop the pain, all of
> them immaterial. Indeed, think back to the sudden slew of alerts in the
> spring and summer of 2002 about attacks on apartment buildings, banks,
> shopping malls and, of course, nuclear plants.

Suskind is only the most prominent of a number of reporters with strong
sources in the intelligence community who argue that the importance of the
intelligence Zubaydah supplied, and indeed his importance within al Qaeda,
have been grossly and systematically exaggerated by government officials,
from President Bush on down.[43]
    Though it seems highly unlikely that Zubaydah's information stopped
"maybe dozens of attacks," as Kiriakou said, the plain fact is that it is impossible, until a thorough investigation can be undertaken of the interrogations,
to evaluate fully and fairly what intelligence the United States actually
received in return for all the severe costs, practical, political, legal, and moral,
the country incurred by instituting a policy of torture. There is a sense in
which the entire debate over what Zubaydah did or did not provide, and the
attacks the information might or might not have prevented—a debate driven
largely by leaks by fiercely self-interested parties—itself reflects an unvoiced
acceptance, on both sides, of the centrality of the mythical "ticking-bomb
scenario" so beloved of those who argue that torture is necessary, and so
prized by the writers of television dramas like 24. That is, the argument centers on whether Zubaydah's interrogation directly "disrupted a number of
attacks."
    Perhaps unwittingly, Kiriakou is most revealing about the intelligence
value of interrogation of "high-value detainees" when he discusses what the
CIA actually got from Zubaydah:

> What he was able to provide was information on the al Qaeda leadership.
> For example, if bin Laden were to do X, who would be the person to

undertake such and such an operation? "Oh, logically that would be Mr. Y." And we were able to use that information to kind of get an idea of how al Qaeda operated, how it came about conceptualizing its operations, and how it went about tasking different cells with carrying out operations. . . . His value was, it allowed us to have somebody who we could pass ideas onto for his comments or analysis.[44]

This has the ring of truth, for this is how intelligence works—by the patient accruing of individual pieces of information, by building a picture that will help officers make sense of the other intelligence they receive. Could such "comments or analysis" from a high al Qaeda operative eventually help lead to the disruption of "a number of attacks, maybe dozens of attacks"? It seems possible—but if it did, the chain of cause and effect might not be direct, certainly not nearly so direct as the dramatic scenarios in newspapers and television dramas—and presidential speeches—suggest. The ticking bomb, about to explode and kill thousands or millions; the evil captured terrorist who alone has the information to find and disarm it; the desperate intelligence operative, forced to do whatever is necessary to gain that information—all these elements are well known and emotionally powerful, but where they appear most frequently is in popular entertainment, not in white rooms in Afghanistan.

There is a reverse side, of course, to the "ticking bomb" and torture: pain and ill-treatment, by creating an unbearable pressure on the detainee to say something, anything, to make the pain stop, increase the likelihood that he will fabricate stories, and waste time, or worse. At least some of the intelligence that came of the "alternative set of procedures," like Zubaydah's supposed "information" about attacks on shopping malls and banks, seems to have led the U.S. government to issue what turned out to be baseless warnings to Americans. Khaled Shaik Mohammed asserted this directly in his interviews with the ICRC. "During the harshest period of my interrogation," he said,

> I gave a lot of false information in order to satisfy what I believed the interrogators wished to hear in order to make the ill-treatment stop. . . . I'm sure that the false information I was forced to invent . . . wasted a lot of their time and led to several false red-alerts being placed in the United States.[45]

For all the talk of ticking bombs, very rarely, if ever, have officials been able to point to information gained by interrogating prisoners with "enhanced techniques" that enabled them to prevent an attack that had reached its "operational stage" (that is, had gone beyond reconnoitering and planning). Still, widespread perception that such techniques have prevented attacks, actively encouraged by the president and other officials, has been politically essential in letting the administration carry on with these policies after they had largely become public. Polls tend to show that a majority of

Americans are willing to support torture only when they are assured that it will "thwart a terrorist attack." Because of the political persuasiveness of such scenarios it is vital that a future inquiry truly investigate claims that attacks have been prevented.

As I write, it is impossible to know what benefits—in intelligence, in national security, in disrupting al Qaeda—the president's approval of use of an "alternative set of procedures" might have brought to the United States. What we can say definitively is that the decision has harmed American interests in quite demonstrable ways. Some are practical and specific: For example, FBI agents, many of them professionals with great experience and skill in interrogation, were withdrawn, apparently after objections by the bureau's leaders, when it was decided to use the "alternative set of procedures" on Abu Zubaydah. Extensive leaks to the press, from both officials supportive of and critical of the "alternative set of procedures," undermined what was supposed to be a highly secret program; those leaks, in large part a product of the great controversy the program provoked within the national security bureaucracy, eventually helped make it unsustainable.

Finally, this bureaucratic weakness led officials of the CIA to destroy, apparently out of fear of eventual exposure and possible prosecution, a trove of as many as ninety-two video recordings that had been made of the interrogations, all but two of them of Abu Zubaydah. Whether or not the prosecutor investigating those actions determines that they were illegal, it is hard to believe that the recordings did not include valuable intelligence, which was sacrificed, in effect, for political reasons. These recordings doubtless could have played a critical part as well in the effort to determine what benefits, if any, the program brought to the security of the United States.

Far and away the greatest damage, though, was legal, moral, and political. In the wake of the ICRC report one can make several definitive statements:

1. Beginning in the spring of 2002 the United States government began to torture prisoners. This torture, approved by the president of the United States and monitored in its daily unfolding by senior officials, including the nation's highest law enforcement officer, clearly violated major treaty obligations of the United States, including the Geneva Conventions and the Convention Against Torture, as well as U.S. law.

2. The most senior officers of the U.S. government, President George W. Bush first among them, repeatedly and explicitly lied about this, both in reports to international institutions and directly to the public. The president lied about it in news conferences, interviews, and, most explicitly, in speeches expressly intended to set out the administration's policy on interrogation before the people who had elected him.

3. The U.S. Congress, already in possession of a great deal of information about the torture conducted by the administration—which had been covered widely in the press, and had been briefed, at least in part,

almost from the outset to a select few of its members—passed the Military Commissions Act of 2006 and in so doing attempted to protect those responsible from criminal penalty under the War Crimes Act.

4. Democrats, who could have filibustered the bill, declined to do so—a decision that had much to do with the proximity of the midterm elections, in the run-up to which, they feared, the president and his Republican allies might gain advantage by accusing them of "coddling terrorists." One senator summarized the politics of the Military Commissions Act with admirable forthrightness:

> Soon, we will adjourn for the fall, and the campaigning will begin in earnest. And there will be thirty-second attack ads and negative mail pieces, and we will be criticized as caring more about the rights of terrorists than the protection of Americans. And I know that the vote before us was specifically designed and timed to add more fuel to that fire.[46]

Senator Barack Obama was only saying aloud what every other legislator knew: that for all the horrified and gruesome exposés, for all the leaked photographs and documents and horrific testimony, when it came to torture in the September 11 era, the raw politics cut in the other direction. Most politicians remain convinced that still fearful Americans, given the choice between the image of *24*'s Jack Bauer—a latter-day Dirty Harry, fantasy symbol of untrammeled power doing "everything it takes" to protect them from that ticking bomb—and the image of weak liberals "reading Miranda rights to terrorists," will choose Bauer every time. As Senator Obama said, after the bill he voted against had passed, "Politics won today."

5. The political damage to the United States' reputation, and to the "soft power" based on its constitutional and democratic ideals, has been, though difficult to quantify, vast and enduring. In a war that is essentially an insurgency fought on a worldwide scale—which is to say, a political war, in which the attitudes and allegiances of young Muslims are the critical target of opportunity—the United States' decision to use torture has resulted in an enormous self-administered defeat, undermining liberal sympathizers of the United States and convincing others that the country is exactly as its enemies paint it: a ruthless imperial power determined to suppress and abuse Muslims. By choosing to torture, we freely chose to become the caricature they made of us.

VIII.

In the wake of the attacks of September 11, 2001, Cofer Black, the former head of the CIA's Counterterrorism Center and a famously colorful hardliner, appeared before the Senate Intelligence Committee and made the most telling pronouncement of the era: "All I want to say is that there was 'before' 9/11 and 'after' 9/11. After 9/11 the gloves come off." In the days after the attacks this phrase was everywhere. Columnists quoted it, television commentators flaunted it, interrogators at Abu Ghraib used it in their cables.[47]

The gloves came off: four simple words. And yet they express a complicated thought. For if the gloves must come off, that means that before the attacks the gloves were on. There is something implicitly exculpatory in the image, something that made it particularly appealing to officials of an administration that endured, on its watch, the most lethal terrorist attack in the country's history. If the attack succeeded, it must have had to do not with the fact that intelligence was not passed on or that warnings were not heeded or that senior officials did not focus on terrorism as a leading threat. It must have been, at least in part, because the gloves were on—because the post-Watergate reforms of the 1970s, in which Congress sought to put limits on the CIA, on its freedom to mount covert actions with "deniability" and to conduct surveillance at home and abroad, had illegitimately circumscribed the president's power and thereby put the country dangerously at risk. It is no accident that two of the administration's most powerful officials, Dick Cheney and Donald Rumsfeld, served as young men in very senior positions in the Nixon and Ford administrations. They had witnessed firsthand the gloves going on and, in the weeks after the September 11 attacks, they argued powerfully that it was those limitations—and, it was implied, not a failure to heed warnings—that had helped lead, however indirectly, to the country's vulnerability to attack.

And so, after a devastating and unprecedented attack, the gloves came off. Guided by the president and his closest advisers, the United States transformed itself from a country that, officially at least, condemned torture to a country that practiced it. And this fateful decision, however much we may want it to, will not go away, any more than the fourteen "high-value detainees," tortured and thus unprosecutable, will go away. Like the grotesque stories in the ICRC report, the decision sits before us, a toxic fact, polluting our political and moral life.

Since the inauguration of President Obama, the previous administration's "alternative procedures" have acquired a prominence in the press, particularly on cable television, that they rarely achieved when they were actually being practiced on detainees. This is especially the case with waterboarding, which according to the former director of the CIA has not been used since 2003. On his second day in office, President Obama issued executive orders that stopped the use of these techniques and provided for task forces to study U.S. government policies on rendition, detention, and interrogation, among others.

Meantime, Democratic leaders in Congress, who have been in control since 2006, have at last embarked on serious investigations. Senators Dianne Feinstein and Christopher Bond, the chair and ranking member of the Intelligence Committee, have announced a "review of the CIA's detention and interrogation program," which would study, among other questions, "how the CIA created, operated, and maintained its detention and interrogation program," make "an evaluation of intelligence information gained through the use of enhanced and standard interrogation techniques," and investigate "whether the CIA accurately described the detention and interrogation program to other parts of the U.S. government"—including, notably, "the Senate Intelligence Committee." The hearings, according to reports, are unlikely to be public.[48]

In February, Senator Patrick Leahy, chairman of the Judiciary Committee, called for the establishment of what he calls a "nonpartisan commission of inquiry," better known as a "Truth and Reconciliation Committee," to investigate "how our detention policies and practices, from Guantanamo to Abu Ghraib, have seriously eroded fundamental American principles of the rule of law." Since Senator Leahy's commission is intended above all to investigate and make public what was done—"in order to restore our moral leadership," as he said, "we must acknowledge what was done in our name"—he would offer grants of immunity to public officials in exchange for their truthful testimony. He seeks not prosecution and justice but knowledge and exposure: "We cannot turn the page until we have read the page."[49]

Many officials of human rights organizations, who have fought long and valiantly to bring attention and law to bear on these issues, strongly reject any proposal that includes widespread grants of immunity. They urge investigations and prosecutions of Bush administration officials. The choices are complicated and painful. From what we know, officials acted with the legal sanction of the U.S. government and under orders from the highest political authority, the elected president of the United States. Political decisions, made by elected officials, led to these crimes. But political opinion, within the government and increasingly, as time passed, without, to some extent allowed those crimes to persist. If there is a need for prosecution there is also a vital need for education. Only a credible investigation into what was done and what information was gained can begin to alter the political calculus around torture by replacing the public's attachment to the ticking bomb with an understanding of what torture is and what is gained, and lost, when the United States reverts to it.

President Obama, while declaring that "nobody's above the law, and if there are clear instances of wrongdoing . . . people should be prosecuted," has also expressed his strong preference for "looking forward" rather than "looking backwards." One can understand the sentiment but even some of the decisions his administration has already made—concerning state secrecy, for example—show the extent to which he and his Department of Justice will be haunted by what his predecessor did. Consider the uncompromising words of Eric Holder, the attorney general, who in reply to a direct question at his confirmation hearings had declared, "waterboarding is torture." There is nothing ambiguous about this statement—nor about the equally blunt statements of several high Bush administration officials, including the former vice president and the director of the CIA, confirming unequivocally that the administration had ordered and directed that prisoners under its control be waterboarded. We are all living, then, with a terrible contradiction, an enduring one, and it is not subtle, any more than the accounts in the ICRC report are subtle. "It was," as Mr. Cheney said of waterboarding, "a no-brainer for me."[50] Now Abu Zubaydah and his fellow detainees have stepped forward out of the darkness to link hands with the former vice president and testify to his truthfulness.

New York Review of Books, April 9, 2009

Into the Light?
Torture, Power, and Us

When we get people who are more concerned about reading the rights to an al Qaeda terrorist than they are with protecting the United States against people who are absolutely committed to do anything they can to kill Americans, then I worry. . . . These are evil people. And we're not going to win this fight by turning the other cheek.

If it hadn't been for what we did—with respect to the . . . enhanced interrogation techniques for high-value detainees . . . —then we would have been attacked again. Those policies we put in place, in my opinion, were absolutely crucial to getting us through the last seven-plus years without a major-casualty attack on the U.S. . . .

—Former Vice President Dick Cheney, February 4, 2009[1]

April 2, 2009

I.

WHEN IT COMES TO TORTURE, it is not what we did but what we are doing. It is not what happened but what is happening and what will happen. In our politics, torture is not about whether or not our polity can "let the past be past"—whether or not we can "get beyond it and look forward." Torture, for Dick Cheney and for President Bush and a significant portion of the American people, is more than a repugnant series of "procedures" applied to a few hundred prisoners in American custody during the last half-dozen or so years—procedures that are described with chilling and patient particularity in this authoritative report by the International Committee of the Red Cross.[2] Torture is more than the specific techniques—the forced nudity, sleep deprivation, long-term standing, and "suffocation by water," among others—that were applied to those fourteen "high-value detainees" and likely many more at the "black site" prisons secretly maintained by the CIA on three continents.

Torture, as the former vice president's words suggest, is a critical issue in the present of our politics—and not only because of ongoing investigations by Senate committees, or because of calls for an independent inquiry by congressional leaders, or for a "truth commission" by a leading Senate Democrat, or because of demands for a criminal investigation by the ACLU and other human rights organizations, and now undertaken in Spain, the United Kingdom, and Poland.[3] For many in the United States, torture still stands as a marker of political commitment—of a willingness to "do anything to protect the American people," a manly readiness to know when to abstain from "coddling terrorists" and do what needs to be done. Torture's powerful symbolic role, like many ugly, shameful facts, is left unacknowledged and undiscussed. But that doesn't make it any less real. On the contrary.

Torture is at the heart of the deadly politics of national security. The former vice president, as able and ruthless a politician as the country has yet produced, appears convinced of this. For if torture really was a necessary evil in what Mr. Cheney calls the "tough, mean, dirty, nasty business" of "keeping the country safe," then it follows that its abolition at the hands of the Obama administration will put the country once more at risk. It was Barack Obama, after all, who on his second day as president issued a series of historic executive orders that closed the "black site" secret prisons and halted the use of "enhanced interrogation techniques" that had been practiced there, and that provided that the offshore prison at Guantánamo would be closed within a year.

In moving instantly to do these things Obama identified himself as the "anti-torture president" no less than George W. Bush had become the "torture president"—as the former vice president, a deeply unpopular politician who has seized the role of a kind of dark spokesman for the national id, was quick to point out. To a CNN interviewer who asked Mr. Cheney in March whether he believed that "by taking those steps . . . the president of the United States has made Americans less safe," Cheney replied:

> I do. I think those programs were absolutely essential to the success we enjoyed of being able to collect the intelligence that let us defeat all further attempts to launch attacks against the United States since 9/11. I think that's a great success story.[4]

To which President Obama a few days later answered, "I fundamentally disagree with Dick Cheney." He went on:

> I think that Vice President Cheney has been at the head of a movement whose notion is somehow that we can't reconcile our core values, our

Constitution, our belief that we don't torture, with our national security interests. . . . That attitude, that philosophy has done incredible damage to our image and position in the world.[5]

The president spoke of justice and reputation and the attitudes of Muslims toward Americans. And he spoke of "the facts"—which, he said of Mr. Cheney, "don't bear him out." It is clear that the president, a former professor of constitutional law and self-professed "optimistic guy" who, when asked whether those who have tortured should be punished, speaks of his preference for "looking forward" over "looking backward," appreciates the political importance of the "great success story" being shaped by Cheney and others out of the recent past, a "success story" that the new president, with his overly "legalistic" concern for the Constitution, is said to be wantonly and foolishly destroying.

Cheney's story is made not of facts but of the myths that replace them when facts remain secret: myths that are fueled by allusions to a dark world of secrets that cannot be revealed. At its heart is the recasting of President George W. Bush, under whose administration more Americans died in terrorist attacks than under all others combined, as the leader who "kept us safe," and who was able to do so only by recognizing that the United States had to engage in "a tough, mean, dirty, nasty business." To keep the country safe "the gloves had to come off." What precisely were those "gloves" that had to be removed? Laws that forbid torture, that outlaw wiretapping and surveillance without permission of the courts, that limit the president's power to order secret operations and to wage war exactly as he sees fit.

The logic here works both ways: If "taking the gloves off" was a critical part of the "great success story" that has "kept the country safe," then those who put the gloves on—Democrats who, in the wake of the Watergate scandal during the mid-1970s, passed laws that, among other things, limited the president's freedom to order, with "deniability," the CIA to operate outside the law—must have left the country vulnerable. And if by passing those restrictive laws three decades ago Democrats had left the country defenseless before the September 11 terrorists, then putting the gloves back on, as President Barack Obama on assuming office immediately began to do, risks leaving the country vulnerable once more.

Thus another successful attack, if it comes, can be laid firmly at the door of the Obama administration and its Democratic, "legalistic" policies. Especially in the case of "the ultimate threat to the country," as the former vice president put it two weeks after leaving office, of

a 9/11-type event where the terrorists are armed with something much more dangerous than an airline ticket and a box cutter—a nuclear weapon or a biological agent of some kind. That's the one that would involve the deaths of perhaps hundreds of thousands of people, and the one you have to spend a hell of a lot of time guarding against.

I think there's a high probability of such an attempt. Whether or not they can pull it off depends [on] whether or not we keep in place policies that have allowed us to defeat all further attempts, since 9/11, to launch mass-casualty attacks against the United States. . . .

If you release the hard-core al Qaeda terrorists that are held at Guantánamo, I think they go back into the business of trying to kill more Americans and mount further mass-casualty attacks. If you turn them loose and they go kill more Americans, who's responsible for that?

Who indeed? Mr. Cheney's politics of torture looks, Janus-like, in two directions: back to the past, toward exculpation for what was done under the administration he served, and into the future, toward blame for what might come under the administration that followed.

Put forward at a time when Republicans have lost power and popularity—and by the man who is perhaps the least popular figure in American public life—these propositions seem audacious, outrageous, even reckless; yet the political logic is insidious and, in the aftermath of a future attack, might well prove compelling. We are returning here to old principles, the post–Cold War national security politics that Karl Rove, scarcely four months after the September 11 attacks, set out bluntly before his colleagues at the Republican National Committee: "We can go to the country on this issue"—the "War on Terror"—Rove said, because voters "trust the Republican Party to do a better job of protecting and strengthening America's military might and, thereby, protecting America." And in 2002 and 2004, just as Rove had predicted, Republicans gathered a rich harvest from this "politics of fear," establishing and adding to majorities in both houses of Congress and managing to reelect a president who had embroiled the country in a deeply unpopular war in Iraq.

Cheney's politics of fear—and the vice president is unique only in his willingness to enunciate the matter so aggressively—is drawn from the past but built for the future, a possibly post-apocalyptic future, when Americans, gazing at the ruins left by another attack on their country, will wonder what could have been done but wasn't. It relies on a carefully constructed narrative of what was done during the last half-dozen years, of all the disasters that could have happened but did not, and it makes unflinching political use of the powers of secrecy. As the former vice president confided to the CNN correspondent John King,

John, I've seen a report that was written based upon the intelligence that we collected then that itemizes the specific attacks that were stopped by virtue of what we learned through these programs. It's still classified. I can't give you details of it without violating classification, but I can say there were a great many of them.

Attacks prevented, threats averted, lives saved—all secret and all ascribed to a willingness to do the "tough, mean, dirty, nasty" things that needed to be done. Things the present "anti-torture president" is just too "legalistic" to do. Barack Obama may well assert that "the facts don't bear him out," but as long as the "details of it" cannot be revealed "without violating classification," as long as secrecy can be wielded as the dark and potent weapon it remains, Cheney's politics of torture will remain a powerful if half-submerged counter-story, waiting for the next attack to spark it into vibrant life.

II.

"Key to what we did" in the "War on Terror," the former vice president told CNN, "was to collect intelligence against the enemy. That's what . . . the enhanced interrogation program was all about." It was not about punishment or pain or degradation but rather about intelligence. The question was, how to gather vital intelligence most efficiently and yet do it—as the former vice president insists it was done—"legally" and "in accordance with our constitutional practices and principles." These "techniques" would not be torture but rather "enhanced interrogation" or "extreme interrogation," or, in President George W. Bush's favored phrase, almost beautiful in its utter and perfect neutrality, "an alternative set of procedures." These "procedures" were "designed to be safe, to comply with our laws, our Constitution, and our treaty obligations."[6]

Working through the forty-three pages of the International Committee of the Red Cross's report, one finds a strikingly detailed account of horrors inflicted on fourteen "high-value detainees" over a period of weeks and months—horrors that Red Cross officials conclude, quite unequivocally, "constituted torture." It is hard not to reflect how officials concerned about protecting the country arrived at this particular "alternative set of procedures," and how they convinced themselves, with the help of attorneys in the White House and in the Department of Justice, that these "procedures" were legal. Thanks especially to pathbreaking reporting by Jane Mayer in *The New Yorker*, to the historical work of Alfred W. McCoy, and now to a partially released report by the Senate Armed Services Committee and a series of leaked and declassified memos by the Bush Justice Department, we have a fairly extensive record of the intricate bureaucratic mechanics of how the program came to be. We can find its roots in various CIA studies of sensory deprivation and induced psychosis and "learned helplessness," some of them more than four decades old, and, in the case of the particular "alternative set of procedures," in the work of consultants and psychologists who had been involved in shaping and administering the SERE ("Survival Evasion Resistance and Escape") "counter-resistance" program developed by the U.S. military.[7]

The effort began early in the days after the September 11 attacks. By December 2001, according to the Senate Armed Services Committee report, the general counsel in the Department of Defense "had already solicited information on detainee 'exploitation' from the Joint Personnel Recovery Agency (JPRA), an agency whose expertise was in training American personnel to withstand interrogation techniques considered illegal under the Geneva Conventions." Two months later, on February 7, 2002, President Bush signed a memorandum stating that the Third Geneva Convention in effect did not apply to prisoners in the "War on Terror." This decision cleared the way for the adaptation of SERE techniques to interrogate these prisoners. As the authors of the Senate Armed Services Committee report explain:

> During the resistance phase of SERE training, U.S. military personnel are exposed to physical and psychological pressures . . . designed to simulate conditions to which they might be subject if taken prisoner by enemies that *did not abide by the Geneva Conventions*. As one JPRA instructor explained, SERE training is "*based on illegal exploitation* (under the rules listed in the 1949 Geneva Convention Relative to the Treatment of Prisoners of War) of prisoners over the last 50 years."
>
> The techniques used in SERE school, based, in part, on Chinese Communist techniques used during the Korean war to elicit false confessions, include stripping students of their clothing, placing them in stress positions, putting hoods over their heads, disrupting their sleep, treating them like animals, subjecting them to loud music and flashing lights, and exposing them to extreme temperatures. It can also include face and body slaps and until recently, for some who attended the navy's SERE school, it included waterboarding.[8]

An awareness of this history makes reading the International Committee of the Red Cross report a strange exercise in climbing back through the looking glass. For in interviewing the fourteen "high-value detainees," who had been imprisoned secretly in the "black sites" anywhere from "sixteen months to almost four and a half years," the Red Cross experts were listening to descriptions of techniques applied to them that had been originally designed to be illegal "under the rules listed in the 1949 Geneva Conventions." And then the Red Cross investigators, as members of the body designated by the Geneva Conventions to supervise treatment of prisoners of war and to judge that treatment's legality, were called on to pronounce whether or not the techniques conformed to the conventions in the first place. In this judgment, they are, not surprisingly, unequivocal:

> The allegations of ill-treatment of the detainees indicate that, in many cases, the ill-treatment to which they were subjected while held in the CIA program, either singly or in combination, constituted torture. In addition,

many other elements of the ill-treatment, either singly or in combination, constituted cruel and inhuman or degrading treatment.[9]

In view of the roots of the "alternative set of procedures," this stark judgment might be dismissed as the chronicle of a verdict foretold. Both "torture" and "cruel, inhuman and degrading treatment" are declared illegal under the Third Geneva Convention, to which the Supreme Court ruled in June 2006 that—President Bush's February 2002 memorandum notwithstanding—the United States in its treatment of all prisoners must adhere. They are also illegal under the Convention Against Torture of 1984, to which the United States is a signatory, and illegal under the War Crimes Act of 1996 (though the Military Commissions Act of 2006 makes an attempt to shield those who applied the "alternative set of procedures" from legal consequences under this law).

Indeed, on the matter of legality the report is admirably explicit and unequivocal:

[T]he ICRC wishes to remind the U.S. authorities that international law absolutely prohibits CID [cruel, inhuman or degrading treatment] and torture. Torture is defined by the 1984 UN Convention Against Torture as: "any act by which severe pain or suffering, whether physical or mention, is intentionally inflicted on a person for such purposes as obtaining from him or a third person information or a confession, punishing him for an act he or a third person has committed or is suspected of having committed, or intimidating or coercing him or a third person, or for any reason based on discrimination of any kind, when such pain or suffering is inflicted by or at the instigation or with the consent or acquiescence of a public official or other person acting in an official capacity." In particular, the provisions of common article 3 to the Geneva Conventions, which reflects elementary considerations of humanity, stipulate that persons taking no active part in the hostilities "shall in all circumstances be treated humanely," and that "cruel treatment and torture," "outrages upon personal dignity, in particular humiliating and degrading treatment" are prohibited at any time and in any place whatsoever.[10]

There is no ambiguity about the writers' use, in describing the "alternative set of procedures" employed to interrogate prisoners at the "black sites," of the words "torture" and "cruel, inhuman or degrading treatment."

What is more, as the report concludes,

The totality of the circumstances in which the fourteen were held effectively amounted to an arbitrary deprivation of liberty and enforced disappearance, in contravention of international law.[11]

It is a testament as much to the peculiarities of the American press—to its "stenographic function" and its institutional unwillingness to report as fact anything disputed, however implausibly, by a high official—that the former vice president's insistence that these interrogations were undertaken "legally" and "in accordance with our constitutional practices and principles" continues to be reported without contradiction, and that President Bush's oft-repeated assertion that "the United States does not torture" is still respectfully quoted and, in many quarters, taken seriously. That they are so reported is a political fact, and a powerful one. It makes it possible to contend that, however adamant the arguments of the lawyers "on either side," the very fact of their disagreement makes the legality of these procedures a matter of partisan political allegiance, not of law.

III.

In the long months of confinement, I often thought of how to transmit the pain that a tortured person undergoes. And always I concluded that it was impossible.

—Jacobo Timerman [12]

Whatever the tangled history of the techniques described in the ICRC report—whatever the sources in Communist China or Soviet Russia or wherever else they might be traced—what was done in the end was quite simple. In setting out after September 11 to "do whatever it takes" in the "tough, mean, dirty, nasty business" of protecting the country against "evil people," Bush administration officials were modern people treading a timeless road. However impressive the advanced degrees of the consultants they hired, the techniques of "enhanced interrogation" are in their essence ancient, for they play on emotions and physical realities that are basic and unchanging. Consider, for example, the "crude but effective" methods of the Soviet State Political Directorate (GPU):

They consisted usually of tying the victim in a strait-jacket to an iron bunk. The strait-jacket was his only clothing; he had no blanket, no food and was unable to go to the lavatory. With a gag in his mouth and a stopper in his rectum he would be given periodic beatings with rubber poles. [13]

Brutal stuff; hard to imagine Americans, however intent on "collecting intelligence against the enemy," engaging in such things. And yet as one looks again at those "crude but effective" procedures, one notices certain unchanging necessities. There is, for example, the basic need to keep the subject helpless and restrained, here accomplished with forced nudity and a straitjacket. In the "black sites," the same end was achieved by forced nudity and what the Red Cross terms, in its chapter of the same name, "prolonged use of handcuffs and shackles." One of the fourteen detainees, for example, tells the Red Cross investigators that

> he was kept for four and a half months continuously handcuffed and seven months with the ankles continuously shackled while detained in Kabul in 2003/4. On two occasions, his shackles had to be cut off his ankles as the locking mechanism had ceased to function, allegedly due to rust.[14]

This technique, like others of the "alternative set of procedures" detailed by the Red Cross, seems to have been consistently applied to many of the fourteen "high-value" detainees. Walid bin Attash told the Red Cross investigators that

> he was kept permanently handcuffed and shackled throughout his first six months of detention. During the four months he was held in his third place of detention, when not kept in the prolonged stress standing position [with his hands shackled to the ceiling], his ankle shackles were allegedly kept attached by a one meter long chain to a pin fixed in the corner of the room where he was held.[15]

As with the GPU set of procedures, prisoners were kept naked, deprived of blankets, mattresses, and other necessities, and deprived of food. As for "the stopper in the rectum," it was supplied by the GPU to deal with the practical problem of how to cope, in the case of a person who is naked and entirely under restraint and at the same time experiencing prolonged and extreme pain, with the inevitable consequences of his bodily functions. The Americans at the "black sites," who had also to face this unpleasant necessity, particularly when holding detainees in "stress positions," for example, forcing them for many days to stand naked with their hands shackled to a bolt in the ceiling and their ankles shackled to a bolt in the floor, developed their own equivalent:

> While being held in this position some of the detainees were allowed to defecate in a bucket. A guard would come to release their hands from the bar or hook in the ceiling so that they could sit on the bucket. None of them, however, were allowed to clean themselves afterwards. Others were made to wear a garment that resembled a diaper. This was the case for Mr. Bin Attash in his fourth place of detention. However, he commented that on several occasions the diaper was not replaced so he had to urinate and defecate on himself while shackled in the prolonged stress standing position. Indeed, in addition to Mr. Bin Attash, three other detainees specified that they had to defecate and urinate on themselves and remain standing in their own bodily fluids.[16]

One turns, finally, to those "periodic beatings with rubber poles" that the GPU administered. No rubber poles are to be found in the Red Cross report. Once again, though, as with the stopper in the rectum and the diapers, the rubber poles simply represent the GPU's practical solution to a problem shared by the CIA at the "black sites": How can one beat a detainee repeatedly without causing debilitating or permanent injury that might make him unfit for further interrogation? How, that is, to get the pain and its effect while minimizing the physical consequences?

Where the GPU responded by developing rubber poles, the CIA created its plastic collar, "an improvised thick collar or neck roll," as the Red Cross investigators describe it in Chapter 1.3.3 ("Beating by use of a collar"), that "was placed around their necks and used by their interrogators to slam them against the walls." Though six of the fourteen detainees report the use of the "thick plastic collar," which, according to Khaled Shaik Mohammed, would then be "held at the two ends by a guard who would use it to slam me repeatedly against the wall," it is plain that this particular technique was perfected through experimentation. Indeed, the plastic collar seems to have begun as a rather simple mechanism: an everyday towel that was looped around the neck, the ends gathered in the guard's fist. The collar appeared later and brought with it other innovations:

> Mr. Abu Zubaydah commented that when the collar was first used on him in his third place of detention, he was slammed directly against a hard concrete wall. He was then placed in a tall box for several hours (see Section 1.3.5, Confinement in boxes). After he was taken out of the box he noticed that a sheet of plywood had been placed against the wall. The collar was then used to slam him against the plywood sheet. He thought that the plywood was in order to absorb some of the impact so as to avoid the risk of physical injury.[17]

How to inflict pain without causing injury that might inhibit or prevent further interrogation? And how to do so in such a way that the pain inflicted might be said not to be akin to that "associated with serious physical injury so severe that death, organ failure, or permanent damage resulting in a loss of significant body function will likely result"? This was of course the legal definition of torture concocted by White House and Justice Department lawyers and codified in what has come to be known as the "Torture Memo," written by John Yoo and signed by Jay Bybee on August 1, 2002.[18] The challenging task set before these lawyers was somehow to "make legal" a set of techniques that had originated in a program developed expressly to prepare soldiers for techniques that were illegal, and thereby to offer officials and interrogators a "golden shield" that would suffice to convince them they would be protected from legal consequences.

In answer to these questions, and with the benefit of experimentation, especially on Mr. Abu Zubaydah, one of the first of the alleged "big fish" al Qaeda captives, the CIA seems to have arrived at a method that is codified by the International Committee of the Red Cross experts into twelve basic techniques, as follows:

- **Suffocation by water** poured over a cloth placed over the nose and mouth . . .
- **Prolonged stress standing position,** naked, held with the arms extended and chained above the head . . .
- **Beatings by use of a collar** held around the detainees' neck and used to forcefully bang the head and body against the wall . . .
- **Beating and kicking,** including slapping, punching, kicking to the body and face . . .
- **Confinement in a box** to severely restrict movement . . .
- **Prolonged nudity . . .** this enforced nudity lasted for periods ranging from several weeks to several months . . .
- **Sleep deprivation . . .** through use of forced stress positions (standing or sitting), cold water and use of repetitive loud noises or music . . .
- **Exposure to cold temperature . . .** especially via cold cells and interrogation rooms, and . . . use of cold water poured over the body or . . . held around the body by means of a plastic sheet to create an immersion bath with just the head out of water.
- **Prolonged shackling** of hands and/or feet . . .
- **Threats of ill-treatment,** to the detainee and/or his family . . .
- **Forced shaving** of the head and beard . . .
- **Deprivation/restricted provision of solid food** from three days to one month after arrest . . .[19]

As the Red Cross writers tell us, "each specific method was in fact applied in combination with other methods, either simultaneously or in succession." A clear picture of this cumulative effect comes from the three long excerpts of interviews with detainees published as annexes at the end of the report, which I have quoted and discussed in the previous essay. To understand the effect one must remember what all experienced torturers know: Dramatic results can be achieved with simple techniques. Forced standing, for example:

Ten of the fourteen alleged that they were subjected to prolonged stress standing positions, during which their wrists were shackled to a bar or hook in the ceiling above the head for periods ranging from two or three days continuously, and for up to two or three months intermittently. . . . For example, Mr. Khaled Shaik Mohammed alleged that, apart from the time when he was taken for interrogation, he was shackled in prolonged stress standing position for one month in his third place of detention. . . . Mr. Bin Attash for two weeks with two or three short breaks where he could lie down in Afghanistan and for several days in his fourth place of detention. . . . Mr. Hambali for four to five days, blindfolded with a type of sack over his head, while still detained in Thailand. . . .[20]

This prolonged forced standing is, again, an ancient technique, and a favorite, notably, of the Soviet intelligence services. It can be difficult, when gazing at the stark descriptions of these procedures, to understand their effect. Secretary of Defense Donald Rumsfeld, for example, when approving in December 2002 a series of interrogation techniques that included forced standing for up to four hours, famously scribbled in the lower margin, beneath his initials: "However, I stand for eight to ten hours a day. Why is standing limited to four hours? D.R."[21] Secretary Rumsfeld, who no doubt was standing at his desk when he scrawled these words, professed to have difficulty comprehending the difference between working at a standing desk in one's office—signing documents, talking on the telephone, speaking to subordinates, drinking coffee—and standing naked in a very cold room with hands shackled to the ceiling for hours and days at a time.

One can begin to gain a sense of the difference simply by rising and standing motionless with one's hands extended directly overhead and trying to maintain the position for, say, thirty minutes. Then imagine maintaining it for several hours, or days, or weeks. The physical effects, as described in a notorious study of Communist interrogation methods by two psychologists, are dramatic:

> After 18 to 24 hours of continuous standing, there is an accumulation of fluid in the tissues of the legs. This dependent edema is produced by the extravasation of fluid from the blood vessels. The ankles and feet of the prisoner swell to twice their normal circumference. The edema may rise up the legs as high as the middle of the thighs. The skin becomes tense and intensely painful. Large blisters develop, which break and exude watery serum . . .[22]

This medical observation is confirmed in the accounts of at least two of the detainees in the ICRC report, including that of Khaled Shaik Mohammed:

> . . . I was kept for one month in the cell in a standing position with my hands cuffed and shackled above my head and my feet cuffed and shackled to a point in the floor. Of course during this month I fell asleep on some occasions while still being held in this position. This resulted in all my weight being applied to the handcuffs around my wrists resulting in open and bleeding wounds. . . . [Scars consistent with this allegation were visible on both wrists as well as both ankles.] Both my feet became very swollen after one month of almost continual standing.[23]

IV.

I fundamentally disagree with Dick Cheney. . . . The facts don't bear
him out.

—President Barack Obama, *60 Minutes*, March 22, 2009

One fact, seemingly incontrovertible, after the descriptions contained and
the judgments made in the ICRC report, is that officials of the United States,
in interrogating prisoners in the "War on Terror," have tortured and done so
systematically. From many other sources, including the former president
himself, we know that the decision to do so was taken at the highest level of
the American government and carried out with the full knowledge and support of its most senior officials.

Once this is accepted as a fact, certain consequences might be expected to
follow. First, that these policies, violating as they do domestic and international law, must be changed—which, as noted, President Obama began to
accomplish on his second day in office. Second, that they should be explicitly repudiated—a more complicated political process, which has, perhaps,
begun, but only begun. Third, that those who ordered, designed, and
applied them must be brought before the public in some societally sanctioned proceeding, made to explain what they did and how, and suffer some
appropriate consequence.

And fourth, and crucially, that some judgment must be made, based on
the most credible of information compiled and analyzed and weighed by the
most credible of bodies, about what these policies actually accomplished:
how they advanced the interests of the country, if indeed they did advance
them, and how they hurt them. For at this point, President Obama's assertion that "the facts don't bear [Cheney] out" remains simply that: an assertion. To that assertion Mr. Cheney and others, including President Bush,
respond and will continue to respond with claims of "specific attacks that
were stopped by virtue of what we learned through these programs"—about
which, of course, they "can't give you details . . . without violating classification." And when public officials do cite specific cases—as President Bush
himself did in describing the use of the "alternative set of procedures" on
Abu Zubaydah, who, the president claimed, "was a senior terrorist leader"
who "provided information that helped stop a terrorist attack being planned
for inside the United States"—other officials, many of them also "in a position to know," leak differing versions to reporters which seem to demonstrate
that the claims that were made are exaggerations or worse.[24]

Unfortunately, these contrary accounts, however convincing—and in the
case of Abu Zubaydah they have been very convincing—generally come
from unnamed officials and cannot serve as definitive proof, or as a sufficiently credible repudiation of what former officials, including the president
of the United States, still assert. Far from ending the discussion about

whether torture really was, as Cheney insists, "absolutely crucial to getting us through the last seven-plus years without a major-casualty attack," these ongoing battles between extravagant claims and undermining leaks will ensure that it persists.

It is because of the claim that torture protected the United States that the many Americans who still nod their heads when they hear Dick Cheney's claims about the necessity for "tough, mean, dirty, nasty" tactics in the war on terror respond to its revelation not by instantly condemning it but instead by asking further questions. For example: Was it necessary? And: Did it work? To these questions the last president and vice president, who "kept the country safe" for "seven-plus years," respond "yes," and "yes." And though as time passes, the numbers of those insisting on asking those questions, and willing to accept those answers, no doubt falls, it remains significant, and would likely grow substantially after another successful attack.

This political fact partly explains why, when it comes to torture, we seem to be a society trapped in a familiar and never-ending drama. For though some of the details provided—and officially confirmed for the first time—in the ICRC report are new, and though the first-person accounts make chilling reading and have undoubted dramatic power, one can't help observing that the broader discussion of torture is by now in its essential outlines nearly five years old, and has become, in its predictably reenacted outrage and defiant denials from various parties, something like a shadow play.[25]

News of the "black sites" first appeared prominently in the press—on the front page of the *Washington Post*—in December 2002.[26] A year and a half later, after the publication and broadcast of the Abu Ghraib photographs—the one moment in the last half-dozen years when the torture story, thanks to the lurid images, became "televisual"—a great wave of leaks swept into public view hundreds of pages of "secret" documents about torture and the Bush administration's decision making regarding it.[27] There have been many important "revelations" since, but none of them has changed the essential fact: By no later than the summer of 2004, the American people had before them the basic narrative of how the elected and appointed officials of their government decided to torture prisoners and how they went about it.

The reports on American torture now fill a shelf next to my desk, beginning with the Taguba Report in 2004, still perhaps the best of them, and then going on to include the ICRC report on Abu Ghraib, the Schlesinger Report, the Fay/Jones Report, the Church Report, the Schmidt Report, and now the Armed Services Committee Report, the full text of which will soon break into the news in all its glory, telling us in much more conclusive detail a story the major outlines of which we already know. More revelations will come from this, and more news, particularly about the mechanics by which prominent senior officials approved use of the "alternative set of procedures" and closely monitored their day-to-day application. We will continue in an endless round-robin of revelation, in which we tell ourselves we are learning something new though in fact, when it comes to the central problem of torture—what we as a society should do about it and whether we will in fact do anything—we are in the end simply repeating to ourselves things, however increasingly detailed and awful, that we already know.

Meantime a number of organizations, including the American Civil Liberties Union in a powerful letter by its director, Anthony Romero, have called on Attorney General Eric Holder—who in his confirmation hearings said bluntly that "waterboarding is torture"—to appoint a special prosecutor to look into possible violations of the law under the Bush administration's interrogation program.[28] As I write, the chair of the Senate Judiciary Committee, Patrick Leahy of Vermont, has called for the establishment of a kind of "truth commission" that will gather information, in part by trading immunity from prosecution for former officials for their truthful testimony, about "how our detention policies and practices . . . have seriously eroded fundamental American principles of the rule of law."[29] And the chair of the Intelligence Committee, Senator Dianne Feinstein of California, and its ranking member, Senator Christopher Bond of Missouri, have announced their own investigation into "how the CIA created, operated, and maintained its detention and interrogation program" and—what is crucial—their intention to make "an evaluation of intelligence information gained through the use of enhanced and standard interrogation techniques."[30]

V.

That is the central, unanswered question: What was gained? We know already a good deal about what was lost. On this subject President Obama in his *60 Minutes* response was typically eloquent:

> I mean, the fact of the matter is after all these years how many convictions actually came out of Guantánamo? How many terrorists have actually been brought to justice under the philosophy that is being promoted by Vice President Cheney? It hasn't made us safer. What it has been is a great advertisement for anti-American sentiment. Which means that there is constant effective recruitment of Arab fighters and Muslim fighters against U.S. interests all around the world. . . . The whole premise of Guantánamo promoted by Vice President Cheney was that somehow the American system of justice was not up to the task of dealing with these terrorists. . . . Are we going to just keep on going until the entire Muslim world and Arab world despises us? Do we think that's really going to make us safer?[31]

This is as clear and concise a summary of the damage wrought by torture as one is likely to get. Torture has undermined the United States' reputation for respecting and following the law and thus has crippled its political influence. By torturing, the United States has wounded itself and helped its enemies in what is in the end an inherently political war—a war, that is, in which the critical target to be conquered is the allegiances and attitudes of young Muslims. And by torturing prisoners, many of whom were implicated in committing great crimes against Americans, the United States has made it impossible to render justice on those criminals, instead sentencing them—and the country itself—to an endless limbo of injustice. That limbo stands as a kind of worldwide advertisement for the costs of the U.S. reversion to torture, whose power and influence President Obama has tried to reduce by announcing that he will close Guantánamo.

The question is how to judge this damage to the country's interests—some of which can be measured by polling data in Muslim countries, by rises in recruitment to violent jihadist groups, and so on—against the claims that attacks have been averted. As is so often the case, the categories are not commensurable. Confronted with former Vice President Cheney's arguments, President Obama says "the facts don't bear him out," but the facts he points to appear to be facts about the political damage caused by torture, or about the difficulties it poses to the country in trying to prosecute prisoners. He appears not to be speaking about the same facts that the former administration officials do—facts that they claim prove that torture, in averting attacks and protecting the country, saved lives.

Investigating what kind of intelligence torture actually yielded—and, most important, whether it produced anything that "traditional methods" of interrogation could not have—is not a popular task: Those who oppose torture do not like to admit that it might, in any way, have "worked"; those who support its use don't like to admit that it might not have. It is a regrettable but undeniable fact that torture's illegality, or the political harm it may do to the country's reputation, is not sufficient to discourage the willingness of many Americans to countenance it. However one might prefer that this be an argument soley about legality or morality, it is also an argument solely about national security and, in the end, about politics. However much one agrees with President Obama that Cheney's "notion" that "somehow . . . we can't reconcile our core values, our Constitution, our belief that we don't torture, with our national security interests" has done "incredible damage" to the country, the fact is that many people continue to believe the contrary, and this group apparently includes the former president and vice president of the United States and many senior officials who served them.

There is a reason that the myth of the "ticking bomb" and the daring, ruthless U.S. agent who will do anything to stop its detonation—anything including torture, a step that proves his commitment and his seriousness—is sacralized in popular culture, and not only in current television dramas like *24* but in *Dirty Harry* and the other movies that are its ancestors. The story of the ticking bomb and the torturing hero who defuses it offers, in the face of pervasive anxiety and fear, a calming message: that no matter what horrible threats loom, there are those who will make use of untrammeled government power to protect the country. It also appeals to uglier and equally powerful emotions: the desire for retribution, the urge to punish and to avenge, the felt need in the face of vulnerability to assert power.[32]

In this political calculus, liberals obsessed by "legalisms" are part of the problem, not part of the solution, and it is no accident that it is firmly in that camp that the former vice president has been seeking to isolate the new president. Cheney's success in this endeavor will not be evident now—he is, after all, the most unpopular member of a deeply unpopular party—but the seeds he is so ostentatiously sowing could, if unchallenged by facts and in the right conditions, flourish dramatically in the future.

The only way to defuse the political volatility of torture and to remove it from the center of the "politics of fear" is to replace its lingering mystique, owed mostly to secrecy, with authoritative and convincing information about how it was really used and what it really achieved. That this has not yet happened is the reason why, despite the innumerable reports and studies and revelations that have given us a rich and vivid picture of the Bush administration's policies of torture, we as a society have barely advanced along this path. We have not so far managed, despite all the investigations, to produce a bipartisan, broadly credible, and politically decisive effort, and pronounce authoritatively on whether or not these activities accomplished anything at all in their stated and still asserted purpose: to protect the security interests of the country.

This cannot be accomplished through the press; for the same institutional limitations that lead journalists to keep repeating Bush and Cheney's insistence about the "legality" of torture make it impossible for the press alone, no matter how persuasive the leaks it brings to the public, to make a politically decisive judgment on the value of torture. What is lacking is not information or revelation but political credibility. What is needed is not more disclosures but a broadly persuasive judgment, delivered by people who can look at all the evidence, however highly classified, and can claim bipartisan respect on the order of the Watergate Select Committee or the 9/11 Commission, on whether or not torture made Americans safer.

This is the only way we can begin to come to a true consensus about torture. By all accounts, it is likely that the intelligence harvest that can be attributed directly and exclusively to the "alternative set of procedures" is meager. But if there was indeed information that might have been gained by these techniques and only by these techniques—that is, that could not have been gathered by other, legal methods—it must be assessed and then judged against the great costs, legal, moral, political, incurred in producing it. Torture's harvest, whatever it may truly be, is very unlikely to have outweighed those costs.

VI.

Such an investigation would have to begin with an inquiry into the broader issue of the Bush administration's detention policies after September 11. These policies, built on a cascading series of reverse incentives, filled United

States facilities, from Guantánamo to Abu Ghraib to the secret "black sites," with tens of thousands of prisoners.

The reverse incentives began with bounties of anywhere from several hundred to thousands of dollars offered by U.S. Special Forces in Afghanistan for any "al Qaeda or Taliban member" whom Afghans might bring to American soldiers—incentives that led to the imprisonment of hundreds of Afghan farmers and even of lower-level Taliban who offered nothing whatever in the form of intelligence but who nonetheless ended up imprisoned in Guantánamo, often for years. They were sent there by young U.S. Army interrogators, many of them reservists with little training and no language skills, who found themselves with the awful responsibility of deciding whether or not to let these prisoners go—and who, whatever their doubts about the prisoners' value as intelligence sources, in the days after September 11 had no practical incentive to release them and every incentive not to. As Chris Mackey, an army reservist who served as an interrogator in Afghanistan in 2002, said:

> In talking to some of the officers at Kandahar and Bagram . . . they all talk about how there was a great fear among them, those who were going to be putting their signatures to the release of prisoners, great fear that they were going to somehow manage to release somebody who would later turn out to be the 20th hijacker. So there was real concern and a real erring on the conservative side, especially early in the war.[33]

This pervasive and understandable concern, together with a lack of competent linguists and interrogators in the combat zone, led to a general policy of rounding up suspects that flooded Guantánamo with prisoners who simply should not have been there. Lawrence Wilkerson, a retired U.S. Army colonel who at the time served as chief of staff to Secretary of State Colin Powell, confirms what other studies have shown: that because of "the utter incompetence of the battlefield vetting in Afghanistan" and "the incredible pressure coming down from Secretary of Defense Rumsfeld and others to 'just get the bastards to the interrogators,'" many or even most of those detained "were innocent of any substantial wrongdoing, had little intelligence value, and should be immediately released." Colonel Wilkerson goes on:

> Several in the U.S. leadership became aware of this improper vetting very early on. . . . But to have admitted this reality would have been a black mark on their leadership from virtually day one of the so-called Global War on Terror and these leaders already had black marks enough: the dead in a field in Pennsylvania, in the ashes of the Pentagon, and in the ruins of the World Trade Towers. They were not about to admit to their further errors at Guantánamo Bay. Better to claim that everyone there was a hardcore terrorist, was of enduring intelligence value, and would return to jihad if released.[34]

These initial errors, and the adamant refusal to correct or admit them, led to an overwhelmed, inefficient, and fundamentally unjust U.S. detention system, one that displayed for the world, in televised images of orange-suited, shackled, and hooded prisoners kneeling at Guantánamo, and naked, grotesquely contorted, and abused prisoners cowering at Abu Ghraib, a kind of ongoing lurid recruitment poster for al Qaeda—a dramatic visual confirmation and reaffirmation of the very claims of an evil, repressive, imperialistic United States that lay at the heart of its ideology. Many studies have confirmed the essential truth that a great many prisoners, probably a majority, were unjustly held, without adequate cause or sufficient investigation.[35] Of the nearly eight hundred prisoners who have passed through Guantánamo, well over half have been released without charge, often after years of detention.

The initial panicked rush to "round up prisoners," which was replicated in Iraq during the first months of the insurgency in the summer and fall of 2003, led to what Wilkerson calls an "ad hoc intelligence philosophy" developed to "justify keeping many of these people, called the mosaic philosophy."

> Simply stated, this philosophy held that it did not matter if a detainee were innocent. Indeed, because he lived in Afghanistan and was captured on or near the battle area, he must know something of importance. . . . All that was necessary was to extract everything possible from him and others like him, assemble it all in a computer program, and then look for cross-connections and serendipitous incidentals—in short, to have sufficient information about a village, a region, or a group of individuals, that dots could be connected and terrorists or their plots could be identified.
>
> Thus, as many people as possible had to be kept in detention for as long as possible to allow this philosophy of intelligence gathering to work. The detainees' innocence was inconsequential.[36]

I saw the consequences of this policy in Iraq, in the fall of 2003, when "neighborhood sweeps" and "cordon and capture operations" in "hot areas" led to wholesale arrests of young men. These men, about whom nothing was known apart from the fact that they were young and lived in a neighborhood deemed "hot," were flex-cuffed, hooded, and promptly sent to Abu Ghraib, where they . . . sat. Interrogators were overwhelmed, mostly with prisoners who simply had no intelligence to impart. The interrogators were well aware of this, of course, but in part because officers of the combat units who made the arrests sat on the boards that had to approve prisoner releases, it was almost impossible to release prisoners once they had been brought to Abu Ghraib. "Certain [Coalition Forces] military intelligence officers told the ICRC," according to a 2004 Red Cross report on Abu Ghraib, "that in their estimate *between 70 percent and 90 percent* of the persons deprived of their liberty in Iraq had been arrested by mistake."[37]

As military interrogators described to me in some detail, these numbers overwhelmed the intelligence collection system that the wholesale arrests were intended to supply and fortify, leading interrogators to spend most of their time working through thousands of prisoners who had nothing to tell them—but who nonetheless could in most cases not be released and had to be interviewed, often repeatedly.

One soon begins to see a pattern: Among officials at the top, panic and fear and incompetence lead to a compensating, self-justifying desire to "do whatever's necessary" to prevent attacks and finally to a consequent injustice inflicted on the innocents at the bottom that is both persistent and politically damaging. Thus the movement from Secretary of Defense Rumsfeld's call to "just get the bastards to the interrogators" to the overflow of innocent prisoners from Guantánamo to Abu Ghraib, innocents who rendered unworkable the very system that the "get tough" directives were meant to snap into effective action.

Chris Mackey, the U.S. Army interrogator, writes of "the gravitational laws that govern human behavior when one group of people is given complete control over another in a prison. Every impulse tugs downward."[38] All evidence suggests that in the days after September 11, 2001, the very officials who should have been ensuring that there were restraints put on such "gravitational laws" were instead doing all they could to augment them. Fear and a compensating desire to prove that nothing would be allowed to stand in the way of the all-important goal of protecting the country—especially not overly "legalistic" notions about international treaties and limitations on presidential power—were allowed to drive policy, and the country is still struggling to cope with the results.

VII.

We know a great deal about the Bush administration's policy of torture but we need to know more. We need to know, from an investigation that will study all the evidence, classified at however high a level of secrecy, and that will speak to the nation with a credible bipartisan voice, whether the use of torture really did produce information that, in the words of the former vice president, was "absolutely crucial to getting us through the last seven-plus years without a major-casualty attack on the United States." We already have substantial reason to doubt these claims, for example the words of Lawrence Wilkerson, who, as chief of staff to Secretary of State Powell, had access to intelligence of the highest classification:

> It has never come to my attention in any persuasive way—from classified information or otherwise—that any intelligence of significance was gained from any of the detainees at Guantánamo Bay other than from the handful of undisputed ring leaders and their companions, clearly no more than a dozen or two of the detainees, and even their alleged contribution of

hard, actionable intelligence is intensely disputed in the relevant communities such as intelligence and law enforcement.[39]

It is important to note that a great many of those charged with the duty to "keep us safe" do not share the former president's view about the necessity of his "alternative set of procedures." Indeed, on September 6, 2006, a couple of hours before President Bush told the nation in his East Room speech about the "separate program operated by the Central Intelligence Agency" where the "alternative set of procedures" were used, and announced that the fourteen "suspected terrorist leaders and operatives" were being sent from the "black sites" to Guantánamo (where they would tell their stories at last to the Red Cross investigators), a very different event was taking place across the Potomac. At the Department of Defense, high-ranking officers and officials were introducing the new *Army Field Manual for Human Intelligence Collector Operations*—the newly rewritten manual for interrogators that was, as Lieutenant General John Kimmons, the army deputy chief of staff for intelligence, pointed out, unique in a number of ways:

> The Field Manual explicitly prohibits torture or cruel, inhumane, and degrading treatment or punishment. . . . To make this more imaginable and understandable to our soldiers . . . we have included in the Field Manual specific prohibitions. There's eight of them: Interrogators may not force a detainee to be naked, perform sexual acts or pose in a sexual manner; they cannot use hoods or place sacks over a detainee's head or use duct tape over his eyes; they cannot beat or electrically shock or burn them or inflict other forms of physical pain—any form of physical pain; they may not use water boarding, they may not use hypothermia or treatment which will lead to heat injury; they will not perform mock executions; they may not deprive detainees of the necessary food, water and medical care; and they may not use dogs in any aspect of interrogations. . . .[40]

Lieutenant General Kimmons's list of procedures is remarkable for including almost all of those that had come to light during the years of the Bush administration, either at Abu Ghraib, Guantánamo, or, now, at the "black sites." Indeed, just before his commander in chief's vivid defense to the country of the necessity of the "alternative set of procedures," the general was declaring that the military had expressly forbidden precisely those procedures—and was explaining, in answer to a reporter's question about whether the prohibitions didn't "limit the ability of interrogators to get information that could be very useful," precisely why:

> I am absolutely convinced the answer to your first question is no. No good intelligence is going to come from abusive practices. I think history tells us that. I think the empirical evidence of the last five years, hard years, tells us that.

And moreover, any piece of intelligence which is obtained under duress, through the use of abusive techniques would be of questionable credibility. And additionally, it would do more harm than good when it inevitably became known that abusive practices were used. And we can't afford to go there.

And yet the "loud rhetoric" of Dick Cheney, as Colonel Wilkerson remarks, "continues even now" and remains a persistent political fact in our debate about national security. What should be a debate about facts remains instead a debate fueled by reckless assertions about "still classified" intelligence and leaks that undermine those assertions. The debate over the supposed importance of intelligence provided by Abu Zubaydah, whose torture, including waterboarding, is related with awful immediacy in the ICRC report, is only the most prominent of these controversies. Though waterboarding has not been performed on prisoners in American custody since 2003, there is a reason we continue to talk about it. Though we have known about the Bush administration's policy of torture for five years, there is unquestionably more debate about it now than there ever has been. We are having, in a ragged way, the debate about ethics and morality in our national security policies that we never had in the days after September 11, when decisions were made in secret by a handful of officials.

Philip Zelikow, who served the Bush administration in the National Security Council and the State Department and who directed the 9/11 Commission, remarked in an important speech in 2007 that these officials, instead of having that debate simply called in the lawyers: The focus, that is, was not on "what should we do" but on "what can we do."[41]

There is a sense in which our society is finally posing that "what should we do" question. That it is doing so only now, after the fact, is a tragedy for the country—and becomes even more damaging as the debate is carried on largely by means of politically driven assertions and leaks. For even as the practice of torture by Americans has withered and died, its potency as a political issue has grown. The issue could not be more important, for it cuts to the basic question of who we are as Americans, and whether our laws and ideals truly guide us in our actions or serve instead as a kind of national decoration to be discarded in times of danger. The only way to confront the political power of the issue, and prevent the reappearance of the practice itself, is to take a hard look at the true "empirical evidence of the last five years, hard years," and speak out, clearly and credibly, about what that story really tells.

The New York Review of Books, April 30, 2009

Postscript

As I write, in mid-summer 2009, there has been no "hard look" at "the last five years, hard years." The public story has reached a disquieting point of suspension. After the release of dozens of official reports and documents (including most recently the exhaustive Senate Armed Services Committee "Inquiry Into the Treatment of Detainees in U.S. Custody" and the four Department of Justice "torture memos"), the road the society traveled to torture has been precisely mapped, and Americans seem to have reached a rough and unacknowledged consensus: Having known for at least five years that their government was torturing, citizens have now collectively relegated torture to the condition of an intermittent but perpetual crisis. The very tumult of debate, the sterile dynamism of revelation and scandal, allows us to deny what is true but cannot be acknowledged: that torture—that our having tortured—is something we have learned to live with.

Though with each new document disclosed, each elaboration of what has long been known, the debate about torture explodes once again into public view, the underlying dynamic persists. Republicans ordered torture and, then as now, supported its use (while calling it something else), thereby reaffirming their status as the party of patriotism, nationalism, and "keeping America safe." Democrats, on the defensive since 9/11 as the party of weakness on national security and now once again wielding power, demand investigations but remain deeply divided about punishing torture's champions, not least because that would mean pressing to its conclusion a cause (the "rights of terrorists") perceived to be deeply unpopular—and even, in the event of a future attack, politically fatal. In the wake of 9/11, "taking the gloves off" was a badge of authenticity, one many remain reluctant to question.

Though the attorney general is now said to be pondering a decision to appoint a special prosecutor—to investigate, in a grim reprise of Abu Ghraib, only interrogators who "went beyond" what the notorious torture memos permitted, not the officials who designed and approved the policies—President Obama continues to affirm his determination to "look forward" rather than "backward." To look forward on torture, when there has been no authoritative, collectively sanctioned judgment on what was done—and when the country remains deeply divided on whether these decisions were right—is in effect to "agree to disagree." To investigate only those interrogators who went beyond the tortures Justice Department lawyers "legalized" in their memorandums, if this is what the new adminstration chooses to do, is in effect to reaffirm that the broader society, not just officials in the Bush Department, has consented to accept the torture they approved as lawful. Stripped bare, these decisions mean the country has collectively consented, however grudgingly, to countenance what was done while hoping to forget it. More practically, they mean that torture will retain its corrosive political power to drive the country's passions on national security—on who has the commitment and will to "keep the country safe."

From a country that did not, at least officially, torture the United States has become a country that tortures only when it feels it needs to. Torture, in passing from the hands of one party to the other, has remained the preeminent frozen scandal: revealed but unpunished, exposed but unexorcised. The cycle of revelation, investigation, expiation has been broken. The dark "state of exception" that the United States entered after the attacks of September 11, 2001—the de facto state of emergency that the Bush administration imposed on the country—has left its permanent shadow. For much of the world the bright mirage of American exceptionalism—that notion Americans cherish of their country as a "city upon a hill" to whose shining example all nations look—has been swallowed up in that gathering darkness.

For Americans living in its shadow the effect is less clear. The high ideological fervor of the post-9/11 months and years—the defiant vow to "rid the world of evil"—feels distant now, an intoxicated dream that elicits guilty looks and unspoken agreement to leave embarrassing acts unmentioned. Iraq, still violent and unstable, still riven by sectarian political passions unresolved, fades rapidly from America's consciousness. The spotlight moves on. The ruins left behind, fading into darkness, seem faraway, foreign. And yet there are ruins here as well, all around us, ignored but unmistakable. The body stripped bare by these years of violence was in the end our own—whether or not we choose to place the stethoscope and track the disorders beneath the skin, or find the will to heal them.

—August 1, 2009

Afterword:
The Erotic Pull of the Strange

March 12, 2003

THE FIRST TIME I WAS KILLED, or nearly so, came just past dawn on election day 1987 at a deserted crossroads in northern Haiti. I had endless time, in the half-second it took to collapse face-first in the dust, to savor the tableau before me: jackknifed in the intersection, a riderless motorcycle, front wheel still spinning; fanned across the ground beside it a sheaf of blackened election ballots, one or two still burning fitfully, the candidate's dark face and white teeth grinning in the flames. I can see it still, this scene; still relish, sixteen years later, the pleasure afforded by its facile symbols. The shooters, though, I hardly glimpsed. A large sedan filled with militiamen, the car had barreled headlong down the street; but now, in my mind's eye, it advances slowly and I see no faces, only the muzzle of the weapon, see no flashes, only the bursts of cement thrown up by the shells striking the walls. As my face thuds against the earth, I feel a feathery caress at the nape of my neck: the drizzle of plaster from the bullets tattooing the wall above.

The second time I was killed, or nearly so, came a few hours later, just north of the capital as we slowed at a roadblock of tree trunks and cinderblocks and old car parts and a crowd of drunken peasants appeared from nowhere and dragged us from the car. The rabble of men with machetes engulfed us, churning and shouting; we argued, pleaded, holding our press cards before us like pitiful shields. Then, after a moment's pause, the scene turned very dark: the tough old man closest to me, small, leathery-faced, narrow-eyed, hissed, "*Kommunis!*" Communist! I'd heard it often that week, shouted at moments like this one; and as he raised his machete and the foot or so between us began to vanish I was startled to feel, behind my fear, a moment of intense narrative pleasure: yes, of course. After a week of standing ogling, cameras and notebooks poised, as Haitians chopped to pieces other Haitians a few feet from us, after a week spent recording precisely what body part and how much of it was hacked off and paraded triumphantly down the street, suddenly on this bloody election day the privileged position we had taken for granted—untouchable, unreachable, white—collapses and we are dragged, mouths agape and fingers clinging with ridiculous desperation to our now useless notebooks and cameras, onto the stage to become

545

props in the bloody play. Surprising yet inevitable, like any good climax. Of course the story would end this way. How perfect.

On the other hand, perhaps it was all a bit too . . . pat, this story of reporters hacked to pieces by their own story. Someone clearly thought so; for at precisely the necessary moment on that utterly deserted road a wealthy man, a diminutive mulatto in a sports shirt driving an expensive four-wheel-drive, happened upon us and, armed with nothing more than his light skin and a half-century's practice in ruling over those darker than himself, commanded the peasants with their raised machetes to "Fuck off out of there!" And they, after an excruciating moment of wide-eyed and near-comic paralysis—however near-revolutionary their drunken mood had been—did just that. On a day marked by the world to let the poorest of the poor take power in Haiti, on a day on which four less lucky reporters died in pools of their own blood on those sun-drenched streets, we owed our lives to our white skins and the Haitian color hierarchy. What better irony than that?

Still, irony is cheap and I must admit a secret preference for the violent outcome. I could tell it that way, of course—I just did, nearly so—but then it would be fiction. And, alas, a funny thing happens to the story on the way to the fiction shelf: it acquires a cheap veneer of melodrama. On the other hand, as a *New Yorker* "fact piece"—which was what I was writing—the story would have worked just fine, for the looming melodrama would have been excused, given a free pass by the fact that these characters and events happened to have counterparts in reality. Of course, if my preferred violent outcome had come to pass—had qualified as fact—I could not have been the one writing it.

We are all storytellers; we all work with narrative. We differ only in the rules we follow. And these rules, when set against the subtlety of narrative modes—the interplay of irony and symbol and structure—are very broad indeed, a breadth perfectly expressed by that most ridiculous of non-category categories: "nonfiction." "There is no such thing as a work of pure factuality," writes Janet Malcolm, "any more than there is one of pure fictitiousness." She goes on:

> As every work of fiction draws on life, so every work of nonfiction draws on art. As the novelist must curb his imagination in order to keep his text grounded in the common experience of man . . . so the journalist must temper his literal-mindedness with the narrative devices of imaginative literature.[1]

Whether employed by a writer needing to "curb his imagination" or a writer seeking to "temper his literal-mindedness," these narrative devices do not change. Plot, character, symbol are the ways we order experience, and the stories we tell, whatever their relation to "fact" or their final address in the bookstore, have these in common. If we persist in organizing works of narrative by their relationship to "truth," we'll find the official genres intersecting, looping back on one another. Place Nora Ephron's

Heartburn next to Ryszard Kapuscinski's *The Emperor* and ask which is "truer to the facts." Ephron's "novel" is a *roman à clef* and many in Washington could identify the "real" original of every character and no doubt the time and place of many scenes. For *The Emperor*, I suspect one would have great difficulty doing the same, though Kapuscinski's book is the "true story" of the fall of Haile Selassie, and no account of those events bears more truth or is told with more art.[2]

Rules constrain but they also help us see. The pleasures that washed through me as I contemplated the riderless motorcycle and the burning ballots—symbols of a leaderless country and a torched election—are narrative pleasures, rooted deep within us. As with all arts unfolding in time, they draw their first life from suspense—from the need to quicken and advance. The sonata form, and its gripping epic of migration from the tonic to the dominant and then back again, is an archetype of this. In narrative, it is plot, story, resolution: the ineluctable move toward climax and denouement. We build these shapes into our world, into our public narratives and our private ones, whether they chart going to war or falling in love.

When we turn to stories of foreign places, to the erotic pull of the strange, it is no mystery that violence and death lie close to the heart of the darkness we find so mysterious—and feel so compelled to understand. As climactic events, violent acts offer the lure of illumination. As a onetime Haitian president told me, "Violence strips bare the social body, the better to place the stethoscope and track the life beneath the skin." He meant, I think, that coups d'etat and revolutions—political violence in general—reveal in their unfolding the true but normally hidden structures of power. By enacting power in motion they show it in reality. And indeed it took only months for my friend's political *bon mot* to be revealed as prophecy, when he was overthrown and exiled by his erstwhile army chief.

He did not die, this president, but in his overthrow others did. He had accomplished little, having accepted power from a handful of disgraced and bloodstained officers in his need to write the conclusion to his own romance, a private tale of grandeur that had been spooling through his head during a quarter century of exile. Drunk with tales of war and triumph from the magical past of his ruined country, he had become desperate to see his own story completed—to see his "destiny fulfilled." And yet despite the struggle for power and the deaths entailed in losing it, his story was in the end a low one, with little to commend it to the chroniclers. Or such, anyway, is the verdict of the writer of "fact pieces"; a fiction writer might see it differently.

The man who killed me, or nearly so—the man who offered guns to those faceless men in the sedan, who had given rum to drink and a roadblock to guard to that band of peasants—had killed hundreds that day, murdered during his life hundreds more; and yet when I met him for breakfast in one of the capital's modern hotels, watched him carefully cut his mango there by the shimmering blue pool overlooking the city, I saw he would fail me as a character. However great his crimes appeared to me—the piles of bodies on election day, the hundreds tortured and murdered during the bloodiest days of the dictatorship—to him they were politics, that's all, the way the system worked. He seemed puzzled by my interest. There was no grandeur there: killing and torture were his day job, the dull mechanics of his profession. His art, on the other hand, was his Ideas—his Vision for the Nation. He cut his mango and in his deep voice set it forth, smiling after each bite. He had killed me, or nearly so, and now we were both disappointed. His art did not interest me.

The third time I was killed, or nearly so, came on an unseasonably warm February day in a crowded market in Sarajevo. The schedule had slipped and we had not yet arrived when the mortar shell landed, leading us to find, moments later, a dark swamp of blood and broken bodies and staggering about in it the bereaved, shrieking and wailing amid an overwhelming stench of cordite. Already two men, standing in rubber boots knee-deep in a thick black lake, had begun to toss body parts into the back of a truck. Slipping about on the wet pavement, I tried my best to count the bodies and the parts of them, but the job was impossible: fifty? sixty? When all the painstaking matching had been done, sixty-eight had died there.

When a few days later I lunched with their killer—the leader of the Serbs, surrounded in his mountain villa by a handful of beautiful bodyguards—he had little interest in the numbers. "Did you check their ears?" he asked. I'm sorry? "They had ice in their ears." I paused at this and took a moment to work on my stew. He meant the bodies had been planted, that the entire scene had been trumped up by Bosnian intelligence agents. He was a psychiatrist, this man, and it seemed to me, after a few minutes of questions, that he had gone far to convince himself of the truth of this scenario. He, too, preferred to speak of his Vision for the Nation.

For me, the problem in depicting him was simple, and familiar: the level of his crimes dwarfed the content of his character. His motivations were paltry, in no way commensurate with the pain he had caused. It is often a problem with evil. Chat with a Salvadoran general about the massacre of a thousand people that he ordered and he will tell you that it was military necessity, that those people were supporting the guerrillas, that they had put themselves in harm's way, and that "such things happen in war." Speak to the young conscript who did the killing and he will tell you that he hated what he had to do, that he has nightmares about it still, but that he was following orders and that if he had refused he would have been killed. Neither is lying. Search for evil there and once you leave the corpses behind you will have great difficulty finding the needed grimacing face.

Talking with mass murderers is invariably a disappointment. Great acts so rarely call forth great character that the relation between the two seems nearly random. The fiction writer is free to correct this imbalance; the writer of fact, alas, is trapped by the rules he purports to follow. I could not make my killer into a great man; I had to fall back, as had Hannah Arendt, on irony—on the fact of this discrepancy between the magnitude of the acts and the banality of the actor. There is compensation, though, in this inequality; what Malcolm calls the reader's "epistemological insecurity," according to which, "in a work of nonfiction we almost never know the truth of what happened." She goes on:

> We must always take the novelist's and the playwright's and the poet's word, just as we are almost always free to doubt the biographer's or the autobiographer's or the historian's or the journalist's. In imaginative litera-ture we are constrained from considering alternative scenarios—there are none. This is the way it is. Only in nonfiction does the question of what happened and how people thought and felt remain open. We can never know everything; there is always more.[3]

Floating in an ocean of "epistemological insecurity," my killer will remain a dynamic element, threatening the reader not only with his vitality but with his refusal to conform to the boundaries of his depiction. The fiction writer might provide motivation, attempt to draw a character interesting enough, com-pelling enough, to justify the acts he has committed. Once completed, how-ever, this portrait is all there is, unmediated, true only to the writer's imagination and on that truth it will stand or fall. Can one construct a charac-ter commensurate with the hundred dead that election day? It is, surely, a great burden—that "this is the way it is." And it is partly to unshoulder that burden that fiction writers experiment so excitedly with point of view, in order to undermine in their narratives—as Ford did in *The Good Soldier*—the unbear-able "epistemological certainty" with which their profession had saddled them.

It is why Conrad constructed his Kurtz, perhaps fiction's most famous mass murderer, almost entirely of suspense, of the primal stuff of narrative itself. Kurtz's words are legendary: "The horror! The horror!"[4] But apart from indirectly reported ravings before he dies, they are nearly all he says. The man is constructed not of dialogue or even direct description but of expectation and, finally, of dread. The dread belongs first to those who know him, then to Marlowe, and finally to us. The problem of evil my murderers could not solve for me is thrown back upon the reader. The "heart of dark-ness" is our own.

To construct the central character out of shadow and dread: it is a feat of narrative virtuosity that the fact writer can only envy. For us, of course, the light would be too bright; readers of "fact," waiting to see the killer, would simply find the reporting a bit thin. Conrad could accomplish his legerde-main only by way of a fictional stand-in: the voice of his storyteller. The drama over evil is painted in Marlowe's mind, so as to instill it in our own. Verisimilitude through point of view is the fiction writers' modern road to truth. Seeking light in worlds that seem impossibly dark, they come to crave some of the doubt taken for granted in writing fact. They long to make it real.

Zoetrope Magazine, July 19, 2003

Coda:
Words in a Time of War [1]

From the totalitarian point of view history is something to be created rather than learned.

—George Orwell, 1946 [2]

May 10, 2007

I.

WE PRIDE OURSELVES in being realists first of all, and thus we know well, or tell ourselves we do, that "the first casualty when war comes is truth." Yet Senator Hiram Johnson's oft-quoted dictum comes down to us from 1918, a more innocent time, when the hopes for truth and transparency at the heart of the Progressive Era were foundering on the rhetorical exigencies of the Great War. [3] What can this truism mean nine decades later, when applied to a war that is itself in large part a rhetorical creation, a war unbounded by space or by time, unlimited in extent and metaphysical in ambition: a forever war launched against evil itself?

Such is the "War on Terror," declared in the wake of the attacks of September 11, 2001, and fought with passionate rhetorical intensity in the half dozen years since. The enemy in this war, the president told Congress and the nation a week after the planes struck, was "heir to all the murderous ideologies of the twentieth century . . . follow[ing] in the path of Fascism, and Nazism, and Totalitarianism" and such a terrible foe called for nothing less than a campaign to "rid this world of evil." Though for a time the war remained mostly "virtual," fought mostly "on the dark side," as Vice President Dick Cheney put it, by intelligence officers, Special Forces, and, in Afghanistan, a large helping of aerial bombardment, this largely virtual conflict shortly gave birth to a real war, the invasion and occupation of Iraq. The stubborn refusal of the Iraq war to conclude on schedule (Pentagon plans called for all but a few tens of thousands of Americans to be out of Iraq by September 2003) and thus supply the promised "shining example of democracy in the Middle East" in time for the 2004 elections resulted in its wholesale absorption, *faute de mieux*, into the virtual war.

And so Iraq, the failed war, now became, as the self-described "wartime president" dubbed it in his reelection campaign, "the central front of the war on terror."

Virtual war begets real war. Failure subsumes real war to virtual. Thus did virtual War on Terror became real, an affair of tanks, weekly casualty counts, and an infinitely receding horizon. As I write, President Bush and the Republican candidates to succeed him, with a losing war on their hands and no place to put it, find themselves working tirelessly, unceasingly, to keep the real war safely sheltered under the virtual canopy of the War on Terror, declaring Iraq "the critical battle" in "the defining ideological struggle of our time," in which defeat will lead to "the terrorists following us home." The Democrats, meantime, struggle equally hard to drag it back out, branding the Iraq war not only a failure but, more seriously still, a "distraction" from "the real war"—by which they mean, to add another twist of paradox, none other than the War on Terror. More surprising, perhaps, than the fact that the struggle over the ontological character of these wars now comprises the central rhetorical battleground of American politics is our own decided lack of surprise, our ongoing willingness to listen seriously to such verbal shadow play. We have come far since Hiram Johnson's simple bromides about war and truth.

George Orwell, it is safe to say, would not have been surprised. It was Orwell, after all, who nearly six decades ago fathered the idea of virtual conflict, creating the perpetual world war between the superstates of Oceania, Eurasia, and Eastasia that forms the background to *Nineteen Eighty Four*. That never-ending, shapeshifting struggle, it is well to remember, was nearly bloodless, a perpetual war that,

> if we judge it by the standards of previous wars, is merely an imposture . . .
> like the battles between certain ruminant animals whose horns are set at
> such an angle that they are incapable of hurting one another. But though
> it is unreal it is not meaningless. . . . [I]t helps to preserve the special men-
> tal atmosphere that a hierarchical society needs.[4]

The comparison, of course, must be inexact. Thousands have died in the War on Terror, and many thousands more in Iraq. These wars are only partly virtual, and it is no accident that the struggle over their reality has attained such a central place in our politics. What Orwell dramatizes is an ideal, the Platonic form of virtual war. What he describes for us—what we must learn from him today—is the power of virtual war to reduce and refine boulders of international armed conflict down to their most valuable political ore. In his conception the great grinding mechanism of modern industrial warfare is stripped of all its material attributes: armies, fighting, even death—all but "the special mental atmosphere" that wars produce. The glittering, priceless ore that remains is the politician's lodestone, for glowing at its heart is that most lucrative of political emotions: fear. War produces fear. But so also does the rhetoric of war. This—Orwell's precious insight—leads to the central lesson he brings us about our own perpetual war: What terrorists ultimately produce is not death or mayhem, but fear; and in a War on Terror the rich political benefits of that most lucrative emotion will inevitably be shared— between the terrorists themselves and the political leaders who lead the fight against them.

II.

Perhaps it would have surprised Orwell, poet laureate of the Cold War, to find himself so much in our thoughts in this second decade of the post–Cold War age. The Soviet Union is fifteen years dead, its imperium in the East long since ended. China has entered into a peculiar economic symbiosis with the American capitalist juggernaut, fabricating most of its consumer goods and holding in payment most of its debt. And in this new post-ideological world no writer is more vital than George Orwell, not least because he helps us see how deeply that earlier struggle has marked us, helps us read the signs it has inscribed on the body of our politics.

Gazing at the solemn White House ceremony on December 14, 2004, watching in inarticulate wonder as the newly reelected president placed the Medal of Freedom around the necks of three high officials, I began to perceive, dancing deep in my memory, a line of Orwell's that I could not quite grasp. Before me on the television screen, neck bent for the president, stood General (ret.) Tommy Franks, who had led the initial "combat phase" of the war in Iraq, that "combat phase" that had never ended. Beside him was L. Paul Bremer, the bold and bumbling proconsul under whose regency the insurgency had taken root and flourished. And beside Bremer, finally, stood George Tenet, the director of central intelligence whose long tenure will be known to history as twice distinguished—by the failure to detect the coming 9/11 attacks and by the certainty about Iraq's bristling arsenal of weapons of mass destruction, those magical objects that, having provided the *casus belli* for the war, turned out not to exist. The three men, dedicated public servants all, had been coauthors of failures quite monumental in their implications, a truth that by December 2004 was quite incontestable, whatever your politics. Now they were receiving from the leader's hands the country's highest civilian honor and basking in the light and warmth of his smile.

That the truth of their failures was incontestable did not matter. The ceremony served not to proclaim truth but rather to assert and embody a proposition that has been central to the current administration: Truth is subservient to power. Power, rightly applied, makes truth. As I watched the television screen and murmured that simple formula, the fragment of Orwell that had been dancing just beyond the grasp of my consciousness finally took shape: "History is something to be created rather than learned." In a few moments, even as the freshly bemedaled heroes on the screen were still smiling and shaking hands, I found the full quotation:

From the totalitarian point of view history is something to be created rather than learned. A totalitarian state is in effect a theocracy, and its ruling caste, in order to keep its position, has to be thought of as infallible. But since, in practice, no one is infallible, it is frequently necessary to rearrange past events in order to show that this or that mistake was not made, or that this or that imaginary triumph actually happened.[5]

These words, written in 1946, are imbued with the anti-totalitarian struggle, the one just ended and the one about to begin. Six decades later, the United States is far from a totalitarian state. But we have seen, during these past half dozen years of perpetual war, more than a little of "the totalitarian point of view" and more than a few attempts to "rearrange past events in order to show that this or that mistake was not made, or that this or that imaginary triumph actually happened." The words might serve as a succinct and elegant description of much of our politics—or, better yet, they might be taken as a caption, ready-made, to be placed beneath a photograph of Messrs. Frank, Bremer, and Tenet receiving their medals from a grateful sovereign.

III.

Nearly five years into the Iraq war, at the beginning of a presidential campaign that may well turn on the question of how to end it, one might be pardoned for forgetting that that war already ended once before. More than four years have passed since that richly choreographed victory scene on the USS *Abraham Lincoln* off the coast of San Diego, when the president, clad jauntily in a flight suit, swaggered across the flight deck, and beneath a banner famously marked "Mission Accomplished," declared: "Major combat operations in Iraq have ended. In the battle of Iraq, the United States and our allies have prevailed."

At first glance, the grand spectacle of May 1, 2003, fits handily into the history of the pageantries of power. Indeed, with its waving banners and thousands of cheering uniformed extras gathered on the flight deck of that mammoth aircraft carrier—which had to be precisely turned so that the skyline of San Diego, a few miles off, would not be glimpsed by the television audience—this grand event, in its vast conception and its clockwork staging, in its melding of event and image-of-the-event, would have been quite familiar to the great propagandists of the last century (most notably Leni Riefenstahl, who achieved a similar grandeur of image in her 1934 masterpiece, *Triumph of the Will*). Indeed, however vast and impressive, the May 1 extravaganza seems a propaganda event of a traditional sort, meant to bind the country together in a second precise image of victory (after the carefully staged dethroning of Saddam's statue in Baghdad two weeks before)—a triumphant image intended to fit neatly into campaign ads for the 2004 election. The president was the star, the sailors and airmen and their enormous dreadnought props in his extravaganza.

For all the historic resonances, though, one can't help detecting something different here, a kind of . . . *knowingness*, perhaps even an ironic self-awareness, that would have been unthinkable in 1934. For we have today leaders who are not only radical in their attitudes toward power and truth, rhetoric and reality, but are occasionally willing, to our great benefit, to state this attitude clearly—at least to members of an elite who are thought to have the wit to understand it and to lack the power to do anything about it. In the annals of such frank expressions of the philosophy of power, pride of place must surely be given to this, my favorite quotation of the present age, published in the *New York Times Magazine* on October 17, 2004, by the writer Ron Suskind, who recounts his discussion with the proverbial "unnamed Administration official," as follows:

> The aide said that guys like me were "in what we call the reality-based community," which he defined as people who "believe that solutions emerge from your judicious study of discernible reality." I nodded and murmured something about enlightenment principles and empiricism. He cut me off. "That's not the way the world really works anymore," he continued. "We're an empire now, and when we act, we create our own reality. And while you're studying that reality—judiciously, as you will—we'll act again, creating other new realities, which you can study too, and that's how things will sort out. We're history's actors . . . and you, all of you, will be left to just study what we do."[6]

These words from "Bush's Brain"—for the unnamed official speaking to Suskind is widely known to have been none other than the selfsame architect of the aircraft-carrier moment, Karl Rove—sketch out with breathtaking frankness a radical view in which power frankly determines reality, and rhetoric, the science of flounces and folderols, follows meekly and subserviently in its train. Those in the "reality-based community"—those such as we—are figures a mite pathetic, for all of our adherence to Enlightenment principles and our scurrying after empirical proof proves only that we have failed to realize the singular new principle of the new age: Power has made reality its bitch.

Given such sweeping claims for power, it is hard to expect much respect for truth (or perhaps it should be "truth," in knowing, self-mocking quotation marks); for when you can alter reality at will, why pay much attention to the matter of fidelity in describing it? What faith, after all, is owed to the bitch that is wholly in your power, a creature of your own creation?

That relativist conviction—that what the unenlightened naïvely call "objective truth" is in fact "a discourse" subservient to power, shaped and ordered by the ruling institutions of our society—is by no means new; on the contrary, it has served for decades as the fertile truism at the root of much fashionable academic discourse. Leading humanist theorists of the last three decades, European and American both, might concede an intellectual kinship, not least in the disdain for the unimaginative drones of the "reality-based community"—though perhaps they would find themselves a bit non-plussed to discover the idea so blithely put forward by a finely tailored man sitting in a White House office. Accusing power is one thing, quite another when power feels comfortable enough to confess.

IV.

We are so embedded in its age that it is easy to forget the stark, overwhelming shock of it: Nineteen young men with box cutters seized enormous transcontinental airliners and *brought those towers down*. In an age in which we have become accustomed to two, three, four, five suicide attacks in a single day—in which these multiple attacks in Iraq often don't even make the front pages of our newspapers—one must make an effort to summon back the openmouthed, stark staring disbelief at that impossible image: the second airliner disappearing into the great office tower, almost weirdly absorbed by it, and emerging, transformed into a great yellow-and-red blossom of flame, on the other side; and then, half an hour later, the astonishing flowering collapse of the hundred-story structure, metamorphosing, in a dozen seconds, from mighty tower to great plume of heaven-reaching white smoke.

The image remains, will always remain, with us; for truly the weapon that day was not box cutters in the hands of nineteen young men, nor airliners at their command. The weapon that day was the television set. It was the television set that made the image possible, and inextinguishable. If terror is first of all a way of talking—the propaganda of the deed, indeed—then that day the television was the indispensable conveyer of the conversation: the recruitment poster for fundamentalism, the only symbolic arena in which America's weakness and vulnerability could be dramatized on an adequate scale. Terror—as Menachem Begin, the late Israeli prime minister and former anti-British terrorist, remarked in his memoirs—terror is about "destroying the prestige" of the imperial regime; terror is about dirtying the face of power.[7]

President Bush and his lieutenants surely realized this, and it is in that knowledge, I believe, that we must find the beginning of the answer to one of the more intriguing puzzles of these last few years: What exactly lay at the root of the almost fanatical determination of administration officials to attack and occupy Iraq? It was, obviously, the classic "overdetermined" decision, a tangle of fear, in the form of those infamous weapons of mass destruction; of imperial ambition, in the form of the neoconservative project to "remake the Middle East"; and of realpolitik, in the form of the "vital interest" of securing the industrial world's oil supplies.

In the beginning, though, was the felt need on the part of our nation's leaders, men and women so worshipful of the idea of power and its ability to remake reality itself, to restore the nation's prestige, to wipe clean that dirtied face. Henry Kissinger, a confidant of the president, when asked by Bush's speechwriter why he had supported the Iraq war, responded: "Because Afghanistan was not enough." The radical Islamists, he said, want to humiliate us. "And we need to humiliate them."[8] For the sake of American prestige and thus of American power, the presiding image of the War on Terror—the burning, smoking towers collapsing into rubble—had to be supplanted by another, of American tanks rumbling proudly down the streets of a vanquished Arab capital. It is no accident that Secretary of Defense Donald Rumsfeld, at the first "war cabinet" meeting at Camp David the Saturday after the 9/11 attacks, fretted over the "lack of targets" in Afghanistan and wondered whether we "shouldn't do Iraq first."[9] He wanted to see those advancing tanks marching across the world's television screens, and soon.

In the end, of course, the enemy preferred not to fight with tanks, though they were perfectly happy to have the Americans do so, the better to destroy these multi-million-dollar anachronisms with improvised explosive devices, so-called IEDs, costing a few hundred dollars apiece. Such is the practice of asymmetrical warfare, by which the very weak contrive to use the strengths of the very strong against them. In the post–Cold War world, after all, as one neoconservative theorist explained shortly after 9/11, the United States was enjoying a rare "unipolar moment." It deployed the greatest military and economic power the world had ever seen. It spent more on its weapons, its army, navy, and air force, than the rest of the world combined. Indeed, the confident assumption of this so-called preponderance was what lay behind the philosophy of power enunciated by Bush's Brain, and what produced an attitude toward international law and alliances that is quite unprecedented in American history. "Our strength as a nation-state," reads the National Security Strategy of the United States of 2005, "will continue to be challenged by those who employ a strategy of the weak using international fora, judicial processes and terrorism."[10] A remarkable troika, these "weapons of the weak," comprising as it does the United Nations and like institutions ("international fora"), international and domestic courts ("judicial processes"), and . . . terrorism. This strange grouping, put forward as the official policy of the United States, is borne of the idea that power is, in fact, everything: the only thing. In such a world, international institutions and courts—indeed, law itself—can only limit the power of the most powerful state. Wielding preponderant power, what need has such a state for law? The latter must be, by definition, a weapon of the weak. The most powerful state, after all, makes reality.

V.

Now consider for a moment this astonishing fact: Little more than a decade-and-a-half into this "uni-polar moment," the greatest military power in the history of the world stands on the brink of defeat. In Iraq, its vastly expensive and all-powerful military has been humbled by a congeries of secret organizations fighting mainly by means of suicide vests, car bombs, and improvised explosive devices—all of them cheap, simple, and effective, indeed so effective that these techniques now comprise a kind of ready-made insurgency kit freely available on the Internet and spreading in popularity around the world, most obviously to Afghanistan, that land of few targets.

Nearly five years into the Iraq war, the leaders of one of our two major political parties advocate the withdrawal of American combat forces from Iraq, and many in the other party are yielding to the growing urge to go along. As for the Bush administration's broader War on Terror, as the State Department detailed recently in its annual report on terrorism, the number of attacks worldwide has never been higher, nor the attacks themselves more deadly. True, the terrorists of al Qaeda have not attacked again within the United States. Perhaps they do not need to. They are alive and, though decentralized and dispersed—transformed into what might be called "virtual al Qaeda"—in numbers they seem to be flourishing. Their goal, after all, notwithstanding the rhetoric of the Bush administration, was not simply to kill as many Americans as possible but, by challenging the United States in spectacular fashion, to recruit greater numbers to their cause and to move their insurgency into the heart of the Middle East. And these things they have managed to do.

Not without help, of course: In their choice of enemy, one might say that the terrorists of al Qaeda had a great deal of dumb luck, for they attacked a country that happened to be run by leaders who had a radical conception of the potency of power. At the heart of the principle of asymmetric warfare— al Qaeda's kind of warfare—is the notion of using your enemy's power against him. How does a small group of insurgents without an army, without heavy weapons, defeat the greatest conventional military force the world has ever known? How do you defeat such an army if you don't have an army? The answer is obvious: You borrow your enemy's. And this is precisely what al Qaeda did. Using the classic strategy of provocation, the group tried to tempt the superpower into its adopted homeland. The original strategy behind the 9/11 attacks—apart from humbling the superpower and creating the greatest recruiting poster the world had ever seen—was to lure the United States into a ground war in Afghanistan, where the one remaining superpower was to be trapped, stranded, and destroyed, as the Soviet Union had been a decade before. (It was to prepare for this war that Osama bin Laden arranged for the assassination, two days before 9/11—via bombs secreted in the video cameras of two terrorists posing as reporters—of the Afghan Northern Alliance leader and U.S. ally Ahmed Shah Massood.)

Well aware of the Soviets' Afghanistan debacle—the CIA had after all supplied most of the weapons that defeated the Soviets there—Bush administration officials confined the American role to sending plenty of air support, lots of cash, and very few troops, relying instead on its Afghan allies, a strategy that avoided a planned quagmire at the cost of letting al Qaeda's leaders escape. Bin Laden would soon be granted a far more valuable gift: the invasion of Iraq, a country that, unlike Afghanistan, lies at the heart of the

Middle East and sits squarely on the critical Sunni-Shia divide—perfectly positioned to fulfill al Qaeda's dream of igniting a regional civil war. It is upon that precipice that we find ourselves teetering today.

VI.

Critical to this strange and unlikely history were the administration's peculiar ideas about power: "We're an Empire now and when we act we create our own reality." Power, untrammeled by law or custom; power, unlimited by the so-called weapons of the weak, be they international institutions, courts, or terrorism—power can remake reality. It is no accident that one of Karl Rove's heroes is President William McKinley, who stood at the apex of America's first imperial moment and led the country into a glorious colonial adventure in the Philippines that was also meant to be the military equivalent of a stroll in the park and that led, in the event, to several years of bloody insurgency— an insurgency, it bears noticing, that was fought with extensive use of torture, notably waterboarding, which has made its reappearance in the imperial battles of our own times.

If we are an empire now, as Mr. Rove insists, perhaps it is worth adding that we remain a democracy. And therein lies the rub. A democratic empire, as the Athenians were first to discover, is an odd beast, like one of those mythological creatures born of man and horse. Its power, however great, depends finally on public support. If its leader longs to invade Iraq to restore the empire's prestige and power, he must first convince his people. And at his peril; for if the menacing weapons vanish, if promised cakewalk turns to long and grinding war, the leader's power wanes and support for his war collapses. The empire's greatest vulnerability—a matter not of arms but of politics—is revealed, to be exploited by a clever enemy. Bin Laden in his writings has long focused on Americans' "lack of will," though one doubts even he could have imagined these self-inflicted wounds.

Herein lies a bit of pathos, or a cruel irony: Officials of the Bush administration, now judged by a good part of the public to have lied the country into war, did believe Iraq had weapons of mass destruction, though they shamelessly exaggerated the evidence they had to prove it and the threat those weapons would have posed. Secure in their belief that the underlying threat was real, they felt they needed only to dramatize it a bit to make it clear and convincing to the public—like cops who, certain they have the killer, plant a bit of evidence to "frame a guilty man." If only a few weapons were found, who would care, once the tanks were rumbling triumphantly through Baghdad? By then, the United States military would have created a new reality.

I have a daydream about this. I see a solitary soldier—a quartermaster, say, or perhaps a cook—breaking the padlock on some forgotten warehouse on an Iraqi military base and finding in a dusty corner a few hundred old chemical artillery shells. They might date from the time of the Gulf War;

they might be corroded, leaky, completely unusable. But still they would be "weapons of mass destruction"—to use the misleading and absurd construction that has headlined our age—and my solitary cook or quartermaster would find himself a hero, for he would, all unwittingly, have "proved" the case.

My daydream could easily have come to pass. Why not? It is nigh unto miraculous that the Iraqi regime, even with the help of the United Nations, managed so thoroughly to destroy its once existing stockpile. And if my private had found those leaky shells, and administration officials from the president on down could point to them in triumph, what would have been changed thereby? In fact, the underlying reality would have remained: that, in the months leading up to the war, the administration relentlessly exaggerated the threat Saddam posed to the United States and relentlessly understated the risk the United States would run in invading and occupying Iraq. And it would have remained true and incontestable that—as the quaintly factbound British foreign secretary put it eight months before the war, in a secret British cabinet meeting made famous by the so-called Downing Street Memo—"the case [for attacking Iraq] was thin. Saddam was not threatening his neighbors and his WMD capability was less than that of Libya, North Korea or Iran."[11]

Which is to say, the weapons were a rhetorical prop and, satisfying as it has been to see the administration beaten about the head with it, we forget this underlying fact at our peril. The administration needed, wanted, had to have the Iraq war. The weapons were but a symbol, the necessary *casus belli*. Or, to shift from law to cinema, they were what Alfred Hitchcock called the Magoffin (and what Quentin Tarantino, in *Pulp Fiction*, in turn parodied as that glowing mysterious object in the suitcase): that is, a satisfyingly concrete object on which to fasten a rhetorical or narrative end—the narrative end being in this case a war to restore American prestige, project its power, remake the Middle East. Had a handful of those weapons been found, the underlying truth would have remained: Saddam posed nowhere remotely near the threat to the United States that would have justified running the enormous metaphysical risk that a war of choice with Iraq posed. Of course, when you are focused on magical phrases like "preponderant power" and "the uni-polar moment," matters like the numbers of troops at your disposal, and the simple fact that the post–Cold War United States had too few to sustain a long-term occupation of a restive and divided country the size of Iraq, must seem mundane indeed. These facts were the reality, and reality had its revenge; and yet Americans live now in a world in which the magical, glowing image of the weapons has been supplanted not by the truth—the foolishness and recklessness of launching an unnecessary war—but by yet another glowing illusion, of mendacious, dastardly officials who knew the weapons weren't there but touted them anyway.

VII.

One of the most painful principles of our age is that scandals are doomed to be revealed—and to remain stinking there before us, unexcised, untreated, unhealed. If this Age of Virtual War has a tragic symbol, then surely this is it: the frozen scandal, doomed to be revealed, and revealed, and revealed, in a never-ending torment familiar to the rock-bound Prometheus and his poor half-eaten liver. All around us we hear the sound of ice breaking, as the accumulated frozen scandals of this administration slowly crack open to reveal their queasy secrets—or rather to reveal that most of them, alas, are not secrets at all.

More than three years have passed since the photographs from Abu Ghraib were first broadcast by CBS News on *Sixty Minutes II* and published by Seymour Hersh in the *New Yorker*; nearly as far back I published a book in which I gathered together Bush administration documents that detailed the decision to use on prisoners in the War on Terror and in Iraq "extreme interrogation techniques"—or, as administration officials prefer to call them, an "alternative set of procedures." A remarkable phrase, this, memorable for its perfect bureaucratic blankness: President Bush personally introduced it to the nation on September 6, 2006, in a full-dress White House speech kicking off the midterm election campaign, at a time when accusing the Democrats of evidencing a continued softness on terror—and a lamentable unwillingness to show the needed harshness in "interrogating terrorists"—appeared to be the Republicans' only possible winning electoral strategy. Indeed, Democrats seemed fully to agree with the president, for they warily chose not to stand in the way of his Military Commissions Act, which appeared to legalize many of these "alternative procedures." And since Democrats did indeed win both houses of Congress, perhaps their victory was owed in part to their refusal to stand in the way of what a less legally and bureaucratically careful politician might call torture. Who can say? What we can say is that if torture today remains a "scandal" or a "crisis," it is so in that same peculiar way that crime or AIDS or global warming or indeed the Iraq war is: that is, they are all things we have learned to live with.

VIII.

I last visited that war in December, when Baghdad was cold and gray, and I spent a good deal of time drawing black X's through the sources listed in my address book, finding them, one after another, either departed or dead. Baghdad seemed a sad and empty place, with even its customary traffic jams gone, and the periodic, resonating explosions barely attracted glances from those few Iraqis to be found on the streets.

How, in these "words in a time of war," to convey the reality of that place at this time? How to punch through the rhetoric of virtual war—to escape the "political language," as Orwell described it, "designed to make lies sound truthful and murder respectable"?[12] Reading his words, I remember an account from a young Iraqi woman of how that war has touched her and her family. On the blog "Inside Iraq," this anonymous Baghdadi offers her personal version of what has become a quintessential Iraqi family ritual: making a trip to the morgue. She writes of what lies behind the headlines and the news reports, and her account is what it is.

> We were asked to send the next of kin to whom the remains of my nephew, killed on Monday in a horrific explosion downtown, can be handed over. . . .
> So we went, his mum, his other aunt and I. . . .
> When we got there, we were given his remains. And remains they were. From the waist down was all they could give us. "We identified him by the cell phone in his pants' pocket. If you want the rest, you will just have to look for yourselves. We don't know what he looks like." . . .
> We were led away, and before long a foul stench clogged my nose and I retched. With no more warning we came to a clearing that was probably an inside garden at one time; all round it were patios and rooms with large-pane windows to catch the evening breeze Baghdad is renowned for. But now it had become a slaughterhouse, only instead of cattle, all around were human bodies. On this side; complete bodies; on that side halves; and everywhere body parts.
> We were asked what we were looking for; "upper half" replied my companion, for I was rendered speechless. "Over there." We looked for our boy's broken body between tens of other boys' remains; with our bare hands sifting them and turning them.
> Millennia later we found him, took both parts home, and began the mourning ceremony.[13]

These are the words of people who find themselves as far as they can possibly be from the idea that, when they act, they "create their own reality"— that they are "history's actors." The voices come from history's objects and it is worthwhile pondering who the subjects are, who exactly is acting upon them.

The car bomb that so changed their lives was not set by Americans; indeed, Americans even now are dying to prevent such things. I remember one of them, a lieutenant, a beautiful young man with a puffy, sleepy face, and the way he looked at me when I asked whether or not he was scared when he went out on patrol—this was in Anbar Province in October 2003, as the insurgency was growing daily more ferocious. I remember him smiling a moment and then saying with evident pity for a reporter's lack of understanding. "This is war. We shoot, they shoot. We shoot, they shoot. Some days they shoot better than we do." He was patient in his answer, smiling sleepily in his young beauty, and I could tell he regarded me as a creature from another world, one who could never understand the world in which he lived. Three days after our interview, an explosion near Fallujah killed him.

Ours is a grim age, still infused with the remnant perfume of imperial dreams. It is a scent Orwell knew well. Contingency, accidents, the metaphysical ironies that seem to stitch history together like a lopsided quilt—all these have no place in the imperial vision. A perception of one's self as "history's actor" leaves no place for them. But they exist, and it is invariably others, closer to the ground, who see them, know them, and suffer them as they must.

Acknowledgments

Reporters, like cops, benefit from the reality that confession is a near universal need, shared by victims, criminals, heroes: People everywhere long to tell their stories. Most deserving acknowledgment are those who, in Haiti, the Balkans, Iraq, and other places near and far spent time and spirit trying to make me understand. I thank them for their patience and humanity, and I hope I have done at least some justice to their stories.

For publishing with loving care my writing on the Balkans, Iraq, the War on Terror, and torture, I warmly thank once again the incomparable staff of the *New York Review of Books*, including, among others, its publisher Rea Hederman, its late co-editor Barbara Epstein, and particularly, especially, crucially, the *Review*'s peerless editor and my longtime collaborator and friend, Robert B. Silvers. God bless him.

I am deeply grateful as well to Robert Gottlieb, John Bennet, and the staff of *The New Yorker*. I thank David Gelber and the staff of *Peter Jennings Reporting* at ABC News; Gerald Marzorati, Alex Star, and the staff of the *New York Times Magazine*; David Shipley of the *New York Times* OpEd page; James Chace, Linda Wrigley, and the staff of the *World Policy Journal*; John F. Burns and the *New York Times* Baghdad bureau; Lawrence Doyle and the CBS News Baghdad bureau; Tamara Straus of *Zoetrope All-Story*; Judith Butler, Ramona Nadaff, and Orville Schell of the University of California, Berkeley; Andras Szanto; and the generous souls at the Nation Institute.

I thank Carl Bromley for editing the book with elegance, skill, and patience. I thank the stars for my tenacious and perfectly named agent, Joy Harris. I thank—and tip my hat to—Hamilton Fish for his unflagging determination and faith: This book would not exist without him.

Far too many indispensable friends have gone. James Chace, my longtime mentor and friend, ordered me to *"Go* to Hispaniola!," published my "Marooned" essay, and stood as indefatigable adviser on where I should be going and how I should be living. Theodore Draper did much to teach me, by his example and his patient words, how to report, how to research, and how to write. Ryszard Kapuscinski read everything and kept pulling me back, always hilariously, to his malaria-tilted view of the world. Czeslaw Milosz, during oceans of miraculous conversation, taught me more about history, politics, and struggle than I could learn in years of reporting. Peter Jennings first brought me to the Balkans, where he argued with me every day and every hour: he was a great newsman and an unceasing pain in the ass. Susan Sontag was generous to me in Sarajevo, impossible everywhere else; both helped. I miss them all.

For friendship, encouragement, and moral support I thank Fouad Ajami, Judith Belzer, Louis Begley, Joan Bingham, Leon Botstein, Ian Buruma, Don DeLillo, Tom Engelhardt, Mathea Falco, John Homans, Cristina Garcia, Les Gelb, David Gelber, Robert Hass, Sy Hersh, Joshua Jelly-Schapiro, Thomas Keenan, Frank Kermode, Catherine Lee, Natalie Marsh, Gerald Marzorati, Kathryn Mintz, Davia Nelson, Michael Pollan, Frank Rich, Donald Richie, Orville Schell, Peter Sellars, Matthew Shechmeister, Robert Silvers, George Soros, Eric Stover, Tamara Straus, Collin Sullivan, Ron Suskind, Peter Tarnoff, Mark Uhlig, Alice Waters, and Maureen Webb.

I thank, with love and gratitude, my father, my first and greatest story-teller. And finally to my mother, Rosalyn Sitrin Danner, whose insistent question—"Why can't you go somewhere *nice* for a change?"—has over twenty-five years become an oft-repeated joke between us, I offer this book. I know, I know: it is not really an answer. Still, the book is for you.

Notes

INTRODUCTION

1. See Allan Bloom (translator), *The Republic of Plato: Second Edition* (New York: Basic Books, 1991), 117.

2. *Wie es eigentlich gewesen*, the phrase belongs to Leopold von Ranke.

3. My friend James Chace, as the movement grew to overthrow Duvalier during the winter of 1986, urged me to "*go* to Hispaniola" for precisely this reason: to see politics contested and created in the streets, politics at its most basic and contingent and brutal. See my appreciation, "Seeing the World: James Chace 1931-2004," *New York Times Magazine,* December 26, 2004.

4. For my writing on Aristide's rise and fall, see my series in the *New York Review of Books*, "Haiti on the Verge," November 11, 1993; "The Prophet," November 11, 1993; and "The Fall of the Prophet," December 2, 1993. See also my earlier report "The Struggle For a Democratic Haiti," *New York Times Magazine*, June 24, 1987.

5. See "X," "The Sources of Soviet Conduct," *Foreign Affairs*, July 1947; collected in George F. Kennan, *American Diplomacy* (Chicago: University of Chicago Press, 1984 [1951]), 125, 119, 120.

6. For the Powell Doctrine see Colin Powell, "U.S. Forces: Challenges Ahead," *Foreign Affairs*, Winter 1992–1993. What is commonly called the Powell Doctrine is more accurately referred to as the Powell Corollary, since it is in effect an elaboration of the Weinberger Doctrine. See Robert M. Cassidy, "Prophets or Praetorians: The Uptonian Paradox and the Powell Corollary," *Parameters*, Autumn 2003.

7. I was not persuaded by this argument to invade Iraq and found myself troubled by what I believed was the dishonesty and self-delusion of the evangelical language in which it was couched. I became convinced that the war would harm the country and its interests and argued against it in the days before the invasion in a series of public debates with, among others, Christopher Hitchens, Michael Ignatieff, and Leon Wieseltier. Recordings and transcriptions of many of these debates can be found on my Web site, www.markdanner.com.

8. I have set out and analyzed the attributes of Bush's "state of exception" in a series of speeches, including "Into the Light of Day: Torture, Human Rights and Bush's State of Exception," the Princeton Theological Union, Princeton University, January 13, 2006 (Scott Horton and Jeremy Waldron, respondents); and "The Politics of the Forever War: Terror, Rights, and the State of Exception," the 2006 Remarque Lecture, The Remarque Institute, New York University, November 14, 2006. Recordings and transcriptions of these and other speeches may be found at www.markdanner.com.

9. See Dana Priest and Barton Gellman, "U.S. Decries Abuse but Defends Interrogations: 'Stress and Duress' Tactics Used on Terrorism Suspects Held in Secret Overseas Facilities," *Washington Post*, December 26, 2002, and James Risen, David Cay Johnston,

and Neil A. Lewis, "The Struggle for Iraq: Detainees; Harsh CIA Methods Cited in Top Qaeda Interrogations," *New York Times*, May 13, 2004.

10. See my essay, "Frozen Scandal," *New York Review of Books*, December 4, 2008. Also "The Iraq Pretext: Why the Memo Matters," *New York Review*, July 14, 2005, included in *The Secret Way to War: The Downing Street Memo and the Iraq War's Buried History* (New York: New York Review Books, 2006), and my speech, "The Age of Frozen Scandal: Power and the Press After 9/11," Willamette University, Salem, Oregon, April 27, 2006, all at www.markdanner.com.

11. For a closer reading of these photographs, see my essay, "Bodies Under Stress," in *Abu Ghraib: Abuse of Power*, a catalogue for an exhibition of works on paper by Susan Crile, The Bertha and Karl Leubsdorf Art Gallery, Hunter College, New York City, September 7–October 21, 2006.

12. See Joe Conason, "Rove Waves Flag for GOP Candidates," *New York Observer*, January 27, 2002.

13. Apart from minor changes the stories are printed here as written. The exception is "The Saddest Story," where the maddening complexity of the Balkan Wars led me, in the hope of clarifying a bit the chronology, to move about a small number of sections of the original texts.

I. BEYOND THE MOUNTAINS

La parenthèse

1. See François-Dénis Légitime, *La République d'Haïti et les races africaines en général: Premier Congrès de races tenu à Londres du 26 au 29 juillet 1911* (Port-au-Prince: Imprimerie de l'Abeille, 1911). Quoted in Julia Llewellyn Smith, *Traveling on the Edge: Journeys in the Footsteps of Graham Greene* (New York: St. Martin's, 2001), 215.

2. See Leslie Francois Manigat, *Haiti in the Sixties: Object of International Concern* (Washington, DC: Washington Center for Foreign Policy Research, 1964), 23.

The Legacy

1. See Henry Adams, *History of the United States of America during the administrations of Thomas Jefferson* (New York: Library of America, 1986), 256.

2. See Justin Girod-Chantrans, *Voyage d'un Suisse dans les colonies d'Amérique* (Paris: Tallandier, 1980 [1785]). Quoted in C. L. R. James, *The Black Jacobins* (New York: Vintage, 1963 [1938]), 10.

3. See M. L. E. Moreau de Saint-Méry, *Description topographique, physique, civile, politique et historique de la partie française de l'isle Saint-Domingue* (Paris : Société française d'histoire d'outre-mer, 1984 [1797]).

4. See James, *The Black Jacobins*, 38.

5. See Adams, *History of the United States of America during the administrations of Thomas Jefferson*, 259.

6. Ibid., 264.

7. See William Wordsworth, "To Toussaint L'Overture" in *The Complete Poetical Works* (Boston: Houghton Mifflin, 1932), and Heinrich Von Kleist, "The Betrothal in Santo Domingo", in *The Marquise of O—, and Other Stories* (New York: Penguin, 1978).

8. See Lyonel Paquin, *The Haitians: Class and Color Politics* (Brooklyn, NY: Multi-Type, 1983), 29.

9. See Mats Lundahl, *Peasants and Poverty* (New York: St. Martin's, 1979), 328.

10. See Bernard Diederich and Al Burt, *Papa Doc and the Tonton Macoutes* (Port-au-Prince: Henri Deschamps, 1986), 38.

11. See David Nicholls, *From Dessalines to Duvalier: Race, Colour and National Independence in Haiti* (Cambridge, UK: Cambridge University Press, 1979), 142–191.

12. See Richard Eder, "Haiti—Land of the 'Big Tontons,'" *New York Times Magazine*, January 24, 1965.

13. See Francois Duvalier, *Mémoires d'un Leader du Tiers Monde: Mes Néegociations avec let Saint-Siège ou une Tranche d'Histoire . . . ,*" 87.

14. See Laënnec Hurbon, *Comprendre Haiti: Essai sur l'Etat, la nation, la culture* (Paris and Port-au-Prince: Karthala and Henri Deschamps, 1987), 15.

15. See Hurbon, *Comprendre Haiti*, 14.

16. See Arthur Schlesinger, Jr. *A Thousand Days: John F. Kennedy in the White House* (Boston: Houghton Mifflin, 1965), 783.

17. See Michel Soukar, *Seize ans de lutte pour un pays normal* (Port-au-Prince, Editions Scolha, 1987), 7.

18. See Leslie Manigat, *Status quo en Haiti?* (Paris: La Technique du Lire, 1971).

19. See Diederich and Burt, *Papa Doc and the Tonton Macoutes*, 397.

The Mountains

1. See Josh DeWind and David H. Kinley III, *Aiding Migration: The Impact of International Development Assistance on Haiti* (Boulder, CO: Westview Press, 1988), 97.

2. Ibid., 100.

3. These institutions did survive, and evolve, until, in the form of Father Aristide's *Lavalas* movement, they took control of the country. See, among others, my series of articles on Aristide in the *New York Review of Books*, "Haiti on the Verge," "The Prophet," "The Fall of the Prophet," cited above.

II. THE SADDEST STORY
How Not to Stop A War

1. See Snjezana Vukic, "Refugees Tell of Women Singled Out for Rape," *The Independent* (London), July 18, 1995.

2. The Mladic quotations are drawn from David Rohde's *Endgame: The Betrayal and Fall of Srebrenica* (New York: Farrar, Straus, Giroux, 1997) except for the second to last, for which see Fawn Vrazo, "Loved ones' final good-byes endure in the minds of families," *The Philadelphia Inquirer*, April 15, 1996, and the last, for which see Laura Silber and Allan Little, *Yugoslavia: Death of a Nation* (New York: Penguin, 1997), 349. The quotation from the Serb soldiers is drawn from the videotape quoted in Jan Willem Honig and Norbert Both, *Srebrenica: Record of a War Crime* (New York: Penguin, 1996), 39.

3. According to some reports, the Dutch peacekeepers videotaped many of these scenes, and perhaps much graver ones later on as well (see note 6, below), but General Hans Couzy, the commander of the Royal Netherlands Army, ordered the tape destroyed presumably because it identified Dutch troops. See John Sweeny, "UN Cover-Up of Srebrenica Massacre," *The Observer* (London), August 10, 1995, quoted in *Bosnia-Hercegovina: The Fall of Srebrenica and the Failure of UN Peacekeeping* (Human Rights Watch/Helsinki), October 1995, 22–23.

4. See *The Fall of Srebrenica and the Failure of UN Peacekeeping*, 23.

5. Ibid., 24.

6. Ibid., 42–43. Though the Human Rights Watch report identifies this survivor only as "N.P.," a number of newspaper accounts, as well as David Rohde's *Endgame*, make it clear that it is Mevludin Oric.

7. And also on the Dutch videotape which, according to John Sweeny's London *Observer* account (note 3, above), showed Serbs herding Muslim prisoners onto a field and making ready their weapons before the tape went abruptly blank.

8. See Michael Dobbs and R. Jeffrey Smith, "New Proof Offered of Serb Atrocities," *Washington Post*, October 29, 1995.

9. See Bob Woodward, *The Choice: How Clinton Won* (New York: Simon and Schuster, 1996), 260.

10. On the senators' machinations on the arms embargo, and the effect the fall of Srebrenica had on them (sending "ten to fifteen senators across the line"), see Elizabeth Drew, *Showdown: The Struggle Between the Gingrich Congress and the Clinton White House* (New York: Simon and Schuster, 1996), 252, and Chapter 19. For Bosnia's anticipated effect on the elections, see Dick Morris, *Behind the Oval Office: Winning the Presidency in the Nineties* (New York: Random House, 1997), 244–256.

11. See Woodward, *The Choice*, 261.

12. See James Gow, *Triumph of the Lack of Will: International Diplomacy and the Yugoslav War* (New York: Columbia University Press, 1997), 298–299.

13. See Warren Zimmermann, *Origins of a Catastrophe: Yugoslavia and Its Destroyers* (New York: Crown, 1996), 7.

14. See Robert Hutchings, *American Diplomacy and the End of the Cold War: An Insider's Account of U.S. Policy in Europe, 1989–1992* (Baltimore: Johns Hopkins University Press, 1997), 304.

15. See Susan L. Woodward, *Balkan Tragedy: Chaos and Dissolution After the Cold War* (Washington: Brookings, 1995), 15.

16. See David Gompert, "The United States and Yugoslavia's Wars," in *The World and Yugoslavia's Wars*, 123.

17. See David Binder, "Yugoslavia Seen Breaking Up Soon," *New York Times*, A-7, November 28, 1990.

18. Interview, January 26, 1994. This and a number of other quotations in these chapters are drawn from interviews I and my colleagues conducted in 1993 and 1994 while preparing an hour-long television documentary for ABC News. See Mark Danner and David Gelber, writers, and Peter Jennings, correspondent, "While America Watched: The Bosnia Tragedy," *Peter Jennings Reporting, ABC-51* (broadcast March 17, 1994).

19. "It cannot be denied that, if the aim is to reduce the number of national minorities in every republic, better borders than the present ones could be devised." See the Dutch draft document, quoted in David Owen, *Balkan Odyssey: An Uncompromising Personal Account of the International Peace Efforts Following the Breakup of the Former Yugoslavia* (New York: Harcourt Brace, 1995), 31–33.

20. See James A. Baker III, with Thomas M. deFrank, *The Politics of Diplomacy: Revolution, War and Peace, 1989–1992* (New York: Putnam, 1995), 479.

21. This statement is drawn from an interview on January 27, 1994 for "While America Watched: the Bosnia Tragedy," *Peter Jennings Reporting, ABC News*.

22. See Silber and Little, *Yugoslavia: Death of a Nation*, 151.

23. See Warren Zimmermann, "Yugoslavia: 1989–1996," in Jeremy Azrael and E. Payan, editors, *U.S. and Russian Policy Making With Respect to the Use of Force* (Santa Monica, CA: Rand Institute, 1997), 185–186.

24. Ibid., 187.

25. *Janez Jansa, Premiki* (Ljubljana: Mladinska Kniga, 1993), 98, quoted in Gow, 209, note 78.

26. See "The Gates of Hell," Program 4 in *The Death of Yugoslavia* (UK TX version), Brian Lapping and Associates; Laura Silber, consultant.

27. Interview with author, January 1994.

28. From a statement broadcast in part on "While America Watched: The Bosnia Tragedy."

29. Quoted in Robert W. Tucker and David C. Hendrickson, *The Imperial Temptation: The New World Order and America's Purpose* (Council on Foreign Relations, 1992), 153.

30. See "While America Watched: The Bosnia Tragedy," *Peter Jennings Reporting, ABC-51* (March 17, 1994), 4.

31. See Wayne Bert, *The Reluctant Superpower: United States Policy in Bosnia, 1991–1995* (New York: Palgrave Macmillan, 1997), 118–119.

32. See Tim Judah, *The Serbs: History, Myth, and the Destruction of Yugoslavia* (New Haven, CT: Yale University Press, 1997), 191.

33. See "Wars of Independence," Program 3 in *The Death of Yugoslavia*.

34. See Maud S. Beelman, "Hear No Evil, See No Evil: Early U.S. Policy in Yugoslavia," *The Reporter*, published by the Alicia Patterson Foundation, Vol. 18, No. 1 (1996), 19.

The Cleansing: A Televised Genocide

1. Roy Gutman broke the story of the camps in an article in *Newsday* on August 2, 1992. But it was not until August 6, when Britain's International Television News (ITN) broadcast the first television pictures from the camps, that President Bush found himself forced to defend his "standoffish" policy toward the former Yugoslavia.

2. Primo Levi, *Survival in Auschwitz* (New York: Simon and Schuster, 1993), p. 90. Perhaps it was this apparent absence of mortal fear, recalling the "supposed fatalism" of the Muslims, that led the SS men to coin the nickname Musulmen; or it may have been the "swaying motions of the upper part of the body," brought on by severe muscle atrophy, which the Germans thought echoed "Islamic prayer rituals." See Wolfgang Sofsky, *The Order of Terror: The Concentration Camp*, translated by William Templer (Princeton, NJ: Princeton University Press, 1997), 329, note 5.

3. Quoted in Roy Gutman, *A Witness to Genocide: The 1993 Pulitzer Prize–Winning Dispatches on the "Ethnic Cleansing" of Bosnia* (New York: Lisa Drew Books, 1993), 47.

4. See Ed Vulliamy, *Seasons in Hell: Understanding Bosnia's War* (Darby, PA: Diane Publishing Co., 1994), 101.

5. See "Omarska Detention Camp," *War Crimes in Bosnia-Herzegovina, Volume II* (New York: Helsinki Watch, 1993), 108.

6. "J." worked in the kitchen at Omarska. See *War Crimes in Bosnia-Herzegovina, Volume II*, p. 103, and, for the earlier quotations about the beatings, 101.

7. *Final Report of the United Nations Commission of Experts Established Pursuant to Security Council Resolution 780*, 1992 (New York: United Nations, 1994), Annexes, 48–49.

8. See *War Crimes in Bosnia-Herzegovina, Volume II*, 110–111.

9. See Raul Hilberg, "The Anatomy of the Holocaust," in Henry Friedlander and Sybil Milton, editors, *The Holocaust: Ideology, Bureaucracy, and Genocide* (White Plains: Kraus International, 1980), 90–91.

10. See Sofsky, *The Order of Terror*, 115.

11. See Rezak Hukanovic, *The Tenth Circle of Hell: A Memoir of Life in the Death Camps of Bosnia*, translated by Colleen London (New York: Basic Books, 1996), 35.

12. See Baker and DeFrank, *The Politics of Diplomacy*, 635–636.

13. See Warren P. Strobel, *Late-Breaking Foreign Policy: The News Media's Influence on Peace Operations* (Washington, DC: United States Institute of Peace, 1997), 150.

14. See Mark Danner and David Gelber, writers, Peter Jennings, correspondent, "While America Watched: The Bosnia Tragedy," *Peter Jennings Reporting, ABC News* (March 17, 1994).

15. See Warren Zimmermann, "Yugoslavia: 1989–1996," in Jeremy R. Azrael and Emil A. Payin, editors, *U.S. and Russian Policymaking with Respect to the Use of Force*, 191.

16. See Arnold Kanter, "Intervention Decisionmaking in the Bush Administration," in *U.S. and Russian Foreign Policymaking with Respect to the Use of Force*, 168–169.

17. See Michael R. Gordon, "Powell Delivers a Resounding No On Using Limited Force in Bosnia," *New York Times*, September 27, 1992, A1.

18. See "While America Watched," 3.

19. Drawn from an unbroadcast section of an interview with *ABC News*, "While America Watched: The Bosnia Tragedy," January 1994.

20. Republished as *The Other Balkan Wars: A 1913 Carnegie Endowment Inquiry in Retrospect with a New Introduction and Reflections on the Present Conflict* by George F. Kennan (New York: Carnegie Endowment, 1993), 151.

21. Drawn from an unbroadcast section of an interview with *ABC News*, "While America Watched: The Bosnia Tragedy," January 1994.

22. See "The Gates of Hell," Program Four (UK TX version) in *The Death of Yugoslavia*, Brian Lapping and Associates; Laura Silber, consultant.

23. See David Rieff, *Slaughterhouse: Bosnia and the Failure of the West* (New York: Simon and Schuster, 1995), 17.

24. See "The SANU 'Memorandum,'" in Boze Covic, editor, *Roots of Serbian Aggression: Debates Documents Cartographic Review* (Zagreb: Centar Za Strane Jezeke Vodnikova, 1991).

25. See Norman Cigar, *Genocide in Bosnia: The Policy of Ethnic Cleansing* (College Station: Texas A&M University Press, 1995), 25.

26. Testimony of Jerko Doko, *The Prosecutor v. Tadic*, case IT-94-I-T, June 6, 1996, pp. 1359–1361, in "Testimony Offered to the International Commission for the Former Yugoslavia," *The Hague*, June 6, 1996.

27. See Adil Kulenovic, "Interview with Vladimir Srebov," *Vreme* (Belgrade), October 30, 1995.

28. See Rabia Ali, "Separating History from Myth: An Interview With Ivo Banac," in Rabia Ali and Lawrence Lifschultz, editors, *Why Bosnia? Writings on the Balkan War* (Stony Creek, CT: Pamphleteer's Press, 1993), 158.

29. See Milos Vasic, "The Yugoslav Army and the Post-Yugoslav Armies," in D.A. Dyker and I. Vejvoda, editors, *Yugoslavia and After: A Study in Fragmentation, Despair and Rebirth* (Boston: Longman, 1996), 134.

30. See Beverly Allen, *Rape Warfare: The Hidden Genocide in Bosnia-Herzegovina and Croatia* (Minneapolis: University of Minnesota Press, 1996), 57.

31. Though "photographs of the bloodbath in Brcko remain unpublished to this day," the authors attribute this description to "an investigator working outside the U.S. government who has seen the pictures. . . ." See Charles Lane and Thom Shanker, "Bosnia: What the CIA Didn't Tell Us," *New York Review*, May 9, 1996, 10.

32. See Honig and Both, *Srebrenica: Record of a War Crime*, 75–76.

33. See Michael H. Sells, *The Bridge Betrayed: Religion and Genocide in Bosnia* (Berkeley: University of California Press, 1996), 65–66.

34. See "The Gates of Hell," Program Four in *The Death of Yugoslavia*.

35. Ibid.

36. See United Nations Report, Annex V, "The Prijedor Report," paragraphs 6–13, 16, 19–20.

37. Drawn from an unbroadcast interview with *ABC News*, "While America Watched: The Bosnia Tragedy," January 1994.

38. Ibid.

39. See Raphael Lemkin, *Axis Rule in Occupied Europe: Laws of Occupation, Analysis of Government, Proposals for Redress* (New York: Carnegie, 1944), 79.

40. Included in Stjepan G. Mestrovic (editor), *The Conceit of Innocence: Losing the Conscience of the West in the War Against Bosnia* (College Station: Texas A & M Press, 1997).

41. See Colin L. Powell, "Why Generals Get Nervous," *New York Times*, October 8, 1992, A35.

42. Even less subtly, Dr. Karadzic, the wily psychiatrist, played the same game, proclaiming that if the West attempted to intervene, "Bosnia will turn into a new Vietnam." Quoted in Judah, *The Serbs*, 212–213.

43. See "Operation Restore Hope," *U.S. News & World Report*, December 14, 1992, 26–30, quoted in Strobel, *Late-Breaking Foreign Policy*, 129. For Eagleburger's statement, see also Strobel, 138.

Toward a Policy of Gesture: The Safe Areas

1. See "People in Glass Houses: Bush Should be Careful Whose Foreign Policy He Calls 'Reckless,'" *Decision Brief* (Center for Security Policy, Washington), July 28, 1992, 1. Also Mark Danner and David Gelber, writers, Peter Jennings, correspondent, "While America Watched: The Bosnia Tragedy," *Peter Jennings Reporting, ABC News*, ABC-51, 9 (March 17, 1994).

2. "People in Glass Houses: Bush Should be Careful Whose Foreign Policy He Calls 'Reckless,'" *Decision Brief*, 1.

3. Quoted in "Method to the Madness," *Decision Brief* (Center for Security Policy, Washington), October 2, 1992, 3.

4. During spring and summer 1992, when Serbs were seizing huge chunks of Bosnia and "cleansing" it of Muslims, State Department analysts were compiling lists of atrocities and tracking deportation to concentration camps. The Central Intelligence Agency later concluded, in a highly classified report, that Serbs carried out 90 percent of all war crimes in former Yugoslavia and that they were the only group to attempt systematically to "eliminate all traces of other ethnic groups from their territory." See Roger Cohen, "C.I.A. Report on Bosnia Blames Serbs for 90% of the War Crimes," *New York Times*, March 9, 1995.

5. See "While America Watched: The Bosnia Tragedy," 8.

6. Drawn from an unbroadcast section of an interview with *ABC News*, "While America Watched: The Bosnia Tragedy," January 1994.

7. See Jean E. Manas, "The Impossible Trade-off: 'Peace' vs. 'Justice' in Settling Yugoslavia's Wars," in Richard H. Ullman, editor, *The World and Yugoslavia's Wars* (Council on Foreign Relations Press, 1996), 43.

8. Dick Morris, *Behind the Oval Office: Winning the Presidency in the Nineties* (New York: Random House, 1997), 245, 253.

9. See Richard Holbrooke, *To End A War* (New York: Random House, 1998), 54.

10. During 1992 and 1993 no fewer than four American diplomats and officials— Marshall Freeman Harris, Richard Johnson, George Kenney, and Stephen Walker— resigned to protest their country's policies in the former Yugoslavia.

11. Quoted in Michael Kelly, "Letter from Washington: Surrender and Blame," *The New Yorker*, December 19, 1994, 44–51.

12. See Owen, *Balkan Odyssey*, 106–107.

13. See Gow, *Triumph of the Lack of Will*, 208.

14. Testimony delivered before the Senate Foreign Relations Committee, February 10, 1993.

15. Drawn from an unbroadcast section of an interview with *ABC News*, "While America Watched: The Bosnia Crisis," January 1994.

16. See Morris, *Behind the Oval Office*, 245.

17. See Noel Malcolm, *Bosnia: A Short History* (New York: New York University Press, 1996), 25, 249.

18. From "Report of the United Nations High Commission on Refugees, February 19, 1993."

19. Drawn from an interview with *ABC News*, "While American Watched," February 1994.

20. See Chuck Sudetic, *Blood and Vengeance: One Family's Story of the War in Bosnia* (New York: W. W. Norton, 1998), 148.

21. See Honig and Both, *Srebrenica: Record of a War Crime*, 78.

22. See Reiff, *Slaughterhouse*, 187.

23. Quoted in Silber and Little, *Yugoslavia: Death of a Nation*, 269–270.

24. Birtley soon ran out of food and batteries, and then, as he watched with UN peacekeepers at an observation post, he was struck with shrapnel from a Serb mortar. His leg was shattered in four places, and an emergency operation just managed to save it (a colleague filmed the operation with Birtley's camera). Birtley was finally smuggled out of Srebrenica on a UN helicopter. See Strobel, *Late-Breaking Foreign Policy*, 122.

25. The official who was not identified, offered this explanation to David Owen. See Honig and Both, *Srebrenica: Record of a War Crime*, 80.

26. See Bert, *The Reluctant Superpower*, 165.

27. See Reiff, *Slaughterhouse*, 174–175.

28. See Colin Powell, *My American Journey* (New York: Random House, 1995), 561.

29. See Reiff, *Slaughterhouse*, 155.

30. For Claes, see *ABC News*, "While America Watched," p. 11. For Christopher, see Elizabeth Drew, *On the Edge* (New York: Touchstone, 1995), 159.

31. See Gow, *Triumph of the Lack of Will*, 220.

32. See Bert, *The Reluctant Superpower*, 199.

33. See Honig and Both, *Srebrenica: Record of a War Crime*, 92.

34. See Owen, *Balkan Odyssey*, 143.

35. See Honig and Both, *Srebrenica: Record of a War Crime*, 96–97.

36. See Gow, *Triumph of the Lack of Will*, 308.

37. See Owen, *Balkan Odyssey*, 134–135.

Explosion in the Marketplace

1. I was in Sarajevo working with an *ABC News* crew to prepare a documentary on Bosnia. See Mark Danner and David Gelber, writers, Peter Jennings, correspondent,

"While America Watched: The Bosnia Tragedy," *Peter Jennings Reporting, ABC News* (March 17, 1994), ABC-51.

2. See Vulliamy, *Seasons in Hell*, 39.

3. See Curzio Malaparte, *Kaputt* (New York: Dutton, 1946; reprinted by Avon, 1966), 257. Tim Judah notes that though the story of the eyes is "for many Serbs the most enduring image of [the Serbian] holocaust," no one can be certain whether it ever actually happened. By now, however, as Judah says, "The scene has become so well known among Serbs that the vast majority believe that it is a description of a real event." See Judah's *The Serbs*, 129.

4. See Zimmermann, *Origins of a Catastrophe*, 121.

5. See Vulliamy, *Seasons in Hell*, 324.

6. See Tracy Wilkinson, "Bosnians Recall Karadzic, a Neighbour Turned Enemy," *Los Angeles Times*, July 23, 1995.

7. See Hukanovic, *The Tenth Circle of Hell*, 55–56.

8. See Deejan Anastasijevic, Massimo Calabresi, Alexandra Niksic, and Alexandra Stiglmayer, "Seeds of Evil: The Opportunistic and Allegedly Criminal Career of Radovan Karadzic May Be Coming to an End," *Time*, July 29, 1996.

9. See Pawel Pawilokowski, *Serbian Epics* (Channel Four 1992).

10. Quoted in Stiglmayer, "Seeds of Evil," *Time* magazine.

11. See David Binder, "Anatomy of a Massacre," *Foreign Policy* 97, Winter 1994–1995, 70–78.

12. See Peter Maass, *Love Thy Neighbor: A Story of War* (New York: Knopf, 1996), 161.

13. See Elaine Sciolino and Douglas Jehl, "As U.S. Sought a Bosnia Policy, the French Offered a Good Idea," *New York Times*, February 14, 1994.

14. See Warren P. Strobel, *Late-Breaking Foreign Policy*, 157.

15. As Tom Gjelten wrote, such charges first came to be taken seriously because of "the persistence of the Serb leadership in making [them], and the readiness of the city's first UN commander, Maj. Gen. Lewis MacKenzie, to believe [them]." MacKenzie declared that "there is strong but circumstantial evidence that some really horrifying acts . . . attributed to the Serbs were actually orchestrated by the Muslims against their own people . . . "—even though, as Gjelten shows, "no physical evidence has ever been found that suggests Muslims purposely shoot themselves." See "Blaming the Victim," *The New Republic*, December 20, 1993.

16. See Owen, *Balkan Odyssey*, 275–276.

17. See Silber and Little, *Yugoslavia: Death of a Nation*, 312.

18. Drawn from an interview for *Peter Jennings Reporting*, "Peacekeepers: How The UN Failed in Bosnia," *ABC News* (broadcast April 24, 1995).

19. Quoted in Silber and Little, *Yugoslavia: Death of a Nation*, 315.

20. The argument over precisely who was responsible for the massacre at the Markela, like many such "controversies" during the Balkan wars, lingered. The Serbs and their advocates argued heatedly from what they called the "facts of ballistics"—in particular, that it would be almost miraculous to hit a target as tiny as the Markela, using a mortar—a highly imprecise weapon—on the first attempt; and thus, they went on, Bosnian intelligence must have planted a bomb in the marketplace. The more plausible explanation is that this was simply a "lucky shot"—or that the Serbs were aiming at a quite different target and the shell fell short. The most likely alternative may be the Sarajevo Synagogue and Jewish Community Center, where a crowd had assembled that afternoon around six buses that were to evacuate several hundred Sarajevans from city, courtesy of the Joint Distribution Committee. From its likely point of firing in the hills the Markela is on a direct path to the Synagogue. I report this theory and discuss the

considerable evidence for it at some length in "Bosnia: The Turning Point," *New York Review of Books*, February 5, 1998, part 7.

21. See Judah, *The Serbs*, 220–226.

22. See Sudetic, *Blood and Vengeance*, 254.

23. See Strobe Talbott, "Clinton Administration and Arms Shipments from Iran to Bosnia," Senate Select Committee on Intelligence, May 23, 1996.

24. See James Risen and Doyle McManus, "U.S. OKd Iranian Arms for Bosnia, Officials Say," *Los Angeles Times*, April 5, 1996, and "United States Actions Regarding Iranians and Other Arms Transfers to the Bosnian Army, 1994–1995," Report of the Select Committee on Intelligence, United States Senate, together with Additional Views, November 1996, 23.

25. The senators add that the general "twice told the Bosnian officials that he had no authority to promise anything, but the positive tone of his remarks . . . may well have given those officials a stronger impression than he intended." See "United States Actions Regarding Iranian and Other Arms Transfers to the Bosnian Army, 1994–1995," 4.

26. See Ed Vulliamy, "How the CIA Intercepted SAS Signals," *The Guardian*, January 29, 1996.

27. See Louis J. Salome, "Ex-U.S. Military Officers Assist Croat Army," Cox News Service, May 26, 1995.

28. See Honig and Both, *Srebrenica: Record of a War Crime*, 144. Though the Tuzla airdrops have been widely reported, and are treated as accepted fact by Honig and Both, whose sources within the United Nations and Western ministries seem strong, the matter has been the subject of considerable dispute. Vulliamy, cited above, writes that "the received wisdom is that there were two such drops, on February 10 and 12, spotted by Norwegian UN personnel," but that "in fact there were four." In an "internal inquiry," NATO's investigators (all of whom were American) claimed the Norwegians had seen civilian traffic in and out of Belgrade—which, as Vulliamy points out, was under sanctions at the time and had no civilian air traffic.

Meanwhile, senators on the Intelligence Committee, who emphasized that they had limited their inquiry to "the recollections of both CIA analysts and senior Defense Department officials" and documents from those agencies, conclude, rather circumspectly, that that evidence "strongly support[s] the conclusion that there was no U.S. role in any clandestine military airlifts." See "U.S. Actions Regarding Iranian and Other Arms Transfers to the Bosnian Army," 13.

29. See Sudetic, *Blood and Vengeance*, 254.

30. See Honig and Both, *Srebrenica: Record of a War Crime*, 149.

31. See Roy Gutman, "UN's Deadly Deal: How troop-hostage talks led to slaughter of Srebrenica," *Newsday*, May 29, 1996.

32. See Honig and Both, *Srebrenica: Record of a War Crime*, 153, 154.

The Great Betrayal

1. See John Pomfret, "Weapons, Cash and Chaos Lend Clout to Srebrenica's Tough Guy," *Washington Post*, February 16, 1994.

2. See Sudetic, *Blood and Vengeance*, 257.

3. See Andreas Zumach, "Western Policy in Bosnia," *Basic Reports: Newsletter on International Security Policy* (No. 46), July 20, 1995.

4. See Honig and Both, *Srebrenica: Record of a War Crime*, 162.

5. Ibid., 164.

6. Bert, *The Reluctant Superpower*, 218.

7. See Roy Gutman, "UN's Deadly Deal: How troop hostage talks led to slaughter in Srebrenica," *Newsday*, May 29, 1996.

8. Whether Janvier "proposed [a] deal" remains a matter of some controversy. Honig and Both say rather laconically that they "have found no evidence of such a deal" (*Srebrenica*, 159), and Rohde concludes a typically extensive and sensible discussion (*Endgame*, 359–364) by observing that, whatever happened, "the very public halting of the . . . air strikes as soon as the hostages were taken made it clear to the Bosnian Serbs that they could stop NATO air attacks by threatening peacekeepers." Further, Janvier's new, restrictive guidelines on the use of air strikes, which the general issued five days before he met with Mladic, "may indicate that there was no secret deal on air strikes—only Akashi and Janvier's unwillingness to use them."

9. See Andreas Zumach, "U.S. Intelligence Knew Serbs Were Planning An Assault on Srebrenica," *Basic Reports: Newsletter on International Security Policy* (No. 47), October 16, 1995. Zumach attributes his story to "sources in the [U.S.] intelligence services"; in a later piece he writes that a German general had confirmed that he had received the same intelligence "through the bilateral information exchange between the USA and Germany"—exchanges which, as Zumach notes, were at the time particularly privileged since the Americans had reduced cooperation with British and French intelligence services in September 1994. See "Intelligence Agencies Fail to Supply Information to War Crimes Tribunal," *Basic Reports* (No. 48), November 20, 1995. For a more nuanced discussion of the role of American intelligence leading up to the Srebrenica offensive, see Charles Lane and Thom Shanker, "Bosnia: What the CIA Didn't Tell Us," *New York Review*, May 6, 1996, especially 12–13.

10. See Gutman, "UN's Deadly Deal."

11. See "Srebrenica: A Bosnian Betrayal," *Dispatches*, Channel 4/BBC, May 29, 1996.

12. See Gutman, "UN's Deadly Deal."

13. See "Srebrenica: A Bosnian Betrayal," *Dispatches*.

14. For the quotation of the "White House aide," see Gutman, "UN's Deadly Deal." For the Vershbow and Delic quotations, see Silber and Little, *Yugoslavia: Death of a Nation*, 352 and 346. For the Americans "directly suggesting" a territorial swap, see Judah, *The Serbs*, 300.

15. See Antun Masle, "Interview with Bosnian Government Army General Joyann Diviak, an ethnic Serb from Sarajevo, and Number Two in the military hierarchy," GLOBUS (Zagreb weekly, No. 234), June 2, 1995.

16. See Barbara Demick, *Logavina Street: Life and Death in a Sarajevo Neighborhood* (Kansas City: Andrews McMeel, 1996).

17. See Andreas Zumach, "New Evidence Further Implicates France in Fall of Srebrenica," *Basic Reports*, February 11, 1997.

18. See Stephen Kinzer, "Bosnian Muslim Troops Evade UN Force to Raid Serb Village," *New York Times*, June 27, 1995.

19. See David Rohde, *Endgame*, 5–6.

20. See Honig and Both, *Srebrenica: Record of a War Crime*, 4.

21. See Sudetic, *Blood and Vengeance*, 269.

22. See Rohde, *Endgame*, 78.

23. See Honig and Both, *Srebrenica: Record of a War Crime,* 15 and 14.

24. See Sudetic, *Blood and Vengeance*, 277.

25. See Andreas Zumach, "New Evidence Further Implicates France in Fall of Srebrenica."

26. See Gutman, "UN's Deadly Deal."

27. These intercepts from Bosnian intelligence are drawn from Gutman, "UN's Deadly Deal."

28. See "The Fall of Srebrenica and the Failure of UN Peacekeeping," *Human Rights Watch/Helsinki Report* (Vol. 7, No. 13), October 1995, 13–14.

29. The buses would this day begin evacuating women and children, and later—to a different destination—some thousand or more men who didn't undertake the trek through the forest, from the Dutch United Nations base at Potocari.

30. See "Srebrenica: A Bosnian Betrayal," *Dispatches*.

31. Gutman, "UN's Deadly Deal."

32. "The Fall of Srebrenica and the Failure of UN Peacekeeping," 30.

33. Quotations and descriptions following are drawn from the "Petrovic video," an hour or so of material photographed by Zoran Petrovic of Belgrade's "Studio B" shot in and around Srebrenica on July 11–14, 1995.

34. See Sudetic, *Blood and Vengeance*, 301–302.

To the Killing Fields

1. See Holbrooke, *To End a War*, 68. Bob Woodward describes the same scene, though with minute differences: Holbrooke appears less deferential, offering, to the President's assertion that he'll "decide that when the time comes," the retort that "Mr. President, it's already been decided." Secretary of State Christopher, rather passive in Holbrooke's rendering, becomes assertive and far-seeing in Woodward's: "That's right," he tells the President. "This is serious stuff. We have to talk further about this." Both men, it seems safe to assume, told their versions to Woodward. See Woodward, *The Choice*, 256–257.

2. See Tom Gjelten, *Sarajevo Daily: A City and Its Newspaper Under Seige* (New York: HarperCollins, 1995), a meticulous and beautifully rendered study of the evolution of wartime Sarajevo as seen through the working of its remarkable newspaper.

3. See Holbrooke, *To End a War*, 68.

4. See Woodward, *The Choice*, 259, and Holbrooke, *To End a War*, 70.

5. The transcripts of Serb radio communications are drawn from Gutman, "The UN's Deadly Deal: How troop-hostage talks led to slaughter of Srebrenica," *Newsday*, May 29, 1996.

6. See *The New York Review*, May 9, 1996, 10.

7. Mr. J. J. C. Voorhoeve, the Dutch minister of defense at the time Srebrenica fell in 1995, took strong issue with Holbrooke's description of the Dutch role in a letter to the secretary dated June 3, 1998, a copy of which the minister sent to this author. Holbrooke, who had just been named U.S. representative to the United Nations, said he would revise this statement in future editions of his book and that he would now say that "European governments" refused to authorize air strikes until the Dutch forces had left Bosnia.

8. "We don't know how many people were killed," according to a Dutch officer quoted by a British journalist. "They were hanging onto the tracks and the wheel arches, like Indians on a train. It could be 10 or 15, maybe more. No one knows." See John Sweeny, "And We Are All Guilty," *The Observer*, December 8, 1996.

9. See O. VanderWind, *Report Based on the Debriefing of Srebrenica* (Assen: Dutch Ministry of Defense, 1995).

10. See Gutman, "UN's Deadly Deal."

11. See Sudetic, *Blood and Vengeance*, 350–353.

12. See *The Independent on Sunday*, July 23, 1995; quoted in *Srebrenica: Record of a War Crime*, 37.

13. See *Report Based on the Debriefing on Srebrenica*, 51.

14. See, for example, Chris Hedges, "Serb Forces Fight Dutch UN Troops in Eastern Bosnia," *New York Times*, July 10, 1995. "But senior United Nations officials also said the Bosnian Serbs . . . may not take the town, filled with refugees as it is. . . ."

15. Like many of the details of this event, the degree of cooperation between Mladic's forces and the Yugoslav National Army remains a matter of dispute. According to a "highly placed NATO officer" quoted by a British television documentary series, "The Bosnian Serb Army couldn't plan an attack like this without the Yugoslav National Army, much less survive without them. The Bosnian Serb Army was not only supported by the Yugoslav National Army logistically, but you have to look at their command and control [and] communications. The Bosnian Serb Army communications were all networked with the Yugoslav National Army, just like the SAM-6 missiles aimed at our planes." See *Dispatches*, June 17, 1996.

16. See Roy Gutman, "Dutch Reveal Horrors of Mission Impossible," *Newsday*, July 24, 1995.

17. See *Report Based on the Debriefing on Srebrenica*, 57.

18. Lane and Shanker, in their *New York Review* piece cited above, attribute this information to an unnamed "intelligence official."

19. See the so-called "Petrovic video," shot by Serb cameraman Zoran Petrovic-Pirocanac, in and around Srebrenica from July 11 to July 16, 1995.

20. See Honig and Both, *Srebrenica: Record of a War Crime*, 34.

21. See Eric Stover and Gilles Peress, *The Graves: Srebrenica and Vukovar* (New York: Scalo, 1998).

22. See Anthony Lloyd, "Srebrenica's Exiles Tell Grimly Familiar Stories of Murder," *The London Times*, July 15, 1995.

23. See Michael Dobbs and R. Jeffrey Smith, "New Proof Offered of Serb Atrocities," *Washington Post*, October 28, 1995.

24. See Sudetic, *Blood and Vengeance*, 310.

25. See Rohde, *Endgame*, 252.

26. Ibid., 226.

27. The words are Dr. Ilijas Pilav's, quoted in Honig and Both, *Srebrenica: Record of a War Crime*, 52–55.

28. Rohde, *Endgame*, 223.

29. Sudetic, *Blood and Vengeance*, 304.

30. Although the initial images of Nova Kasaba were identified, when U.S. Representative Madeleine Albright unveiled them to the United Nations Security Council, only as "aerial photographs," it seems generally agreed that they were drawn from satellite imagery. According to William E. Burrows, for example, "On July 13 or 14 a U.S. reconnaissance satellite downlinked imagery showing several hundred people gathered at a soccer field in the area." See "Imaging Space Reconnaissance Operations during the Cold War: Cause, Effect and Legacy," on the Cold War Forum Web site (www.fas.org). Both the *New York Times* and the *Washington Post* agree with this,

though Honig and Both write that the photographs were taken by an "American U-2 spy plane."

31. Drawn from an interview in the "Petrovic video," cited above.

32. See Human Rights Watch/Helsinki, *The Fall of Srebrenica and the Future of UN Peacekeeping* (October 1995). This account, by a man identified only as I. N., and those of other survivors below, are drawn from this report, 36–45.

33. See "War Crime: Five Days in Hell," *Panorama* (BBC, 1996), quoted in Honig and Both, 56.

34. "On 15 July, [Dutch] military personnel . . . saw 'clean-up teams' (these people were wearing rubber gloves) as well as tipper trucks and lorries carrying corpses." See *Report Based on the Debriefing on Srebrenica*, 51.

Operation Storm and the Cold Peace

1. Quoted in Marcus Tanner, *Croatia: A Nation Forged in War* (New Haven, CT: Yale University Press, 1997), 299.

2. See "THE AFTERMATH OF THE KRAJINA CONFLICT: A VISIT TO KNIN," declassified reporting cable from the U.S. Embassy, Zagreb, August 14, 1995.

3. See *Report to the OSCE: The International Helsinki Federation for Human Rights Fact-Finding Mission to the Krajina*, August 17–19, 1995, 1.

4. See Tanner, *Croatia: A Nation Forged in War*, 298.

5. Quoted in Silber and Little, *Yugoslavia: Death of a Nation*, 356.

6. See Holbrooke, *To End a War*, 73.

7. See *Stern*, August 17, 1995.

8. See Alborghetti, *Globus*, October 20, 1995.

9. See Powell, *My American Journey*, 149.

10. See Drew, *Showdown*, 252.

11. For the Vershbow and Lake quotations see Silber and Little, *Yugoslavia: Death of a Nation*, 352.

12. Joseph Kruzel, deputy assistant secretary of defense for Europe, and Air Force Colonel S. Nelson Drew of the National Security Council were also killed.

13. See Demick, *Logavina Street: Life and Death in a Sarajevo Neighborhood*.

14. See Holbrooke, *To End a War*, 104.

15. Ibid., 385.

16. See Chris Hedges, "Serbs in Bosnia See No Peace for Their Dead . . . ," *New York Times*, January 18, 1996.

17. See Stephen Kinzer, "Muslims to Take a Sarajevo Suburb Sooner Than Expected," *New York Times*, February 20, 1996.

18. See Chris Hedges, "Postscript to Sarajevo's Anguish: Muslim Killings of Serbs Detailed," November 12, 1997.

19. See Stephen Kinzer, "As Leaders Urge Them On, Serbs Clog Roads Out of Sarajevo," *New York Times*, February 22, 1996.

Coda: Endgame in Kosovo

1. See "The Knock on the Door: Letter from Pristina," by an anonymous correspondent, *Global Beat Syndicate*, NYU Center for War, Peace, and the News Media: www.nyu.edu/globalbeat/syndicate, April 1, 1998.

NOTES FOR PAGES 318–341   581

2. See John Daniszewski and Elizabeth Shogren, "With Refugees From Kosovo, Tales of Terror," *Los Angeles Times*, April 2, 1999, AS.

3. At this writing it appears that the Serbs have so far limited their massacres of military-age men to villages and towns, while in Pristina and other cities they have been more selective, murdering politicians, human rights lawyers, and other members of the intelligentsia, while in some cases detaining large numbers of men in police stations and military barracks.

4. These stories are drawn from Christiane Amanpour's report broadcast on "Strike on Yugoslavia," *Cable News Network*, April 3, 1999.

5. See Lawrence S. Engleburger, "NATO, In A Corner," *New York Times*, April 4, 1999.

6. Quoted in "Method to the Madness," *Decision Brief* (Center for Security Policy, Washington), October 2, 1992, 3.

7. See David Binder, "Bush Warns Serbs Not To Widen War," *New York Times*, December 28, 1992. Mr. Eagleburger's recent statement that "NATO may no longer feel it has [the] choice" to avoid intervening in Kosovo seems further evidence that the "Christmas Warning," however uncompromising its language, was hardly a firm commitment to "employ military force."

8. See Stephen Engelberg, "Weighing Strikes in Bosnia, U.S. Warns of Wider War," *New York Times*, April 25, 1993.

9. See Holbrooke, *To End a War*, 357.

10. See *Kosovo: A Short History* (New York University Press, 1998), 353.

11. See "U.S. Warns of 'Serious Action' Against Belgrade on Kosovo," Agence France-Presse, March 4, 1998, and "U.S. State Department Press Briefing," March 5, 1998.

12. See Julius Strauss, "Massacre Evidence Mounts Against Milosevic," *Sunday Telegraph*, January 31, 1999.

13. See "Massacre of Civilians in Racak," Kosovo Verification Mission, January 17, 1999.

14. See Craig R. Whitney with Eric Schmitt, "NATO Had Signs Its Stragegy Would Fail Kosovars," *New York Times*, April 1, 1999, A1.

15. See George Stephanopoulos, *All Too Human: A Political Education* (Boston: Back Bay, 2000), 214.

III. MAROONED IN THE COLD WAR

1. See Kennan, *American Diplomacy*, 101.

2. See Percy Lubbock (editor), *The Selected Letters of Henry James* (New York: Scribner, 1920), 384.

3. See *Confirmation Hearings before the Senate Foreign Relations Committee,* January 9, 1996.

4. See *Statement by Secretary Madeleine Albright to the North American Council Special Ministerial Meeting,* Brussels, February 18, 1997.

5. The term is Michael Mandelbaum's. See *The Dawn of Peace in Europe* (New York: Twentieth Century Fund, 1996), 113.

6. See Michael Dobbs, "Wider alliance would increase U.S. commitments," *Washington Post*, July 5, 1995.

7. Richard Holbrooke gives his own extensive version of his role in planning and executing NATO enlargement in a letter in response to this essay. See "Marooned In the Cold War: An Exchange between Mark Danner and Richard C. Holbrooke," *World Policy*

Journal, Winter 1998. See also "Marooned in the Cold War: An Exchange between Mark Danner and George F. Kennan, Strobe Talbott and Lee H. Hamilton," *World Affairs Journal*, Spring 1998. Available at www.markdanner.com.

8. See Henry Kissinger, "Expand NATO now," *Washington Post*, December 19, 1994.

9. See Henry Kissinger, "Helsinki fiasco; What previous president could ever bring himself to say that NATO was 'basically a mirror image of the Warsaw Pact'?," *Washington Post*, March 30, 1997.

10. See David Lloyd George, *Memoirs of the Peace Conference* (New Haven, CT: Yale University Press, 1939), 139.

11. See John Maynard Keynes, *The Economic Consequences of the Peace* (New York: Harcourt, Brace and Howe, 1920), 43.

12. Quoted in Barbara Crossette, "A political diplomat: Madeleine Korbel Albright," *New York Times*, December 6, 1996.

13. See Kennan, *American Diplomacy*, 78.

14. See Martin Walker, *The Cold War: A History* (New York: Macmillan, 1995), 12.

15. See Dean Acheson, *Present at the Creation: My Years in the State Department* (New York: W. W. Norton, 1987 [1970]), 243.

16. See Walter Lippmann, *U.S. Foreign Policy: Shield of the Republic* (Boston: Little, Brown & Co., 1949), 9.

17. Quoted in Ronald Steel, *Walter Lippmann and the American Century* (Boston: Little Brown, 1980), 348.

18. See Theodore Draper, *A Present of Things Past: Selected Essays* (New Brunswick, NJ: Transaction, 2001 [1990]), 72.

19. See "Tapes show Johnson saw Vietnam War as pointless in 1964," *New York Times*, February 15, 1997.

20. See George F. Kennan, "A Fateful Error," *New York Times*, February 5, 1997. For an expanded account of Kennan's views and his response to this essay, see "Marooned in the Cold War: An Exchange between Mark Danner and George F. Kennan, Strobe Talbott and Lee H. Hamilton," *World Affairs Journal*, Spring 1998. Available at www.mark danner.com.

21. See Jim Hoagland and David Hoffmann, "NATO plans worry Russia's premier; Chernomyrdin says growth could bring arms buildup," *Washington Post*, February 4, 1997.

22. See Peter Rodman, "4 more for NATO," *Washington Post*, December 13, 1994.

23. See Vaclav Havel, "NATO's quality of life," *New York Times*, May 13, 1997.

IV. LOST IN THE FOREVER WAR

How Not to Win a War

1. Department of Defense news briefing, July 16, 2003.

2. See Scott Johnson and Evan Thomas, "Still Fighting Saddam," *Newsweek*, July 21, 2003, 22.

3. Anthony Cordesman, "Iraq and Conflict Termination: The Road to Guerrilla War?" Center for Strategic and International Studies, July 28, 2003.

4. See "War and Aftermath," *Policy Review*, August and September 2003, 9.

5. See Mark Fineman, Robin Wright, and Doyle McManus, "Preparing for War, Stumbling to Peace," *Los Angeles Times*, July 18, 2003.

6. See Jeffrey Sachs, "The Real Target of the War in Iraq Was Saudi Arabia," *Financial Times*, August 23, 2003, and Robert Badinter, "La vraie raison de la guerre qui

s'annonce," *Le Nouvel Observateur*, February 20, 2003. As both authors make clear, the administration was reluctant to discuss publicly the displacement of the Saudis as a motive for the war.

7. See Dana Milbank, "Patience on Iraq Policies Urged," *Washington Post*, August 26, 2003, 1.

8. See "Deputy Secretary Wolfowitz Interview with Sam Tanenhaus, *Vanity Fair*," Department of Defense Web site, May 9, 2003.

9. See Rolf Ekeus, "Iraq's Real Weapons Threat," *Washington Post*, June 29, 2003, B7, who argues convincingly that Iraq destroyed its remaining weapons and focused "on design and engineering, with the purpose of activating production" in the event of war with Iran.

10. For my public discussions about Iraq, including debates with Christopher Hitchens, Michael Ignatieff, Leon Wieseltier, and others, see www.markdanner.com.

11. See "Deputy Secretary Wolfowitz Interview on PBS with Charlie Rose," August 4, 2003, Department of Defense transcript.

12. Quoted in Robert Baer, "Will Lebanon's Horror Become Iraq's?" *Washington Post*, August 24, 2003.

Delusions in Baghdad

1. See Mohammad Bazzi, "Saudis Suspected in 2 Iraq Attacks," *Newsday*, November 11, 2003.

2. See Susan Sachs, "U.S. Is Set to Return Power to Iraqis as Early as June," *New York Times*, November 15, 2003.

3. See Jonathan S. Landay, "CIA Has a Bleak Analysis of Iraq," *Philadelphia Inquirer*, November 12, 2003.

4. Christopher Hitchens made the comment, in a debate with me at the University of California at Berkeley on November 4, 2003. See "Has Bush Made Us Safer? Iraq, Terror and American Power," at webcast.berkeley.edu/events /archive.html and www.mark danner.com/orations/view/87.

5. See Michael Hirsh, Rod Nordland, and Mark Hosenball, "About-Face in Iraq," *Newsweek*, November 24, 2003; and Douglas Jehl, "Plan for Guerrilla Action May Have Predated War," *New York Times*, November 15, 2003.

6. See Mark Fineman, Robin Wright, and Doyle McManus, "Preparing for War, Stumbling to Peace," *Los Angeles Times*, July 18, 2003; and David Rieff, "Blueprint for a Mess," *New York Times Magazine*, November 2, 2003.

7. See Ahmed S. Hashim, "The Sunni Insurgency in Iraq," Middle East Institute Policy Brief, August 15, 2003, who notes that the "elimination of Saddam and his dynasty may demoralize pro-regime insurgents but may actually embolden anti-regime and anti-U.S. insurgents who may have held back in the past . . . because of the barely submerged fears that the regime could come back."

Abu Ghraib: Hidden in Plain Sight

1. See Edward Cody, "Iraqis Put Contempt for Troops on Display," *Washington Post*, June 12, 2004.

2. I first wrote about Abu Ghraib in "Torture and Truth," *New York Review of Books*, June 10, 2004, and "The Logic of Torture," *New York Review of Books*, June 24, 2004. All can be found collected, along with several hundred pages of government documents,

depositions, reports, and photographs, in my book, *Torture and Truth: America, Abu Ghraib and the War on Terror* (New York: New York Review Books, 2004).

3. See Maj. Gen. George R. Fay, *AR 15–6 Investigation of the Abu Ghraib Detention Facility and 205th Military Intelligence Brigade* (*The Fay Report*), 25–26.

4. See Press conference with Members of the Independent Panel to Review Department of Defense Detention Operations, August 24, 2004.

5. See Osama bin Laden, "Jihad Against Jews and Crusaders," February 28, 1998, in *Voices of Terror*, edited by Walter Laqueur (Reed, 2004), 410–412. See International Committee of the Red Cross, *Report of the International Committee of the Red Cross (ICRC) on the Treatment by the Coalition Forces of Prisoners of War and Other Protected Persons by the Geneva Conventions in Iraq During Arrest, Internment and Interrogation*, February 2004, 7.

6. See *The Fay Report*, 37.

7. See my "Torture and Truth" and "The Logic of Torture," in the *New York Review of Books*, June 10 and June 24, 2004, respectively.

8. See Final Report of the Independent Panel to Review DoD Detention Operations (*The Schlesinger Report*), August 2004, 29.

9. See *The Fay Report*, 37.

10. Ibid., 39.

11. See *The Schlesinger Report*, 11.

12. See James Risen, David Johnston, and Neil A. Lewis, "Harsh CIA Methods Cited in Top Qaeda Interrogations," *New York Times*, May 13, 2004.

13. See Risen, Johnston, and Lewis, "Harsh CIA Methods Cited in Top Qaeda Interrogations."

14. See Dana Priest and Barton Gellman, "US Decries Abuse but Defends Interrogations," *Washington Post*, December 26, 2002.

15. See *The Gangrene*, translated by Robert Silvers (Lyle Stuart, 1960), 81–82.

16. See John Conroy, *Unspeakable Acts, Ordinary People: The Dynamics of Torture* (University of California Press, 2000), 170–171.

17. See Richard A. Serrano, "Prison Interrogators' Gloves Came Off Before Abu Ghraib," *Los Angeles Times*, June 9, 2004.

18. See Maj. Gen. Antonio Taguba, Interview with Lt. Col. Steven Jordan, *AR 15–6 Investigation Interview*, February 21, 2004, 111. See also Maj. Gen. Antonio Taguba, *Article 15–6 Investigation of the 800th Military Police Brigade* (*The Taguba Report*), May 2004.

19. See "The Logic of Torture," *New York Review*, June 24, 2004, and *Torture and Truth*, 12–14.

20. See *The Fay Report*, 74–75.

21. For Detainee 7's full and detailed account of what was done to him—originally posted on the Web site of the *Washington Post* in 2004—see "The Logic of Torture," *New York Review*, June 24, 2004, and my book, *Torture and Truth*, 247–248.

22. See *The Fay Report*, 70.

23. See *The Schlesinger Report*, 5.

24. See Alberto R. Gonzales, Memorandum for the President, January 25, 2002, included in *Torture and Truth*, 83–87.

25. See *The Schlesinger Report*, 34.

26. See *The Fay Report*, 25.

27. Anthony Cordesman, "Goal in Iraq Is to 'Get the Best Compromise You Can,'" interview with Bernard Gwertzman, Council on Foreign Relations, May 11, 2004.

28. See *The Schlesinger Report*, 13.

A Doctrine Left Behind

1. See Powell, *My American Journey*, 149.

2. See Powell, "U.S. Forces: Challenges Ahead," 38. As mentioned in an earlier note, some refer to this as the Powell Corollary to the Weinberger Doctrine.

3. Ibid.

We Are All Torturers Now

1. See *Report of the International Committee of the Red Cross (ICRC) on the Treatment by the Coalition Forces of Prisoners of War and Other Protected Persons by the Geneva Conventions in Iraq During Arrest, Internment and Interrogation*, February 2004, 4.

2. See *Final Report of the Independent Panel to Review DoD Detention Operations* (*The Schlesinger Report*), August 2004, 9.

3. See "Email from [REDACTED] to [REDACTED]," August 2, 2004, available at the ACLU Web site.

4. See Jay S. Bybee, *Memorandum for Alberto R. Gonzales*, Counsel to the President, August 1, 2002. See my *Torture and Truth*, 115–167.

5. See (Ret.) Gen. Joseph Hoar et al, "An Open Letter to the Senate Judiciary Committee," January 5, 2005.

The Real Election

1. See Steven Metz, "Relearning Counterinsurgency," a panel discussion at the American Enterprise Institute, January 10, 2005. I have slightly edited the language of the rough transcript.

2. See *Iraq Index: Tracking Variables of Reconstruction and Security in Post-Saddam Iraq*, Brookings Institution, March 25, 2005 (updated). The index gives a total of 220 "mass casualty bombings" of which 136 "reported so far were suicide bombings." The death toll from these "mass casualty bombings," including suicide bombings, Brookings estimates at 2,290, with 5,059 wounded. Though estimates vary a good deal, these numbers are certainly on the low side.

3. See "Sources Say Hundreds of Iraq Attacks Planned," *CNN*, January 20, 2005.

4. See my chapter "Delusions in Baghdad," above.

5. See Edward Wong, "American Jails in Iraq Bursting with Detainees," *New York Times*, March 4, 2005.

6. "Never have elections been held under such difficult conditions, with a level of violence so high that the country had to be locked down for several days in order for the vote to be held." See Marina Ottaway, "Iraq: Without Consensus, Democracy Is Not the Answer," *Policy Brief*, Carnegie Endowment for International Peace, March 2005.

7. See Dexter Filkins, "On Bus, Bicycle and Foot, Suicide Bombers Aim at a Shiite Holy Day," *New York Times*, February 20, 2005.

8. See *Iraq Index*, 12. The real wave of kidnappings of foreign nationals began in April 2004, when forty-three were seized.

9. See especially Robert Fisk, "Curbs Leaving Big Holes in Reporting about Iraq," *The Independent*, January 17, 2005.

10. See John F. Burns, "U.S. Shouldn't Cut Force Soon, Iraqi Leaders Say," *New York Times*, February 2, 2005.

11. The percentage, much reduced from election-day estimates of 72 to 80 percent, remains "soft," for it is unclear precisely how many Iraqis are registered to vote, and what

percentage the Iraqis who are registered represents of those eligible. In any event it seems likely that fewer than half of those Iraqis eligible to vote did so. See Greg Mitchell, "Update: Officials Back Away from Early Estimates of Iraqi Vote Turnout," *Editor and Publisher*, February 2, 2005, and Howard Kurtz, "The Spinners, Casting Their Versions of the Vote in Iraq," *Washington Post*, February 1, 2005.

The Secret Way to War

1. See "The secret Downing Street memo," *The Sunday Times*, May 1, 2005. The text was first published in the United States in the *New York Review of Books*, June 9, 2005, and later appeared with seven related memoranda, in Danner, *The Secret Way to War*.

2. See Ken Roth, "War in Iraq: Not a Humanitarian Intervention," *Human Rights Watch*, January 2004.

3. See Bob Woodward, *Plan of Attack* (New York: Simon and Schuster, 2004), 162.

4. Ibid., 177–178.

5. See "Chirac Makes His Case on Iraq," an interview with Christiane Amanpour, *CBS News*, March 16, 2003.

6. For a further discussion of this point, see my "'The Moment Has Come to Get Rid of Saddam,'" *New York Review of Books*, November 8, 2007, an analysis of a transcript of President Bush's meeting, on February 22, 2003, with Prime Minister José Maria Aznar of Spain.

7. See Hans Blix, *Disarming Iraq* (New York: Pantheon, 2004), 86.

8. See Ron Suskind, "Without a Doubt," *New York Times Magazine*, October 17, 2004. See also the Afterword, "Words in a Time of War," below.

9. This paragraph, though widely attributed to Goebbels himself, is in fact an amalgam of Goebbels's words and a quite precise paraphrase of his words by his editor, Hugh Trevor-Roper. See Trevor-Roper's introduction to *Final Entries 1945: The Goebbels Diaries* (New York: Putnam, 1978), 20. For a discussion of press coverage of the war and the Downing Street Memo, see two long exchanges, with the journalists John Walcott and Michael Kinsley, respectively, that followed on the publication of this article: "Why the Memo Matters," *New York Review of Books*, July 14, 2005, and "The Memo, the Press, and the War," *New York Review of Books*, August 11, 2005. The exchanges are included in *The Secret Way to War* and can be found at www.markdanner.com.

Taking Stock of the Forever War

1. See Julia Spinola, "Monstrous Art," *Frankfurter Allgemeine Zeitung* (English Language Edition), September 27, 2001. I have slightly altered the translation.

2. See "Rumsfeld's war-on-terror memo," *USA Today*, October 16, 2003. The memorandum was addressed to General Richard Myers, the chairman of the Joint Chiefs; Paul Wolfowitz, deputy secretary of defense; General Pete Pace, deputy chairman of the Joint Chiefs; and Douglas Feith, Undersecretary of defense for Policy.

3. See Dana Priest and Josh White, "War Helps Recruit Terrorists, Hill Told: Intelligence Officials Talk of Growing Insurgency," *Washington Post*, February 17, 2005.

4. See "Text: President Bush Addresses the Nation," *Washington Post*, September 20, 2001.

5. See *Report of the Defense Science Board Task Force on Strategic Communication*, Office of the Under Secretary of Defense for Acquisition, Technology, and Logistics, September 2004, 42.

6. See *Report of the Defense Science Board Task Force on Strategic Communication*, 43.

7. See "Declaration of Jihad Against the Americans Occupying the Land of the Two Holy Places," in Robert O. Marlin IV (editor). *What Does Al-Qaeda Want? Unedited Communiques* (Berkeley, CA: North Atlantic Books, 2004), 10.

8. See Bill Blum, "Interview with Zbigniew Brzezinski, President Jimmy Carter's National Security Advisor," *Le Nouvel Observateur,* January 15–21, 1998.

9. See Menachem Begin, *The Revolt: Story of Irgun* (Jerusalem: Steimatzky, 1977), quoted in Bruce Hoffman, *Inside Terrorism* (New York: Columbia University Press, 2006), 50.

10. See "Bin Laden Video Tape: An Online NewsHour Report," *PBS Online NewsHour,* December 13, 2001. Quoted in Gambetta, *Making Sense of Suicide Missions*, 265.

11. See Fuad Hussein, "Al Zaqawi: The Second al Qaeda Generation," excerpted in *Al Quds al Arabi*, June/July 2005. Quoted in Peter L. Bergen (ed.), *The Osama bin Laden I Know: An Oral History of al Qaeda's Leader* (New York: Free Press, 2006), 308–309.

12. See "Declaration of Jihad Against the Americans Occupying the Land of the Two Holy Places," 12–13

13. See Amin Tarzi and Kathleen Ridolfo, "Afghanistan/Iraq: Al-Zarqawi, Al-Qaeda, And the New Islamist Front," *Radio Free Europe/Radio Liberty*, June 10, 2005, quoting Hussein, *Al-Zarqawi: The Second Al-Qaeda Generation*.

14. Quoted in Hoffman, *Inside Terrorism*, 54.

15. See Begin, *The Revolt*, quoted in Hoffman, *Inside Terrorism*, 53.

16. See "Text from Abu Mus'ab al-Zarqawi Letter," February 12, 2004. GlobalSecurity.Org. Text originally released by the Coalition Provisional Authority, Iraq.

17. See Stephen D. Biddle, *American Grand Strategy After 9/11: An Assessment* (Carlisle, PA: Strategic Studies Institute, April 2004), 29–30.

18. See Peter Baker, "In Iraq, No Clear Finish Line," *Washington Post*, August 12, 2005.

19. See "Bush Speaks to Idaho Military and their Families," *Good Politics Radio—Idaho,* August 24, 2005.

20. For "Jihadi Iraq: Hopes and Dangers," also known as "The Madrid Blueprint," see Brynjar Lia and Thomas Hegghammer, "FFI explains al-Qaida document," The Norwegian Defense Research Establishment, http://www.mil.no/felles/ffi/start/article.jhtml?articleID=71589. The forty-two-page strategy document, apparently completed in September 2003 and dedicated to the Saudi al Qaeda member Yusef Al-Ayeri, was first discovered, translated, and analyzed by researchers at the Norwegian Defence Research Establishment. Ron Suskind suggests some in the CIA believe the document was partly written by al-Ayeri before his death in May 2003. See *The One Percent Doctrine: Deep Inside America's Pursuit of Its Enemies Since 9/11* (New York: Simon and Schuster, 2006), 302–303.

21. See Marc Sageman, "Understanding Terror Networks," *E-Notes*, Foreign Policy Research Institute, November 1, 2004.

22. See, for example, Colin Freeman, "How best to blow up people on a bus—the chilling video circulating on terrorist websites," *The Telegraph*, July 10, 2005. The video was originally brought to public attention by members of the Search for International Terrorist Entities Institute, or SITE, in Washington, DC.

The War of the Imagination

1. See Albert Eisele, "George Kennan Speaks Out About Iraq," *The Hill*, September 26, 2002.

2. See "Rumsfeld Ruminates on Tenure at Pentagon," MSNBC, November 9, 2006.

3. See "Defense Secretary Donald Rumsfeld's Colleagues Debate His Legacy," *The NewsHour with Jim Lehrer*, November 9, 2006.

4. See "Transcript for September 10: Dick Cheney," *Meet the Press with Tim Russert*, September 10, 2006.

5. See Bob Woodward, *State of Denial: Bush at War, Part III* (New York: Simon and Schuster, 2006), 408.

6. See Suskind, *The One Percent Doctrine*, 123.

7. Among those taking part in "Bletchley II" discussions, according to Woodward, were Fouad Ajami, Reuel Marc Gerecht, Steve Herbits, Bernard Lewis, Mark Palmer, James Q. Wilson, and Fareed Zakaria.

8. See Woodward, *State of Denial*, 84–85.

9. "The Struggles of Democracy and Empire," *New York Times*, October 8, 2002: See above, 371–374.

10. Here are the number of daily attacks on U.S. forces at each of the Iraq war's purported "turning points": July 2003: Bremer Appoints Iraqi Governing Council, sixteen attacks per day; December 2003: Saddam captured, nineteen attacks per day; June 2004: Handover of sovereignty to Iraqis, forty-five attacks per day; January 2005: Elections for Transitional Government, sixty-one attacks per day; June 2006: Death of Abu Musab al-Zarqawi, ninety attacks per day. See Anthony Cordesman, *Iraqi Force Development: Summer 2006 Update* (CSIS, 2006), 7.

11. See Michael R. Gordon, "Military Team Undertakes a Broad Review of the Iraq War and the Campaign Against Terror," *New York Times*, November 11, 2006.

12. See Woodward, *Plan of Attack*, 154–155.

13. In the first year of the war Iraq saw 109 "terror related bombings"; in the second year 613; in the third year, 1,037; in the last six months, 1,002. See "The Geography of War," *Newsweek*, November 6, 2006. These numbers do not include attacks on American troops with improvised explosive devices, of which there were 2,625 in July alone (nearly double the 1,454 IED attacks in January). See Michael R. Gordon, Mark Mazzetti, and Thom Shanker, "Insurgent Bombs Directed at GI's in Iraq Increase," *New York Times*, August 17, 2006.

14. See "Civilian Deaths Soar to Record High in Iraq," *The Guardian*, September 22, 2006.

15. See the statements of Manfred Nowak, "Torture in Iraq 'Worse than Under Saddam,'" *The Guardian*, September 21, 2006.

16. The current rate of killing of one hundred Iraqis a day would be the equivalent, adjusting for population, of 1,100 Americans a day, or 33,000 dead a month. In the decade-long Vietnam War, about 58,000 Americans died.

17. See "Declassified Key Judgments of the National Intelligence Estimate 'Trends in Global Terrorism: Implications for the United States' dated April 2006," found at www.dni.gov/press__releases/Declassified__NIE__Key __Judgments.pdf.

18. See Woodward, *State of Denial*, 144–145.

19. See James Risen, *State of War: The Secret History of the CIA and the Bush Administration* (New York: Free Press, 2006), 133–134.

20. See Ron Suskind, "Why Are These Men Laughing?," *Esquire*, January 2003, and *The Price of Loyalty: George W. Bush, the White House, and the Education of Paul O'Neill* (New York: Simon and Schuster, 2004).

21. See Suskind, *The One Percent Doctrine*, 227.

22. Ibid., 225.

23. Ibid., 225–226.

24. Ibid., 227.

25. See Woodward, *State of Denial*, 162.

26. Ibid., 193–194.

27. Ibid., 194.

28. See L. Paul Bremer, *My Year in Iraq: The Struggle to Build a Future of Hope* (New York: Simon and Schuster, 2006), 39.

29. See Woodward, *State of Denial*, 194–195.

30. Ibid., 197–198.

31. Ibid., 198.

32. Ibid.

33. See "We're Not Looking for an Exit Strategy, We're Looking for Victory," *Time*, October 30, 2006, 35.

34. See "Weekend Update," *Saturday Night Live*, November 11, 2006.

35. See John F. Burns, "Stability vs. Democracy: Could a New Strongman Help?," *New York Times*, November 12, 2006.

36. See "This Week with George Stephanopoulos," *ABC News*, October 22, 2006.

37. See "This Week with George Stephanopoulos," *ABC News*, November 12, 2006.

38. See Eisele, "George Kennan Speaks Out About Iraq."

Voices from the Black Sites

1. See "Restoring Trust in the Justice System: The Senate Judiciary Committee's Agenda in the 111th Congress," 2009 Marver Bernstein Lecture, Georgetown University, February 9, 2009.

2. See "ICRC Report on the Treatment of Fourteen 'High Value Detainees' in CIA Custody," (February 2007) by the International Committee of the Red Cross, 81. I obtained a copy of the report in March 2008 and made the full text public on the Web site of the *New York Review of Books* the following month. Though the report drew on interviews conducted at Guantánamo in the fall and winter of 2006, and though many of its details had appeared in the press—most notably in the work of Jane Mayer of *The New Yorker*, particularly in her book, *The Dark Side: The Inside Story of How the War on Terror Turned into a War on American Ideals* (New York: Doubleday, 2008)—the text of the report had remained secret until the appearance of this essay. The full text can be found at www.markdanner.com, and at www.nybooks.com.

3. See "President Discusses Creation of Military Commissions to Try Suspected Terrorists," September 6, 2006, East Room, White House, available at cfr.org.

4. See, for the authoritative account, Dana Priest, "CIA Holds Terror Suspects in Secret Prisons," *Washington Post*, November 2, 2005.

5. See "ICRC Report on the Treatment of Fourteen 'High Value Detainees' in CIA Custody," 59.

6. See "ICRC Report," 6.

7. See Raymond Bonner, Don Van Natta Jr., and Amy Waldman, "Interrogations: Questioning Terror Suspects in a Dark and Surreal World," *New York Times*

8. See Jonathan Alter, "Time to Think About Torture: It's a New World, and Survival May Well Require Old Techniques That Seemed Out of the Question," *Newsweek*, November 5, 2001.

9. See "President Discusses Creation of Military Commissions to Try Suspected Terrorists," September 6, 2006.

10. See "ICRC Report," 3–4.

11. Ibid., 5.

12. Ibid., 30.

13. "President Bush's News Conference," *New York Times*, September 15, 2006.

14. This and subsequent quotations from Kiriakou drawn from "CIA—Abu Zubaydah. Interview with John Kiriakou, 8–9." This is an unedited, rough and undated transcript of a video interview conducted by Brian Ross of *ABC News*, apparently in December 2007, and available at abcnews.go.com. Quotations from this document have been edited very slightly for clarity. See also Richard Esposito and Brian Ross, "Coming in from the Cold: CIA Spy Calls Waterboarding Necessary But Torture," *ABC News*, December 10, 2007.

15. See "ICRC Report," 32.

16. See "Working Group Report on Detainee Interrogations in the Global War on Terrorism: Assessment of Legal, Historical, Policy, and Operational Considerations," April 4, 2003, in Danner, *Torture and Truth*, 190–192. A great many of these documents, collected in this book and elsewhere, were leaked in the wake of the publication of the Abu Ghraib photographs, and have been public since late spring or early summer of 2004.

17. See "CIA—Abu Zubaydah. Interview with John Kiriakou," 12–13.

18. See David Johnston, "At a Secret Interrogation, Dispute Flared Over Tactics," *New York Times*, September 10, 2006.

19. See Mark Hosenball, "How Good Is Abu Zubaydah's Information?," *Newsweek* Web exclusive, April 27, 2002.

20. See "CIA—Abu Zubaydah. Interview with John Kiriakou," 15–16.

21. See "ICRC Report," 33.

22. See Johnston, "At a Secret Interrogation, Dispute Flared Over Tactics."

23. See "ICRC Report," 33.

24. See *KUBARK Counterintelligence Interrogation—July 1963 and Human Resource Exploitation Training Manual—1983*, both archived at "Prisoner Abuse: Patterns from the Past," *National Security Archive Electronic Briefing Book No. 122*. For the historical roots of the "alternative set of procedures" see Alfred W. McCoy, *A Question of Torture: CIA Interrogation, from the Cold War to the War on Terror* (New York: Metropolitan, 2006); and Jane Mayer, *The Dark Side*, especially 167–174. See also my "The Logic of Torture," *New York Review of Books*, June 24, 2004, and *Torture and Truth*.

25. See "ICRC Report," 33.

26. See "CIA—Abu Zubaydah. Interview with John Kiriakou," 20–22.

27. See Jan Crawford Greenburg, Howard L. Rosenberg, and Ariane de Vogue, "Sources: Top Bush Advisors Approved 'Enhanced Interrogation,'" *ABC News*, April 9, 2008.

28. See "ICRC Report," 34.

29. See McCoy, *A Question of Torture*, especially 33–42.

30. See "ICRC Report," 35.

31. Ibid.

32. Ibid., 36.

33. Ibid., 37–38.

34. Ibid., 38.

35. Ibid., 38–39.

36. Ibid., 39: The bracketed comment appears in the ICRC report.

37. Ibid.

38. Ibid., 39–40.

39. Ibid., 40.

40. Ibid.

41. See Bob Woodward, "Detainee Tortured, Says US Official: Trial Overseer Cites 'Abusive' Methods Against 9/11 Suspect," *Washington Post*, January 14, 2009.

42. See "CIA—Abu Zubaydah. Interview with John Kiriakou," 16–17.

43. See Ron Suskind, "The Unofficial Story of the Al Qaeda 14," *Time*, September 10, 2006. See also Suskind's *The One Percent Doctrine: Deep Inside America's Pursuit of Its Enemies Since 9/11* (New York: Simon and Schuster, 2006), 99–101, and Mayer, *The Dark Side*, 175–177.

44. See "CIA—Abu Zubaydah. Interview with John Kiriakou," 18–19.

45. See "ICRC Report," 41.

46. See "Statement on Military Commission Legislation: Remarks by Senator Barack Obama," September 28, 2006.

47. Black supposedly made this comment on September 19, 2001, to CIA officers heading to Afghanistan. He recounted it to a Congressional committee a year later, on September 26, 2002. See John Barry, Michael Hirsh and Michael Isikoff, "The Roots of Torture," *Newsweek*, May 24, 2004. For the comment by the Abu Ghraib intelligence officer—"The gloves are coming off gentlemen regarding these detainees . . ."—see "Abu Ghraib: Hidden in Plain Sight," above.

48. See "Feinstein, Bond Announce Intelligence Committee Review of CIA Detention and Interrogation Program," U.S. Senate Select Committee on Intelligence, March 5, 2009.

49. See "Getting to the Truth Through a Nonpartisan Commission of Inquiry," Statement of Senator Patrick Leahy (D-Vermont), chairman, Senate Judiciary Committee, March 4, 2009.

50. See "Interview of the Vice President by Scott Hennen, WDAY at Radio Day at the White House, "Office of the Vice President, October 24, 2006.

Into the Light? Torture, Power, and Us

1. See John F. Harris, Mike Allen, and Jim VandeHei, "Cheney Warns of New Attacks," *Politico*, February 4, 2009.

2. See "ICRC Report on the Treatment of Fourteen 'High Value Detainees' in CIA Custody by the International Committee of the Red Cross," February 2007. The report is based on extensive interviews, carried out in October and December 2006, with fourteen so-called "high-value detainees," who had been imprisoned and interrogated for extended periods at the "black sites," a series of secret prisons operated by the CIA in a number of countries around the world, including, at various times, Thailand, Afghanistan, Poland, Romania, and Morocco.

3. See "Inquiry Into The Treatment of Detainees in U.S. Custody: Report of the Committee on Armed Services United States Senate," November 20, 2008. Meanwhile, a Spanish judge sent to a prosecutor a case against Alberto Gonzales, the former White House counsel and attorney general, and five other senior Bush officials, including John Yoo and Jay Bybee. See Marlise Simons, "Spanish Court Weighs Inquiry on Torture for 6 Bush-Era Officials," *New York Times*, March 28, 2009. In the United Kingdom, the Crown Prosecution Service has begun an inquiry into allegations of the torture of Binyam Mohamed during his detention by the CIA. In Poland, prosecutors have reportedly begun an inquiry into allegations that the CIA made use of an abandoned military facility as a "black site" to torture prisoners.

4. "Interview with Dick Cheney," State of the Union With John King, *CNN*, March 15, 2009.

5. See "Obama on AIG Rage, Recession, Challenges," *60 Minutes*, March 22, 2009.

6. See "President Discusses Creation of Military Commissions to Try Suspected Terrorists," September 6, 2006, East Room, White House, available at cfr.org.

7. See, for the definitive account, Jane Mayer, "Outsourcing Torture," *The New Yorker*, February 15, 2005, and *The Dark Side*; and also Alfred W. McCoy, *A Question of Torture: CIA Interrogation, from the Cold War to the War on Terror* (New York: Metropolitan, 2006).

8. See "Executive Summary and Conclusions," Inquiry into the Treatment of Detainees in U.S. Custody, Senate Armed Services Committee, xiii. Emphasis added.

9. See "ICRC Report on the Treatment of Fourteen 'High Value Detainees' in CIA Custody," (February 2007) by the International Committee of the Red Cross, 30.

10. Ibid., 27–28.

11. Ibid., 30.

12. See Jacobo Timerman, *Prisoner Without a Name, Cell Without a Number* (New York: Knopf, 1981), 32.

13. See Robin Bruce Lockhart, *Ace of Spies* (New York: Penguin, 1984 [1967]), 176.

14. See "ICRC Report," 18.

15. Ibid.

16. Ibid., 13.

17. Ibid., 13–14.

18. See "Memorandum for Alberto R. Gonzales Counsel to the President, Re: Standards of Conduct for Interrogation under 18 U.S.C 2340–2340A," in Danner, *Torture and Truth*, 182.

19. See "ICRC Report," 9–10.

20. Ibid., 12–13.

21. See "General Counsel of the Department of Defense Action Memo," November 22, 2002, in *Torture and Truth*, 182.

22. See Lawrence E. Hinkle Jr. and Harold G. Wolff, "Communist Interrogation and Indoctrination of 'Enemies of the State,'" *A.M.A. Archives of Neurology and Psychiatry*, Vol. 76, No. 2 (August 1956), 134.

23. See "ICRC Report," 39. The interpolated words in brackets are as they appear in the Red Cross report.

24. I discuss the Abu Zubaydah case more fully in the previous essay. Nearly three years ago, author Ron Suskind offered an extensive account of Abu Zubaydah and the exaggerations that officials had made about him, from President Bush on down—both about his rank and importance in al Qaeda and about the value of the information he supposedly offered after the application of the "alternative set of procedures." See Suskind's *The One Percent Doctrine*, especially pages 99–101 and 115–118. The debate about the case has continued to be pursued furiously in the press, an indication of the strong feelings of many, mostly unnamed officials within the intelligence and law enforcement communities. See, for example, Peter Finn and Joby Warrick, "Detainee's Harsh Treatment Foiled No Plots: Waterboarding, Rough Interrogation of Abu Zubaida Produced False Leads, Officials Say," *Washington Post*, March 29, 2009.

25. Jane Mayer, in her article "The Black Sites," *The New Yorker*, August 13, 2007, and in her book, *The Dark Side*, published many of the details of abuse contained in the ICRC report, though not texts from the report itself.

26. See Dana Priest and Barton Gellman, "U.S. Decries Abuse but Defends Interrogations: 'Stress and Duress' Tactics Used on Terrorism Suspects Held in Secret Overseas Facilities," *Washington Post*, December 26, 2002.

27. In October of that year I published several hundred pages of those documents in my book *Torture and Truth*. A few months later Karen J. Greenberg and Joshua L. Dratel published their more comprehensive collection, *The Torture Papers: The Road to Abu Ghraib* (New York: Cambridge University Press, 2005).

28. See "Transcript: Senate Confirmation Hearings Eric Holder Day One," *New York Times*, January 16, 2009. See also Anthony Romero, "Letter to the Honorable Eric Holder," March 17, 2009.

29. See "Getting to the Truth Through a Nonpartisan Commission of Inquiry," Statement of Senator Patrick Leahy (D-Vt.), chairman, Senate Judiciary Committee, March 4, 2009.

30. See "Feinstein, Bond Announce Intelligence Committee Review of CIA Detention and Interrogation Program," U.S. Senate Select Committee on Intelligence, March 5, 2009.

31. See "Obama on AIG Rage, Recession, Challenges," *60 Minutes*, March 22, 2009.

32. These emotions affect government officials as well, as this description of those who insisted on the torture of Abu Zubaydah suggests: "They couldn't stand the idea that there wasn't anything new," the official said. "They'd say, 'You aren't working hard enough.' There was both a disbelief in what he was saying and also a desire for retribution—a feeling that 'He's going to talk, and if he doesn't talk, we'll do whatever.'" See Finn and Warrick, "Detainee's Harsh Treatment Foiled No Plots."

33. See "Interview: Chris Mackey and Greg Miller discuss their book, *The Interrogators*," *Fresh Air*, National Pubic Radio, July 20, 2004. See Chris Mackey with Greg Miller, *The Interrogators: Inside the Secret War Against Al Qaeda* (Little, Brown, 2004). The name "Chris Mackey" is a pseudonym.

34. See Lawrence Wilkerson, "Some Truths About Guantánamo Bay," *The Washington Note*, March 17, 2009.

35. See, for example, Corine Hegland, "Who Is at Guantánamo Bay," *National Journal*, February 3, 2006.

36. See Wilkerson, "Some Truths About Guantánamo Bay."

37. See "Report of the International Committee of the Red Cross (ICRC) on the Treatment by the Coalition Forces of Prisoners of War and Other Persons Protected by the Geneva Conventions in Iraq During Arrest, Internment and Interrogation," February 2004, reviewed in my article "Torture and Truth," *The New York Review*, June 10, 2004.

38. See Mackey and Miller, *The Interrogators*, 471.

39. See Wilkerson, "Some Truths About Guantánamo Bay."

40. See "DoD News Briefing with Deputy Assistant Secretary Stimson and Lt. Gen. Kimmons from the Pentagon," September 6, 2006.

41. See Philip Zelikow, "Legal Policy for a Twilight War," Annual Lecture, *Houston Journal of International Law*, April 26, 2007.

Afterword: The Erotic Pull of the Strange

1. See Janet Malcolm, *The Journalist and the Murderer* (New York: Knopf, 1990), 152.

2. See Nora Ephron *Heartburn* (New York: Knopf, 1983) and Ryszard Kapuscinski, *The Emperor: Downfall of an Autocrat* (New York: Harcourt, 1983).

3. See Janet Malcolm, *The Silent Woman: Sylvia Plath and Ted Hughes* (New York: Knopf, 1994), 154–155.

4. See Joseph Conrad, *Heart of Darkness and The Congo Diary* (New York: Penguin, 2007 [1899]), 86.

Coda: Words in Time of War

1. This essay was first delivered as a commencement address to the Department of Rhetoric of the University of California, Berkeley, on May 10, 2007, and was later published, in its present form, in Andres Szanto (editor), *What Orwell Didn't Know: Propaganda and the New Face of American Politics* (New York: PublicAffairs, 2007), 16–36.

2. See George Orwell, "The Prevention of Literature," in *The George Orwell Reader: Fiction, Essays and Reportage* (New York: Harcourt, 1961), 371.

3. The quotation is attributed to Senator Hiram Johnson of California, who uttered it in a speech to the Senate during World War I, though it remains a matter of some controversy on precisely what date—or whether indeed it was in 1917 or 1918. See, for example, Philip Knightley, *The First Casualty: The War Correspondent as Hero and Myth-Maker From the Crimea to Kosovo* (Baltimore: Johns Hopkins, 2002 [1975]).

4. See George Orwell, *Nineteen Eighty Four* (New York: Everyman's Library, 1992 [1949]), 205.

5. See Orwell, "The Prevention of Literature," 371.

6. See Ron Suskind, "Without a Doubt: Faith, Certainty and the Presidency of George W. Bush," *New York Times Magazine*, October 17, 2004.

7. See Begin, *The Revolt*. Quoted in Bruce Hoffman, *Inside Terrorism* (New York: Columbia University Press, 1998), 52.

8. Quoted in Woodward, *State of Denial*, 408.

9. See Bob Woodward, *Bush at War* (New York: Simon and Schuster, 2002), 137.

10. See "National Defense Strategy of the United States of America," Department of Defense, March 2005, 3–4.

11. See "The Downing Street Memo," in Mark Danner, *The Secret Way to War*, 90.

12. See "Politics and the English Language" in *The George Orwell Reader*, 366.

13. See "At the Morgue," *Inside Iraq*, McClatchy Washington Bureau, February 15, 2007. Accessed at http://washingtonbureau.typepad.com/iraq/2007/02/at_the_morgue.html.

Selected Bibliography

I. BEYOND THE MOUNTAINS

Adams, Henry. *History of the United States of America during the administrations of Thomas Jefferson.* New York: Library of America, 1986.

Aristide, Jean-Bertrand. *Aristide: An Autobiography.* Maryknoll, NY: Orbis, 1993.

———. *In the Parish of the Poor: Writings from Haiti.* Maryknoll, NY: Orbis, 1990.

———. *Dignity.* Charlottesville, VA and London: University Press of Virginia, 1996.

———. *Théologie et Politique.* Montreal: CIDIHCA, 1992.

———. *Tout Moun se Moun, Tout Homme est un Homme.* Paris: Seuil, 1992.

Avril, Prosper. *Vérités et Révélations, Tome I: Le Silence Rompu.* Port-au-Prince: Août, 1993.

Ballard, John R. *Upholding Democracy: The United States Military Campaign in Haiti, 1994–1997.* Westport, CT, and London: Praeger, 1998.

Barthelemy, Gérard. *Les Duvalieristes après Duvalier.* Paris: l'Harmattan, 1992.

Barthélemy, Gérard and Christian Girault. *La République Haïtienne: État des Lieux et Perspectives.* Paris: Karthala, 1993.

Courlander, Harold. *The Bordeaux Narrative.* Albuquerque: University of New Mexico Press, 1990.

Dalvius, Gerard. *Une Armée pour la Démocratie en Haïti.* Port-au-Prince: Le Natal, 1987.

Davis, Wade. *Passage of Darkness: The Ethnobiology of the Haitian Zombie.* Chapel Hill, NC, and London: University of North Carolina Press, 1988.

———. *The Serpent & the Rainbow: A Harvard Scientist's Astonishing Journey into the Secret Society of Haitian Voodoo, Zombis and Magic.* New York: Simon and Schuster, 1985.

de las Casas, Bartolomé. *A Short Account of the Destruction of the Indies.* London: Penguin, 1992.

Deren, Maya. *Divine Horsemen: The Living Gods of Haiti.* New Paltz, NY: McPherson & Company, 1953.

Diederich, Bernard and Al Burt. *Papa Doc and the Tonton Macoutes.* Port-au-Prince: Henri Deschamps, 1986.

DeWind, Josh and David H. Kinley, III. *Aiding Migration: The Impact of International Development Assistance on Haiti.* Boulder, CO: Westview Press, 1988.

Duvalier, François. *Mémoires d'un Leader du Tiers Monde: Mes Négociations avec le Saint-Siège ou une Tranche d'Histoire.* Paris: Hachette, 1969.

Farmer, Paul. *The Uses of Haiti.* Monroe, ME: Common Courage, 1994.

Fass, Simon M. *Political Economy in Haiti: The Drama of Survival.* New Brunswick, CT, and London: Transaction, 1990.

Fox-Genovese, Elizabeth and Eugene Genovese. *Fruits of Merchant Capital: Slavery and Bourgeois Property in the Rise and Expansion of Capitalism.* Oxford: Oxford University Press, 1983.

Franketienne. *Les Affres d'un Défi.* Port-au-Prince: Henri Deschamps, 1979.

Genovese, Eugene D. *From Rebellion to Revolution: Afro-American Slave Revolts in the Making of the New World.* New York: Vintage, 1981.

Gold, Herbert. *Best Nightmare on Earth: A Life in Haiti.* Upper Saddle River, NJ: Prentice Hall, 1991.

Haïti Solidarité Internationale. *Haïti 1990: Quelle Démocratie?* Port-au-Prince: Haïti Solidarité Internationale, 1990.

Heine, Jorge and Leslie Manigat (eds). *The Caribbean and World Politics: Cross Currents and Cleavages.* New York and London: Holmes & Meier, 1988.

Heinl, Robert Debs, Jr., and Nancy Gordon Heinl. *Written in Blood: The Story of the Haitian People, 1492–1971.* Boston: Houghton Mifflin, 1978.

Hoffmann, Leon-Francois. *Haiti: Couleurs, Croyances, Creole.* Port-au-Prince: CIDIHCA and Henri Deschamps, 1990.

Hurbon, Laënnec. *Comprendre Haiti: Essai sur l'Etat, la nation, la culture.* Paris and Port-au-Prince: Karthala and Henri Deschamps, 1987.

———. *Pour une sociologie d'Haiti au XXIe siècle: La démocratie introuvable.* Paris: Karthala, 2001.

James, C. L. R. *The Black Jacobins: Toussaint L'Ouverture and the San Domingo Revolution.* New York: Vintage, 1963 [1938].

L'Ouverture, Toussaint. *The Haitian Revolution.* London and Brooklyn: Verso, 2008.

Laguerre, Michael S. *The Military and Society in Haiti.* Knoxville: University of Tennessee Press, 1993.

———. *Voodoo and Politics in Haiti.* New York: St. Martin's, 1989.

Lionet, Christian. *Haiti: L'année Aristide.* Paris: L'Harmattan, 1992.

Lundahl, Mats. *Peasants and Poverty: A Study of Haiti.* New York: St. Martin's, 1979.

———. *The Haitian Economy: Man, Land and Markets.* New York: St. Martin's, 1983.

Manigat, Leslie. *Haiti in the Sixties: Object of International Concern.* Washington, DC: Washington Center for Foreign Policy Research, 1964.

Malone, David M. *Decision-Making in the UN Security Council: The Case of Haiti.* Oxford, UK: Clarendon, 1998.

Mathon, Alix. *Haiti, un Cas: La Société des Baïonnettes, un regard nouveau.* Port-au-Prince: Le Natal SA, 1985.

Métraux, Alfred. *Voodoo in Haiti.* New York: Schocken, 1972.

Moreau de Saint-Méry, M. L. E. *Description topographique, physique, civile, politique et historique de la partie française de l'isle Saint-Domingue.* Paris: Société française d'histoire d'outre-mer, 1984 [1797].

Nicholls, David. *From Dessalines to Duvalier: Race, Colour and National Independence in Haiti.* Cambridge: Cambridge University Press, 1979.

Opération Lavalas. *La Chance qui Passe.* Opération Lavalas, 1990.

Paquin, Lyonel. *The Haitians: Class and Color Politics.* Brooklyn: Multi-Type, 1983.

Perusse, Roland I. *Haitian Democracy Restored, 1991–1995.* Lanham, MD: University Press of America, 1995.

Ridgeway, James. *The Haiti Files.* Washington, DC: Essential, 1990.

———. *The Haiti Files: Decoding the Crisis.* Washington, DC: Essential, 1994.

Rodman, Selden and Carole Cleaver. *Spirits of the Night: The Vaudun Gods of Haiti.* Dallas, TX: Spring, 1992.

Romulus, Marc. *Les Cachots des Duvalier: Marc Romulus, ex-Prisonnier Politique Témoigne.* Port-au-Prince: Kopirapid, 1991.

Rotberg, Robert I. (ed). *Haiti Renewed: Political and Economic Prospects.* Washington, DC: Brookings, 1997.

Rotberg, Robert I. *Haiti: The Politics of Squalor.* Boston: Houghton Mifflin, 1971.

Schacochis, Bob. *The Immaculate Invasion.* New York: Viking, 1999.

Schlesinger, Arthur M. Jr. *A Thousand Days: John F. Kennedy in the White House.* Boston: Houghton Mifflin, 1965.

Schmidt, Hans. *The United States Occupation of Haiti: 1915–1934.* New Brunswick, NJ: Rutgers University Press, 1995.

Seabrook, William. *The Magic Island.* New York: Paragon, 1989.

Soukar, Michel. *Entretiens avec l'Histoire, tome 2.* Port-au-Prince: Le Natal S.A., 1993.

———. *Seize ans de lutte pour un pays normal.* Port-au-Prince: Magiques, 1987.

Stotzky, Irwin P. *Silencing the Guns in Haiti: The Promise of Deliberative Democracy.* Chicago and London: University of Chicago, 1997.

Trouillot, Michel-Rolph. *Silencing the Past: Power and the Production of History.* Boston: Beacon, 1995.

Weinstein, Brian and Aaron Segal. *Haiti: The Failure of Politics.* Westport, CT, and London: Praeger, 1992.

Wilentz, Amy. *The Rainy Season: Haiti Since Duvalier.* New York: Simon and Schuster, 1989.

II. THE SADDEST STORY

Allen, Beverly. *Rape Warfare: The Hidden Genocide in Bosnia-Herzegovina and Croatia.* Minneapolis: University of Minnesota Press, 1996.

Azrael, Jeremy and E. Payan (eds). *US and Russian Policy Making with Respect to the Use of Force.* Santa Monica, CA: Rand, 1997.

Baker, James A. III with Thomas M. deFrank. *The Politics of Diplomacy: Revolution, War and Peace, 1989–1992.* New York: Putnam, 1995.

Bert, Wayne. *The Reluctant Superpower: The United States Policy in Bosnia, 1991–1995.* New York: St. Martin's, 1997.

Cigar, Norman. *Genocide in Bosnia: The Policy of Ethnic Cleansing.* College Station: Texas A&M University Press, 1995.

Cushman, Thomas and Stjepan G. Mestrovic (eds), *This Time We Knew: Western Responses to Genocide in Bosnia.* New York: NYU Press, 1996.

Demick, Barbara. *Logavina Street: Life and Death in a Sarajevo Neighborhood.* Kansas City: Andrews and McMeel, 1996.

Drew, Elizabeth. *Showdown: The Struggle Between the Gingrich Congress and the Clinton White House.* New York: Simon and Schuster, 1996.

Gjelten, Tom. *Sarajevo Daily: A City and Its Newspaper Under Siege.* New York: Harper-Collins, 1995.

Gow, James. *Triumph of the Lack of Will: International Diplomacy and the Yugoslav War.* New York: Columbia University Press, 1997.

Gutman, Roy. *A Witness to Genocide: the 1993 Pulitzer Prize-winning dispatches on the "ethnic cleansing" of Bosnia.* New York: Macmillan, 1993.

Helsinki Watch. *War Crimes in Bosnia-Herzegovina, Volume II.* Helsinki Watch, 1993.

Holbrooke, Richard. *To End A War.* New York: Random House, 1998.

Honig, Jan Willem and Norbert Both. *Srebrenica: Record of a War Crime.* New York: Penguin, 1997.

Hukanovic, Rezak. *The Tenth Circle of Hell: A Memoir of Life in the Death Camps of Bosnia.* New York: Basic Books, 1996.

Human Rights Watch. *Bosnia-Hercegovina: The Fall of Srebrenica and the Failure of UN Peacekeeping.* Helsinki, Finland: Human Rights Watch, 1995.

Hutchings, Robert L. *American Diplomacy and the End of the Cold War: An Insider's Account of U.S. Policy in Europe, 1989–1992.* Washington, DC: Woodrow Wilson Center Press; Baltimore, MD: Johns Hopkins University Press, 1997.

Jansa, Janez. *Premiki.* Ljubljana: Mladinska Kniga, 1993.

Judah, Tim. *The Serbs: History, Myth, and the Destruction of Yugoslavia.* New Haven, CT: Yale University Press, 2000.

Levi, Primo. *Survival in Auschwitz.* New York: Simon and Schuster, 1993.

Mestrovic, Stjepan G. (ed). *The Conceit of Innocence: Losing the Conscience of the West in the War Against Bosnia.* College Station: Texas A&M University Press, 1997.

Morris, Dick. *Behind the Oval Office: Winning the Presidency in the Nineties.* New York: Random House, 1997.

Owen, David. *Balkan Odyssey: An Uncompromising Personal Account of the International Peace Efforts Following the Breakup of the Former Yugoslavia.* New York: Harcourt Brace, 1995.

Rieff, David. *Slaughterhouse: Bosnia and the Failure of the West.* New York: Simon and Schuster, 1995.

Rohde, David. *Endgame: The Betrayal and Fall of Srebrenica.* New York: Farrar, Straus and Giroux, 1997.

Sells, Michael A. *The Bridge Betrayed: Religion and Genocide in Bosnia.* Berkeley: University of California Press, 1998.

Serotta, Edward. *Survival in Sarajevo: How a Jewish Community Came to the Aid of its City.* Vienna: Christian Brandstrae, 1995.

Silber, Laura and Allan Little. *Yugoslavia: Death of a Nation.* New York: Penguin, 1997.

Sofsky, Wolfgang. *The Order of Terror: The Concentration Camp,* translated by William Templer. Princeton, NJ: Princeton University Press, 1997.

Stephanopoulos, George. *All Too Human: A Political Education.* Boston: Back Bay, 2000.

Stover, Eric and Gilles Perress. *The Graves: Srebrenica and Vukovar.* Zürich, Switzerland: Scalo, 1998.

Strobel, Warren P. *Late-Breaking Foreign Policy: The News Media's Influence on Peace Operations.* Washington, DC: United States Institute of Peace, 1997.

Sudetic, Chuck. *Blood and Vengeance: One Family's Story of the War in Bosnia.* New York: W. W. Norton, 1998.

Tanner, Marcus. *Croatia: A Nation Forged in War.* New Haven, CT: Yale University Press, 2001.

Tucker, Robert W. and David C. Hendrickson. *The Imperial Temptation: The New World Order and America's Purpose.* New York: Council on Foreign Relations, 1992.

Ullmann, Richard H. (ed). *The World and Yugoslavia's Wars.* New York: Council on Foreign Relations, 1996.

Vulliamy, Ed. *Seasons in Hell: Understanding Bosnia's War.* New York: Simon and Schuster, 1994.

Woodward, Bob. *The Choice: How Clinton Won.* New York: Simon and Schuster, 1996.

Woodward, Susan L. *Balkan Tragedy: Chaos and Dissolution After the Cold War.* Washington, DC: Brookings, 1995.

Zimmermann, Warren. *Origins of a Catastrophe: Yugoslavia and its destroyers—America's last ambassador tells what happened and why.* New York: Times Books, 1996.

III. MAROONED IN THE COLD WAR

Acheson, Dean. *Present at the Creation: My Years in the State Department.* New York: W. W. Norton, 1987.

Draper, Theodore. *A Present of Things Past: Selected Essays.* New York: Hill and Wang, 1990.

Kennan, George F. *American Diplomacy.* Chicago: University of Chicago Press, 1984.

Keynes, John Maynard. *The Economic Consequences of the Peace.* New York: Harcourt, Brace and Howe, 1920.

Lippmann, Walter. *U.S. Foreign Policy: Shield of the Republic.* Boston: Little, Brown & Co., 1949.

Lloyd George, David. *Memoirs of the Peace Conference.* New Haven, CT: Yale University Press, 1939.

Lubbock, Percy. *The Selected Letters of Henry James.* New York: Scribner, 1920.

Mandelbaum, Michael. *The Dawn of Peace in Europe.* New York: Twentieth Century Fund, 1996.

Steel, Ronald. *Walter Lippmann and the American Century.* Boston: Little, Brown & Co., 1980.

Walker, Martin. *The Cold War: A History.* New York: Macmillan, 1995.

IV. LOST IN THE FOREVER WAR

Agamben, Giorgio. *State of Exception*, translated by Kevin Attell. Chicago and London: University of Chicago Press, 2005.

Ajami, Fouad. *The Arab Predicament: Arab Political Thought and Practice Since 1967.* Cambridge, UK: Cambridge University Press, 1981.

———. *The Dream Palace of the Arabs: A Generation's Odyssey.* New York: Vintage, 1998.

———. *The Foreigner's Gift: The Americans, the Arabs, and the Iraqis in Iraq.* New York: Free Press, 2006.

———. *The Vanished Imam: Musa al Sadr and the Shia of Lebanon.* Ithaca, NY, and London: Cornell University Press, 1986.

Allison, Graham. *Nuclear Terrorism: The Ultimate Preventable Catastrophe.* New York: Henry Holt, 2004.

Arquilla, John and David Ronfeldt. *Networks and Netwars: The Future of Terror, Crime, and Militancy.* Santa Monica, CA: Rand, 2001.

Aussaresses, Gen. Paul. *The Battle of the Casbah: Terrorism and Counter-Terrorism in Algeria, 1955–1957.* New York: Enigma, 2002.

Bacevich, Andrew J. *The Imperial Tense: Prospects and Problems of American Empire.* Chicago: Ivan R. Dee, 2003.

———. *The Limits of Power: The End of American Exceptionalism.* New York: Metropolitan, 2008.

Baer, Robert. *See No Evil: The True Story of a Ground Soldier in the CIA's War on Terrorism.* New York: Three Rivers, 2002.

————. *Sleeping with the Devil: How Washington Sold Our Soul for Saudi Crude.* New York: Three Rivers, 2003.

Baker, James A., III, and Lee H. Hamilton. *The Iraq Study Group Report: The Way Forward–A New Approach.* New York: Vintage, 2006.

Bell, J. Bowyer. *The Dynamics of the Armed Struggle.* Portland, OR, and London: Frank Cass, 1998.

Benjamin, Daniel and Steven Simon. *The Age of Sacred Terror.* New York: Random House, 2002.

Bergen, Peter L. *The Osama bin Laden I Know: An Oral History of al Qaeda's Leader.* New York: Free Press, 2006.

Berman, Paul. *Terror and Liberalism.* New York and London: W. W. Norton, 2003.

Blix, Hans. *Disarming Iraq: The Search for Weapons of Mass Destruction.* New York: Pantheon, 2004.

Bremer, L. Paul. *My Year in Iraq: The Struggle to Build a Future of Hope.* New York: Simon and Schuster, 2006.

Brisard, Jean-Charles. *Zarqawi: The New Face of al-Qaeda.* New York: Other Press, 2005.

Carr, Edward Hallett. *The Twenty Years' Crisis, 1919–1939.* New York: Perennial, 2001.

Carr, Matthew. *Unknown Soldiers: How Terrorism Transformed the Modern World.* London: Profile, 2006.

Chandrasekaran, Rajiv. *Imperial Life in the Emerald City: Inside Iraq's Green Zone.* New York: Knopf, 2006.

Cockburn, Andrew and Patrick Cockburn. *Out of the Ashes: The Resurrection of Saddam Hussein.* New York: HarperPerennial, 1999.

Cockburn, Patrick. *The Occupation: War and Resistance in Iraq.* London and New York: Verso, 2006.

Cole, David and Jules Lobel. *Less Safe, Less Free: Why America is Losing the War on Terror.* New York and London: New Press, 2007.

Coll, Steve. *Ghost Wars: The Secret History of the CIA, Afghanistan, and bin Laden, from the Soviet Invasion to September 11, 2001.* New York: Penguin, 2004.

Conroy, John. *Unspeakable Acts, Ordinary People: The Dynamics of Torture: An Examination of the Practice of Torture in Three Democracies.* Berkeley: University of California Press, 2000.

Cordesman, Anthony H. *The Iraq War: Strategy, Tactics, and Military Lessons.* Washington, DC: CSIS, 2003.

Cronin, Isaac (ed). *Confronting Fear: A History of Terrorism.* New York: Thunder's Mouth, 2002.

Daaleder, Ivo H. and James M. Lindsay. *America Unbound: The Bush Revolution in Foreign Policy.* Washington, DC: Brookings, 2003.

Danner, Mark. *The Secret Way to War: The Downing Street Memo and the Iraq War's Buried History.* New York: New York Review Books, 2006.

————. *Torture and Truth: America, Abu Ghraib and the War on Terror.* New York: New York Review Books, 2004.

Delegates of the International Committee of the Red Cross. *ICRC Report on the Treatment of Fourteen "High Value Detainees" in CIA Custody.* February 2007

————. *Report of the International Committee of the Red Cross (ICRC) on the Treatment by the Coalition Forces of Prisoners of War and Other Protected Persons by the Geneva Conventions in Iraq During Arrest, Internment and Interrogation.* February 2004.

Devji, Faisal. *Landscapes of the Jihad: Militancy Morality Modernity*. Ithaca, NY: Cornell University Press, 2005.

Diamond, Larry. *Squandered Victory: The American Occupation and Bungled Effort to Bring Democracy to Iraq*. New York: Times Books, 2005.

Dodge, Toby. *Inventing Iraq: The Failure of Nation Building and a History Denied*. New York: Columbia University Press, 2003.

Fallows, James. *Blind into Baghdad: America's War in Iraq*. New York: Vintage, 2006.

Fay, Major General George R. *AR 15–6 Investigation of the Abu Ghraib Detention Facility and 205th Military Intelligence Brigade*, August 2004.

Feldman, Noah. *What We Owe Iraq: War and the Ethics of Nation Building*. Princeton, NJ, and Oxford, UK: Princeton University Press, 2004.

Friedman, George. *The Next 100 Years: A Forecast for the 21st Century*. New York: Doubleday, 2009.

———. *America's Secret War: Inside the Hidden Worldwide Struggle Between America and Its Enemies*. New York: Broadway, 2004.

Fromkin, David. *A Peace to End All Peace: The Fall of the Ottoman Empire and the Creation of the Modern Middle East*. New York: Henry Holt, 1989.

Frum, David and Richard Perle. *An End to Evil: How to Win the War on Terror*. New York: Random House, 2003.

Frum, David. *The Right Man: The Surprise Presidency of George W. Bush*. New York: Random House, 2003.

Gaddis, John Lewis. *Strategies of Containment: A Critical Appraisal of American National Security Policy During the Cold War*. Oxford and New York: Oxford University Press, 2005.

Galbraith, Peter W. *The End of Iraq: How American Incompetence Created A War Without End*. New York: Simon and Schuster, 2006.

Goldsmith, Jack. *The Terror Presidency: Law and Judgment Inside the Bush Administration*. New York and London: W. W. Norton, 2007.

Gordon, Michael R. and Gen. Bernard E. Trainor. *Cobra II: The Inside Story of the Invasion and Occupation of Iraq*. New York: Pantheon, 2006.

Gray, John R. *Al Qaeda and What It Means to be Modern*. New York and London: New Press, 2003.

Greenberg, Karen J. and Joshua Dratel (eds). *The Torture Papers: The Road to Abu Ghraib*. New York: Cambridge University Press, 2005.

Gunaratna, Rohan. *Inside al Qaeda: Global Network of Terror*. New York: Columbia University Press, 2002.

Hashim, Ahmed S. *Insurgency and Counter-Insurgency in Iraq*. Ithaca, NY: Cornell University Press, 2006.

Hersh, Seymour M. *Chain of Command: The Road from 9/11 to Abu Ghraib*. New York: HarperCollins, 2004.

Hiro, Dilip. *Neighbors, Not Friends: Iraq and Iran After the Gulf Wars*. London and New York: Routledge, 2001.

Hoffman, Bruce. *Inside Terrorism*. New York: Columbia University Press, 1998.

Hoge, Jr., James F. and Gideon Rose (eds). *Understanding the War on Terror*. New York: Council on Foreign Relations, 2005.

———. *How Did This Happen? Terrorism and the New War*. New York: Council on Foreign Relations, 2001.

Kaplan, David E. and Andrew Marshall. *The Cult at the End of the World: The Terrifying Story of the Aum Doomsday Cult, from the Subways of Tokyo to the Nuclear Arsenals of Russia*. New York: Crown, 1996.

Kennan, George F. *American Diplomacy*. Chicago and London: Chicago, 1984.

Kepel, Gilles. *Jihad: The Trail of Political Islam*. Cambridge, MA: Belknap, 2002.

———. *Bad Moon Rising: A Chronicle of the Middle East Today*. London: Saqi, 2003.

———. *The War for Muslim Minds: Islam and the West*. Cambridge, MA, and London: Belknap, 2004.

Kiesling, John Brady. *Diplomacy Lessons: Realism for an Unloved Superpower*. Dulles, VA: Potomac, 2006.

Kissinger, Henry. *Crisis: The Anatomy of Two Major Foreign Policy Crises*. New York: Simon and Schuster, 2003.

———. *Diplomacy*. New York: Touchstone, 1994.

Korb, Lawrence J. *A New National Security Strategy in an Age of Terrorists, Tyrants, and Weapons of Mass Destruction: Three Options Presented as Presidential Speeches*. New York: Council on Foreign Relations, 2003.

Laqueur, Walter. *No End to War: Terrorism in the Twenty-First Century*. New York and London: Continuum, 2003.

———, (ed). *Voices of Terror: Manifestos, Writings and Manuals of al Qaeda, Hamas, and Other Terrorists from Around the World and Throughout the Ages*. New York: Reed, 2004.

———. *Guerrilla: A Historical and Critical Study*. Boston and Toronto: Little, Brown and Co., 1976.

Lawrence, Bruce (ed). *Messages to the World: The Statements of Osama bin Laden*. London and New York: Verso, 2005.

Lewis, Bernard. *From Babel to Dragomans: Interpreting the Middle East*. Oxford: Oxford University Press, 2004.

———. *The Crisis of Islam: Holy War and Unholy Terror*. New York: Modern Library, 2003.

———. *The Middle East: A Brief History of the Last 2,000 Years*. New York: Touchstone, 1997.

———. *What Went Wrong?: Western Impact and Middle Eastern Response*. Oxford: Oxford University Press, 2002.

Lockhart, Robin Bruce. *Reilly: Ace of Spies*. New York: Penguin, 1984 [1967].

Luttwak, Edward N. *Strategy: The Logic of War and Peace*. Cambridge, MA, and London: Belknap, 2001.

———. *Coup d'État: A Practical Handbook*. Cambridge, MA: Harvard, 1979.

Makiya, Kanan. *Republic of Fear: The Politics of Modern Iraq*. Berkeley: University of California Press, 1998.

Mann, James. *Rise of the Vulcans: The History of Bush's War Cabinet*. New York: Viking, 2004.

Marr, Phebe. *The Modern History of Iraq*. Boulder, CO: Westview Press, 2004.

Mayer, Jane. *The Dark Side: The Inside Story of How the War on Terror Turned Into a War on American Ideals*. New York: Doubleday, 2008.

McCoy, Alfred W. *A Question of Torture: CIA Interrogation, from the Cold War to the War on Terror*. New York: Owl, 2006.

McGeough, Paul. *In Baghdad: A Reporter's War*. Crows Nest NSW, Australia: Allen and Unwin, 2003.

Merry, Robert W. *Sands of Empire: Missionary Zeal, American Foreign Policy, and the Hazards of Global Ambition*. New York: Simon and Schuster, 2005.

Miller, John and Aaron Kenedi (eds). *Inside Iraq: The History, the People, and the Modern Conflicts of the World's Least Understood Land*. New York: Marlowe and Co., 2002.

Nakash, Yitzhak. *Reaching for Power: The Shi'a in the Modern Arab World*. Princeton, NJ: Princeton University Press, 2006.

———. *The Shi'is of Iraq*. Princeton, NJ, and Oxford: Princeton University Press, 2003.

Nance, Malcolm W. *The Terrorists of Iraq: Inside the Strategy and Tactics of the Iraq Insurgency*. Charleston, SC: BookSurge, 2007.

Nasr, Vali. *The Shia Revival: How Conflicts within Islam Will Shape the Future*. New York and London: W. W. Norton, 2006.

National Commission on Terrorist Attacks. *The 9/11 Commission Report: Final Report of the National Commission on Terrorist Attacks upon the United States*. New York: W. W. Norton, 2004.

Phillips, David L. *Losing Iraq: Inside the Postwar Reconstruction Fiasco*. Boulder, CO: Westview Press, 2005.

Podhoretz, Norman. *World War IV: The Long Struggle Against Islamofascism*. New York: Doubleday, 2007.

Pollack, Kenneth M. *The Threatening Storm: The Case for Invading Iraq*. New York: Random House, 2002.

Posner, Gerald. *Secrets of the Kingdom: The Inside Story of the Saudi-U.S. Connection*. New York: Random House, 2005.

Prados, John. *Hoodwinked: The Documents that Reveal How Bush Sold Us a War*. New York and London: New Press, 2004.

Rashid, Ahmed. *Taliban: Militant Islam, Oil and Fundamentalism in Central Asia*. New Haven, CT, and London: Yale University Press, 2000.

Reuters. *Afghanistan: Lifting the Veil*. Upper Saddle River, NJ: Prentice Hall, 2002.

Rich, Frank. *The Greatest Story Ever Sold: The Decline and Fall of Truth from 9/11 to Katrina*. New York: Penguin, 2006.

Ricks, Thomas E. *Fiasco: The American Military Adventure in Iraq*. New York: Penguin, 2006.

Rieff, David. *A Bed for the Night: Humanitarianism in Crisis*. New York: Simon and Schuster, 2002.

Risen, James. *State of War: The Secret History of the CIA and the Bush Administration*. New York: Free Press, 2006.

Riverbend. *Baghdad Burning: Girl Blog from Iraq*. New York: Feminist Press, 2005.

———. *Baghdad Burning II: More Girl Blog from Iraq*. New York: Feminist Press, 2006.

Robinson, Linda. *Tell Me How This Ends: General David Petraeus and the Search for a Way Out of Iraq*. New York: PublicAffairs, 2008.

Rosen, Gary (ed). *The Right War? The Conservative Debate on Iraq*. Cambridge, UK: Cambridge University Press, 2005.

Rosen, Nir. *In the Belly of the Green Bird: The Triumph of the Martyrs in Iraq*. New York: Free Press, 2006.

Rothkopf, David. *Running the World: The Inside Story of the National Security Council and the Architects of American Power*. New York: PublicAffairs, 2004.

Roy, Oliver. *Globalized Islam: The Search for a New Ummah*. New York: Columbia University Press, 2004.

Sageman, Marc. *Understanding Terror Networks*. Philadelphia: University of Pennsylvania Press, 2004.

Scheuer, Michael ("Anonymous"). *Through Our Enemies' Eyes: Osama bin Laden, Radical Islam, and the Future of America*. Dulles, VA: Brassey's, 2002.

Schlesinger, James R., Harold Brown, Tillie K. Fowler and General Charles A. Horner (USAF-Ret.). *Final Report of the Independent Panel to Review DoD Detention Operations* (*The Schlesinger Report*), August 2004.

Sick, Gary. *All Fall Down: America's Tragic Encounter with Iran*. New York: Penguin, 1985.

Stewart, Rory. *The Prince of the Marshes and Other Occupational Hazards of a Year in Iraq*. Orlando, FL: Harcourt, 2006.

Suskind, Ron. *The One Percent Doctrine: Deep Inside America's Pursuits of Its Enemies Since 9/11*. New York: Simon and Schuster, 2006.

Taber, Robert. *War of the Flea: The Classic Study of Guerrilla Warfare*. Washington, DC: Potomac, 2002.

Taguba, Major General Antonio M. *Article 15–6 Investigation of the 800th Military Police Brigade* (*The Taguba Report*), May 2004.

Telhami, Shibley. *The Stakes: America in the Middle East: The Consequences of Power and the Choice for Peace*. Boulder, CO: Westview Press, 2002.

Timerman, Jacobo. *Prisoner Without A Name, Cell Without A Number*. New York: Vintage, 1988.

Traub, James. *The Freedom Agenda: Why America Must Spread Democracy (Just Not the Way George Bush Did)*. New York: Farrar, Straus and Giroux, 2008.

Tripp, Charles. *A History of Iraq*. Cambridge, UK: Cambridge University Press, 2000.

Visser, Reidar and Gareth Stansfield (eds). *An Iraq of Its Regions: Cornerstones of a Federal Democracy?* New York: Columbia University Press, 2008.

Whitney, Craig R. (ed). *The WMD Mirage: Iraq's Decade of Deception and America's False Premise for War*. New York: PublicAffairs, 2005.

Whittaker, David J. (ed). *The Terrorism Reader*. London and New York: Routledge, 2001.

Woodward, Bob. *Bush at War*. New York: Simon and Schuster, 2002.

———. *Plan of Attack*. New York: Simon and Schuster, 2004.

———. *State of Denial: Bush at War, Part III*. New York: Simon and Schuster, 2006.

Wright, Lawrence. *The Looming Tower: al-Qaeda and the Road to 9/11*. New York: Knopf, 2006.

Zizek, Slavoj. *Iraq: The Borrowed Kettle*. London and New York: Verso, 2004.

Index